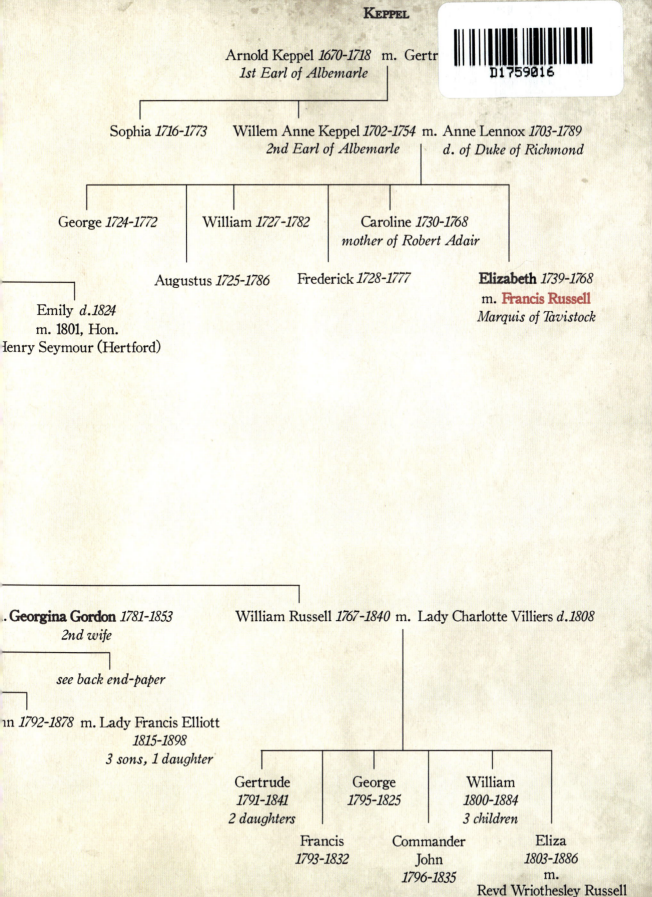

Arnold Keppel *1670-1718* m. Gertr
1st Earl of Albemarle

Sophia *1716-1773*   Willem Anne Keppel *1702-1754* m. Anne Lennox *1703-1789*
2nd Earl of Albemarle   *d. of Duke of Richmond*

George *1724-1772*   William *1727-1782*   Caroline *1730-1768*
mother of Robert Adair

Augustus *1725-1786*   Frederick *1728-1777*   **Elizabeth** *1739-1768*
m. **Francis Russell**
Marquis of Tavistock

Emily *d.1824*
m. 1801, Hon.
Henry Seymour (Hertford)

. **Georgina Gordon** *1781-1853*   William Russell *1767-1840* m. Lady Charlotte Villiers *d.1808*
2nd wife

see back end-paper

n *1792-1878* m. Lady Francis Elliott
1815-1898
3 sons, 1 daughter

Gertrude   George   William
1791-1841   *1795-1825*   *1800-1884*
2 daughters   *3 children*

Francis   Commander   Eliza
1793-1832   John   *1803-1886*
1796-1835   m.
Revd Wriothesley Russell

Improbable Pioneers
of the Romantic Age

The Lives of John Russell, 6th Duke of Bedford,
and Georgina Gordon, Duchess of Bedford

Improbable Pioneers of the Romantic Age

The Lives of John Russell, 6th Duke of Bedford,
and Georgina Gordon, Duchess of Bedford

Keir Davidson

Pimpernel
Press Ltd

Pimpernel Press Limited
www.pimpernelpress.com

Improbable Pioneers of the Romantic Age
The Lives of John Russell, 6th Duke of Bedford,
and Georgina Gordon, Duchess of Bedford
© Pimpernel Press Limited 2022
Text © Keir Davidson 2022
For copyright in the illustrations see page 560

FRONT ENDPAPER Details of Lord John Russell's
family, that of his first wife, Georgiana Byng, and their
children

BACK ENDPAPER Details of the family of Georgina
Gordon, Lord John Russell's second wife, and their
children

HALF-TITLE 'Two Birds', the central image of the
ceiling decoration in the Garden Room, Woburn Abbey

TITLE PAGE Humphry Repton, Red Book for Endsleigh
(1814), Plate XI, 'View from the Library' (after)

ABOVE H.W, Burgess, Drawings of the Evergreens at
Woburn Abbey (1837), Plate 9

Keir Davidson has asserted his right to be identified
as the author of this work in accordance with the
Copyright, Designs and Patents Act 1988 (UK).

A catalogue record for this book is available from the
British Library.

Designed by Anne Wilson
Endpapers, maps and special artwork by Jas Davidson
Typeset in Bembo and Bliss

ISBN 978-1-910258-25-5
Printed and bound in China
By C&C Offset Printing Company Limited
9 8 7 6 5 4 3 2 1

Contents

Foreword

F OR A LONG TIME I was not sure where my fascination with, and thirst for knowledge about, my ancestor the 6th Duke of Bedford and his second wife, Georgina Gordon, began . . . it was an indistinct trail of breadcrumbs that only became visible in retrospect. I finally realised, once we started to really explore the idea of writing this story, that I had been following the trail ever since my family moved into Woburn Abbey in 1976, after my grandfather, the 13th Duke, handed over the reins of the estate to my parents.

All of the clues: Covent Garden, the Walled Kitchen Garden at Woburn, Repton, Red Books, Kew, Landseer, tea huts, hillside seats, log cabins, the Bedfords' close relations with key figures of the Enlightenment and the Romantic Age – they were all parts of that invisible trail which permeated my life at Woburn . . .

And then came the very first time I drove down the drive at Endsleigh, the Devon 'cottage' built by the 6th Duke and Duchess. Having heard about Endsleigh from my parents, and reading little bits over the years, I thought I would quickly drive by and visit while I was in Devon. I very distinctly remember the moment I turned into the long drive, I felt energized and inspired by the beauty and the tranquillity – and then, when I finally turned the corner and saw the house the spell was well and truly cast. I was transfixed immediately by this picturesque architectural gem . . . there was so much atmosphere and so much seemingly tangible energy. I was completely entranced.

I still had not put the pieces together, I was still following the breadcrumbs . . . However, this was the biggest clue so far and from that moment (in the mid-1980s) I actively followed the trail with more intensity, hungry for as much information as possible about this wondrous place. Over the next few years, and more trips to Endsleigh with Stephanie, my wife, getting up at first light to wander around the magical garden, sitting quietly in front of the fire or out on the terrace with a cup of tea, I became more and more fascinated by the 'force' that I felt in this place. At the time it was still owned by the Endsleigh Fishing Club, who had kept it relatively untouched, and the history permeated every corner of the house and garden – it was an unseen force that just kept getting stronger.

Finally, twenty-four years ago, after an afternoon in the library at Woburn leafing through the Endsleigh Red Book, Stephanie and I invited our friends Keir and Linda Davidson to Endsleigh for the weekend. I knew Keir would 'get' the landscape and the stunning water garden. And 'get it' he did . . . he too felt the energy and knew this was a very special place. For Keir and me it all came together late one afternoon when, after a long walk along the river, we walked back to the house and into the Stable Courtyard, and stood in front of the fountain looking at the plaque installed by the 6th Duke a few years after completion, to commemorate the construction of the house and the contribution of Duchess Georgina to both the selection of the site and the decision to build a house inspired by her early life in the Scottish Highlands; reading the inscription, we shared an ah-ah moment . . . We agreed right there that the story of the people who created this house – and so much more – had to be told. At that moment I understood the breadcrumbs and looked back at the trail that led to this spot – and the book was born.

We have had so much fun researching and writing this book, and travelling to the many places where the 6th Duke and Duchess left their mark. We have met so many people, many of whom have added vital elements to the story, uncovered new information and deciphered old information to reveal previously unknown facts . . . along the way discovering forgotten letters and drawings and paintings and books that have now finally been analysed together to reveal how full and rich, bohemian and pioneering John and Georgina Bedford were, and how what they achieved and created has had a wide influence on so many lives in the fields of science, politics, agriculture, architecture, botany and art; an influence which continues to this day.

This book is being published at a point when humanity is becoming ever more disconnected from the natural world. Maybe, set as it is in a time when the realization of previously unseen links was just starting to bloom – with the convergence of science, art, literature, botany, politics, nature and humanity all being recognized – it might help shine a light back on to this interconnectedness.

I would like to add my huge thanks to everyone who along the way has guided, helped, facilitated, opened doors, shone lights and made this book possible. Keir has listed all of the many people whose invaluable help is very greatly appreciated and it just leaves me to say my biggest thank you to Keir for taking on this challenge and for writing this exceptional biography . . . thank you so very much for revealing their story. Keir has exceeded everything I hoped for with this book. He has brought John and Georgina's story so fully to life, and uncovered and exposed and explained and confirmed so much detail and information . . . enabling us, the readers, to see, explore, understand, feel and experience the lives of these Improbable Pioneers.

Lord Robin Russell
Woburn, 2021

Introduction

A WEDDING TOOK PLACE on the afternoon of 23 June 1803 at Fife House, Whitehall, London. It was initially an intimate affair, largely members of the bride's family and their friends, and when the ceremony and lunch were over, the newlyweds left to begin a short honeymoon. As their carriage pulled away, the next phase of the celebrations got underway as the house and the street outside were prepared to host some five hundred family, friends and leading lights of the 'ton' – the most important and popular members of London's fashionable society – for supper and dancing. Supper began at ten o'clock, and by two in the morning the rooms had been given over to the dancers. Starting perhaps with a few sedate minuets, it was not long before things started to liven up as the dancers turned their attentions to a succession of Highland strathspeys and reels. Once underway, the tempo of the night changed as dancers flew round the rooms accompanied by claps and shouts of encouragement, 'rough' Highland accents grating on refined London ears, and the infectious mood carried the dancers and musicians on until seven o'clock the next morning. By this time the drinking and dancing had long since spread to the street outside, where a crowd had gathered amidst what *The Times* described as 'excessive delight and rejoicing'. One correspondent of Lord Fife described the night as a 'midnight orgy', and it was only later that day that the house and its neighbourhood returned to some sort of normality as the last stragglers left for home: 'the ladies depart half stupid with fatigue and dissipation, and their naked arms dangling out of their carriage windows.'[1]

Complaints were later heard from the Earl of Fife concerning damage to his house and furniture, and from the neighbours concerning the behaviour and language of many of those in the street all night, but none of these could spoil the night's success for the bride's mother, Jane Maxwell, Duchess of Gordon, the ringmaster of the entertainments. For Jane this was not simply a celebration of a daughter's marriage, although she was inordinately proud at having secured

George Garrard's portrait of the Duke of Bedford sitting in Woburn Abbey park, 1806, the year of his appointment as Viceroy of Ireland.

a third duke for her daughters; it was also a defiant statement, in the heart of London, of personal and national identity, a celebration of a culture and way of life long under threat.

The bridal pair that afternoon had been John Russell, 6th Duke of Bedford (1766–1839), and Lady Georgina Gordon (1781–1853), but the duke's family party at the wedding had been sadly small. He and his brothers, Francis, Marquis of Tavistock, and Lord William, had lost their parents while they were still very young, and they had been largely brought up in the quiet splendours of Woburn Abbey or Bedford House in London by their grandparents, John Russell, 4th Duke of Bedford, who died in 1771, and Gertrude, Duchess of Bedford, who died in 1794. While the eldest, Francis, had succeeded as the 5th Duke of Bedford in 1787, he too had died suddenly in 1802, leaving only the new duke's younger brother, Lord William, to attend as immediate family. On his brother's death, Lord John Russell had succeeded unexpectedly as 6th Duke, but his life had been overshadowed since 1801 by the death of his first wife, Georgiana Byng.

On the other side, however, were the Gordons. Lady Georgina was the daughter of Alexander, 4th Duke of Gordon, and Jane Maxwell, Duchess of Gordon, and was

Georgina, Duchess of Bedford, 1803, engraving. It is possible that this celebration of Georgina's new status was commissioned by her proud mother, Jane, since a very similar image of her sister Charlotte, as Duchess of Richmond, also exists.

one of the youngest of seven children, brought up in the busy world of Gordon Castle in Morayshire, and part of a complex web of families and landholdings that spread across the Highlands from Aberdeenshire through Moray and Banff, up Strathspey through Badenoch and beyond into Lochaber. Georgina's Gordon relatives included not just those of the Duke of Gordon's family, but also those of the Earls of Aberdeen and the Earls of Aboyne, the Lords Haddo, the Lords Huntly, the Gordons of Gight and, by marriage, the Dukes of Richmond and Sutherland, not to mention the numerous cadet branches of the Gordon line and the Maxwells of her mother's family.

It was thus a strangely mismatched pair who got married that day. The duke was thirty-seven, a father of three who had been widowed just two years before, and in deep mourning for both his first wife and his elder brother. A shy and introverted second son with few ambitions beyond running his country estate in Hampshire, Lord John had suddenly found himself responsible for three young sons and for filling the shoes of his dominant elder brother as Duke of Bedford, and of all this new responsibility, most pressing of all, perhaps, were the commitments he had made to his dying brother. He had given his word that he would continue the work on the estate of their family home at Woburn Abbey to make it the leading centre for 'national improvement' in the field of modern agriculture, and also to become an active supporter of the Foxite faction of the Whig party in Parliament. Previously only ever on the periphery of his brother's circle of acquaintances and his contacts in the social, political and agricultural worlds, the new duke was at something of a loss to know where to begin or whom to turn to first, but he was determined to fulfil the commitments he had made.

Lady Georgina Gordon, on the other hand, had celebrated her twenty-second birthday just two months before the wedding.[2] Although at the time they were estranged and living apart, her father and mother were both present, as were a good number of her family – siblings, cousins, aunts and uncles – and their friends. Her mother, fiercely ambitious for her daughters' marriages, had introduced Georgina to London society at the first opportunity, where she had become popular for her vivacity, humour and sense of fun. Far from shy, she nevertheless also appears to have had a quieter side to her nature: a reflective young woman equally happy living with her mother in the simplest of cottages in the Highlands, where she clearly felt at home. The youngest daughter still at home, Georgina had spent much of her teenage years with her mother after the latter had moved out of Gordon Castle, and had been a witness to her mother's bitter struggle to secure what she considered to be her share of the estate following the breakup of the marriage. By the time of her own marriage, Georgina had no doubt become a practised and compassionate listener, just the person perhaps to bring the reserved duke out of his sad interior world and into a brighter future – but at the time, few saw it like this.

For the duke's family and wider circle of friends the marriage seemed precipitously sudden, given that the pair had only known each other for about a year, and rumours swirled round London's salons that, only a year before, Georgina had been in love with Napoleon's step-son Eugène de Beauharnais before becoming engaged to marry the duke's elder brother, Francis; the truth of either of these things remains a mystery to this day. In addition to the difference in their ages, there were several other reasons for consternation among the duke's friends and London society, including the unseemly speed at which it happened following the loss of his first wife and the unusual location for the ceremony – a rented house belonging to neither ducal family. Above all, perhaps, it was the fact that the head of one of the country's most prominent aristocratic families – guests of royalty, key members of London's social world and established leaders of the Whig party – should choose to marry someone from outside their 'set', let alone a Scot who was also a Gordon, part of a distant Highland clan that was wrapped in mystique and wild tales, and whose loyalty to the crown during the two Jacobite rebellions had been at best questionable, and some of whom had fought for the Stewart cause to the bitter end at Culloden. Beyond this, some twenty years before, Georgina's uncle Lord George Gordon had led the series of riots in London to which he gave his name, associating the clan forever with the days of uncontrolled violence and destruction that followed. Worst of all, as far as London society was concerned, Georgina was the daughter of Jane Maxwell, Duchess of Gordon, a woman who had scandalized London when she first arrived from the north in 1787 with her disrespectful attitude towards society's unwritten rules and conventions. She was seen as vainglorious and unscrupulous, brash and loud, her speech obscene, manly in mien, her style showy, ignoring the proscription on tartan and Highland dress. Above all, she was shamelessly ambitious, challenging prominent hostesses by hosting increasingly active political gatherings on behalf of the Tory party and the Pitt government. It was viewed as a huge risk and many predicted disaster.

Yet, in spite of all this, it proved to be both a long and a successful marriage, as its unusual nature turned out also to be the secret of its success. Each brought something radically new into the life of the other, and perhaps a rapid, intuitive recognition of this initially brought them together so quickly, since a large part of the success of the marriage lay in the fact that they shared a curious and Romantic nature, one which enabled them to look beyond the familiar into the unknown natural world around them with a sense of wonder as to what lay out there waiting to be discovered. Beyond this, they were both drawn to actively experience that world and to participate in the processes of discovery, whether personally or thanks to their positions as patrons, and it is this circumstance that adds complexity to their story.

In effect, because of the extraordinary prominence of the aristocracy in society of their time, this is really a book about four people: the 6th Duke and Duchess of Bedford, John Russell and Georgina Gordon. In each case, one was a high profile role and one was the person themselves. The duke and John Russell were different people, with subtly different priorities and personae, as were the duchess and Georgina Gordon. This becomes clear as we read contemporary accounts, which differ sharply depending on the context in which the commentator met or knew them. Many of the more critical accounts were the result of a visitor expecting to meet one version and becoming caught up with the other. For the 'duke' and 'duchess' there was a constant tension between their sense of nobility, which was very much a part of both of them, coupled with the civic duties and responsibilities which came with their privileges, and their sense of responsibility to their private and family lives. This was made all the more extreme by the fact that, during their lifetimes, the aristocracy occupied the same place in the public interest as participants in the modern entertainment industry do now – their comings and goings, looks and fashions, marriages and scandals, were every bit as scrutinized and criticized in contemporary newspapers as today's singers, musicians, actors and social media personalities. The only real difference between their circumstances was that the duke and duchess lived in a time when how much land you owned was the ultimate test of a person's value and identity rather than simply money.

Nevertheless, their lives were ones of extraordinary privilege based on the traditional respect accorded to those who held land and the access this provided to power and position within the hierarchies of British society. Although the lives of individuals like the duke and the duchess, and indeed their times more generally, seem thoroughly worldly and informed, there was, as one writer has put it rather beautifully, 'a golden thread of early nineteenth century naivety' running through them, which sprang from a systemic lack of self-awareness concerning both themselves as individuals and the results of their actions on others at home and abroad and, as it turns out, the planet. Rarely actually bad, they were people who could, for example, abolish the slave trade but still own slaves since the status quo was pre-ordained, both from 'on high' and by history, and accept it even though many were 'conscious … of the inequality of the system responsible for their mode of existence'.

When writing about his brief *Autobiography,* Thomas Huxley noted that 'Autobiographies are essentially works of fiction, whatever biographies are.'[3] By this he seems to have meant that someone writing about their own life is drawing on a memory of self created by what they choose to remember at a given time in their past, or what they remember at the time of writing, and that may be distorted by hindsight. Even when an autobiography is based heavily on diaries or memoranda, it is still selective according to what the individual chose to record and to leave out. The result therefore is an edited memory of self, a version of their life, which Huxley saw as 'essentially works of fiction'. It would seem that he could in fact also have classified biography in the same way, since it too is edited, both by the selective nature of the archives and sources that have survived and of the claims of other writers, and the creative choices that have made up the biographer's point of view. This seems inevitable, particularly since the strict chronological narrative of a person's life can, perhaps, only be made interesting and comprehensible if placed in the context of, as one biographer has put it, some 'creative connections across time'.[4]

This biography was conceived as part of a communal effort, helping to create a fuller picture of John Russell's and Georgina Gordon's lives, and the story of their marriage, by building on the work of those who have gone before. In particular, it owes much to the largely unpublished research into the childhoods of Lords Francis, John and William Russell, and the adult life of Francis, 5th Duke of Bedford, undertaken by Gladys Scott Thomson, Archivist at Woburn Abbey 1927–40, during the 1940s and 1950s, and most directly to the work of Rachel Trethewey in her pioneering biography of Georgina Gordon, *Mistress of the Arts: The Passionate Life of Georgina, Duchess of Bedford* (2002).[5] In addition, this book is indebted to the knowledge and expertise of the current Archivist at Woburn, Nicola Allen, and her team, the Curator, Matthew Hirst, and his assistant, Victoria Poulton, as well as to Martin Towsey, Estate Gardens Manager, and his team of gardeners at Woburn. While the validity of some of the 'creative connections' made in this biography may be the subject of debate, it is hoped that the distinction between fact and commentary will be clear, and that the exploration of these lives through their engagement with the Romantic age and their sense of wonder, reflecting as it did the spirit of the time, will add to the work that has gone before and edge us closer to a more complete picture.

In Chapters 1 and 2, we take a close look at the early life and first marriage of Lord John Russell; in Chapters 3 and 4, we turn to Georgina Gordon's early life, her family, the story of her mother, Jane Maxwell, and her upbringing in the Highlands – looking closely in turn at these two individuals to better understand just how different were the worlds which they came from. Following this, in Chapters 5 and 6, as their married life begins, we see them growing into their roles as duke and duchess, taking on the responsibilities that went with their positions, starting a family, fulfilling the duke's promises to his elder brother, and completing the work begun on Woburn Abbey: furnishing and decorating its interiors and landscaping the gardens, pleasure grounds and parkland. At the same time, we can also follow the duke's political career and his dedication to his brother's ideal of turning Woburn into an innovative and respected centre for, on the one hand, modern scientific agriculture and arboriculture, and, on the other, art and culture. A place of beautifully landscaped parkland and pleasure grounds, model farms and cottages, comprehensive libraries, art collections of old and modern masters, a sculpture gallery full of the glories of the classical and ancient world, it was to be a model of enlightened liberal taste and a grand celebration of the Russell family and their historic dedication to the sacred cause of 'Liberty'.

Throughout these chapters, amidst all this activity, we also start to get insights into their shared tastes and interests, and nothing illustrates the emergence of these better than the creation between 1810 and 1814 of an entirely new location for family life, a large picturesque *cottage ornée* at Endsleigh, part of the Russell family's Devon estates. This was a brand new house, and it was built specifically as a private holiday destination for the family. It represented something new and the first time the family had undertaken such a project; the use of the picturesque style reflected in turn the new Romantic aesthetic sense at work and the influences that formed part of Georgina's world.

The mid-1820s see the completion of many of these projects, and from this time on there was a permanent shift in the couple's interests and activities from the formal to the personal. The chapters that follow recount what happened as they began what were, in their own ways, pioneering explorations of those things that appealed to their curious and Romantic natures: their 'sense of wonder'.

Richard Holmes offers us some useful hints as to exactly what this phrase means when he writes in *The Age of Wonder* of the arrival at this time of a 'new sensibility, the dreaming inwardness of Romanticism', of 'the search for new worlds – inspired by the Romantic revolution of science', and of a new 'scientific passion, so much of which is summed up in that child-like, but infinitely complex word, *wonder*'.[6] The first of these phrases gives an insight into the aesthetic sense that Georgina brought with her to the marriage, the second to the emerging interests of the duke at this time as he fought to be free of the projects inherited from his brother, and the third to the sheer excitement of an era when it seemed that anything was possible and before all the new areas of science – geology, chemistry, astronomy, botany and so on – were separated out into distinct and detached areas of study. For a brief period, all these scientific disciplines were simply part of a new box of tools that along with others – such as literature, art, horticulture and gardening – were suddenly available to help make sense of the natural world and our relationship to it. The duke himself was deeply engaged in this, and came increasingly to look on Woburn as one of 'the meeting places of science and art' in an era of 'discovery and wonder'.[7]

In Chapters 7 to 9, this engagement with discovery and wonder dominates the story up to four years before the duke's death in 1839, as we look in detail at his horticultural and botanic activities at Woburn and, equally, at their lives in the Highlands, a region which effectively became their second home. Just four years after they were married, Georgina took the duke to Scotland for the first time, and would probably have done so sooner if he had not been required to move to Dublin on his appointment as Lord Lieutenant of Ireland (1806–7). Once in

Scotland, however, his reaction was ecstatic, Georgina's mother reporting that 'the Duke is delighted with everything,' and within ten years they had taken a long-term lease on an estate in Badenoch with shooting rights in Glen Feshie. While the family's initial stays in Scotland consisted of the customary two or three weeks shooting in late August and early September, it was not long before these visits, especially those of the duchess and the younger children, were extending to months at a time, and during the last decade of the duke's life, when he was well enough to travel, he would join the family there for up to five months, returning with them for Christmas and New Year at Woburn Abbey. While the common perception of the Bedfords in Scotland is that their trips were fun-filled social occasions during which they hosted large parties of family and friends who, when not out shooting deer and other game, were entertained with the novelty of camping in bothies, donning Highland dress, and dancing the night away, the truth is that, with the exception of two or three years, the family were largely alone and visited now and then by a few close friends. Something much more interesting than simply holidaying was going on, and much of their time was spent living in a series of simple huts up in Glen Feshie itself. In Scotland they had found a place where they were able to engage individually with the landscapes, communities and way of life that surrounded them, in a deeply personal way, far from the roles and pressures of their formal lives. Here, their experience was shared privately with a few relatives and friends, some of them artists, poets, writers, gardeners and botanists.

Of particular significance was the Bedfords' patronage of the young portraitist and animal painter Edwin Landseer (1802–1873). The artist came to the duke's attention in the early 1820s, and in 1821 he was invited to execute some drawings of the family's dogs. Following this, he visited Woburn on several occasions over the next few years and painted portraits of the some of the younger children. It was in 1824, however, that the relationship really developed when the Bedfords met up with Landseer in Scotland, where he instantly shared their fascination with the landscape, creating, seemingly for the first time, a series of paintings that included completed views of the Highland landscape. He subsequently both visited Scotland and stayed with the Bedfords on the estates they leased almost every year over the next thirty years. He was particularly enamoured with the scenery of Glen Feshie, producing a series of paintings in which he learnt how to capture those emotive qualities of romance and wonder which so drew them all to the area.

In addition to the landscape, it is clear that Georgina and Landseer were also drawn to each other, and over the years they spent an increasing amount of time together, particularly at the huts, until the affair became public knowledge. None of them ever spoke about, wrote about or acknowledged either the affair or the suggestion that Landseer may have been the father of Georgina's youngest daughter, Rachel. We are not ever likely to know the full story; if there was an affair it did not disrupt either the Bedfords' marriage or the duke's close friendship with Landseer, which was maintained until the former's death. The lasting legacy for us from Landseer's closeness to the family is that we have the most wonderful collections of illustrations, both formal paintings and informal sketches, of them and the places and people they knew. Beyond this, the duke was one of most significant early patrons who helped to launch Landseer's career.

The Bedfords together held leases in Scotland at two different properties in Badenoch between 1818 and the duke's death in 1839, first at Invereshie Lodge until 1829, and then at The Doune, Rothiemurchus, where circumstances allowed the duchess to retain the lease until 1852, the year before she died. Suitably, perhaps, the house was also the place where the duke died, having spent his last days at his desk in his library, surrounded by collections of plants, the latest books and journals on botany, and firing off letters as he lobbied hard to achieve a long-held dream – the establishment of a national garden in the old royal gardens at Kew. He did not quite live to see this happen, but the establishment of the Royal Botanic Gardens at Kew, and Sir William Hooker's appointment as its first director in 1842, remain one of the great legacies of the duke's scientific, horticultural and botanical activities that dominated the second half of his life.

Although the duke himself had withdrawn from active politics following his year in Ireland, he remained interested and supportive of his three sons from his first marriage as they entered the political arena. The eldest son, Francis, Marquis of Tavistock, took over management of the Bedford political interest, and sat as

Member of Parliament for Peterborough and then Bedfordshire, before entering the House of Lords in 1833. Lord George William, as a serving soldier in the Peninsular War and then a diplomat in Europe, was less active, and less interested, in Parliament, sitting briefly for Bedford, but the baton of national political leadership was really passed to the youngest, Lord John, who was returned for Tavistock in 1813, before entering government in Lord Grey's Whig administration in 1830, and eventually serving as prime minister. In an era of rapid change, this generation of politicians took on some of the great social issues of the time, dragging an often reluctant country into modern times. Briefly put, these included Catholic emancipation, abolition of the slave trade, the Parliamentary Reform Bill and the repeal of the Corn Laws, all issues which required the Whig aristocracy to take a long hard look at what they stood for, especially those who controlled the notorious pocket and rotten boroughs in Parliament, or who were, or whose friends were, owners of slave plantations. In many ways, this period saw a profound change in the assumptions of aristocratic status as the urgent interests of the nation's industrialized communities began to overwhelm the invisible boundaries of privilege that had seemed unassailable at the time the duke was born.

Chapter 10 covers the years up to the duke's death in 1839, and afterwards we see how life changed for Georgina, now the dowager duchess. Everything pertaining to the dukedom was, of course, inherited by Francis as soon as he became 7th Duke of Bedford, and while she kept the use of her London home at Campden Hill for her lifetime, Georgina's complicated relationship with her three stepsons meant that nothing was ever the same again; she became, at best, an occasional visitor to Woburn, and seems never to have been able to visit Endsleigh again. Apart from a burst of social activity on the London scene when her youngest daughter, Rachel, came of age in 1847, Georgina spent increasing amounts of time in Scotland, unless her failing health required a visit to the kinder climate of the resorts of Brighton, Worthing and Bognor along the south coast of England.

In spite of the fact that Georgina had organized numerous events in 1847 at her villa in Campden Hill to which all the eligible young men and their mothers were invited, Rachel does not seem to have been tempted and, in the end, did not marry until after her mother's death. Instead, as her mother had done before her, she remained with the duchess, acting as a companion and, in Rachel's case, a point of contact between her mother and her half-brothers. In the end, it was not until 1856, three years after her mother died, that Rachel finally married, aged thirty, and went to live with her husband in Ireland; this chapter is, therefore, also partly an account of what little is known of Rachel's life after her father died.

Yet, however much Georgina may have wished to stay in Scotland towards the end of her life, only the guaranteed dry, warm weather of the south of France gave her any sustained relief from her various ailments, and so it was there, in Nice, that she died in 1853. Although the duke was buried, along with so many of his ancestors and their wives, in the family mausoleum at Chenies Manor in Buckinghamshire, she did not join him. Whether this was her stated choice or whether his successor and his family did not extend an invitation for her to join him is not entirely clear. Instead, although her burial in the grounds of the English Church in Nice is recorded, the grave site, in a tidied up cemetery, is now lost.

Finally, Chapter 10 looks at the legacy of the lives of John Russell and Georgina Gordon, in the first case as individuals and in the second as the Duke and Duchess of Bedford. Their legacy as two individuals lies largely in their engagement with 'the dreaming inwardness of Romanticism', sharing that intuitive state of mind which embraced opportunities to experience the unfolding wonders of the natural world and a life spent as close to it as possible. This aspect of their lives is most clearly revealed in what they created at Endsleigh, where they deliberately avoided all the standard signs of 'civilized' taste by creating not a stately home but a rustic lodge, a setting that embraced and accessed the picturesque landscapes beyond the terraces rather than parterres and flower gardens.

This engagement is also seen in John Russell's growing desire to create at Woburn not just a fine showcase for the Russell family and what they represented, but also a 'meeting place of science and art' for himself and his friends, to participate not just as a patron but as an informed amateur in the discovery, classification, display and publicizing of the new discoveries, personally publishing at least eight beautifully produced catalogues of both plants and art. Equally, in his patronage of young British artists, actively supporting and encouraging careers such as Landseer's, Russell was interested also in the opportunities it gave him to participate in the processes of art, choosing subject matter, style, size and framing. And, above all perhaps, he wanted to see scientific botany and horticulture placed at the centre of the national agenda, to create a national garden that could be accessed by the public, and secure the future of grand collections that, unlike so many private collections (and indeed his own), could not be arbitrarily sold and dispersed, and could carry on the regular funding of plant collectors, bringing the world's treasures to these shores.

Georgina's legacy, however, is more difficult to define, largely because much less was written about her during her lifetime, but also because, apart from letters, she seems not to have kept diaries, notebooks or scrapbooks (unless they have been lost or destroyed). Her legacy, though, is very much alive today, and if it is not discernible from her own writings, it can be pieced together from the writing of others, in what draws people to her and their descriptions of what she left behind in Scotland and in Devon.

Georgina herself described the huts she had built in Glen Feshie and the glen itself: 'a little paradise there is in that lonely Glen, and I flatter myself that I improve it every year.'[8] Her life there, by reputation, clearly caught the imagination of many people. Take, for example, the following extract from Queen Victoria's journal, in which she describes a visit with Prince Albert to Glen Feshie in September 1860, to see the huts that had been the focal point in Georgina's life in Scotland seven years after her death: 'a most lovely spot – the scene of all Landseer's glory – and where there is a little encampment of wooden and turf huts, built by the late Duchess of Bedford; now no longer belonging to the family, and alas!, all falling into decay – among splendid fir-trees, the mountains rising abruptly from the side of the valley. We were quite enchanted with the beauty of the spot.' Indeed, they were so enchanted that they returned again a year later: 'The huts, surrounded by magnificent fir-trees, and by quantities of juniper bushes, looked lovelier than ever, and we gazed with sorrow at their utter ruin. I felt what a delightful little encampment it must have been, and how enchanting to live in such a spot as this beautiful solitary wood, in a glen surrounded by high hills. We got off, and went into one of the huts to look at a fresco of stags of Landseer's, over a chimney-piece. Grant on a pony led me through the Fishie.'[9]

To some extent the royal family were following in the steps of the Bedfords as they created a place for themselves in Scotland at Balmoral; it is clear that the queen knew all about what Georgina had created during her years in Scotland, and – sharing her delight in the romance of experiencing the Highland landscapes – perhaps also understood why. She knew all about Landseer's relationship with Georgina and the impact the Highlands had had on his work, and having met the artist in 1837, the royal couple commissioned a succession of paintings from 1842 onwards.

Equally, the power of Georgina's other great legacy, the house and grounds at Endsleigh, is apparent in the comments of any number of visitors there, including Victoria herself. When she arrived in 1856, the queen wrote: 'Endsleigh is approached by a pretty lodge and avenue of Evergreens, and suddenly a most magnificent and extensive view opens up before one – a perfect basin of woods, closed in by wooded hills,' and what she saw retained its impact in the twenty-first century:

> Visiting Endsleigh for the first time, I found myself caught in a seamless web of past and present. As we drove past the ornate gatehouse down the long, heavily wooded drive to [the house,] it was as if the years had fallen away and I had travelled back almost two hundred years … Wandering around the gardens … I realised this was a very special, secret place. I had never experienced anything like it before, where the past was so palpable; I was enchanted and I wanted to know more about Georgina, Duchess of Bedford, the inspiration behind this magical house and gardens.

This is from the Introduction to Rachel Trethewey's biography of Georgina, *Mistress of the Arts*, and conveys vividly the impact that her legacy can still have. Trethewey goes on to explain that this visit convinced her to write the book: 'Once away from the house, Georgina's spell remained unbroken. I felt that a woman with such a powerful, creative spirit must have lived an extraordinary life, and I wanted to know more about her.'[10] A similar experience of Endsleigh was also the catalyst for the present book.

In the second case, their legacy as the Duke and Duchess of Bedford is most clear at Woburn Abbey. Here, completing the work started by the duke's grandfather and brother, they were responsible for creating the grandest set of buildings, the most complete pleasure grounds and flower gardens, the most elaborate infrastructure of roads and walks in the park, and the most diverse and interesting attractions in every corner of the park for the family and visitors to enjoy. It was their vision, taste, energy and willingness to spend money that created the Abbey and grounds seen by Victoria and Albert during their four-day visit in 1841. They were suitably impressed.

The intervening years, for different reasons, took their toll on their achievements, in particular the years during which the Abbey, gardens and park were requisitioned by the secret services, and then the army and air ministry during the run-up to D-Day, during the Second World War. Much remains, however, of their legacy, particularly since the recent programme of garden restorations, bringing back many of the features created for the 6th Duke by Humphry Repton, and the refurbishment of the displays within the house which will feature a number of the historic room arrangements from John and Georgina's time.

In trying to understand how and why this legacy came about, we turn first to look at who these two individuals were, but it should be noted that in the late eighteenth and early nineteenth centuries the spelling and punctuation of English had not been codified the way it is today. Depending on who is writing, both of these elements can vary widely, sometimes within the same letter. On occasions, the lack of basic punctuation makes letters very hard to follow, and so, in an attempt to clarify things, the punctuation in the quotations used has been modernized where possible. In terms of spelling, however, where the meaning of a word is still clear, the original spellings have been left in order to give a sense of the period. A typical example is the word 'Duchess', which can appear in this spelling or as 'Dutchess'.

PART ONE
Lord John Russell

After Sir Joshua Reynolds, *His Grace, the Duke of Bedford, with his Brothers Lord John Russell, Lord William Russell and Miss Caroline Vernon*, 1778.

CHAPTER ONE
1766–1786

I N 1770, three young boys, Chuff, little Johnny and baby William, went to live permanently at Woburn Abbey with their grandparents, John Russell, 4th Duke of Bedford, and Gertrude, Duchess of Bedford; the move marked the end of a period of crisis, illness and death which had so far dominated the boys' short lives. Lord Francis Russell, known as Chuff, was the eldest at five years old; Lord John Russell, or little Johnny, was a year younger, while Lord William Russell was three. It had been a very difficult period for everyone – grandparents, family and friends – watching as a marriage of such promise was devastated, first by the death of the boys' father, Francis Russell, Marquis of Tavistock, in March 1767, then in April 1768 by the arrival of smallpox among the children, and later that year by the steady deterioration of the health of their mother, Lady Elizabeth Keppel, Marchioness of Tavistock, her eventual departure in October for Portugal in the hope the warm, dry weather would help her, and her death there in November 1768.

Since neither of them referred to it again, it is difficult to say just how much Francis and John would have remembered of these early years, or their parents, or the family home at Houghton House, some six miles from Woburn Abbey. William, who was born five months after the hunting accident which killed his father, will have remembered even less, since he never knew his father, his mother had left for Portugal when he was just over a year old, and he never lived at the family home. Houghton House was a substantial structure, originally a seventeenth-century red brick hunting lodge that had steadily been enlarged, and by the time the Duke of Bedford bought it in 1738, Italianate loggias and classical doorways had been inserted between the twin-spired corner towers of old Jacobean facades. If the

W. Kimpton, Houghton House, south front, 1788.

older boys did remember Houghton, it is likely to have been for its fairy-tale appearance, its spectacular setting on the edge of Bedfordshire's greensand ridge, the views stretching away to the north, and, in the grounds, all the excitement and bustle associated with their father's passion for hunting.

Francis Russell (1739–1767), Marquis of Tavistock,[11] who was just twenty-eight when he died, left little behind to indicate what he might have achieved had he lived to become the 5th Duke of Bedford. He was, however, by his own account prone to sudden, all encompassing, enthusiasms, the first of which was a great passion for the army. After leaving Cambridge in 1760, Tavistock signed up with the Bedfordshire Militia, and told his parents that he had a 'rage for everything that has a connection for military life … I am more militia mad than ever.' His second great passion was for fox hunting, and following his marriage to Elizabeth Keppel (1739–1768) in 1764, and once settled at Houghton, he declared himself now 'mad' for hunting, something he pursued at every opportunity after co-founding the Dunstable Hunt.[12] Whether he would have continued with this interest to the same extent in later life is uncertain,

Houghton House today, the roofless ruins overlooking the spectacular view of Bedfordshire.

but there are indications that even before his passions for the military and hunting, he had become interested in collaborating with his father on the architectural and landscaping projects that the latter was undertaking at Woburn Abbey.

At the time, Tavistock did not pursue this interest further, but it appears to have developed rapidly during his subsequent two-year Grand Tour of Italy between 1761 and 1763. He had left Cambridge and attained his majority and was now encouraged to travel to complete his education, and although he did not react to Italy with the same immediate 'mad' passion he had shown for the military, it does seem that the experience engaged his imagination at a more fundamental level. While in Rome he reported that he felt 'an awakening interest in art and architecture', and fortunately for us, following the fashion of the day, he commissioned a portrait of himself in Rome by Pompeo Batoni (Colour Plate 1).[13] Completed in 1762, Batoni's portrait is in some ways typical of any number he completed for young English tourists commemorating their visits, particularly the smart clothes and the heroic pose set against the ruins of Rome. In this sense, Russell's portrait was very much a typical Batoni image, but beyond Batoni's trademark content and style, we do catch a glimpse of Russell's growing interest.

Although the background and setting of the painting is similar to many of the others, with the ruins of the Coliseum filling the background, the statue of the goddess Roma (the personification of the city of Rome) and the tree branches hanging down on the upper right, there are also subtle differences. Compared to other subjects, although he is smartly dressed in a new red jacket and breeches, the Tavistock portrait is far less flamboyant in dress and pose, and it seems to try to integrate him into the scene rather than simply pausing to pose in front of it. Rather than being placed in the background, the statue of Roma is part of the central composition with Tavistock: his hand and cane are resting on the plinth, and fallen pieces of the classical masonry surround his feet. The items are highlighted as part of the painting rather than simply as incidental, background props. Tavistock's picture is more subdued and he appears more serious about his interest in Rome, and certainly, once home, he began to work with his father on significant new features in the park at Woburn, designs influenced by his interest in Italian architecture and his travels. In fact, as early as 1756, the duke notes that he is implementing Tavistock's design for an 'Arch' at the Bason Pond. This arch with a cascade emerging beneath it appears to have been located at the head of the duke's New Pond, and to have been designed to be seen from the new approach road to the Abbey as it passed over a bridge beside the Bason Pond. Much of what the structure may have consisted of is now under water, lost when Humphry Repton subsequently raised the water level, so we do not know exactly what Tavistock's design looked like, but the surviving arch perhaps indicates the direction he would have taken the development of the house, grounds and gardens had he not died so young.[14]

Following the example of his father, who was the leader of the Bedford faction of the Whig party in Parliament, Tavistock initially committed himself to an active political career, sitting for the constituency of Armagh in the Irish House of Commons between 1759 and 1761, before standing for the Russell interest in Bedfordshire in 1762. It would seem, however, that in spite of his father's activities and holding various government posts as Lord Lieutenant of Ireland and then as

Lord President of the Council, Tavistock had little time for the business of politics, as is suggested in correspondence with his relative and neighbour, Lord Ossory. In one letter he seems to hint that he would leave politics as soon as possible: 'I am not quite in good humour with London, and what is called the world, but I am extremely so with myself and all those whom I love and esteem. I own fairly that parliament and politics help to make me dislike it; but the former I only wait to get rid of till you are of age, and can succeed me in the county.' He did not in fact resign at this time, retaining his Bedfordshire seat until his death, but he was clearly happier away from both Parliament and London, occupying himself with his country pursuits, as the beginning of this letter makes clear:

> I long to hasten to Italy (in idea only I mean); for I amuse myself extremely in thinking over all the fine things there, and doubly so when I can communicate those thoughts to you who are on the spot … As to home news, I am too much a country gentleman to know any out of Bedfordshire: my house in Houghton takes up most of my attention; … the outside will be beautiful; and the farm (which I am going to take into my own hands) will, I think, make my principal amusement. I don't mean absolutely to bury myself in the country, but I am not quite in humour with London.[15]

The *Biographical Catalogue of the Pictures at Woburn Abbey* compiled by Adeline Marie Tavistock and Ela M. S. Russell in 1890 tells us that the marriage to Lady Elizabeth was one of 'unclouded happiness', and, certainly, as the couple settled down to life at Houghton everything seemed set fair (Colour Plate 2).[16] The son and heir, Francis, was born the next year, and Tavistock was busy organizing his own estate, its farm and parkland at Houghton, helping his father with developments at Woburn and hunting as much as possible. The second son, Lord John, was born in 1766, and Elizabeth was pregnant again when in March 1767 suddenly tragedy struck. Horace Walpole reported what happened: 'Lord Tavistock, the Duke of Bedford's only son, has killed himself by a fall and a kick from his horse as he was hunting … No man was ever more regretted … The news came about 2 hours before Lady

Tavistock was to go to the Opera: they did not dare tell her the worst so abruptly so the Duke and Duchess were forced to go too, to conceal it from her.'[17]

It was Tavistock's parents, the Duke and Duchess of Bedford, who had to break the news to Elizabeth, and she seems never to have recovered from the shock. Heavily pregnant and distraught by her husband's death, Elizabeth was persuaded to leave Houghton and go with the children to live with her in-laws at Bedford House in London to have the baby. Lord William was duly born that August, but his mother's health rapidly declined. Up to the time of William's birth she had struggled on, but from that time, although the nature of her complaint was still unclear, it became apparent that she was very unwell. Over that winter, life at Bedford House must have been very difficult, and was further complicated by the duke's own worsening health. He had recently undergone surgery to remove cataracts from both eyes, and his gout had become so severe that in 1768 his doctors suggested he visit Bath for a few months to take the waters. He left in April and was to stay until August, but in his absence the duchess had yet another emergency to deal with when the baby William contracted smallpox.

Letters from those at Bedford House to the duke in Bath kept him updated. The first from Elizabeth Wrottesley, Gertrude's niece, on 16 April 1768 tells him that 'The eldest little Boy is quite well, but Lord William has got the small-pox with the most favourable symptoms,' before the duchess writes on 19 April: 'The little William goes on as well as possible and Johnny has no appearance of illness. Chuff coloured for joy when he saw his little brother, and said now Lord Johnny will come, Lady Tavistock's cold is much better … I have just had a visit from Chuff and his mother, he is more delightful than ever.'

This is followed a few days later by a letter from Elizabeth in which she tells the duke that 'the oldest is thank God as well as ever, quite the good-humoured little Angel he always was, and my pretty little William goes on as well as possible, he has suffered from being full and very sore, and now I hope he will very soon get quite well.' Little Johnny, however, 'has hitherto escaped it', and Elizabeth goes on: 'I flatter myself, as I ever wish to meet with your approbation in any steps I take, particularly regarding my sweet Children, that you will not disapprove of my having determined to inoculate him. The physical people have no objection to it, I really think it is my duty, seeing how much slighter and easier the distemper is from inoculation. It will be done tomorrow. The infection is to be taken from William.'[18]

By the 25th, the inoculation has been carried out and little Johnny has been quarantined at Bedford House, while Elizabeth and the other two are taken off to her sister Caroline's house at Chalk Farm. Elizabeth Wrottesley writes again to the duke from Bedford House where they are keeping an eye on little Johnny:

> Dear Duke of Bedford,
>
> I return you a thousand thanks for your very gallant letter … Lady Tavistock is very well and all her children. We have got little Johnny still at Bedford House, and he is to stay till the small-pox comes out. His elder brother came to see him yesterday and they were both delighted to see one another. The Duchess and I were at Court yesterday morning and were as usual very graciously received. Both their Majesties enquired very much about your Grace.[19]

By August, however, there is renewed concern for Elizabeth, and the duchess reports to the duke that 'I was in hopes by staying in London last night to have had more intelligences of poor Lady Tavistock's health but Miss W[rottesley]'s account is as confused as Lady Albemarle's the night before. So far it is certain that her condition is very dangerous, but I hope not desperate, they will none of them speak until they have seen more of her.' Soon afterwards the duke's political agent and family friend, Richard Rigby, writes on 4 August:

> I went to see Lady Tavistock yesterday at her sister's … and was very sorry to find her so much out of order that she could not see me … I have been again this morning and sat an hour with her. She had a very good night and was a great deal better … Her spirits are pretty good this morning and she has promised me and her brother and sister to follow implicitly whatever the Physical people shall direct … I have heard no mention of Lisbon, but a hint in your letter but that Climate recovered her brother William.

When the doctors came to examine Elizabeth again, she was found to be clasping a miniature of her husband that she said she had 'kept in my bosom or my hand ever since [his death] and thus I must indeed continue to retain it till I drop after him into a welcome grave'. The doctors had confirmed that by now she was dying of consumption, and commented that prescriptions would be useless 'while sorrow wasted her thus', and Rigby tells the duke, 'Poor Lady Tavistock is not long for this world.' Finally, 'As a last hope, a voyage to Lisbon was agreed upon, and her brother Captain Keppel and her sister Lady Caroline Adair, conveyed her there in a frigate, but she survived the voyage only a few days and died in November, 1768.' In a further tragedy, her sister, Lady Caroline, 'contracted the same fatal disease' and died a year later.[20]

How much of all of this the boys were aware of when they finally arrived at Woburn Abbey in 1770 is not clear. Although the duke in particular was not in very good health, the atmosphere at Woburn must have been so different, particularly since life there was enlivened by a number of the duchess's young nieces who had become part of the family. In 1763 she had been made guardian of the children of her two sisters, Lady Evelyn Fitzpatrick and Lady Mary Wrottesley. By her first marriage to John Fitzpatrick, Lady Evelyn had two daughters, Mary and Louisa, and by her second to Richard Vernon, three: Henrietta, Caroline Maria and Elizabeth. In 1764, following the death of their mother, Lady Evelyn's daughters had arrived, and then, five years later, in 1769, following the death of their father, Sir Richard Wrottesley, Lady Mary's daughters arrived: Mary, Elizabeth ('Bessy') and Harriet. With the exception of Mary, who remained with the Russells until her early death, the girls all left when they got married, but seem to have remained close to the duke and duchess.[21]

Thus, in 1770, when the boys arrived, for the first time in two years in a 'comfortable place', they were surrounded by doting cousins, and a year or so of peace for everyone ensued. Throughout this period the duke had been engaged in developments centred on the Abbey itself, the park and plantations, the gardens round the house, and the pleasure grounds to the east. In the first place, working with the architect Henry Flitcroft, they substantially rebuilt the west wing with its grand entrance and state rooms, and then added two courts to the east: the south court, consisting of offices and carriage houses, and the north court, with stables, a laundry and accommodation, and crucially, for the first time, they laid these new structures out in a symmetrical relationship with the Abbey: the two courts set equidistant from a central axial line that ran down the Great Avenue from the west, through the centre of the new west wing and out to the limits of the pleasure grounds beyond. This line became the focal points for the garden features added later by the boys, Francis and John, as 5th and 6th Dukes of Bedford.

Alongside this work, undertaken between 1738 and 1758, the 4th Duke also initiated a major new feature in the north-west corner of the park, where a wide ride was laid out between plantations of evergreen trees, running from Crawley Gate, round through the Dean Hills and down the side of the park below the slopes of the old warren and past Drakelow Pond. Created from 1743 to commemorate the birth of the duke's daughter Caroline and known as the 'Evergreen Ride', it was then, as 'The Evergreens', greatly enlarged by both the 5th and 6th Dukes, and remains a major feature of the park today. In addition to this, the duke developed the pleasure grounds, with temples, seats, nine-pin bowling, greenhouses, flowers gardens and a small menagerie, and also, just outside the pleasure ground's fences, created two large 'shrubberies'. Known as 'Parson's Wood' and 'Somerley Grove', they were areas of the park that were fenced off to keep the deer out, and the pre-existing grand old oak trees were underplanted with flowering shrubs and trees over which honeysuckles were encouraged to spread alongside the serpentine paths. Additional interest was added to Parson's Wood when a decorative 'Temple' was built, with chairs, tables and beds – everything the family would need for an overnight stay (Map 3).

In August 1770, the duke reports that 'My grand-children came to live with us' and by this time the gardens and park were full of interesting places; the duchess tells him that 'in hot weather [she and the children] have breakfasted upon the pavement', but unfortunately recently 'the weather is really cold which is a great misfortune to my little companions and me, for we have lived out of doors and not found the hay too long.' Indeed, the duchess, while seeming to enjoy the company of the little boys, also gave them considerable freedom to roam and explore, and her remarks offer a glimpse of the boys' upbringing. We can imagine them setting out for the temple in Parson's Wood to spend a day, playing among the honeysuckles and sweet briars of the ornamental woodland, riding in a carriage with their grandmother through the long grass of summer, along the open spaces of the park or round through the dark woodland of the Evergreens, taking a boat trip on Drakelow Pond. Living out of doors also meant accidents, as the duke noted in his Memorandum Book, 'My little grandson John fell from the swing and broke his arm; a simple fracture, which was immediately set by Mr Stubbs, and is in a fair way.'[22]

Suitably, perhaps, the one image we have of the three boys around this time shows them at play out in the park, entertaining their cousin Caroline Vernon. Certainly, both of the older boys as adults had a very close connection with Woburn and were dedicated to building on the legacy of their grandfather.

Just as the boys' life was starting to settle down, however, they suffered another severe loss when, following a stroke the year before which had left him partially paralysed, the duke died in 1771. Outliving her husband by some twenty years, their grandmother Gertrude, working with the other trustees of the Russell Estate − Caroline Russell, Duchess of Marlborough, Anne (Lennox) Keppel, Lady Albemarle and Robert Palmer, the duke's agent − took on the responsibility of looking after the three little boys, but it was their grandmother who played the central role in their lives. In the duke's will she was appointed guardian of Woburn Abbey and Bedford House, and the related estates, until Lord Francis reached his majority and and took control of his inheritance in 1786. There is no doubt that, given the circumstances and the make-up of the trustees, one thing that the boys lacked from this time on was an adult male role model they could turn to, both as individuals and, particularly for Francis, in terms of watching and learning about the roles that he now had to play.

The one figure of authority they did have to deal with was Robert Palmer, who had day-to-day responsibility for running the estates, and whom Gertrude used as her contact point with the boys once they left the Abbey. This placed Palmer in a difficult position, being an employee rather than a member of the family, since he was required not only to control the boys' expenditure as they grew older and attended university, but also to pass on their grandmother's wishes, remonstrations and advice. He became effectively a mentor for the boys, which did not always make him popular. Summing up Palmer's unique position in the family, Scott Thomson writes that his role 'combined the offices of Trustee and that of Agent-in-chief and … as such, he had somewhat overstepped the mark in the opinion of the 5th Duke and his brothers,' concluding: 'no one was ever given the position and supreme authority Palmer had enjoyed again.'

Scott Thomson undertook extensive research in the archives for her account of the 5th Duke's life and Gertrude's trusteeship, trying to uncover the story of this period, but concluded: 'Very little has appeared of how life went at the Abbey in these years. Even the accounts which Gertrude must have kept, or were kept for her, have disappeared.' As a result, until the boys started writing to each other in the 1780s, we hear almost nothing about their grandfather or grandmother, and the correspondence that has survived between these two is consistently impersonal and rather formal; the duchess's letters to the duke, for example, while headed 'My dear Love', were otherwise largely businesslike, giving nothing away about their relationship.[23] Thus, it is only through the writings of others that we are able to catch a glimpse of the kind of people the 4th Duke and Duchess were.

The historian John Langton Sanford, for example, tells us: 'It would seem that the duke was a man of some ability and considerable powers of application to business, though he often neglected it, owing, he himself said, to his natural indolence, but seemingly because he preferred country life at Woburn; so that, as far as his own advancement was concerned, his temperament was stronger than his personal ambition, and led him to be inclined to refuse rather than seek office.' In the *Biographical Catalogue* the authors add: 'He delighted in the amusements of country-life, especially in cricket and theatricals. He almost entirely rebuilt Woburn Abbey on a plan of great extent, formed there a large gallery of historical portraits, and delighted in laying out anew the plantations at Woburn'; they also tell us in turn that Gertrude was a 'shrewd and able woman'. Horace Walpole, however, had a slightly different take, noting that 'the warm little Duke' was 'always governed – generally by the Duchess; though immeasurably obstinate when once he had formed or had an opinion instilled into him', confirming in part Gertrude's reputation as a 'hard woman', a no-nonsense person, 'a woman of iron will, great ambition, and singular capacity', and for whom 'the atmosphere of politics, or rather of factions, was her native element.'[24]

Although Gertrude 'resided usually at Bath in the late summer and autumn', she also 'entered the political and social life of the day with great zest', and at Woburn 'she held perpetual court', with large numbers of people coming to stay. The *Biographical Catalogue* states, 'The bitter political animosities of the day [especially between Bedford and Bute] were intensified by the part she took in them, and there is little trace, beyond that of her complete identification with her husband's interests, of a more amiable side to her character,' and suggests that only the death of the Marquis of Tavistock seems to have deeply affected her.[25]

Scott Thomson, in turn, writes that Gertrude was 'a personality and it must be admitted a personality that aroused dislike', and she quotes various commentators to this effect. Mrs Delany, for example, who met the Bedfords at Dublin Castle, wrote that Gertrude was 'very stately in her drawing room but also very condescending'; Lord Charlmont called her 'artful and dangerous' in his *Memoirs*, while the *Whig Club* considered her 'stingy and avaricious'.[26] One thing everyone seemed to agree on, however, was that Gertrude loved to play and wager on card games and was a renowned whist player, usually for money. There seems little doubt, though, that while the children seem to have enjoyed a close relationship with Gertrude when young, as they grew older, resentment of her control of their lives and money, and her treatment of them, grew steadily, to the extent that by the time of the duke's majority, both he and Lord John were ready to openly defy her. Scott Thomson writes, 'There is little to contradict the unpleasing and malicious estimates of the Duchess,' and considers that by this time the relationship with the boys had become openly hostile. She notes: 'Family tradition says that the devotion that the three orphaned boys were to display one to another was in part founded on detestation of the grandmother under whose rule they were for so many years.'[27]

It was evidently a very complex situation, and it seems that, Gertrude's character aside, there were specific aspects of her actions which the boys came to view with growing resentment. Evidence for this spilled out in a letter written by Lord John following his brother's death in 1802, in which he defends his brother's actions as duke, placing much of the blame for any shortcomings he may have had on their upbringing at Woburn, largely under Gertrude's care. Writing to his old friend Francis Randolph, Bishop of Bristol, after the funeral, Lord John, now the 6th Duke of Bedford, says:

> I cannot any longer delay in answering that part of your letter, which so nearly concerns the character of my regretted Brother. You say you have heard much talk of his want of religious sentiments. The charge is a serious one, and I am proud to add an unmerited one. The statement shall be short, and I hope satisfactory – He, as well as myself, laboured under all the disadvantages of a mistaken education. We went to Church every Sunday, it is true, but we were not instructed as to the motives or causes of such attendance. We regarded it as a compliance with custom and nothing more.
>
> We both left Westminster School very early, he went to Cambridge, and by an ill-judged kindness was encouraged to attend Newmarket, Brooke's &c. &c. and to enter into all the follies and dissipation of worldly amusement. I was sent to Germany, and you found me at Gottingen my own master, and not sixteen years of age.

He goes on to note that in his estimation, in the case of his brother Francis, his 'mind was gradually rising superior to the disadvantages of Education, and I have only to lament that he was not more constant in his attendance here on divine Worship.'[28]

The letter makes clear that the new duke was very touchy about criticism, particularly of his late brother, which he feels unjust, since as far as he is concerned they were the victims of 'a mistaken education', not just in spiritual matters but also in terms of a proper scholastic education, and one senses that they felt the dowager duchess had always been more interested in cards and her social life than them. There is certainly no doubt that this feeling of a lack of proper education stayed with the duke for the rest of his life, during which he suffered a sense of inadequacy – 'my weak nature' as he once referred to it – and a lack of confidence in his own judgement. Alongside his naturally shy nature, he never developed a protective sense of self-confidence, remaining easily hurt by criticism, partly because he seems to have felt it might be justified.

Although by the time he reached his majority and succeeded as duke, Lord Francis had 'acquired social assurance', Scott Thomson notes that 'with that assurance went a certain oddness, an abruptness of manner' which many saw as rudeness.[29] This may well have been his way of covering deeper insecurities, but Lord John, on the other hand, coped by projecting a sociable, self-depreciating and noticeably deferential approach to people, even to those who, like himself, were largely self-taught (as were many of the most brilliant people of his time), while William, as we shall see, seems never to have been able to shoulder the responsibilities of adulthood, let alone parenthood, and to have drifted off into his own strange, rootless, internal world. All three were clearly damaged to some extent by the circumstances of their childhood, and however much Gertrude may have tried, she does not appear to have been able to provide much emotional support or, it would seem, a satisfactory education.

It is not just Lord John who referred to this circumstance. In 1786, the 5th Duke of Bedford came of age and entered the House of Lords (Colour Plate 3), and when he first rose to speak, 'it was commonly said that even as, for all his social assurance, his manner in private life was still too often abrupt and awkward, so was his style when he spoke in public, a defect attributed to neglect of having profited by the education' he had been provided; he also 'admitted he had not used his opportunities as he might have done'. Lord Holland went further, claiming that the duke was prone always 'to treat the understandings of his adversaries with contempt, and the decision and even the good will of the audience which he addressed with utter indifference'.[30]

To understand what happened here a little better, it is interesting to look more closely at exactly what kind of education Gertrude and Palmer did arrange for the boys. It is possible that it was limited to private tutors, and little else, after they first moved to Woburn if one is to understand this newspaper report correctly: 'The Duke of Bedford and Lord John Russell – boarded with Dr Smith, and had Beresford as a home tutor. It is not even known how much they have to boast of in the Duke!' Following the death of their grandfather in 1771, however, it seems that as each one reached the age of six, they were successively enrolled at a boarding school known as Loughborough House, in Lambeth Wick, south-west London, where they stayed until moving to Westminster School. From Westminster all three then went to a different university. Although none of them left any record of their schools and universities, it is possible to give some account of Loughborough House thanks to a memoir written by one of their fellow schoolboys, Sir John Stanley.[31]

Described as 'a superior academy for young gentlemen', it seems the boys were taught the basics of Latin, history, geography and English. Stanley tells us:

> The House was let by Lord Holland a few years before I went there [1774] to a French Protestant Clergyman, M. Perney, who had recently come to England … [He] was appointed one of the preachers of the chapel near St. James's Palace, and was induced to attempt to establish a school for very young children on a scale of show and expense exceeding any others then existing. The occupation of a nobleman's villa, for the purpose, the purchase of a service of plate for the use of the scholars, the providing beds for each of them separately, with the conversion of an extensive walled garden into a playground had their effect, and he soon had 80 or 90 boys of the higher classes of society placed under his care [a year's board and tuition was £52].

Stanley goes on: 'The playground retained the vines and fruit trees which had been planted along the walls, and it was singular proof of the good discipline in which the boys were kept that grapes, apricots, peaches, and cherries were allowed to remain un-gathered, … and Rose trees, which had grown to the size of large bushes, blossomed unmolested.' He then lists among his 'school fellows … the

Duke of Bedford and his brothers – Lords John and William Russell', confirming that all three did attend the school. Stanley continues:

> Before I left Loughborough House I had got through the Latin Grammar, and had translated and learned by heart part of Ovid. I had picked up a little French, and drew tolerably for my age. M. Perney left it to his ushers to make religion a part of education if they pleased. I remember [my teacher] Rev Mr Reynolds Davies often speaking to us of God as a Being who saw everything everywhere, but more as One who was watching to see our faults than to guide us to good and protect us from evil. It is possible that, fear being a passion, more easy to excite than love … Mr Davies succeeded in making us tell fewer lies, and keep our hands off M. Perney's fruit.

Stanley's comments on his religious education are particularly interesting considering the Duke of Bedford's comments in the letter to Randolph quoted above, but his description below of his 'fellow-prisoners' and his comparison of the teaching at Loughborough with his next school are, perhaps, most telling:

> The confinement within walls in which I spent so much of my early years was perhaps rather a stimulant than otherwise of my love of nature. I know every flower that blossomed in our playground, and the impression they made on me was so strong that I have them all now before me each in their respective place. Whenever I see polyanthus, crocuses, snowdrops, wall-flowers, lilies, the fellows of my old fellow-prisoners, I think of Loughborough House … The boys were seldom allowed to take walks in the country.

Overall, Stanley's short account does not suggest that Loughborough house was a very positive experience, and he seems to confirm this when he tells us: 'I was sent to Mr James's school in Greenwich after the Christmas holidays in 1777. Mr Jones was a scholar, and so far was a better master than M. Perney' – and, presumably, than the Revd Reynolds Davies and, almost certainly, than the ushers.

For the Russell brothers, arriving in 1771, 1772 and 1773, one suspects that the strange world of Loughborough House to which they were suddenly exiled must have come as something of a shock. Given the access they had had to the gardens, pleasure grounds, shrubberies, park and rides at Woburn, the lack of walks in the country and the confines of the walled playground must have been very hard, not to mention being suddenly wrenched from the privilege and security of the Abbey and the gentle company of their indulgent cousins. While Stanley goes on to relate some of the teasing inflicted on him by fellow pupils, he does not mention either bullying or the specifics of the 'good discipline in which the boys were kept', both of which would have made up so much of the boys' experiences. There must have been many occasions over the years at Loughborough House when having your own bed, a service of plate and access to a playground did little to compensate for the sense that they had been dumped, conveniently out of the way. Later in life the duke showed a keen interest in improving the kind of education children received at this early age, supporting in particular the reformer Joseph Lancaster, an interest that may well have stemmed from his experience at Loughborough House.

From Loughborough House all three boys went on to Westminster School, Francis in 1774 aged nine, John in 1776 aged ten, and William in 1778 aged eleven. While Loughborough may have been chosen by Gertrude or Palmer, the boys were always destined for Westminster, it being the family choice of school since the 1st Duke's time. It is not clear why William spent five years at Loughborough, but it may suggest that it took him a little longer than everyone else to learn his Latin grammar and Ovid by heart. Unfortunately, there are no references to their careers at Westminster, but Francis's remark when he was twenty-four, that he had never read a book, tells us something about both schools, and with the exception of William, who seems to have done well, Francis and John needed constant encouragement from Palmer to concentrate harder on their studies once at university.

Looking back on his education in 1828, Lord John had formed some very definite opinions. Writing to his daughter-in-law on the subject of her son Hasting's education, he wrote that, given 'the difficulties [of] what to do with him when he should be removed from under your immediate eye – my own opinion is in favour of a *small* private [school] in a healthy situation by the seaside – a private tutor at home is a great hazard,' but that, given Hasting's 'delicate constitution', perhaps he should 'wait until nine'. After that, although he clearly dislikes them intensely, he feels obliged to recommend a public school: 'A public school in England is one of the greatest evils I know of, but I fear in some respects it is a necessary evil, with our habits of public life, our free Constitution and the habitual intercourse of men of all professions.'[32] Perhaps, like Stanley, there had been things about Loughborough House he had liked, but, also like Stanley, the sense of confinement actually served to stimulate his love of nature, which came to dominate John's adult life.

Whatever the boys thought of their guardians' choice of school and although at the time they resented the restrictions placed on them, there was little reason for complaint about the way in which the duchess and Palmer had managed the estate finances throughout the duke's minority. Indeed, with careful budgeting, shrewd investment and careful development of the Bloomsbury Estate, Gertrude was able to leave the 5th Duke an estate in outstanding financial condition. As Scott Thomson notes, 'at no time did the thrifty trustees, even when subject to pressure from the young men as they began to grow up, spend anything like the total income they had to handle; an income from the estates that normally fluctuated on an average, between £28,000 and something over £30,000 a year [*c*.£1,800,000].' She adds: 'It is to the credit of the dowager that there is no sign whatsoever that she ever exceeded her allowance or demanded that it should be raised.'[33]

Besides Gertrude's fixed allowance of £3,500 a year for the upkeep of the house and gardens at Woburn Abbey and Bedford House, the 4th Duke's will provided her with £350 a year for personal use. Francis was given an allowance of £200–£300 once at school, while John and William received £150–£200. It was these modest and tightly controlled allowances that became a major source of friction between their guardians and the boys as they grew older. Circumstances changed for the younger brothers once Francis became duke, and we can get a better picture of what they had at their disposal from Palmer's letter to the duke about his brothers' allowances in June 1785 in which he writes: 'I received your Grace's letter in which you are so good as to say you would allow each of your brothers £400 to be added to the £400 a year each is to have under his late Grace's Will.' Palmer was optimistic that this should be sufficient for their needs and tells them so, but both of them immediately overspent regularly, requiring additional requests for money which were usually indulged.[34]

Francis was the first to move on to university when he followed his father to Trinity College, Cambridge, aged just sixteen, in 1780. Alerted by his own comment the he had never read a book and Lord John's remark that, once there, his brother 'by an ill-judged kindness was encouraged to attend Newmarket, Brooke's &c. &c.', we see him, increasingly free from the control of his guardians and never under that of his tutors, start to pursue his own interests rather than academic study. Perhaps inevitably, given the proximity of Newmarket, it was horse racing and the fast-paced, thrilling world of winners and wagers, trainers and tipsters that claimed his interest, and a key influence on his life at this time was the 'father of the turf' Richard Vernon, his grandmother's brother-in-law and father of his cousins Henrietta, Caroline and Elizabeth.

Due to his connections by marriage to Lady Evelyn Fitzgerald, Vernon had been a close political associate of Francis's grandfather, sitting in Parliament in the Bedford interest for Tavistock (1754) and Bedford (1764), and serving as his private secretary when the 4th Duke was appointed Lord Lieutenant of Ireland (1757–61). He was, however, best known for his activities in the Jockey Club at Newmarket. Walpole described him as 'a very inoffensive, good-humoured young fellow, who lives in the strongest intimacy with all the fashionable young men', among whom was the young duke newly freed from boarding school and ready for some adventures. After having moved to Newmarket in mid-1750, by means of betting and breeding horses Vernon is stated to have converted a 'slender patrimony of three thousand pounds into a fortune of a hundred thousand' before quitting the turf as an owner. He was 'one of the original members of the Jockey Club', who were his tenants 'at the old coffee-room at Newmarket', and went on to have considerable success with his horses.[35] It was the duke's first real introduction to fashionable society and he rapidly became a popular participant in

Vernon's heady world of excitement and fast money. In fact, horses, whether racers or hunters, became a life-long interest, and he went on to establish his own stud at Woburn breeding and racing horses with some success, while also founding the Oakley Hunt and building substantial kennels at Woburn to pursue his growing interest in hunting.

Given these circumstances it is perhaps inevitable that most of the letters we see passing between the duke and Palmer during his time at Cambridge concern the latter's dismay at the duke's expenditure rather than encouraging him to pursue his studies:

> I must desire you will speedily make a payment to Mssrs Child & Co. on account of the balance ... that ought to have been paid long since. Also I do desire that you will send your accounts. There is no Steward employed in the Duke of Bedford's affairs in arrears like as yourself ...
>
> I have sent your Grace £420 in Notes ... Permit me to desire your Grace to recollect the several sums you have received since Midsummer, and to request you to reflect if it is proper or fitting for you in your 18th year, or even at any time during your minority, to spend so much Money; I beg leave to appeal to your own good understanding; I fear you are imposed upon by experienced artful Men.
>
> I lay before your Grace the inclosed account that you may see the sums of Money you have had for your Pocket Expenses ... they amount to a sum (I believe) much larger than you would imagine ... I hope you will reflect on the Largeness of the sum and consider whether it is not too much for your Grace to spend. Your expenses last year are larger, and amount to about £4500.[36]

In the event, in spite of Palmer's regular remonstrations about expenditure, the money was always found to cover his debts, but the duke, and later his brothers for similar reasons, began increasingly to resent what they saw as unnecessary restrictions imposed on them financially, the constant criticism of the friends they were making and the interests they chose to pursue. From the start, they saw their grandmother's hand at work behind Palmer's actions, and the relationship between them steadily soured during these years.

Just two years after his brother went up to Cambridge, it was Lord John's turn to pursue his further education, and so it was that in January 1782 he enrolled at Göttingen University in southern Germany. In 1734, George II, when he was Elector of Hanover, founded a major new library at Göttingen, and three years later a new university was established in association with it. One of the key elements of the new university was that it should be free from religious censorship: 'the Faculty of Theology did not hold a dominant position over the other Faculties, as was usual up to this time.' The university rapidly gained a reputation for a curriculum inspired by the Enlightenment which featured high quality academic teaching and scientific research in the newly emerging disciplines, and which began to attract students from all over Europe. By the end of the eighteenth century, 'more than two hundred students had arrived from England, Scotland and Ireland,' and the university had become a popular option that combined some academic study with the opportunity to travel abroad. The university also broke with tradition by encouraging the students to use the large library, a place usually reserved for the professors and visiting academics.

Exactly whose choice Göttingen was is not clear, and we have no word from Lord John about it. It is possible he was attracted by the university's cutting-edge curriculum and the opportunity to study under some of Europe's leading professors, but more likely he was drawn to it by the university's reputation in England. In the first place its Hanoverian connection was popular, and in addition the university's co-founder, Gerlach Adolph von Münchhausen, had explicitly sought to build on this connection and attract British students: 'It is my intent to invite the English gentlemen to Göttingen, where they can certainly live as well as in Holland, where they often use up all their money.'

Göttingen was already popular before the Seven Years War (1756–63), and afterwards, once peace was established, student numbers from Britain began to rise steadily again, leading to 118 enrolling between the end of the war and 1786.

Partly this was down to the quality of the teaching staff, a number of whom were also members of the Royal Society, but alongside this Baron Münchhausen had made life particularly friendly to the British. Many of the lecturers spoke English and in addition to their academic duties they also played the role of 'Hofmeister', each taking on the 'the general supervision of several students', arranging accommodation and tuition for British students, and smoothing 'the ruffled feathers of local officials irritated by their youthful exuberance and occasional rowdiness'. Finally, and perhaps most importantly, they spent 'countless hours managing the financial affairs of [their] pupils'.

Gordon Stewart tells us that Göttingen 'was a distinctly British milieu', with English newspapers and books on sale in the university bookshop, and relates that so popular did Britain become that 'When news of Admiral Rodney's defeat of the French fleet in April 1782 at St Domingo, reached Göttingen, the town rejoiced. The English students proudly paraded about the town in … Marine-uniform.' No doubt the recently arrived Lord John was also part of that jubilant march, and he seems to have been a willing participant in some of the 'occasional rowdiness'. It was his first real taste of personal freedom, and this may well suggest why he chose Göttingen over following his brother to Cambridge. He may simply have wanted to get out of England for a while and, as he travelled to Germany in early 1782, he was ready for a more independent life. In the end, although all three brothers remained very close, Westminster was to be the last of their closely shared experiences.[37]

Once again, as with the duke at Cambridge, it is largely through Robert Palmer's letters that we can follow Lord John's progress at Göttingen, but before looking at these there is one other source which provides a glimpse not just of life at Göttingen at this time, but also of the world of 'manners' that Lord John may have been trying to escape. In his memoir of 1801, George Hanger, who enrolled at Göttingen in November 1770, relates both why he went there and why he soon left. After leaving Eton, 'as I had resolved on being a soldier, a German education was best suited to the profession I had chosen,' and in addition, 'Had I been placed at Oxford or Cambridge, not being of a studious disposition, my health might have suffered from every species of riot and dissipation … I was accordingly sent into

Germany, to Göttingen, which is one of the most celebrated universities in the world … the finest teachers in every science are there [and] public lectures in all branches of learning are delivered by the most experienced and learned professors.'

In spite of this, although he had escaped the dangers of Oxford and Cambridge, Hanger soon found a series of defects in the social world at Göttingen. 'Göttingen', he writes, 'is not a proper place, in my opinion, for the character of a young militant (particularly an Englishman). For a soldier, for whom no talent, after courage, can recommend so much … as good-breeding, and elegant and polite manners, is not likely to acquire those fascinating accomplishments from a reclusive set of learned professors.' In addition, among other defects, was the problem that, at Göttingen, 'There are too many English there, who herd together, and, by always talking their own tongue, never acquire a fluency in that of the country, which can only be obtained by associating with the natives.'[38]

Dissatisfied with the situation, Hanger 'quit Göttingen for Hanover and Hesse Cassel', but if Palmer's letters are anything to go by, Lord John seems to have found the university and society of Göttingen suited him perhaps rather too well. Palmer's first letter, dated 18 January 1782, sets the scene and names Dr Erxleben as Lord John's tutor and mentor:

I am obliged to you for your letter of the 2nd instant and am very glad to hear you are arrived safe and well at Göttingen; I hope you will find the place, the mode of your education and Instruction agreeable to you, as you wish it to be; I have inclosed a letter which will furnish you with a Credit of £100 sterling – I am informed that all Gentlemen residing at Göttingen are supplied with money from Hamburgh and that Doctor Erxleben will assist you in recovering the money without any trouble to yourself.

If there is any better method of conveying money to you, than the present method now made use of by me, please let me know it, and I will adopt it.

Dr Erxleben, as Lord John's tutor, had now become responsible for his studies, his finances and his progress, but Palmer's letters in April indicate that in terms of the last there is soon concern at Woburn about how things are going. On the 16th for example, Palmer writes: 'I hope you apply yourself to your studies, Her Grace the Dutchess of Bedford is anxious about you, having heard in some companies that there [are] many English Gentlemen at Göttingen, and that some of them spend their time in pleasures and amusements and do not attend to their Studies and Improvement. Her Grace trusts you will not follow their example but set a good one.'

Clearly under pressure from Gertrude to find out what is happening, he follows this with a letter, also on the 16th, to Dr Erxleben asking about his pupil:

The occasion of giving you this trouble is to enquire after your pupil Lord John Russell … I trust and hope his behaviour and application meets with your approbation and that I shall receive such an account from you as will give pleasure to the Dutchess of Bedford and satisfaction to me … the reason of making these enquiries is occasioned by the Dutchess of Bedford having heard in some of the first Companies that there are many young English Gentlemen at Göttingen who give up all their time to pleasure and amusements and neglect their Studies and Improvement.

I hope there is no foundation for such a Report, and that you will enable me to contradict the Report which is Injurious to your University. I beg you will supply Lord John Russell and his Servant with such money as appears to you to be proper and reasonable and please to draw on me for the same which Drafts shall be punctually paid.

By 26 April, Palmer seems a little apologetic about the previous letters and more conciliatory, being careful as to what he says to Lord John and seeking to reassure him: 'My Lord, … I shall take care have your draft paid … and I trust in your prudence not to be extravagant – I hope you know that everything I say to you is intended to be for your benefit and service; I am wishing you good health.' However, a letter of the same date to William Rohloff, Lord John's manservant, who had accompanied him to Germany, would seem to indicate that, whether or not our student had been studying hard, he had certainly been enjoying himself on a trip to Hanover:

> Lord John writes to me that he will pay his bills and your wages every Quarter punctually – I shall pay your Wife quarterly or as she wants the money … I am glad to hear Lord John was pleased with his Journey to Hanover …
>
> I would not have Lord John or yourself want for anything that is fitting and proper, but I wish you to be Oeconomists and to act with prudence … I request that you take care of Lord John now he is not well and be particularly careful that he has skilfull and good advice and attendance, and that you will not mention his complaint to any one in any of your letters as I should be very sorry to have it known here, let me know when he is well, I hope it will be a warning to him.

As the year went on, things seem to have settled down a bit as Lord John recovered from his complaint and his studies continued under Dr Erxleben's beady eye. Exactly what these studies were is something of a mystery, partly because he never referred to them, and in an almost unique exception to all the other entries in the enrolment lists, which specify 'Med', 'philus', 'math', 'Artus Liber' and so on, there is no entry for him under the heading of 'Faculty'. The only hint we have that he was studying anything more than a broad-based foundation course of some sort comes in a letter from Palmer in November, in which he advises Lord John to 'be content to stay quietly where you are and study Languages in order to lay the foundation for further Improvements – I am persuaded it has fallen within your observation that a Child wants to run before it walks.'

This advice was given as a reaction to the suggestion that Lord John may have been planning on travelling in Europe with friends. The reaction from home was immediate. In October, Gertrude continued to keep a typically close eye on expenditure: 'the Dutchess thinks you are spending too much Money and directed me to tell you so.' Palmer, with his usual patient tact, also writes: 'Permit me to request you to be attentive to your Studies which will be the best method you can put in practice to avoid spending Money,' but by November there are signs that indicate this might not be happening. The beginning of this letter tells us that concern was growing about both his expenditure and, it would seem, plans to start travelling; in another letter Palmer indicates that Gertrude was involving Daniel Beaumont, an estate officer based in London, in the effort to guide the young sixteen-year-old abroad in the wide world:

To Lord John Russell, Göttingen.　Nov 26 1782

… I am favoured with your letter of the 12 instant; it is proper you should be informed that the purport of what I added at the Bottom of Mr Beaumont's Letter was by the direction of the Dutchess of Bedford.

I am very much pleased by your saying you will diminish your Expenses. It is very prudent and commendable, whoever advises you to pursue pleasure instead of Study is not your Friend; lost time is the most difficult of all things to recover and is of more value than you are aware. Don't my Lord be led into a desire to see places at present, you are too young to edify from it, the expense will be as great now as if you was 20 years of age, but the observations you will now make will be of little advantage … and permit me as a friend to give you one word of advice, which is, before you do any Act or undertake any new thing, examine your own reason candidly, Consider if it is right and fit for you to do it … The uprightness of your mind and the goodness of your understanding will guide you right if you receive no improper bias from some pretended Friend.[39]

At this stage we have no indication as to whom Lord John had befriended at Göttingen or what his intentions were, and unfortunately no letters have survived in the archives from 1783 to enlighten us. Perhaps at this point Lord John took Palmer's advice and settled down to finish his two-year course, and certainly, in later life, beyond the Latin and the Greek he would have learnt at school, he spoke and read French, Italian and German proficiently or even fluently. It is also possible, however, that the lack of letters and activity between 1783 and 1784 related to the catastrophic volcanic eruptions that ripped apart the Lakagigar fissure in Iceland during that period. One of the largest such events ever recorded, it created a thick toxic haze that blanketed Western Europe, causing widespread deaths and crop failures, and one of the hottest summers on record. When describing the extraordinary effects of this occurrence in England, Gilbert White wrote that things got so extreme that 'The country people began to look with a superstitious awe, at the red louring aspect of the sun; and indeed there was reason for the most enlightened person to be apprehensive,' suggesting that everyone was simply waiting to see what was going to happen.[40]

The next letters start in the summer of 1784, once the lingering haze had cleared, and by this time Lord John has left Göttingen and is travelling round Europe with a friend from university, Francis Randolph, and his manservant William Rohloff. Randolph is of interest because he was one of the five British students who enrolled at Göttingen the same year as Lord John, and it seems that Lord John made a good friend of Randolph, a classics and theology student. Randolph was some fourteen years older and had already graduated from Cambridge, and he seems to have been someone the duchess and Palmer approved of. Although those back in London had initially opposed Lord John's plan to travel in 1782, news of his 'complaint' seems to have convinced them it might be better if he did stay abroad for a while, and when the plans to travel were approved, Randolph was engaged to accompany him as a paid companion and perhaps to keep him out of further trouble. Thus, it was to Randolph that Palmer sent a number of letters concerning the need to keep expenses down as the pair made their way round France and Belgium between 1784 and 1786.[41] His later career, in fact, remained closely linked to the Bedford family as he gained livings, among others, at Chenies in Buckinghamshire and St Paul's Covent Garden, both granted by the Duke of Bedford.

Another individual of interest at this point was George Byng, who had enrolled at Göttingen in 1780 aged eighteen to study philosophy and was still there when Lord John arrived in 1782. Byng, or 'Byng-go' as he was known, was a member of a leading Whig family based at Southill Park, not far from the Russells at Woburn, and although George was brought up at his father's house, Wrotham Park, Hertfordshire, he may well have met the young Russell brothers when visiting his cousins at Southill. Those cousins, the children of the diplomat George Byng, 4th Viscount of Torrington, were numerous – three boys and four girls – and in 1782, when Torrington was appointed as the British Minister in Brussels, the girls all moved there with their parents.

By July 1784 Lord John was in a position to start travelling, and over the course of the year he and Randolph travelled through France, reaching Montpellier on the south coast by November. On 24 July we catch up with the travellers in two letters sent to Palmer, the first from Rohloff in Angoulême, between Poitiers and Bordeaux. It is clear that Lord John was still not in the best of health, and Rohloff reports, 'at present everything goes on very well, and think if they had stayed here a little longer his Lordship would have found benefit by it; to be sure there is very little amusements nor women to be met with here … the place where we are going is a Water Drinking place, where they expect to find a great deal of Company.'

He is clearly wary of what may happen if they do meet 'Company', and the reason for this is clear from the second letter, from Randolph in Bordeaux: 'We arrived here on Aug 6th … My dear friend improves daily in Health and Strength and for his and my sake I had rather at this moment have him anywhere but in a great City. All venereal complaints have long since ceased, and I do not wish to place him in Temptation's Way to risk another. I flatter myself he is perfectly happy out of Temptation, and that is as much as I should hope for.'[42] Randolph goes on to report to Palmer, 'I have only two Faults to complain of in my little Friend, a too great Partiality for his Bed, and rather a puerile fondness for Trinkets and Baubles. I hope to make his Curiosity amidst the new and mountainous Scenes of the Pyrenees subservient to my purposes in weaning Him from the first, and Time and Ridicule will I trust cure him of the latter.' Palmer and Gertrude were clearly hoping that, apart from regaining his health, Randolph's influence might also cure a few of Lord John's undesirable habits.

At the same time, in England, while Lord William was enrolling at Christ Church College, Oxford, the duke, having graduated in 1783, left Cambridge and the delights of Newmarket aged eighteen, and in the interlude before he came of age he planned to set out on an elaborate Grand Tour. If the newspaper articles are right, this was to be more than the usual visits to France and Italy because, from Europe, he intended to travel on through the East India Territories and carry on as far as China; all in all, 'The Duke of Bedford's voyage to China, if he is accompanied by a suite of learned men, may be productive of the greatest advantage to the literary, as well as commercial world … With his Grace's vast fortune and high rank, he may command every advantage, go where he will.' Scott Thomson may well be right in suggesting that 'it is tempting to connect this [plan] with the interest in the East India Trade, and part ownership of some of the East Indiamen which the Russells had acquired when, a century earlier the [duke's] grandfather had married the grand-daughter of the great East India Company magnate, Josia[h] Child.'[43]

By the time the duke left, however, this grand plan had been replaced by something all together different, and when he finally sailed for Flanders in April 1784, it was not with a 'suite of learned men' but someone much more interesting – a beautiful and beguiling older woman. The newspapers reported: 'The scandalous rumour of yesterday was, that a certain young Duke is attended on his present tour by Lady M___, but we hope such report has no foundation in truth.' It was, however, quite true and the lady in question was Lady Maynard, wife of Lord Maynard, but before this marriage she had been the infamous Nancy Parsons, a much admired beauty and wife or mistress to a number of men, including the Dukes of Dorset and Grafton. Beyond this she was highly intelligent, widely read and a renowned conversationalist, and the duke was totally captivated. The *Morning Herald* tells us what happened next: 'Lord Maynard is going abroad as soon as the parliamentary business will let him. Her Ladyship accompanied by the Duke of Bedford, is, for the benefit of her health, gone before to Flanders.'

So, for the benefit of Lady Maynard's health, the duke's travels began, as he was swept into a strange *ménage à trois* that was to continue for over two years, in spite of the fact that by 1784, although passing for twenty-nine, Nancy was at least forty-nine. As is suggested by the newspaper quoted above, Lord Maynard, himself a younger man, seems to have been quite comfortable with the arrangement; he went about his own business, happily carried on affairs of his own, and remained a close friend of the duke to the extent that for some time he had his own room at

Woburn Abbey. From Flanders, the couple moved on to the Paris area, where the *Morning Post* gives us a colourful glimpse of their life:

> His Grace the Duke of B___ is not visiting the different Courts upon the Continent, studying their politics, and storing his mind with knowledge, to render him serviceable to his native country when he takes his place in the Senate. He lives within thirty miles of Paris, accompanied by a sage female companion, where his expenses do not exceed one thousand Pounds a year. Such rigid economy in a person of his age and immense fortune, has made him in France an object of public curiosity, insomuch, that both ladies and gentlemen come into the neighbourhood where he lives, to gratify themselves with a sight of so extraordinary a character. [44]

While we know very little as to what they actually did, or how they spent their time during the next two or three years, it would seem that under Nancy's guidance the young duke began to widen his world, to leave behind for now the fast, careless life of drinking clubs and high stakes gambling, and take an interest in literature and culture generally, but, perhaps even more importantly, she seems to have settled him down, listened to him and encouraged him to take himself seriously. Scott Thomson quotes Lord Glenbervie, writing that 'in his opinion … her attraction for young men [was that] … she had "the peculiar art of seeming to take an interest in them, listening to them with complacency, their concerns and pursuits, making them seem important in their own eyes, the only object of her thoughts and attention".' We do not know if the word 'seeming' is justified here, but if taking an interest is what Nancy was able to do for the duke, she was probably the first adult in his life to have done so; if his earlier grand travel plans had fallen by the wayside, perhaps in the end they were replaced by something more valuable to him in the long run. The anonymous dowager duchess quoted in the *General Advertiser* in January 1785 catches what was likely to have been the reaction of many to what they considered to be simply a youthful fling, when she 'heard that his juvenile Grace … had made an elopement with a Lady turned the period of forty, she blessed his prudence, in forming an *amour* which could not be productive of children, and the expenses consequent thereof.'[45]

Meanwhile, by November 1784, as the duke and Lady Maynard reached Nice, Lord John and Randolph were also on the south coast of France at Montpellier enjoying the warm weather. The relationship between the brothers was at this point rather distant, and Lord John does not seem to have really understood, or perhaps approved of, the duke's relationship with Nancy. Either way no attempt was made to meet up. Palmer, writing to Randolph in November, is as ever concerned about money: 'I trust no more money will be spent than is necessary … I hope Lord John will establish his Health, and be sensible it is worth preserving to make his life happy,' but 'It is always pleasing to hear that Lord John and yourself are well and that the places you visit afford Entertainment and Comfort.'

By February 1785 Lord John and Randolph were in Paris, where they separated before Lord John travelled to London in March to join Gertrude at Bedford House, Bloomsbury. It is not clear why Gertrude wanted to meet with her grandson, but the fact that Randolph was let go may suggest that she considered that this was enough travelling and it was time for Lord John to settle down. Equally unclear at this time is the nature of the relationship between Gertrude and the three brothers as individuals, but the following letter concerning his immediate plans would seem to indicate that Lord John, at least, preferred to use Palmer as a go-between rather than discuss things with his grandmother directly. Whatever his grandmother's plans for him may have been, Lord John was determined to 'go abroad again', as he explained to Palmer:

I do not know whether you have acquainted the Duchess of my final determination of going abroad this summer; however if you have not I wish you would as my wish is to leave England about the end of June, being thoroughly convinced that I shall spend my time much more profitably and to greater advantage than I should in England (where I am firmly persuaded I shall only lead a life of idleness and dissipation), and also I shall be more likely to live upon my present income of £800 a year. I should wish to order my post-chaise immediately as it will be some time making.[46]

Why he should then have chosen Brussels as his first destination is an interesting question, and it seems possible that now, for the first time free from the watchful gaze of schoolmasters, tutors, staff from the Bedford office, his grandmother and a travelling companion, he had decided to follow up on a suggestion from George Byng at Göttingen that he should visit Brussels and call on George's cousins there. Whatever the reason, this is what he did, and settling himself at 'l'Hotel d'Angleterre, Bruxelles', he soon became a frequent guest at Lord Torrington's residence, where he was introduced to the minister's four daughters, Lucy (25), Georgiana (17), Isabella (12) and Emily (6). For the nineteen-year-old Lord John, somewhat adrift in the world, a bit lost and probably lonely, being welcomed into a large, warm family must have been a revelation after those long years at boarding school and university. It was perhaps inevitable that the young visitor should rapidly have become close to one of the girls in particular, and he soon writes excitedly to a close friend, quite possibly Randolph: 'Believe me, my heart is in no imminent danger, yet I blush not to own that its strings are gently touched by an object I have seen. I have been but ten days in this town, in fact a short period of time, but yet long enough to have enabled one to distinguish a most sweet and amiable person.' She is, he says, 'mild, gentle, affable, good tempered, and thoroughly amiable' and has 'a goodness of spirits, a pleasing and gentle timidity so distinguishable in the female mind'. He had met the British minister's second daughter, the seventeen-year-old Georgiana Elizabeth Byng.

Over the next few months the relationship developed rapidly, and writing again to his friend a short while later, he declares: 'I feel an unconscious desire, even an absolute want, of communicating my feelings to you, indeed they are not the same as they were but a few weeks ago. I feel not the undisturbed calm of indifference that so lately flowed gently in my veins – I feel happy but when I am near the woman I love. Yes! my friend, I firmly believe I love.' He cannot 'but feel the merits of this heavenly Soul, this all accomplished Woman'.

But he is still not sure if his feelings are reciprocated, 'I feel I am not destined to possess the heart of so amiable a Woman,' and half-heartedly prepares for the worst: 'But alas! I go on vainly talking, vainly hoping, forgive me good and generous friend. You feel for me and pity me. Yes! pity me for I shall possibly never see her more after I quit Bruxelles. My stay here will be short. I propose going from hence to Spa, from whence god knows where I shall seek consolation.'

His friend feels duty bound to warn him of 'Two Rocks' on which he must 'avoid to split'. First, the possibility that this will be a passing feeling, that he will realize it to be a mistake and seek to escape, but 'By your constant attention and assiduities you might possibly create a flame which would grow into an unconquerable passion and would render an amiable person miserable for her life.' And second, he must be sure this is not a 'light and superficial Passion – I mean a slight and temporary frenzy of love created by external Beauties and allurements. Nothing in nature is so slight and inconsistent, it quickly evaporates and subsiding leaves no impression but Remorse and stings of Conscience.' He ends by urging caution: 'You are young and inexperienced, yet you want not for sense … But yet, my Friend, you might from want of thought, be led to actions that you would afterwards repent of. On these motives alone then am I prompted to what I have already said to you.'[47]

In the end, Lord John did not have to leave for Spa to sooth a broken heart in the warm waters, because by December the couple have become engaged, and Lord John, determined to marry as soon as possible, has written a series of letters to his elder brother, his grandmother and Palmer. Only the last of these letters has survived, but it conveys his new, animated excitement. Writing on 6 December 1785, he informs Palmer of his intention:

> I take the liberty of troubling you with this letter to inform you that I have fixed upon a partner for life. I am soon going to enter into the married state which I hope will meet with your approbation. The lady is Miss Georgiana Byng second daughter of Lord Torrington, perfectly accomplished, and endowed with a heavenly mind.
>
> I wish Sir, to request a favour of you which I hope with your usual goodness to me you will grant – it is to undertake the marriage settlements and get them drawn up immediately. I wish to have them as handsome and advantageous to her as possibly can be, and such as her rank and amiable

qualities require; but I will leave them wholly to you. In regard to my fortune being paid to me now, suppose that cannot be, however, I am thoroughly convinced we can live upon a very little. She is an excellent oeconomist and I hope will reform me – I have written to the Duke and the duchess upon the subject. I beg you will favour me with an answer by return of the post and am with great regard …

John Russell.

If you could conveniently let me have £200 I should be extremely obliged to you.

Having sent this letter off, it seems then to have dawned on Lord John, or perhaps it was pointed out to him by his prospective father-in-law, that it was not going to be that simple to make such financial arrangements as he was still underage, and a few days later he follows up with another letter: 'I am sorry to trouble you so often with letters, but part of the contents of the last I wrote to you are, I believe, unnecessary. I understand that being under age, I can make no settlements – of which I knew nothing, and as I am perfectly unacquainted with everything concerning it, I leave it entirely up to you,' adding hopefully, 'I can make no doubt of everything meeting with your approbation as well as that of the Duchess.'

Whether Lord John could have suspected it or not, 'everything' was not received with universal approbation, since there was 'much opposition from relatives' and, as Scott Thomson points out, 'there were rumours that Lord Torrington was heavily in debt.' Ever cautious, the trustees wanted to be sure before any marriage took place what they could expect Georgiana's marriage settlement to be. These concerns were conveyed to Lord John in Palmer's reply, in which he points out Lord John's financial situation to him:

I am favour'd with yours of 6th December … I sincerely wish you were 21 years of age that I might make a Settlement which would be of benefit of the Lady and your Children.

> You should consider how you are to live when married until you are 21, you know you have only £400 a year until that time. Your brother has proposed to allow you £400 a year … Give me leave to ask what Lord Torrington proposes to do for his daughter, towards making you in any degree comfortable in circumstances.

Taking his lead from Lord John's admission – 'of which I knew nothing, and as I am perfectly unacquainted with everything concerning it' – Palmer then emphasizes the problems:

> I should be wanting in Friendship and duty to you if I did not tell you in the plainest terms – that if you do not live to be 21 years of age you have not one single Guinea under your father's settlement or your Grandfather's Will. Let me ask you to consider these matters well. My zeal to be of benefit to you and any one whom you choose to make a partner for life, makes me say that to you, that I should do if you were my son, consider well what you are going to do, and of a proper time to do it …
>
> After saying these things … Let me prevail upon you to have your Brother's approbation before you proceed further, whose Goodness and Judgement (in so young a man) has often astonished me.
>
> I think it behoves yourself as well as Lord Torrington to consider how you are to live till you are 21. I shall trouble Lord Torrington with [a letter] by this Post.

True to his word, Palmer writes to Lord Torrington explaining Lord John's situation, and asking him what he 'proposes to do for your daughter'.[48]

Beyond his unfailing politeness to Lord John, Palmer's real feelings about the proposed marriage are clear from his letter of 20 December to the Duke of Bedford, who was still in Nice:

> On the 12th I received a letter from Lord John Russell which gives me great uneasiness, in which he says that he has fixed on a partner for Life,

Lord Torrington's 2nd daughter. The Duchess received a letter from Lord Torrington by the same post acquainting Her Grace that Lord John had proposed … and hoped it would be approved by Her Grace. I wrote a letter to Lord John in the strongest terms not to think of marrying whilst he was under age … I also pressed him to proceed no further without your knowledge and unless he had your approbation. It appears to me to be so improper a measure as to give me great vexation which made me ill for three days. Pardon me, My lord, if your Grace is of a different opinion.

Unfortunately for Lord John, it would seem that the duke was very much of the same opinion. Judging from a letter he was to send his brother early the next year, it seems Lord John did eventually write to the duke, but rather than asking for advice, he simply asked for the duke's approval. Writing from Nice in January 1786 the duke replies:

> I shall begin by informing you I still continue to be very averse to your match and am determined not to give my consent, but as your Guardians have given theirs, I shall not try to throw any impediment in the way … I am still of the opinion you have used a great deal of deceit … I will now give you a piece of advice on that subject. If you continue acting upon other occasions in the same manner you have done upon this, you will make a good worldly man, but you will never be cited for an upright character.[49]

If not exactly on his brother's side, the duke did not stand in the way of the marriage; Palmer could do little except patiently point out the problems that could arise from a quick marriage in Brussels, and does so in an exchange of letters. Since Lord John is intending to marry abroad, and is still a minor, they will need to apply for a special licence, which will take some time to arrange, and beyond that, there is also an issue as to whether the church ceremony he is proposing in Brussels will be recognized in English law. In view of all of this, he tries again to convince Lord John to wait until he is twenty-one, when these obstacles will be removed and when he will have far more money available. His increasingly exasperated tone gives an indication of the strain the relationship between the boys and the trustees of the estate was under:

> I perceive you are acquainted with the Marriage Act. It will require a much longer time than you imagine to obtain a License. The Lord Chancellor must be applied to before any License will be granted … [and] the consent of the Duchess of Bedford and the Duchess of Marlborough [Lord John's aunt and a trustee of the estate] must both be obtained … I do not know what difficulties may arise. I can't help saying that in my Judgement you ought to wait until you are 21, it is no long time to wait …
>
>   I will now proceed to answer your [question] about raising money. By no means, my Lord, think of borrowing money before you are entitled to your Fortune, you must pay very extravagantly for what you borrow … You ask me what other Method you must take, the answer is that you must live on £800 a year, no great hardship … You tell me it is [difficult for you to contact] your Brother to ask his Advice, but, as you will not follow it, or to the same effect, Pray my Lord consider how can you ask your Brother to do anything for you or even expect it, as you will not ask or take his advice.

Palmer will, however, do his best, since

> My desire for you doing well and to prevent that fatal evil of raising money before you are of age has induced me to join with your kind and indulgent Grand Mother to let you have the Money you have imprudently spent to avoid the evil that attends borrowing money in the way that you propose.
>
>   If it is in my power to do you real service you may command me, but I hope you will not ask me to aid you in ruining yourself, for that I cannot do.

Palmer then lays out the options facing the couple if they do marry in a candid letter to William Rohloff:

To Mr Rohloff, Brussells   Dec 25 1785

The Business you mention is likely to go forward but to accomplish it needs more time than the Parties [wish]. If it takes place they will either live in Brussells, or go to the south of France but which I can't say. I am glad to hear Lord John is in good health.[50]

In January 1786, Palmer writes to the duke in Nice updating him on the situation, especially since he has ascertained the likely size of Georgiana's settlement:

As Lord John is determined to marry Miss Byng, I intend by the next post to acquaint your Grace with the [terms] of an Agreement relating to the £50,000 left to him by his Grandfather's Will if he lives to 21. Miss Byng's fortune is very little, there being only £10,000 provided for all the younger children.

I much wished to prevail upon Lord John to have delayed Marrying … but I find all my endeavours and advice had no effect. Therefore I must hope your Grace will think it right to secure the £50,000 [providing he] promises to live within his income …

The Marriage Act will give some delay to his being married as the requisites of that Act must be complied with. I understand that Lady Albemarle as well as the duchess of Bedford thinks favourably of Lord John's choice and expect it will have an effect on his Conduct which will in the event give satisfaction to his friends.

Thus, with the tacit approval of the duke and the trustees and access to the interest accumulating on his inheritance secured, the marriage arrangements could go ahead, and the ceremony in Brussels would be followed by a second in the church at Streatham when the couple returned to England. Writing to Lord John in Brussels on 14 February, Palmer says: 'The business you wish to compleat is proceeding on with every degree of attention and dispatch. I am sorry that you will not come to England to be married. It is of more consequence than you at present imagine.

After you are married I do hope you and the Lady will come to England and be married according to the English Laws before you go to the south of France. I desire to know your determination as to that matter.'

Lord John agrees with this solution and, postponing their planned travels in France, arrangements for the visit to England are made instead:

February 21 1786

The Duchess of Bedford received your letter yesterday and thinks Streatham will be a proper place for you to go to for a few days until you have been married a second time and then for you and your Lady to retire to Micheldever until her Grace goes into the Country – Your Guardians are appointed and the settlement is going on with utmost diligence.

Micheldever was one of the Russell properties in Hampshire, not far from the larger estate at Stratton Park. In the end the latter was settled on John and Georgiana, but that house was not ready for occupation at this time, and so the smaller house was furnished for their arrival. The biggest question facing everyone, however, was what would happen when the duke came of age in July and finally returned from France, and whether Gertrude would seek to remain in any of the properties. For now, then, it was considered best that the newlyweds take a house that would not interfere with any of their grandmother's plans, 'until her Grace goes into the country' – that is to say, until she relinquished her role in running the estates.

With the arrangements made, Palmer signs off on 28 February with a final word of advice: 'Your Lordship has my best wishes that the Union may be attended with mutual Happiness and Comfort. To make it so in the Extent, I wish it you must be an Oeconomist, live within your income … I wish you and the Lady a safe journey to England and will trouble you to make my respectful Compliments to Lord and Lady Torrington.'[51]

The anxiously awaited marriage took place on 21 March 1786 at the Anglican Church, Oostende, West Viaaneren, Belgium, followed by a celebration which 'took place in the house of the British Minister in Brussels' (Colour Plates 4 and 5). Within a week or two the couple made their way to England to stay at Streatham, where Dr Bullock married them in the local church for a second time on 17 April. Although his life so far had been one of considerable privilege, in which the opportunities open to him bore no relation to his abilities or academic achievement, it had also been one of great loss, and at times must have been very difficult, if not harsh, for a shy, uncertain and lonely boy. He will also have steadily become aware that with privilege came very real responsibilities and expectations to which he would have to respond, even if, at this time, he had no idea how or in what way he would be able to do so. There is no doubt that throughout his life he respected and sought to learn from those people he met whose vocations, interests in life and the career they might follow were clear to them from a young age. It must have been a salutary process for him at Göttingen to be surrounded by brilliant and inspired professors, sitting in the great library listening to his fellow students caught up in the excitement of the worlds of science, maths, physics, philosophy and the arts that were opening up across their various disciplines – to catch a glimpse of the world these people saw ahead and yet have no idea how he could be a part of it. Reflecting on this, it really comes as no surprise that he should have responded so rapidly to the 'mild, gentle, affable, good tempered, and thoroughly amiable' girl he met in Brussels; she was nice, she was interested, no doubt she listened intently, and she encouraged him – it all seemed so promising.

With Lord John safely married, Palmer was now able to turn his attention to the other important event which was imminent: the preparations for the transfer of authority over the Bedford estates from the trustees to the duke on his twenty-first birthday. First and foremost, he was concerned about how smooth the transfer might be. Although the duke came of age in July, there were no signs that he was preparing to return from France, leading the *Morning Post* to ask, 'Where is the Duke? In minority or majority is it all the same?' It appears that the duke, in turn, was worried as to if and when his grandmother would vacate Woburn Abbey and Bedford House, and whether he would have to battle her for possession. In August, however, while visiting Plombières with Lady Maynard, he was cautiously reassured by a letter he received from Gertrude which took him by surprise: 'I was very much surprised at receiving a letter from the Duchess confirming she meant to give me up Woburn in October … I intended being in England by this time had Woburn been given up … I shall avoid going to Woburn after my first visit as I am sure that the Duchess will do nothing but plead me to let her live there and if not let her take away half of the furniture.'

Reassured, and clearly intending to carry on as he had done in Nice, the duke arrived back in England, as he tells the Earl of Ossory: 'Lord Maynard arrived with me last night in London. My brother William [who had been in Paris] has been so good as to stay and accompany Lady Maynard. They will be here in about eight days.' Lord William was to graduate from Oxford three years later, and when he then got married, the duke gave his brother the house in Steatham to establish his presence there so that he could be returned in the Bedford interest for Surrey, a seat he held until 1807.

It was the end of an era, the long period of the minority, and in a letter to the duke, Robert Palmer seems happy to be able to hand over all his responsibilities:

I feel great satisfaction that I have lived to congratulate your Grace on your attaining the age of 21 years; it is an event that your Grandfather much wished for … Your affairs are in a fine situation, I trust your Grace will take the time to examine all the accounts during a long minority, and that you may feel satisfaction that they are all exactly correct … and that [you] may have a further information how greatly the estates … are improved. That information I wish your Grace to have … the news writers have taken pains to exaggerate your Estate which can be of no service to you … I wish your Grace a long and happy life accompanied by good health.[52]

CHAPTER TWO
1786–1803

A pleasing form, a firm yet cautious Mind, Sincere, tho' Prudent; Constant, yet Resigned ... Fixed to one side, but moderate to the Best ... A Scorn of Wrangling, yet a zeal for Truth, a Generous Faith, from superstition free; A Love of Peace, and Hate of Tyranny; Of Modest Wisdom ... Good without noise, without pretentious Graces. Just to his word, in every thought Sincere ... Of softest Manners, Unaffected mind ... Friend of Humankind.[53]

THIS IS PART of a long 'Memorial' on 'The Character of the right Honble Lord John Russell, addressed to him by his best Friend, Brusselles, February 12, 1786', almost certainly Georgiana Byng, and it gives us a snapshot of both the differences in the couple's personalities and their relationship at the start of their marriage. We see Georgiana at her exuberant best in this open and humorous description of her husband, and it stands out in its generosity and sense of fun when compared to his description of her given to his friend when announcing his intention to marry, which describes her as 'mild, gentle, affable, good tempered, and thoroughly amiable' with 'a goodness of spirits, a pleasing and gentle timidity'. She would no doubt, both then and in the future, have appreciated a little more from him.

Finally, by June 1786 the two weddings and the formalities were all behind them, and the couple set out from Streatham to visit Lord John's aunt and guardian, Caroline, Duchess of Marlborough, partly because it was best they stayed out of the way once the duke got back and until the succession was complete. Lord William seems to have acted as contact point between his two older brothers, and while staying with the duke in Plombieres, which he found far more 'interesting' than studying at Oxford, he wrote to Lord John:

I suppose as the Duke of Marlborough has invited you to Blenheim, you will pass some of the summer there ... I fancy it is my brother's intention to return to England sometime in August and I believe to go to Woburn immediately, so that you may suppose it cannot be convenient either to the Dutchess or him for her to remain there all that time ... I would advise you by all means to profit from your invitation to Blenheim as both Woburn and Bedford House must be at present a perfect scene of confusion which must be disagreeable to both Lady John and you.[54]

Quite happy to stay away from both Woburn and Bedford House during this transition period, Lord John and Georgiana spent much of August at Blenheim with Caroline and her husband, the 4th Duke of Marlborough, Lord John being no doubt eager to introduce his wife to this important member of his family and his Spencer cousins, and perhaps to learn more about the duke's interest in astronomy.[55]

From Blenheim, the couple's next priority was to pay a visit to the Duke of Portland and his wife at Bulstrode in Buckinghamshire, a visit both personal – the duchess was a relative of Georgiana – but also political. Although by this time the structure of the Whig faction as it had been in Lord John's grandfather's day had largely broken up, the process of establishing a new and more effective opposition to the Pitt government had begun, and by the early 1780s this process was headed by the Duke of Portland and Charles James Fox. Encouraged by the sudden support of the eighteen-year-old Prince of Wales, who, in opposition to his father, had begun interacting with and supporting the Devonshire House circle of Whigs which coalesced around Georgiana, Duchess of Devonshire, they began organizing for the 1784 election. Donald Ginter points out the key players in this process: 'the Whig opposition had centralized and organized itself under the formal leadership of the Duke of Portland ... [and] its organizational activities had come under the central control of a political manager, William Adam.' Under Adam an unprecedented degree of party organization was put in place for internal communications and political canvassing, increasing the party identity, and a number of political clubs 'with both a parliamentary and a broad extra-parliamentary membership' were established in London and across the counties based on Fox's Whig Club, founded in 1784. The Whigs may have had organization, but their major weakness at this point was a lack seats 'at the disposal of … members of the party or their friends'.[56]

It was into this more optimistic and energized political atmosphere that the Russell brothers came of age and started their political careers, just as the push was on to start leveraging the landed and financial power of the aristocratic houses to challenge local Tory interests in both rural and urban constituencies and to make more seats available for a variety of Whig candidates. The old Bedford interest, although continued by Russell loyalists such as Richard Rigby, had lost some of its influence and ability to promote candidates over the sixteen years that had passed since the 4th Duke of Bedford's death and his successor came of age; a revitalized Bedford interest with the new duke was one of the prime targets on Portland and Adam's list as sources of potential seats and his brothers as influential members of Parliament. Closely aligned with Fox from the start, the new duke was immediately encouraged to rebuild and start expanding his family's areas of influence, a process that began in September 1786 when he arrived back in England from France.

Since both of them had spent a considerable time abroad – Lord John some four years and Georgiana nine years from the age of nine until she was eighteen – now that they were back living in England and entering society and politics as a couple, the visit to Bulstrode must have been both interesting and exciting. Lord John had no doubt already been made aware of the political ambitions of his brother and the Whig party, and the fact that, with the duke in the House of Lords, he and Lord William would be required to represent the family interests and the new opposition in Parliament. For Georgiana it was possibly even more interesting. On her father's side she came from a line of politicians and had been brought up in Brussels among the dramas and intrigues of the diplomatic world, and would seem to have been actively drawn to both. If her husband was uneasy about what participation in politics might bring, Georgiana saw her role as supporting and encouraging her husband; she was ready and eager to be involved, and Bulstrode was the place to see it all in action. In addition, the visit will have been interesting for her because Dorothy Cavendish was a cousin through her mother, and judging from the visits that were to follow, often with the children, the Russells very much enjoyed their time with the older couple.

With immediate legal and political business in England out of the way, John and Georgiana returned in October to Brussels to see her family for one final piece of business: the details of her settlement from her father. When these had been worked out, they were at last able to enjoy their long postponed honeymoon as they set off to travel through France, aiming to spend the winter in Nice; as the newlyweds travelled south through the autumnal countryside it must have been a moment of intense joy, clouded only by the issue that had come between Lord John and his elder brother the year before. A letter from Lord William, now back at Oxford but clearly written for the duke, explains the problem:

> My Dear John,
> I take up my pen in order to mention a subject by no means agreeable … [but] when I first heard that you meant to pass your winter at Nice, I felt some uneasiness at the account as Lady Maynard … would certainly go there … and in several conversations I have had upon the subject with my Brother … he appears to be very uneasy and his mind seemed so full of anxiety respecting the part Lady John and you would act with regard to her.[57]

William ends by expressing the hope that they would be civil if they met Lady Maynard, even if they did not become friends.

This intervention cannot have eased any tensions between the brothers and was no doubt ignored by Lord John. Quite apart from feeling he did not need William's advice on how to conduct himself if he met Lady Maynard, whom we have no reason to believe he disliked personally, he had only just, for the first time in his life, been able to break the cycle of obeying the wishes and will of others. He had faced down those who had governed every step he took until this moment, overcome the duke's disapproval, and had finally taken control his own life by securing access to at least some of his money, and was determined to be happy. Most importantly, like the duke a year or so before, he had found someone who actually took an interest in him, who was sympathetic and who took him seriously. It was, perhaps, one of the happiest moments of his life so far; certainly, later in life, he was to remember their time in Nice as such. Similarly, for Georgiana this was a period of great happiness as she contemplated the future, life with a husband she clearly adored and the anticipation of the great political battles they would fight together; some six years later, as ill health started to dominate her life, Georgiana too remembered this trip: 'The happy manner in which we passed one year in travelling round France rendered me anxious to see other countries in the same way.'[58]

In the end, the couple reached Nice in November, but there is no indication they met Lady Maynard or experienced any difficulties. In February 1787 they retraced the route he had taken with Randolph, along the coast to Montpellier before journeying through the Pyrénées and on to Bordeaux, returning to England later that year. An earlier letter from Georgiana to Lord John confirms that they had a good, if cautious, relationship with Gertrude, and on their return the dowager duchess offered them a place to live, inviting them to join her at her house in Pall Mall. Georgiana wrote to her husband:

I have communicated the contents of the Dutchess of Bedford's letter to my Father and Mother. They both join in thinking that after her kind behaviour, it would be highly wrong not to acquiesce in whatever is her wish and besides that on leaving them I might be under her protection. That is their opinion, as to mine – feeling as sensibly as I do all her kindness – I can only wish to acknowledge my Gratitude for it. The only reason which could make me against going to England to her, is the dread of not meeting with her approbation … But I am perfectly of your opinion that you [sometimes] show her too much how desirous you are of complying with her wishes.

All of this would seem to indicate that Lord John had come to terms with his grandmother some time before. Georgiana, presumably, also played her part and clearly passed that first test on meeting Gertrude, and it would appear that the latter's subsequent kindness to his wife had helped to ease his own relationship with his grandmother, the only family member who appears to have been supportive of his marriage from the start. The invitation to Pall Mall was not simply a question of niceties; it had a lot to do with the fact that 112 Pall Mall lay at the very heart of fashionable London at the time and was very much in the public eye. Nearby Buckingham House had been taken that year by Jane, Duchess of Gordon, in town with her eldest daughter Charlotte, who was nineteen and a star of the London season, and where she had established her salon as a gathering place for Tory politicians. Her parties were legendary and she was a favourite of the Prince of Wales, who lived round the corner at Carlton House. Georgiana, watching all the goings on from down the street, wrote disapprovingly that year, 'The gaiety of the night, … the Prince of Wales keeping the Duchess of Gordon [in] English Society, is sad sad stuff.'[59]

In June 1787, Robert Palmer died after a long illness, and this event, combined with the revival of the family's political interests, marks the end of the long minority; a month later, when Lord John turned twenty-one, his inheritance became available and the future must have seemed bright. As Lord John, and then Lord William a year later, came of age and were eligible to stand for Parliament, the duke was clearly ambitious to revive their political fortunes with their participation, but for Lord John none of the Bedford family seats were currently vacant, having been retained for the family interest by Russell loyalists. Instead of waiting for a vacancy, at their meeting with the Duke of Portland the year before it appears that a decision had been made to take advantage of a by-election at Windsor to stand Lord John for Parliament there. Although this was unsuccessful, he was returned for the family seat of Tavistock in the 1788 general election, when Richard Rigby stood aside.[60]

Although John and Georgiana had still to decide where they were going to live in the long run, by October 1787 Georgiana was pregnant and it was at Gertrude's house that she gave birth to their first son, Francis, in May 1788. For the moment, though, Lord John had little time to contemplate their future, since at the end of the year the duke took his seat in the Lords and politics became the top priority. Letters from Georgiana to her husband at this time and into the next year are largely addressed to him at Woburn Abbey, which tells us that, along with Portland and Adam, the brothers, besides taking time for some shooting and visits to Newmarket, were busy planning their political strategy. It was also the first extended period of time that the brothers had spent together since their schooldays, and although they seem to have put behind them any problems or misunderstandings that had occurred in recent years, there can be no doubt that their relationship had to be substantially reconstructed to allow for the extraordinary change in circumstances that came when one inherited everything, including all the responsibility, and the others had to either walk away entirely or play whatever role was open to them.

At this stage, with a career in Parliament in the offing, Lord John chose the latter, and had been working closely with the duke, often at Woburn, before being returned for Tavistock in April 1788. While Lord John was engaged with his brother, Georgiana seems to have been enjoying her social life in Pall Mall, but one undated letter of this period also clearly indicates that she was fully supportive of his choice to concentrate on politics: 'I'm sure if you could have wrote me more you would have, I long like madness to see you, but stay as long as the Duke likes for Heaven's Sake and I wish you had told me if he was friendly to you; you know how I wish for that … and how little for anything else from him.'[61]

The note seems to confirm that, although engaged in a common purpose, Lord John's relationship with his elder brother was not entirely comfortable, and that the duke was somewhat unpredictable. Following his marriage and return to England in 1786, Lord John became an integral part of an organized effort led by the Duke of Portland to build Whig opposition interests in the west and south. As part of this effort the Duke of Bedford determined to reach beyond his pocket boroughs such as Tavistock, and he sought to use his Hampshire properties, Micheldever and Stratton Park, as the base for a new area of influence in Hampshire (Map 1). He determined that Lord John should lead this effort, and activity in June 1789 at Micheldever House suggests that this was to be their base to establish Lord John as a resident of Hampshire before standing him for election there in 1790. The contract for this work, however – that it should be 'no more … than is absolutely necessary for the temporary purpose of this summer and may be of the plainest useful sort, [it is] not required to be new' – indicates that the duke was not looking at this as a permanent home for the couple.[62]

In January 1789, the house at Streatham was settled on Lord William, who had come of age the year before, in preparation for his candidature for the Surrey constituency. No letters have survived from 1789 and so, other than the fact that Georgiana was pregnant again by August, there is something of a gap in the records, but the repairs on Micheldever House suggest that Lord John and Georgiana moved there in the late summer of this year, and stayed until the parliamentary session began in January 1790, at which point they moved back to London, having taken a house in Harley Street. With a general election coming in June 1790, Lord John was expecting to spend a lot of time travelling around the constituency in his attempt to take the Hampshire seat, and in anticipation of this, plans were made for them to move to the larger house at Stratton Park as their primary residence.

As Lord John began his election tour from a base in Winchester, Georgiana writes to him from Harley Street, 'The House is excellent,' and although she is not happy at the separation, she is 'resolved to be cheerful … how all adorable you are. Best of Men!', and busies herself with the opera and visits to the theatre. Yet beneath her apparent cheerfulness, something of her sensitive nature is glimpsed in a letter from February, when she tells him: 'Most truly and warmly has your kind letter (written when your room smoked and your candle was nearly burnt out) affected my feelings and left a quiet but soft melancholy throughout my mind,' a melancholy prompted by his revelation in a letter to her of his 'hidden thoughts'. Her reply continues: 'The Hidden Thoughts, which your kind confidence in me has caused you to record, pain me, altho' my Friend, I have long known it to be the case – but I imagine it was nearly destroyed by better Health and more contented Spirits – but we will exterminate its existence.'[63]

As the pressures of the election and political activity had begun to build, it would seem that Lord John, in an unguarded moment, had revealed 'hidden thoughts' about his awareness of an underlying 'melancholy' ever present in his wife that he found perplexing. Her reply appears to confirm that, beyond a recurring pain in her side, exacerbated now by her pregnancy, there was also a melancholic or depressive side to her nature, one which was to persist in spite of her promise to 'exterminate' it, and which, as their marriage went on, her husband found increasingly difficult to live with. Highly sensitive to the effects of illness and depression that had dogged his mother during his childhood, he appears to dread their reappearance in his marriage as well.

In April, when Lord John has just crossed to the Isle of Wight, Georgiana writes to reassure him that all is well, 'My side is so astonishingly better that it quite surprises me, I think the little unborn child moves near … I am sure that it is a boy.' In the letter she also includes some small pressed flowers to 'prove how very much I am formed to be happy at Dear Stratton, if we can ever go and establish ourselves there in peace and comfort', before going on to discuss at some length the election candidates for Southampton.[64] While she waited, she began keeping a close eye on politics, and while closely involved in the Hampshire election race, she was also following her father's negotiations with Portland concerning the borough of Wigan. Lord Torrington's interest in the borough stemmed from the fact that the constituency returned members of the Bridgeman family, into which his eldest daughter, Lucy, had just married.[65]

In 1788, just before the birth of her first son, Georgiana had written a will, and now in May 1790 just before she gave birth again, she wrote a second because of 'the great danger I was in after my first lying-in having justified my apprehension of another'. In the second will she emphasizes her concerns, raised in the first, about what happens to daughters if the mother dies in childbirth. She repeatedly requests that Lord John should not 'part with a daughter of your Georgiana'. She says that if people suggest 'taking charge of our poor girl, if we have one', he must refuse. Should the baby be a girl, 'Oh, keep her, educate her, and never never part with her.'[66] Having, as she says, nothing other than her sentiments to leave anyone, the only thing she asks is that he promises to raise all their children; it is a salutary reminder of the inequalities that in so many ways dominated women's lives, privileged or not. Fortunately, the precautions were unnecessary, and on 8 May a healthy baby, George William Russell, was born in London.

By 1 June Lord John, back from the Isle of Wight, has moved into the house at Stratton Park and is clearly expecting Georgiana and the boys to join him from London to await the election results. She writes to say that she is 'obliged' to stay in London a little longer because her sister Isabella is being presented at court, precipitating an angry letter from him accusing her of preferring to stay in London with her family and friends to joining him at Stratton Park: their first recorded disagreement. Georgiana, hurt but ever understanding, placates him, and arrangements are made for them to meet up at Highclere Castle to await the election results, and she appears to be full of confidence: 'I hear you are quite sure of success in dear Hampshire.'[67]

Unfortunately, others disagreed and a fascinating insight into Lord John's chances in the election comes from remarks made by a lady called Mrs H. M. Bramston to her niece, who said she was 'heartily sorry for Lord John Russell, who is a very amiable, worthy young man, his constitution delicate and loaded with bile, which added to his natural shyness, makes him a very unfit person for so rigourous an undertaking'.[68] He too may have felt this, and after joining the family briefly at Highclere, Lord John appears to have left for London, possibly summoned to join the duke, and Georgiana writes to him, 'Your mind is worked and harassed by this Election, I know you are anxious about it, and eager to succeed … we have talked of nothing tonight but of your election – Lord Porchester thinks that you are not anxious about it, how much does he mistake you!' She adds, 'We drove all over the Park after dinner to see the cows, the sheep and the Colts … I like all those sorts of things and it therefore pleased me – I long to see Stratton.'[69]

By now, both of them are looking forward to a stable family life and she is clearly anxious to see the house and get settled into their own home. Although the house had been substantially rebuilt by Lord John's grandfather in 1732, and he in turn had settled the house on Lord John's father, neither of them had ever lived there, so by this time the house and grounds would have needed some refurbishment.

On 16 June some of the results were initially encouraging; Lord William was returned for Surrey by a 'considerable majority', but then came news that Lord John had lost heavily, a distant third.[70] The result called for a quick change of plan,

Stratton Park, 1790s. The village of East Stratton lay in front of the house, and the gardens stretched up the hill behind.

and Lord John headed immediately for Devon to be returned for the duke's pocket borough of Tavistock in the election later that month. This at least ensured John's presence in Parliament, although it meant no real gain had been made in Whig numbers and, as Georgiana pointed out, all at some expense to the duke. Following the elections, Portland summed up the results in a letter to Adam: 'You will see that all Our Western Speculations have failed completely, as I expected, & I am sorry to add that those in the South have been equally unsuccessful, at which perhaps You will not be much disappointed.' He added, 'I am not dissatisfied with the results in general.'[71] Just how disappointed or dissatisfied they really were is not clear, but there is no doubt that the 1790 results took much of the steam out of the Whig revival, and by the late 1790s leadership of the party had inexorably drifted into different hands.

While Lord John was busy in Devon for the election, Georgiana and the boys moved into Stratton Park, and were established there by the end of the year. Although in November Lord John had to leave again for the new session of Parliament, she set about making herself at home and, after the concerns of the election campaign, was now focused on their domestic arrangements, and began thinking about the gardens. Beyond this she tells her husband, by now in London, 'I don't like your using the Hunter the Prince gave you as a Hack, I don't think it looks well, but you know best … I think like you that you will get no more hunting this year and that the Prince will come but little more to Kempshot, your not being here must make a great difference to him.'[72]

The ensuing seven months during the parliamentary session were difficult for Lord John. Confined largely to London and living in a succession of hotels, he had a lot of time to reflect on what his life had inexorably become. Governed again by factors he had little control over, and clearly against his deeper instincts, he had been swept up into a political life which he was not comfortable in and which called for long separations from the family he had fought so hard to establish. On top of this, the fact that, for whatever reason, he was living in hotels rather than staying at Bedford House in Bloomsbury suggests that the relationship between the brothers continued to be as uneasy as ever, and the strain soon started to show. Georgiana did her best to keep his spirits up with news of home and encouraged him to visit whenever possible – 'A good hunt would have taken away the smoke and bad air of London' – and in 1791 advised him on how the refurbishments of the house are proceeding.[73]

Following Lord John's return in June, the family were finally living together full-time for the first extended period since spring 1790, and began making serious plans for their life together at Stratton, redecorating the house, recovering the overgrown gardens, planning new features, taking control of management of the farm and extensive parkland. Lord John applied for a game licence to facilitate shoots, and the family started attending local social gatherings, such as Winchester Races. In addition, at the end of 1791 Georgiana was pregnant again. In January 1792, after what seems to have been a peaceful and productive six months, Lord John returned to London for the new session of Parliament due to end in June. This period is almost entirely silent, with no letters surviving, and can perhaps be explained by the fact that Georgiana lost her mother very suddenly, aged forty-eight, and her two surviving brothers, William Henry Byng, aged seventeen, and George Byng, aged fifteen. Devastating though this must have been for Georgiana in the middle of her pregnancy, these events are not mentioned and the dates and circumstances of these deaths are not clear, but the fact that no letters survive from 1792 perhaps indicates how difficult things had been.[74]

The toll these circumstances took would seem to be reflected in the fact that the baby, John Russell, was born prematurely in Mayfair, London, in August 1792, but though he was physically small and never very strong, young Lord John was to become one of the family's most successful politicians, playing a leading role in Whig politics in the 1830s. For now, though, the birth seems to have left Georgiana increasingly weak and prone to her melancholy episodes. Although they were both still young – Lord John twenty-six years old and Georgiana twenty-four – they had no more children, which might suggest that her health and physical delicacy following the birth were beginning to impact their relationship.

Although there is no correspondence to help illuminate life at Stratton in these years, some light is shed on their lives when, the next year, Georgiana began a series of diaries that cover the period between 1793 and 1795. Beyond the details of everyday life, these diaries tell us a lot about the things that caught her eye and her other great interest, painting, which she seems to have taken up with enthusiasm.

The first part of the first diary, and perhaps the reason she decided to keep it, was a proposed trip the family took in the summer of 1793. After being joined at Stratton by the duke and leaving the children at home, they set off to visit Hampshire and the Isle of Wight, where they met up with Lord and Lady William.[75] The purpose of the trip is unclear, although the island was already a fashionable summer destination, but by 10 August they were staying in a small house in Cowes. The duke, Lord John and possibly Lord William were not there, having gone to some pre-arranged meeting – most likely concerning their future election prospects in the county – which may well have been the reason behind the trip. Back in Cowes, Georgiana was awaiting Lord John's return and trying to find accommodation for her father and sister Isabella, who were also about to arrive. It would seem that for their father and the two girls this may have been something of a pilgrimage, a chance to remember happier family times and revisit places they had known when the children were all young, staying at a cottage their father had rented in Sandown Bay.

Arriving in Cowes they find it full of visitors, and she is 'in anxiety as to lodgings for [her father], and a house for Lord William who came on Friday. All houses are taken, it is almost impossible to get one, there are few, and none good, the village is of itself dirty and stinking which is a pity,' since the setting is so pleasant. Apart from this anxiety the rest of her 'day has passed in perfect calm … and a book I have resolved to read, thro having attempted to read so often in vain.' The book she wants but has failed to read is *Clarissa*, and so 'I must try *The Inconstant Lover*, or *The Happy Moment*, or *The Error of High Life*, or some such stupid stuff.' It is one of the first, and few, glimpses we have of Georgiana in 'perfect calm', entertaining herself.

On the 12th, 'Ld John came home today – and we passed the rest of the day in great comfort … walked out & sat in the shade of the Yew trees by the [Cowes] Castle … but my side is bad today & my chest.' In spite of this, the next day they visited Newport and 'went to Mr Rogers' shop, as he had been a friend to Lord John in the Election'. The next entry on 22 August was written at Lyndhurst in the New Forest, and from here they made their way back to Stratton Park, but Georgiana ends the initial diary by giving an account of two other trips they had taken before leaving. The first, a tour with Lord and Lady William in a chaise round the Isle of Wight to Seaview, Sandown Bay, Brading and back though Ryde, gives us a hint of why the area meant so much to her.

In spite of riding in the 'roughest Buggy which shook us so completely that I still feel the bruised marks on my shins', they 'proceeded through a fine Country mostly over downs and thro' lanes, looking down from each side, to a woody and well cultivated Country terminated by the Sea and on one side the Sussex Hills, Spithead, St Helens, Portsmouth' before arriving at Sandown Bay. Here they 'obtained leave from Mr --- to see his Cottages … we walked over it, and found it much altered and improved since the time it belonged to my Father, where the novelty of the scene had attracted me as a Child and fixed in me a pleasing recollection of the few months that we had passed in it, which made me see it again with a lively interest – it is cheerful and pretty.' After Sandown they visited Brading for lunch and returned through Ryde, the day ending with a visit to Carisbrook Castle.

The second trip, the next day, takes on some significance in the light of Lord John's later activities. Once again, they take to the rough buggy to better see the passing landscape and proceeded to Appuldurcombe, home of Georgiana's cousin Sir Richard Worsley, who had sent over 'a ticket of Admission' to see his collection of antiquities displayed in the house. They 'stopped there to see the House, which is good, but much neglected, & the Park is in a miserable abandoned state and is not in any way pleasing'; afterwards they drove on 'to Sir Richard's Cottage at St Laurence. He received us very kindly and showed us the place … The spot is well chosen, and the place made entirely by himself.'[76]

Although Georgiana does not mention it, the main feature of Sir Richard's house at Appuldurcombe was his notable collection of antiquities, one of the largest in the country at the time, which had been assembled on his four years of travel, during which he visited Spain, Portugal, France, Athens, Rhodes, Cairo, Contantinople, Troy, Crimea and Rome. Throughout his travels he avidly collected statues, reliefs and other antiquities which he then carefully displayed in the house. Having arranged and displayed the collection, he went on to publish the *Museum Worsleyanum* (1798 and 1802), a fully illustrated description of the collection, and a *Catalogue Raisonnée of the Principal Paintings, Sculpture and Drawings at Appuldurcombe* in 1804.

The description in the diary of the house at Appuldurcombe and its contents is unfortunately very brief, suggesting that this was primarily a social visit to family, but given the amount of time and money that Lord John would later expend on similar collections at Woburn Abbey, and also on publishing similar catalogues, it seems the visit may well have planted a seed of interest which was later able to grow once he had the resources as Duke of Bedford.

On 25 August they arrived back at Stratton with Lord and Lady William and were joined there a day later by her father and sister. Once home Georgiana writes,

Far different were my reflections when I reached this Dear Place … The cheerful[ness] of the Pasture, the foliage of the old trees, the foresty wildness of the woods make it a most pleasing habitation and I should be content to pass the remainder of my life confined in this small but comfortable habitation.

I found my dear children all in Health and Spirits, my John had forgot me, but I hope to regain his affection when I have fed him two or three times … and I expect my father here with Isabella on Tuesday. I continue suffering from both my Cough and the pain in my Breast.

From the diary it is clear that her cough and her pain were relentless, and by 3 September her peaceful life was turned upside down when her doctor 'determined on the necessity of my passing the winter in a warm climate, Alas! Alas! How contrary to my wishes. Our destination is not yet determined, but I fear a sad sea voyage to conduct us to it.' When Portugal was decided upon, she writes, 'Not for one instant have I been able to conquer the heavy dejection that hangs like a weight on my Heart.'

At the end of the month they went to London 'to prepare for our Journey to Lisbon' and then travelled to Woburn where it had been arranged that they will leave the baby, Lord John, to be looked after by the duke, being too young to travel. In town, they spent time at Carrington Place and met with friends, particularly Georgiana, Duchess of Devonshire, and her companion, Elizabeth Foster, with whom, frequent records of meetings suggest, Georgiana had a close friendship. Finally, on 16 October they left with Francis and William for Falmouth.[77]

After a delay in Falmouth waiting for the winds to change, during which Georgiana records that 'My heart is heavy and my spirits quite exhausted,' they had an uneventful passage and arrived in Lisbon in late November and stayed for the winter. Although they seemed to enjoy the cosmopolitan social life in Lisbon, they were looking forward to somewhere quieter so that Georgiana could convalesce, and in April the family made the 30 km/18 mile journey to Cintra [Sintra], an area of renowned beauty, where they stayed for the next sixteen months, a time that proved to be one of the happiest periods of their marriage. Free of distractions and comforted by the warm weather, Georgiana felt better than she had for a long time, and putting all the baggage of life at Stratton and Parliament behind them, they began to enjoy both each other's company and long walks and donkey rides through the idyllic surroundings. Even on the journey from Lisbon to Cintra,

Georgiana started noticing and writing about the countryside again, remarking initially on its lack of woods and trees, but then, 'after winding around the great Rock of Cintra … one can have an idea of this enchanting Place, with which I am every hour more delighted. Covered with trees on the uneven ground of the rock, rivulets streaming down on all sides. Birds in abundance singing on every Tree. The whole forming a most cheerful and pleasing Scenery, and the more astonishing as everything beyond is a dreary waste.'

They immediately started exploring the area, curious to see everything around them, and Georgiana was disappointed by a neighbour's garden: 'it is all stiff and walks with statues and stiff fountains … not the best part of Cintra.' She was often with the Duchess of Northumberland, who may well have helped them in their house hunt because Georgiana reported later that month: 'We conclude the bargain for our little cottage at Cintra.'[78]

On 6 June they moved into the 'cottage', and something of her new mood of relaxed contentment is caught in a diary entry from late May: 'At night nine ships came up the Tagus by the brightest moonshine I ever beheld. The effect was beautiful. The night was so still and the sky so blue and full of stars.' She relates a story about eating frogs and Lord John reminding her that this dish 'had been customary in Brussells'; privately, in the diary, she corrects him, 'I ought to know the habits of my second country … where I deny the eating of frogs, but on the contrary believe it a French kind of food and that very good.' She settled down into life in Cintra, and although she gives us no details of the house or how the boys and their nanny fit into their lives, we find her waiting for the morning fogs to lift and for the news of home – domestic, political and international – to arrive on the packet ships, the arrivals and departures of which were surrounded by uncertainty since they were at risk of being intercepted and captured by the French. One such piece of news marked the passing of an era, when they heard that Lord John's grandmother, Gertrude, had died in London on 7 July, aged seventy-nine.

Beyond entries like these, the diary records the peaceful days passing. On 5 July: 'We took a ride on our burros yesterday which was more beautiful than all those I have seen before. Parts of it were so picturesque [heavily wooded with evergreens] the tree tops covered with Vines hanging and twisting from tree to tree … little white houses … bridges grown over with ivy. The whole way as we were in the bottom, we looked up on these Hills covered with Wood and behind them the bold straggling rocks with their Moorish walls of palaces.' By August, the hot dry summer and peaceful burro rides seem to have worked their magic as her health had improved dramatically, and finally able to relax together, the couple started to explore their shared and growing interest in botany:

> I took a long ride with Lord John this morning and came home perfectly enchanted with the country which is inconciously [*sic*] beautiful and so much sheltered that in a cold and dismal day everything felt warm and cheerful. The lanes are so green from the Hedges that one can hardly believe that it is winter. They are composed of Prickly Pear evergreen with various creepers that twist from branch to branch, and the myrtle, the Holly, the Oak, the Cistus, the perrywinkles, and millions of plants and shrubs under the sides of the roads. So beautiful that one can almost fancy oneself in made gardens in the midst of summer. The Cistus is in full flowering, the Heaths are loaded with flowers, the furze, the rosemary and various others are in their richest beauty. Besides all these, there are many large trees in the Hedges … trees which from their great age and their old picturesque trunks have a better effect than I thought they could have from their appearance in other places.

And in January 1795, one particular entry is of some interest: 'I took a long walk with Lord John, the day was delightful and the abundance of wild flowers which the rains have produced make the fields look as if they were painted. It is a fine country for a Botanist. I wish I understood the science as much as I like it.' This is the first sign of the two of them taking a growing interest in botany and horticulture, which they would pursue once back in England and would become one of the central interests of Lord John's later life.

As the new year got under way, there is still a sense that things 'felt warm and cheerful'. Georgiana's diary recounts burro rides and walks with the boys, and she records herself, for the first time, being 'very busy painting', and a short time later, when the weather is bad, she writes: 'My painting occupies much of my time and as the weather has been too bad even for Lord John to go out I have spent the whole morning most comfortably in hearing him read whilst I paint.' This, like the interest in botany, is new, and she was to pursue it further once she was back at Stratton. The relaxed and happy time in Cintra is the first opportunity we have had to catch sight of Georgiana beyond the wife, mother and political cheerleader, and it becomes clear that her sensitivity extended into a curious and creative consciousness. As some of the passages quoted above indicate, she clearly enjoyed both writing and art, and some of the longer, detailed descriptions of the landscape are written as though, as a painter, she was analysing the composition of what she was looking at. Indeed, an enjoyment of writing should not really come as a surprise when we consider some of the individuals in her mother's family, particularly her maternal grandfather, John Boyle.[79] Writing certainly was in the family, and Georgiana's diaries are more than simply records of events; they also contain thoughtful passages such as this, written about a view near Newport on the Isle of Wight:

> The Country at each side of the River is pretty and looks well at this time of year being mostly cornfields … some very pretty groups of trees, and a Parsonage House in the middle of one of them. A little white Cottage singularly situated on a rising eminence, in the middle of trees looking on a river. It must be enchanting and it gives one the idea of peace and comfort. [The owner spends little time there] but those who have it not, think they should be content to live there always – Men pass their lives in searching for happiness and wishing for what they have not.[80]

Overall, the family appear to have been very close during their stay in Cintra, enjoying a period of freedom from the expectations on them, and, in particular, Georgiana enjoyed both her husband – 'his merits are not of a common order and I wish that he knew himself better' – and her children: 'I have been trying to amuse my dear Boys … I can more entirely devote my time to them.' She added, 'William has been very ill today, if it was not for my angelic Francis I believe my courage would fail me, but I never saw such a Boy.' By February, however, there appears to be pressure on Lord John to return and attend Parliament, now in session for two months, and with this comes the need to arrange the journey home, which was not a straightforward proposition. The long established packet service from Falmouth to Lisbon was run by three or four boats, of which the *Hanover* and the *Jane* were two, but the regularity and punctuality of the sailings were very much subject not only on winds and weather, but also the activities of the hostile French fleet, based in Brest and constantly active in the Bay of Biscay. The uncertainties and the dangers of the trip had been underlined for the Bedfords when, in June, Georgiana had received letters from her friend Lady Ann Fitzroy, who had been captured by the French on one of the packets and imprisoned in Quimper, where she was waiting, hoping at some point to be freed.[81] Such risks were very much a part of travel during this prolonged period of war, and Georgiana writes in March, 'the uncertainty of Packets renders it difficult at all times to say when one ought to expect them.'

Waiting in Cintra for news of the packets, after a period of storms the weather improved along with Georgiana's spirits: 'The sky without a cloud and the air mild, with scarcely any wind. I felt as if I had regained new Life and the beauty of the Country gave me that happy feel which nature alone is able to bestow. I took a long ride on a little burro, Lord John and my Dear Francis were my Conductors on foot and William met us with nanny.' A week or so later they finally got the news they had been waiting for: 'We leave this place tomorrow.'

By 9 April they were on board the *Hanover*, along with '2 Captains from the Engineers' returning home, and were on their way to Falmouth. 'Fortunately,' Georgiana notes, 'I am grown so bold a sailor as to attempt writing on Board a ship,' and we are able to catch a glimpse of the uncertainties and frustrations of their journey. A few days into the voyage the dangers of crossing the Bay of Biscay became apparent as the sails of two vessels appear on the horizon and, rather than waiting to identify them, the captain immediately turned out to sea: 'I was most alarmed yesterday evening by the cry of "A Sail", "A Sail" from the masthead … One was a brig but the other being a ship, Capt. Harris thought it most prudent for us to tack, fortunately we were not chased.' In spite of several days of calm, followed by westerlies which took them off course, by 13 April they had made some progress, but danger still lurked as their sea room narrowed in the mouth of the Channel: 'The wind continues favourable and we have made 107 miles…[and] we will pass the Lizard in 3 or 4 days … My fears of being taken [grow] as I get nearer the Channel [and] we lost many miles this morning by seeing a ship which as usual we avoided.' They finally arrived at Falmouth on 16 April after a week of incident and adventure.[82]

The journey home from Falmouth took them to St Austell and Plymouth, where 'The bells rang for our arrival, which was a compliment we could neither expect nor wish for … We crossed the Tamer at Tor Point.' From here they visited Mount Edgcumbe and met the Duchess of Devonshire, Lady Bessborough, Mrs Elizabeth Foster and the children before travelling on and reaching 'Dear Stratton' by 1 May. At Stratton the welcome from the village was even more exuberant, reminding us of the status, unimaginable today, accorded to the aristocracy at this time, and Georgiana was overcome with 'joy' when 'I heard the poor people of the village ringing the church bells for our return, I felt unable to support myself. Joy may occasion tears as with my grief and mine relieved me.' In return, 'Lord John has had Bread and cheese and beer distributed in the Park to the people of the village who were still huzzaring and as merry as we wished to see.'

A few weeks later Georgiana travelled to London, and then to Woburn to pick up Lord John, who was now three: 'I have been passing two days most delightfully at Woburn, I went there to see my Dear Child and found him a little good humoured Angel [very] fond of the Duke of Bedford, whose goodness to him certainly deserves some tenderness. The Duke of Bedford had the goodness to ask both Isabella and Lord Weymouth to go with me.' The 'goodness' displayed by the duke, both to her son and her family, clearly touched Georgiana, and she was noticeably more 'tender' to him over the coming years. Once home at Stratton, Georgiana settled down to country life, attending Stockbridge Races and then

Winchester Races with the associated balls, while Lord John turned his attention to running Stratton home farm, and for a couple of months entries in Georgiana's diary indicate that life at Stratton settled into a comfortable rhythm.

In early August, however, their 'comfortable' life came to an end as Georgiana's health started to fail again just as Lord John was obliged to travel to Tavistock to meet with the duke. It would appear that he too had health issues, quite possibly early symptoms of the gout which was to plague his later life, and planned to combine his trip to Devon with one to Cheltenham to take the waters; he left Stratton by early September. On her doctor's advice, Georgiana took the opportunity of Lord John's visit to Devon to travel with the children to Bristol for a change of air, expecting to meet up with him when he travelled on from Devon to Cheltenham. In a series of undated letters from her to Lord John we see her writing from Devizes and then Bristol, where she was looking for a suitable house in Clifton in order to 'take the air' on the Downs (presumably the Clifton and Durdham Downs), before returning to Stratton Park in late October. There is a strong sense of emotional separation in these letters, as though they are trying to get through a difficult period – she was consistently unwell and he suddenly appeared particularly unsupportive, to the extent that he bypassed Bristol on his way to Cheltenham and did not visit the family. It was the start of a pattern of behaviour that continued throughout his life: when illness struck the family, he removed himself for one reason or another and avoided the situation.[83] In this case, that situation was exacerbated by the fact that her doctors were hinting that she would probably have to go abroad again if her chest pains and discomfort did not improve.

On her way to Bristol, Georgiana wrote from Devizes reporting that the children were well, but told him just how challenging seven-year-old Francis's 'schoolboy' behaviour was becoming. The next letter was from Bristol and we sense her impatience with her husband, who had not joined them to help find a house: 'I should have written to you, yes, if I could have given a you a better account of myself but I am still on the first floor of a street house full of people, so tormented with messages to get a House by Ld Randolph that I really could not have wrote anything which you would have read with patience.'

Writing to Tavistock a few days later, she seems more relaxed and is focusing on the Clifton area of the city to find a house. She sends on letters from Francis and William, and tells Lord John to take the waters as long as he likes when he gets to Cheltenham, before informing him that she has 'got a home in Boyce's Buildings, Clifton Hill … too public to be comfortable, but where I shall be happy to see you.'[84] Once she has the house, the tension between them eased a little, and her subsequent letters to Cheltenham become a little more relaxed: 'I have nothing to say but that I thank you for your kind letter and that I shall be happy to return to Stratton on Saturday … I hope to be able to remain there and not have to leave England. I must request you not to name the subject and believe me that it is the wish of my heart to make your happiness.'

Clearly, this had been a difficult few weeks for Georgiana, travelling with the children, arriving in the city of Bristol, trying to find a house in the right area, not feeling very well at all, and now returning to Stratton without him; in the face of all this, Lord John's behaviour is difficult to understand. The journey from Tavistock to Cheltenham would have taken him directly past Bristol, and yet he seems not to have stopped, or even told her of his future plans; she has to ask him to 'let me know how long you think of remaining in Cheltenham … and whether you mean to go to Stratton or to return here', before adding, 'I am sorry to tell you that you have lost a Desert Spoon, and a Tea Spoon, best coat and hat. The House was broke upon in the night and it is fortunate they took no more and did not alarm us.' Perhaps Lord John felt a prick of conscience as he took the waters at Cheltenham, but soon enough, after the summer's travels, he returned to London for the parliamentary session, and in a series of letters Georgiana kept him up to date with the estate and the children.[85]

In October she reports, 'The weather is dreadful – John goes on well, the other two angels are busy painting as the day is too bad for them to go out,' and 'Francis wrote you a little letter … he writes quick and with great ease to himself and spells tolerably considering how little time has been spent in study.'[86] At Stratton, during her husband's absence, Georgiana was running the house, and one of her main concerns was working on continuing the developments of the gardens, which she admits is shockingly weedy but is delighted to tell him that 'the Heaths is in full bloom.' No doubt these heaths remind them both of those they saw in Cintra, and she confirms that they have 'the same smell'. The garden seems to be so weedy because there are clearly tensions with their gardener, Mr Lamb, whom she can only deal with 'when he is reasonable'. Lamb is evidently not at all comfortable dealing with her and not Lord John, and she ends by saying, 'Lamb has done nothing but remove Plants, and he is anxious to receive your orders.' Georgiana's final comment on Lamb was that he 'is not the sort of man I like or that you will ever like as a Gardener, at least I think not, but we must have patience … another season will enable you to judge'; Lamb was soon to be let go, having never altered his ways.

For all her evident engagement with Stratton and for all her domestic contentment, Georgiana also had one eye on London, and kept abreast of political developments through letters and newspapers. She read the latter regularly and was starting to miss not just her husband but also the excitements of the parliamentary session, something she was always asking him for news about: 'Oh! Heaven, what a state this country is in. Pray write me what you really think, whether these Bills are likely to go off quietly,' and 'I fear last night's debate could not be classed amongst the number, it must have been painful to you to see Human Nature so degraded.'[87] As we have already seen, if there was one big difference between them, it was that, unlike her husband, she was definitely drawn to the dramas and tensions of the House of Commons and political life, and was keen to stay up to date. As a close friend of Georgiana, Duchess of Devonshire, she no doubt participated in some of the gatherings of Whig politicians at Devonshire House, and with the Portlands at Bulstrode, and the discussions of personalities, policies and strategies that took place there. It is from this time that, in spite of herself, she encouraged him towards a deeper, more committed involvement, becoming increasingly bothered by his seeming lack of ambition: 'Pray take care of yourself and don't let a false opinion of yourself check your merits.' And, 'As you will know I often displease you by venturing to rate your abilities as highly as I think they deserve.'

While her letters at this time were largely concerned with encouraging her husband, a passage in one of them offers a rare insight into their assumptions about the world, the lack of self-awareness and naivety identified in the Introduction to this book, and how running the estate at Stratton had opened her to new experiences. She related a visit she received, and her words illustrate just why it took so long to achieve reforms that extended the electoral franchise: 'Farmer Sankins sent to speak with me and placing himself in an arm chair next the fire with a glass of Port, he really talked so ably on Politics … I really did not suppose it possible that Farmers were so enlightened.' Following this, she told Lord John: 'My side is better, so is my Cough … I am very glad that you are better,' but in December her pain and discomfort started to manifest themselves again, and she was 'tormented with visits and Lord William had stayed with me till I was quite worn out.' Then, following a visit from her doctor, Farquhar, she faced renewed discussion of her going abroad again: 'Farquhar was here twice … You know what I think of those orders for a foreign Climate − in this case it is the simple wish to get a case of which he has little hopes out of the way.'

Uncertain of her doctor's motives and reflecting on his advice she went on, 'The more I think of it … the less I feel determined, therefore we will, if you please, leave it to further consideration.' But 'at all events I would not again have you leave England, that I am absolutely determined against.'

By the end of 1795 or early 1796, however, Georgiana had indeed left Stratton. Perhaps as a compromise, not wanting to take her doctor's advice that she should go abroad again but aware that things were not right, she seems to have been persuaded to move to London for closer treatment. Once there, forbidden to travel by her doctors, Randolph and Farquhar, who were convinced that the physical consequences of travelling in a coach would exacerbate, perhaps fatally, whatever was causing the steadily increasing pain in her left side, she was now lodged uneasily with the Duke of Bedford at Bedford House, and missing her children very badly. She remained at Bedford House until at least May 1796, and they were six long months. Lord John, once again it seems reluctant to confront illness, visited London and Bedford House only occasionally, content to busy himself at Stratton. Indeed, the years 1794–6 marked his poorest period of attendance in Parliament, partly, of course, because of the family's travels to Portugal, but also it appears that he was working towards his preferred future: a quiet life of farming at Stratton.[88]

Bedford House, c.1730. At this time, Bedford House and Bloomsbury Square were an outlier of urban development north of the Strand, with open fields stretching from the gardens of the house towards the hills of Hampstead and Highgate. Although the surroundings had changed by the time Georgiana lived there, Bedford House itself was little changed from how it looked in the 1730s.

Georgiana's life at Bedford House cannot have been very comforting. The enormous house had not been a family home since the boys' childhood, and then only periodically; since their grandfather's death in 1771, and although used by Gertrude when she was in London, whole wings of the house must have been closed down, curtains drawn and the furniture draped in covers. Outside, although the house still overlooked gardens and the double avenue of elms stretching north towards the fields and hills of Hampstead, the views were changing rapidly. Ongoing development of the Foundling Estate was beginning to encroach on the views to the east, and the duke and his surveyors were already drawing up plans to develop the entire property; by the spring of 1796, the very future of the house itself seemed increasingly uncertain. While Georgiana was there, the duke seems rarely to have been at home, and, when he was there, seems not to have interacted with her very much at all. She reported in March:

The House has no particular charms in it – I suffer to give trouble and to be an inconvenience to your brother and his society, which certainly will always give me pleasure, cannot be an inducement as he is so little in Town, and you know the life he leads is totally different from mine. He has never breakfasted lately till near 3 – he has come to dinner only at 8 and gone out as soon as dinner is over. This you know as well as me – and you likewise know how little society I have of any sort.

Even dinner itself does not seem to have been very special. At one point she thanked Lord John for sending mushrooms and flowers from Stratton, but warned that 'the Caterer here does not deal in variety. She was Cook to the Dowager Duchess of Bedford and has much of her style of cooking – nothing very nutritious.'[89]

Although she rarely saw the duke, she appears totally reconciled with him since his care and attention to young Lord John while the family were in Portugal, and she was a keen supporter of his political stances. We can imagine that what gatherings there were at Bedford House, when the duke and his friends returned from the Lords, gave her at least a sense of proximity to the big political issues of the day. More immediately, however, the long months were difficult for Georgiana. A hostage to her doctors' advice, very unwell, stranded in a doomed house that lacked any elements of home, desperate not to 'inconvenience' her host, separated from her children and 'dear Stratton', she also found herself required to console a husband who was at home but starting to feel sorry for himself and complaining that he felt abandoned, and had to defend herself against charges of selfishness. In addition to everything else, Lord John had been particularly upset when, on 24 February, Edmund Burke published his 'Letter to a Noble Lord' in reply to speeches by Duke of Bedford and Lord Lauderdale in the House of Lords attacking the pension of £1,200 granted to him by the crown; the attack was based on the fact that Pitt had arranged this grant without parliamentary consent. The issue blew over, but Lord John never forgot or forgave Burke for his reply, in which he had characterized the Russell family as stemming from 'a minion' of a 'tyrant king Henry VIII', and, as we shall see, some thirty years later this still rankled.

The letters that followed reflected all of these issues, and reveal a great deal about the depth of Lord John's insecurities and his need for consistent emotional support: the very thing he clearly felt was being compromised, once again, by the illness of someone he depended on to supply it. In February 1796, although clearly unwell, Georgiana did her best to encourage him, warning him to be wary of 'the distress of your imagination … There is nothing in your situation that is not favoured to your content. Your income is not only clear but likely to remain so … You are fond of the Country, and are partial to Stratton which is rendered doubly interesting to you by the different works you have done there … You have got hunting … and you will now have the additional Pleasure of Farming which will be a constant resource.' Even so, she continued to feel that his greatest rewards will come from supporting the duke's political initiatives: 'of all the cares to which your natural inclinations lead you, none is more suited to your disposition than Politics.' She added:

> There is one reason which I think should add to your zeal on that subject – I mean the part that your Brother has taken, which ought to animate you more than ever in a cause you have ever supported right … These are not times to trifle with the Publick Good, and every honest and zealous individual who loves his Country should do his utmost in the most forsaken and suffering cause which is English Freedom. And where can it ever flourish if the House of Commons is abandoned by Honest Men?

Yet her insistence seems by now to have become a source of friction, since he was more intent on settling down at Stratton to a farming life, and, no doubt aware of this, she reassured him: 'I am sure you will be an excellent farmer in a short time,' and whatever the future holds, 'one thing I do assure you that if I should recover I am equally willing to lead the life of a Farmer's wife as any other which may be agreeable to you.'[90]

The one thing that kept her spirits up was the children, 'Pray talk to the Dear Boys of me, tell them how tenderly I love them – I feel anxious that they should never forget me or cease to love me,' and in spite of her insistence that they should not inconvenience the duke, the children joined her at Bedford House in early March. Their arrival clearly lifted her spirits, and in a more cheerful vein she wrote to Lord John about Stratton and instructions for Henry Holland, who appears to have been carrying out some of the refurbishments there: 'I long to hear particulars of Stratton and all your occupations. The Children are very well. I hope you will come back soon. Your brother went out of town this morning. I have not seen Lord William. [Henry] Holland was with me and desired to know what you thought about giving directions for the papering of the room.'[91]

Letters continue thus, sharing ideas on gardening work and the dismissal of Lamb, but then a few weeks later the mood darkened dramatically, when his growing irritation with her continued absence and her criticism of his apparent lack of political ambition boiled over. He seems to have accused her of using her health as an excuse to stay in London, that she had changed since being there and was now more interested in politics and socializing than in him and her family. Unfortunately, we do not have a copy of his letter, only her hurt and dispirited reply. In this letter she insists that he is wrong about her having changed, but accepts that

It is unlikely that I should ever recover my Health sufficiently to be again to you what I was, and therefore I with the heaviest regret relinquish all hopes of undeceiving you, for till you see me able to resume every accustomed endeavour to promote your happiness, you will always suppose me changed though I declare positively that it is not the case and that in no moment of my life have I felt greater warmth and affection for you, or more anxiety to promote your happiness, than I at present do and have invariably – more than this I will not say … With regard to Farquhar's decisions I can say little – you know I asked him to let me go to you as soon as you left Town, [and] he thought it would be exposing my life to the utmost danger … to remove me during the cold weather would probably shorten an Existence hardly worth the trouble it has given.

She is hurt by his accusations: 'Certainly I ought not to be supposed to stay here for my Pleasure. I do not even allow myself to see those friends whom I love as often as I might do – There is no person whom I see enough of to be supposed to remain for my pleasure. The distance is great from most of the people whom I love.'

She goes on to lament that

you have seemed continually hurt and angry at my wishing you to go out and to take exercise … I have always wished you to go out, to go into Society, to take a bit more active part in Politics … To your judgement and to your fair and impartial justice do I leave the opinions you may now form of my past conduct. During the short time I may be suffered to remain in this world those exertions will be lessened – I now find they are disagreeable to you … I have lost all influence with you as to your Happiness … I have written this with fatigue to myself and probably too ill to be understood … My health is a little better today. The Children are very well. Ever most faithfully yours, Georgiana.[92]

'Ever most faithfully yours': patiently and painfully polite, clearly he had hurt her, and the sense of lonely despair that she felt seeps into her words. This was a very difficult moment, and it is not known exactly what happened next, but the sense that it took some time for their relationship to come together again is perhaps indicated by the lack of letters covering the rest of 1796 and early 1797. In addition, when her letters do resume again in March 1797, they have a very different, much more distant tone; very few open with any kind of greeting, they are brief and they are all are signed 'G. E. Russell' or simply the initials 'G.E.R.' The other noticeable difference is that a great deal of the contents concern her increasing ill health, which appears to have dominated her life over this period. There is no record of the exact date that her doctors finally allowed her to return to Stratton Park, possibly when the weather warmed up over the summer of 1796, but by spring 1797 their locations had reversed: she was at Stratton with the children and he was in London attending Parliament.

A typical letter at this time is from March 1797, in which she writes: 'I am so sorry that your Bile is disturbed by the state of Public Affairs. I suppose you do not return tomorrow as I see your name as Steward of the Whig Club Tuesday, and you have not been there so long that you will probably stay for it,' before advising him to stay calm and not attack his opponents however much they goad him. Then in a most matter of fact way she tells him, 'The feverishness I have had for some days has ended in a spitting of blood which is of no consequence … in a day or two I will be as well as ever,' and adds a few days later, 'I have slept so ill … my Chest is in much pain … I dare say I shall be well in a day or two.'[93] By the summer, in an attempt to ease her symptoms, she was advised to visit her father and sister Emily beside the sea at Brighton, and is clearly aware of the effect her health is having on her husband. Writing to him at Stratton she says, 'I cannot express how much I feel obliged to you for having written to me. It has been such a comfort to me … Kiss the dear children for me. G.E.R.'

Throughout this period, and once back at Stratton, Georgiana consistently encouraged her husband's participation in the affairs of the Whig Club, and also endeavoured to convince him to take a London house rather than staying in hotels so that she and the children could visit – 'I should be there with you as you dislike being in London alone' – an idea he never adopted.

Up to this point, recent Whig opposition to Pitt had been focused around the leadership of the Duke of Portland, Charles James Fox, and the political gatherings at Devonshire House that we have noted before, but by the late 1790s the energy generated around the 1790 election had begun to dissipate. Following Fox's secession from Parliament in 1797 new leaders had arisen, new venues had become the key meeting points, and new issues were dominating the agenda. Hints of what was to come start to appear in Georgiana's letters, none more so than these from January 1798, in which she seems more abreast of developments than her husband: 'Lord Holland was in the chair [for a special dinner] on Reform' and 'I see you laugh at my friend Lord H[olland], very justly … but these are great times for little men.'[94]

By the late eighteenth century, politics was changing rapidly, and alongside facing changes in the party itself, two issues in particular were becoming increasingly pressing for the Whig opposition, issues that would require them, both personally and in their discussions, to look very closely at assumptions which they had grown up with and make some hard choices – parliamentary reform and the abolition of slavery.[95] To fulfil either of these ambitions they would have to examine aspects of their 'civilized' world of the Enlightenment, a place which, while apparently founded on precious liberties, still sought to limit suffrage on the basis of wealth and, perhaps even more disturbing, to exclude the populations of entire countries from 'civilization', even from humanity itself, on the basis of racial identity. In addition to these considerations, it steadily became clear to the Whig aristocrats and their allies that some of the privileges they took for granted had begun to seem untenable, particularly their entitlement to office based on pedigree and 'character' alone and the traditional control of parliamentary representation and political influence based on land holdings. They were going to have to make decisions that might go against their interests and against the assumptions that would have been made by their fathers and grandfathers.

Political change was in the air: 'related to the humiliation of the American War, the growing sense that something fundamental was amiss with the British political system, and the emerging parliamentary reform and revitalised economical reform movements which aimed at purifying the political life of the nation'.[96] Political change was mirrored by changes in the scientific and artistic worlds, both now propelled by the sudden removal of traditional certainties and the revelation of new ideas and new possibilities. So too in politics and governance, where ideas previously unimaginable became realities: a form of stable government shorn of a monarchy and aristocratic control was established under the American Constitution in 1787, and universal suffrage – male, of course – suddenly became a reality in France in 1792. While the American Constitution did not in itself establish who had the right to vote (qualification was left to individual states), it did open up wide discussions about new systems of government and governance.

When the Society of the Friends of the People was founded by Charles Grey and others in 1792 specifically to promote parliamentary reform, Lord John initially joined the society, but he resigned two weeks later, quite possibly under pressure from his elder brother, who did not support its aims. In spite of this Lord John remained committed, voting in favour of Earl Grey's unsuccessful reform motions in 1793 and 1797, though by the end of 1798 he had decided that continued parliamentary activity was futile, and professed a willingness to resign his seat if his brother gave the nod, and was more than ever convinced 'that an adequate representation of the people in parliament' was 'the only real remedy to all our grievances'.[97] His brother, needless to say, did not give the nod, and Lord John remained in Parliament until 1802, after which he went on to support his son Lord John Russell, and proudly watched him successfully introduce the Reform Bill of 1832.

On the other hand, by the late 1790s relentless work by abolitionists had forced the issue of slavery to the forefront. Since 1663 'modern' slavery, as illustrated by the British example, had seen slaves traded as part of a commercial enterprise sanctioned by the crown which involved human beings given a monetary value and being held on the basis of their racial identity, an identity seen as so base that it was considered that being an indentured slave was actually of benefit to them, since it helped expose them to European culture. In the eighteenth century, the impact of the writings of people like David Hume, who had stated in 1748 that he was 'apt to suspect the negroes to be naturally inferior to the whites', was rapid and profound, creating a racism that was conceived to provide 'the necessary moral justification … for enslaving black people … when it was no longer permissible to enslave white people'. This point of view created the circumstances which, just thirty years later, made possible an event so inhuman that it shook to its core the compliant complacency in England that had allowed the slave trade to flourish.[98] In September 1781 the slave ship *Zong*, owned by a Liverpool syndicate, ran low on drinking water in the Atlantic on its way to Jamaica, and to ease the situation the crew threw 130 slaves overboard alive. Little would have been known about this incident had it not been for the fact that the lives of the slaves had been insured and the ship's owners duly claimed compensation. During the ensuing court case, the Solicitor General, Justice John Lee, 'insisted that it was a matter of property, that Africans were not human beings, and argued … against bringing criminal charges'. Although the judge found for the insurers, stating that 'in some circumstances the killing of slaves was legal,' the finding was rapidly overruled on appeal by Lord Mansfield.[99] In the end no compensation was paid, but the story was out, and the widespread publicity around the horrors of the case led inexorably to the founding of the abolitionist movement a few years later. Led by individuals such as Granville Sharpe, Hannah More and William Wilberforce MP, the 'Society for Effecting the Abolition of the Slave Trade' was founded in 1787 with the aim of abolishing slave trading to British colonies and the emancipation of the slaves already trafficked, and the campaign took off in print and in Parliament.

By June 1788 the government responded to growing pressure by passing the Slave Trade Act, which limited the number of slaves per ship, but the next year Wilberforce introduced before Parliament the first motion for total abolition. It was unsuccessful, as was a second motion in 1791, and in his speech on this occasion Lord John Russell, no doubt reflecting the views of his peers and friends, was perfectly satisfied that former slave trader Henry Ellis's 'equitable' suggestion of regulating the 'term of servitude' made in a letter of March 1788 to the Board of Trade would indeed address the issue. Lord John then went on to make the case against abolition, considering it more 'practical' for the trade to be regulated in some way, and, in so doing, presumably accepted the premise that slaves were property with none of the rights of civilized human beings.[100] Fortunately others did not, and from 1791 onwards Wilberforce introduced a new motion almost every year until 1799, when support fell away as the war with France intensified.

Regrouping, with new ideas and new sponsors such as Henry Brougham, renewed pressure on the government led to the ineffective Slave Trade Act passed by the Whig government ('Ministry of All the Talents') in 1807, which outlawed the slave trade in the British Empire but made no provisions for effective enforcement. The issue, however, was not about to go away, and four years later the government passed the Slave Trade Felony Act (1811), which made participation in slavery a felony, and which was given some teeth when the Royal Navy established the West Africa Squadron to patrol the Atlantic. In the end, though, it took another twenty-two years before the Slavery Abolition Bill became law in 1833, abolishing slavery throughout the British Empire, and passing just three days before William Wilberforce died.

As Lord John was negotiating his way through these difficult issues, by the summer of 1798 it was clear that changes were afoot for his family. Georgiana had been in London and often visited Bulstrode, where she clearly felt very comfortable, but Lord John was spending increasing amounts of time at Woburn Abbey with his brother, where, along with regular visits to Newmarket races, they appear to have been working on a new political strategy and developing their plans for agricultural improvement; it was this summer that the duke held the first of what became the annual Woburn agricultural shows, or 'Sheep Shearings'. Writing to him from London, Georgiana told her husband: 'Our three Boys are now sitting by me … they are as amiable as ever and you only are wanting to make them supremely happy,' and passed on news of the Duchess of Gordon, who 'has sent you another invitation for tonight'. The duchess had spent the London season looking for a suitable husband for her seventeen-year-old daughter, Georgina. Georgiana wrote: 'Lady Isabella Thynne went with me to the Opera, and then to a farewell supper at the Duchess of Gordon's, she is gone, and tho' the Prayer Book was ready on the table, I fear no match was completed.'[101] By October, Lord John was still at Woburn Abbey, and before he could rejoin the family, Georgiana received news from him that rather turned her life upside down again:

> Nothing could surprise me more than the letter I received from you this morning, that you should have accepted the offer of Oakley under the present circumstances appears to me so incomprehensible that I believe something must have happened to make you change your Plans … You are very right not to consult me and I am really obliged to you – whatever can make you happy will please me and whatever may be Your determination I am as convinced of their Wisdom as I am desirous to do what I can to contribute to your content – I passed a delightful morning at Bulstrode.[102]

By this time, the duke appears to have given up on any progress in Hampshire and was turning his attention to the Bedford interests down in Devon. This meant, of course, that Stratton Park was no longer politically useful, yet it remained a considerable expense. Whether he already had plans to sell Stratton Park is not clear, but following the offer of Oakley, the family moved out and the house at Stratton was stripped, and three years later the entire property was sold. Clearly, the decision to move them came as a complete surprise to Georgiana, but it is not clear what she meant by 'under the present circumstances'. Nor is it clear what she really thought about the move. In the first place the family was moving from a major estate with a large house, extensive gardens and large park to a much smaller 'villa' on a small estate beside the River Ouse. In the second place, instead of being in deepest Hampshire, they were now living within an hour or so of Woburn, uncomfortably close, perhaps, to the duke and his activities. Yet the move had one very positive outcome, because it was here that the couple met Revd Charles Abbot, a renowned local botanist, and with him they not only developed the gardens but also began to pursue a serious interest in botany.

J. P. Neale, engraved by T. Matthews, *Oakley House, Bedfordshire*, 1818.

Oakley House had been bought by Lord John's grandfather as a 'hunting box' on the banks of the Ouse a few miles upstream from Bedford. In those days the river at this point flowed through a wide valley with large margins of reed beds, which were seasonally filled with wild duck, and Oakley remained a popular hunting spot for the dukes and their families well into the nineteenth century. Whatever the immediate reasons for the move, by April 1799 the family had moved into their new home and Georgiana had begun work on the new furnishings and the gardens. She tells Lord John in October: 'The weather is worse than ever. Lord O[rford] says you must get the *Flora Rustica* and pray look at a book entitled *Observations of Modern Gardening*. Lord Orford quotes it in the book he gave me.' The small size of the grounds and gardens at Oakley compared to Stratton is illustrated by the accounts, which for 1799–1802 record three different managers, indicating the job was not full-time, assisted by two to three boys.[103]

Charles Abbot was the vicar at Oakley Raines and a keen botanist who seems to have encouraged both Lord John and Georgiana to pursue their interest in the subject that had first developed during their stay in Cintra, and Abbot now introduced them to the science as they began to develop their new gardens at Oakley. Lord John was to write later that Abbot was a man whose 'botanical enthusiasm used to afford me both instruction and amusement',[104] and these few years at Oakley sparked an interest that was to become one of the great passions of Lord John's later life.

In August 1800 Georgiana spent the month in Tunbridge Wells, hoping that regular drinking of the waters there would ease some of her symptoms, but it seems the pains in her chest and side were relentless. She steadily became an invalid, worried as ever about the impact of her ill health on her husband's spirits, but determined to enjoy life at Oakley as much as possible. Her boys were twelve, ten and eight and under the care of a tutor while Lord John was busy in Parliament or on call at Woburn, and her letters over the winter into 1801 suggest she was busy with the gardens, her botanic studies and painting, and making the most of family life before her eldest son went off to Westminster School.

By June 1801, however, the doctors advised she move to Bath, once again in the hope that the waters would be of benefit, and in the hope she could avoid another trip abroad. It was not to be, however, and in October 1801 she died in Bath – away from her family but finally out of pain. We get a sense of the difficulties of her last few months when Lord John later wrote that he had been 'engaged since the commencement of the last year in attending the progress of a painful and lingering illness which by the will of the Almighty God terminated fatally on the 10th October and has deprived me of the society, the comfort, the enduring kindness and affection of one of the best women that [ever] was'. He felt it a 'heavy, a dreadful heavy infliction' but wondered if he had really done his best: 'I now find myself able and willing to review within my own heart those melancholy past transactions, and must find that I have to accuse myself that my attentions to a suffering angel in a bed of sickness and sorrow, were far very far from what they ought to have been, and I humbly implore pardon and remission of God, and if the sainted spirit of my beloved and lamented wife – looks down upon me that she will see my contrition thro' my repentant tears.'[105]

If the doctors had been unable to provide any useful diagnosis of what was causing her growing ill health during her lifetime, the autopsy result was equally vague. The report noted that everything appeared normal except that 'There was, at first view, no appearance of any Lungs on the left side … the left Pulmonary Artery, at the distance of an inch from its entrance into the corresponding Lung' was contracted and 'the left Auriele of the Heart was preternaturally small'; the blood vessels 'were contracted in the manner before described of the left Pulmonary Artery'. No conclusions or immediate cause of death were recorded.

The fact that the whole left lung and its associated blood vessels were very small would indicate a long-standing problem, if not from birth then perhaps from early childhood, possibly some sort of pneumonia or infection causing a collapsed left lung that was never diagnosed or treated. A collapsed and dysfunctional left lung would have left her feeling breathless and susceptible to fatigue and suffering recurrent chest infections and pneumonia as a result, in keeping with the description of the painful cough and pain in her side. Pericarditis generally also causes significant chest pain and, once enough fluid accumulates, stops the heart pumping effectively and results in catastrophic heart failure. So, in essence, this sounds like a chronic lung problem, probably becoming more frequent as she got older and the damage from recurrent bouts got worse. Although not specified, the actual cause of death could have been pneumonia, heart failure or pericarditis, possibly from an infection of the pericardium.[106]

The duke's reaction was warmer than might have been expected; writing to a friend he said:

> Since I last wrote to you, I have had a sad source of regret … My poor brother has lost his amiable Wife, his more than amiable Wife … I never met her like: a heart so warm, a mind so stored, and principles so settled, and with these, the most amiable modesty and an almost unexampled diffidence … My brother, however, sets us the example, he bears his loss with a noble fortitude, and tho' the wound is deep … I try to imitate him … but I can find no other consolation than the reflection that for years she had looked forward almost with impatience for the moment that would release her from this world and all her sufferings in it.[107]

For the remainder of 1801, we hear nothing of Lord John or the boys. He clearly felt considerable remorse for some of his treatment of Georgiana – his impatience, accusations, absences and apparent indifference at times to her suffering and need for support – and reflection on all or any of these things may have lain behind his 'repentant tears'. During this time it would seem that his greatest source of comfort was not his own family, but rather his two sisters-in-law, Lucy, Lady Bradford, and Isabella, Lady Bath. In January 1802, after all the formalities had been taken care of, Lord John left Oakley with his boys to visit them at Weston Park and Longleat respectively. Over the next three months we can follow their progress in a diary he kept: his first, and perhaps another legacy of his wife, it also illustrates just how serious an interest he and the duke were taking in agricultural improvements at this time.[108] Once at Weston, Lord John made a series of 'agricultural excursions' with his brother-in-law Lord Bradford to farms in the neighbourhood, where they inspected new styles of farm buildings, farm management, stock breeding programmes, machinery, quality and style of water meadows and tree planting programmes.

Unfortunately, he reports, 'The frost still continues – a great disappointment to the boys who are anxious to get some hunting – but they bear with it with their accustomed good humour.' By 19 January, 'Lord Bradford and the boys are gone to hunt with Sir George Pigot's harriers – the first time since the frost – I have walked over Lord Bradford's farm, most of it light worthwhile land, but in very poor condition,' and he is particularly disappointed with the water meadows and woods, both 'under unprofitable management'. The next day he also visited Sir George Pigot at his farm at Pattishall, where 'I viewed his stock, both of which pleased us much, he has some good new Leicester sheep, & some good cattle of the long-horned breed … He has a capital threshing machine worked by water, which performs the several operations of threshing, winnowing, grinding and chaff catching … Sir George is making some very valuable water meadows for his tenants.'[109]

Another day, while the 'Boys have all been hunting this morning and have had good sport', they visited Mr Monckton, who 'showed us his farm, he had done much with water draining and with good effect,' and he 'has planted about 60 or 70 trees about his house … and a fine oak in front of his house he has transplanted at the age of 70 or 80 years.' The following day, Lord John 'walked … to Blymhill to look at some willow plants, with a view of ascertaining the species of Leicestershire willow…[the proprietor] seems of the opinion that it is no other than *Salix fragilis*.'

It had clearly been both an interesting and a very comforting time for Lord John, and by 27 January, 'The 3 boys set out for London with their cousins to proceed to their respective schools' and he 'proceeded to Longleat'. Looking back at the visit, he writes, 'I feel deeply impressed with the unvarying kindness [to] my children … Lord Bradford has shown us every attention which friendship could suggest,' before making this observation: 'In Lady Bradford I see the counterpart of my Georgiana, all her mild virtues, all her solid attainments of moral and mental excellence – a fond and indulgent mother.'

At Longleat, with Isabella and Lord Bath, 'I have again to notice with gratitude the warm and friendly reception I have met with from Georgiana's family,' and he settled in for another comforting stay. Taking things day by day, he visited Stourhead, where he accompanied the farm manager to see the newly constructed water meadows, but then, suddenly, on 27 February news arrived from Woburn that was to change his life forever. His brother, the duke, 'suffered a strangulated rupture' incurred when playing tennis and appealed to Lord John to travel to Woburn. By the time he arrived, the duke had been operated on, but as Lord John tells us he was 'seized with very violent pain about 5.00 o'clock on Friday 26th'. The next day things deteriorated further and on 1 March, 'about noon my poor brother sent for me into his room, and with enduring affection, every tender solicitude, endeavoured to console me from the fresh calamity I was about to sustain. He then with the utmost calm and composure … delivered to me all his wishes, requests and instructions on every subject.' The duke died the next day in Lord John's arms, and at that moment the latter succeeded as 6th Duke of Bedford.

To Georgiana, Lord John and many others the 5th Duke had been a somewhat secretive individual and much of his private life remains unknown; on his deathbed he gave strict instructions to his brother that everything personal should be burnt or destroyed. His social life had either been very public – racing at Newmarket, partying with the Duchess of Devonshire's circle, hosting dinners, joining clubs – or very private: secret liaisons with several women and fathering at least two children.[110] And on his death, he left behind one more enduring mystery: had he or had he not just proposed to Lady Georgina Gordon?

—•—

PART TWO
Lady Georgina Gordon

CHAPTER THREE
1767–1785

I N 1785 a proud mother wrote that her four-year-old daughter 'astonishes Edinburgh with her cleverness'. The little girl in question was Georgina 'Georgy' Gordon, born on 18 April 1781 at Gordon Castle, the youngest daughter of Alexander, 4th Duke of Gordon, and Jane Maxwell, Duchess of Gordon. From the very start, Georgina appears to have been a gregarious and spirited child, her mother reporting from their remote hunting lodge in Glenfiddich in 1783, 'from morning until night Georgina's cheerful note is to be heard, talking of mama, and all her new friends, the Goats, the Kids, the Deer, and sisters, papa … to be heard in her interesting Rhapsodies.'[111] Although largely raised amidst the formality of the household at Gordon Castle, Georgina and her siblings spent a good number of their childhood summers with their mother at Glenfiddich, and for all her cleverness in society, she was thoroughly at home among the mountains and moors of the Highlands, for which she came to share a passion reflective of her mother's. She was very much the product of both the complexities of her background and those of the landscapes in which she was raised.

Although initially uncommitted, Sir Adam Gordon, a Lowland laird from Berwickshire, had supported Robert the Bruce following his success at Bannockburn in 1314, and after helping the king to consolidate his position in 1315 was rewarded with a 'grant of the lands of Strathbogie, Aberdeenshire, in the far north forfeited by the Earl of Athol'. Based at Huntly Castle, the Gordons steadily expanded their lands and built up an enormous holding that stretched across Moray and Aberdeenshire. The Huntly line nearly became extinct in the mid-fifteenth century, but when Elizabeth Gordon married into the Seton family and insisted her descendents adopt the Gordon name, the family name was secure.

Her son, Alexander Seton, changed his name to Gordon, claimed the leadership of the clan, and was raised to the title of 1st Earl of Huntly in 1445.

The 6th Earl was subsequently to become the 1st Marquess of Huntly in 1599 and his great-grandson, George Gordon, became the 1st Duke of Gordon in 1684. In turn, Elizabeth's Gordon cousins acquired Haddo House in 1469, and while part of their lineage, as the Lords Haddo, became the Earls of Aberdeen in 1682, the 2nd Earl of Huntly's younger brother, William Gordon, founded the House of Gight before he died at Flodden in 1513. Other branches of the Gordon family became the Barons of Stanmore, the House of Lesmoir and the Earls of Aboyne. In turn, the 'notorious Gordons of Gight in Aberdeenshire', 'a crazy crowd who so terrorized their neighbours for centuries', became the ancestors of Lord Byron.[112] In the fifteenth century the Gordons fought a prolonged battle for local power in Aberdeenshire with the Clan Douglas, and following their eventual success in 1454, the Gordon chiefs earned the enduring name of 'Cock o' the North'.

By the eighteenth century, the Gordons had helped to define the idea of a Highland clan, fiercely loyal to their chief but also violent, in almost perpetual feud, operating by their own codes and laws in the remotest, roadless places and, unlike their southern equivalents, largely beyond the control of national authorities. The Highland clan territories were seen by Lowland Scots, polite society of Edinburgh and the English as uncivilized, barbaric places, best known for their primitive smoke-filled hovels, poverty and lack of literacy, and superstitious and credulous nature: communities mired in violence, ignorance and idleness.

By the mid-eighteenth century, Alexander Gordon's ancestors of the ducal line had built up an enormous landholding, the estates eventually stretching from the Moray Firth and the east coast of Aberdeenshire to Badenoch, largely running west along the banks of the Spey, and then further west to the coast of Lochaber and Loch Eil. Alexander had succeeded to 'immense landed possessions – the largest in Scotland at the time',[113] and as the estates grew, the clan seat, Gordon Castle, first established for defensive reasons on land known as the Bog of Gight near the mouth of the Spey in 1479, was then enlarged by the 4th Earl in the sixteenth century, and finally by Alexander, transforming the old fortress tower in the late 1760s into one of the grandest country houses ever built in Scotland (Map 2).

Although the Gordons had a reputation for 'forcefulness and restlessness' with a tendency to 'action rather than contemplation', and as a family who 'produced very little literature', Alexander seems to have been something of an exception. He inherited the dukedom aged nine, and while the estates were handled by trustees until his majority in 1764, he was 'extensively educated' and attended Eton before travelling to Switzerland, France and Italy between 1761 and 1764. At this point, while in Rome, the young duke's portrait by Pompeo Batoni shows Alexander with a horse, gun and dogs, standing over a pile of dead animals and birds, reflecting not so much 'forcefulness and restlessness', but rather one of the lasting passions of his life – hunting. During his travels, he seems to have had little interest in either 'the ancient sites or classical learning'.[114]

However, if he was not a man of forceful action drawn to the legacy and symbols of Rome, he did show signs of a contemplative and artistic nature. When in Rome 'he commissioned several copies after the old masters by Angelica Kauffmann', displaying them later in Gordon Castle, and throughout his life he continued to enjoy art, music, dance and poetry.[115] For all this, however, records indicate that hunting and hunting society remained his principal interest, and his year revolved around the hunting calendar. During the spring of 1767, for example, in his first improvement of the castle grounds, 'the Duke [gave directions] to erect and inclose a large space of the new Park', to include a hare warren, along with 'a Canal in which his Grace designs a Decoy for Ducks and Teals &c', and 'went to his Highland country to Hunt for some time [with] … Tents and all other Hunting and Fishing Equipage, as the weather was favourable'.[116]

In mid-September of the same year, Alexander set off for London, where he was to take his seat in the Lords as one of the Representative Peers for Scotland. It was soon apparent, however, that while the young duke was very conscious of his rank, enjoyed the pomp and ceremony that accompanied it, and was ambitious to surround himself with trappings that reflected his status, particularly in terms of the grandeur of Gordon Castle, he was, as one writer has put it, 'a man of easy habits …

He interfered little in politics, his time being principally occupied in rural affairs, field sports, with an occasional trifling with the Muses, as is evidenced by his well-known song *Cauld Kail in Aberdeen*.' He also seems to have enjoyed poetry and on one occasion is recorded translating a poem from the Latin.[117]

In terms of the Gordon estates, rather than working consistently with his agents on long-term plans and strategies which would consistently improve and build up the infrastructure, income potential and, in particular, resilience of the tenanted farms at a time of momentous changes in traditional Highland life in a post-Culloden world, the duke largely left matters to drift, intervening only when estate revenues began to regularly fall short of his financial needs, and then took short-term, unsustainable measures such as selling land and raising rents.

Equally, rather than engage with the business, bother and cost of electioneering and sponsorship of candidates to maintain a power block in Parliament, the duke surrendered his political 'interests' to the control of Scotland's Lord Advocate, Henry Dundas, later Lord Melville, in 1783, and with the exception of using his position to encourage support for some of Dundas's candidates in local elections, the duke took little further active part in political affairs.[118] Dundas was an ambitious and powerful figure in Scottish politics, having used his position to build up a network of connections to create his own political interest controlling parliamentary candidates and their seats. Holden Furber tells us that by 1783 Dundas, who had already achieved his aims in the Edinburgh region and the Borders, was now newly committed to the Tory cause and keen to 'increase his influence in the North'. To this end, in December 1783 he wrote a letter to the Duke of Gordon in which he offered to become the duke's 'political guide and mentor', and take control of the duke's 'vast political interest across three counties' in the north: effectively, putting himself in a position to select and nominate MPs across the duke's extensive land holdings. Clearly, the proposal was not a complete shot in the dark, and it suggests that Dundas already knew the duke well and felt that this was an idea he would entertain, and, sure enough, 'the Duke replied on the 6th December gratefully accepting Dundas's offer,' thus ending his active participation in politics.

In May 1767, however, the young Duke of Gordon's carefree life changed forever when he stopped off in Edinburgh on his way to attend his sister Susan's wedding in London.[119] Taking the time to attend a ball at the Old Assembly Rooms he met and danced with Jane Maxwell, a young seventeen year old whose beauty and vivacity had made her the toast of Old Town society; swept up into her exuberant world of dance and fun, the reserved young duke did not stand a chance. They were married at her brother-in-law's house at Ayton outside Edinburgh some four weeks later, and it was not until December that the duke finally made it to London, and when he did so, he was accompanied by his new duchess.

The new Duchess of Gordon was not a fellow Highlander, but came instead from the Maxwell family of Wigtownshire. In 1760 her father, Sir William Maxwell, sold much of his estate to pay off debts, and the family had moved to his town house at Shrub Hill on Leith Walk, Edinburgh, when Jane was eleven. The circumstances around selling the estates and moving to Edinburgh could not have been easy for the family, and James Boswell, meeting Sir William two years later, described him after the move as having been 'formerly … a genteel, pretty-looking man. Now he looks like an overgrown drover. He entertained us with many of the exploits of his youth, which were however a little too marvellous.'[120] Soon after the move, it appears that the stresses involved exacerbated existing tensions in their marriage and caused Jane's parents to separate, her mother taking an apartment in Hyndford's Close, off the Royal Mile, where Jane grew up with her two sisters, Catherine, thirteen, and Eglantine, nine. Our first eye-witness account of Jane comes from a story involving her and younger sister Eglantine told to the author of the *Traditions of Edinburgh* (1847), and included in his section on Hyndford's Close, which was

At the bottom of the High Street, on the south side … The entry and stair at the head of the close on the west side was a favourite residence, on account of the ready access to it from the street. In the 2nd floor of this house, lived … Lady Maxwell of Monrieth, and there brought up her beautiful daughters, one of whom became the Duchess of Gordon … Lady Maxwell's daughters were the wildest romps imaginable. An old gentleman, who was their relation, told me that the first time he saw these beautiful girls was on the High Street, where Miss Jane, later Duchess of Gordon, was riding upon a sow, which Miss Eglintoune thumped lustily behind with a stick.[121]

A number of stories suggest that the girls, particularly Jane and Eglantine, pretty much had the run of the streets around Hyndford's Close and became well known in the area for their high spirits and adventurous natures. As a young teenager Jane clearly grew up confident, very streetwise and quite capable of giving as good as she got among the denizens of Old Town, with a sharp tongue to match her attitude; part of polite society's disapproval of her in later years stemmed from the fact that she never lost some of these traits and appeared among them as an exotic presence from another world. In 1763, her high spirits caused her to lose part of a finger on her right hand, when she slipped jumping on to the back of a passing cart and caught it in one of the wheels. It was something she remained very conscious of and always ensured that the damaged finger was kept hidden in all subsequent portraits. Fortunately, some order was imposed on the girls' lives by a family friend, Henry Home, later Lord Kames, a central figure in the Scottish Enlightenment who, according to one source, 'customarily invited intelligent young people to his house for reading and discussions. Home encouraged his "pupils" to read and study, and among his other protégés were Boswell and Adam Smith, and Home remained a friend and correspondent of Jane's until his death in 1782.'[122]

In November 1767, following her marriage, Home wrote to congratulate Jane: 'Madam, It gave me solid satisfaction, nay joy, to hear that you had drawn so great a stake in the Lottery of Life … Formerly your Business was to please all the world: it is now to please one man and to study every art for making him happy.' He then apologizes for passing on advice, but does so because 'I have long been in the habit of considering you as my adopted daughter. As I was not young enough to be a Lover, the next character of importance was to assume the guardian … and you always took kindly to my ambitions.' Finally, he writes, 'in time, I shall learn to know my distance and to treat you with the deference which is due to a person of the first rank … Your Friend[,] Henry Home.' He then adds a postscript: 'Perusing a second time your *billet douce*, I discover a circumstance that flatters my vanity extremely, which is that it bears the date of the very day of the celebration. How could my Child be so good as to think of me upon that important occasion?'

Among the things that Home warned young Jane about following her marriage was 'Play', or cards and gambling, and in reply she hopes an account of her conduct 'since I came to this vile city [London]' will set his mind at rest: 'I have gone to very few publick places … I find more satisfaction in being at home with the Duke than in going to any publick places in the World. I have never play'd at Cards but one night since I came to London.'[123]

The other person from whom Jane received advice at this time was her father. In a long, affectionate letter to congratulate her on her impending marriage, he too had advice:

My dear Jeany,

I assure you it made me altogether Happy to find the long and variously told story of your marriage confirmed by yourself. I must now as it is probably the last time I shall have ane [*sic*] opportunity of offering you any advice. The man who is soon to Honour you with his hand, is by Birth and Fortune, a match for any Lady in Britain, but that is little … and men of sense say he is a pattern of those virtues now almost lost, which can only constitute Romantick Happiness … but never, my dear Jeany, lose sight of yourself. Consider that Charms are only attractions, and from various causes and accidents may be impaired or fade away … and Titles only enoble where properly placed. As I hope you shall always find Happiness at Home, I shall say nothing of that distracted, gay Hurry which you will soon be call'd to, where you will see Pride, and Envy, Rancour and Falsehood reign without control … London is not the High Road to Heaven.

I am my dear Jeanie's

Sincere and affectionate father,

Willm Maxwell[124]

Although her parents were separated, it seems clear that her father remained a presence in her life and that she also kept in contact with the family in Wigtownshire.

Quite apart from her new status and the sheer extent of the Gordon estates, one other aspect of the world into which Jane entered that is very important in this story is the location of a significant proportion of the estates along the 'Highland Line'. This was a distinct cultural boundary that ran, and still does to some degree, from Helensburgh (just beyond Dumbarton) and Nairn (on the Moray Firth), marking 'the boundary between Gaelic and English speaking Scotland'.[125] 'Lowland' in this context means the predominantly non-Gaelic-speaking areas of Scotland, with the 'Highland Line' the hazy, liminal boundary separating these Lowlands from the Gaelic-speaking Highlands, creating a very interesting interface where the traditions, languages, histories and cultures of both interacted, throwing up new cultural forms and a society which was subtly different from those to the north and south.

Most interesting for us is that Gordon Castle and much of the Gordon lands, including Kinrara, lie within this boundary zone. Indeed, as Strathspey runs north-east from Kingussie towards Grantown-on-Spey, it forms part of the Line itself. While the Gordons considered themselves Highlanders and participated in Highland society and culture, much of their time was actually spent in the Lowlands, particularly Aberdeen and Edinburgh – and, indeed, in London – participating fully in Lowland and English society and culture, and from the eighteenth century onwards they represented an interesting mixture of both. While Alexander Gordon may have had a Highland background, Jane Maxwell's family was from Wigtownshire in Galloway and she grew up in the centre of Edinburgh, subjecting her to a very different set of influences. What for Alexander may have been a simple process of rediscovery of Highland culture, after much of it was proscribed and banned following the defeat of a Stuart restoration at Culloden, for Jane represented a dynamic and exciting discovery of a culture she knew only by repute, and their mother's zealous adoption of Highland ways was a dominant factor in the upbringing of the Gordon children. Particularly influenced by these circumstances was Georgina, the youngest daughter, and the one who spent the most time living on the Highland Line in Strathspey with her mother; it was to have a considerable impact on both her and, after their marriage in 1803, on her husband, John, 6th Duke of Bedford, who seems to have fallen in love with her romantic background perhaps as much as Georgina herself. It was a background created by fluid interaction of people and culture, where norms of society to the north and south did not apply so rigidly; it threw up behaviour and attitudes which, transposed to places in the south, appeared eccentric, irrational and even threatening to the status quo.

Given Alexander's laissez-faire approach to estate affairs once he became duke, much of the burden of the day-to-day management fell on his staff, and some of these became important figures in the lives of the Gordon children. Two in particular who were members of the household staff had a lasting influence on the younger children: William Marshall and James Hoy.

William Marshall was born locally and went to work at Gordon Castle as a boy, rising rapidly through the household with 'ever increasing responsibilities – first as Butler and then as House Steward', until eventually he ran the Gordon households in both Scotland and London. He was clearly a man of extraordinary talents, and he 'strove to master the basics of astronomy, horology, architecture and falconry, taking advantage of the opportunities for learning he found at Gordon Castle'. He went on to 'acquire a reputation for fashioning precision instruments … including an astronomical clock'. In 1790, he left Gordon Castle aged forty-two, moving eventually to a farm at Keithmore, near Auchendoun Castle, when he became factor to the duke, with responsibility for estates in Banff and Aberdeenshire. Retiring in 1817, aged sixty-nine, Marshall 'spent the last years of his life in Dandaleith, near Craigellachie Bridge'.[126]

In addition to taking a great interest in a range of scientific subjects, perhaps most importantly of all, he was one of the finest traditional fiddle players of his generation. Scottish music at this time fell into two categories, defined by Dr John Gregory as 'one for the learned in the science, and another for the vulgar'. The 'vulgar', he continued, 'is perfectly suited to dancing, and the plaintive music particularly expressive of that tenderness and pleasing melancholy attendant on distress in love' – and we know it as 'folk music' – while the music 'learned in the science' is 'composed art music', or 'classical'. While classical music, much of it imported from London and the Continent, was very much part of polite society in Edinburgh, rural Scotland, including the Highlands, had remained a repository of vernacular folk music traditions, and with the possible exception of a few minuets newly introduced from France, for the seasonal balls, barn dances and gatherings where servants and family members shared the dance floor, the traditional reels, jigs, hornpipes and gallops were danced to folk tunes. And key to all of this was the rise of the fiddle, which coincided, and in part created, a 'boom in dancing in Scotland, which called into being a completely new repertory of fiddle dance music'.[127]

At Gordon Castle William Marshall was the key figure in placing folk music at the centre of dance entertainments, since he was not only a very talented fiddle player, but also a prolific composer of original dance tunes, and encouraged by the duke and duchess, some twelve or so of these were composed to mark the birth of the children and for family members. In addition to traditional reels, sometime after 1730 a new style of dancing emerged 'designed to go with Scottish folk songs': a 'new type of slow reel, the strathspey, originally presumably from the Spey valley … appeared in the Lowlands during the 1760s and caught on very quickly.' The precise origins of the strathspey are a hotly debated topic, but it is generally agreed that its emergence was the result of a fusion of influences from north of the Highland Line, particularly the unique Scots 'snap' in the rhythmic pattern, and from the south, from Continental instruments (the violin/fiddle) and dance forms, especially the minuet. The name of the dance is, no doubt, an indicator of where it originated.

In addition to dance music, Marshall 'also wrote recital pieces of a new type which he invented, the "slow strathspey", pieces in the strathspey rhythm but too slow for dancing; they were usually nostalgic in character.' Thus, Marshall was not just an innovative and influential musician; he, alongside Jane, was also responsible for helping to popularize the strathspey dance, typical of the kind of music Georgina grew up with, as well as being a central figure in the Gordon household, responsible for much of the management and the entertainments for the Gordon

Castle parties. He was also close enough to Jane to have been included among the assembly at George Square commemorated in the painting 'Meeting of Burns and Jane Maxwell in Edinburgh, November 1786'.[128]

Equally, James Hoy, who was employed at Gordon Castle between 1781 and 1827, became an important part of the family. As a young man Hoy had shown an early interest in science, and although employed as librarian and literary companion to the duke, Hoy had wide scientific interests, sharing an interest in astronomy with the duke, as well as entomology and botany, and he 'made almost daily observations of the heavenly bodies, and from his having undertaken the regulation of the clocks at Gordon Castle and Fochabers, it was a matter of notoriety that his was the only accurate kept time in the north of Scotland.' When Hoy arrived at Gordon Castle, William Marshall was thirty-three years old, and it may be that from this time he was able to 'take advantage of the opportunities for learning' and studying both horology and astronomy under Hoy. Beyond the possibility that he helped Marshall, Hoy's role seems also to have included acting informally as a kind of tutor to the children, especially the girls, who were not sent to school and who did not leave home until they were married. In addition to all this, he almost certainly also helped with finishing the work on the new village built at Fochabers and the further landscaping of the park and gardens. Hoy is remembered as a 'singular and original character' whose business was 'to devote his forenoons to reading [the newspapers] when they arrived; and then he was enabled, as they sat tête-à-tête over their bottle of claret together after dinner, to fill the duke with all that was worth remembering'. When 'Robert Burns visited Gordon Castle, he was particularly delighted with Hoy's blunt manner, and perhaps the circumstance of his being a native of the Borders gave him additional value on the poet's estimation.'[129] In addition, while the duke was away or otherwise busy, Hoy joined Jane and her daughters, as in this instance in late autumn 1788: 'The Duke has been for some days hunting, feasting, and dancing in Banff … The surrounding mountains, indeed the plains, are white with snow, but we have no company and are very happy. I and my girls work, Mr Hoy reads aloud. I wish you were of the party.'[130]

By November 1767, following their marriage and visit to London, the couple travelled up to Gordon Castle, and their arrival is recorded in the 'Diary of Events at Gordon Castle': 'His Grace returned to Gordon Castle with his Dutchess, in company with his Mother, his two Sisters Lady Anne and Lady Kate, Colonel Morris, and Lady Maxwell, her young Grace's mother and Mr Maxwell, a brother to her Grace.'[131]

It is clear from this that, from the very beginning of Jane's life at Gordon Castle, her parents and other family members were welcomed by the duke, and we see Jane's mother in particular regularly staying at the castle over the years, sometimes for as long as five months. Indeed, it would seem that even though her parents were not living together, they still met up and appear to have been on good terms, and both her parents and her brother-in-law are all recorded as being present the next year at the christening of Jane's first child, Lady Charlotte.[132]

In 1768, with the Gordons' married life and family underway, Jane wrote again to Henry Home. She thanks him for his advice and goes on: 'My experience in Life is small but … I value your kind hints as they may assist me to be what of all things I wish most – A good Mother and a good Wife to the best of Husbands.'[133]

The same year work began in earnest on the enlargement of Gordon Castle, and continued on and off for the next twenty years or so. At this point the duke commissioned John Baxter Jr, an Edinburgh architect, to enlarge the castle; a new four-storey block was built around the original six-storey tower, and subsequently two new two-storey wings were built on either side. James Beattie described the resulting building in 1777 as 'one of the finest in the kingdom, being no less than 568 ft in length'. By June 1769, 'being the anniversary of his Grace's Birth, 1743, was laid the Foundation Stone of the new Addition and further Improvements of Gordon Castle in the presence of His Grace, Her Grace, Lady Maxwell and many Gentlemen Free Masons.' Following this in June 1773: 'His Grace laid the Foundation Stone of the Western Addition to the Castle, which is to be exactly like the Eastern one now finished.'[134]

Externally not much had been done since floods 'the like had never been seen' destroyed part of the park in September 1768. The Spey 'quite altered its channel', but fortunately these did not affect 'a new Garden at some distance from the Castle, in a fine well air'd field', created some five months before, where in 1772, 'his Grace erected, in the Garden mentioned above, a Parnassus, or Pleasure Romantic House, from which is a visto or Prospect of a part of five counties in Banff, Murray, the mountains of Loch Cathness[?] and Aberdeen.'[135]

It was not until 1775 and 1776 that the Gordons turned their attentions to the landscapes of the parkland to the south and west of the castle previously devastated by the floods, and in 1775 masons were employed 'making an extensive and very necessary Drain'. With precautions against further flooding underway, one of the first decisions was to move the village of Fochabers, which in its original location limited the potential for development. Designed largely by John Baxter, it was rebuilt south of the castle between 1776 and 1780 on the line of the Aberdeen to Inverness main road, and provided the location for the bridge built later over the Spey. With the old site cleared, the landscaping included the 'New Park', complete with plantations, a lake and Jane's private gardens.

We also catch an early glimpse of family life at the castle, when the 'Diary of Events' records that in March 1775 a dancing master was called to teach the marquis (aged seven) and his sisters, and that in December 'her Grace called from Fochabers the whole children Boys and Girls (about his age) to a Ball (about 40 in number).' After the dancing, 'Her Grace treated at supper all the children with her own hand.' We can, perhaps, assume that since 'with her own hand' is specified like this, it may have been considered unusual. In July the next year, the family returned from London 'and all their servants, even such as had come by sea, landed at Garmouth … [The duke] has bought three ships for amusements'; in August the 'Duke of Buckclough arrived at Gordon Castle … to pass some time Deer hunting in the Duke's Forrests', and 'both their graces amus'd themselves in joining the Masons in erecting a new Stair from the bottom to the top of the Castle.'

Between 1775 and 1779, Jane does not appear to have been active at the castle, but in 1779 accounts suggest she began to take an interest again. Rosemary Baird tells us that Jane chose a particular lime tree 'whose branches she trained to form an arbour in which she could sit' and quotes Jane's comment to Henry Home: 'I go

Lady Louisa Tighe, *Gordon Castle*, 1850s, from her album 'Views of Scotland'. Louisa was the daughter of Charlotte Gordon and the 4th Duke of Richmond, and her picture indicates the sheer scale of building undertaken by her grandparents, the 4th Duke of Gordon and Jane Maxwell.

every Morning before breakfast to visit the Shrubbery.' Baird goes on: 'She also had her own summer house at Cotton Hill, in which the plasterers created a special decorative trophy of garden implements on the wall.'[136] This summer house may well have been the 'Parnassus' erected by the duke seven years earlier.

Against a background of severe crop failures and famine between 1770 and 1776, life at Gordon Castle and all this expenditure did not come without a price, as the estate managers, without a long-term improving plan in place, steadily raised the rents to keep up with the growing cost of the massive building works at the castle, the landscaping and the new village, not to mention the personal expenditure of the growing family. In the face of the great debts that were building up, the duke 'took a trip to his estates of Inverness and Lochaber and Badenoch. The whole possession of all these countries are to be set and leased at this occasion, as well as the Glens and Grazings, the Black Water and Glen Fidich in Auchendoun, Glentruin in Strathavon, Glen Feshie and Gaik in Badenoch, several more in Lochaber, and one or two in his Castle lands of Inverness; this must make a considerable addition of Rent … to his Grace's yearly income.' Not only does this list give us an interesting glimpse of the sheer size and geographical spread of the Gordon estates the duke had inherited, but the leasing of such large areas also indicates just how much 'addition of Rent' was required at this time.

As Jane adjusted to her new life during these early years of the marriage, we also catch glimpses of her development as both duchess and an individual. For example, in a letter to Home in January 1769, she asks him for help 'in laying down the plan for establishing some sort of manufacture here, to add greatly to my happiness and that of all the poor peoples in the country', perhaps 'some sort of one established in Fochabers thru making of Linen Cloth', and since 'a very clever man' already makes it in Huntly, and they could sell what they produce to him.[137]

Following this kind of initiative, Charles Fraser-Mackintosh notes that, after their marriage and before they got busy at Gordon Castle, 'the Duke of Gordon brought Jane Maxwell, the new duchess, to the north, and they visited all his estates. She was not taken with Gordon Castle, but was so much struck with Kinrara that she at once made up her mind that it should become her Highland residence, and she stuck to it to the last, ordering that her remains be there laid.' The place which had had such an impact on her was an old farmstead at Kinrara on the west bank of the Spey a few miles south of Aviemore. The old 'but and ben' bothy stood among its meadows and haughs running down to the river, with rougher grazing and woodland above on the steep slopes of Tor Alive. It was a minute part of the Gordon lands in Badenoch, but what made Kinrara particularly special were the wide open views across the Spey, out towards the Cairngorm Mountains. Whether she made up her mind there and then that it should become her residence is not so clear, but two years later in 1770, 'a clearance order for North Kinrara, signed in Feb 1770 by the Duke of Gordon "warned out" over 24 families, involving at least 100 people, from Kinrara and Dellifour.'[138] It is also not clear, however, whether this clearance was actually carried out in full at this time.

Whether or not Jane 'chose' this site at this time, she certainly came back to it and occupied the Kinrara farmstead from about 1792, but for the time being her gardens at Gordon Castle served as suitable retreats from the increasingly busy household in the castle itself. Not only were there many guests, including Sir William Maxwell, Jane's father, and her aunt, on a six-month-long visit, but over the next few years an heir to the duke, George, Marquis of Huntly, in 1770, and two more daughters, Madelina, in 1772, and Susan in 1774, were all born.[139]

From 1775, however, Jane also found a new place of retreat at Glenfiddich, which, being much closer to the castle than Kinrara and more convenient for quick visits, became of increasing importance to her. Here, the upper reaches of the river Fiddich run through a remote and intimate glen, before flowing out into

Glenfiddich Lodge, 1788, from Revd Charles Cordiner, *Remarkable Ruins &c.*, 1788. This shows the lodge as it was enlarged for family visits, and with the exception of the ramp down to the river Fiddich, the scene is remarkably similar today.

more open country below the ruins of Auchindoun Castle and eventually joining the Spey at Craigellachie. It was one of the duke's favourite locations for hunting on his estates at this time, and the 'Diary of Events' records that in August 1772, 'His Grace went to Glenfidich in Auchindoun to Hunt, where he caused to be built a House to lodge in while there … and stayed some weeks.'[140] The lodge was completed by 1774, the year that Jane is first recorded as visiting the glen, and although it was a very different place to Kinrara, with none of the Spey valley's grandeur and wide views, the narrow, winding glen of the Fiddich seems to have had much the same effect on her. Once the duke had built the lodge, almost certainly replacing or adding to existing bothies, Jane was able to visit with the children; indeed, it became a summer ritual for her to visit with the girls for at least a month in June every year between 1775 and 1779, and during this period we first witness her growing excitement as she becomes increasingly drawn into the world of the Highland landscapes.

Although much is known about the chronology of Jane's life and how she spent her life as a duchess, there is a lot less information about the process by which the streetwise teenager of Hyndford's Close was drawn into a more solitary life in such landscapes, or how she gained the knowledge, insights and sensibilities to become a central figure in the Romantic literary world of Edinburgh in the last decades of the century. In Edinburgh both Home and those in his circle will have provided opportunities to learn, but with a husband at Gordon Castle largely disinterested in literature and culture – his family motto was 'By Valour, not by Craft' – opportunities to pursue such an interest would have been few. Yet, as she navigated the early years of her marriage, Jane clearly felt an awakening of what she described in one letter as the 'sensibility, I called a fatal Gift of Heaven (which I still think it is)', and a growing awareness of the qualities of the physical world around her. She does not appear to have been particularly religious, but under certain circumstances and in certain places she began to sense the presence of the numinous. Sitting beside Loch Lomond on a calm summer evening, for example, she wrote: 'I never saw such a setting … with the lovely Hills, which light and shade made of a thousand different colours … At last, the Moon rose in unclouded

Majesty and "a flood of Glory – Burns from all the skies" … I don't think we spoke a word in half an hour. I felt a reverence as if superior beings must inhabit, or at least visit, such bewitching scenes.'[141]

One key to understanding the process by which this awareness grew is the friendship that Jane formed with the poet and philosopher James Beattie from 1770 onwards. They became life-long friends, and in Beattie Jane had finally found someone who, having been through a similar process, understood her instinctive awareness of, and interest in understanding, the manifestations of the numinous in landscape; Beattie, rather than Edinburgh figures such as Home, was the key influence on Jane's deepening relationship with the landscapes of the Highlands. This aspect of her life was, in turn, a seminal influence on Georgina, who spent so much of her life before marriage alone with her mother in such landscapes.

In 1770 Beattie published the work which was to catapult him to fame, *Essay on the Nature and Immutability of Truth, in opposition to Sophistry and Scepticism*, and such was the demand for the book that a second edition was published in 1771. Beattie had told William Forbes that he was planning his *Essay on Truth* since 'I own it is not without indignation, that I see sceptics and their writings … so much in vogue in this present age,' and sought to make a robust defence of Christianity in answer to David Hume's metaphysical treatises and the subsequent popularity of scepticism.[142]

Jane seems to have been immediately drawn to Beattie, and while the *Essay* will have been one of the topics of conversation that came up when he met the Gordons, she was no doubt equally intrigued to hear about another work Beattie was working on and published the first part of early the next year: the largely autobiographical first canto of his epic poem *The Minstrel*. This was by no means his first poetic work, and while trying on the one hand to establish a lasting basis for his profession as a philosopher, he also had a highly developed sensitivity to the poetic aspects of the natural world and, like Jane, the liminal periods of dawn and dusk.

The Minstrel, planned as a three-part epic, was to tell the story of 'Edwin', a young man drawn by forces he does not really understand to leave his everyday life behind and spend as much time as possible roaming the wild landscapes around his home in an attempt to understand what 'Nature's light' would reveal, and then to express what he discovers through poetry. Book I illustrates this initial process in action, and in Book II Edwin will meet 'the minstrel', the traditional trustee of a community's cultural knowledge, who will provide him with the background education and poetic skills he will need to harness and understand his experiences and create the poetry. A third book would then identify and explain the specific place and role available to the poet/minstrel figure within the wider fabric of society. In the event, Book I was published anonymously in 1771 and became an instant success, even a sensation, but Book II took another three years to write and was less well received, and Book III was never even started. The reasons this grand project faltered and was never completed are not clear, but it would seem that the poem rather fell between two stools: one, Beattie's desire to express as completely as possible his own unique experiences in the natural world, and the other, his desire as a poet to envelop these into a wider poetic concept and to create a 'great poem'. His problem seems to have been that the groundbreaking style and content of Book I largely achieved his main goal, making further elaboration unnecessary, and after its completion Beattie himself acknowledged that the rest of the poem would probably never be finished; as Margaret Forbes puts it, 'The Minstrel was laid aside and never resumed.'[143]

Finished or not, the first canto of the poem had a considerable impact on Jane, particularly the line 'Lo! Where the stripling, wrapp'd in wonder, roves …'. She seems to have instinctively understood what Beattie meant by 'wonder', a state of mind that helped to articulate her own reactions to landscape and validated both the excitement and sense of freedom she experienced when she saw Kinrara and Glenfiddich; she had found someone who understood her better than anyone. As Jane became a regular visitor to Glenfiddich between 1776 and 1779, and continued to visit less regularly until 1792, just what the glen came to mean for her is reflected in some of the letters she sent over the years.

Writing to Henry Home in March 1776, she set the scene, 'I propose going early in the spring to a <u>Shealing</u> with my children, not for Health, but to enjoy the rude Beauties of Nature in greater perfection. I prefer it to London'; the attractions

The remote setting of Glenfiddich Lodge, in the bottom of the valley, as seen today from the east side of the glen.

of the glen were by now superseding even those of London's summer season. In 1778, she writes to Beattie that 'I am to leave [Gordon Castle] with all my little girls, to fly to peace and solitude, and I am sure our pleasant Glen will have charms for you,' and the same year, 'I never tire alone, so that I have no body with me, I find it much easier to amuse myself then.'[144] It is at this point that we start to see the extraordinary influence that the *Ossian* cycle of poems published by James 'Fingal' Macpherson in the early 1760s were beginning to have on the way in which the Scots saw the Highlands.[145]

By the 1770s, those Highland landscapes that had previously been seen as barren wastelands populated by backward and savage people were now viewed as filled with glamour and romance. They were becoming central to the rediscovery of Scottish cultural identity and Highland people as keepers of those traditions, following the post-Culloden proscriptions on language, dress and customs. Beattie's own choice of the traditional minstrel figure as the culture-bearer and central figure of his second canto reflects this new interest.

Before Jane left Glenfiddich in 1779, however, we get a glimpse of just how 'delighted with the place and life' she was there, and how engaged with the landscape of the glen she had become, in a letter to her old friend William King of Newmill. Unfortunately, Jane's letter is lost, but we have King's reply in which he is thanking her for

a copy of the Letter, in the manner of Fingal, which I read twice over … I value it much. Tho' the imitation is inimitable, I admire those parts most where you have not confined yourself to it – 'Fiddick's Glen – the Fragrant Birch – the blue stream winding along – the Green, tho' narrow Vale – the peaceful Cottage in all its mildness – the Sun, trembling at thoughts of his departure – and the parting Beams – upon the dark brown thatch' – are so justly described, so happily blended, as well as many other parts of it, that it loses the appearance of imitation, and is a true picture of the scene alluded to.

He goes on: 'I never see the appearance of Thunder, or Rain in the Hills, without putting in a Petition for the precious and lovely inhabitants of the Glen – it is recorded as the most lovely of Glens,' before apologizing: 'I have somehow made this letter of a most unconscionable length, but when your Grace is tired [of] reading drown it in the stream or give it to some Goat to gnaw.'[146]

King's letter makes clear that the poetry of Fingal Macpherson's *Ossian* had set a tone, presenting the landscapes through a heroic Romantic lens, but what he admires most in Jane's letter are her own descriptions of the glen, a style of writing influenced by Beattie and the emerging Romantic poetry. Jane had shown an early interest in the romance of vernacular Scottish poetry, dating from the time in 1775 when, through Beattie, she had met Alexander Ross, the 'Poet of Loch Lee' at Gordon Castle, and later supported publication of his poem 'The Fortunate Shepherdess' in 1780.[147]

It is an indication of how radically tastes were changing at this time when we compare Jane's association with this new Romantic aesthetic to what happened when she and the duke paid a visit to Lord Temple's house and grounds at Stowe in the summer of 1776.[148] Although the Grenville-Temple family had been leading Whig politicians and many of the features in the grounds at Stowe reflected Whig iconography, it is perhaps reflective of the duke and duchess's Tory sensibilities that, out of the large selection of well-known features that were available in the gardens, this visit should have centred on just one, the 'Grotto', a place of sensibilities rather than of politics. The Grotto, built by William Kent in 1739, was described in 1744 as 'furnished with a great number of Looking-glasses both on the Walls and Ceiling, all set in artificial Frames of Plaister-work, set with Shells and broken Flints – a Marble Statue of Venus on a pedestal stuck with the same,' and a few years later an anonymous French visitor described the interior as 'adorned in a way that dazzles and that charms', and the effect of the mirrors as 'multiplying the perspectives of the garden and your own figure'.[149]

During the visit, Lord Temple and Earl Nugent conveyed the visitors 'in a chaise round the gardens of Stowe' before entertaining them in the Grotto, which had been lit up especially for the occasion. Letters also indicate that the purpose of the visit to the Grotto was specifically to use the strange, otherworldly atmosphere created by the multiple mirrors as a suitable setting to discuss the mysteries of life and death and immortality, of dreams, nightmares and spectres, and to use the supercharged sublimity of the experience to enrich the reading of suitable 'graveyard' poetry, such as 'The Complaint, or Night Thoughts on Life, Death and Immortality' by Edward Young, as a source of inspiration for the group to write poems of their own.[150] Young's poem is referred to by Temple as being Jane's 'favourite', and it served to popularize the attractions of 'moonlight and melancholy' and the 'melancholy and gloomy mysteries'.

'Lord Temple and [Earl Nugent] both composed verses after this time addressed to the same object' and 'these two aged Peers presented some couplets of their respective composition to the late Duchess of Gordon, then in the meridian of her charms, when Lord Temple, having entertained her and the Duke, her husband, at

Stow, lighted up the grotto for her reception.' The visit had clearly meant a great deal to the 'aged peers', and a month later Temple thanked Jane for confirmation of their safe arrival home: 'I have taken refuge in the poetry of your favourite Young's "Night Thoughts", imagining I should thereby become better and more fully acquainted with the inner most recesses of yours'; he goes on to complain, 'Nights – indeed there are none in Town, and consequently no night Thoughts,' before concluding, 'these melancholy and gloomy mysteries therefore only suit the Rocks, the Precipices, the Storms, the aged oaks, the solitude &c. of the Highlands, so well described by Mr Pennant, who has confirmed in me an ardent wish to visit all these romantic scenes even from Gordon Castle to the Cave of Fingal.'

Yet, if he was not to visit the Highlands, he was encouraged by the Gordons' promise to return next year, writing, 'How richly are my noontide Fancies hung / With gorgeous Tapestry of pictur'd Joys?', before adding, 'it is a Fairy Land of your own Creation, will you condescend to be the Queen Mab of it?' He continues, 'Your Grace is remarkably fond of Dreams' and 'In dreams one may be allowed to be a little Romantic … Romantic sensibilities, in a great variety of instances, lead to Good. Their progeny are Virtue, Courage, Generosity, and all the nobler exertions of the Mind.'[151]

Just what Jane made of all of this is hard to gauge, but the fact that they did not return before Temple's death a few years later suggests that she had not been overwhelmed by the attentions of the 'aged peers' or their poems. That is not to say that she had not been a responsive and participatory guest at the time, since we know from a number of sources that one of her charms was the ability to seem interested in another person's life and enthusiasms.[152]

Above all, perhaps, Jane at this point had moved on from 'graveyard poetry' of the mid-eighteenth century to be most at home among the landscapes of the natural world; far from being 'no enemy' to the sensations of the Romantic, she fully embraced these as the lens through which she would experience those landscapes. It is also significant that her daughter Georgina should have grown up with a very similar sensitivity, not to the febrile atmosphere of dreams, grottoes, melancholy and fairy worlds, but to the presence of the landscape itself, and would go on to become as strongly attached to life among the natural world in the glens as her mother.

Jane's ongoing engagement with Scotland was, of course, not limited to the landscapes or even the emerging dialect poetry – she was also very interested in both music and dance. Although the children all learnt the 'polite' forms of dance, such as the minuet, for formal balls, most of their dancing at Gordon Castle and also later at Kinrara revolved around Scotland's traditional reels and jigs, and the important element of servants, family members and guests all sharing the dance floor. Jane, in fact, became particularly associated with popularizing the 'strathspey', the new slower form of the traditional Scots reel; working with the dancing master George Jenkins in the 1780s and early 1790s, she helped iron out some of the rough edges and add 'grace' to the dances with music provided by William Marshall. As David Johnson has put it, 'The advent of the Strathspeys in the 1760s set off a further wave of composition … Marshall's reconstruction of the song tune *The Lowlands of Holland* as *Miss Admiral Gordon's Strathspey* set the scene.' A chance meeting with another leading fiddle player in late July 1777 further deepened Jane's interest in the music.[153]

The author of *Public Characters* recounts the meeting: 'At Athol House … her Grace first saw Niel Gow, the father of the present Scotch ball music. To this circumstance may be traced the origin of the introduction of Scotch dancing into the fashionable world'; in particular, 'One of his productions', too plaintive for dancing, 'attracted her Grace's notice, from the taste, genius and feelings which it exhibited' when it was, 'for the first time, performed by the orchestra of Niel's patron, the Duke of Athol, to the exquisite delight of the company, and especially [the Duchess of Gordon]'. Indeed, Jane was so impressed by Gow that she 'proposed to him to attend the Leith races, of which she was to be a spectator the following week'.[154] It was the start of a long relationship with the Gow family, and either Gow himself or his sons, Nathaniel, John and Andrew, played at numerous parties for Jane in Edinburgh and London – and, indeed, at Georgina's wedding.

Unfortunately, behind the facade of their comfortable lives, by October 1780 the finances of the estate had once again reached crisis point. With no serious programme of improvements put in place to modernize and improve the estates, rental incomes could not keep up with expenditure and it became necessary to impose restrictions by 'selling the London residence, [and for] the Duke and duchess to receive only £400 personal allowance each, total expenses limited to £5,000 per annum'. The situation became even more acute in 1782, when a year of exceptionally bad weather once again caused widespread crop failures and severe food shortages.[155]

An additional financial burden had been incurred in 1778 when the duke received a government mandate to raise the Northern Fencibles, a regiment of ten companies, a very expensive proposition. The 'Fencibles', young men from tenant farms and villages, were for 'the internal protection of North Britain' while so much of the regular army was serving abroad and to aid regular soldiers in the event of an invasion. Five other Fencible regiments were created at this time, all at the expense of those raising them, and the Duke of Gordon had to be granted several extensions as he struggled to fill his quota. Jane had already had experience of recruiting for the army when in 1775 she raised 'a company [100 men] for the Fraser Highlanders … on behalf of her brother Captain William Maxwell', and no doubt she helped out now.[156] Eventually the quota was reached and the Northern Fencibles mustered at Fort George in 1778, only to be disbanded five years later in 1783, possibly due to the duke's ballooning debts.

It was at this point that the duke was approached by Henry Dundas with his offer to take over the Gordon political interest, and as we have seen, the duke accepted Dundas's offer with alacrity; his reasons, apart from his lack of interest, may well have been financial. Holden Furber, in his biography of Dundas, has concluded that the duke accepted the offer because he was 'absorbed in the task of paying off his huge debts by reorganizing his estates', and was living exiled by these debts at Gordon Castle 'because he had too much Scotch pride to go to London and be obliged to live beyond his means'. The fact that the duke and duchess were able to relocate to London just four years later, taking a house on Pall Mall, would suggest that either the reorganization had been extremely successful in paying off his debts, or that Dundas's offer also came with undisclosed financial incentives. If so, this might explain why, in his reply to Dundas, the duke promised 'that not even … the Duchess … should see the letter'.

Either way, the duke recognizes in his reply that 'You have long known that I am the very worst politician in the world,' and was, as Furber writes, immediately 'willing to resign himself in the hands of a political expert for the present'. In spite of not being allowed to see the original letter, it is doubtful that the duchess remained ignorant of the deal for very long, and certainly by the next year she writes, 'We are going up to town to support Dundas with all our power. You will hear of the wonders he has done in Elegance and Politicks.'

With his control of large parts of Scotland's politics in place, Dundas's next move was to ally himself with William Pitt in 1784, becoming 'the friend and confidante of the new Prime Minister', and a year later James Boswell summed up what Dundas had achieved by giving him the title of 'the uncrowned king of Scotland'. Once in power, Dundas became one of the most implacable opponents to change, leading him to be both anti-reform and against the abolition of the slave trade, stances which brought him into line with the major Scottish Tory families and which reflected the position of both the duke and duchess.

Dundas, by now Lord Melville, went on to achieve notoriety during his term as Home Secretary between 1791 and 1794 for his sustained attack on those he saw as sympathetic to the French Revolution, and Jane became closely associated with him by providing active support in her social and political salons in London, Edinburgh and the Highlands. By 1805, however, Dundas faced political ruin when he was charged with being part of a corrupt scheme in the office of the Paymaster of the Navy. His vulnerability due to his waning political influence, coupled with his defiant attitude to the authority of the investigation and the whiff of corruption, all came together to create a perfect storm as all those people of whom he had made enemies in the past moved in for the kill. The scam that had been uncovered concerned Alexander Trotter, Paymaster of the Navy under Dundas, who had 'constantly speculated with the public money by placing it in his own account at Coutts Bank'. Trotter then settled the naval accounts with this money but kept the interest, and in 1795 he was shown to have 'drawn the staggering sum of £1,000,000 from the Bank of England and placed it all with Coutts'.

Although not accused of taking money directly, Dundas was drawn into the mess: 'first, by refusing to answer questions he was perceived to be shielding Trotter, second, he had borrowed money from Trotter which was in all probability public money, and third he occasionally diverted funds specifically appropriated for the Navy to other public services.' Above all, however, it just seemed wholly unlikely that a man such as Dundas, who maintained such meticulous control over his sprawling political interests, would not have known what was going on in the Paymaster's office, and would have known how Trotter was able to accumulate the large sums of money from which he could borrow to finance his various activities.

Loudly proclaiming Dundas's innocence, Jane assiduously attended the ensuing trial, which began in April 1806 and lasted fifteen days, and although in the end Dundas was personally acquitted, his credibility was gone and he had to resign – the long reign of the 'uncrowned king of Scotland', who had also dominated the British Parliament, was over. The end of Dundas's career also marked not just the end of Jane's participation in politics, but also perhaps the end of a long-standing affair between the two. Furber is particularly adamant that the widely repeated suggestion that Dundas and the Duchess of Gordon were lovers is totally erroneous, and suggests that his real interest was not in the women but how they could further his political ends: 'He was a past master of the art of charming women whom he wished to use for his political ends, [and] the Duchess of Gordon is a case in point.' Furber then dismisses all the other gossip at one go by insisting that Dundas was far too busy a man 'to live the scandalous private life attributed to him by the gossips', adding: 'On the whole, we have a feeling that the gossip about Dundas's private life deserves to be entirely ignored.' Whether or not Dundas really was too busy for affairs, it is hard to believe that Jane would have allowed herself to be used in this way and to have been so active in supporting him simply because he was charming.[157]

In the midst of their financial problems, however, in 1781 there was some good news. While Jane's first five children had arrived with great regularity every two years, by now there had been a gap of five years since the birth of Louisa, but in the spring of that year Lady Georgina was born. Jane's last child, Alexander, was born in 1785, but he appears to have stayed at Gordon Castle to be educated by Hoy, who had just arrived at the castle, before joining the army aged sixteen, after which he was away in the military most of his short life.[158] For Georgina, however, the gap in age turned out to have some significance since she was the only one who accompanied her mother when she moved to live in Kinrara around 1792 and shared the experiences of living in both the original bothy farmhouse and the new lodge built there a few years later. There is no doubt that these years, together with her experiences at Glenfiddich, which she first visited aged two, exerted a huge influence on Georgina as an adult.

The years and subsequent ownership have not been kind to either Glenfiddich or the lodge. It is not quite clear who built or designed the original lodge, but by the time Jane stopped visiting it had been enlarged by John Baxter, and remained, as Mary Miers comments, 'a somewhat more rudimentary affair than the unbuilt Palladian scheme for the site illustrated by Plaw in his Rural Architecture or Designs (1796)'.[159] The fact that Plaw's scheme was not used indicates that either the duke or Jane was not looking to create a Palladian villa in such a landscape, but rather something more modest and sympathetic to both place and purpose; today, in contrast, although still occupied just forty years ago, the buildings lie sadly derelict and ruinous, and on the high moors beyond, a cluster of wind turbines dominate the skyline.

Approaching the upper part of Glenfiddich, the road from Dufftown to Cabrach sweeps to the left and crosses the bridge over the river at Bridgehaugh, and from this point a track leaves the road to run up the west side of the glen. If the visitor can ignore the dark, dense blocks of commercial forestry and the access roads to the turbines on the opposite side, walking up the track it is still possible to understand just what was so special about this place for Jane and her children. After the ride down from Gordon Castle, we can imagine their excitement on arriving at this point. While on a map the two and a half miles of the glen up to the site of the lodge appear to be essentially straight and featureless, with the river running down between the gently sloping plantations and open moor, on the ground the glen is revealed in at least four different sections, before the track and river follow a long sweeping curve to the left that seems to go on and on until finally the long low run of buildings that make up the lodge come into view perched on a wide open area just above the river; then, after more of the buildings have steadily come into view, the high ridge of moors beyond can be seen and the setting of the lodge is complete.

One can almost feel the growing sense of excitement and anticipation the children must have felt as the glen closed in behind them, closing off one kind of life and promising something new as they approached each turn in the track ahead. There is something about the way in which the geography of the glen delays the first sight of the lodge and steadily creates a growing sense of anticipation that is very special and makes the distance from the road seem further and the sense of remoteness of the place more intense. It is easy to imagine the children exploding from the carriage and 'skipping off amidst the Heath', and Jane 'hurrying to every spot'.

Here was what Arthur Young had described as 'the mountain many miles from Gordon Castle', where the children could be seen 'running up and down hills barefooted … and being delighted with the place and life', and where Jane heard the 'Rocks, Woods, Torrents and Mountains' preach – 'Ten miles frae ony town this shealing lies', as the Poet of Loch Lee had written, a place where

> … Till on a high brae head she lands at last,
> That down the how burnie pathlins past.
> Clear was the burnie, and the bushes green,
> But rough and steep the brae that lay between …[160]

The long, slender single storey of the main block of the lodge, a run of four or five rooms linked by a corridor down one side, lies at right angles to and maybe 3 metres/10 feet above the river as it flows past the bay window of the large drawing room at the end. This room, with wide windows giving views up and down the glen and a large fireplace, seems to have been the only 'grand' room in the lodge; bedrooms, kitchen, store rooms, boot room and game larder made up most of the rest. This serves to confirm the simplicity that Jane, at least, seemed to value, and it set the pattern for the farmhouse at Kinrara. Outside the lodge, while a few ornamental structures and a garden fenced off beside the building were added to the grounds later on, for now all Jane needed were the features of 'Fiddick's Glen' itself, the 'Fragrant Birch', the 'blue stream winding along', the 'Green Vale', the 'peaceful Cottage', the 'parting beams' of the setting sun, and her growing sense of wonder.[161] In this context, one other incident recorded by Jane, which occurred during a trip to Loch Lomond in August 1784, is also of interest. Late one evening, as the moon rose over the loch, she describes suddenly feeling 'a reverence as if superior beings must inhabit, or at least visit, such bewitching scenes'. It is almost as though she feels herself to be following in the footsteps of Beattie's Edwin in *The Minstrel*, roving the landscape 'wrapp'd in wonder'.[162]

Although the years 1781–5 saw the birth of her last two children (Colour Plate 6), reflecting perhaps a period of harmony between Jane and the duke, in the same period Jane lost one of her most ardent supporters when, in 1783, Henry Home died at the age of eighty-three: a great loss for Jane since Home was without doubt one of the most important figures in her early life. Her own father had died a decade before, but Home had continued to provide a constant source of unconditional support, and even love. One of the last letters from Home to Jane gives an intimate glimpse of just how close that relationship had become, and the depth of feeling he felt for her. The letter begins 'My Darling', and he goes on:

> There has been much talk of you coming to town about this time, and all my friends concluded that you would certainly put me to death by making me exert spirits far beyond my power. I told them gravely that I could not die in a better cause.
>
> While alive, I am your Grace's property,
>
> Henry Home.

Yet around the same time we also hear, for the first time, of another rather different individual close to Jane: her sister-in-law Lady Anne Gordon, one of the duke's three sisters. We first met Anne at Jane's eldest daughter Charlotte's christening, and since then she had been living, unmarried, at Huntly, and a letter to her from Jane to congratulate Anne on her marriage in 1782 suggests that they had had a close friendship; they were, after all, two women of the same age coping with life in an overwhelmingly masculine environment for whom a mutually supportive friendship would have been of some importance. Jane writes from Kinrara, 'I spent a great many of the happiest days of my life in your society, dear Lady Ann and have always been interested in your happiness.'[163]

The letter is also of interest because Jane wrote it from Kinrara. This is her first recorded visit back to the farmhouse beside the Spey since she had been so taken with it twenty years before, and the fact that she should visit it now suggests she wanted to refresh her memory of the place and possibly assess its potential as a replacement for Glenfiddich should she need one in the future.

In June 1785 a new figure appeared at the castle in the form of Matthias D'Amour, who had been hired to serve as 'groom of the chamber' for Jane. Hired for his skills as a hairdresser, D'Amour is of particular interest because in 1836 he published his *Memoirs*, a portion of which relate to the ten or eleven years he worked for the Gordons. From the day of his arrival, he gives a vivid picture of life at Gordon Castle and the central role of William Marshall, the butler, in everyone's lives. Sitting after dinner in the staff quarters of the castle and sharing a bottle of wine with the butler and others, he writes:

> when each had taken a moderate quantity of wine, instruments of music, which hung against the wall, were taken down by the different individuals, and all of a sudden the steward's room was converted into something like a concert hall … I was pleased beyond measure … The butler, particularly, was an amateur of the first class; not merely being a performer but a composer, and actually was himself the author of many excellent Scotch reels, which were not only played in Gordon Castle, but which I have often heard far south of the Tweed.
>
> The music was so unexpected by me, and sounded so sweet, that I sat for a considerable time raptured with delight. And while the butler was playing by himself on the violin, he did it so charmingly that I was fairly overcome, and

starting upon my legs, commenced dancing a hornpipe … They, in their turn, were as much charmed by my dancing as I had been with their playing; and information of my performance being carried to the females, who had retired, they all re-entered the room, and I was desired by all parties to repeat what I had done, with which request I willingly complied.[164]

In the end it was three days before D'Amour was called for by Jane, and still it seemed there was little for him to do: 'The Duchess of Gordon was an uncommonly fine looking woman … and informed me in the general of the nature of what my duties would be, and that on the Monday following she was going to Peterhead, for the purpose of sea-bathing; that I was to go with her, and that until we got there she did not require me to do anything.'

It was not long, however, before the Gordons discovered that he had a particular talent: 'It happened one morning that the Duke was complaining of the coffee, how wretchedly thick and unpleasant it was, and his Grace addressing me said, "D'Amour, could you not make coffee?" I replied that I had no doubt of it … I hastened to the kitchen, and procuring the necessary ingredients, made it after the manner I had learnt in Paris. It was the most excellent imaginable and my praises for coffee-making were repeated on many occasions.'[165]

In late summer 1785, with D'Amour as a new member of her retinue, Jane and the family travelled to Edinburgh for the birth of Lord Alexander, but due to an outbreak of smallpox it was necessary to move the children away. D'Amour tells us: 'The temporary residence was a cottage belonging to Mr. Dundas … [and I] was sent along with them as a kind of provider and governor of the whole. Here I had the honour of superintending the whole delightful little colony, and of several times preparing dinner … for her Grace herself, when she came to see the children.' While staying there, building work was underway at Melville Castle, and 'our duchess was requested to lay the first stone, which she did. The cottage was within a mile of the place, so we were all allowed to be present. The little Lady Georgiana, now Duchess of Bedford … was then two years of age, and I carried her in my arms to see the ceremony.'

With the birth of Alexander in November, Jane's family was complete, and to her delight her precocious four-year old, Georgina, was by then charming the world at large: 'Huntly [then 15] is here, much improved in body and mind. Georgina is his delight, but she is not yet reconciled to the intrusion of this little stranger. She always insists on calling Mr Dundas Mr Beattie and no care can prevent it … she still says, "Well, Mr Dundas, you are so like my friend Dr Beattie."'[166]

While back in Edinburgh in 1785 and waiting to give birth, Jane had begun entertaining in the house the Gordons had taken in George Square, where among her neighbours was Henry Erskine, the Lord Advocate, who had known Jane since the days of Hyndford's Close. The house soon became a central location of the Edinburgh social season and Erskine's biographer notes 'the brilliancy of the Edinburgh season with dancing, cards and company' under the guidance of the 'fascinating Duchess of Gordon'.[167] Now, in addition to these card and dancing parties, she initiated something more significant. These were regular literary evenings, usually accompanied by a substantial dinner, where Edinburgh's literary figures and academics could meet and talk with Jane's friends, particularly those interested in literary and cultural patronage, and where they could all meet new talent – and in November 1786 they were introduced to a young man from Ayrshire whose poetry had recently attracted much attention.

CHAPTER FOUR
1786–1803

ONE EVENING IN 1786 the literary gathering at Jane's house in Edinburgh was introduced to the poet Robert Burns. He was twenty-seven, and this event proved to be not only a key meeting in ensuring the credibility and longevity of his career, but also one of the key moments in the process by which Edinburgh's cultural elite embraced the previously neglected genre of poetry written in Scots vernacular, helping to elevate it to a status similar to that of poetry written in English. With a series of love affairs, children and growing debts behind him, Burns had accepted the offer of a job as an assistant overseer of slaves on a sugar plantation in the West Indies, and in the hope of making sufficient money to fund his travel, Burns approached a publisher in Kilmarnock, John Wilson, who, in July 1786, published *Poems, Chiefly in the Scottish Dialect* (known as the Kilmarnock volume). With the book out, his friend, the influential Dr Blacklock, suggested he should make an immediate visit to Edinburgh to promote both the book and himself, and Blacklock lost no time in mentioning him to Jane, who in turn invited them both to attend her salon in George Square. The evening was a great success, and Jane was evidently delighted that they had found such a good young poet writing in the kind of broad dialect, the 'rustic terms', she had grown up with and sought to promote. Her reaction was shared by a number of others who were present, including the critic Henry Mackenzie, who wrote a favourable review of Burns's book in *The Lounger* magazine, and Burns remained in touch with Jane and visited the family at Gordon Castle (Colour Plate 7).

Yet, in spite of her role in bringing Burns to the attention of Edinburgh society and her continuing efforts to encourage such talents, it is symptomatic of the type of criticism Jane attracted throughout her life that questions were immediately raised about her credentials for the role, her seriousness, and what was perceived as a blurring of the line between Edinburgh's renowned cultural forums and purely social gatherings. Mrs Grant of Laggan may have been reflecting a common view when she wrote the following about Jane's salon:

> Her Grace's present ruling passion is literature, – to be the arbitress of literary taste, and the patroness of genius, – a distinction for which her want of early culture, and the flutter of a life devoted to very different pursuits, has rather disqualified her; yet she has strong flashes of intellect, which are, however, immediately lost in the formless confusion of a mind ever hurried on by contending passions and contradictory objects, of which one can never be attained without the relinquishment of others.[168]

Such was the attitude of many who saw Jane as a brash and presumptuous interloper into worlds in which she did not belong, and yet, as in many other cases, on better acquaintance Mrs Grant came to see those qualities that had attracted Beattie, to value Jane's friendship and, like Burns, to benefit from her literary patronage. Burns was to leave a poem at Gordon Castle following his visit in 1787, which included the following lines in its final verse:

> Wildly here, without control,
> Nature reigns and rules the whole …
> She plants the forest, pours the flood …
> Where waters flow and wild woods wave,
> By bonie Castle Gordon.

No mention here of the grand, expensive castle, the art, the library or the carefully laid out parkland and gardens, and Jane would no doubt have understood that.

In spite of the perception that Jane's 'formless confusion of mind' compromised her value as a literary hostess, no one ever doubted or questioned her sustained focus on the task of finding good husbands for her daughters or her interest in

PLATE 1: Pompeo Batoni, *Francis Russell, Marquis of Tavistock*, 1762. Painted in Rome and reflecting Russell's 'awakening interest in art and architecture', the image suggests the goddess Roma is offering the wisdom of the Roman world to the young marquis.

PLATE 2: Sir Joshua Reynolds, *Lady Elizabeth Keppel, c.*1764. Her marriage to the Marquis of Tavistock was one of 'unclouded happiness' until his untimely death in 1767. She died less than two years after her husband.

PLATE 3: John Hoppner, *Francis Russell, 5th Duke of Bedford, c.*1786. The portrait shows Francis in his ducal robes on the occasion of his entering the House of Lords. Like his parents the duke died young, and his sudden death in 1802 left many of his ambitious plans for agricultural improvement to be finished by his brother Lord John Russell, who became the 6th Duke of Bedford.

PLATE 4: Sir William Beechey, *Lord John Russell*, 1786. Painted the year he married Georgiana Byng, the picture shows the twenty-year-old Lord John as he must have looked as a student at Göttingen and while he travelled through France with Francis Randolph.

PLATE 5: Samuel Coates, *Lady Georgiana Byng*, c.1790. She was described by Lord John as 'mild, gentle, affable, good tempered' but, beyond her demure appearance, Georgiana was a fierce advocate of Whig political principles and ambitious for her husband's career in Parliament.

PLATE 6: Anon., *Alexander, 4th Duke of Gordon and his Family*, *c.*1785. Painted soon after the birth of their last child, the picture shows (left–right) Charlotte, George (Marquis of Huntly), Jane Maxwell, Duchess of Gordon, with baby Alexander in her arms and Georgina at her feet, Madelina, Susan, Louisa (seated in front), and Alexander, Duke of Gordon. Georgina was four years old, and this appears to be the only picture of her until she turned twenty-one in 1802.

PLATE 7: Charles M. Hardie, *Burns in Edinburgh 1786*, 1887. Hardie's picture captures the atmosphere of Jane Maxwell's literary evenings in Edinburgh. Jane sits on the right watching Burns recite his poem 'Winter Night'. On Jane's left sits the renowned Scottish poet Revd Dr Blacklock, who had encouraged Burns to publish *Poems largely in the Scottish Dialect*, while Henry Mackenzie, whose enthusiastic review of the poems in the *Lounger* magazine had brought Burns to the attention of Edinburgh's literary community, stands immediately to the right of the table in the centre, arms crossed. In another indication of Jane's interests, standing in the background pouring drinks is William Marshall, butler to the Gordon household and one of the leading fiddle players of the time.

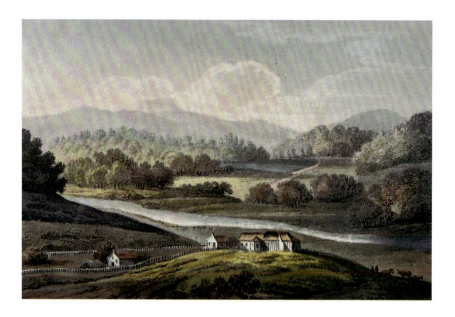

PLATE 8: John Claude Nattes, engraved by J. Merigot, *Kinrara Farmhouse*, 1801. John Stoddart caught the atmosphere of life at Jane Maxwell's Kinrara farmhouse when he wrote of his visit, 'In the evenings our time was passed with authors most interesting in such a situation – with Ossian, the painter of Highland scenery – with Burns, the still more animated painter of Scottish feelings.' This setting inspired the Bedfords to build the house at Endsleigh.

PLATE 10: Anon., *Kinrara*, *c*.1804. The new villa built for Jane Maxwell, *c*.1804, seen across the Spey from the Rothiemurchus estate, with Tor Alvie rising to the right. The original bothy farmhouse stood above the river just out of sight to the left.

PLATE 9: John Hoppner, *Lady Georgina Gordon*, 1802. It is telling that in this image, painted as she came of age, rather than being in an architectural or domestic setting, Georgina is seen walking along a woodland path, reflecting Sarah Murray's description on meeting her a few years before beside Loch an Eilein: 'on seeing us, [she] came bounding from rock to rock so light and airy.'

PLATE 11: After George Garrard, *Sheep Shearing at Park Farm, Woburn*, c.1810. Although the trees and some of the buildings are now gone, the setting of this image of the Sheep Shearings in full swing is still recognizable today. The duke sits on his horse watching the sheep shearing exhibition, while Garrard sells his prints and busts from a table in the bottom left-hand corner.

PLATE 12: J. C. Bourne, *Hundreds Farm*, 1815–16. Bourne's lovely image illustrates the Romantic picturesque style of the new cottages built on the Woburn estate by the duke and duchess. Hundreds Farm was occupied for some time by the duke's youngest son by his first wife, Lord John Russell.

PLATE 13: Humphry Repton, Endsleigh Red Book, east view, 1814. This is the clearest contemporary image we have of the view from the duke and duchess's apartments at Endsleigh. Comparing this image with that of the view today from the site of Jane Maxwell's bothy farmhouse at Kinrara, it is clear why Georgina and the duke were so excited when they first visited Endsleigh in 1809.

PLATE 14: View from the Kinrara bothy farmhouse site today. The view down the grassy slope to the Spey, the wooded foothills immediately beyond, and the patterns of peaks in the distance bears an uncanny resemblance to the view to the Tamar and out towards the Cornish moors in Repton's painting.

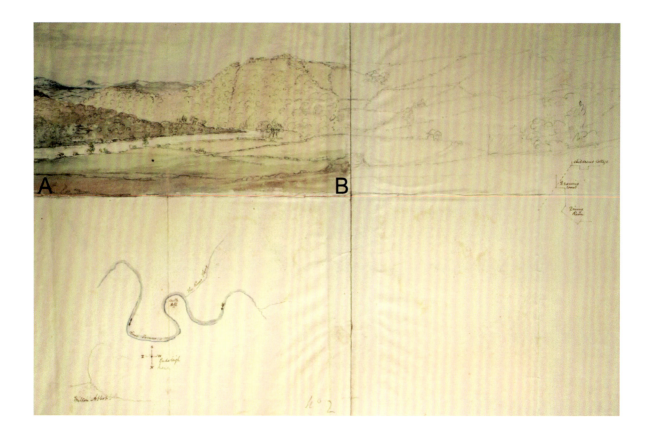

PLATE 15: Jeffry Wyatville, Endsleigh, 'Worksheet No. 2', late 1809 – early 1810. This image indicates the lengths Wyatville went to in situating the new house at Endsleigh exactly where the Bedfords wanted it. One of two sheets (No. 1 is now lost), the landscape shown represents the view to the right of the north–south arm of the compass associated with the map below, and suggests that No. 1 showed the views to the left on this line. The compass marks the exact location of the house in relation to the map, and, to the right, the outline indicates the proposed location of the house on the ground, articulation of the house permitting views to the left, centre and right. Points A and B relate to the view indicated in Colour Plate 16.

PLATE 16: Jeffry Wyatville, Endsleigh, 'Worksheet No. 2', detail. Superimposing the outline of the house as built on to the compass allows us to see how the location and orientation of the apartments on the east end of the house provided views of the landscape between points 'A' and 'B'.

PLATE 17: 'Endsleigh Cottage, July 1828', seen some ten years after completion and by now a place of peace and privacy, from Ackerman's *Repository*, 1 July 1828, engraving. With the children's cottage to the left, the curving wall of the garden runs round in front of the bay windows of the duke and duchess's sitting rooms with their bedrooms above, overlooking the view to the south-west. Beyond these, the library and drawing room run along the south front to the dining room, which was turned away to face south-east.

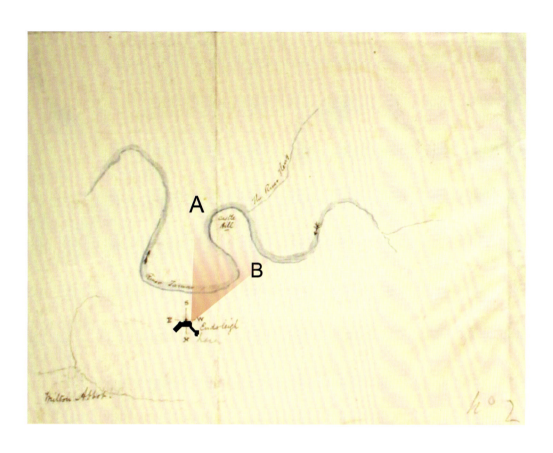

PLATE 18: Jeffry Wyatville, *The Duke of Bedford's Dairy at Endsleigh Cottage*, c.1814. In addition to the house itself, buildings such as Wyatville's dairy and Hundreds Farm at Woburn provide a glimpse of the practical yet Romantic and decorative atmosphere the Bedfords sought to create.

PLATE 19: The grand chimney of the Ferryman's Cottage still survives today in the woods opposite the house at Endsleigh and it is still possible to see just how visible it was from the private apartments of the house.

politics. These processes began in 1787 when her eldest daughter, Charlotte, turned nineteen and Jane introduced her into Edinburgh and London society. To facilitate the latter, in early July the duke and duchess made an extended visit to London and leased Buckingham House, Pall Mall, from Lord Temple's son, the Marquis of Buckingham. Once there, Jane was able to use the house not only to introduce Charlotte into London society, but also as the base from which she could become involved in Tory politics, actively supporting the Pitt government and positioning Buckingham House as the focal point for Tory gatherings that 'led the war against the Whigs and their leading lady, Georgiana, Duchess of Devonshire'.

Even D'Amour was taken by surprise by the lavishness of the entertainments at this time. He says that in London, 'I found that my lady was one of the tip-tops among the fashionables. Our house, indeed, was the rendezvous of all the moving and gay spirits which at that time floated in the political atmosphere of Great Britain.' He adds, 'I have frequently known us have not less than five or six hundred individuals in the house at once, comprehending, of course, the most fashionable and gay of all the nobility and gentry about town.'[169]

Jane's arrival in London, her rapid development of a close relationship with Pitt and the attention of the Prince of Wales, who had required an 'undressed' party at Buckingham House for Scots Reels to be danced, were raising a few eyebrows, especially among the friends and admirers of her rival Whig hostess, the Duchess of Devonshire, and judgements about her were rapidly made. This is the period, for example, when Georgiana Russell, down the road at Gertrude, Dowager Duchess of Bedford's house, was watching and writing disapprovingly of visits of the Prince of Wales to Buckingham House.

Lady Mary Coke, commenting on Jane's influence on Pitt, said: 'It will not be the first time that a man of great understanding has been the dupe of a designing woman,' adding: 'The Duchess of Gordon ... scruples nothing to gain her end, such a person must always be dangerous,' while the Earl of Fife's brother had this to say, 'What do you think of our northern Dutchess and her tartan ball? I daresay the same as I do, that great people by courtesy and etiquette seem entitled to play the fool in any stile they please.' Yet, although there was 'little sympathy between Jane and the Prince of Wales' and 'despite her opposition to his aspirations, the Duchess remained on friendly terms with [him], and never lost her custom of treating him in conversation, with the utmost freedom, even upon points of great delicacy.'

While many of these comments may be by those opposed to Jane's political programme, there is no doubt that her seeming disregard for London's social formalities, her outspoken language, 'rough' accent and undisguised enthusiasm for all things Scottish offended much of polite London society, and Amanda Foreman quotes a typical piece of doggerel by a 'Scottish wit': 'The Duchess triumphs in a manly mien; Loud her accent, and her phrase obscene';[170] the same groups of people for the same reasons were equally determined to be offended by her youngest daughter some twenty years later.

By 1788, when not in London for social and parliamentary reasons, Jane was also in the Highlands where she started taking in interest in local affairs, economic and social, as well as hosting large gatherings at Gordon Castle. This year Jane used her government connections to promote the creation of the Caledonian Canal, a scheme which eventually became a reality in 1803, while also becoming a founding patron of the 'Northern Meeting', of which the inaugural meeting was held in Inverness in June 1788. Its purpose was to provide a vehicle to 'promote social intercourse' among the remote communities in the Highlands, and provide an alternative venue for gatherings to those in Edinburgh. Designed entirely as a social event, with a central focus on music and dancing, all political discussion was banned even at dinner. Jane and her family attended every September, joining fellow landowners and professional people from Inverness and the surrounding areas. Its popularity, and in particular that of its annual piping competitions, has continued to this day, giving some indication of the role it played in local life.

Meanwhile, at Gordon Castle itself, the gatherings continued, and on occasions several hundred people would be staying for a week or more, during which guests came together in the evenings to celebrate Scottish music, song and dance. Led by William Marshall, dancing in traditional dress would last for hours, as the Poet of Loch Lee had put it:

> When dinner's o'er, the dancing neist began,
> And throw they lap, they flang, they ran:
> The country-dances and the country reels,
> Wi' streaked arms bob'd round, and nimble heels …[171]

Such occasions became central to family life.

Over the winter Beattie had been unable to visit Gordon Castle and so Jane sent him an account of the family and their lives: 'The Duke had been for some days hunting, feasting, and dancing at Banff. We were expected, but a little influenza and a great desire to enjoy the last days of the loveliest season of the year in the country kept us at home. I like to walk amongst the rustling leaves and plan future forests … The surrounding mountains, indeed the plains, are white with snow, but we have no company and are very happy. I and my girls work, Mr Hoy reads aloud. I wish you were of the party.'[172]

Unfortunately, their mother does not specify exactly what her girls were 'working' at, but it would appear that, other than drawing, it was not particularly educational, beyond Mr Hoy reading aloud. None of them went to school as the two boys did, as ambition for the future of the girls was strictly limited to making a 'good' marriage and then being a wife, mother and accomplished social hostess. In later life Georgina was very self-conscious of her lack of formal education, but it is an indication of the strength of social attitudes that did not consider an education for girls as one of the important qualifications for making a good marriage that she in turn, many years later, failed again to secure anything but the most basic schooling for her daughters.

By 1789 Jane's efforts on behalf of her daughters began to pay off when, within a few months of each other, her two eldest daughters married. Interestingly enough, although Jane had spent the last few years concentrating on finding a suitable match for her eldest, Charlotte, it was Madelina, the next one down, who found herself a husband – it seems without much help from her mother. If her mother's subsequent letter to her long-time friend Major Ross is anything to go by, it appears that Jane had left it up to her sister Catherine to guide her daughter, even though 'Maddy' was just sixteen: 'Sir John Sinclair is "delighted" at the prospect of my daughter Madelina being his daughter-in-law. She is much too young – but I left her some weeks with my sister Mrs Fordyce, during which period they fixed their own future fate.'[173]

Sir John's son was Sir Robert Sinclair, the Lieutenant Governor of Fort George, and from Jane's letter it would appear that the Sinclairs were close family friends, so it seems likely that the couple had known each other for some time before they were married at the Fordyces' house in Ayton in April 1789. This event was followed some six months later when Charlotte married Charles Lennox, later 4th Duke of Richmond, at Gordon Castle in September. The marriage had had to be postponed from the summer because Lennox had recently wounded a man in a duel – at least the second he had fought – and they all had to wait in London until the wounded man's survival was assured, since, had he died, Lennox would at the very least have been required to exile himself abroad. Finally, they set off and arrived at Gordon Castle, where the marriage happened right away, in the duchess's best dressing room: 'The Duke was not at home. Nobody in the house but the Duchess and two women servants, no one besides the immediate parties knew of the wedding, not even the Marquis of Huntly … Lady Charlotte's brother, until the third day after. The reason, I believe, was to avoid tedious parade.'[174]

D'Amour may well be right about the reason for the speed and secrecy of the wedding, but it was part of a pattern whereby, once an engagement had been secured, Jane ensured there was no delay before the wedding, and before anyone could call it off, even if it meant that there was no lavish ceremony and subsequent celebration. The only apparent exception to this was Georgina's wedding, the last Jane would be required to organize, where, once the couple had left, the infamous 'midnight orgy' broke out.

For all this social and family success, however, it is at this point in 1789 that we first start to become aware that there were serious strains building up in the duke and duchess's relationship. George Gordon notes that this year 'relations between the pair – at least on the surface – were not entirely hostile,' but at the same time everyone had the sense that there were growing problems.[175] The reasons are not straightforward, and while expenditure was clearly a problem, there is a sense that there was also something more serious, and that the duke's 'one fault' was that his attentions had been drawn elsewhere. We have seen that as early as 1778 extravagant expenditure had reached crisis point and that restrictions were imposed, but both bore responsibility for this. Jane's social and political activities in London and Edinburgh had been expensive, as were the duke's ambitious plans for Gordon Castle, which had proved enormously costly, but it was the combined expenditure of the family as the children grew up in the late 1780s and early 1790s which created a renewed economic crisis for the estates. Their lifestyle could no longer be sustained by their income, and additional money was constantly needed to pay off the relentlessly high debt burden.[176] Yet beneath these economic concerns, hints had been appearing that all was not well on a personal level between the couple. Even Beattie found the relationship complex and wrote this very carefully worded summary of the duke and duchess following his two-month stay at the castle in summer 1783 in reply to Mrs Boyd's enquiry about the Gordons:

> Your sentiments of the Duchess are perfectly just. I have had the honour to know her long, and I think I know her well. A perfect character I have never yet met with; but of her I will venture to say that the more it is known the more it will be admired, and that nothing but prejudice, or envy, or ignorance, or pure malice, can be insensible to it. The Duke, though more inclined to a retired life, is in no respect inferior … His passion for astronomy and other parts of science, his abhorrence of drinking and gaming, and his attachment to his children, keep him at a distance from the dissipations of high life, and give him in the eyes of some people an appearance of reserve; but that wears off entirely when one becomes acquainted with him.[177]

Reading between Beattie's carefully worded lines, he is clearly indicating the widening split between the two, the effervescent and social Jane, the retired and reserved duke, both still living at Gordon Castle but pursuing increasingly different lives. In his book, *The Last Dukes of Gordon*, George Gordon considers that 1787 was the year it became clear that she 'had "lost" her Duke … the differences in personal habits and inclination were far too wide to be easily bridged.'[178]

Typically, perhaps, in December 1789 the duke was at Gordon Castle while Jane was in Edinburgh, and the mood appears to have darkened since Jane's happy letter of the summer. A relative of the duke, Mr George Gordon of Cluny, tells Beattie in a letter about his role in persuading her to return to the castle for the winter:

> The Duchess of Gordon left this place for Gordon Castle yesterday morning, and seems determined to pass the winter there. I said everything in my power to confirm her Grace in that resolution; and all her true friends will, I flatter myself, be of my opinion. Her residence in the North is not only for the good of her own family, but of the country in general, where she promotes a spirit of mirth and hospitality to a degree beyond any person I know. I never saw her in greater beauty than she is just now.

This is interesting because it strongly suggests that Jane was perhaps in two minds about returning to Gordon Castle, a clear sign of tensions. It would seem that the friends were encouraging her to continue as normal a life as possible for the good of all, but relations became increasingly 'hostile' from this time on.[179]

Looking beyond the economic reasons for this hostility, in the light of what happened within a few years, it seems clear that the duke had, or was about to initiate, a relationship with one of the Gordon Castle staff called Jean Christie, the daughter of one of the housekeepers. If so, it would not have been the first time, since his first 'natural' son, George, was born to another woman on the staff, Bathia Largue, just before he married Jane. As the Gordon marriage broke up, the duke developed his relationship with Jean Christie to the point that she gave birth to a daughter, Catherine, in 1791. Jane spent that winter in London with her daughter Susan, and by the next year had accepted that, even though she still spent some time with the duke and the children, she needed to leave permanently.

Although, as we will see, she remained on speaking terms with the duke at this point, and remained involved with the family and to some extent life at Gordon Castle, the Gordons' relationship was over and her biggest concern, which increasingly poisoned relations over the next ten or twelve years, was securing a decent settlement for herself and the children, especially the girls. Subsequent to Jane's departure, Jean Christie continued to live in Fochabers with two more of the duke's children, until he finally moved her and the children into the castle in 1804. Two more children followed over the next eight years or so, and finally, following Jane's death in 1812, Jean became the Duchess of Gordon.[180] At this time, however, although it might have appeared that everything was well, it is clear that Jane was rarely at the castle, and that the two passed like ships in the night, never quite being together any longer; the commencement of an annual annuity in 1792 suggests the widening rift.

The separation must have had some impact on the children who were still at home, no doubt fully aware of what had been going on: Susan (seventeen), Louisa (fifteen), Georgina (ten) and Alexander (six). In 1791 and 1792, Susan, who was Jane's next target for marriage, appears to have been travelling with her mother, certainly to Edinburgh and London, and in October 1793 Jane's efforts paid off when she married William, 5th Duke of Manchester, once again at the Fordyce house in Ayton. Huntly was away in Europe and, interestingly enough, only the duke and Louisa seem to have been present, since there is no mention of Jane or the others. At this point we rather lose sight of Alexander, who was destined for the army, but in 1792 Jane took the opportunity to visit Glenfiddich once more, and she, Louisa and Georgina enjoyed one more carefree summer there. Jane recounts that summer in letters to Beattie and Ross, and these also suggest that the duke visited, no doubt to hunt. Writing to Beattie in 1792 she is clearly enjoying the summer and is still delighted to have secured a second duke for one of her daughters: 'I have spent most of my time in Glenffidoch [sic]. The "Lonely Cot" has still ten thousand charms for me. I never was so delighted with its wild beauty as after being so long [at Gordon Castle] where I spent the winter … The Duke of Manchester is everything I could hope … How I would like to spend some days with you, and have one more walk upon the solitary shore, where we used to be so happy.' She then continues with the following news: 'I go tomorrow … I am going to build a Shieling in Badenoch; perhaps you and Montagu [Beattie's son] may come next summer and view those tremendous mountains covered with fragrant birch and gloomy pine.'[181]

This 'Shieling in Badenoch' was the old farmhouse at Kinrara which she had admired so much since first seeing it when she toured the Gordon estates with her new husband. Now, perhaps, its distance from Gordon Castle suited her perfectly, and she seems to be increasingly resigned to the fact that she will not be able to visit her 'romantic Glen' Glenfiddich again. In September she writes to Ross from Glenfiddich, but appears now to be looking to the future at Kinrara:

I have been for some weeks in this Dear romantic Glen – you cannot think how delightful it is, the stillness, the fragrance, after the tiresome bustle of a London life … I have taken a Farm, and intend to build a sheiling for Goat's Whey … It is in the most beautiful part of Badenoch Mountains, Woods, Lakes and Rivers. I hope you will be tempted to come and see us.

Louisa is the first Botanist in the world and constantly climbing amongst the Rocks to look for plants. Georgina has the care of the Goats and a pretty little Dairy Maiden she is – in short it is perfect rural felicity – surrounded by every beauty of nature.[182]

She had returned to Kinrara during the summer of 1782 for another visit, but now Jane is talking about actually moving there to build a house and take a farm. In her letters, Jane states repeatedly that '92' was the year she was first paid an annuity of £4,000 a year with additional 'pin money' for expenses agreed in her settlement, and it was probably part of the deal that she spend more time away from Gordon Castle. Some efforts were made to present a united front, such as in October 1793 when Jane and the duke appeared at the Northern Shooting Club meeting in Aberdeen, before the family returned in November to Gordon Castle, 'where

[Jane] got up theatricals. In November, 1793, the play *No Song, No Supper* was given, with the whole family taking part, including the 7 yr old Lord Alexander, who sang duets with his sister Georgina.'[183]

It would seem that the 1792 visit to Glenfiddich was her last, and with Louisa spending time at home and Alexander also there to prepare for entering the army, it was from this time that she started to spend increasing amounts of time with 'my little Georgie'. Jane's family at this difficult time was reduced to her eleven-year-old daughter and the company of the staff at the new shieling at Kinrara. This situation was to last for the next nine or so years, but fortunately Georgina seems to have thrived; their life in Badenoch, the farmstead, gardens, walks and long pony rides, building on that in Glenfiddich, provided an experience that laid the foundations for the rest of her life (Colour Plate 8). Even after she left Scotland in 1803 when she became Duchess of Bedford, she was back to visit with her new husband just four years later, and from 1818 onwards spent a large part of every year in Badenoch for the next thirty-four years, with only occasional breaks for Continental travel or illness.

From this time on we find Jane at a variety of addresses including Kinrara, some of them belonging to members of her family, such as her mother's house at Shrub Hill, Edinburgh, and some to the extended Gordon family, indicating that although no longer part of the duke's immediate circle or Gordon Castle, she remained on good terms with some of his family, 'occupying herself … with exerting her influence in the interests of those whom she considered worthy of promotion' in politics, the army and, in particular, the military and commercial worlds of the East India Company.[184] And, when 'Gordon' duty called, as in 1794, Jane and her daughters helped the duke in his quest to raise the 92nd, Gordon Highlanders from Gordon lands, the regiment parading for the first time in June 1794 in Aberdeen; her contribution to this effort is commemorated today at the Gordon Highlanders Museum in Aberdeen, where exhibits include her recruiting bonnet and wedding ring.

By 1793 Jane and Georgina were established at Kinrara with her footman and factotum Lang James and a French cook, and with the essential and sympathetic help of the Gordon estates factor in Badenoch, Revd John Anderson, who had responsibility for the Kinrara estate and farm. If the date of 1770 for the original clearance ordered by the duke is correct, the buildings of the Kinrara farmstead will have been in some disrepair, and so over the next few years alterations were made to the original 'humble farmhouse', adding extra rooms to the two of the 'but and ben' design, creating what was described as a 'small farm *cabin*', and converting some of the surviving outbuildings into a kitchen and store houses and extra accommodation. Meryl Marshall estimates that the settlement may originally have had up to nine buildings before clearance and reports that a detailed site survey between 2006 and 2011 identified the remains of five buildings on the site that are likely to be those associated with the farmhouse Jane occupied, including the main house.[185]

One neighbour who caught Jane's attention was Anne Grant, an interesting and unusual woman, who was married to James Grant, the minister for the parish of Laggan. Born in Glasgow, Anne moved with her family first to America where her father had a small estate, and then, following their return, to Glasgow and later Fort Augustus when he was appointed barrack master in 1772. In 1773 she met 'the clergyman of the place', Revd James Grant, and they were married six years later following his appointment to Laggan. Their new home at Gaskbeg, Laggan, 'the Pastor's cottage', came with a farm 'which affording us every necessary of life, we [only] send to Inverness for elegancies and superfluities'.[186] Once established, Anne immediately set about learning to speak Gaelic, and steadily won the 'respect and affection' of the local people for her commitment as a 'parish-helper'. Certainly, part of that respect and affection came from her activities as the minister's wife in the locality, but part also came from her unconditional and committed adoption of local life and her successful management of their small farm, which much impressed the local women. Yet above all, it seems, she had time for people, was interested in them, young and old, and had an awareness of who they were and their circumstances. Her respect and interest in the people she went to live with is clear in her letters. In 1773, for example, she writes:

I love the good old people: there is something so artless, primitive, and benevolent about them ... [they accept] being poor with a better grace than other people. If they want certain luxuries or conveniences, they do not look embarrassed, or disconcerted, and make you feel awkward by paltry apologies ... they rather dismiss any sentiment of that kind by a kind of playful raillery, for which they seem to have a talent ... [and] the moment tea was done, dancing began. Excellent dancers they are, and in music of various kinds they certainly excel.

There was clearly much that she valued in Highland life and culture, and the subtleties of the women's existence in particular caught her attention. Although Mrs Grant herself had a shepherd to take the sheep up into one glen and a dairy-maid to take cattle to another during the summer months, she noticed the effect life in the shielings had on the women and children, giving 'a romantic peculiarity to their turn of thought and language'.[187]

As something of an outsider coming into these mountains, she was drawn to immerse herself in local life, its attitudes, language, pleasures and challenges, and would seem to have been an influence not only on Jane when she arrived to live in her farmstead, but even more so on the young Georgina, who in time would go one step further and travel herself to live seasonally in the glens with her children.

Although never a part of her regular social life at Kinrara, Jane clearly knew all about Mrs Grant from her efforts for local people and her penchant for poetry, especially after discovering their shared interest in Beattie's poems. Jane was also clearly touched when, on the departure of her son, the Marquis of Huntly, to Holland with his regiment in 1799, Anne wrote the poem 'Lord Huntly's Farewell', which included the line, 'Oh, where, tell me where, is your Highland laddie gone?' In a letter to a friend, Jane subsequently slightly altered this line to 'Where, tell me where, has my Highland laddie gone?' when writing about her son's departure abroad, leading some to credit it to her, but it seems much more likely that she first saw it in Anne's poem.[188]

All this suggests a degree of acquaintance, if not friendship, between the two, and in 1801, when Grant's husband died of tuberculosis – like four of their young children before him – she was well enough known by the duke and duchess to be let a small cottage on Gordon lands, and for the duchess to be a prominent subscriber to the volume of Grant's poems published in 1803 with the aid of 3,000 subscribers, many of whom had been recruited by Jane. Her husband's death had left Anne homeless with eight surviving young children but without an income, and although she tried to make ends meet by farming, she was soon deep in debt. The success of the book of poems paid off her debts and enabled her to move to Stirling where she began a successful career as a writer.

One other thing that Mrs Grant has left us, in addition to her assessment of Jane's pursuit of her literary salon in Edinburgh quoted at the beginning of the chapter, is the following: 'Having said all this of her Grace, it is but fair to add, that in one point she never varies, which is active, nay, most industrious benevolence. Silver and gold she has not, but what she has – her interest, her trouble, her exertions – she gives with unequalled perseverance.'[189]

Another neighbour who would have added interest to the area for Jane was James Macpherson of Fingal and *Ossian* fame. She records in February 1787 that 'Fingal has bought the estate of Raitts,' adding, 'I hope it is for him,' looking forward perhaps to some interesting evenings, while Mrs Grant puts an altogether more poetic slant on the news in a letter to Mrs Brown: 'The bard of bards, who reached to mouldy harp of Ossian … and awakened the song of other times, is now moving, like a bright meteor, over his native hills … [he has] has bought three small estates in this country within these two years, given a ball for the ladies, and made other exhibitions of wealth and liberality. He now keeps a Hall at Belleville, his new purchased seat.'[190]

Jane's other great preoccupation at this time was the lack of a proper communal focal point in the area, and she was working with the Revd John Anderson on the creation of a new village at Kingussie, a project which became 'my favourite child'. David Taylor tells us that by 1793, 'there was already a school, courthouse, post office, and a lint mill on the proposed site of the village,' and Stoddart notes in

1799 that 'Her Grace has planned the establishment of a village … whose bakers, butchers etc. may serve all the adjacent country.'[191]

As Taylor also notes, however, for all the good projects such as these might have done for some in the area, such improvements came at an extravagant cost for an estate already in debt, and for the estate tenants the ongoing rent increases 'aggravated the very poverty she was trying to alleviate … a paradox the Duchess never quite grasped'. The lack of money also affected Jane too, because although she had been granted the annuity of £4,000 a year in 1792, it appears from a later letter that even by 1795, 'all I ever received from his estate was my then pin money of £500.' It has been pointed out that, with very few exceptions, nobody was ever 'cleared' from Gordon lands in the manner that was so common at this time across the Highlands, but the advantages this gained them were largely negated by the fact that no cohesive plan was ever put in place to help those tenants adapt in rapidly changing times and circumstances; the outcome was therefore often no better, and relentless rent increases and diminishing access to land led many to voluntary emigration, especially to Canada.[192]

Meanwhile, although in February 1794 another of the castle servants, Isobel Williamson, had given birth to duke's third 'natural child', family life went on; in July 1795 Thomas Young visited the Highlands with 'letters of recommendation', and left this account of Georgina's fourteenth birthday being celebrated at Gordon Castle:

> It was Lady Georgina's birthday; the flag was hoisted. Lord Alexander's regiment of little boys was paraded, and employed in racing and dancing on the green, and in the evening a ball was given to the servants; all the family … amused themselves with observing the agility of the lads and lasses … The Duchess proposed that Sir George Abercrombie and I should dance a reel with the two younger ladies; for they danced nothing but reels. Afterwards the Duke danced with one of the upper servants … [and] when it was late, and Sir George was tired, we took a girl in his place and resumed the sport. Lady Madeline (Sinclair) sat by, and made the music play till the other sets quitted the field.[193]

Following the birthday party, it would appear that Jane spent much of 1795 staying with the duke in London while she sought a husband for Louisa, who, 'in her mother's opinion, was "ripe for marriage"', and she soon settled on Charles Cornwallis, Viscount Brome. Brome, however, 'hesitated, due to old rumours of insanity in the Gordon family', but she assured him 'there was not a drop of Gordon blood in Louisa.' This remark, while it seems to have persuaded the Cornwallis family, has never been fully explained. Whatever the truth of Louisa's parentage, the duke received a letter from Lord Brome in March 1797, taking this opportunity 'of acquainting your Grace with my attachment to Lady Louisa, which I am happy to say she approves of', and the marriage finally went ahead at Jane's house in Piccadilly in April 1797.[194] With Louisa safely and happily married, Jane returned north in August, stopping off at The Burn in Kincardineshire, the home of the duke's uncle, Lord Adam Gordon. At this time, Lord Adam was Governor of Edinburgh Castle, but he had also been very busy in the development and improvement of the house and grounds at The Burn, where 'the picturesque beauties of the place far exceed most of the sceneries of the kind in Scotland.'

That August, however, the 'picturesque beauties' of The Burn had a different effect on Jane's mood, even though she was clearly delighted to be travelling north:

> Every step as I advanced towards the Grampians added to my hopes of once more seeing you, my dear sir. They tell me you are at Peterhead, and I hope when you return you will come and see me in these wild scenes such as you admire … Have you ever been here? It is a creation of Lord Adam's; Nature has done much, and he has only made it comfortable, without robbing it of one beauty. The house is most excellent, and rocks, woods, and torrents in great perfection; but to me they awaken a thousand painful ideas, they heighten every feeling of mind; and as mine is dark and gloomy as the grave, these dark, brown mountains and solemn scenes, though most delightful, are not good for me at present.[195]

This passage from a letter to Beattie tells us a great deal about Jane's state of mind as her relationship with her husband continued to unravel, and with it any certainties she may have been counting on for her future. That the very things that had brought her the most happiness over the years – rocks, woods, torrents and mountains – should now appear to her as 'dark and gloomy as the grave' suggests the fragility of her confident exterior, and that Beattie was the one, and perhaps the only, person in whom she could ever confide in this way. There was, however, one other individual upon whom she had been relying for support, and who no doubt also had some awareness of Jane's fears and sadness – her daughter Georgina. But by now the latter was no longer 'little Georgy'; she was sixteen and Jane faced the task of finding her a suitable husband and launching her into life. Since Jane was living much of the year in either Kinrara or Edinburgh, her access to the London social scene was now more limited, and so it is not until the next year that we get a hint as to whom she has in mind.

In March 1798 Lady Georgiana Russell sent her husband, Lord John, a note to say that the Duchess of Gordon has sent him 'an invitation to tonight' to a dinner in London to which she had also invited his bachelor brother, the Duke of Bedford. Clearly, Jane was catching up on her acquaintances with eligible young men, and later in the year Georgiana tells Lord John that the duchess 'has sent you another invitation for tonight', following her return to London after a summer in Scotland. Jane had her eye on Francis Russell, the Duke of Bedford, and, knowing they were close, was keen to make a friend of his brother Lord John as well, but, as we have seen, at this time 'no match was completed.'[196]

No match at this point, but in February 1799 the pace began to pick up for Georgina, starting with a ball given by her mother in London. The excitement of the evening was recorded in *The Times*:

The Duchess of Gordon's Ball.
The festive portals of the bonny Duchess … received upwards of 300 of the most fashionable company in town. The fête was given to introduce Lady Georgina … into fashionable life, her Ladyship having been presented the

preceding day to Her Majesty. Her Ladyship opened the ball with Lord Petty, the youngest son of the Marquess of Lansdowne. Her fascinating form, grace of gesture, and pleasingness of manner, aided by the animating strains of Gow, quickly inspired the whole company … The Country Dances continued without interruption till about 3.00 o'clock when the Supper room opened.[197]

The ball was followed by Georgina's eighteenth birthday in July.

Later that summer Jane returned again to her 'Highland Cottage', but Georgina does not appear to have been with her when John Stoddart visited Kinrara during his tour of Scotland late in 1799. He reaches The Doune and then Kinrara, where he stays 'several days' at the bothy 'in the middle of November', just as snow starts to fall on the Cairngorms.[198] Stoddart's account, although breathlessly deferential in tone, is most interesting because it is the only description of any length of life at the farmstead that was written from direct first-hand experience more or less at the time; even the account of the 'Highland Lady', Elizabeth Grant, was based on second-hand accounts and written from memory decades later. Stoddart reports:

From Rothiemurchus to Kinrara … is a walk as simply beautiful, as any part of the Highlands can be, where objects are on so grand a scale. The Spey flowing under a long wall of mountain crags and fir plantations embraces in its sweep a verdant plain which is close shut in, on the opposite side, by the hill of Tor Alive … In this very spot, on a knoll commanding the small plain … stands the cottage of her Grace, the Dutchess of Gordon. Around it are the birch woods … The house was a mere Highland farm … Her Grace has taken it, as it stood, its thatched roof, its out-houses, its barn and byre, and with the addition of only a single room, and some alteration of arrangements in the others, has converted it into a summer residence … in Badenoch, one of the wildest places of the Highland Districts … the house itself was by no means well built, and the construction of the chimneys in particular was so faulty, as to fill the rooms frequently with smoke. The task of improvement was therefore one great occupation. Her Grace has planned the establishment of a village, at a little distance …

From what I have said, it will easily be imagined, that there was little room for tedium, or ennui; notwithstanding the neighbourhood afforded very few visitors, and her Grace had no other companions, but her grand-daughter, Miss Lennox, and her friend Mrs Rose of Inverness.

… In the evenings our time was passed with authors most interesting in such a situation – with Ossian, the painter of Highland scenery – with Burns, the still more animated painter of Scottish feelings; nor should I forget Mr Price's *Essay on the Picturesque*, which served as a textbook to all our discussions on local improvement. The most amiable light, in which the Dutchess appeared, was that of a benefactress to the surrounding country. She visited individually the separate cottages of the peasants; at one time she prevailed on a great number to have their children inoculated under her inspection … The affability of her manners, still more than the extent of her benevolence, rendered her name universally beloved …

While her Grace was thus occupied, we wandered with delight, from prospect to prospect, among these grand and varied scenes … The autumn was far spent, and the wind storms, which come off the tops of the mountains, frequently brought passing showers of snow.

Then, as winter rapidly approached, Stoddart set off up Glen Feshie and over into Braemar to continue his tour. Since he arrived in late November, it is clear that Kinrara was already far more than simply 'a summer residence' as he reports, and, fortunately perhaps, a few years later Jane's circumstances at Kinrara changed radically when a new, much grander house was built for her between 1800 and 1804 a mile or so further downstream along the Spey on higher ground and with wider views. However, it was in a spot adjacent to the original farmhouse that Jane that chose to be buried and where her memorial can be seen today.

It was in 1803, some three years after Stoddart's visit, that Elizabeth Grant came to live with her family at The Doune, Rothiemurchus, and it was another year before they met Jane and Georgina. By this time the latter were living in the new 'cottage villa' as she describes it, and the account she gives of life at the 'old' Kinrara farmhouse in her *Memoir of a Highland Lady* was based on that of her mother, the events being 'quite beyond my memory': 'She inhabited the real old farmhouse of Kinrara … where I have heard my mother say that the Duchess was happier and more agreeable, and the society she gathered around her far pleasanter, than it ever was afterwards in the new cottage villa she built about a mile nearer to us.' Grant describes the 'backwoods life' at the old farmhouse as

> a dramatick emancipation from the forms of society that for a little while every season was delightful, particularly as there was no real roughing it. In the but and ben, constituting the small farm *cabin* … she and her daughter Lady Georgina dwelt in, by the help of white calico, a little white wash, a little paint, and plenty of flowers they made their apartment quite pretty.
>
> Her favourite footman, Lang James … an excellent servant for that sort of wild life, able to put his hand to any work, played the violin remarkably well, and there was no difficulty in getting up a highly satisfactory band on any evening that the guests were disposed for dancing.

She then tells us, 'Half the London world of fashion, all the clever people that could be hunted out from all parts, all the north country, all the neighbourhood from far and near without regard to wealth or station, and all the kith and kin both of Gordons and Maxwells, flocked to this encampment in the wilderness during the fine autumns to enjoy the free life, the pure air, and the wit and fun the duchess brought with her to the mountains.'

Yet, one thing that Stoddart's account makes clear is that Jane was at Kinrara in late November, clearly spending more than 'a little while every season' at the farm, and although Elizabeth puts the number of visitors at 'half the London world of fashion', 'all the clever people', 'all the neighbourhood' and many family members, even if this was true, which seems unlikely, it would not have applied outside the summer season. Beyond a few weeks in the late summer when visitors arrived, life at Kinrara is much more likely to have reflected Stoddart's recollection of just three other visitors huddled in the smoke-filled rooms. In addition, given the fact that there are no other accounts of visits to Kinrara at this time at all, one has to wonder if Elizabeth's mother's memory had not somewhat exaggerated things. Certainly, there would have been a steady stream of visitors over the years, although the person Jane really wanted to see, James Beattie, was never able to make the trip, but, as at Glenfiddich, it seems that it was the quiet and seclusion of Kinrara that she really valued.

Elizabeth Grant, who was only seven when she met Jane and Georgina in 1804, then passes on her mother's memories of Georgina in earlier times:

> Lady Georgina Gordon, the youngest of the fair sisters … and the only one unmarried, was much liked; kind hearted she has through her life shown herself to be; then, in her early youth, she was quiet and pleasing, as well as lively. Unchangeable in amiability of manner, she was very variable in her looks; one day almost beautiful, the next day, almost plain; so my mother described her when she described those merry doings in the old cottage at Kinrara in days quite beyond my memory. Lady Georgina had been some years married to the Duke of Bedford, and the Duchess of Gordon was living in her new house in this summer of 1804 when I first recollect them as neighbours.[199]

This last bit of information gives us further reason to wonder just how well Elizabeth knew the Bedfords, since in the summer of 1804, when Georgina was in England, she had been married exactly one year. Nevertheless, it is an invaluable glimpse into both Jane's and Georgina's life at Kinrara, and the relationship between the Bedfords and the Grants was to continue for some forty years.

Before Georgina left with her mother to go south in late summer 1801, however, we can catch one more glimpse of her in the Highlands, in a short description by Sarah Murray of meeting Georgina and Jane on a visit to Loch an Eilein in Rothiemurchus:

we came to another lake called Loch-in-Eilan, the island lake. We there entered a boat and rowed towards the ruin on the island. The scene was such, that I began to fancy myself in a state of enchantment, and to assist the delusion, we saw through the branches of the trees on the banks of the lake, a milk-white flag flying, and heard a voice claiming attention. We turned out of our course, and on reaching the shore, her Grace the Duchess of Gordon presented herself. Lady Georgiana, now the Duchess of Bedford, was at some distance from her mother, and on seeing us, came bounding from rock to rock so light and airy, I fancied her Elegance personified.

Perhaps more than any other description of her, Sarah Murray caught something of Georgina's personality here (Colour Plate 9). We see a young woman as equally at home among the rocks beside a remote loch in Scotland as in the ballrooms and supper parties of Edinburgh and London, but the scene Murray conjures up also suggests something more. Many years before, missing his company, Jane had written in one of her letters to Beattie, 'I wish for someone who would admire the silent Beauties of this Glen with the same enthusiasm I do and that regret embitters the finest romantic walks in the world.'[200]

It was a theme which ran through a number of her letters, and Sarah Murray's brief description of Jane and her daughter on the banks of Loch an Eilein would suggest that Jane had finally found someone with whom she could share 'the silent Beauties of this Glen', which had come to mean as much to her daughter as they did to her.

Although Georgina would return to the area around Kinrara before too long, in 1801, back in the south, she became caught up not just in the search for a husband, but also with her parents' increasingly acrimonious separation. It seems that by the summer tensions in their marriage, precipitated by the birth of Jean Christie's third child by the duke, led Georgina to be caught in the middle of a series of difficult and stormy meetings. During the first, in London, Lord Adam Gordon of The Burn, the duke's uncle and a sympathetic friend to Jane, laid out the terms to prepare the ground for a settlement, terms that the duke was to ratify the following day. Unfortunately, at the second meeting things did not go well. Writing from Margate, where Georgina had subsequently taken her, Jane described what happened:

> Lord Adam told me he [Duke of Gordon] would pay all the [bills] but grant no allowance of more, which I thought the times required. They begged me to go on and said he would pay the taxes, [to which] I consented to prevent bustle and exposing the family it had been my pride and glory to raise to the pitch of favour and glory it finally possessed. [The duke] called the day Lord Adam went and, after much abuse of former imaginary extravagance, told me by God he should take off £800 a year. I told him only a Court could do that. Then he says 'I shall order you to Gordon Castle'. I said nothing but begged to be told what to do. These scenes … made me very ill. Georgina begged that I would leave town, [so] we came to this solitary island.

A Deed of Separation was drawn up 'taking off £800 now, and £500 more if Georgina wed … that I rejected … The Duke today sends me an order to Gordon Castle, which I certainly do, rather than accept this offer, but I shall be Duchess of Gordon, neither commanded by servants nor favourites.' She goes on to say that if it goes to court, she has her story ready: 'First, why I was afraid to live at Gordon Castle, tho' I did it for the good of my family. How I was turned out of the House, [and] I went to find his relations, who after an examination of his affairs … gave me £4.000 a year and my house rent of £500.'

But circumstances then changed again when Louisa married Cornwallis and the duke deducted an additional £100, leaving Jane to ask, 'If any Court sees honour and justice in that, I am mistaken, and, alas, what an awful exposure of a family that, were it not for him, would be the first in the world. I shall show what I have done for the family … I am too ill and too wretched to think of anything else.'[201]

At this time, however, there was to be no easy solution, and agreeing the terms of the settlement was to drag on for another four or five years. In the meantime, Jane's efforts to find Georgina a suitable husband brought her into direct competition with her old rival on the political and social scene, Georgiana, Duchess of Devonshire. Amanda Foreman in her biography of Georgiana sets the scene with this quote from the French *Bon Ton* magazine, 'The Duchess of Gordon had taken Georgiana's place as the leading political hostess in society, although the press made fun of her attempts to set the fashion.'

This, of course, made things rather personal since both duchesses had their eye on Francis, Duke of Bedford, as a suitable husband for their daughters: Georgina Gordon being twenty and Georgiana Devonshire just turned eighteen. Fortunately for Jane, perhaps, the friendship between Bedford and the Duchess of Devonshire broke down that year over her failure to repay a loan from the duke to cover her gambling debts, and this left the field clear for Jane. It would seem Jane had come close to success the year before when 'Lord Morpeth had almost proposed to Lady Georgiana Gordon', but now she was concentrating on Bedford, and in early 1802 news reached the Duchess of Devonshire that Bedford was 'courting the Duchess of Gordon's youngest daughter Lady Georgina. The thought that her ... rival might steal the greatest prize in the Whig matrimonial field made Georgiana weep with frustration ... Indeed we are all undone,' she wrote, 'no possible event could have so thoroughly overturned the habit of our society as this.'[202]

In the end, of course, the courtship was doomed, since a few months later, on 2 March, the Duke of Bedford died at Woburn and his brother Lord John Russell became 6th Duke of Bedford. The question that remained, however, was how far the 'courtship' of Georgina had progressed before the duke's death, and whether or not the duke had actually proposed to her – had there been an engagement? While Jane insisted that they were and instantly put Georgina into full mourning, the new duke, who had spoken to his brother before he died, said not, and wider society's view depended largely on their like or dislike of Jane. There seems to be no surviving evidence either way, and perhaps the clearest, although inconclusive, version of events comes in a letter from Granville Leveson-Gower to his mother around April 1802:

The conversation of London is wholly turned upon the story of the Duke of Bedford having been engaged to marry Lady Georg. Gordon. The duchess of Gordon last night related to me all the Circumstances, and, as it appeared to me, embellished and exaggerated many things. I hear from good authority that the present Duke declares that he was commissioned by his brother upon his Death-Bed to give a message to Lady Georgiana, but that his Brother was under no positive engagement of Marriage. I think myself that a message sent is in itself evidence that he did intend to marry her. The Duchess of Gordon says that he was not only under a private engagement, but that a few days before his Illness he had sent to the Duke of Manchester declaring that obstacles which had hitherto prevented his Marriage (that is his connection with a Mrs Palmer, by whom he has two children) were at an end, and that he waited only for Lady Georgiana's arrival from Scotland to declare it, and from his death-bed he sent her a lock of his Hair as the most precious Legacy he could leave her, and she is on this account to go into Mourning for the Duke. The conduct of the Duchess is very foolish, for she is going about everywhere telling her Story, and is furious at the incredulity of the World, which indeed is very general. Lady Georgiana is remaining quietly with her sister at Culford, oppressed beyond Measure with Grief.[203]

So perhaps, in the end, in their own way, both sides were right, but it is very difficult to assess to what extent Georgina was 'oppressed' by grief or was simply overwhelmed emotionally by the often difficult events of the past year. Not only had she been dealing with some very difficult family issues and angry scenes, having spent the last couple of years trying to look after her mother while maintaining a relationship with her father, she had also had to leave the relative seclusion of Scotland, the people and places among which she felt at home, to perform in the uncomfortable and often hostile glare of court and London society, while also trying rapidly and under pressure to process her feelings for, and imagine life with, first one suitor and then another chosen for her by someone else. One thing is evident, however: as the year went on, reports of her being oppressed by grief are replaced by reports that she is very ill, and the line between her being in deep mourning and in ill-health becomes very blurred, particularly after her mother sweeps her off to Paris that summer.

The other person deeply in mourning for the late Duke of Bedford at this time was, of course, his brother Lord John as he faced life without the 'adult' who had given it structure, stability and direction since they were young. Now, following the deaths of his wife and brother, any plans he had had for his life were torn up and he had to rapidly learn an entirely new role in an entirely new reality. After deciding not to attend his brother's internment in the family mausoleum at Chenies, the new duke spent a few days with his brother Lord William at Streatham, before setting off at the end of March to visit Lord and Lady Bradford at Weston Park, the people he had also turned to after his wife's death. He was, he told Lord Holland, trying 'to obtain a few days respite from Business which comes upon me with such accumulated pressure that it almost exhausts my body and mind', a sentiment which might also aptly sum up Georgina's state of mind.[204]

On his return to Woburn, the duke dealt with a few pressing matters. Most importantly, on his brother's advice and to ensure a smooth transition and that the estates continue to run properly, he appointed the Whig party's political manager William Adam as chief agent of the Bedford estates. Following this he met with Thomas Coke and Arthur Young at Woburn to decide whether or not it would be suitable to hold the annual agricultural show, the 'Sheep Shearings', that summer; perhaps because the duke was not ready to host such a large gathering or perhaps out of respect, they chose to cancel the event for that year.

With these immediate issues taken care of, the duke now turned his attention to another of his brother's last wishes – that he should personally carry a message to Georgina. He had so far made no public comment at all on the question of the engagement but, anxious to his keep his word, the duke duly met up with Georgina at the house where she was staying with her mother in Barnes in late June. Although we do not know what was said, or what comfort he could give Georgina, it appears he had also been asked to give her a lock of his brother's hair to be worn as a token of the late duke's feelings. It would seem that he was not able to provide the lock there and then, but promised to deliver it at a later date, and soon after the meeting he received a letter from Jane thanking him for his words to Georgina, but disappointed that he still said nothing publicly. Part of this reads:

> Clouded by your silence which the World judges as a denial of what they are pleased to call my assertions – the malignancy of some envious wretches when they first discovered her engagement to your brother, made it necessary to show this engagement did exist ... I never doubted in your loudly agreeing to every word I advanced – 'that she had every consolation a woman in her situation could have, being remembered with affection in his last moments and desired to wear his Hair'– it raised her above all others in my opinion, and proved it was not the proud partiality of a Mother.[205]

The duke's reply neither confirms nor denies the suggestion of an engagement:

> I feel myself at a loss in answering your Grace's letter and enter as fully upon the subject as you seem to expect and desire. It has been a painful one for me, and has cost me many moments of regret and disappointment. Regret that it should have afforded a topic of Conversation ... to the public, and disappointment that the part I had taken in it should not have met with your Grace's approbation.
>
> You may rest assured that it was dictated only by the respect that I owe to the memory of a much loved and lamented brother and by ... the indispensible and impervious obligations of [confidentiality]. What he communicated to me in his last moments was in strict and total confidence and as such will find a faithful sanctuary in my heart to my dying day. No one has heard anything from me on this subject, except that when he named your daughter to me it was in terms of the most unfeigned and unbounded respect. Consequently no person can have been authorized to affirm or deny any of the stories that have been circulated.

Lady Georgiana Gordon's character is dear to me because I know it was so to him; but surely your Grace would not call upon me to publish to the World the confidential death-bed communications of a beloved Brother on account of the supposed censure of a few misjudging individuals … and no one who had the slightest knowledge of my Brother could for a single instant doubt that that his object, his views and his intentions were most … honourable.

… When I saw Lady Georgiana at Barnes my motives were as openly stated to her, and I had the consolation to learn … that they were sanctioned by her approbation.

Jane clearly remained unhappy about the uncertainty and, on impulse it seems, decided to take advantage of the Treaty of Amiens to travel to Paris, to get Georgina out of London and have a chance to meet some new people. It seems, however, that following their meeting in Barnes, Georgina and the new Duke of Bedford kept in touch and on 12 August, as she was leaving for Paris, Georgina wrote to him on black bordered mourning paper, 'It is with the utmost regret I leave England without seeing you once more, and receiving the beloved and ever valued Hair you were so good as to promise me, as I leave London in a few hours I must relinquish that hope, but entreat that you will preserve it for me. They may carry me to new scenes and different climes, but nothing will obliterate the awful events of this year. Pray let me have a place in your remembrance … Georgiana Gordon'[206]

It is not clear why Georgina should suddenly be calling herself 'Georgiana', and we do not know if that more formalized version of her name had been adopted when she 'came out' in London on turning eighteen, but it is hard not to suspect that, adapting rapidly to changed circumstances and knowing the name of Lord John's first wife, her mother might not have suggested it. She was also no doubt responsible for Georgina adopting full mourning dress while in Paris, which caused some amusement: 'with the engagement fiasco fresh in their memories, all eyes were on Georgina to see how she was behaving … On 14 October, Lady Bessborough wrote to Lord Leveson-Gower: Lady G Gordon is consoling herself with Lord Hinchinbroke and danced at the Salon in her weeds.'

It seems, however, that the 'weeds' were soon set aside when Jane spotted another possible candidate for Georgina in Paris, Eugène de Beauharnais, the son of Napoleon's wife Joséphine. Lady Bessborough was by now reporting that 'Lady Georgiana Gordon appeared out of mourning', and commented on what good company she was for her daughter Caroline. Unfortunately, whatever the young couple may have thought of each other, Napoleon had other plans for Eugène, who went on to marry the daughter of the Elector of Bavaria, and so, once again, Jane's hopes were dashed and Georgina suffered 'another romantic disappointment'.[207] At this point Georgina appears to have slumped into some kind of depression due, as Trethewey suggests, to the 'constant emotional strain' of the past few years, and it was thus a rather teary, vulnerable and lost soul that the Duke of Bedford encountered when he too arrived in Paris in October to complete his mission of delivering the famous lock of hair. Sitting in their rented rooms in Paris after being on display day and night in front of crowds of people, many of whom were not her friends, how distant must the soothing calm of the shores of Loch an Eilein have seemed to Georgina.

Although the duke was extremely busy at this time as he became more and more engaged in the running of Woburn Abbey and the Bedford estates, and he and William Adam were also busy managing the Bedford political interests, the fact that he made time to travel to Paris is interesting. Certainly, he was anxious to carry out his brother's wishes, but one suspects too that there was already 'place in [his] remembrance' for Georgina after their earlier meeting in Barnes, and that meeting her again in Paris in such broken spirits touched him deeply, given what he had just been through with the death of his wife and brother. No accounts have emerged of this meeting – perhaps he passed over the lock of hair, or perhaps that now seemed unimportant as the couple were drawn together at this difficult moment in both of their lives. Georgina had met a man who seemed to unconditionally embrace who she was, and her family, and who appeared to be as lost as she was. In turn, the duke had met someone who listened and sympathized and sought to console him, who had many of the qualities of his first Georgiana, yet who seemed not to share his first wife's political and social ambitions. On the contrary, she seemed to offer something much more mysterious and exciting: the chance to share a world so different from his own. He was dazzled, and as Jane watched the relationship blossom, she could probably not believe her luck – she was to secure a third duke after all. Whatever had occurred, the duke left for England in December to return again in January or February 1803. Society in Paris and London waited with baited breath to see what would come of this relationship.

It had proved to be a pivotal year for the duke. In March 1802 he had written to Lady Bradford:

I think I wrote twice to you before I left Woburn, but my head has been sadly confused and is so still. Pray to god, my friend, to give me the strength to get through this trial. I have a world of Cases upon me, too much for my weak nature to bear. I know you would have cheerfully gone to Woburn, to assist and soothe me with your Consolations, I know too the comfort I should have derived from your presence – kind and gentle Being! Best loved sister of my lost Georgiana! … The Church Bell is now tolling in melancholy solemnity. With a sorrowful heart then, I will only add that I am your truly grateful, affectionate and faithful friend – pray with me here.[208]

Almost a year later, by late January or early February 1803, although we still have no news about an engagement, the duke is back in Paris where the foreign visitors are by now wondering nervously whether they should leave before the peace treaty breaks down. As he explains to Lady Bradford, 'I trust I shall not be obliged to leave Paris before my appointed day, in fact we know nothing more of the Peace … than you do on the other side of the Water, nor does anyone I believe, except the Negotiators themselves, not even Tallyrand.' He then adds, 'I have seen the Dss of G. who has received me most graciously and has not ever given a hint upon any subject which could be unpleasant to me … Lady Georgiana Gordon looks very ill, she has been so seriously.' In fact, both the duke and the Gordons appear to have stayed on in Paris a few more weeks. The Gordons returned to

London as soon as Georgina recovered, while the duke stayed long enough to do some shopping in Paris, receipts from the time indicating that he bought clothing in addition to 'furniture, bronzes, lamps, clocks'.[209] All of which suggests that something, perhaps his rapidly developing relationship with Georgina, had lifted his spirits, and certainly they all met up again once back in London. In the event, the Treaty of Amiens finally broke down on 13 May 1803, at which point the last of the British left Paris; Britain declared war on 18 May, and the twelve years of the Napoleonic Wars began.

By 2 May there was a new development, when the duke wrote the following note to the Duke of Gordon:

> My Lord,
>
> I take the earliest opportunity of acquainting your Grace that I have been fortunate enough to obtain Lady Georgiana's consent to unite her lot with mine, and as my object will now be to promote and secure her happiness, I am induced to flatter myself that it may meet with your Grace's approval.

To which Gordon replies:

> I have had the honour to receive your Grace's letter, and feel highly flattered that my daughter Georgina has been so fortunate as to be the object of your Grace's choice. I can only add that nothing in this world could have given me greater satisfaction, …
>
> Gordon.[210]

At much the same time, the duke also sat down to write a much more difficult letter – to Lady Bradford –which could not be more different from the one he sent her some fourteen months before when still lamenting the loss of Georgiana:

> I should think myself wanting in every feeling of gratitude towards you after the marks of friendship and affection you have ever shown me … were

I to delay communicating to you an Event which affects my happiness, and it would be a matter of sincere and painful regret to me were you or your Sister to be first apprised of it from any other quarter. I am about to exchange my lot for one which promises me more happiness than I have of late enjoyed.

I trust, my kind and amiable friend, you will not blame me if I seek for tranquillity and ease in my future life, and that you will not consider it as a want of respect or affection for the memory of our lost, ever loved and ever lamented angel. No! My dear Lady Bradford, my sorrows and regrets for her have taken a deep and lasting root and are never to be removed, but I feel a reasonable and well grounded belief that she to whom I have determined to unite my Lot, will feel for and sympathise with my afflictions … I have formed no wild or visionary schemes of happiness … Since the sad loss I sustained, my situation has been most comfortless and attached to Domestic Life I have every day felt more and more the want of someone to share my occupations and interests, accustomed to this from the early age of nineteen it had grown into a fixed habit of the mind, and without it my home became cheerless and miserable.

You know Lady Georgiana Gordon, I have more reasons than one to believe her to be most amiable. I have seen her in the most trying situations acting with the utmost propriety, and with a feeling and dignity of Conduct … and I think I am not mistaken in my judgment when I believe her to be formed to give comfort and happiness to domestic Life. I feel that the world will be busy in Conversation and Conjecture, the arts and intrigues of the Dss of G[ordon] will give rise to many, and I shall in all probability be pronounced to be the dupe of them. To this I must make up my mind, but the virtuous and estimable part of Society will know how to distinguish between the Daughter and the Mother … Will you have the kindness my dearest friend to communicate the subject of this letter to your sisters, and to Lord Torrington, and not to name it to anyone else for a day or two. God bless you![211]

It was both an awkward and a revealing letter, walking the thin line between being too happy and showing respect for his first wife, and while he looks forward to sharing his 'occupations and interests', he tactfully limits his list of Georgina Gordon's merits to those of providing cheer, comfort and happiness to his domestic life. The relationship had clearly developed rapidly once they were back in London, and two months later they were married. In the interim Jane, lacking access to a suitable house in London, was able to prevail on the Earl of Fife to make Fife House in Whitehall available for the wedding, and George Gordon relates how she did it, writing that Jane 'desired the coachman to drive to Fife House. My Lord was *not at home*, but she made her way upstairs and found him at late breakfast, "My Lord, you were in love with me five and twenty years ago, and I am now come to ask a favour of you [and] nor will I stir from this chair till it is granted." He was out within a week, and her Grace took full possession.'

Finally, after all the dramas and uncertainties, the couple were married on 23 June 1803, the certificate stating simply that John Russell, Duke of Bedford, and Lady Georgiana Gordon 'married in the Dwelling House of Lord Fife by special license of the Archbsp of Canterbury; witnessed by Gordon, Charles Seymour, Brome'.

Although they left for Woburn after the marriage, they briefly rejoined Jane when she organized one final spectacular event in London on 8 July, the details of which were caught by *The Times*:

> The Duchess of Gordon, on Wednesday evening, attended Vauxhall with a numerous party of Nobility. They came down the river from Richmond in barges, rowed by watermen in rich scarlet dresses, and entered the Gardens at 11.00 o'clock, where they were met by His Grace of Norfolk, Lord Galway and several persons of distinction. The noble party completely filled the Pavilion, in which we observed the Duke and Duchess of Bedford, the Duke and Duchess of Manchester, the Duchess of Rutland, Lady Essex, &c. Nothing could exceed the splendour of the illuminations, which were so arranged that the Gardens appeared to form one continued blaze of fire.[212]

Following this spectacular day, and now very much alone, Jane left London for the seclusion of Kinrara, where in August, just two months after the wedding, a letter arrived postmarked Aberdeen and sealed with black wax used for mourning. It was the news that she had been expecting and dreading in equal measure: James Beattie had died. Beattie had been seriously ill for some time, but prepared as she was for this outcome, his death must have left her in a darker, less friendly world, one she had now to face without Georgina or her 'guardian angel', as she referred to Beattie. Indeed, the effect of these losses are reflected over the next couple of years as we witness Jane's increasingly desperate and at times vicious struggle with her husband, his lawyers and Gordon estate staff to secure the respect she felt due to her, and a settlement that reflected this. She kept her composure in her reply to Beattie's niece, Mrs Glennie, and her husband, but we sense what the end of this thirty-three-year and unconditional friendship meant to her:

Kenrara [*sic*] Cottage September 1803

Though we had nothing to hope when we parted, yet the black seal and the Aberdeen postmark gave me a sensation you can feel, though I cannot describe it. At this time of year, and in the happiest days of my eventful life, he used to come to Gordon Castle. He not only enjoyed the gay scenes, but was the gayest of the gay. That voice I shall never hear again still vibrates in my memory, and I often draw a picture of him, surrounded by my children, playing his violoncello with that benign countenance … When I first saw these wild scenes of delight, which possess everything in Nature that is sublime and beautiful, I pleased myself to think how he would admire them … He certainly believed that the grave was not a dark and dreadful region of forgetfulness, but that those objects that interested us in this world of care would be revealed as far as would be conducive to our happiness.

'May many an evening sun shine sweetly on his grave.'

I feel a pleasure in conversing with one who knew Dr. Beattie, loved him as I do, and, indeed, soothed the last moments of a long, long-lingering illness.[213]

It is interesting that, while Beattie would regularly visit Gordon Castle and sometimes spend months on end there, he never managed to join Jane at either Glenfiddich or Kinrara. This may have been because the opportunities to visit were never convenient, but it also raises the possibility that he was not attracted to the landscape of the Highlands in the same way as he had been to the much gentler hills of Kincardineshire or Aberdeenshire. Nevertheless, even before they met, Jane had immersed herself in Beattie's poetry and *Essay on Truth*, and her subsequent letters to him tell us how close the two were. Reading them in the light of this relationship, we can sometimes hear what must be echoes of conversations they had had in the terms she used: 'sensibility', 'another world', 'superior beings must inhabit, or at least visit, such bewitching scenes' – her recognition of the numinous in nature.

Beattie's crucial role on a personal level seems to have been in supporting Jane's natural instincts, encouraging her interaction with the natural world as the necessary antidote to the artificiality, secrecy and hypocrisy of the court and society at large, to treat both the natural world and the 'people' as objects of interest, to develop and trust one's 'vivacity of perception'.[214]

But as she mixed with the wider world, with Enlightenment Edinburgh or high society and the court in London, Beattie also had another influence on Jane and those around her. As we have seen, while he fulfilled his role as Professor of Moral Philosophy and published the *Essay*, he was also on a different, more personal, trajectory which caused him to pull away from many of the emerging strands of the Scottish Enlightenment, as he explained to Dr Blacklock:

There is a little Ode of yours on the refinements of metaphysical philosophy, which I often read with peculiar satisfaction:
'You, who would be truly wise,
To Nature's light unveil your eyes …'[215]

Beattie understands 'Nature's light' to mean both the truths about life and reality revealed by engagement with the natural world and the 'inner light' provided by our own nature, our intuition, as sources of wisdom to guide our lives and make sense of our existence.

In pursuing this endeavour, Beattie was modifying the central role given to reason and the 'rational' by those philosophers and writers of the elites of Edinburgh and Aberdeen among whom Jane moved, many of whom, including himself, he felt had become overrun by metaphysics and intellectual constructs: lost in 'literary weeds' as he put it. Increasingly aware of this tendency, he sought to counterbalance it by going back to those things that had been revealed to him during his youth. By doing so, although he had many critics, and *The Minstrel* itself failed as a project because the inspiration behind it could not sustain the conventional superstructure of a 'great poem', Beattie nevertheless emerged as one of the earliest voices that sought to explore our world in a new way, 'wrapp'd in wonder'. This approach to the world around us came into sharper focus towards the end of the century and manifested itself as the Romantic era – an approach which called on new science, new art, new literature and new poetry to express a new view of the world. Those who took this view forward embodied a new incarnation of Beattie's minstrel figure, individuals who pioneered an inclusive comprehension of culture made up of combinations of the different aspects of science and art, and the faculties that inspired them.

In science, this approach really came into focus between 1768 – Cook's mapping of the southern oceans, which finally dispelled the Ptolemaic myth of the 'great southern continent' – and 1802 when William Herschel confirmed that 'The universe was … almost unimaginably older than people had previously thought.' In between those dates, Herschel had also discovered the planet Uranus, suggesting an infinite universe beyond the known stars, while in geology James Hutton, who published his ideas in 1785, saw 'no vestige of a beginning, no prospect of an end' in the formation of the rocks of the Earth, and William Smith in 1801 mapped the rock strata of Great Britain for the first time. This work laid the foundations of a cross-discipline revolution in our perception of both the Earth and the universe beyond, and the world was introduced to the wonder of the intertwined concepts of 'deep space' and 'deep time', both ideas unimaginable a generation earlier.[216]

In the arts, this new consciousness of the integrated fabric of the world was captured by Samuel Taylor Coleridge when he wrote of seeking a subject for a poem 'that should give equal room and freedom for description, incident, and … reflections … yet supply in itself a natural connection to the parts and unity to the whole'. Although he wrote this in 1817, Coleridge was actually referring back to his time in Somerset with William and Dorothy Wordsworth between 1797 and 1798, when the poets were looking for the new poetic forms and subject matter that became the *Lyrical Ballads*; both poets were influenced by Beattie's work and were inspired by the figure of Edwin from *The Minstrel*. Malcolm Elwin quotes Stanza XXII from Book I of *The Minstrel*, a description of Edwin, which begins,

> In truth he was a strange and wayward wight,
> Fond of each gentle, and each dreadful scene;
> In darkness, and in storm, he found delight …

Elwin continues: 'This verse by James Beattie, "always reminded me of him", Dorothy Wordsworth declared referring to her brother William; indeed the whole character of the hero of Beattie's *The Minstrel* … "resembles much what William was when I first knew him after my leaving Halifax." Doubtless Wordsworth had not neglected to suggest to her this supposed resemblance, and Beattie was one of the poets to whom he acknowledged indebtedness in the footnotes to *An Evening Walk*.' It would seem that Wordsworth was introduced to *The Minstrel* 'probably about the age of 14 or 15, by his schoolmaster Thomas Bowman at Hawkshead', and he went to 'use a quotation from the *The Minstrel* as a motto, and there are important borrowings in the poems, "The Vale of Easthwaite", "An Evening Walk", "The Excursion", etc.'

According to Roger Robinson, 'the greatest appeal of the poem was in the portrait of Edwin. Edwin was the young nature poet in the making, and other poets were moved by his communion with nature and his freedom of imagination. They were also moved by the exploration of Edwin's childhood: by the growth of a poet's mind.'

In the case of Coleridge, 'although there is no direct quotable instance' in his poetry, Robinson points out that in his Third Lecture on Revealed Religion Coleridge used a stanza from *The Minstrel* (Book I, Stanza LI) as part of his argument, and knew the poem well enough to actually 'do a bit of rewriting'.[217] It seems certain that Coleridge knew Beattie's poetry at least as well as the Wordsworths did, and it is likely no coincidence that once the Wordsworths joined Coleridge in Somerset in 1797, they should have immediately set out on walks of their own into the landscapes around them, and often in the late evening or at night, as Beattie had done, and then used their experiences as material for poetry. It is also likely no coincidence that the year before Beattie died, Coleridge had just completed a groundbreaking series of walks on his own in the Lake District between 1799 and 1802. These walks mirrored Edwin's expeditions in so many ways, and through such similar terrain and in all weathers, but with one major difference which reflected the changed times: they were recorded not in poetry but in free-flowing, descriptive prose. Contained in his notebook and in letters to friends, this prose, explaining what he had been doing and what he had seen and experienced, was part of the first stirrings of a new genre – nature writing.

Responding to what he saw and experienced among the Lakeland fells, Coleridge wrote of becoming aware of conversations between mountains and sky, of 'lakes, the Vale, Rivers, & mountains, & mists, & Clouds, & Sunshine [which] make endless combinations, as if heaven & Earth were forever talking to each other', and that he became aware of 'a *oneness*, not an intense Unity but an Absolute Unity', that 'Nature has her proper interest; & he will know what it is, who feels and believes, that every Thing has a Life of its own.' Like Beattie, Coleridge felt that 'A Poet's Heart & Intellect should be combined, intimately combined and unified, with the great appearances of Nature.'[218] Reading Coleridge's language, we sense echoes of both Beattie's poetry and Jane's prose descriptions of what she had found and had been tutored to look for by Beattie himself.

While Beattie's influence can be detected in the wide-ranging cultural developments of the times, it also formed the backdrop to Jane's retirement to the farmhouse at Kinrara, which became the focus for her life following her separation from the duke, and where she could feel at home; that this should be the case sums up to some extent the complexity of Jane's character and her life. As David Taylor has put it, 'The word enigma barely does justice to Lady Jane: friend to both king and local peasantry; elite society hostess and hands-on social reformer; political intriguer and practical farmer,'[219] and her enigmatic quality and apparent contradictions have intrigued people down to the present. She was entitled, indulged, profligate but also strangely mercurial, yet beneath the mercurial, flighty exterior, Mrs Grant notes that Jane gave 'her interest, her trouble, her exertions – with unequalled perseverance', acknowledging a deep, sustained sense of humanity and compassion. Combined with her insecurities about her own place in life, this compassion informed Jane's interest in, and identification with, people in whom she instinctively saw those moral qualities that she admired, whether they were lords or labourers, ladies or maids, politicians, poets, musicians or farmers. We see this side of Jane's character find expression in the life she created at Kinrara and also in the life her daughter Georgina created following her marriage.

In 1792, when writing to Beattie and Ross about her new 'shieling', she also made it clear that she had 'taken a farm', alerting us to the fact that, from the start, Kinrara was to be a very different place to Glenfiddich. Whereas the latter was a place to visit, enjoy for a few weeks in isolation and leave again, Kinrara was to be a home where Jane could stay, actually *live* among the 'romantic glens' and, as far as possible, experience life as part of the community. Clearly, to some extent, she was forced by her straightened circumstances to live a simpler life than before, and also, given who she was, she was never going to merge into local life as Mrs Grant of Laggan had done, but one senses that this was something that she wanted to do and embraced the opportunity. Mrs Grant seems to have recognized this and records Jane's new life sympathetically: 'The Duchess of Gordon is a very busy farmeress at Kinrara … She rises at five in the morning, bustles incessantly, employs 20 to 30 workmen every day and entertains noble travellers from England in a house very little better than our own, but she is setting up a wooden pavilion to see company in.'

If Mrs Grant is right about the number of workmen every day, Kinrara clearly became a substantial undertaking, and this is reflected in an agricultural review of 1808:

> The vale, in which the [river Spey] flows, is narrowed considerably at Kinrara. The banks on both sides are richly wooded by a variety of trees … Some beautiful fields are formed by the serpentine course of the river, which glides by with an equal, but not rapid motion, on its pebbled bed … The garden is closely embosomed in wood, sheltered from every blast … The drilled turnips, and the other crops, demonstrate the variety of talent and strength of mind, which are the springs that move all the operations about this singular place.

In addition to the fields, Jane began other improvements with a series of plantations: 'On the south west side of Kinrara, the late Duchess, thirty years ago, planted an extensive piece of barren moor with Scotch firs, mingled with some larch trees,' and 'a few years later, she planted, on the north drive, a piece of equally barren ground … with the same kind of wood which is considerably advanced in growth.'[220] Besides the farm and plantations, Jane was also determined to make the most of the setting. As she had said, 'I like to walk amongst the rustling leaves and plan future forests.'

In terms of improving the house, Stoddart tells us, 'The Duchess has … received several designs … but her taste is too correct to adopt any, whose simplicity does not accord with the surrounding scenery.' Elizabeth Grant writes that, in the end, the original 'but and ben' was where Jane and Georgina lived, and that what once had been the kitchen was simply 'elevated by various contrivances into a sitting room; a barn fitted up as a barrack for ladies, a stable for the gentlemen'; a kitchen was created in one of the outhouses, and all was done in a simple style. Outside, however, Jane's ambitions for the grounds were initially a little more elaborate. In 1799 Stoddart identifies two areas around the farmhouse that Jane is interested in:

To the westward of the knoll on which the cottage stands, is a small plain rendered marshy by a brook which flows through it; the draining and ornamenting of this spot, with a due regard to its natural capabilities, will form no unpleasant exercise for a lover of the picturesque … With a similar view, her Grace has planned a garden, in a hollow of the hill, which at the same time serves to shelter its productions, to screen it from sight, and to produce the effect of a pleasing surprise on its discovery. The neighbouring declivities are clothed with woods, among which she has opened several walks and drives. In directing their formation, and often in pruning the trees with her own hand, she finds her morning employment no less healthful than entertaining.

In spite of the ideas Stoddart tells us were provided by 'Mr Price's Essay on the Picturesque, which served as a textbook to all our discussions on local improvement', actually 'draining and ornamenting' what the 1771 plan of Kinrara describes as a 'morass occasioned by the River Spey' seems to have been beyond the resources available, and there is no record of any significant landscaping to the 'westward of the knoll'.[221] The garden in the 'hollow of the hills', however, was created, and would appear to refer to the garden area beyond the existing house, tucked away under Tor Alive and which still exists today.

There was, however, also a third area which appears to have become increasingly important to Jane: the open field, or haugh, which runs along the bank of the Spey between the two house sites. Two points located on edges of this field are very interesting and appear on the earliest Ordnance Survey maps as 'St Eata's Chapel' and 'St Eata's Well'; the chapel stood a few hundred yards north of the original farmstead, while the well stood at a point beyond the chapel where a spring rose from the steep bank on the north side.[222] How or why St Eata's cult became established in the Kinrara area is not clear, but the presence of these features seems to have meant something to Jane, and she chose to be buried on the site of the ruined chapel. Today the spot is marked by her monument, standing among a later planting of rhododendrons, and the well site – although any structures have gone – is visible today as a neglected bog, another morass, from which the water seeps down to the field below. Whether any traditions or rituals associated with the chapel or the well still survived, even in memory, when Jane arrived, we will never know, but it is not hard to imagine that their presence overlooking the large 'haugh … pretty good dry soil and free from the river' – one of the best pieces of pasture land on the original farm – added another dimension to the landscape around her new home, one which made it 'seem like another world' and a place where she could eventually rest in peace.[223]

PART THREE

BECOMING DUKE AND DUCHESS

CHAPTER FIVE
1803–1810

Johnny and Georgy, the new Duke and Duchess of Bedford, arrived at Woburn Abbey late in the afternoon on 23 June 1803, tired and excited after their wedding that morning. Both had experienced a difficult couple of years leading up to this day, but now, as their carriage passed up Park Street in Woburn village, the street lined with cheering well-wishers, and entered the park, a great new adventure had begun. As they drove through the park to approach the Abbey itself, the rewards and challenges of what lay ahead became clear. Everywhere, there were signs of great activity – new buildings, new roads, new trees and new plantations – and everywhere there were also signs of unfinished projects. After leaving the London road at Hockcliffe, for example, they had passed Henry Holland's unfinished London entrance to the park, the expansive structure still shrouded in scaffolding, the ground around covered in piles of timber, rubble and cut stone, and the wooden formwork for the grand central arch soaring overhead, promising great things to come, as perhaps did everything that day.

By August, the couple had spent a week or so at the Abbey, attended Jane's celebratory party at Vauxhall, taken a quick 'honeymoon' trip to the duke's estates in Cambridgeshire and Northamptonshire, attended Bedford Races, and were now back at Woburn, with the reality of what had happened setting in: two people who knew very little about each other and who were both new to their role, but who were suddenly on the same shared adventure. The relationship that developed at the heart of the marriage took a little time to emerge, but two narratives quickly became apparent, both of which endured. Georgina soon discovered that her key role was to support, encourage and comfort her husband – as Georgiana had done before her – a man full of self-doubt who was now under even more pressure as duke; in addition to this, from the carefree girl Mrs Murray had met by Loch an Eilein just two years before, Georgina had suddenly become a stepmother to three young strangers, Lord Francis (fifteen), Lord George William (thirteen) and Lord John (eleven), who lived with them at the Abbey when not in school at Westminster. This would not be straightforward since not only had the children recently lost their mother, they also had to adapt to a very different woman, and the boys, who had needed to make allowances for their mother's ill-health and fragility for many years, were now confronted by someone brimming with life and mischief, and who expected everyone to keep up.

The second narrative, and its impact on the couple, was more subtle. Georgina had grown up socially at ease with the adult world, had since early childhood interacted with confidence with her parents' guests and even counted them as her 'friends', had often been left to her own devices, and had experienced much more personal freedom than Georgiana Byng. As a result, she was a more independent individual with a strong sense of self-identity, ideas and interests, and brought a new aesthetic vision, a new world of experience, and new possibilities into her husband's life. This strength of character took a while to become apparent, but when it did a few years later, it created a balance in the marriage which was to be the key to its success: space within a close and loving relationship which also allowed each individual to continue to develop and pursue their own interests. Within a few years, as we will see, a shared outlook had been established between the two whereby she too could influence developments, and do so significantly and at some speed.

In considering how their relationship evolved, it is also worth noting that the duke was thirty-seven when they married and the duchess twenty-two, a fifteen-year difference which may not have had much significance early on, but which may have played a role later on, particularly as the duke's health became increasingly fragile. As the newly married couple arrived at Woburn in 1803, however, they both still had something to prove to themselves and those around them – that this marriage could work. This part of the book, then, concerns the establishment of this underlying balance, the start they made on finishing what had been begun by others, the process of becoming the duke and duchess, and discovering what interested them and what sort of a world they would make for themselves and the children.

Over the last few years of his brother's life, and while Lord John was living nearby at Oakley, he had spent a considerable amount of time at Woburn and witnessed the duke putting his ideas for 'national improvement' into action. It is clear that the younger man shared much of that vision, at the heart of which lay agriculture, the bedrock on which the country was built and which ensured its future and that of the aristocratic landed estates (Map 3). Thus, the new duke was also committed to establish 'a thoroughly modern agricultural and sporting estate built around the enlarged and updated Abbey and the Park Farm', the latter a model of its kind, and 'to create an estate which would set new national standards of efficiency and productivity, securing their position and status at the centre of an invigorated rural economy, increasing and stabilizing food production, and steadying the country at a time of great social unrest and radicalization'. It was an era which believed 'that science [and improvement] could help restore stability and maintain the status quo'.[224]

For the duke this meant fulfilling the common vision of his class, one he shared with his brother, of securing the future of the landed estate at the heart of the country's social and political worlds, but also, of course, at the heart of the economic and cultural structure of the English countryside, in this case Bedfordshire. In a smaller way, it was something he had begun to express at Stratton Park, but now on a grander scale and with increased responsibilities. It would seem that what gave this vision its real authority for the new duke, whose self-image was far more literary than his elder brother's, was its direct links back to the classical worlds of Rome and Greece in the form of Virgil's *The Georgics: A Poem of the Land*.

It is a long poem and although ostensibly about farming techniques and the cycles of the farming year, it is far more than simply a 'farming manual'.[225] On the surface it seems to present an idealized vision of the Roman landed estate, the villa set among gardens and surrounded by productive agricultural land, but the great subtlety of Virgil's work is that instead of simply presenting a fixed image of the farming year and farming techniques, it provides an image of a world that is also constantly in flux. The poem's language and themes reflect the uncertainties and ever-changing nature of this life, the successes and the disasters, the need for adaptation and experimentation required to survive and succeed.

For the duke's era the importance of *The Georgics* lay in pointing out the essential fragility of this way of life and the need to continually experiment, change, adapt and develop; in addition, through repeated references in the poem to art, literature, national mythology, astrology and history, Virgil was embedding the world of agriculture, arboriculture and horticulture in the wider context of culture and civilization in order to help anchor this way of life in the face of all these existential threats. It was a literary vision of a world that people like the duke sought to emulate. Thus, it was a complex literary image of agriculture as a key part of a country's wider culture, which to some degree served to sanction the way of life of the aristocratic landowners by linking it to the wider patterns of classical history, and at the same time giving it a sense of a timeless higher purpose.

So it was with a sense of himself as an inheritor of this literary world view that the duke set about the task of completing his brother's works, and there was a lot to be done. There were questions about new senior staff and the continuity of bookkeeping for the wider estates, decisions to be made in the Abbey, and the projected Temple of Liberty in Holland's conservatory to be completed. Outside in the gardens, the ground around the new south front needed to be landscaped, the pleasure grounds, parkland and plantations were also incomplete, as were the entrances to the park and associated roadways and bridges. At Park Farm, the agricultural experiments, creation of water meadows, land draining, stock rearing programmes and annual agricultural show – the 'Sheep Shearings' – required to be seen through. In addition, in London the first phase of the development of the Bloomsbury estate, begun in 1800, was still underway and there were decisions to be made about the next phase; beyond all this, the new duke had to engage afresh with the Bedford political interest and decide whether he was going to continue his brother's strategies for expansion or not.

In the first case, estate management, he was keen to follow his brother's advice, and appointed William Adam, the 5th Duke's personal solicitor, whom we have already met as political manager of the Whig party, as chief agent, as confirmed by the following letter from the solicitors Gotobed and Brown to the agent for the Dorset estate at Swyre: 'The Duke of Bedford has appointed W. Adam Esq. of Lincoln Inn to superintend his Estates in the Country … He is a gentleman of great character and respectability.'[226]

John Gotobed and Thomas Pierce Brown, who had been the solicitors for the Bedford estate during the 5th Duke's time and for the trustees before that, were the key point of continuity for the new duke, knowing as they did so much about the estate and the people, and they seem to have organized the transition period, keeping the various agents, stewards and leading tenants up to date with developments. The letter above indicates that Gotobed established Adam's authority and smoothed his way into the organization, while Adam in turn, as the 5th Duke's personal solicitor, knew many more of the personal details.

With these arrangements underway, the duke was able to turn to completing work on the Abbey. The neoclassical style had suited the 5th Duke's utilitarian, unsentimental and direct approach to life, and when working with Henry Holland on Woburn Abbey, he had attempted to rationalize the old building, providing some overall balance (since total symmetry was not possible) to the outlines of the historic structures of the north and west wings. By creating new south and east wings, he completed the transfer of private family apartments from the north to the sunny south side of the building that had been started by his grandfather.

The 6th Duke, however, had a far more comfortable relationship with the past and tradition than his brother. The clean lines of the neoclassical had a decorative appeal for him, but beyond the utilitarian, the romance of historical architecture and of the context of his position better reflected his taste. His tastes, in contrast to his brother's, were more literary and artistic, reflecting, as one writer has put it, 'the full flood of picturesque enthusiasm and romantic historicism'.[227] Georgina also instinctively understood this vision, not perhaps through the lens of classical scholarship, but through her experience of life in the Highland world of Gordon Castle and from her teenage years spent among the communities of the Gordon estates, where, as described by Elizabeth Grant, one could still 'catch the remains of all the noble feelings of the Highlander … the romance of that beautiful country' and where 'the recollection of past events and the ages of connection between Chieftain and vassals, or rather clansmen, excited every warm and every noble feeling.'[228] These elements of Georgina's identity were further strengthened by her mother's determined promotion of traditional Scottish culture, creating a Romantic historical vision similar in many ways to the duke's. Instinctively then, albeit for different reasons, both were drawn to the picturesque and to the world of wonder opened up by the Romantic sensibilities which followed. In terms of the Abbey itself, in Georgina the duke had also found someone who shared his taste for the aesthetic of the Regency style, one that appreciated classicism but with a more theatrical air, providing a sense of decorative formality realized in harmonious proportions, quiet colours, ornamentation and specifically designed furniture and fittings.[229]

Although the bulk of the new construction work was completed by 1803, it is not at all clear just how much of the interior decoration of the Abbey was finished by the time the newlyweds arrived. It seems that some of the staterooms, such as the Dining Room and the South Drawing Room (now the Canaletto Room), had been decorated and furnished, but work was needed to provide apartments for the new couple and the children to come. Matthew Hirst says that 'the 6th Duke and his new Duchess set about a programme of wholesale redecoration that lasted well into the 1830s … Beginning in their private apartments, which had only been constructed in the last ten years, they gradually worked their way around the whole building – no room was left untouched.' Indeed, the earliest entry in the Abbey accounts for this period tells us this work began in the Duchess's room: 'painting, gilding and fixing mouldings in Her Grace's Room'.[230] The couple each had a suite of three rooms: a sitting room/study, a dressing room and a bedroom on the principal floor on the east end of the south corridor (all now demolished along with the adjoining east wing), which had direct access out on to the gardens on the south side of the building. In the staterooms, the major work begun at this time was a refurbishment of the Long Gallery in the west wing.

Immediately upon his appointment, William Adam began his work as the new chief agent, and with accounting business taken care of, Adam set off in July on a tour to visit the different estates. He started in Bedfordshire, visiting Ampthill, Houghton Regis and Dunstable, before travelling to Cambridgeshire and Northamptonshire to visit Thornhaugh and Thorny in early August, and finally left Woburn in late August to visit Dorset and Devon.[231]

After visiting Berwick Manor in Dorset, the original home of Russell family, Adam moved on to Tavistock, where he met with the agent for the Devon estates, Edward Bray, visited the church, mines, canal, forge and Market House, which he noted is 'much too small' and should be extended. He then assessed the town's housing stock, which he considered generally to be 'of poor construction', and suggested possible remedies before mentioning what he saw as another problem relating to the market, 'than which nothing can be more inconvenient … The Cattle are brought into the streets and occupy these so completely that it is both Dangerous and Difficult to pass … and houses are obliged to shut their outward shutters to save their windows during the whole day. A convenient field within the limits of the Borough might surely be found.'

Clearly, he felt that at the moment Tavistock, the economic and cultural centre of the Devon estates, reflected badly on the estate as a whole, and the duke himself, from previous visits connected to elections, may well have agreed with Adam; it was not long before upgrading the housing and infrastructure of the town became a priority. Following this, after visiting Morwellham Quay, the highest navigable point on the Tamar and supply point for Tavistock, Adam travelled further afield, visiting the manor of Milton Abbot, which he described as 'the most fertile and productive ground I have ever seen', adding that, while the rich pastureland is 'all or chiefly let … the part of Milton Abbot Estate which lies next to the Tamar is beautiful, some very handsome Woods with Timber trees as well as copse.' This observation was to have some significance seven years later.

Once back in Tavistock, Adam mentioned plans for 'the Tunnel and Canal' to be built across the Duke of Bedford's land to connect Tavistock with Morwellham Quay, which will, he concluded, be 'a very great encouragement to improvements' – and how right he was. The mineral rights connected to the Peter Tavy estate and the opening of the Tavistock canal in 1817 were soon to have a significant impact on the fortunes of the estate as new silver, lead and copper mines and slate quarries were opened and the produce transported by the canal to boats at Morewellham Quay.[232]

After further discussion of housing, both in Tavistock and out on the various farms, where he had found houses 'all of mud and thatch and their condition … most deplorable', Adam's final visit was to Launceston, where he met with both Bray and Mr Hawk, the agent for the Launceston area. On 7 September he 'went from Launceston to Camelford, in the Chaise with Bray, Hawk, and with my nephew'. Although most of this trip was to do with the Devon estate, its condition and management, this visit had a more complex purpose since the constituency of Camelford had lain at the heart of the 5th Duke's drive to increase the scope of his political interests in the west. As early as 1796, eager to revive the long dormant Bedford interest, the 5th Duke sought to challenge the control over the two seats returned for the constituency by the Phillips family, supporters of the government. This challenge, which involved making deals with the managers of the rival interest – Carpenter, an attorney, and Jago, the town clerk – to support his candidates, in addition to paying the mayor £300, the aldermen £200 and the freemen £100, had only secured one of the seats, for family friend Robert Adair, but the duke had been ready to try again for both in 1802. His death left the situation up in the air, and it fell to Adam on this trip to try to complete the takeover. After visiting Camelford that August, Adam reported his doubts for success to Gotobed, and looked for guidance as to whom he should appoint and, indeed, whom he should trust, and continued: 'I feel [this] business very weighty and delicate. The situation of it very critical and my un-acquaintance with the people will be a great disadvantage to me.' Gotobed replied: 'The Business at Camelford is very delicate' and gave Adam the names of those to be appointed Freemen that Adair left with him. He advised Adam to talk to the agent Jago about what he knew of Adair's opinions, but warned him, 'Jago is not to be trusted with every secret relating to the last Election. He is ignorant of it and must continue so, and of other matters.'[233]

When the issue was presented to the 6th Duke in November, however, he took a very different view from his brother's, and his letter to Adam concerning

Camelford is very revealing about himself as well as the way landed interests could manipulate political power through their pocket boroughs:

> At all events I am not ambitious of any increase of parliamentary interest; to one who has nothing to expect from any minister, it is of little consequence, except to oblige a friend who may wish to be in Parliament, and as long as the representation continues as it is, Tavistock and whatever influence arising from property I may possess in other places, will, I trust, always enable me to return those of my own family who may be desirous of it; I have little taste for the election contests, more especially those of the nature of which a contest in a borough like Camelford must ever be.[234]

Unlike his brother, who one rather suspects thoroughly enjoyed the rough and tumble of political contests, the duke seems to have wanted nothing to do with the underhand secrecy, the 'other matters' of bribery and scheming, not to mention the cost and dealing with the kind of people involved. Nevertheless, although he did not seek to increase the number of seats he controlled in Camelford, the duke maintained his interest and used the one seat in 1810 to return Henry Brougham, the rising star of the Whig party. Camelford marked the end of the duke's participation in his brother's political plans, although he sought to maintain 'whatever influence arising from property I may possess in other places' and remained committed to the Whig cause.

Following Adam's visits to the estates, a series of meetings and reports, decisions made about the political situation, and new systems of accounts and household books for the estates in place, the duke was able to turn his attention to Woburn's park, farms, plantations and gardens. In March 1802, in the aftermath of his brother's death, the duke had written to the agriculturalist Arthur Young 'on a subject, deeply interesting to me, because it occupied the last thoughts of my much lamented brother … and on his death bed with an earnestness expressive of his character … he strongly urged me to follow up those plans of national improvement [in agriculture] which he had begun … He referred me to Mr

Cartwright and to you for explanation and details … I trust it will not be long before I may have the satisfaction of seeing you at Woburn, desirous as I am in every point of view to fulfil the best wishes of my departed brother.'[235]

As the duke and duchess drove into the park on their way to the Abbey in 1803, one thing they cannot have missed will have been Park Farm, the new focal point of the 5th Duke's plans. Built between 1795 and 1802 by Robert Salmon, who had come to Woburn as Holland's clerk of works, Park Farm was not simply a model farm in itself, with newly designed buildings reflecting the latest ideas of animal husbandry, it also formed with Speedwell, another farm built by Salmon at this time just outside the park, the centrepiece for a collection of yards, workshops and laboratories where new machinery was invented and built and experimental agricultural chemistry was carried out by some of the leading figures in their fields. Altogether, the farm complexes reflected the interest at this time in harnessing the emerging sciences of chemistry, horticulture and botany in the cause of improving the quality and output of the nation's agriculture.

In charge of the park and farms, and working alongside Robert Salmon, John Farey was tasked with putting in place new management structures, running the day-to-day business of the park and farms, and engaging the tenant farmers with the 5th Duke's new ideas. As the duke's interest in the new areas of scientific investigation grew, Salmon and Farey were joined by a succession of individuals, largely self-taught, who were at the forefront of establishing new disciplines in agricultural and forestry science. In 1790, for example, the 5th Duke had hired William Pontey, a Huddersfield nurseryman and landscape gardener, to 'direct a series of experiments … on [the Duke's] extensive fir plantations', and these experiments enabled Pontey to develop a system he called 'close pruning' which he subsequently outlined in his influential book *The Profitable Planter*.[236]

Eight years later, another series of experiments were begun at Park Farm by a friend and neighbour, George Biggin of Cosgrove Priory. Biggin and the 5th Duke, who had known each other at Trinity College, came to share an interest in the chemistry of tanning, and in 1799 and 1800 Biggin carried out a series of experiments 'to determine the quantity of tanning principle and gallic acid contained in the bark of various trees', the results of which were published later that year. Biggin was involved in something altogether more exciting and groundbreaking that had also caught the duke's attention. In November 1783 the Montgolfier brothers had caused a sensation by conducting the first manned hot-air balloon flight, to be followed a month later by Dr Alexandre Charles's ascent over Paris in the first hydrogen balloon. It was just over a year later that the excitement reached England when, in September 1784, the dashing Vincent Lunardi flew in a balloon from Moorfields in London to Ware in Hertfordshire.

Eager to capitalize on his success, Lunardi organized a second flight for June the following year, this time accompanied by George Biggin and the well-known actress Mrs Letitia Sage. Sure enough, the publicity generated a huge crowd to the launch site at Hyde Park, but unfortunately they had underestimated Mrs Sage's weight, and it was not until Lunardi himself jumped out that the balloon took off. Left to themselves, Biggin and Mrs Sage sailed off, 'the two of them lunching peacefully off sparkling Italian wine and cold chicken', before landing near Harrow on the Hill to great acclaim and instant celebrity. Among those who were both engaged and entertained by this venture was Biggin's friend the Duke of Bedford, who was clearly following the development of ballooning closely, and was also eager to participate: 'The Duke of Bedford has declared, that he will be at the expense of a balloon, for any philosopher that will rise in it; and if he goes as high as Monsieur Charles, will reward him handsomely besides.'[237]

Whether any philosophers attempted to take up this offer is unknown, but after 1801 two other figures of some importance arrived at Park Farm, both hired for their specialist knowledge. William 'Strata' Smith, the geologist and canal engineer, later to win lasting fame for the first geological map, 'A Delineation of the Strata of England and Wales' (1815), was initially recommended to the duke by Thomas William Coke of Holkham. After conducting a geological survey, he then undertook the drainage of the 'infamous Prisley Bog on the Woburn estate. This he managed with such speed and ingenuity – and, moreover, published a brief monograph in 1806 on how he had done it – that the Society of Arts awarded him a medal.' In addition, Edmund Cartwright, the inventor of the spinning jenny, 'received an offer from Francis, Duke of Bedford, to undertake direction of an experimental farm he was about to establish', and went on to conduct 'some curious experiments on the application and fertilizing effects of different substances used as manure, the results of which he had double-checked with Sir Humphry Davy'.[238] Cartwright brought considerable mechanical expertise and experience in patent applications, useful to the Park Farm workshops, and expanded the range of experiments in everything from manure, soil chemistry, innovative crop rotations, new seeds types and stock breeding programmes to new machinery. He went on to work as tutor to Lord John in 1803, before leaving Woburn in 1807.

With the arrival of the new duke, Pontey, Farey and Smith all left, leaving him able to temporarily streamline staffing at Park Farm under Salmon's leadership, and to allow Cartwright to complete his studies on manures. In June 1803, the duke authorized the continuation of the Woburn 'Sheep Shearings' after a hiatus following the 5th Duke's death, and held a typically ambitious three-day event that included the judging and sale of sheep and cattle, demonstrations of new farm machinery, a ploughing contest, an exhibition of turnip sowing and a shearing competition; each day lunch and dinner were served at the Abbey. The events were designed to provide an opportunity for landowners, farmers, stock breeders, herdsmen and dealers from all over the country to come together, socialize, exchange ideas and see the latest techniques and machinery in action. First held at Woburn *c.*1798, it had steadily grown in popularity until it attracted huge crowds, and some two hundred people or more would sit down to meals in the Abbey. On 20 June the next year, the *Morning Chronicle*, reported:

Woburn Sheep Shearing,

Monday 18th June, 1804: This morning at an early hour the company began to assemble at the Park Farm … about eleven o'clock his Grace of Bedford, and several Noblemen and Gentlemen with him at the Abbey being arrived, the exhibition of the new Leicester rams began … In the course of the forenoon, a party repaired to the Duke's mill, where a steam engine, perhaps the first ever applied to the purposes of agriculture, has lately been erected by Mr Cartwright.

It was also this year that the artist George Garrard produced his painting of the Sheep Shearing, which hangs to this day in the Abbey, showing the proposed monument to the 5th Duke and the gathering filling the yard at Park Farm, while the better known engraving, with its key of some eighty-seven numbered portraits but without the monument, followed in 1810. The latter was essentially a record of those who had attended over the years up to that time rather than an image of the gathering in that particular year. Missing from the image, however, is the duchess, and the *Morning Chronicle* explains why: 'The Duchess of Bedford left Woburn to spend the time of the Sheepshearing with her noble sister, the Duchess of Manchester, at Kimbolton Castle.'[239] It is quite possible, therefore, that she did not attend any of the Sheep Shearings, keen perhaps to avoid the long days traipsing round the farmyards and fields, visiting cattle, sheep and pig pens, watching seed drills and ploughs pass up and down the fields, and the long noisy meals listening to earnest discussions about water meadows and draining bogs or how long to leave your manure.

As work got underway on their living accommodation at the Abbey, the duke and duchess turned their attention to the surrounding grounds which, like the London entrance, were still to some extent a building site. Perhaps the most significant aspect of the 5th Duke's and Holland's work on the Abbey, in terms of its relationship to the area around it, was the fact that they had radically altered the ground level on two sides of the building. Both the south and east sides of the Abbey had faced rising ground, and given this situation it was perhaps inevitable that when Holland was designing his grand new south and east wings, he chose to lift his principal rooms up out of the basement, aligning them on the same level as the old staterooms, opening up the views, and providing direct access to them by filling in the ground in front. This major alteration in turn provided the opportunity to run a new approach road into a wide entrance court in front of the porte cochère and reception rooms of the east wing above the old stables, and

Henry Holland's additions to the Abbey and grounds, 1790s. The shaded portions of the Abbey, the covered walkway and the buildings to the east indicate those added by the 5th Duke of Bedford and Henry Holland.

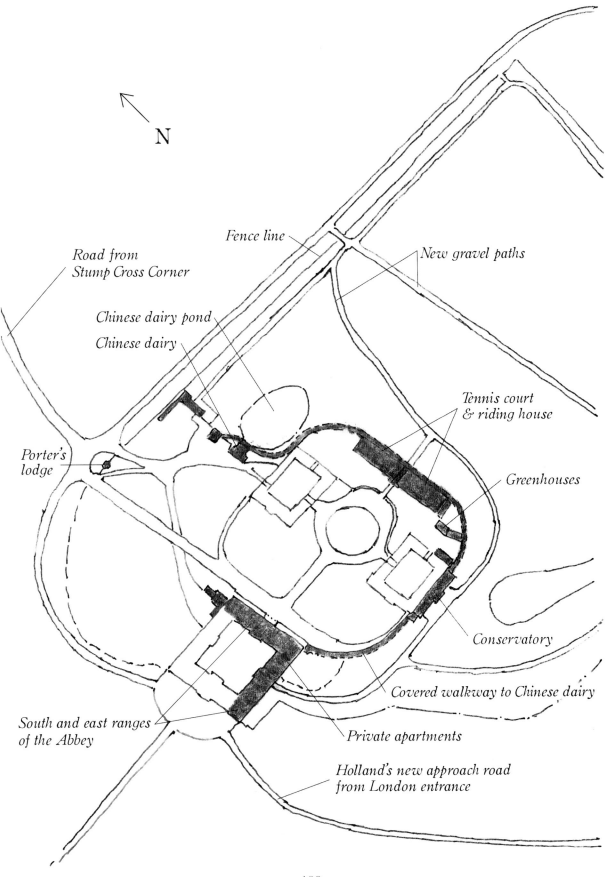

N

Road from
Stump Cross Corner

Chinese dairy pond

Chinese dairy

Fence line

New gravel paths

Porter's
lodge

Tennis court
& riding house

Greenhouses

Conservatory

South and east ranges
of the Abbey

Private apartments

Covered walkway to Chinese dairy

Holland's new approach road
from London entrance

to create new gardens running out to the park ha-ha in front of the south wing rooms and apartments, a process which had only just begun when the new duke and duchess arrived. Also recently installed were the two approach roads through the park to the Abbey, one from Holland's new London entrance and one from the Woburn entrance. Both of these were in place, but both needed new entrance lodges. The London entrance lodge was under construction, but the Woburn entrance still needed a design.[240]

Working with the 5th Duke, Holland had also added a number of buildings to the north and south court complex, and these new buildings included the conservatory attached to the south side of the south court, a stand-alone building just to the east of the two courts which housed an indoor riding house and tennis court, and the ornate Chinese dairy beside the existing pond to the north of the north court. All the new buildings were then linked up by a new covered walkway which ran from the private apartments in the south wing all the way round to the Chinese dairy. Brightly painted and festooned with scented climbing plants, this elegant and decorative feature linked Holland's work together and allowed the family to enjoy the gardens whatever the weather.

As the duke and duchess settled into their new apartments, they began to think about designs for new gardens south of the Abbey and conservatory, and for the rather dated and neglected pleasure grounds. They were not altogether happy with some of what Holland had already done, and keen to engage fresh eyes, they soon determined to call upon Humphry Repton, the designer the duke had used at Oakley a few years before, to produce some new ideas.

For Repton the duke's invitation in 1804 represented a major opportunity, and he went on to create one of the largest and most beautifully designed of his 'Red Books' of proposals. He paid his first visit to Woburn in September 1804 and reported the duke's instructions as follows: 'much had been done here, but much remains to be done, and some things I think to <u>undo</u>. I am not partial to destroying works recently executed, but sometimes cases will occur … Freely give me your opinion as to what alterations or improvements suggest themselves to your judgment, leaving the executing of them to my own discretion or leisure.'[241]

Since we know from Repton's Red Book that 'the Duchess of Bedford exercised a strong influence on the grounds' and the duke had strong opinions of his own, it appears that when it arrived in January 1805, the Red Book was a combination of ideas suggested to him or modified by the duke and duchess, and Repton's development of these ideas with additions, details and ideas of his own.

One suspects that, for a man who often questioned his own abilities, the duke was comfortable dealing with Repton, who never knowingly failed to elaborately praise a client's taste and artistic eye, and interestingly enough, as we will see, a number of the projects that Repton undertook at Woburn during this period (1805–c.1810) did not form part of the Red Book, but would seem to have originated in subsequent discussions between the two. Work started in June 1805 on the initial projects approved by the duke, which included rerouting of the London approach road, a new bridge at the Bason Pond, alterations to the ground levels created by Holland outside his new south wing rooms, adding complexity and interest to the shape of the Bason Pond, a new ornamental plantation of thorn trees out in the park, and a far-reaching redesign of the neglected pleasure grounds, an area which had remained largely unchanged since the alterations made when Flitcroft built the north and south courts for the 4th Duke in 1757.[242]

As these works began, Georgina was also becoming involved with family life. Her eldest stepson, Francis, who out of the three probably remembered his own mother best, was already about to leave Westminster to attend Trinity College, Cambridge. This meant that Georgina never developed the same close relationship with him that she did with the younger two, Lord William, an affectionate but needy and insecure boy, and Lord John, who, with her help, overcame his physical frailties and thrived in Georgina's informal and playful world.[243] In addition, by September 1803 the duchess was also pregnant, and on 11 May 1804 Lord Wriothesley Russell was born, the first of their ten children over the next twenty-two years.[244]

As life got underway at Woburn, one other important area of activity initiated by his brother came to occupy the duke's attention: the development of those parts of Bloomsbury that had been occupied by Bedford House and its extensive contiguous grounds to the north along Southampton Terrace (now Southampton Row), and the area around Bloomsbury Square to the south. The future of Bedford House had become an issue as development of the New Road (Euston Road) to the north and the Foundling Hospital estate to the east began to threaten the views in the late 1780s, but a decision on this could not be made until the 5th Duke came of age, and it was not until the mid-1790s that he turned his attention to Bedford House and the Bloomsbury land. Although in 1795 he initially considered laying out new gardens overlooking the 'Long Fields' which ran up towards the Euston Road, a decision on the future of the house was not long in coming; in 1799, bowing to the inevitable, the duke made an agreement for the demolition of the family's last grand home in London, and took a house for himself on Arlington Street. Although, as Donald Olsen tells us, 'the reason for the change of plan is not clear … the potential value [of the Long Fields] as building land of so large an area was obviously too great for the Duke to ignore.'[245]

By May 1800, with the house demolished and the unwanted materials and contents put up for sale, the duke commissioned a plan for the redevelopment of the land. In turn, both the 5th and 6th Dukes were keen to replicate the example of the imposing style and spacious garden of the Bedford Square and Gower Street development, which had been overseen by Gertrude and the trustees, over the whole estate. For both aesthetic and economic reasons, they concentrated on creating residential squares of unified facades with integrated mews and stables as the centrepieces for a development which could capitalize on the economic opportunities provided by making them attractive to upper class and professional families.[246]

The 'Plan of Intended Improvements on the Estate of his Grace the Duke of Bedford' (1800) sets out an ambitious agenda to develop the entire area from Great Russell Street north to the Duke of Grafton's proposed 'Nursery' gardens on the south side of the Euston Road, bounded on the east by Southampton Terrace and on the west by Gower Street, and, while the plan itself was drawn up by James Gubbins, the duke's surveyor, the key figure in seeing it carried out was the architect and builder James Burton. The overall plan, a regular grid layout of streets

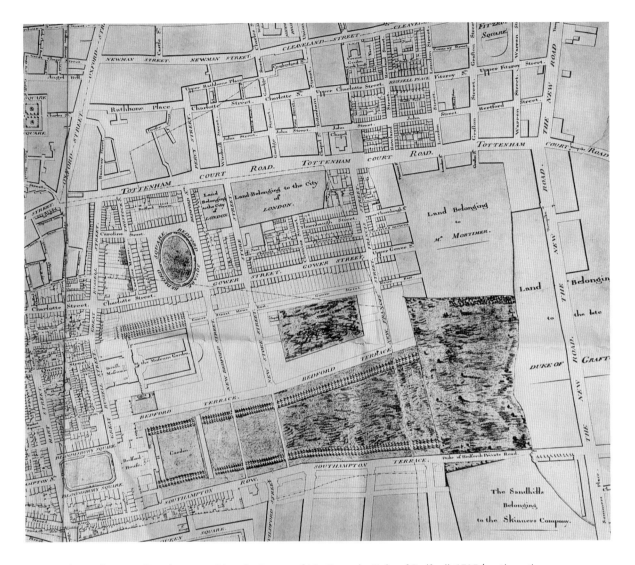

'Part of a Map of London comprising the Estates of His Grace the Duke of Bedford', 1795 (north on the right), detail showing Bloomsbury Square and Bedford House (bottom left) and the 'Long Fields' beyond the garden before development. East of Bedford House, the British Museum and its gardens have already been built and new streets have been laid out west of Southampton Row, as has the 'New Road' (Euston Road) to the north.

enclosing straight-sided blocks of housing, was broken only to include two garden squares, Russell Square and Tavistock Square, and clearly reflects the 5th Duke's utilitarian taste.[247]

Work began on the new plans in the summer of 1800, and by 1805 James Burton had completed the north side of Bloomsbury Square, Bedford Place, the east side of Woburn Place, Woburn Place north, two sides of Tavistock Square, and Russell Square, where the houses had also been complemented by the 'extensive enclosure in the centre … a miniature landscaped garden, combining beauty and variety'.[248] James Gubbins had included details of the garden designs for both Russell Square and Tavistock Square on his plan, but while those in Tavistock Square were not completed until 1825, the Russell Square garden was worked on at the same time as the buildings. Clearly, establishing Russell Square as the centrepiece of the whole development had become the priority, and was taken up immediately by the new duke, its importance being reflected in the trouble taken with the design of the gardens.

From the start, the 5th Duke had clearly wanted to make the square special, and according to Lady Holland, he wanted to erect a statue of his ancestor Lord William Russell, executed in 1683 for his part in the Rye House Plot, and whose marriage to Rachel Wriothesley, daughter of the Earl of Southampton, had brought Bloomsbury into the Russell family. Lady Holland writes that the Duke of Bedford 'has some idea of erecting a statue of Lord Russell', but adds that 'Sergeant Lens[?] surprised me by saying that should this statue be erected, the populace would in all probability pull it down. If so, public opinion has undergone a strange revolution, he was a martyr whom patriots worshipped.'[249]

Whether or not there was really a danger of the statue being pulled down, it would seem that the plan was not pursued at this time, since Gubbins shows a relatively simple design, two concentric circles of paths separated by a ring of planting enclosing a central lawn and flower bed, but with no indication as to

Bloomsbury I: 1800–20, the first phase of proposed development following the demolition of Bedford House (north at the top).

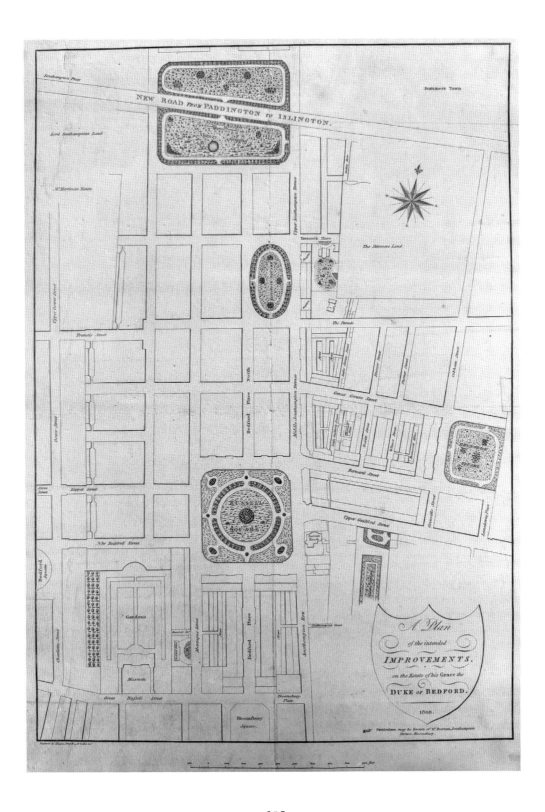

where a statue might stand. By 1801, as work on the square moved on, the garden area seems to have been left up to James Burton, who had agreed to 'enclose and plant Russell Square … either according to his own plan or according to the more elaborate plan of James Gubbins'.[250] Like much of the Long Fields area, the ground was naturally uneven, and extensive digging for brick clay had exacerbated the problem by leaving the area covered with waterlogged pits. While this situation only really became an issue as development reached the northern part of the estate, the area enclosed by Russell Square was large enough to need levelling out, a job which Burton undertook. Beyond this work, it remains unclear whether or not Burton took the landscaping of Russell Square much further, or what plans might have been in place by the time the 5th Duke died in 1802; the priority may well have been to complete the buildings.

The 6th Duke, having a keen interest in landscape design and working with the committee of residents, determined to complete the gardens, and sometime in late 1805 or early 1806 called on Humphry Repton, who was still busy at Woburn, to provide a plan. In this case Repton did not provide a Red Book, but a plan survives in the Woburn archives which would seem to be by Repton, and he wrote at length about the design in his *Enquiry into the Changes in Taste in Landscape Gardening* (1806): 'The ground of this area had all been brought to one level plain at too great an expense to admit of its being altered.' He goes on to approve of placing 'the fine Statue of the late Duke of Bedford, now preparing by the ingenious Mr. Westmacott, on one side of the square facing Bloomsbury, and forming an appropriate perspective, as seen through the vista of the streets crossing two squares'.[251]

Clearly, by this time, the duke had determined that a statue would be appropriate as an important element of the square, but instead of seeking to memorialize their ancestor, Lord William Russell, he settled on his brother, and perhaps in an attempt to avoid any possibility of the populace 'pull[ing] it down', he is presented holding a sheaf in one hand, the other resting on a plough, celebrating a champion not of liberty but of agricultural improvement – a much safer option. The plans for this statue had been displayed at the Sheep Shearing in June 1804, and although the statue was not installed until 1809, Repton suggested a planting of shrubs and trees to separate it from the gardens. He then proposed a 'compact hedge' to screen the gardens from the streets outside, a broad gravel walk running round the perimeter inside the hedge, and a 'margin of grass' surrounding the central area that was outlined by 'a walk under two rows of lime trees, regularly planted at equal distances, not in a perfect circle', but finishing 'towards the statue in two straight lines directed to the angle of the [statue]', creating a decorative knot shape, while a final touch was to 'provide some seats for shade or shelter'. Repton ended his description of the design hoping that the resulting garden will be seen not as a mere caprice, but as a design founded 'on a due consideration of utility as well as beauty'. No doubt the 5th Duke would have approved, and in 1805 James Malcolm wrote of these developments: 'Squares, and spacious streets of the first respectability, are rising in every direction … which [have] entirely obliterated every vestige, except two poplar trees, of the house and gardens of the Duke of Bedford, and a great part of the verdant fields between them and the New Road.'[252]

Now, with the statue of the 5th Duke installed and the completion of Russell Square, the key statement of the whole development had been made, but it was, in fact, to be a considerable time before the rest of 'the squares and spacious streets' were completed, as a post-war recession, difficulties with the site, changing tastes, new fashionable suburbs elsewhere and the increase in commercial traffic in the area slowed development.

There must have been moments during these early years of their marriage when this legacy of projects started by the 5th Duke must have seemed almost overwhelming for both the new duke and duchess. With so many people and projects urgently needing his attention, and decisions to be made over issues he would not necessarily have chosen to involve himself in, the duke must have felt more than ever the relentless pressure 'from Business which comes upon me', as he had written immediately following his brother's death. Similarly, for Georgina this must have been a challenging time as she adjusted to her new role as wife, duchess, stepmother and now mother of her own children. Something of the couple's vulnerability at this time is caught in contemporary portraits. At this critical point in John Russell's life, we can catch a glimpse of him in 1806, when he was forty years old, in a small, informal portrait by George Garrard that shows him sitting in the park at Woburn with the Abbey in the distance, and it is a noticeably different image from that caught by Beechey twenty years earlier at the start of his first marriage. In Beechey's image we see a confident young man looking directly at us, meeting our eye, in notable contrast to the later image, in which he is perched rather uncomfortably on a bench and looking away to the side as if he would rather be reading the book in his hand, reflecting perhaps his discomfort in his new role (Colour Plate 4 and page 10).

Such differences can also be seen in portraits of Georgina: Hoppner's of the twenty-one-year-old before her marriage, a full-length portrait set among the trees and looking confidently straight at us (Colour Plate 9), and the first image we have of her as duchess. In this second picture we see a far more demure, vulnerable head and shoulders almost engulfed by the trappings of her new status that include her coronet, a lion and unicorn, the Bedford family armorial shield and motto. Amidst all this, the young duchess is looking pointedly to one side, no longer at us, perhaps actively avoiding our gaze, weighed down by people's expectations (page 11). Fortunately, however, we also have a fascinating eye-witness account of both John and Georgina at this time, as they attempted to balance the demands of being a duke and duchess, and those of being a couple who knew little of each other starting married life.

In August 1804 the Bedfords joined house parties at Cirencester Park, home of Lord and Lady Bathurst, and the duke's old family friends, the Baths, at Longleat, and a fellow guest at both houses that summer was Mrs Elizabeth Hervey.[253] Hervey was fifty-six by the time she met Georgina, and was a woman whose husband, Colonel Thomas Hervey, had died some twenty-five years before. Since that time, Mrs Hervey (as she was always known) had written a succession of six novels, largely about women's lives, but it was not until 1817 that her sixth and final novel, *Amabel, or Memoirs of a Woman of Fashion*, was published under her own name. Reading her journal account of August 1804, we meet a thoughtful, observant and interested woman. She had clearly heard all the gossip about Georgina but, unlike so many others, she actually took the time to make up her own mind about the young duchess. Georgina, meanwhile, took immediately to the older woman, instinctively intrigued perhaps by meeting someone whose books she knew of or had read, and was determined to make her a friend.

When they first met at Cirencester Park in mid-August, while complimenting Georgina's 'beautiful figure, fine eyes and teeth', Elizabeth did not consider her a 'fine woman', but rather 'affable, free and apparently good humoured', noting also that she was 'accused of being contrary' and lacking a 'little … dignity in her manner'. Meeting up again later that month at Longleat, however, Hervey notes how 'uncommonly civil and even kind' Georgina is towards her, and observes that, while 'it is supposed the Russell boys hate her', from what she saw, Georgina's 'behaviour to them is apparently amiable and proper'. A few days later she adds, 'I protest I think she behaves exceedingly well to all the boys.' During the stay at Longleat, on a particularly 'glorious day' and while 'the ladies amused themselves on the banks of the lake', Hervey 'meditated in the cottage porch', and we have a sense of her watching the interactions of the other guests amusing themselves, quietly making up her own mind about Georgina. A few days later, during an evening of cards, she watched Georgina 'lose her money and her temper at once', appearing 'very unamiable & teasing at the D:', and concludes that while she 'has many good points', her 'spirits are too great & lead her into actions inconsistent with dignity, to divert herself she is apt to amuse herself at the expense of others': shrewd comments that others were to repeat over the years.

Whatever she made of the duchess, Georgina appears to have been drawn to befriend Elizabeth, who goes on: 'Never was there anything like the Dss of B's civilities to me! She has pressed me in the warmest manner to visit her at Woburn,' adding that before the end of the visit, 'the Dss on taking leave of me last night again warmly pressed me to come to Woburn, adding that the D: wished it too, & I promised to go.'

The next time they met was in October when the visit to Woburn went ahead. On her arrival for a five-day visit, she was shown to her apartment, where Georgina greeted her 'heartily shaking my hand' and 'expressing much pleasure at seeing me' before 'leaving me to dress'. During her subsequent descriptions of her stay, we get a clear impression of the enormous challenges that faced the Bedfords as they struggled not only to create a home for themselves in the enormous, largely neglected Abbey, where the 'long passages in this house are noble but seem endless', but also to form a lasting, mutually accommodating relationship with each other. Although, of course, the suite of staterooms built by the 5th Duke and Holland were new, Hervey tells us there were at least 130 other rooms, most of them, she discovered, still decorated 'in the old fashioned style' with 'furniture of very ancient date', and many others, although very grand, were decorated 'in the style of 30 or 40 years ago'.

On her first evening, heading for dinner, she became 'quite bewildered seeing nothing but passages of an immeasurable length' and had no idea which door she should open, but 'Fortunately I at that instant met the groom of chambers … who conducted me … to a spacious library. Here I sat until the Duke appeared, who was in one of his silent moods, but the Dss. arriving she was chatty enough, and we proceeded without any other company to dinner, attended by a host of servants.' The next day only the duchess appeared and after breakfast took Hervey for a drive through the park 'in a chaise with four tiny ponies not much bigger than dogs … the Dss first drove herself', visiting the Evergreens, 'such a winter drive can I believe scarcely be paralleled', and on to Park Farm, which contained so many buildings 'it looked like a town.' Ignoring most of it, Georgina 'hastened to the poultry yards where there is a garden and a running stream' and the 'Dss says the poultry man is the best in the world.'

Hervey was delighted the following day when they were joined by Lord John and to hear that Lord William was expected. She reports that during the summer the family occupied only the south wing, their private apartments, the inner library, the library, the map room (for breakfast) and an eating room, but that in winter the suite of staterooms in the west wing were occupied, and that over the winter months, even when the family were away, '100 fires are made' every day. Although her visit included a drive over to Ampthill to meet the Ossorys, beyond the descriptions of the Abbey, her account of the duke and Georgina is very interesting. Invited to see the couple's respective private apartments, she is most taken with the fact that 'throughout the windows are French, down to the ground and open to the Duchess's flower garden.' Beyond this, much of the decoration is also French, the duke's rooms being 'less recherché and elegant'. Over breakfast, which they ate alone, Hervey describes having tête-à-têtes with the duchess and, sitting in her apartment on a wet day, records Georgina talking 'very confidentially and feelingly of the late Duke whose picture … is constantly on the sopha [*sic*] in her boudoir'.

She also recounts that, visiting Ampthill, she travelled 'wrapped in a famous green shawl given by young Beauharnais to the Dss before her marriage, when he was much in love with her, and she kindly brought this shawl from Woburn purposely for my use.' Clearly, the excitement and romance of these two early suitors, Francis, the 5th Duke, and Eugène de Beauharnais, Napoleon's stepson, still meant a great deal to Georgina, as she began her marriage to a man known for his 'silent moods'. When not silent, however, it seems the duke could be very entertaining, and one evening after Georgina had, as usual, retired to bed, 'the Duke and I had a long tête-à-tête during which he was very agreeable telling me several curious anecdotes'; on other evenings she notes that the duke would read to them while the ladies 'worked', particularly poetry, which he read 'remarkably well'. Although Hervey was probably not aware of it, Georgina's behaviour during her stay will have been to some extent conditioned by the fact that she had just become pregnant for the second time, and no doubt required rest, but in spite of this, the lasting impression of the couple is that they were to some degree still strangers. Hervey writes that 'The Dss spends much time in her apartment, and the Duke when in the house lives the whole morning in his'; they were still in the process of becoming both collectively a married couple and individually a duke and a duchess. In due course, on 24 April 1805, Georgina's second son, Lord Edward Russell, was born.

Over the spring and summer of 1805 activity in the park and gardens picked up as work began on Repton's designs, and moved sequentially from the south front to the Bason Pond, the pleasure grounds, the new London approach, the Thornery and all the associated plantings. By April, however, just as it seemed that life for the family at Woburn was settling down into some kind of routine, priorities suddenly changed when the duke, at the urging of Fox, accepted the post of Lord Lieutenant of Ireland, and the family left at short notice for Dublin.[254]

This appointment represented one of the most challenging episodes in the duke's life and also a significant turning point. Although he had withdrawn from an active political career after entering the Lords and from aggressive expansion of the Bedford political interest, he had remained engaged with the political scene, and his commitment to complete his brother's Temple of Liberty, a shrine to the legacy of their father-figure Charles James Fox, reflected his continuing involvement with the attempt to revive the Whig party's fortunes and thereby restart Fox's political career. On becoming duke he also took on the role of a patron of Fox's Whig party in the fading years of the Pitt government, and if he did not see himself actually participating in parliamentary matters again, he embraced his role as a figure around whom Whig politicians could now coalesce and Woburn's place alongside Holland House as a location where this could happen. Everything changed, however, when Pitt died in January 1806, his administration fell, and the king called on Lord Grenville to form an administration, the 'Ministry of all the Talents'. When Fox was appointed Foreign Secretary in the new ministry, he immediately asked the duke to take on the sensitive role of Lord Lieutenant of Ireland, and out of loyalty to Fox but against his own better judgement, the duke agreed. It proved to be a very testing time for the duke, and he was not unduly sorry when, within a year, the new government fell, a casualty of the intractable problem of Catholic emancipation. This was an issue the duke had focused on over that year, lobbying the government, meeting all sides to urge patience, and giving his word to people that progress would be made, but in the end he had been unable to deliver, and as the government fell, he left Ireland unthanked, deeply hurt and disillusioned. Once home he never took an active role in politics again.

It is clear from the duke's letters at this time that he took the post only out of loyalty to Fox:

My mind is entirely made up. If you wish it, and think I can be of use, I will go to Ireland – no other Consideration upon earth would tempt me to do it … I have a confident expectation that I can do some good there … I understand that I am to carry out a system of kindness, of conciliation, and of justice to the people of Ireland … that I am to hold out to Ireland a complete union, not just in name but in substance, with England. All I have to wish is a free, unreserved, and confidential communication with <u>you</u> … Bedford.[255]

Since the duke sometimes lacked confidence in his own judgements and was not close to many members of the new administration, even suspecting there were some who actively opposed his appointment, it is clear that it was only the guarantee of a 'free' and 'confidential' communication with Fox that persuaded him to take the post. Nevertheless, just how much he doubted his 'fitness' became clear in a letter he wrote to Lord Howick in September 1806, following the death of Fox, 'I came to this country [Ireland] at the earnest solicitation of Fox – the partiality of his friendship and that indulgence so natural to his nature gave me a fitness for the office I undertook, which I felt an unaffected conviction did not belong to me.'[256]

Governing Ireland at this time was not a straightforward business, since serious matters of governance and religious emancipation remained unresolved by the Act of Union, and in some cases were exacerbated by it. Passed in 1800, it had been an attempt to contain Catholic unrest and opposition, which as recently as 1798 had led to an armed uprising supported by a French invasion force. The defeat of the French immediately doomed the uprising, but the British suppression of the rebels and subsequent reprisals were still brutal, and this, in addition to the hated 1796 Insurrection Act, which had imposed the death penalty for acts deemed to promote rebellion and remained in place, renewed resentments which soon turned to anger when the promised measures of Catholic emancipation never materialized.

Effectively the Act had formed a new country – 'The United Kingdom of Great Britain and Ireland' – which seemed to promise to the Irish a union of equals, whereas in reality it removed all of Ireland's traditional legislative independence and left discrimination against Catholics and Presbyterians in place, even though it had been promised that this would be abolished. Once this became apparent, another uprising in Dublin in 1803 was once again suppressed by the military. The first Lord Lieutenant charged with imposing the union and taking control of the fractious situation had been Philip Yorke, Earl of Hardwicke, who was appointed, according to one historian, for his 'genial and easy-going disposition, [and] it was thought that he would eradicate, with the assistance of his wife, the ill-feeling caused by the union.' His effectiveness, however, was fatally compromised by the initial lack of clarity concerning the scope of his powers, which led to infighting within the new administration and hampered his efforts at diplomacy. Although Hardwicke favoured Catholic emancipation, he was caught unawares by the rising tensions and subsequent uprising in 1803, and this, plus the handling of the subsequent trials, led to charges of callousness and inefficiency. The government in London was not long in responding to these circumstances, and although it was arranged for Hardwicke to be replaced, his chosen replacement refused to serve, and he had to remain in position until the government changed and Fox persuaded the duke to take on the role in April 1806.

Yet, if her husband had struggled to make a mark in Ireland, his wife, Lady Elizabeth Hardwicke, clearly took the new role of Vicereine very seriously, and taking her lead from the social activities associated with the royal family, she set out to establish an equally visible and glamorous social world in Dublin. Charles O'Mahony notes, she 'certainly did her best, and cultivated every class of Dublin society … and for five years [Dublin Castle] remained at the centre of the social life of the city.' Thus, by the time the duke and Georgina arrived in 1806, the social season of the vice-regency in Dublin had been firmly established, and one of the early tasks facing the new arrivals was to continue and develop it. As we know, unlike Hardwicke, who 'dearly loved a good story and a good Dinner', such socializing did not come naturally to the duke; but it did not take long for Georgina to fill the role. While Lady Elizabeth is described as 'pointedly conservative', it became clear, from the very first ball following the duke's inauguration, that things would be different under the new, much younger, fashionable and vivacious

Vicereine; The *Dublin Evening Post* reported: 'The people of Dublin immediately responded to her warmth and her first drawing room was more numerously and splendidly attended than we have witnessed these many years.'[257]

Whatever the duke and duchess may have been expecting as they arrived in Dublin, they were immediately confronted with the reality, noted by Trethewey, of the role of 'public relations as politics at this time because, after the Act of Union, the Irish were very sensitive to any suggestion that they were inferior to the British. Part of the Viceroy's responsibility was to hide the loss of Dublin's political status by increasing the trappings of power.' This meant that 'as real power ebbed away from Dublin the pomp and pageantry increased.' Their first taste of this came a short while after landing as they were caught up in the elaborate theatrical performance concocted for the duke's inauguration.

The instructions sent to Hardwicke outlined meticulously the details of the costume pageant that had been created to lend pomp and circumstance to the role of Viceroy. After an elaborate procession from the boat to Dublin Castle along streets lined with the 'Regiments in Garrison' to hold back the crowds, 'His Grace upon quitting his Coach is to be … conducted to the Presence Chamber, where the Lord Lieutenant is to receive His Grace sitting covered under the Canopy as Chief Governor.'

After a 'short conference' Hardwicke and the duke 'process to the Council Chamber', 'all the Privy Councillors being seated and with their Hats on and the Duke standing uncovered on the right Hand of the Lord Lieutenant's Chair', while 'His Majesty's Letters Patent appointing him to be Lord Lieutenant of Ireland' are read, followed by the delivery of the Sword of State to the duke, the investing of 'his Grace with the Collar of the Order of St Patrick as Grand Master', and the 'retirement of Earl of Hardwicke'. At this moment, a fifteen-gun salute is fired as the duke proceeds back to the Presence Chamber 'during which time the State Trumpeters are to sound their Trumpets, the Ordnance upon Signals are to fire three rounds of twenty-one Guns, and to be answered by a Volley of the Foot in College Green'. Finally, at 4 o'clock a levee was held at the castle, followed by illuminations and a grand ball.[258]

We have no record of what the couple made of all this, but it is quite difficult to imagine the uneasy figure in his top hat seated on a bench in the park at Woburn of Garrard's picture forming the focal point of this spectacle, especially given his own doubts about his fitness for such a role. It was just four years since Lord John had become the duke, and now he found himself thrust into another role he had neither foreseen nor wanted. Watching on, Georgina must have wondered exactly what lay ahead.

Following the duke's inauguration, the family moved into Dublin Castle, their home during the Dublin 'season' between January and March, and into the viceregal lodge, their 'country retreat' in Phoenix Park. Since there was no fixed term for the Lord Lieutenancy, it was possible that the family could be in Ireland for an extended period, and so for the second time in three years, Georgina now set about creating a home for the family, their two boys and the coming baby.

When the king appointed the duke to Ireland, he also provided a set of 'Private Instructions' authorizing 'conversations with the leading members of the Roman Catholic Communion' to state that 'the sentiments of … the administration who supported the Catholic Question in the last session remain unchanged' and that, given this, the administration 'cannot but be anxious to seize any favourable opportunity for the completion of a measure which they consider as essential to such important ends'. Long a supporter of emancipation for the Catholics, with these specific orders the duke seems to have felt that he could really achieve something significant on this issue. The instructions then went on to insist that he must also 'seize any favourable opportunity of conciliating and securing the attachment of the Protestant part of the community', and to warn that all this would require 'a spirit of moderation' and everything should 'appear best directed to contribute to the consolidation of the Union'.[259]

The instructions seemed clear enough, but from the moment of his arrival, the duke faced the true complexity of the situation. The Catholics, who had initially supported the union and its promise of emancipation, had become increasingly disillusioned with the slow rate of progress, and were determined to keep the pressure on a new administration which seemed to be sympathetic to their cause.

At the same time, the Protestant Orangemen, fearing what might be coming, began to organize and consolidate their opposition to any alterations in the status quo. Equally, rural unrest, focused on the agrarian population's growing resentment of high levels of tithes due on their harvests, whether corn or potatoes, and the dues levied on every household by the Catholic priesthood, became a persistent problem as resentment festered under the surface in the meetings of secret societies. This erupted periodically in localized outbreaks of violence against property and persons, and when the duke arrived, it was the 'Thrashers' in Connaught who were causing particular outrage. Apart from the continuing disruption caused by the violence, he was also alarmed when, in response, the Orangemen, as the local sheriffs, called for the use of militia under the Insurrection Act, calls he repeatedly turned down, unwilling to allow the use of the army against the civilian population, let alone permit the execution of rioters.

Early signs were that, in the relative calm following his arrival, the duke felt he was up to the task ahead, and writing to Lord Holland in May, he appears to be almost enjoying himself: 'I am pleased with the manner in which we are going on here and am fully persuaded that the system we are pursuing will render Ireland a far far different country from what it has heretofore been, both as to its internal prosperity and its … connection with England … I feel in better spirits than I have done for a considerable length of time.'[260]

Yet the mood was short-lived as the duke soon faced a raft of complex issues: the continuing Thrasher violence against rents and tithes, the depressed state of farming, the Catholic question, the loss of support for the government and particularly, given French success on the Continent, the increasing danger of another invasion attempt from France and his ongoing concerns about the lack of available troops in Ireland should that happen. In addition, further tension was added by the rising hostility of the Orangemen to the government's conciliatory attitude to the Catholics and, more generally, by the underlying fears of loyalists about the existential fragility of the foundations of the occupation of Ireland.

Over that summer, while Georgina reinvigorated Dublin's social scene, setting fashions and hosting parties in Phoenix Park, family life also continued and in August her stepsons arrived for their holidays.[261] It was a generally happy, occasionally carefree time until in mid-September some very serious news arrived: on 13 September Charles James Fox died after a long period of illness. Beyond its implications for the ministry and the Whigs generally, for the duke this was a disaster, and he suddenly felt very exposed as he lost his trusted confidante. He still had friends in the administration – Earl Spencer, his son Viscount Althorp, Charles Grey, Lord Howick (later Earl Grey), who replaced Fox as Foreign Secretary, and Lord Holland, who joined the administration in October 1806 – but none of them could replace Fox. Replying to Lord Holland's letter informing him of Fox's death, the duke appears almost overwhelmed by the situation: 'Every day and every hour bring with them fresh reason to deplore his great and irreparable loss, and I can barely bring my mind to contemplate it with any degree of calmness and reason.' And, writing to Lord Howick at the same time, the duke stresses that he will only stay in Ireland providing he is assured of the backing of 'the Prince of Wales and of the Cabinet at large'.[262]

As his mood darkened and his confidence started to slip, Georgina's support became crucial. This was a real test of their marriage and we get the sense that this was also the moment that finally consolidated its foundations, as the duke became aware of the true depth and strength of character of the woman he had married at such speed and on whom he now depended for sympathy and encouragement. In spite of a successful agricultural tour of Sligo, Mayo and Connaught, visiting farms, giving speeches at meetings and dinners, reviewing cattle and livestock, his underlying self-doubt still left him very vulnerable during this difficult time. Even though she was herself struggling with a difficult pregnancy, Georgina's unfailingly supportive and optimistic letters proved a constant source of comfort. In some, such as the earliest of 4 October, we hear loud echoes of those written to Lord John some twenty years before by Georgiana:

> why my own Johnny will you give way to unpleasant thoughts when you have so many cheering reflections, that you ought to make and so many bright prospects before you … is there a father in the world more beloved

by his Children or a husband more adored by his wife than you are … [and who is] more calculated to restore peace to a disturbed Country, happiness to its inhabitants, and respectability to its degraded Government. Then why, best of men, allow too much humility to prevent your 'shining in all your Glory.' Rouse yourself and shake off your false notions, rely on my word, that the more you are known the more you must be loved, respected and admired.

Yet, beyond any similarities there are to his first wife's letters, we see a distinct and telling difference in the confident, teasing, broad humour of the letter as it continues, almost daring him not to cheer up, if not actually smile:

when in spirits you are the most pleasing and the most agreeable Creature in the world and I beg you will talk incessantly out of compliment to me, pray do … and recall that I am too much interested in your fame to recommend anything to you, that would not show you in the most advantageous light. Make *love* to all the Ladies, but keep your dear heart for me, tell *naughty* stories to the Gentlemen, but keep their *effects* for me, handle all the Cattle with pleasure, but keep the tender pressure for me.[263]

While Georgiana's letters of encouragement had also often included the heartfelt lament that her own health and dark moods prevented her from truly supporting Lord John, that she could not be what he needed, Georgina's letters display an unswerving confidence in both herself and her husband.

A few days later, Georgina left Dublin and travelled to the coastal suburb of Clontarf, where she went to bathe in the hope of relieving some of the discomfort of her pregnancy away from the bustle of their official residences. In one undated letter, avoiding any mention of how she felt, of the aches, pains and spasms this pregnancy caused, she passes on upbeat news of their children, 'Our dear boys are quite well and happy. Wrio [two] sends "my *love* and my *kiss* to Papa". Edward [one] walks delightfully, the little thing is jumping about, and I suppose by that, means his love as well.' She goes on, 'Oh! My own Johnny, how it warms my heart towards this Country … that they value, and look up to, the first man certainly now in the world, you darling … your principles are not to be shaken, your manners are most pleasing, and your temper gentle. This is not half what I think, but all that I dare tell you for fear of appearing what I abhor – a flatterer.' She ends with the following endearing apology, 'Forgive any mistakes I have made – I do not have my Dictionary with me.'[264]

While this may seem to be simply a humorous reference to her spelling, it actually indicates something much more significant and provides a glimpse of the doubts and fears that lay behind Georgina's confident exterior. Throughout her life, Georgina was very aware of just how deficient her formal education had been and she never lost the fear of exposure to ridicule any mistakes might bring, particularly now that she moved in such rarefied social and intellectual circles. As a result, she spent her much of her adult life not only endeavouring to catch up through reading, but also, when she felt insecure, adopting an impatient and dismissive attitude designed to preclude the possibility of being publicly humiliated. Humiliation, real or imagined, had stalked her mother's life, stemming often from that same lack of education and everything that went with it, and Georgina fought her whole life to avoid it happening to her; she could be a vicious, even duplicitous, enemy to those people who she felt threatened to expose her to it.

On the duke's return to Dublin, seemingly intractable problems faced him in every direction, but he felt increasingly unsupported by the government. One fear was that everything could suddenly spiral out of control and that he did not have the military support he had asked for, but more generally he felt a crisis coming on the issue of Catholic emancipation, a measure he considered essential to the future of Ireland.

In the face of all this, he could do little except lobby ministers in London, and in letters from November 1806 he tells Spencer that while he is 'extremely unwilling to resort to the extreme measure of proclaiming under the Insurrection Act', dreading 'to place such a formidable engine in the hands of such men, which may be used as a means of gratifying the most evil and inveterate passions', he also acknowledges that, if the uprisings 'assume a more vigorous aspect … we may feel ourselves under the painful necessity of adopting the vigorous measure which has been so vehemently ... called for'. He seeks reassurance about his actions: 'It will be a satisfaction to me, to know whether my conduct under the difficult circumstances in which I am placed is approved by Your Lordship and the rest of His Majesty's confidential Servants ... I am apt to distrust my own judgements.' He ends his letter with a stark warning to Spencer that, if things do escalate, he will need up to 2,000 troops to be sent to Ireland immediately to get control of the situation.[265]

Amidst all this gloom, there was at last some good news in February 1807, when the duchess successfully gave birth to another son, Lord Charles James Fox Russell, a welcome opportunity for the duke to celebrate the memory of the man who had dominated the political lives of both himself and his brother. After this brief respite, however, the issue of allowing Catholics to occupy senior ranks in the army and navy – a measure the duke agreed was a good first step towards eventual full emancipation – suddenly brought down the government at the end of March and ended their stay in Ireland. Encouraged by the duke, the ministry had introduced a bill to this effect which was then immediately opposed by the king, who not only insisted it be dropped, but also required an undertaking from the government not to introduce any such bill again, stating that it would breach his coronation oath should he approve any measure of emancipation for Roman Catholics. The result was inevitable: the government resigned in April, and the Bedfords left Dublin to return to England – a swift and for the duke a rather unsatisfactory end to his labours. He had clearly invested a great deal of his political capital and made personal commitments to the people he had been negotiating with to ensure good faith. He had committed his credibility and good name to the process all for nothing.

In spite of these events, however, he soon became engaged in a new crusade around which he hoped they could all coalesce, but once again, as with the case of slavery, while approving the goal he was opposed to the means proposed, and asked Grey for his opinion: 'Major Cartwright perseveres ... to induce me to countenance in some mode or other in his Plans of Reform, but however disposed

I may be to promote the measure of Parliamentary Reform, in any way which may lead to practical good, I confess I have no inclination to adopt the proceeding proposed by Major Cartwright of going [to] a King's Closet with a Petition.' He believed such an action would simply harden opposition and cause an outcry, and hoped Grey agreed with him.[266]

While the Irish experience ended his political and public career, it cemented the foundations of his marriage, the Bedfords emerging from the experience in a deeper, more balanced and mutually supporting relationship than had existed when Mrs Hervey had visited. The manner in which Georgina had carried off her role as Vicereine deeply impressed the grateful duke, and despite being pregnant for most of their period in Ireland, she provided constant emotional and social support for him at a challenging time in his life. In his 'Moral Reflections', written on their return from Ireland about men and women's relationships in general, and his with Georgina specifically, he says, 'The woman I have described, is one whom I repeat <u>ought</u> to be happy – if this not so, with a heart and mind and soul like hers, it is her own fault. She is beloved by all who know her intrinsical worth by none more than by myself, and if I can make her happy, whilst god gives me my health and strength, she shall be so – August 12, 1807.'[267] In the four years since their marriage, the duke seems to have learned a lot about his wife, and while the years put great strains on their relationship, it appears that she was happy, and the relationship both survived and gained in strength.

Arriving back at Woburn in 1807, the Bedfords must have been disappointed with progress, since elements of the landscaping projects had been slowed down by a lack of supervision. The main reason was the fact that as soon as the duke and duchess left, Repton turned his attentions to writing his *Enquiry*, publishing it before the end of 1806, and pursuing the possibility of a royal commission from either George III or the Prince of Wales at Brighton. To the exasperation of Adam, Salmon and the others charged with completing the work, Repton missed appointments and failed to provide details for finishing the excavation at the south front and for path layouts in the pleasure grounds, until reappearing when the duke and duchess arrived home. Nevertheless, they were pleased with much of what had been done – the work around the Bason Pond, the 'viaduct' design for the new bridge, the creation of the central terrace in the pleasure grounds – and looked forward to the creation of the Menagerie. Eager to move on, the duke and Repton were also discussing further projects not included in the Red Book: a cottage to be built at the Thornery, the creation of a new pond between Drakelow Pond and Park Farm (Upper Drakelow), the refurbishment of the park keeper's house and garden, and the addition of a new 'porch' room on the north-west corner of the Abbey. All of which were carried out.

For the duke and duchess, the late spring and summer of 1807 were a time of relative peace and quiet during which they could relax a little and enjoy themselves, not only at Woburn, where they began work on the refurbishments of the dated staterooms, starting with the Long Gallery, but also in London where in June and July they stayed with Georgina's mother at 15 St James's Square. The duke had needed to be in London for the negotiations on the allocation of parliamentary seats for the general election, but clearly enjoying themselves, they stayed on. Jane's lease on the house was soon to run out and she was about to return to Scotland for the summer; it seems likely that at this point she invited the Bedfords to join her there. The timing was perfect, and the invitation accepted. Travelling with the teenage Lord John, they set out in early September on a new adventure which, in the event, would change the course of their lives; Georgina was going home, but for the duke and Lord John this was to be their first experience of Scotland.

Also travelling north were Lord and Lady Holland, similarly freed from government commitments by the fall of the ministry, and who in turn had left for 'our Scottish Tour' in late August. By different routes both couples reached Inverary Castle by 9 September, and one wonders what the duke made of his first trip to Scotland as they battled through the 'storm of hail, rain, wind and sleet' which, as Lady Holland described it, greeted them at Inverary. Their host, the 6th Duke of Argyll, was another of the leading Whig politicians of the day, a close associate of both Lord Grey and Lord Holland – and many years before, as Lord Lorne, had been smitten by the sixteen-year-old Georgiana Byng, but was swept away by his mother before 'it was too late'. Lady Holland's only complaint about their stay was 'to the mode of life is the extraordinary lateness of the hours, and the subsequent inability to do anything; some wags have called it the Castle of Indolence.'[268] A few days later, the Hollands set off for a tour along Loch Tay to Blair Atholl before turning south to Perth and meeting the Bedfords again in Edinburgh in early October. Although the route the Bedfords took is not recorded, it is likely they all travelled together as far as Blair Atholl, at which point the Bedfords would have travelled on over the pass of Drumochter heading for Badenoch and Kinrara.

Even though, when they arrived, Jane was in the midst of her court battles with the Duke of Gordon and the weather was not the best, the visit proved to be an outstanding success. By this time Jane had moved into the new house at Kinrara (Colour Plate 10), and although we have no details of the visit, it is hard to imagine that Georgina did not take the duke for the short walk down through the woods and along the river to see the original bothy farmhouse which meant so much to her, and once there had pointed out to him and his son the view spreading away in front of them that she knew so well – in the foreground the meadow running down to the Spey, beyond this low rounded wooded hills rising on either side and, beyond these, the high hills and moors of the Cairngorms stretching across the horizon. It is clear that the experience opened up an entirely new world for the duke, and the impact of this visit on him is reflected in the fact that, from a few years later onwards, the Spey valley in Badenoch and the surrounding glens and mountains became a central part of the Bedfords' year. Following their departure for Edinburgh, Jane summed up the mood of this visit: 'We had rivers, mountains and society… [and] I never saw any body so delighted as the Duke of Bedford was with every inconvenience, no cook, no servants, nothing but sheep heads, a hearty welcome, and an affectionate desire to please on all sides … the dear Bedfords left us on Sunday, and often declared no time in their life they would sooner live over again than the time they spent in my palace.'[269]

This must have been a triumphant moment for Georgina: to have finally connected her new life with her old. As they travelled down to meet the Hollands in Edinburgh, we can only imagine the plans they were making, since it would seem that these months in the immediate aftermath of the Irish experience were a key moment in the duke's life. Together the Bedfords had come through a very difficult experience strengthened as a couple and eager to start building their own lives. It was as if, on their return from Scotland, the duke had suddenly caught a glimpse of a world of new possibilities, interest and challenges that lay beyond his brother's legacy, that engaged his sense of curiosity and that he could explore on his own terms. Ireland, it seems, had provided a clean break from the world he had been so suddenly caught up in and encouraged him to follow his own interests; from the moment they returned from Scotland we start to see the duke doing just that. It was as though he had been mesmerized by the enormity of the deaths of his wife and his brother, and that by stripping away all that was familiar, his experience in Ireland had broken the spell, and that, far from being lost, Georgina had been able to immediately introduce him to new alternatives for their lives ahead.

During this trip to Scotland the Bedfords and the Hollands seemed to have developed a much closer personal relationship, young Lord John having previously become particularly close to the Hollands when he travelled with them to Spain between 1802 and 1805. As they left Edinburgh in mid-October, the Bedfords were looking forward to welcoming the Hollands to Woburn later that month. One of the reasons for this was that travelling with the Hollands was their 'Librarian', a Scot, Dr John Allen, whose conversation the duke in particular seems to have enjoyed, as he writes to Lady Holland, 'I neglected to say to Mr Allen before I left how happy I should be to see him at Woburn … The Dss desires me to say everything most kind from her.'

Although Allen had been recommended to the Hollands as a physician, 'it was as a scholar, rather than a doctor, that he entered the household of Holland House' in 1802.[270] Born near Edinburgh, Allen was a polymath who wrote about a wide range of subjects from politics, constitutional history and historical research to metaphysics and philosophy, and his informed conversation clearly attracted the duke, who was impressed enough by the stimulating intellectual atmosphere he found in Edinburgh to send Lord John to the university there between 1809 and 1812.

After visiting Georgina's sister, Mrs Fordyce, at Ayton, the Bedfords returned to the Abbey, where they were joined by the Hollands and Allen, but it was the arrival of another Scot at this time that gives some indication of the impact of the duke's first visit, with his appointment of the gardener George Sinclair. Sinclair, born in Edinburgh, had been working for a member of the extended Gordon family, and is likely to have been recommended to the duke during his trip; his arrival proved to be the catalyst for the duke's new interest in botanical and horticultural science, which he pursued with increasing passion for the rest of his life. Although only twenty years old, Sinclair's precocious interest in chemistry and soil science, combined with his practical experience, made him a perfect fit for Woburn; working there from 1807, he became overall Head Gardener in 1814, combining management of the pleasure grounds with that of the Froxfield kitchen gardens, and stayed until 1825, when he left to form his own seed and nursery company.[271]

Together, as we shall see, the duke and Sinclair, through a shared interest in the meticulous details of scientific investigations, plant collections and related publications, combined to put Woburn on the map as a centre for serious and groundbreaking horticultural science. The duke had found his true passion, the scientific exploration of aspects of the natural world through methodical study and observation, practical experimentation, literary endeavours, art and landscape gardening, and in Sinclair he had found someone who shared his curiosity and his enthusiasm for the new sciences and the possibilities of what could be achieved at Woburn. For Georgina, it must also have been nice to hear a familiar accent in the halls of the Abbey.

The Sheep Shearings resumed at Woburn in 1808, and this summer's was one of the grandest gatherings of all (Colour Plate 11). Attendees included Sir Joseph Banks, the duke's brother Lord William, 'the American Minister', Mr Coke of Holkham, Georgina's brother Lord Huntly, Arthur Young, Humphry Davy, William Adam and, among many others, '2 Mr Reptons'. In December, the duke chaired another great agricultural event, the Smithfield Club Cattle Show, and this, plus a flurry of activity at Park Farm and similarly large Sheep Shearing gatherings over the next two years, suggest that the years 1808–11 represented the period of the duke's most intense pursuit of agricultural matters, commissioning papers from tenants and papers and plans from those working for him on a variety of subjects, as though impatient to complete his brother's work before turning to his own interests.[272]

Over these years, work was finished on the new London entrance, the new roads and bridges in the park, and attention became focused on the pleasure grounds. As the family had grown, the duke and duchess sought to make these places for children as well as adults to enjoy, and over the next few years this became one priority. One of the first actions the duke had taken in 1803 after his marriage was to 'put up the netting' and prepare his brother's indoor tennis court for action again, to bring it back to life after the injury his brother had sustained there which led to his death. He appointed James Cox as the Tennis Master in 1809; Cox stayed for thirty years, coaching the adults and teaching successive members of the growing family. Also added to the pleasure grounds was a 'labyrinth', now known as the Maze, the layout of which was 'worked out' by the duke using a plan which Lord George William had brought back from Cintra, and to which a few years later a 'Chinese' pavilion was added.[273]

In addition to this, work continued on the Menagerie, designed to house a collection of exotically plumaged birds and, in many ways, to provide an entertaining and instructional centrepiece to the gardens. Around it were the serious plant collections, new arboretums, greenhouses and flower beds, but the Menagerie – with its playful entrance (on one side a formal Doric doorway, on the other a rustic wooden pavilion built over the water), its rows of intricate wire cages full of perches of twigs and nesting boxes filled with moss, the aviary and picturesque fence of netting and rough posts – had been designed to delight, surprise and entertain both adults and children.

By this time, however, the duke's rapidly changing priorities meant that, beyond the layout of gravel paths, little more of the detail in Repton's Red Book proposals was added. Instead, something very different appeared in the pleasure grounds which had nothing to do with Repton: an elaborate layout of small plots featuring different varieties of grasses. Although he did not become Head

Gardener at Woburn until 1814, George Sinclair was clearly working very closely with the duke immediately following his appointment. Their first collaboration began with 'levelling new Grass Ground' in March 1808, to scientifically test the efficacy of different soils and soil mixes on the nutritive value of a variety of grasses. To achieve this, 'The different species in this Grass Garden, have each a square space of ground allotted to them, bordered with cast iron edgings; gravel walks intervene betwixt the beds. The whole compartment is enclosed by a Hornbeam-hedge, bordered with Moss Roses.'[274]

The duke's purpose was to investigate the nutritive qualities of grasses in order to provide the best pasture for cattle, and Sinclair was instructed to carry out the necessary enquiries, using Humphry Davy to assist with the assessments of the grass species, to 'provide a method for analyzing grasses' and give advice on equipment. It was Sinclair, however, who made the project possible, and it was his mastering of Davy's experimental techniques and meticulous recording of data over the next eight years which led to its success. Some of the data gathered was published in the appendix to Davy's lecture series in 1813, but recognition of the significance of the work Sinclair had done came with a full account in his groundbreaking book *Hortus Gramineus Woburnensis* that the duke published in 1816. It was typical of the depth of the duke's curiosity and engagement with these projects that he 'decided to enlist the aid of chemistry to help with this project', and although not a chemist, it was the sort of detailed investigation he so enjoyed, and kept himself up to date with the work of Davy, who was also a guest at the Sheep Shearings.[275]

What is so interesting about this is that we see here the new directions which the duke's and duchess's interests were taking, and the imaginative promotion of detailed research and enquiry into the world around us. Discussing Coleridge's understanding, at exactly this time, that 'science and art [were] not mutually exclusive', Kathleen Coburn writes: 'The imagination for Coleridge contains both conscious and unconscious elements, and far from being an escape into illusion, is a means of ordering the chaos of reality, and one of the ways to access truth.'[276] This was to be very much the spirit in which the duke began to pursue art and science at Woburn, and it illustrates how he hoped the resources there, in terms of both patronage and the contents of the collections within the Abbey and the gardens and grounds, could be exploited in the pursuit of imaginative scientific and artistic enquiry into a world of wonder opening up around them. It must have been a tremendous encouragement to the duke in these endeavours when, in the 'Advertisement' for his published lectures, Davy wrote, 'The Duke of Bedford has enabled me to stamp value upon this Work, by permitting me to add to it the results of the experiments instituted by His Grace upon the quantity of produce afforded by the different grasses.' The plan of the pleasure grounds, published in *Hortus Woburnensis* (1833), indicates that as the family and visitors left the sculpture gallery gardens and made their way round the main gravel path towards Repton's playful Menagerie, the first feature they came across was the grass ground. While the contrast between the two features could not have been clearer, this juxtaposition served to emphasize, for all to see, the duke's vision of a world to be explored by both the artistic and the scientific imagination.[277]

In June, following the Sheep Shearing, the duke and duchess and the three boys set off for a visit to Leamington Spa. This was to be the first of a number of visits he made to the spa as he sought relief from his gout and other ailments, but this trip may also have been for Georgina's benefit in the midst of her latest pregnancy. According to one source, however, the duke had also been 'persuaded by his relations, the Warwick bankers of Russell & Tomes, to invest profits from his Bloomsbury estates' in the development of the town, adding that the duke 'had an interest in the Bedford Hotel, opened 1811, and recommended friends and relations to take the waters'. For the Bedfords, besides bathing at the spa, there were fishing expeditions on the river Leam for the children, and for Georgina there was another point of interest since her mother had been 'a frequent visitor there in the early 1800s and had a modest house built [Gordon House] which still stands off Russell Terrace, at the rear of George Street'.[278] By late the next month, while the family returned to Woburn, Georgina made an 'excursion' to Bognor, suggesting perhaps that, halfway through her pregnancy, she was once again feeling the strain and looking for some relief from sea air; in the end, another son, Lord Francis Russell, or 'Franky' as he became known, was born safely in October.

As 1809 got underway, work continued on completing all the new landscaping at Woburn, and there were increasing signs that the duke and duchess were continuing to pursue other interests.[279] In June, he received a letter from the Society of Antiquities informing him that 'at the Meeting of the Society at Somerset Place, you are duly elected a Fellow of that Learned Body', a development that reflects his growing interest in both the romance of historical architecture and understanding the genuine style and details of its construction. We see this again in April 1810, when Repton visited Woburn and Oakley for a week of meetings, and subsequently wrote that 'The Duke of Bedford … one day observed, that out of the numerous Cottages called Gothic, which everywhere present themselves near the high roads, he had never seen one that did not betray its modern character and recent date. At the same time his Grace expressed a desire to have a Cottage of the style and date of buildings prior to the reign of Henry VIII.' Repton goes on, 'A communication of some curious specimens of Timber-houses was made to the Society of Antiquaries in 1810, which was ordered to be engraved and printed for the *Archæologia,*' and adds that 'by the recent works of professed Antiquaries, a spirit of inquiry has been excited.'[280] At Woburn, the results of this 'spirit of inquiry' produced five such historic and highly picturesque cottages, two built within the park at Woburn – the Thornery (1806) and Purret's Hill Lodge (1834) – two, Aspley Lodge (1810) and Hundreds Farm (1815), (Colour Plate 12), built 'near the high road' from Woburn Sands to Woburn, while Ivy Lodge (1825) was built where the Great Avenue crossed the London road. Although Repton does not mention it, in a guide to the Abbey written some twenty years later, Georgina's involvement in this new enquiring spirit is explicitly acknowledged. Writing about Aspley Lodge, the writer says it is a 'lofty and handsome building … in the Gothic style, of about 1500; adjoining which are a shrubbery, and maze. For this ornamental erection the neighbourhood is indebted to the taste of her Grace the Duchess of Bedford.'[281]

With her fourth son safely delivered and her health recovered, Georgina was clearly enjoying herself during this time when so many new projects had been completed and others were underway, and we get a sense that the new-found equilibrium in their relationship that developed in Ireland now extended to their shared interest in exploring the world of new ideas. It was an exciting time, and this was very much the frame of mind they were in when they left Woburn that summer to travel down to the Devon estates, where the duke was keen to follow up on William Adam's concerns and suggestions following his visit in 1802.

By August 1809, the Bedfords were in Tavistock, where he had arranged for Repton, with his architect sons John Adey and George Stanley, to work on developing new buildings in the marketplace and begin the process of improving facilities in the town. With these improvements underway, the family set off for a few days fishing on the upper Tamar, staying in a large farmhouse at Longbrooke outside the village of Milton Abbot. From here, they set out on their ponies to visit 'the part of Milton Abbot Estate which lies next to the Tamar', a place Adam had described as 'beautiful, [with] some very handsome Woods'. Whether or not they actually did any fishing, this turned out to be a momentous morning, because as they emerged from the woods and approached the small cluster of buildings of Endsleigh Farm, the view suddenly opened up to reveal a spectacular spread of landscape stretching out beyond the river below them and off over rolling hills to the rugged outline of the Cornish moors on the horizon. Judging from what happened next, this revelation stopped the duchess in her tracks, lost in wonder at what she saw, silent for a moment, before calling her husband back to look again. Before them lay a view that, while not identical, was uncannily similar in layout and extent to one they had seen together two years before when visiting the bothy farmhouse at Kinrara. Almost instantly, it seems, Georgina had a vision of building a house here for family holidays, of recreating in this place the experience of seasonal trips to the Highland moors with her mother, of her children in turn benefiting from the freedom and rewards of regular exposure to the natural world which had been so much a part of her childhood.

It is equally clear that the duke understood her vision, because Edward Bray, the duke's agent in Tavistock, was immediately instructed to relocate the tenant farmer, to secure the view on the far side of the river by taking a lease on the woods there from the Duchy of Cornwall, and to commission Repton and his sons to visit the site and draw up plans for a cottage. By November these plans had arrived and been turned down as unsuitable, and another architect, Jeffry Wyatville, was similarly briefed. He produced plans over the winter which were adopted, and construction started on the house in early spring 1810, with the builders under strict instructions to complete work within two years. It seemed there was no time to be lost. As we shall see, things did not go entirely smoothly, but as they left Devon at the end of August, their world, which had so recently expanded to include Scotland, now included an entirely new location, a custom-built new house – the first ever in the history of the duke's family – and a place that reflected who they were and the wonderful possibilities that lay ahead for them.

CHAPTER SIX
1810–1818

'ENDSLEIGH COTTAGE was built and a residence created in this sequestered valley by John, Duke of Bedford, the spot having previously been chosen from the natural and picturesque beauties which surround it by Georgiana, Duchess of Bedford. The first stone of the building was laid by her four eldest sons, Wriothesley, Edward, Charles Fox and Francis, Sept, 1810.' So reads the commemorative plaque still on display in the stable yard at Endsleigh, which, besides emphasizing Georgina's role in choosing the site, also indicates the shared nature of this endeavour and the landscapes they were interested in. Today the 'natural and picturesque' views from the house are much more limited due largely to the growth of trees beyond the river, but the sequestered scene still retains much of the special atmosphere that drew the Bedfords to it. The only contemporary image of the view that has come down to us today is from Repton's Red Book for Endsleigh, and comparing this image (before the woods had grown to maturity) with the view from the doorway of the bothy foundations at Kinrara today, we can get a sense of what drew Georgina, in particular, to the site. In both pictures we are looking down a long grassy slope to a river running from the right to the left. Beyond that, in the middle distance, the low wooded foothills following the far bank of the river are very similar, as is the range of hills in the distance beyond; it just remains for us to substitute the Spey for the Tamar, and the outlines of the Cairngorm range with that of the Cornish moors, and, unlikely as it may seem, the views have a similar sense of composition and extent, and atmosphere of remoteness (Colour Plates 13 and 14).

The distinct influence of Scotland was also felt in the house that was built. It was not a typical country villa, or even a decorative thatched *cottage ornée*, and the fact that both the Repton and Wyatville designs had a similar theme of connected cottages suggests also a strong echo of the Highland lodges Georgina had known from a young age, and specifically of the original building at Kinrara, which also featured a corridor joining two buildings. The other key element of the design was that it should be articulated in order to take advantage of the full sweep of the views, those to the west overlooked by the duke and duchess's private apartments, the central rooms, library and drawing room looking directly south out towards the distant moors, and the view to the east seen from the large dining room window. Here we may well be seeing the continuing influence of Uvedale Price, whose work had proved so useful to Jane for landscaping at Kinrara:

> if Endsleigh lacks the uninhibited rusticity of the ideal cottage ornée it is, in its planning and siting ... possibly for the first time, Uvedale Price's idea of designing houses for aspect instead of for symmetry ... given practical expression: 'If the owner of such a spot, instead of making a regular front and sides were to insist on having the windows turned towards the points where objects were most happily arranged, the architect would be forced into inventing a number of picturesque forms and combinations which otherwise might never have occurred to him ... [and] accommodate his building for the scenery, not make that give way to the building.'[282]

It is quite possible that such considerations played a part in how Jane had altered and added to the original bothy at Kinrara, including the use of a bay window, but whatever influences were at work, from the moment Wyatville set to work on the design and submitted it by early 1810, things moved very fast (Colour Plates 15 and 16). As soon as the tenant of the existing farmhouse vacated the property on 25 March, work started immediately on clearing the site, and negotiations were begun with the Duchy of Cornwall to lease Wareham Wood across the river to secure the view from the house. Huge quantities of timber were felled and transported from the duke's various woodlands around Milton Abbot and Tavistock, new quarries to supply the stone were opened, and a brick kiln was established in a field on Milton

Jeffry Wyatville, well-house and rustic seat, c.1816. This image indicates that the well-house on the bank of the pond had been carefully positioned to form part of the view from the duke and duchess's apartments on the hill above.

Down that remained in use until 1814. As all this work got underway, another very interesting task was undertaken: the relocation of the surviving parts of a medieval well-house and rustic seat from neighbouring Leigh Barton to Endsleigh, where the old pieces of stone were set in a new rubble stone exterior covering a spring beside the pond just below the house. The structure survives intact today.

Leigh Barton, an old hunting lodge for the abbots of Tavistock Abbey, was part of the Bedford estate, and the well-house was a medieval structure covering what was likely to have been a much older holy well.[283] Long out of use for formal religious purposes, it seems that the duke and duchess had seen the old well and wanted to include the structure as a part of the Endsleigh site, and by doing so they added another significant element to a location that already reminded them both of Kinrara. A key element of the landscape at Georgina's old home was the survival of St Eata's Well, and, clearly, the addition of a structure with similar associations to the Endsleigh site would have provided an echo of the spiritual dimension that pervaded the old site at Kinrara.

Another significant event that summer was the birth in June of Georgina's fifth child, and this time to her delight, after four boys, it was her first daughter, Georgiana. Just how much having a daughter meant to Georgina soon became clear as her reluctance to end breastfeeding began to cause concern. Rachel Trethewey notes that months later, in December, Georgina 'constantly nursing her daughter was affecting her health' and quotes the duke writing to Lady Holland: 'She has been far from well and … fainted dead whilst we were at dinner, but rallied again with her accustomed spirits and came back into the room, only to faint a second time – she is still very languid but I cannot prevail upon her to wean her little girl.'

At the same time, while there were causes for concern about Georgina's health, we see the first signs of health problems for the duke when Georgina tells Lady Holland: 'I know your anxiety about the Duke … he is very unwell [but] I do not see anything serious at present, however, every precaution has and shall be taken to prevent any mischief. His complaint he says has nothing to do with the Champagne etc etc, tho' neither him nor I doubt that.'[284] This may well have been the first signs of the gout which was to plague him, and indeed Lord Holland, as the years went on, and, like his first wife, Georgina constantly reminded him of the need for exercise.

As we have already seen, while Repton was at Woburn that spring completing the bulk of the work to be done based on his Red Book, the duke had requested additional work. One element of this was the creation of the 'Keeper's Cottage' at Aspley Wood, while another, perhaps at the request of Georgina, was the design for the children's garden in the Woburn pleasure grounds, the inspiration for which may have been Wyatville's addition of a similar garden at Endsleigh. In that instance it was included as an integral part of the house design, emphasizing again the idea that the house was built for and around the family, unlike Woburn where the family apartments were peripheral to the public staterooms.

In August 1810, the family set out to visit Endsleigh again, and on this occasion were accompanied by the duke's niece Lady Gertrude Russell and her brother John, travelling via the New Forest and Dorset. On the 15th the party were in Sidmouth, where 'we saw Lord Le Despenser's Cottage' before going on to Plymouth and Tavistock.[285] News about 'Knowle Cottage', a sprawling forty-room thatched structure with roof dormers, Gothic-style windows and rustic verandas, must have spread rapidly after its completion in 1809, and this visit may have been the reason the Bedfords took such an unusual route to Endsleigh. Although the architect is unknown, Christine and Rab Barnard have found evidence that Sir John Soane's office was involved to some extent, probably as project managers, but whoever designed it, judging from the list of decorative items included at Knowle – 'stone grotto flinting, pebble paving, thatching, work on a dairy, coach houses, greenhouse, hot houses, and 2 Rustic Seats' – it may well have been the source for some of the decorative details at Endsleigh. Unfortunately, we will never know for sure how influential this house may have been, or what these decorative details may have looked like, since the house had already been altered by 1812. Nevertheless, it would have been fresh in their minds when the Bedfords reached Endsleigh and met up with Wyatville, whose surviving plan of the house indicates a number of alterations were made to the design.

Once at Endsleigh, the family visited the building site where Richard Facey & Co., 'Miners', had spent the summer clearing the site, excavating and removing rock, making roads and room for the stockpiles of slate, stone and timber being delivered from all corners of the Devon estate.[286] Work was just about to start on the children's cottage, and the visitors stayed long enough for the four boys to lay the foundation stone for the house, after which they left for a three-week visit to Torquay, before returning to Woburn for Christmas. Here they were joined by the

Hollands, and Lady Gertrude Russell, writing about the New Year holidays for 1811, gives us a glimpse of Woburn over the festive period, mentioning among the visitors William Adam, Georgina's sisters Louisa and Madelina, the Hollands, Gertrude's brothers William and Francis Russell, and the Fitzpatricks, and that they played Blindman's Buff and 'had a little masquerade among ourselves'. She also notes that on Christmas Day the family was joined by Jane, Duchess of Gordon, and her granddaughter Lady Jane Montagu.[287]

By February 1811, however, the duke's holiday was interrupted by discouraging news from Edward Bray, the agent in Tavistock, who passed on letters from the site manager at Endsleigh, William Walker, concerning progress on the house. Not only had terrible winter weather made the roads impassable and brought building to a halt, but there were problems with building materials. Walker had been given rooms at Longbrook Lodge, and his letters from there over the next few years provide a vivid and often gloomy picture of the difficulties they encountered bringing this unusual house to completion. In February, for example, he wrote, 'Nothing has been built since I have been here … When the weather proves fair, no time shall be lost in forwarding the work as fast as possible … I take the liberty of informing you that the rain comes in at several places at Longbrook house particularly in the room that I sleep in. The two privies are in a bad state the plastering is all falling down.' Little, it seems, was going right, but in March the news was, if anything, even gloomier:

> Be pleased to inform His Grace the Duke of Bedford that the buildings at Endsleigh are going on very slowly. If His Grace wishes to go faster with the work – it entirely rests with Mr Martin as Carpenter – Mr Sanders as Mason and Capt. Hitchings as conductor of raising stone … I understand by Mr Wyatt that the buildings at Endsleigh were to be finished in 2 years – but I am very clear if there is not greater exertions made than what there is at present – the buildings will not be finished in 7 years.

By April, although work had begun on the children's cottage, Walker was ready to leave, frustrated as much as anything by Bray's unease about his candid assessments of progress: 'As the last report I made of the work at Endsleigh has given offence … I beg leave to decline saying anything more about the progress of the buildings, when the Duke of Bedford comes down if His Grace finds I have given a false report of the works, I am ready and willing to meet my discharge from a very unpleasant situation.'[288]

Beyond the terrible weather, the leaking roof at Longbrook, the poor site conditions, the two-year deadline, problems with the poor quality of some of the stone supplies, the complexity of the design, and ongoing changes that were being made, one of his most immediate problems was the lack of skilled masons. In May he writes, 'I really must give up the setting out of the building … for I can't find a man that knows how to place a single stone without I am with him.' In his next letter he says, 'I had great expectations from the foreman of the masons, but I conceive he is no better judge of business than his Master – he actually does not know how to build a flue of a chimney.'

By July little had improved and Walker reported that 'there is scarcely a part done but what is altered perhaps twice'; by the end of the month, although he was hopeful of roofing the children's cottage, to have a chance of completing the rest, 'I am of the opinion that the best remedy for the evil we labour under (with respect to the mason work) will be for Mr Wyatt to send a man from London – one who is capable of conducting the mason's work throughout.'[289]

This was duly arranged, but work on the house still overran by two years, and it was not until 1814 that the site was cleared, driveways completed and work begun on the landscaping around the house. Yet, in spite of what must have seemed like endless delays on the house, these months seem to have been a period of great happiness, particularly for Georgina, who was enjoying her new daughter, as she told Lady Holland: 'I never saw Woburn in such beauty the scenery really is like my idea of fairy land and my little girl to me represents Mistress of those fairies, she is so elegant, lively and beautiful; forgive this rhapsody.'[290]

This mood continued through the early summer when the family went to London in June for the season, taking up residence in a house in Hamilton Place overlooking Hyde Park and Hyde Park Corner, the fashionable meeting place for rides in the park, and which remained the family's town house until 1820.[291] Georgina, making the most of a short break from pregnancy, seemed determined to enjoy herself, and entries in the cash book for this year indicate that she attended the Countess of Jersey's concert with the duke and Lord John, joined several thousand other invitees to the grand fete given by the Prince of Wales at Carlton House in honour of the king's birthday, and then later in the month hosted a dinner and ball at Hamilton Place.

At the end of the summer of 1811, the duke and duchess were in Leamington again for the waters, 'by way of precaution and to fortify myself against the winter', but by September they were back at Woburn and ready for another adventure, as the duke tells Lord Grey, 'The Duchess … this morning started for Scotland to execute the project she had so much in mind when you left us, of once more visiting the Highlands. She said she would write to you … and will probably ask you to receive us at Howick on our return southwards in October … I leave tomorrow.'[292]

This second trip saw them join Jane for almost a month at Kinrara before travelling to Gordon Castle for the duke's first visit there, and then to Huntly Lodge and Aberdeen before returning via Howick. For the duke, who was clearly as enthusiastic and enchanted by Scotland as he had been on their first journey, this was largely an extended shooting trip, his exploits all carefully recorded in game books, and it probably helped the duke's good mood that, when in Aberdeen, he was presented with a certificate and seal for the Freedom of the City of Aberdeen.[293] Quite apart from immersing the duke in the world of the Highland grouse moor, this visit also served to introduce him to a large number of people and places from Georgina's past. We do not have a record of how Georgina spent her time – she had always been a keen angler – but it is very possible that 'the project she had so much in mind' went far beyond introducing the duke to family and the moors, and that taking a house in Badenoch may well have been her ultimate goal. In this context, it is interesting that instead of travelling directly down the Spey to Gordon Castle, they headed up the road to Inverness, stopping for two days' shooting at Freeburn near Tomatin before travelling on to the castle. This route would have given them an opportunity to visit Mackintosh of Mackintosh at Moy Hall, Tomatin, who held land at Kincraig on the Spey and in Glen Feshie, Badenoch. The duke's exposure to the Highland shooting season this year may also have convinced him that an estate in the Highlands would be the perfect way to immerse himself in this exciting new place, and would add new moors for family and friends to visit.

Following their return to Woburn in late October, Georgina discovered she was pregnant again, her brief respite over, and the winter holidays passed quietly, broken only with the duke's visits to shooting parties at Holkham in Norfolk in November and Uppark in Sussex in January 1812. As expenditure at Endsleigh steadily increased, work at Woburn slowed right down, and apart from the construction of a new greenhouse in the 'yard' between the conservatory and the riding house, little new work began. This may also have been because the duke's mind was on the complications inherent in the development of Endsleigh, where (for the first time ever, perhaps) he had to get agreement from neighbours before he could put his plans into action. As much of the contiguous land around the farm at Endsleigh, although part of the Bedford estate, had been let on long-term leases to the Edgcumbes by the 5th Duke, his brother now found himself hemmed in, unable to make the changes he wanted. An example of this came up in March 1812. Following his visit the year before, the duke must have been mulling things over, and that March he wrote to Richard Edgcumbe: 'As it is very essential to render the approach to Endsleigh cottage as perfect as I could wish it to be, that one side of the land should be planted, I flatter myself that you will not have any objection to alienate from your lease that part of the ground you hold which lies immediately to the right of the line of approach and contiguous to the road – as the quantity is so very trifling I trust it will not be any inconvenience to you to part with it, which involves me in less difficulty to request this favour of you.'[294]

It came as something of a surprise to the duke that Edgcumbe did indeed have an objection and was not interested in alienating any of the land; within a few months, a number of similar issues came up concerning rights of way, particularly by foot from Endsleigh to Milton Abbot, and who could legally divert streams. The duke rapidly changed his tone, emphasizing he wanted to be a 'good neighbour' and seeking accommodation through agreement, but it still took all his tact and Adam's hardball negotiating to secure what they wanted, and before they could start on the driveway plantations which still make such an impression today.

The next month witnessed the end of an era when on 14 April 1812 Jane Maxwell, Duchess of Gordon, died at Pulteney's Hotel, Piccadilly. Jane had arrived in London earlier that year, having spent her last months at Kinrara in 'quietness', and Bulloch recounts that the Duchess of Gordon 'had been summoned to Carlton House to a reception given by the Prince Regent. She got a new gown for the occasion … and threw open her apartments in the hotel for a reception of her own. She was seized with a bad cold and died in a few weeks, surrounded by members of her family.' She was sixty-three.

Before her death, Jane had left explicit instructions about where she was to be buried at Kinrara and the wording on the memorial plaque – a detailed list of her children and their spouses as a record of what she felt she had contributed to the family: not just raising the children, but also securing three dukes for her daughters. Bulloch then goes on to describe the funeral procession arriving in Kingussie: 'in a hearse drawn all the way from London by six jet-black Belgian horses'. On crossing the Drumochter Pass, Jane lay in state at Dalwhinnie, the first stage within the family estates, for two days, and then for another two days at Pitmain, 'and was subsequently followed by an immense concourse of Highland people to the resting-place at her beloved Kinrara'.[295] After leaving Pitmain, the solemn procession then left the road to proceed down the driveway to Kinrara House, before turning down a track, passing through the trees, and emerging on to the wide haugh beside the Spey. There, within sight of the old bothy farmhouse, St Eata's Well and looking out towards the Cairngorms, Jane was buried within the site of the old chapel.

In 1815 Elizabeth Grant described the scene as she saw it: 'The charming Duchess, whose heart was in the highlands, had left orders to be buried on the banks of the Spey … Lord Huntly planted a few larch around the enclosure, but Lady Huntly laid out a beautiful shrubbery and extended the plantation, making paths through it. The grave was covered by a plain marble slab, but behind this rose

Jane Maxwell's burial site at Kinrara today. The inscription lists all Jane's children, their spouses and her grandchildren.

a stunted obelisk of granite, bearing on its front by way of inscription the names of all her children with their marriages; this was by her own desire.'[296] For our purposes, however, perhaps her most lasting memorial was the profound gift Jane left for her daughter Georgina, summed up by Stoddart in his description of Jane's life as he had found it in 1799: 'Those, whose notions of enjoyment are built only upon city life, and who know the spirit and animation, which the Dutchess of Gordon infuses into the circles of fashion, will probably be astonished at her being able to derive enjoyment from so different a source. They will not believe, that a mind habituated to all the polish and splendour of courts … can give place to the calm and cool air, the soft and tranquil shade of a Highland cottage.'[297]

Reflecting on these events, Elizabeth Grant, in whose young life at The Doune Jane had loomed so large, wrote, 'Both my father and mother grieved sincerely for the death of their old friend and neighbour with whom they had spent so many happy hours. Indeed, the whole of the highlands mourned for her, as with all her oddities she was the soul of our northern society.'

On Jane's death, Kinrara passed to the Marquis of Huntly, and Grant laments, 'We had no Kinrara; that little paradise had been shut up ever since the death of the Duchess of Gordon, except just during a month in the shooting season, when the Marquis of Huntly came there with a bachelor party.' Two years later she described meeting Huntly and his new wife Elizabeth when they paid a visit to The Doune: 'He in his shabby old shooting dress ... and she in a beautiful baby phaeton drawn by four goats', adding that Huntly 'got very fond of her, and so did I; the rest of the family never took to her ... remembering her predecessor, the beautiful brilliant Duchess.' She concludes, 'Kinrara too was different, a more elevated and very stupid society, dull propriety, regularity, ceremony ... a flow of wine but not of soul.'[298]

Another consequence of Jane's death was the arrival at Woburn of Georgina's niece Lady Jane Montagu (the eldest daughter of Susan, Duchess of Manchester), who had been living for the past few years with her grandmother. It would seem that when in 1811 Jane returned from Kinrara to the hotel in London and her health began to fail, the question came up as to where her granddaughter should live. Her paternal grandmother, Elizabeth Montagu, Dowager Duchess of Manchester, appears to have insisted on the girl returning to live with her other siblings under her care at Kimbolton, and her aunt Georgina, who would have taken her in, deferred to her wishes. Thus, Trethewey tells us that Lady Jane had initially 'returned to her father's house at Kimbolton to live with her sisters and their governess, but she was not happy ... and suffered from depression which she called "the blue devils"'. It is clear from a letter Lady Jane, then eighteen, wrote to the duke in January 1812, when an invitation to her to visit Woburn had been brusquely turned down by her grandmother, that she had come to realize it would in fact have been better if she had been at Woburn all along. She writes to apologize:

My dearest Johnny,

Perhaps, indeed I am sure, what you say about my going to Woburn is right, and I am afraid it showed a want of feeling in me not to have thought so before … If grandmamma had shown any consideration for my wishes, or feelings, I should have had a still greater regard for hers, but she did not, and her motives for refusing me seemed to be so selfish that I was angry with her, and my disappointment made me cross – It was really wrong of me to say what I did to Aunt Georgy and I hope you will believe me when I say I have blamed myself very much for it since … I think when Grandmama said it, she did not mean she disliked my going to Woburn, but the truth is she was afraid of my liking it too much and she thought there was less chance of my wishing to remain at Kimbolton than at Woburn … Pray tell Aunt Georgy this for I am afraid that speech made her more angry with Granny than anything else and I hope she will not remain angry with her … I trust neither you or Aunt Georgy will never let any circumstance make you doubt of my affection, attachment and gratitude to you both … your affectionate, Jenny [Janey].[299]

A decision was finally made once the Duchess of Gordon died, and at Woburn, where Jane clearly had a very close and informal relationship with her aunt and uncle, her life settled down for a while, before ill health intervened.

Another family member going through difficult times that summer was the duke's younger brother, Lord William, whose life had been rocked by the sudden death of his wife in 1808. Although his eldest daughter, Gertrude, had moved to Woburn in 1810, his eldest son, Francis, was already in the army and the next two sons, George and John, were serving in the navy, he was having difficulties with the youngest two. Lord William explained to the duke: '[of] the difficulties that surround me – those which press hardest on me, relate at this moment to my two youngest children. The truth is William's behaviour has disallowed me from attention to any other point, and for him, I am yet without any plan to rest on.'[300]

Although we do not know what young William's behaviour involved, or what the duke and duchess could do to help, he went on to have a successful career in London, but they were able to assist with the youngest girl, Eliza, who immediately joined the ever-growing family at Woburn. Then, in July, Georgina gave birth to another daughter of her own, Louisa, and soon after this the family left Woburn to spend two weeks at her aunt Fordyce's house overlooking the Thames in Putney while Georgina recovered. Set in leafy grounds, the villa was an excellent place for Georgina to rest, and for the duke to sit in the gardens and read his newly ordered books. Although the Sheep Shearing had been held at Woburn that summer, these new books give an early indication, alongside the building of the new greenhouse, of the direction of the duke's new interests, as his bookseller, James Webb, supplied books on 'Mineralogy' and 'Botanical Publications'.[301]

As the family regrouped at Woburn that December, we get a vivid, if horrified, account of an evening's entertainment there from the diary writer Lady Frances Shelley, who was visiting with her husband. They were invited perhaps as friends of the Spencers, but Lady Shelley clearly did not enjoy herself. In a letter to Lady Spencer she wrote, 'a formal reception prepared the way for a silent dinner of twenty people ... during dinner every one whispered to his next neighbour ... But when evening came, God knows ... for such a scene of vulgar noise, and riot, I never beheld! ... As soon as we left the dining-room, the Duchess went to her nursing employment (after an edifying conversation on the subject) and we dispersed ... through an *enfilade* of six rooms.' Some men played billiards in one room, while in another 'Lady Asgill established herself in an attitude lying on a sofa with Sir Thomas Graham at her feet.' Elsewhere some sat at whist, while in the next room

Lady Jane and Miss [Eliza] Russell at harp and pianoforte (both out of tune) playing 'The Creation'! ... it was chaos ... In the Long Gallery, a few pairs were dispersed on the sofas; others sauntered from room to room. I joined the latter, and talked of furniture, china and ormolu, till the subject was exhausted. I was bored to death ... Scarcely was I seated [in the card room] when the Duchess entered; and, collecting her romping force of girls and young men, they all seized cushions, and began pelting the whist players. They defended themselves by throwing the cards and candles at her head; but the Duchess succeeded in overthrowing the table, and a regular battle ensued with cushions, oranges, and apples. The romp was at last ended by Lady Jane being nearly blinded by an apple … Shelley … had been almost smothered by the female romps getting him on the ground, and pummelling him with cushions. To this succeeded Blind Man's Buff. *Trieste*, disgusted and cross … I stole off to bed … Living as he does, in the languor created by the dearth of intellectual amusement, can you wonder that [the duke] should, in despair, try to enjoy the physical distraction of Blind Man's Buff?

In the end though, all the romping and pummelling aside, she appears to have been expecting not to approve, and what the good lady really 'thought impossible' was the 'disgusting familiarity of Lady Asgill and Sir Thomas Graham, who, though in the field a hero, is in love, a dotard', and she sums up the visit as a 'parade both new and disgusting'.[302] Had she not been so disgusted and cross, Lady Shelley might well have paused to admire the new scarlet and crimson decor of the Long Gallery, the only one of the six staterooms worked on so far.

The year 1813 found the family at Woburn, where, still nursing baby Louisa, Georgina discovered she was pregnant again. With the exception of the short break between her two daughters, she had now been pregnant every year since her marriage, and with the strain beginning to tell on her health, she seems to have spent most of her time quietly at Woburn until she joined the duke on a trip to the Isle of Wight in July. For him, the ongoing projects in the Abbey grounds, other than maintenance, were limited by the expenditure at Endsleigh to completing the London approach road, the London entrance, the new 'rough bridge' beside the Hop Garden Pond and the plantations that surrounded it.

At Endsleigh itself, Walker was having a better year. With the children's cottage largely complete, work began on the main building, the private apartments occupying the west end, comprising a pair of drawing rooms with bedrooms above for the duke and duchess looking out over the area for the children's cottage and garden, and beyond towards Castle Head and the moors. In the central area work began on the library and drawing room, both with bay windows looking south, and an anteroom with access to a roofed veranda paved with sheep knuckles and, finally, the dining room with a large window looking out across the slope to the Leigh Woods in the east. Around the house, the grounds were levelled, some gravel paths created, and work was done on 'Levelling the Marsh in front of the Cottage by the Tamar, and Stoning by the River'.[303]

Things really began to move, however, with the duke's arrival in May, which coincided with that of James Langley, who travelled down from Woburn with his 'father, wife and child' to take up an appointment as the new farm manager, including Dunterton, Endsleigh, Harrowgrove and Elwells, all of which supplied the house. With new staff in place and building on the house continuing, the duke turned his attention to the grounds, to setting up the pheasant shoot and expanding the plantations, ordering thousands of new trees, including '2,200 English Oaks, 2,200 Birch, 2,200 Larch and 875 Scotch Firs'. Also this year, the first 'Abstract of Expenditure' at Endsleigh arrived and it made sobering reading for William Adam, laying out that between 2 February 1811 and 4 September 1813 a total of £21,741.18.4 had been spent.[304] With the house less than half finished, Adam could see that drastic reductions in expenditure would be needed in expenses elsewhere if the Endsleigh project was ever going to be finished.

Whether or not this looming economic problem was apparent to the duke and Adam that summer, on his return to Woburn the duke made a decision that took many by surprise: that summer's Sheep Shearing would be the last to be held at Woburn. As the *Monthly Review* reported: 'The Resolution of the present Duke of Bedford, respecting the discontinuance of the annual Sheep-Shearing festivity at Woburn, is the subject of deep regret with gentlemen-agriculturalists.' At the same time, it also published an anonymous satirical poem, 'Woburn Abbey Georgics; or, The Last-Gathering: A Poem in four Cantos'. Full of double entendres and in-jokes, the poem suggests that Georgina was responsible for the decision – 'Tis thus the lovely woman wills' – and imagines her saying to the duke,

> … On Monday! How I dread the hour –
> I wish this clod-pole meeting o'er,
> Of Farmer and of Grazier.
> Ah, Johnny! Thee it ill befits,
> Wool-gathering to send thy wits …
>
> It will not vex thy brother's ghost,
> Which, well I know, thou think'st of most,
> By saving all this senseless cost,
> On ram, and bull, and hog …

And, at the end of the final dinner all his guests will

> … smile, that he must drop the plan,
> Because he is – a married man.[305]

While it is entirely possible that Georgina helped persuade the duke to end the Sheep Shearings and 'all this senseless cost' may by now have been a consideration, it is also likely that the duke himself no longer felt justified in spending so much time and money every year on matters he was now less interested in. Equally, he will have been relieved to be free from the obligation to entertain hundreds of people, something he had never enjoyed, and whose dedication to agricultural improvement he no longer shared.

Whatever the reasons, it marks a decided shift in the duke's activities away from those inherited from his brother and towards horticulture and botany. Although Lady Shelley had portrayed the duke as languishing in a 'dearth of intellectual amusement', this actually marks the start of his truly productive period as he became deeply involved in original scientific research, reading extensively and committing ever increasing time and resources to establish Woburn as an important player in the rapidly expanding world of botanical and horticultural science; these interests lay at the heart of his activities for the rest of his life, and had an enormous influence on the way the pleasure grounds at Woburn developed in the years after Repton's work.

Altogether, this summer was not an easy one for the family, as Georgina suffered from ongoing problems related to a particularly difficult pregnancy, and Lady Jane had, as Trethewey reports, 'started to cough up blood and consumption was diagnosed … and in a bid to boost their health Georgina and her niece' joined the duke on the trip to the Isle of Wight. In early October, however, Georgina started to haemorrhage and then gave birth to a premature son, who died less than two days later; the duke, who had gone on ahead, described Georgina as 'much affected and very low' when she and her niece finally arrived back at Woburn. In spite of her own problems, Georgina's real concern was for Jane rather than for herself, and as soon as she returned to Woburn, she and the duke began to make plans for a trip to Portugal in an attempt to relieve Jane's symptoms. The duke was no doubt very aware that his mother had undertaken such a trip under very similar circumstances, and remembered the comfort and relief that it had given to his first wife, Georgiana, when her health was bad, and the decision was soon made.

While these plans were being put in place, the duke was able to witness an important milestone in Lord John's life when, having attained his majority, he was returned to Parliament as member for Tavistock (although he was abroad). Of the duke's three elder sons, Lord John was perhaps closest to his father and Georgina and the world of Woburn at this time, and it may have been in recognition of this that, two years later, the duke gave his son the idyllically picturesque new house at Hundreds Farm, which became Lord John's bolthole from London and the parliamentary sessions. It was here that he was able to build up his library, study and write, and has been described as 'the place in which his mind was formed'.[306]

Although at this time Lord John remained close to his family, the older boys, for different reasons, were more distant. The eldest, Francis, Marquis of Tavistock, had been at away at school when Georgina first arrived, but due to his position in the family as the duke's heir, he had a more proprietary attitude towards the Abbey. But for his mother's death, he might have been more involved in running the estates, and he clearly found it very hard not to resent its occupation by

Georgina's children. Perfectly suited to the role of rural aristocrat and landowner, he inherited the enthusiasm of his grandfather and uncle for fox hunting, but had no interest in politics; his life drifted indecisively as he waited patiently to inherit and he was plagued with ill health. Although he toyed with the idea of joining the army, he eventually followed his uncle Francis to Trinity College, Cambridge, in 1807, but was not a great scholar. By December that year, his tutor, Revd Greenwood, reported to his father, in the most tortuously diplomatic letter, that the marquis 'complains that he cannot fix his mind sufficiently upon any subject', but 'if your Grace would have the goodness to prevail upon him to favour me a little more with his company, and that regularly, I am sure it would eventually be for his advantage, as regularity itself would generate attention.'[307] Yet despite dropping out of lectures on Greek, maths and astronomy, he somehow graduated as a Master of Arts a year later, immediately married Anna Maria Stanhope and set up home at Oakley.

In 1809, when the marquis attained his majority, the duke returned his son to Parliament for the family's seat in Peterborough, but politics seems to have had no more appeal than university. A year later his father bemoaned that 'I fear the charms of fox-hunting are greater than Tavistock's political zeal,' and his wife confirmed that he 'has no ambition' for politics or serving in government.

Blakiston describes the marquis as 'a man of great integrity but not much warmth of heart', and quotes John Cam Hobhouse, who wrote, 'Lord Tavistock … is a good man, but not a happy man,' and once he was settled at Oakley, his 'favourite pursuits were hunting, racing and shooting'.[308] Although Francis always treated Georgina with respect and recognized her central role in his father's life and happiness, beyond their shared care for the duke, he and Georgina had nothing in common and the relationship was never warm or relaxed.

Lord George William, 'Billy', was eleven when his mother died, and consequently, like his younger brother John, remembered less of his mother and welcomed a new mother figure into his life. Georgina in turn became very fond of Billy, and their relationship was particularly close over the next six years until his military career took him away. Small in stature, he was bright but insecure, lacked any real self-awareness, and never came to terms with what he saw as the appalling injustice of being a second son to whom nothing came by right, all the wealth and properties forever just out of his reach. He later allowed his wife's disapproval of Georgina to poison their relationship, to the enduring exasperation of the duke. Describing him in 1817, Countess Granville wrote, 'Lord William Russell, with his demure look, is a gay deceiver.'[309]

Unlike his elder brother, William needed to make his own way in the world and, entering the army as a cornet in the Dragoons in 1806, served initially on his father's staff in Dublin, before being posted the next year to serve at the siege of Copenhagen. From here he went to Spain at the start of the Peninsula campaign, arriving in June 1809 and serving under General Wellesley at the Battle of Talavera in July. A few weeks later news reached the duke at Longleat that Lord William had been badly injured when his 23rd Dragoon Guards were part of an 'undisciplined' cavalry charge following the defeat of the initial French attack. The duke passed on details of William's injuries to Lord Grey: 'he had a narrow escape, poor fellow … he received a wound in one of the most desperate charges ever made … The squadron he commanded was almost entirely annihilated [and] men and horse were either killed or taken prisoners, himself and one man only escaped. One shot hit his eye, one his pouch, another went through his cloak, and a fourth (grapeshot) grazed his side, and carried away a part of his flesh. His horse was shot.'[310]

Lucky to be alive, and in spite of such serious injuries, William returned to Spain in 1811, where he served as an aide-de-camp to General Sir Thomas Graham, Lord Lyndoch (whose behaviour had so upset Lady Shelley), participating in the Battle of Barossa (Chiclana) in March that year, and after a period of leave during which he was elected to Parliament for Bedford, William returned to Spain for a third and final tour in 1813–14.[311] During this period, when his enthusiasm for politics to some extent made up for his older brother's lack of interest, William remained in close contact with his family, and he seems to have been particularly attracted to Georgina's niece Lady Jane Montagu, whom he described to Lord John as 'Beautiful as the morning sun – with a temper more heavenly sweet than ever was known. I never met her equal. But she is destined for a Duke at least.' Some kind of closeness between the two is hinted at by Jane in her January 1812 letter to the duke: 'I have enclosed a letter for William. Do not you have the same ideas as Grandmama. But if there is any impropriety in my having written to him, tell me, but I should think there was no greater than in my corresponding with John.'[312] If a relationship was on the cards, it was not able to withstand his return to Spain and her growing ill health.

There is no doubt that Georgina's relationship with both Lord William and Lord John was much warmer than that with Tavistock. John, nine years old when his mother died, had been born prematurely, and he remained a small and frail boy, growing to no more than 5 foot 4 inches. He was at Westminster along with Lord William when Georgina arrived, but she 'saw that he was physically unfit for the rigorous life of that public school' and ensured that he was brought back to Woburn to be tutored by Revd Cartwright. Along with Lord William he was a favourite at Holland House, and had thrived during his eleven-month journey in Spain with the Hollands, caught up in the complexities of diplomacy and strategic manoeuvrings that preceded the Peninsula campaign, and even found time to visit his brother William on the eve of the Battle of Talavera and to travel to Elba to meet with Napoleon. On his return, his father was keen to further his education and arranged for John to spend the next two years in Edinburgh. It was clear, however, that he was impatient to start his parliamentary career, and as soon as he turned twenty-one, after his father threw a lavish party for him at Richmond, complete with fireworks staged from barges in the river and the Duke of Gloucester's Band, he was duly returned for Tavistock in 1813.[313]

With the Marquis of Tavistock married, his brothers launched on their various careers, the building at Endsleigh finally underway, and the younger boys at school, the Bedfords left England on 7 November headed for Lisbon. Although the duchess was to become increasingly tied up with nursing Jane, the couple were hopeful her health would improve, and the duke recorded much of this trip in his 'Travel Diary'.

During this period we also see the friendship between the duke and Lady Holland start to develop through their letters to each other. His letters from Spain and Italy indicate the relaxed, flirtatious kind of friendship the duke established with several safely married women: my 'great favourites', as he called them. These included Lady Holland, Lady Frances Villiers, Lady Elizabeth Harcourt, Lady Louisa Sandwich and Lady Emily Cowper, with whom he connected largely through letters; they were entertained by his elaborate, courtly praise and provided a sympathetic ear when, although unfailingly loyal to Georgina, he would complain of being ignored by his wife or children, or was out of sorts with the world. 'Again and again, my dear Lady Holland, I must report that you are the best, the most admirable, and the most entertaining correspondent I have,' he writes in June 1814.[314] In turn, Georgina had male correspondents, such as Lord Holland and Lord Grey, to whom she would write under similar circumstances and in similar terms.

Reading the travel diary and the duke's and duchess's letters to friends, we are reminded of just how hazardous this journey was, as it had been some years before when he visited with Georgiana. From the moment they left Portsmouth, there was always a risk of running into the French navy in the Channel or the Bay of Biscay, and even in sight of Gibraltar and into the Mediterranean, privateers from North Africa, recently so active through the long years of the siege, were still a constant danger; once on shore, cholera, incubated by the crowded, unsanitary conditions on the Rock during the siege, remained a threat. In addition, once in Italy, there were still safety concerns, as Georgina reported to Lord Grey, 'We hear that the Hollands and many others are detained at Geneva, the accounts of the *Bandittis* are so formidable that they are afraid of proceeding.' Yet, in spite of all of the danger and disease, and travelling with Jane and three young children, there is no suggestion of abandoning the trip and returning home; indeed, Georgina (referring to the Hollands) goes on, 'But however, I still flatter myself with the hopes of passing the winter with them in Rome.'[315]

So it was that on 1 November 1813 the family left Algeciras, arriving in the Leghorn Roads in Italy ten days later. Following this, the duke reports, 'Jane was apparently very well during the whole of our voyage, but less so when we landed, and on the 4 December had a return of hemorrage [*sic*] more considerable than she had had before.'

After visiting Pisa, where they were 'highly gratified by the Cathedral, the Baptistry, the *falling tower*, and the Campo Santo', and Florence, where there were 'numerous interesting objects to be seen', on 20 December they finally reached Rome, where to their great relief, 'we were met on the road by Lord Holland, who conducted us to the Porto del Poplo, and thence to our lodging. Lady Jane was a good deal fatigued by the journey, and we were painfully convinced that her Disease was from the time of our leaving Leghorn evidently making fast progress.'

The Hollands had arrived in Rome just before the Bedfords, after running the gauntlet of the *banditti*, and the families, who were joined by Lord William and his cousin Orlando Bridgeman, settled down in their lodgings near the Piazza del Popolo at the foot of the Pincian Hill, ready to enjoy Rome. The duke records that Lord John 'had left us at Florence, to pay a visit to the Emperor Napoleon in his little island of Elba … and rejoined us again at Rome', no doubt full of stories. In spite of everything, Napoleon had retained a fascination for many people following his abdication and exile in April 1814, and inspired by Lord John's adventure, the duke and Lady Holland were also hoping to visit Napoleon themselves at some point. It is worth noting here that both the Hollands, and to some extent the duke, were all experienced Continental travellers who spoke Italian and knew Rome and Italy very well. Georgina, on the other hand, had not travelled widely in Europe when younger, and was very aware that, as with so much of her education, both her Italian and her knowledge of Italy were lacking compared to the others; always by her side at this time was her well-thumbed copy of the *Nouveau Dictionnaire de Poche François, Italien et Anglais*, one of her first purchases on landing in Leghorn. To some extent, as she dedicated herself to taking care of her increasingly unwell niece, she was also trying to catch up with the language and the excited conversations going on around her among seasoned travellers.

At this point the duke writes in his travel diary, 'As I wish only to note the different places we have been at on the Continent, with reference to Jane's health, marking the progress of her melancholy disease, I shall say nothing of the various interesting objects which engaged our attention at Rome.'[316] One such 'object' that we do know about, however, relates to their growing friendship with the sculptor Antonio Canova. On a visit to his studio the duke had been smitten by Canova's statue of the 'Three Graces', and seeing the group as a perfect focal point for his idea for a sculpture gallery at Woburn, he commissioned a version of it. For the duke the experience of actually meeting the sculptor face to face, of discussing a commission with a living artist, and of experiencing the atmosphere of the studio, the blocks of marble and the creative process was exciting, and one he was to actively pursue over the coming years as his focus and interest moved from old masters to contemporary artists. Trethewey captures the mood of these weeks in Rome: 'During their stay … the Duke and Duchess became friends with Canova. They enjoyed informal dinners together and one evening Georgina felt so relaxed and happy that she waltzed and danced with castanets in front of the sculptor.'[317]

Also in Rome at this time, and also friends with Canova, were Mrs Elizabeth Rawdon and her twenty-two-year-old daughter, Elizabeth (widely known as Bessy), and it is possible that the Bedfords met them at Canova's studio. The Rawdons – and particularly Bessy, who was a celebrated beauty – were leading lights in a diverse group of British expatriates, military and diplomatic families who drifted back and forth across Europe, equally at home at the court in Vienna, the salons of Paris or any number of spas, resorts and capital cities from Germany to Italy. The duke's brother, Lord William, became associated with this group after leaving England following his wife's death. It was a milieu, at once worldly and intensely self-centred, in which Bessy Rawdon thrived, her beauty, wit and cultured conversation creating a point of focus wherever she went. Young Lord William, facing the reality of Lady Jane's situation and the loss of another woman close to him, was drawn inexorably into the glamour and promise of the Rawdons' world.

In February 1815 Bonaparte escaped from Elba and returned triumphant to France; given the rapidly changing situation, the duke decided it was time to move, writing: 'The extraordinary political events which occurred about this time made it absolutely necessary that we should decide upon some plan for the summer.' Considering Naples a safer location for the family, they travelled there in early April, but the duke reports that 'poor Jane grew progressively weaker.'[318] By 1 June the situation had changed, and the duke writes: 'I left Naples for England with Wrio and Edward and Mr. Roy,' a move evidently prompted by the renewed fighting in France, which also meant they were forced to take the eastern route, up through Italy into the Tyrol, on to Stuttgart heading for Brussels via Cologne and Liege. By the time they left Stuttgart, events had come a head when, on 18 June 1815, Wellington brought about Napoleon's final defeat at Waterloo. The duke heard the news as they passed through Liege, where 'we met Bonaparte's Carriages and horses, the whole of his *Necessaire*, which had been taken by a Prussian officer at the Battle of Waterloo … I visited Waterloo, and went over the Field of Battle.' They finally reached England by 19 June, and arrived back in Woburn on 5 July amidst the ringing of the church bells 'upon the event of His grace's arrival at Woburn Abbey after an absence of 600 days. N.B. abroad', an event repeated the next day to celebrate the duke's forty-ninth birthday.[319]

Needless to say, the duke's sudden departure left Georgina with little Georgiana and Jane in a very difficult situation. With the situation in Naples growing increasingly tense, she too had decisions to make. It is not clear why the duke decided to accompany the boys home; he may have feared that the long-suffering tutor, Mr Roy, would not cope, or he may have received word from Adam that, after such a long absence, the duke needed to return as issues were arising at Endsleigh that needed his attention. Equally, as we have seen previously, he may simply not have been capable of supporting Georgina as Jane's death became imminent. As with Georgiana many years before, when there was illness in the family, he opted to absent himself.

Although newly preoccupied with Bessy Rawdon, Lord William's bond with Georgina was still strong, and it was he who duly arrived in Naples to help escort the ladies home. Arriving in late September in Genoa, the little party stopped for a few days, during which Jane finally and mercifully died. The duke's diary records the last days:

The accounts I had from the Duchess of her poor suffering patient … were every Mail worse … till her exhausted frame was actually worn out by it, and her sufferings were closed on the 27th September at Genoa – God rest her

Soul!, a purer spirit never went to Heaven – my poor wife who loved her with real warmth and Tenderness, and whose attentions to her were unremitting to the last, sent me word that as soon as her earthly remains were consigned to the grave, she should set out with William for England, by Paris, and on Friday the 13th Oct. I left London, with the intention of meeting them in Paris.[320]

At Endsleigh, although work on the house was by now largely complete, issues had arisen that needed to be addressed by the duke once he got home, particularly those related to access to the site and to water. In the first case, it seems to have been assumed that there was a public right of way across Richard Edgcumbe's land from the village to Endsleigh; this was hotly disputed and the duke had to come to an accommodation with the Edgcumbes. More seriously, part of the water supply for the stream that flowed from Milton over land leased to the Edgcumbes to enter the Dairy Dell at Endsleigh, and provided water for both the house and irrigation, had been diverted to other Edgcumbe fields, and it required letters and ominous legal threats from Adam to get it reinstated. Thus, in August the duke, accompanied by Adam, made a four-day visit to Endsleigh to see the house, resolve these outstanding issues and discuss the landscaping with Repton. Before leaving for the Continental trip the duke had authorized Adam to commission a report from Repton concerning the plantings along the driveway, the landscape around the house and possible improvements to lie of the land running down from the house to the river. After conducting his surveys and marking out features with the Endsleigh gardener Mr Forrester, Repton sent an informal report to Adam covering these items, which included tree pruning along the drive to open up existing views, and the replacement of Wyatville's 'bastion' retaining wall below the house with a 'broad grass terrace' in front of the house. This was to be created with a retaining wall curving round directly below the house and straight out along the slope to the west and ending at a terminal bastion in the middle distance, the view beyond it ending at the towering forms of the rock crags in Leigh Woods in the distance. This terrace would in turn be adorned with a flower garden, a conservatory and an arched pergola supporting climbing plants, along with gravelled walks.[321]

After sending the rather hasty report to Adam, on his return home Repton set about organizing his ideas and bulking them up into a proper 'Red Book for Endsleigh' (1814) with additional theoretical material, discussions of the flow of water in streams and rivers, what is and what is not picturesque, 'playthings' for children, and the value of children as a 'defence against the gloom of Solitude'. In addition, it contained design proposals for further improvements to the wider views from the house across the river and to the Dairy Dell, the site he had originally chosen for the house, which he still sought to turn into a 'romantic valley'. Although in his report he writes that the sheer 'Grandeur' of the landscape surrounding Endsleigh means that 'there is so little I can do', he nevertheless makes trying to improve these views central to the Red Book. Key to this attempt was his telling phrase 'frame maker', since he presented the ideas in an image which compressed the wide sweep of the landscape into a single viewpoint, an image he could then frame and treat as a picture. This, in turn, allowed him to tidy up the composition, and add features to the view that would mitigate the 'bleak situation' by creating new pastures for grazing cattle, a homely cottage with smoke drifting from its chimney, and a rustic seat in the form of a temple complete with waterfall on the far side of the river (see title page and Colour Plate 13).[322]

Although the Red Book was addressed to the duke in Spain, it is not clear whether he saw it until he returned home, but in the end, other than the work done in the Dairy Dell, almost nothing in it was used beyond what had already been covered in the report. In addition, invoices indicate that work on some aspects of the report, particularly the terrace wall in front of the house, had already started by the summer of 1814 when Repton submitted the Red Book.[323] There is no doubt that the duke and duchess knew exactly what they valued in the views from the new house, and Repton, for all his discussion of the picturesque, had never been to Scotland and did not appreciate that they thought the views did not need 'improvement'. This seems borne out by the fact that all work subsequently undertaken at Endsleigh in the 1830s was focused not on 'improving' the landscape but on providing more convenient access to it, embracing the natural landscape not as a picture but as a recreational resource, as Georgina had known it during her childhood. In this context, Stoddart's 1799 observation of work done by Jane at Kinrara around the farmhouse is very interesting: 'The neighbouring declivities are clothed with woods, among which she has opened several walks and drives.' Their purpose was to facilitate not just walking but also pony and pony cart rides through the woodland, and as such appear as a prototype for those developed at Endsleigh, and subsequently in the evergreen plantations at Woburn.

As that summer turned to autumn, after his return to Woburn the duke continued to pursue his new interest in shooting, spending time in September at Shugborough and Beaudesert in Staffordshire while, far away in Genoa, Georgina had been watching over the last hours of her niece Jane. After seeing her 'into her grave', Georgina finally set off for Paris to meet the duke. He duly arrived there on 16 October, reporting to Lady Holland that 'Paris is not what it was. France is not what it was,' and an exhausted Georgina arrived five days later. Once back in England, while they picked up the threads of family life, one enjoyable task that faced them was unpacking and sorting the cases of purchases made in Spain and Italy which were starting to arrive. As early as May, four cases from Leghorn arrived at Hamilton Place containing silver ornaments for Georgina, 'three unbound books with Prints and a tin case with valuable Prints' for the duke, and for Georgina's aunt Madelina and her husband, Charles Fsyche Palmer, '24 bottles of Liquors and a bottle of comfits' and '2 Alabaster vases'.

In June another shipment arrived, this time from Malaga, consisting of '2 Boxes of Clay Images and a box of Herbs'. The box of herbs was landed in Plymouth and sent on to Endsleigh, while the 'Clay Images' arrived at Woburn via the Port of London. John Docwra Parry records these figures at Woburn in 1831 in the south corridor, where a 'glass case contains a variety of clever figures, illustrating the costumes, sports and manners of Italy, Spain and Portugal'. These shipments were followed by forty-seven cases of antiquities and contemporary sculptures sent from Italy including, among other things, large marble Medici-style vases, a bust of Napoleon, marble figures, a pair of marble Apollo-figure candelabras, two large Alabaster Medici-style vases, a figure of Hebe in alabaster by Canova, an alabaster vase for 'la Signora Duchessa', and four alabaster urns for Lord John

Russell.[324] A number of these items were dispersed among the personal apartments at the Abbey, and others used as decorative elements in the newly refurbished Inner Library, South Drawing Room and South Corridor, but their arrival, along with the Canova commission, alerts us to the duke's new interest in collecting sculpture, which he shared with his son William. Perhaps it was something he had long had in mind, going back to the days of his visit to Sir Richard Worsley's house at Appuldurcombe on the Isle of Wight, but it is likely that the idea to create his own collection of antique and contemporary sculpture came into focus as he toured the cities and grand houses of Portugal, Spain and Italy. In addition to this, the experience of meeting Antonio Canova – to sit and discuss art with a contemporary master, to commission a work and to experience the atmosphere and industry of the working studio – all seem to have helped to open a new realm of possibilities for the duke to complement his growing interest in science and botany in a wider context that included art and culture; contemplating these matters over the winter of 1815–16, he chose a location and directed Wyatville to convert his brother's conservatory into a custom built sculpture gallery, to include at one end his brother's Temple of Liberty, and at the other a special 'temple' in which the *Three Graces* could be displayed once they arrived.

Amidst all this activity, family life started again at the Abbey, and the theatre reopened in late November for performances by 'Henry Jackman playing the Comedy of *Hit & Miss*', with nineteen seats given to the servants, followed by Jackman performing 'Dramatic Pieces by desire of The Lords Wriothesley and Edward Russell, *Agreeable Surprise, Killing no Murder* and *Beehive*'.[325] Finally, by the end of the month, Georgina discovered she was pregnant again.

In contrast to the extraordinary capital expenditure of the previous five years, 1816 was somewhat quieter, since building at Endsleigh was largely complete, but as the duke's range of interests began to expand, a number of new projects got underway at Woburn, and William Adam was becoming increasingly concerned. While his annual report for 1815 indicated that, due to the family being abroad for so long, household expenses at Woburn fell by £5,000, for 1816 Adam calculated that just finishing work on the interiors and on the grounds at Endsleigh and the alterations, decoration and 'furnishing of the new rooms at Woburn' would require expenditure of £57,000, which would leave a deficit of at least £2,000 in 1816: 'It is only therefore by reducing the expenditure that the income for the present year can be made equal to the expenditure, and every exertion consistent with the Duke's situation should be made to attain this reduction … If any diminution can be made in the Expenditure of the Household department it would certainly be most desirable.' After reviewing possible savings in the Household and the Extraordinary Works budgets, Adam ends by saying, 'His grace will consider what can be done to diminish the Drafts in matters not referable to any of the preceding heads. Of this I can form no opinion.'[326] It was, of course, Adam's job to be careful, but for the duke and duchess this was the time when a new vision of Woburn began to come into focus, and they were both determined to fulfil it. There is little to indicate that Adam's suggestions were acted upon, as designs for the new Sculpture Gallery, with its 'Temple of the Graces', began to take shape.

In the early months of 1816 there was a general concern about Georgina's health, as once again she was experiencing a very difficult pregnancy. In the end, a boy, Lord Henry Russell, was born safely in London on 17 August, but it left Georgina very unwell and she was not strong enough to travel to Endsleigh until the following May. While this may have been a holiday for their parents, William Roy, their redoubtable tutor, had drawn up 'Proposed' Regulations' for the 'Lords Russell', Charles and Francis, which involved rising at 7 a.m., breakfast followed by three and a half hours of lessons, alternating with play and meals, and bed by 7 p.m.[327]

Back at Woburn and in spite of Adam's warnings, as work on the Inner Library and the Drawing Room was being completed, the duke and duchess started that summer on the 'transformation' of the State Saloon and the 'redecoration' of the State Dining Room, neighbouring reception spaces at the heart of the Abbey's west wing. Work in the Saloon, 'the great room of the house', included new 'carved ornaments' for the window shutters, 'new stove grates for the fireplaces', new 'furniture, decorations and elaborate window dressings'. The draperies were made of 'a new blue silk woven with an "amure" ground and hand brocaded with alternating posies of stylised flowers and ears of wheat', the fabric also used

The west end of the Sculpture Gallery and the 'Temple of the Graces' in 1887. The inscription above the entrance is dedicated to 'the Daughters of Jove / From them flow all the decencies of life: / Without them nothing pleases ... / ... Those on whom they smile, / Great though they be, and beautiful, and wise / Shine forth with double lustre.'

to cover the walls. Work on this room continued until 1820, and the result was a luxurious and 'full-bodied Regency scheme of decoration'.[328] It represented a major statement by the Bedfords of their commitment to the status and legacy of the family.

In many ways, however, a further development at this time related to the duke and his gardener George Sinclair's scientific inquiries in the pleasure grounds best epitomizes the direction in which his interests were leading: the appearance of Sinclair's book *Hortus Gramineus Woburnensis*, published by the duke in 1816. A groundbreaking work in its own right in the range and accuracy of the data, it also illustrated perfectly the duke's inclusive interest in agricultural and botanical science, and his shared interest with Sinclair in horticultural science. Many years later, the leading botanist Sir William Hooker was to write of the book, 'seldom has it happened that a publication has appeared on any agricultural subject, comprising an equal portion of real science, joined to so much valuable practical information.' In addition, the fact that the grass garden had always been included as part of the pleasure grounds points up an interesting aspect of the duke's character. Although on one level this was a strictly scientific project, it had not been banished to the distant regions of the kitchen gardens or to Park Farm, as other such experiments had been. This one was undertaken in the midst of the pleasure grounds, forming part of the decorative displays, indicating that the duke also found aesthetic qualities in the endeavours of 'improvement'. Not only was the grass garden itself given a prominent place in the gardens, but further embellishment of the entrance gate by Wyatt as late as 1838 gave it a sense of permanence and grandeur matching the other additions to the gardens at the time.

Equally, instead of the data collected being presented as a simple pamphlet or published as an article, it was given pride of place in the duke's and other libraries in the form of a smart leather-bound volume, accompanied in the first edition by dried grass specimens and subsequently by beautifully painted images of the grasses – stems, flowers and seed heads. *Hortus Gramineus Woburnensis* was the first of a series of eleven such books the duke was to publish, covering all aspects of his collections and interests from grasses and trees to horticultural technology, sculpture, art and the family's history, placing the scientific discovery of the natural world alongside art and literature as he engaged in collaborative exploration of the world. Such collaboration lay at the heart of research at this time before professional specialization separated scientific endeavour into distinct disciplines later in the century. Sinclair acknowledges this, noting in turn the contributions of Humphry Davy, for his 'kind and liberal assistance in furnishing the simple chemical process, from which I derived the confidence to realize the idea', the duke, whom he credits with suggesting the idea, Thomas Greg Esq. of Coles for 'many valuable communications', James Sowerby Esq. for 'promoting the knowledge of different agricultural soils', Andrew Wilson, manager of Park Farm at Woburn, and Thomas

Gibbs, seedsman to the Board of Agriculture. For the duke, it is clear that promoting, funding and watching these experiments unfold gave him pleasure and a deep satisfaction, and as these programmes continued through the 1830s, he increasingly sought to integrate them into the fabric of the Abbey and its surroundings, to celebrate them beside all the other indicators of culture and beauty on display.

It is, perhaps, an indication of the quality and relevance of the research Sinclair was carrying out at Woburn at this time that the data he collected with Davy's help should later have been mentioned by Charles Darwin in his discussion of 'Divergence of Character' included in *Origin of the Species*, published in 1859. In this discussion, Darwin wrote, 'It has been experimentally proved, that if a plot of ground be sown with one species of grass, and a similar plot be sown with several distinct genera of grasses, a greater number of plants and a greater weight of dry herbage can be raised in the latter than in the former case.' This passing reference would clearly have given the duke enormous satisfaction and pleasure had it happened during his lifetime and had he known the contribution his efforts had made to this aspect of Darwin's work. It has recently been suggested, however, that the grass ground research can be seen in retrospect as 'the world's first ecological experiment', but it is less clear whether either the duke or Sinclair would have understood at the time the connection to what became the discipline of ecology, first defined in the 1860s, or indeed whether either could be said to have had such sensibilities or an 'ecological' awareness.

Indeed, even twenty years later, the duke, Hooker and Forbes showed few signs of such sensibilities. Writing to Hooker from The Doune in 1836, while noting the scale of wild plant collecting underway in the Highlands – 'The Sow of Atholl is now completely denuded of *Menziesia caerulea* by travelling Botanists' – the duke goes on to mention that he had been told of 'a hill within twenty miles of this place which abounded with [it]' that could be collected, and that 'My gardener brought me a large supply of *azalea procumbens* yesterday, but these you say Mr Murray does not want.'[329] Clearly, the denuding of the Sow of Atholl (particularly vulnerable given its proximity to Drumochter Pass) and the duke's activities at The Doune reflect the extent of the collecting that was going on, and indicate that there was still little awareness of the impact wild plant collecting on this scale would have on the fragile ecosystems of the Highlands. Vast quantities of plants were being taken for which, in the case of those collected for the duke, there was no immediate use.

While for the duke this was a time of activity and excitement, Georgina was once again suffering the effects of pregnancy and childbirth, and by the end of 1816 the duke reported to Lord Grey, 'The Duchess has been unwell for sometime past, and is now so weak in consequence of the starving system she has been condemned to, but she says she must trust wholly to me.' Nevertheless, the Greys, the Hollands and George Tierney were all due for the 1817 New Year festivities, and the duke airily assured Grey: 'There is plenty of room for as many of your children as you will bring.'[330] Although this was largely a seasonal social gathering, from the people invited one also gets the sense that the Whig grandees are working to bring the party together and use their patronage in the most effective way in the build-up to the election due in 1819. It is probably no coincidence that the duke had also just offered one of his Tavistock seats to John Peter Grant of Rothiemurchus (Elizabeth Grant's father) to occupy until one of his sons needed it. Grant was someone they judged would be a 'friend' in Parliament.

Politics aside, this year marks the first recorded performances in the Woburn 'Theatre' by members of the family, when, on 11 January, the playbill announced: 'This Theatre presents … the Juvenile Company of Performers lately arrived … who will perform … *The Watch-word* … a Melo-Drama now at the Theatre Royal, Drury Lane.' The cast included Lord Wriothesley Russell (thirteen), Lord Edward Russell (twelve), Lord Charles James Fox Russell (ten) and Lord Francis John Russell (nine), with the 'Price of Admission: Plenty of Applause to the Actors'. This first playbill catches the spirit of relaxed social interaction and communal fun that Georgina brought with her to Abbey life, reflecting the atmosphere of the Highland gatherings she had known from childhood.

Over the next few months Georgina's health continued to improve, and she was well enough at Easter to host the Hollands at Woburn, where the assembled guests and family put on 'a masquerade and tableaux in frames in the dress and attitude of pictures', but the visit also caused one of the occasional spats between these two forceful ladies when 'it reached the Duchess's ears that Lady Holland had complained about the noisiness of her room at Woburn.' While 'the Duke gently admonished Lady Holland, he also tells her " … The Duchess is very much amused with a joke of Lord Eynmouth. The world you know will have it, that you and the duchess have quarrelled, and about the foolish story of the room. Lord E calls it the Feuds of Elizabeth Queen of England and Mary Queen of Scots."'[331] The ability to be amused with each other's foibles lay at the heart of the relationship between the Bedfords and the Hollands, which, if anything, grew even closer when they became neighbours in Bedfordshire on Lord Holland inheriting Ampthill Park following the death of his maternal uncle John FitzPatrick, 2nd Earl of Upper Ossory, in February 1818.

Of much more consequence to life at Woburn, however, was the marriage on 24 June 1817 of Lord George William and Elizabeth 'Bessy' Rawdon. After meeting in Rome, their romance had blossomed as William became entranced by this popular, beautiful star of Europe's salons, and she was struck by the handsome, heroic soldier whose family seemed to offer the chance of a secure and comfortable future. She had lived with her parents on the Continent since the age of four and her father's retirement from active military service, and through his brother the Earl of Moira's connections, the young girl grew up to become the toast of the aristocratic, military and diplomatic circles of Vienna and Rome. Blakiston describes Bessy at various points as 'beautiful', 'clever', 'extremely intelligent', and as someone who developed a life-long passion for Austria and Italy as the zenith of European culture, while 'remaining all her life ignorant of English literature' and disdainful of English and Irish culture and society. Growing up in this rarefied atmosphere, Bessy was lionized, adored and confided in by those around her – august older figures from the worlds of politics, diplomacy, the military, art and culture, who invariably felt themselves to be in love with her. While on the surface the Rawdons led 'a life of comfort and amusement', in reality her young life was full of tension, anger and violence, as her father's alcoholism led to her mother keeping a diary in which she 'minutely detailed … the number of blows she received from her husband when drunk'. This darker side also informed the person Bessy became, who Blakiston also describes as 'selfish', 'arrogant' and capable, in turn, of 'uncompromising cruelty'.

Lady Holland, who knew Lord William as well as anyone, wrote: 'Married to a stronger character than Lord William … [his wife] might with her practical and intellectual gifts have succeeded … but unhappily her husband's indolence and want of self-confidence provoked her, and [she treated him with] contempt, harshness and lack of loving-kindness.' Inevitably, the marriage became increasingly unhappy, not just for Lord William but also for his family, because although, as Blakiston suggests, 'William appears to have loved [Georgina] dearly until his marriage, when his wife chose to find something almost improper in their relationship … taking his cue from his wife he saw only the faults of his step-mother, and his coldness to her became the subject of her reproaches, though her letters to him remained stubbornly affectionate in spite of the rebuffs she received from him.'[332]

Georgina and Bessy, it seems, clashed almost from the start, since, for all her intelligence, Bessy, perhaps sensing the vulnerabilities behind Georgina's social confidence, particularly related to her education, appears to have set out to compete with her mother-in-law, and to challenge her position both at Woburn and as William's confidante and friend. At the same time, she seems also to have resented Georgina's emotionally close relationships with her younger stepsons William and John and, indeed, with her own children, which Bessy was never able to replicate with those close to her or her children. In turn, Georgina felt the implied disrespect of her position as duchess very deeply; she had seen her mother treated this way, and was fierce in defence of what she had created. Whatever the reasons, over the years the feud simmered, occasionally erupting in behaviour that did neither of them credit, and which left the duke, who was unswervingly loyal to Georgina, struggling in the middle to maintain peace and any kind of relationship with the one son who shared so many of his interests.

The duke was initially upbeat about the marriage, dazzled no doubt, like so many others, by his new daughter-in-law: 'I have no doubt … with all the qualifications she has for rendering the marriage state happy, united to your own good sense and amiable feelings, I can have no fears on the subject.' He does, however, warn

William that 'you will not be rich, but with prudence and economy you will have *de quoi vivre*,' adding: 'you are careless and thoughtless in money matters, and this you must endeavour to correct. If you have any debts still unpaid, let me know, and I will discharge them before your marriage so that you may start clear.' He then invited the newlyweds to Woburn 'for as long as you please, and till you are ready to go abroad'. It was during this stay that Bessy wrote to Canova with news of the new temple at Woburn: 'Yet every day we talk of Canova, and in what part of the world is he not talked of? But chiefly here, in this spot, where the three goddesses are awaited and have a beautiful temple ready for them.'[333]

By July, although William invited Mrs Rawdon to Woburn to join them, her behaviour began to cause difficulties for the young couple. Since the marriage Mrs Rawdon had taken to her bed, and now wrote to Bessy asking her to return to London to look after her. William immediately responded to his mother-in-law: 'You allow me to marry your daughter & then you endeavour to seduce her away from me. Indeed I am obliged to watch her constantly to prevent her … going off to you.' He then asked her to 'conceal your feelings from her as much as you can. Telling them to her can do no earthly good, and it makes her very wretched … What is done cannot be undone … strive to see joy and happiness where you now only see gloom & misery.'[334]

Reading this letter, written barely a month after the marriage, indicates clearly the intense and unhealthy emotional relationship between mother and daughter, and sets the tone for his entire, ultimately miserable, marriage as his wife's behaviour came increasingly to replicate that of her mother.

In June the couple and her mother left Woburn to take up William's posting to Wellington's staff in Cambrai, and meeting them in Paris the Countess Granville commented: 'I have been interrupted by visits from Mrs Rawdon and Lady William Russell … [they] do nothing but sigh. This sounds brutal, but the fact is there is a great deal of affectation and selfishness in the sort of display of grief they never cease detailing to one. Lady William's turns chiefly on the dullness of Cambrai.' Two months later, meeting them again, she added: 'Lady William is very pretty, very pleasing; Lord William looks quiet and pleased, but a little small between his accomplished bride and *exigeante* mother-in-law, who talks all the time as if Lady William were dead – "From the time I lost my poor Bessy …" It is clear that Lord William will not love Mrs Rawdon.'[335]

While William and his new wife honeymooned at Woburn with her mother, the duke and Georgina, pregnant once again, had retreated to the peace and quiet of Endsleigh (Colour Plates 17 and 18). After all the difficulties entailed in creating it, the house now began to fulfil its role as a private retreat for them. Two important events, both the result of long negotiations, awaited the duke that summer, and both were causes of some celebration. In the first case, by May William Adam had finalized the lease for Wareham Wood from the Duchy of Cornwall: 'all impediment is removed to the proposed reversionary Grant of Wareham Wood to the Duke of Bedford,' a matter which had taken some very careful negotiation; the Bedfords were now able to take control of the woods facing the house across the river for the first time.

In the second case, the duke attended the opening of the canal and Morwell Down tunnel. Begun in 1810, the canal ran for four and a half miles from Tavistock Weir, across an aqueduct and through a long tunnel, to Morwellham Quay, and proved a crucial element in the subsequent development and economic prosperity of the Devon estate, first by providing a faster and cheaper way to bring goods from Morwellham to the Tavistock area, and second because copper ore was discovered during the process of cutting the tunnel. Following the opening of the mine to exploit this find, it is estimated that 'about 70,000 tons of copper ore [were] sold … at a value of about £500,000.' Given the fact that the Bedford estate owned both the land the canal was built on and the extraction rights on the copper ore that was subsequently mined and transported down it, the subsequent royalties, particularly as more mines opened during the 7th Duke's time, provided a considerable windfall. Work on the canal and the tunnel was completed in 1816, and it opened with great ceremony on 24 June 1817. The duke arrived that morning by river, the boat then being loaded on to a wagon which could be drawn up the hill to the canal, where he joined the ceremonial procession of boats along the new waterway.[336]

The benefits to the local community of having the family living locally for a few months of the year also became apparent in a number of smaller ways as the duke and duchess began to provide both patronage and financial support to local institutions; that summer we find them attending a meeting of subscribers to Tavistock Public Library, and a subscription for the duchess to the 'Tavistock Dorcas Society'. The duke also made arrangements at this time to ensure that he was in touch with local and national issues when at Endsleigh, taking out yearly subscriptions for the *Western Luminary* and its local competitor, Trewman's *Exeter Flying Post*, while, more immediately, the duchess also paid a year's subscription to the 'Tavistock Lying-in Society'; perhaps she had needed assistance while still at Endsleigh, but, in the event, the family was back at Woburn in time for the birth of Lord Cosmo in July.[337]

During their stay, some of the rooms at Endsleigh were still being fitted with furniture and bookcases, while outside work was being completed on the fountain and its 'circular moorstone basin' in the children's garden, the sundial was erected on Repton's grass terrace, and in the stable yard masons were 'fixing the Basin [on its Portland stone pedestal] and Lion's Head'. This arrangement is still in place, as is the engraved inscription quoted at the start of this chapter, which was carved and installed on the wall above the water basin two years later. Elsewhere on the grounds, in June further work was underway clearing stones and rubbish from the head of the Dairy Dell, probably related to securing the flow of water into the reservoir pond which fed the leats and stream, and in September some 150 apple and cherry trees were delivered.[338] Most of the activity, however, had moved away from the house itself to the wider estate, where the masons, thatchers and carpenters were engaged on other buildings for James Langley, the duke's farm manager.

The family was at Woburn for the New Year in 1818, and in a further sign of his changing priorities, the duke retired from local politics by withdrawing when challenged in the election for the lord lieutenancy of Bedfordshire, long an automatic Russell appointment, and endorsed the election of his challenger, Lord Grantham. At Woburn itself, the duke purchased 'Parts 2–4 imprint folio with portfolio Neale's Woburn Abbey', reflecting his growing interest in formally

J. P. Neale, engraved by W. Wallis, *Woburn Abbey*, *c*.1820. This view shows the staterooms of Holland's south front, the dining room and libraries, with Repton's narrow terrace running along in front. Hidden by the trees on the right are the duke and duchess's private apartments with Georgina's flower garden laid out in front of them. It was to be another decade before the ha-ha was filled in and the extended south terrace laid out.

memorializing the achievements of the family, and the collections at Woburn, in bound albums, an interest which later led him to commission the first detailed family history.

By 20 March, however, the family was on the move again as the duke, duchess and little girls travelled to Paris to be with William and Bessy, who was imminently expecting a baby. In late March, following concerns about Georgiana's and Louisa's health, the duchess returned briefly to England with the girls, before travelling back to Paris to be with Bessy, whose pregnancy was proving to be increasingly difficult. On 9 April the duke tells Lady Holland, 'we have been so much alarmed about poor Lady William … She was brought to bed at 8 o'clock this morning of a girl, but has since been so ill that we have been under the most serious apprehension for her life … The Dss has been with her.' However, a week later he is able to reassure her, 'I thank God that Lady William is now doing perfectly well … The Dss commends in the highest terms [the doctor's] skill … I understand he on his part says he really knows not what he should have done without the Dss's assistance. She never left Bessy for 24 hours.'[339] Unfortunately, after the long struggle, the baby, a daughter, died soon after birth, and two months later William and Bessy returned to England. This was also the time when Georgina discovered that she was pregnant yet again, and while she still felt fit and well, they decided to stay on in Paris before travelling to the south of France and Milan.

Before leaving, the Bedfords met up with the Duke of Wellington at Fontainebleu, and 'forming a *partie carrée* [a party of four persons] with the Duchess and Lady C. Greville, have been in a vortex of pleasure & amusement. The Duchess proposed to end it by giving a dinner to the Duke of W[ellington] at Versailles, & on asking for it, Louis le Gros Tyran said, *no, he* would give the dinner.'[340] It seems to have been a fun and carefree time, and this mood continued in the charming letters the duke and duchess sent to Louisa from various places on their trip. Written on colourfully illustrated French notepaper, they were in reply to letters written to them from the girls. The first letter in June reads:

My dear Louisa,

Many Thanks for your pretty letter and pray tell dear little Georgy that I thank her for hers … Your mama came back to me quite well – I hope to see you all at W.A. next month – Pray tell Georgy with my love, that I sent her a French purse, and I will send you one soon, if you have money to put in it. I send a thousand kisses to you both, and am your affectionate father,

    Bedford.

Pray give my love to Eliza and my compliments to Miss Hanson [the girls' governess].

Following this, they sent Louisa two playful letters wishing her a happy birthday, the first from Milan, in which the duke adds, 'I know you can write and spell very well with Miss Hanson now, but I am afraid you will not be able to read my bad writing – God bless you!, Your affectionate Father, BEDFORD,' to which Georgina has added, 'How do you do Mistress Pussy Cat? How are all your dolls, I hope they talk French with Mamselle Clarisse, et qu'elles sont très sage, from Mama.'

This is followed by a second undated letter from Calais, sending 'Happy returns' and noting, 'I send you a necklace like your sister's because you are now a great Girl, and seven yrs old. Be a good Child,' and a third: 'Ma chére Louise, Comment te porte tu? Nous aurons bientot le Plaisir de t'embrasser à Woburn Abbey – Adieu! soyez toujours sage – Your affectionate Father, Bedford. P.S. I have got a very pretty purse for you.'[341]

The Bedfords finally returned to Woburn on 1 August, having taken the time during their stay in Paris to buy furniture and fittings for the Abbey. It is also possible that they met the artist Louis Parez in Paris at this time, since in August 1818 he is recorded as 'Drawing Master for the Nursery' at Woburn, while also providing in September '20 lessons in Drawing' for Eliza Russell and '6 lessons in Drawing' for Wriothesley Russell, fifteen and fourteen respectively at the time.[342] Parez went on to become a valuable asset to the duke as an illustrator.

No sooner had the duke and Georgina returned to Woburn, however, than they set off at short notice for Edinburgh on a visit that would change their lives, and which may have represented the realization of the 'project' Georgina had so long 'had in mind'. Although the lawyers were still sorting out the details in December, it would seem that on this trip the Bedfords made the decision to take a lease on Invereshie House in Badenoch and the associated shooting rights in the Forest of Feshie from George Macpherson-Grant of Ballindalloch (Colour Plate 34). For many of their friends this must have seemed a strange decision, especially given the opportunities they had to shoot at Woburn and any number of other estates in England, but there is no doubt that the reasons behind it were complex, and as the years went by, with the exception of their sons as they grew up, it became clear that access to the moors for shooting played a secondary role to much deeper emotional and personal motives.

From the start, the Bedfords looked forward to using Invereshie as a home from home, and, as at Endsleigh, they wanted it as another alternative private world they could occupy with their family and pursue their personal interests away from Woburn Abbey and their formal life. For the duke, Scotland represented the promise of an intriguing new world of wonders to discover, a place he could raise new and different livestock, discover new wildlife, plants and trees, sit peacefully in his library among his books on Scottish history, Highland flora and fauna, folklore, superstitions and the supernatural, and, in addition, watch his wife, whom he had only really known in the context of the London season and the provincial societies of rural Bedfordshire and Devonshire, thrive among the people and the places she had known before her marriage.

For the duchess, she could finally relax again among people who knew her and her family, no longer an oddity. It was an opportunity for her to pick up the threads of her own life, enjoy again the landscapes and the rich dialect of the Highlands, and have the opportunity to introduce them to her own children. Endsleigh had much to offer, but now she was once again in a place which Devon could only, at best, remind her of. As her mother had done, she went on to enjoy hosting large parties of friends and guests, and exploring the mountains with them, but, also like her mother, most of her time in Scotland was in fact spent either alone or with just those closest to her, thriving in 'the calm and cool air' and 'the soft and tranquil shade of a Highland cottage'. Over the nineteen years the duke was to visit, and the thirty years the duchess was able to, their stays steadily extended from four to five weeks in late August and early September to over three or four months, way beyond the 'season', often only arriving back at Woburn just in time for Christmas. And it seems only appropriate, given how much the area came to mean to the duke, that it would be where he died, amidst his books and the glories of a Highland autumn.

Before returning to Woburn in September, perhaps to mark the occasion, the duke bought himself 'a Cairngorm Seal handle, and fitting for Seal stone, both in fine Gold', and Georgina purchased '4 yds broad 42nd Plaid Satin ribbon' and '4 yds broad 42nd Tartan satin ribbon', in celebration of the 42nd Highland Regiment of

Foot, which was more widely known as the 'Black Watch', and was the regiment in which her brother the Marquis of Huntly was currently serving.[343]

Invereshie House stands to this day in an elevated position above the river Feshie as it nears its junction with the river Spey. In 1818 the land of the Invereshie estate stretched away to the south on both sides of the river Feshie watershed, up to the Cairngorm massif on the east and to Glentromie on the west. On the east side of Glen Feshie, the estate lands surrounded an outlier of the Mackintosh estates, and to the south the boundary ran along the ridgeline bordering the Duke of Atholl's lands. Macpherson-Grant had completed his control of the Feshie watershed when he bought the Forest of Feshie in 1815 from the Duke of Gordon, land his estate had previously only leased and which comprised the south-east portion of the glen.

While much of the land in Badenoch was originally part of the enormous Gordon estates – and suffering from the lack of investment and development we noticed under Georgina's father – by contrast, when the Bedfords arrived in 1818, the Invereshie estate was in a much better condition. Bought from the Duke of Gordon as early as 1637 by the Macpherson family, through the late eighteenth and early nineteenth centuries it had benefited from the management of George Macpherson and his son, Captain John Macpherson. George Macpherson, 'driven by the desire to preserve the estate both intact and in credit', had secured its long-term stability by offering nineteen-year improving leases to every tenant from as early as 1734, carefully tailoring the improvement demands of each lease to the circumstances of the farm itself and what needed to be done there, and he had further guaranteed the general welfare of the estate by calling on traditional feudal labour services from his tenants for larger estate-wide projects, maintaining and developing the essential infrastructure such as buildings, roads, bridges and flood defences along both the Feshie and the Spey.

Although the estate was never totally 'cleared' of the tenant population, 'improvement' by way of the consolidation of small farms into larger units had inevitably caused social upheaval, but 'significantly … all tenants held their own land directly from the landowner with security of tenure and moderate rents –

far superior to their sub-tenant neighbours on the Gordon lands'; in these ways Macpherson and son had 'transformed the estate'.[344] From 1812 the estate had been inherited by Captain John's son, George Macpherson, who in 1806, on the death of his great-uncle General James Grant of Ballindalloch, also inherited the Ballindalloch estates, changing his name to Macpherson-Grant and moving with his wife from Invereshie to Ballindalloch Castle. The Invereshie estate had leased the Forest of Feshie since the mid-eighteenth century to provide some game shooting but also, more crucially, summer grazing lands for Invereshie tenants in Badenoch. When the lease was due for renewal in 1812, the cash-strapped Gordon estates, seeking a more lucrative deal, advertised it in the *Inverness Courier* as the 'forest of Glenfeshie consisting of 13,706 acres … either for a summer grazing to black cattle or for a shooting ground to a sportsman who might wish to preserve the tract for deer, moor game and ptarmigan, all of which abound in the adjoining hills and with which it would be abundantly stocked in a very short time, if carefully kept for this purpose'. A lack of interest, caused partly by the lack of farm or residential buildings anywhere in the forest as a base for either enterprise, meant that in the end the Macpherson-Grant lease was renewed, though at almost twice the rent. Given this, it made economic sense for Macpherson-Grant to buy the property when the opportunity arose three years later.

Although the farm at Invereshie and the fields around it continued to function as part of Macpherson-Grant's wider estates, once he left for Ballindalloch, the house had no real purpose until the decision was made in 1818 to combine it with the recently purchased Forest of Feshie and lease them together as a sporting estate, at this time primarily for grouse shooting. As such, it formed one of the two or three earliest such estates in the area following the Duke of Gordon's lease in 1784 of 'Dalenlongart … to Robert Dundas, for the sport and "a spot to build a shooting hutt [*sic*] upon" on Loch Ericht'. At Invereshie, to ready it for leasing in 1806 when Macpherson-Grant left for Ballindalloch, extensive refurbishments were undertaken on the main house, gardener's house and stables, a new driveway was laid down, the ground in front of the house was levelled and tidied up, new plantations were laid out and stretches of the flood dykes were repaired.[345]

The impact on the communities in Badenoch of sporting estates leased for seasonal use to non-resident sportsmen is complex and represents one of a series of episodes in the ongoing transformation of the area during the eighteenth and early nineteenth centuries. As David Taylor tells us, the geography of the Spey valley in Badenoch and the glens of its watershed, lacking large areas of open, workable farmland, had led to the development of an 'indigenous agricultural system' that was 'dependent on pastoralism and transhumance'. Thus, the 'eighteenth-century Badenoch farm was a closely integrated eco-system, generally running in a narrow strip from the river to the distant mountain top'. While far from perfect, this vertical system provided access for subsistence farming families to 'the essentials of self-sufficiency: the riverside for hay meadows and winter pasture … the lower slopes for arable and grass … the moorlands for grazing, peat, turf and heather [and] the higher mountains for shielings', the location used during the summer grazing of cattle.[346]

Access to both summer and winter grazing was the key to enabling this degree of self-sufficiency, and the loss of either one of these elements made it impossible. As the opening up of the Highlands in the post-Culloden era led to development and change, and economic pressure grew on landlords to 'improve' their tenant farms, the creation of 'sheep walks', which ranged right across the moors from the 1770s onwards, and the deer forests which followed from the 1830s, spelt the end of this traditional system by eliminating the traditional vertical boundaries. Although local landlords such as the Duke of Gordon and Macpherson-Grant resisted wholesale clearance of tenants from the hills to make room for sheep, widespread social dislocation was inevitable as the vertical system of access broke down and was replaced by barely viable small farms. By 1818, the subsequent breakdown of the traditional communities, already susceptible to cyclical crop failures and famine, was thus well underway and had led many from those communities to follow the example of those mentioned in the following letter of 1807: 'Unfortunate Jas. Macpherson … taking his last farewell of Badenoch I am told, he went straight to Greenock and is bound to America,' while 'Alex Campbell is … going to America along with George Macpherson's family, but

I hear of none else … I am sorry to inform you that the old ground is growing worse every day since you left the country.'[347]

Emigration from Badenoch, particularly to Canada, by individuals and whole families had become a regular occurrence and continued well into the second half of the nineteenth century, and it was into this steadily evolving world, fortunately one spared some of the trauma and dislocation of forced clearances elsewhere, that the Bedfords arrived in 1818. For the Invereshie tenants in Glen Feshie, however, these developments had serious consequences. Initially, seasonal grouse shooting in the forest had co-existed with summer grazing rights, but once shooting took priority, the presence of sheep or cattle grazing on these moors throughout the summer led to increasing conflicts between the farming tenants and the sportsmen. Inevitably, the more lucrative shooting leases soon took precedence over the farmers, who were then totally excluded from the moors once the sporting emphasis switched from game birds to deer stalking during the 1830s.

Although the details are not clear, it seems likely that, besides the main house, the duke's Invereshie lease included the access road which ran from the Feshiebridge road, past Invereshie Mill, before dog-legging round the walled kitchen gardens to the house, and that the land extended to include the woodland plantations around the perimeter of the site, enclosing land to the extent of about 19.42 ha/48 acres. This consisted of a large open area in front of the house, which became the 'Duke's Park' of c.6.43 ha/15.89 acres, a large field surrounded by woodland, and a smaller pasture beside the walled garden, while other buildings included the gardener's house, stables, barns and sheds.[348] Although the lease was signed and the property handed over in 1818, for various reasons it was not to be until 1821 that the family paid their first visit.

This eventful year drew to a close with a grand shoot at Woburn, at which they were joined by the Duke of York, something he seems to have enjoyed so much that it became an annual event for the next few years. Yet, while the duke was subsequently at particular pains 'to bring the preservation of game on his estate to perfection' for such occasions, Blakiston tells us he 'did not enjoy the great organised *battues*, infinitely preferring to take his gun and wander along the hedgerows by himself'; Lord William wrote in 1825 that 'now I never saw him do otherwise than retire from the contest, & shoot the stray game that went back to him.'[349] This suggests that the duke increasingly preferred a quiet shoot on his own, and in Scotland as time went by he came to value the experience of being out on the moors looking as much for interesting plants as birds to shoot.

As 1818 drew to an end, one other individual who was to prove of great significance to the duke's ambitions arrived at the Abbey. Jeremiah Wiffen was the son of a Quaker ironmonger from Woburn, who at fourteen had been apprenticed in Yorkshire as a schoolmaster. In 1811, aged nineteen, he returned to Woburn to found a school in Leighton Street, where he also started writing and publishing poetry, and the same year he travelled with his brother to visit Southey and Wordsworth in the Lake District. It is hardly surprising that this bright young teacher and poet soon attracted the duchess's attention, and in November 1818 she engaged Wiffen as a tutor for Edward and Francis. By February 1819 his duties had expanded to include the other children as he became 'Writing Master of the Nursery' and gave lessons to Wriothesley and Charles.[350] Wiffen clearly thrived at Woburn and over the next few years, as the boys grew up and began to leave home, he started to work with the duke on other projects, bringing some organization to the enormous collection of family papers that had been stored in the vaults at Woburn and the Bedford estate office in London. During this period, the duke, perhaps aware for the first time of the extent and significance of this archive beyond matters of estate management, conceived the idea of having Wiffen research the material and write up the first history of the family. To this end, in 1821 Wiffen was formally appointed the duke's librarian, and established himself in the vaults below the west wing. Although working largely out of sight, Wiffen became, along with Sinclair and then Forbes, the duke's constant companion, as well as his secretary and author of the *Memoirs of the Russell Family*, published by the duke in 1833.

PART FOUR
ENGAGING WITH WONDER

CHAPTER SEVEN
1819–1824

ON 5 JANUARY 1819 the duke reported to Lady Holland: 'The Dss was very [unwell] last night on account of a tormenting headache ... God bless her!' He might have added that Georgina was in fact reaching the end of another difficult pregnancy. Although the family had welcomed the Greys to Woburn Abbey over the New Year, Georgina was by now exhausted and she travelled to Brighton to recuperate; it was here that the baby was born, only to die a month or so later at Woburn having never gained strength: her second baby boy to die young. Also that month, after losing their youngest, the duke and duchess 'lost' Edward, who became the first of the children to leave home when he joined the navy as a midshipman, aged fourteen.[351]

Early in the year the duke was 'confined to the house' on doctor's orders, but he remained busy at Woburn. The Sculpture Gallery and 'Temple of the Graces' had been completed, and they were now awaiting the arrival of the figures and Canova, who was to install them in person. Throughout 1819 work also continued in the gardens, where a new greenhouse (now the Camellia House) was added, linked to the east end of the Sculpture Gallery; outside, work was done on the west end of the 'Greenhouse Pond' beyond. In front of the Sculpture Gallery, the gardeners were set the task of creating a new parterre garden 'to the Duchess's designs', an early indication of Georgina's growing interest in the design of the flower gardens, and which led the following year to the creation of 'Her Grace's Garden', a private space set in front of their private apartments.[352] In another interesting development, this year they were also 'preparing stonework for the entrance to the Grass Ground', creating a decorative setting for the test plots Sinclair had spent so long monitoring, and marking the beginning of the process by which the duke sought to integrate this scientific endeavour into the wider decorative scheme of the pleasure grounds, combining science and art to demonstrate his developing sense of the integrated nature of the natural world.

Early that summer, the duke and duchess were in London for the first of three or four years' intense participation in London's social season, before travelling down to Endsleigh.[353] Once there, they were both eager to continue bringing their ideas to life as they moved on from landscape gardening to embracing the 'natural and picturesque qualities' of this wild, romantic landscape. They did not want to simply sit and look at the view from the house; they intended to explore it, and it was to be a productive summer. Now that Wareham Wood had been secured and they had control of the entire sweep of the middle-distance views, when meeting with Wyatville in August they were looking for ways to make the landscape more accessible to the family. Attention was turned initially on the single most picturesque aspect of these views: the large outcropping of rocks in Leigh Woods on which Repton had focused the view down his grass terrace. Wyatville had already added the Rock Seat at the foot of the rocks, and they now sought to integrate this with other features at the top of the hill above the rocks and below beside the river. To this end, part of their discussions this summer concerned the construction of a decorative Alpine-style chalet, the 'Swiss Cottage', above the rocks, which would have wide views out across the Tamar; Wyatville submitted plans later that year, and work began on the structure in January 1820. To illustrate the overall plan, Wyatville produced a pencil drawing of the river below the woods showing the Rock Seat among the trees half-way up, the outcrop of rock above this, and the Swiss Cottage as it would look on the crest of the hill.[354]

A steep flight of stone steps was then added, zigzagging their way down through the trees and past the rock face and linking the cottage to the seat below. From here, people could turn right and make their way round the track across the hillside to the driveway, or to go the end of the grass terrace and so to the house. Alternatively, they could turn left and make their way gently down through the woods to the river, or carry straight on down a further flight of steps directly to the river below, where other recreational features were to be created. Although out of use for a very long time, parts of these flights of steps still survive in places under layers of leaf mould and confirm the route down from the cottage to the river.

BELOW Jeffry Wyatville, *Swiss Cottage and Seat in Leigh Woods from the Tamar*, 1819. Wyatville's study for the developments in Leigh Woods at Endsleigh, seen from the river. It would seem that Georgina and, perhaps, Eliza Russell were producing sketches of their own. Visible in the woods beyond are the Rock Seat halfway up (left of centre) and the Swiss Cottage on top. The zigzag steps led from the cottage to the river below.

OPPOSITE F. C. Lewis, 'From a Seat under the Rock', *Views of the Tamar Valley*, 1823. Lewis's image shows the view from the Rock Seat at Endsleigh, looking back across the valley towards the house, which is at a similar elevation above the river. Nothing remains of this structure.

By August work had begun on the new riverside features, when Samuel Chubb (miner) began 'Blowing Rock in making the Cold Bath in the Tamar on the side of the Leigh Woods and taking out some Rocks where the Fly Bridge crosses'; by the end of year, the carpenters had billed for work 'at the Fly Bridge'. Unfortunately, there are no surviving images of either feature, and their exact sites have been lost.[355] Although these sites have been lost, a new route from the house directly down to the bend in the river was laid out around this time, running down the slope through a new plantation called the 'Georgy', completing the networks of paths and tracks designed to provide access to and from the house and all the new features. While Repton had suggested a bridge to access Wareham Wood directly below the house, the location of the Fly Bridge, further downstream, enabled this access to be combined with that from the Swiss Cottage and the Rock Seat, linking the various paths together. To the east, about a half mile upstream towards

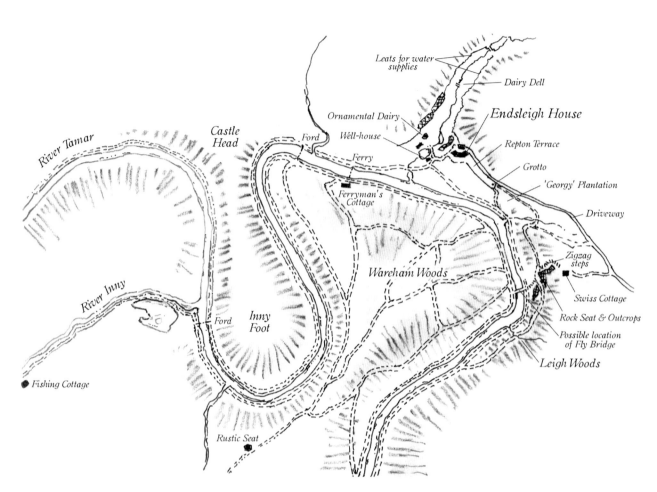

Plan of Endsleigh grounds, 1819, with the location of the features added to the landscape by Wyatville. Before the growth of trees in Wareham Wood, the Rustic Seat, the Rock Seat and the house would all have been visible from each other and at much the same elevation.

Castle Head, access across the river was, and still is, provided by a ford, but at this point the river is out of sight and distant from the house. So a new ferry point nearer the house was established to provide more convenient access to the wood, which also linked up with the paths from the house and the Dairy Dell.

From either the Fly Bridge or the new ferry point, paths then led uphill through Wareham Wood, climbing steadily until they came to a dramatic viewing point almost 49 metres/160 feet above the river as it twisted its way round the foot of the Dunterue Wood promontory. From the top of the sheer rock cliffs above the river the view opens up across Innyfoot, past Cartha Martha Rocks and out towards the Cornish moors beyond, and it was here, a year later, that Wyatville placed his picturesque 'Rustic Seat', an octagonal seat with a thatched roof that overlooked the view, a spectacular and unexpected climax to a walk or ride up through the woods. Finally, to complete the overall design, Wyatville provided a series of suggestions for an eye-catching castle ruin to be built on Castle Head; while this was not built, two years later, in 1822, a new cottage was built in the woods just uphill from the new ferry point, the 'Cottage in Wareham Wood', known later as the 'Ferryman's Cottage', to provide accommodation for the ferryman, stables for the children's ponies, and a sty for the pigs kept to exploit the pannage in the woodland. It is not clear if this was also a Wyatville design, and there are no surviving plans or sketches for the cottage, but a late nineteenth-century photograph and the remains visible today suggest that it was essentially an enormous chimney which rose from a thatched, conical roof covering a modest – perhaps one up and one down – dwelling set among a series of outbuildings. The chimney, which is still standing to full height, complete with its pots (identical to those on the house), helps to provide the key to understanding this strange little building, since it was carefully positioned to be clearly visible from the duke and duchess's apartments on the west end of the house (Colour Plate 19). Also, quite apart from operating the ferry and looking after the ponies and pigs, the other main duty of the occupant was to light the fires in the cottage just before the family arrived and keep them burning during their stay, so that, in a nod to Repton's original idea, the smoke could be seen rising up through the trees, providing a homely sight from the house. It is said that this arrangement remained in place until the estate was sold in 1956.

Looking at these developments and the reasons behind them, it is clear that this was an imaginative and well-thought-out plan, but its true subtleties only emerge when it is recognized that, before the trees grew to their present heights, the main components – Endsleigh House, the Rock Seat and the Rustic Seat – were all visible, more or less at eye level, to and from each other. This arrangement provided a visual connection, and with it a sense of intimacy, across an otherwise wild and expansive landscape, which helped to unify the house and its setting, and illustrates the unique opportunities that this site offered.[356]

Excited by all the developments at Endsleigh, and also looking forward to a planned visit to Vienna, the Bedfords returned to Woburn in late August, where Lord William and Bessy had become frequent visitors. Following their marriage, the couple had taken a small house in Curzon Street in London; from here they liked to visit Woburn, in spite of Bessy considering it 'the *gloomy* Abbey', while William, living on half-pay from the army, first began to attend Parliament as a member for Bedford. Although elected to the post as long ago as 1799, his military career and travels in Europe had intervened, and it was only now that he began to attend, joining Lord John and drawn partly by his brother's new interest in parliamentary reform. Meanwhile, Bessy was pregnant again, and in October gave birth to a baby boy named Hastings, an event which began what Blakiston describes as 'perhaps the happiest year of [their] marriage'. By this time, the Bedfords had left for the Continent, and we catch sight of them when their path crossed with that of Elizabeth Grant and her parents, who were in Liège that October and recorded the meeting: 'the Duke and Duchess of Bedford on their way to one of the German Spas for his health, without any of their children, but with Upper Servants and Under Servants, and their Doctor, good Mr Wolridge. I had gone up to my Mother and did not see them, but the rest were glad to meet – at least there was great chattering.'[357]

Yet, for all the good news, a letter at this time suggests the difficulties which seem always to have been a part of the duke's relationship with William, who, in spite of sharing so many of his father's interests, was often outspoken about perceived faults in his father's behaviour. This was partly the result of the ever-present sense Georgiana's boys had that their father put them second to his new wife and her children, and partly because William in particular always thought more was owed to him as a duke's son than was forthcoming – that, at the very least, a London residence at a smart address and a house in the country should have been provided (a feeling encouraged by his wife). For him, rooms being made available at Woburn, for example, were no substitute for Tavistock's estate at Oakley

PLATE 20: Jeffry Wyatville, 'Entrance for the Grass Ground'. Completed in 1820, the new entrance reflected the duke's determination to integrate this scientific endeavour with the aesthetic experience of the pleasure grounds enjoyed by both family and visitors. The covered entrance way and the name 'Hortus Gramineus' above the decorative iron gate, complemented by a bench seat on either side and beds of roses planted in front of the hedge, all suggest that something important and interesting lay within.

PLATE 21: W. H. Taylor, *The Menagerie, Woburn Abbey*. This is a coloured version of *Hortus Woburnensis*, Plate X, executed in the 1850s. By this time, with the roofed rustic 'seat' overlooking the small pond, the rows of wire cages running round the perimeter fence, the keeper's cottage on either side of the central aviary, and the colourful birds, Repton's Menagerie had become one of the family's favourite places in the gardens.

PLATE 22: Charlotte Augusta Sneyd, *Panorama of Almack's*, 1821–22. Charlotte Sneyd's remarkable panorama of the 'seventh heaven of the fashionable world' – shows more than 150 figures, a composite of attendees over a summer season, and catches for us one of the evenings attended by Georgina, in the pink top (123), with Eliza Russell behind her (124), seen here forming a group with Marchioness Conyngham, with pink wrap over her arm (121), Elizabeth Conyngham (122) and Frederic Seymour, holding his hat (125).

PLATE 23: Jeffry Wyatville, Bedford Lodge, Campden Hill, south front, design for new offices, 1823. Having leased the house for three years, the duke bought it in 1823 and immediately asked Wyatville to draw up plans to add new offices and staff quarters on the right-hand side. This house was situated beside Holland House and Park, with long views from these south-facing windows to the Surrey hills, and Georgina occupied it when in London until her death.

PLATE 24: Edwin Landseer, *Scene on the River Tilt*, 1824. The year marks Landseer's first visit to Scotland, and the first time he met and spent time with the Bedfords there. The image is set in the grounds of Forest Lodge, Glen Tilt, on the Duke of Atholl's estate, and is significant since it appears to be Landseer's first painting to feature a completed landscape. Waiting for the meal to cook are (left–right) Francis (sixteen), Louisa (twelve), Cosmo (seven) and Georgiana (fourteen).

PLATE 25: Edwin Landseer, *Lord Cosmo Russell on his Pony Fingal*, 1824. It is likely that the rider and horse were painted at Woburn and the moody Highland landscape was added later.

PLATE 26: Edwin Landseer, untitled, known as *Fishing Scene, Endsleigh*, *c*.1824–6. This little painting shows a boy (possibly Cosmo) fishing on the Tamar, the view looking upstream towards Leigh Woods where the Swiss Cottage emerges from the trees at the top of the slope. The chimneys and roof of Endsleigh House are just visible emerging from the trees in the upper left. The picture was important enough to Georgina to be among her possessions when she died in Nice.

PLATE 27: Edwin Landseer, *Shooting Party at Woburn Abbey*, 1828. The figures are identified by Lord William Russell as, left to right, Lord Spencer and the duke (white hat) on horses, Mr Chester, Francis Russell (cigar and whiskers), Lord Jersey, Hon. John Talbot (tall figure), the duke's sons John and Charles (the latter with his arm around John Shelley of Maresfield). Francis was the son of old Lord William.

PLATE 28: Edwin Landseer, *A Scene in the Highlands*, *c*. 1825–8. This picture shows Georgina with her youngest son, Alexander, who has been fishing, meeting up with her brother, the Duke of Gordon, who has been shooting with his ghillie. Once again, the figures are set in a Highland background, but this has the added interest of being Landseer's earliest painting of Glen Feshie, the huts at Ruigh Fionntaig being visible beside the river in the distance.

PLATE 29: Garden room in the new kitchen gardens, interior looking north, 1827, a reconstruction based on William Atkinson's coloured drawings and photographs of the surviving decoration on the ceiling. In this picture we see the green serpentine chimney piece round the fireplace, the china cupboards on either side of it and the decorative oak flooring.

PLATE 30: Garden room, looking south. This image shows the view over the walled kitchen gardens, with the rows of fruit trees shown on plans and, on the horizon, the gap in the trees which marks the point where the 'Gallop' reaches the end of the pleasure grounds. The blue glass in the doors survives, as do the window shutters and parts of the ceiling, but the fireplace, cupboards, floor and pictures are all gone.

PLATE 31: The Doune today. On the right is the 'old' wing dating back to the late seventeenth century, and rising immediately behind it is the tree-clad 'dun', or fortified mound, which gives the house its name. On the left is the 'new' wing that was completed c.1821, showing the duke's study on the ground floor nearest the camera and the bay windows of the dining room beyond it and drawing room above.

PLATE 32: Sir George Hayter (1792–1871), *Portrait de 6ième Duc de Bedford*, *c*.1830. Hayter's sympathetic portrait of the duke was possibly commissioned to mark his appointment as Knight of the Garter by Lord Grey in 1830; the insignia is pinned to his jacket. The French title of this version suggests that it may have been another of the works that Georgina had with her in Nice in the last years of her life.

PLATE 33: Edwin Landseer, *Georgina, Duchess of Bedford*, 1830. The portrait shows Georgina in her prime. Although the painting is unfinished, the artist still has been able to capture in the dignified, confident pose much of her character.

OVERLEAF PLATE 34: Map of Badenoch and Atholl, 1820–40, showing land ownership on either side of the River Feshie, the deer forests associated with the houses the Russells leased, the relationship of Glen Feshie to the Atholl estate, and the route taken from The Doune to Loch Avon in 1833.

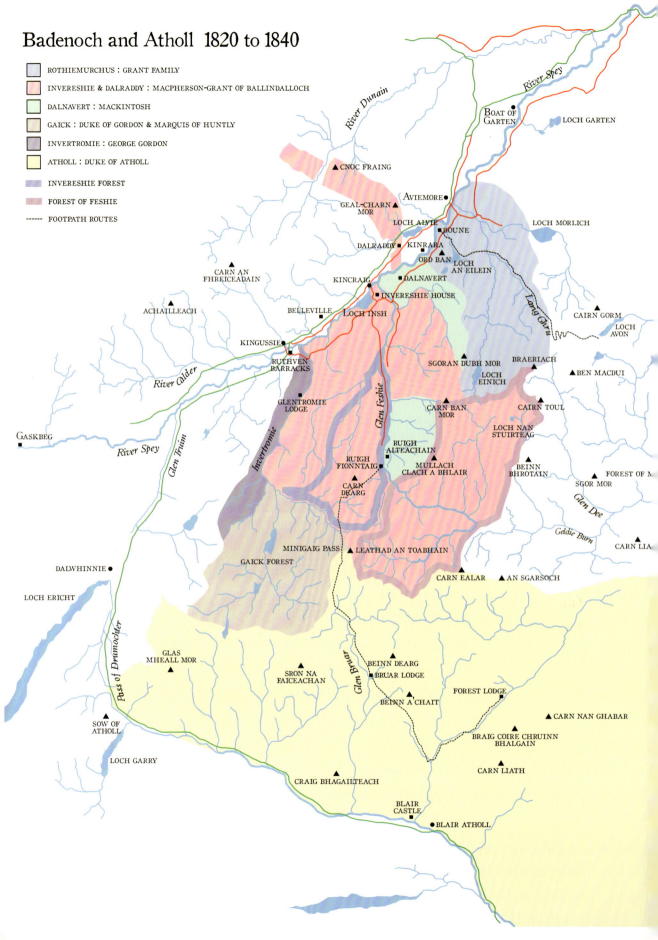

Badenoch and Atholl 1820 to 1840

ROTHIEMURCHUS : GRANT FAMILY

INVERESHIE & DALRADDY : MACPHERSON-GRANT OF BALLINDALLOCH

DALNAVERT : MACKINTOSH

GAICK : DUKE OF GORDON & MARQUIS OF HUNTLY

INVERTROMIE : GEORGE GORDON

ATHOLL : DUKE OF ATHOLL

INVERESHIE FOREST

FOREST OF FESHIE

‑‑‑‑‑ FOOTPATH ROUTES

River Dunain

River Spey

Boat of Garten

LOCH GARTEN

CNOC FRAING

GEAL-CHARN MOR

AVIEMORE

LOCH ALVIE

LOCH MORLICH

DOUNE

DALRADDY

KINRARA

ORD BAN

LOCH AN EILEIN

CARN AN FHREICEADAIN

KINCRAIG

DALNAVERT

INVERESHIE HOUSE

ACHAILLEACH

BELLEVILLE

LOCH INSH

Lairig Ghru

CAIRN GORM

LOCH AVON

KINGUSSIE

SGORAN DUBH MOR

BRAERIACH

BEN MACDUI

RUTHVEN BARRACKS

LOCH EINICH

River Calder

GLENTROMIE LODGE

Glen Feshie

CARN BAN MOR

CAIRN TOUL

LOCH NAN STUIRTEAG

GASKBEG

River Spey

Glen Truim

Invertromie

RUIGH ALTEACHAIN

RUIGH FIONNTAIG

MULLACH CLACH A BHLAIR

BEINN BHROTAIN

FOREST OF M

SGOR MOR

CARN DEARG

Glen Dee

Geldie Burn

CARN LIA

DALWHINNIE

MINIGAIG PASS

LEATHAD AN TOABHAIN

CARN EALAR

AN SGARSOCH

LOCH ERICHT

GAICK FOREST

Pass of Drumochter

GLAS MHEALL MOR

Glen Bruar

BEINN DEARG

SRON NA FAICEACHAN

BRUAR LODGE

FOREST LODGE

CARN NAN GHABAR

BEINN A' CHAIT

SOW OF ATHOLL

BRAIG COIRE CHRUINN BHLALGAIN

CARN LIATH

LOCH GARRY

CRAIG BHAGAILTEACH

BLAIR CASTLE

BLAIR ATHOLL

or Lord John's cottage at Hundreds Farm. A letter from the duke and Georgina to William congratulating them on their son indicates both the tensions between father and son and that Georgina had begun to sense a growing chill in William's attitude to her. The duke wrote, 'I congratulate you on the birth of your son and heir and on Bessy's safety … I wrote to you soon after my arrival at this place and I have received your Jobation on my absenting myself from England, to which I shall pay proper attention'; Georgina added, 'My dearest Billy, I … rejoice more than I can express that everything has gone on so well, and that your dear and amiable wife is safe … I always feel delighted when I have it in my power to prove the unalterable affection I have, from my first acquaintance … felt for you; the coldness of your manner towards me, is always a subject of regret, particularly since I know it to be a great injustice to me, for if I have any merits, sincerity is one of the many … Pray write to Paris – not a *scold* to me or your father though that is better than nothing … I send a kiss and a blessing to my grandson. I am impatient to see his little round chin.'

While 'William loved the house and park' at Woburn, 'he kept his hunters in the stables, and he enjoyed the company and conversation of his father and his brothers,' he also seems to have felt such access to be his by right, and when other benefits such as a house of his own or a generous allowance were not forthcoming, he bitterly attacked his father.[358] For the most part, however, the tensions between father and son reflected the irritations of all people of similar natures who see their faults mirrored in the other, but were never serious enough to threaten the foundations of their relationship. Unfortunately, the growing tensions between Georgina and Bessy, although caused by similar circumstances, were not so easily overcome, and lacking any deep foundations their worsening relationship came to place enormous strains on the family and caused lasting harm.

As 1820 dawned, William Adam again warned the duke about expenditure, and with work going ahead at Endsleigh and in Scotland, Woburn was limited to schemes already begun: inside the Abbey, the State Dressing Room and the Billiard Room 'were each redecorated and furnished en-suite',[359] while, outside, further work was limited to the completion of the greenhouse, the installation of the dome on the Sculpture Gallery, the addition of balustrades to the parterre gardens in front of it, and the refurbishment of the covered walkway, which by now required new plaster and whitewashing on the interior walls. In the park, 1820 saw the completion of the 'rough bridge' on the new road from the London entrance and the addition of plantations around it – the final tasks that completed the projects started all those years ago by Holland and Repton. One other item this year alerts us to the direction Georgina's interests were leading: her purchase of 'an account book for the Chinese Dairy'. From this time on, apart from its occasional use as an entertainment for guests, Georgina 'rented' the dairy from the estate and used it to run a hobby business, with her own small herd of Devon cattle.

During the spring of 1820, Lady Holland was staying at the Bedfords' new house in St James's Square before they moved in on their return from Endsleigh, and she was there when the duke wrote to her in March. In this letter he corrects her on an observation she had made to Wriothesley that some of the paintings at the house were 'copies', insisting this was not true, but the letter's real significance lies in the fact that it is the duke's first reference to an eighteen-year-old artist who was fast emerging as one of the brightest stars of a new generation of British painters and was to play a central role in their lives: Edwin Landseer. The time and place where Landseer first met the duke and duchess are not recorded, but in the letter the duke mentions that one of the pictures on display at St James's Square is a 'a pretty little sketch of Cosmo on his Shetland pony and in his highland garb by Edwin Landseer'.[360] The date of this unidentified sketch, currently untraced, suggests that Landseer had met the Bedfords and visited Woburn Abbey either in late 1819 or very early in 1820. Whatever the exact date, beyond this being the moment when the duke began his significant patronage of new British artists, it was also a time of major changes in the British art world; the British Institution had been founded in 1805 with the objective of opening up the art market, and access to it, by alternating exhibitions of Old Masters with those dedicated to contemporary British artists, a process that led in time to the founding of the National Gallery in 1824.

The significance of this was not simply to open up art to an ever widening public, but it also allowed those patrons to interact with the artist, most for the first time, in the creation of art, rather than simply buying it as a finished product, whether this was choosing subjects, suggesting compositions or specifying details, and it was this element of direct participation which had such an appeal for the duke. It reflected the same intense interest he had begun to show in the processes and details of botanical and horticultural science and his growing curiosity in the world around him in all its artistic and scientific forms. This moment is caught for us in the catalogue for Christie's sale of art on 30 June 1827. Referring to the Duke of Bedford, the catalogue states, 'The following 44 pictures are the property of a Nobleman of High Rank and removed from his Mansion in the country,' before adding that the sale is organized to 'make room in his mansion for works of distinguished Living British Artists'.[361]

On a personal level, for the Bedfords and Landseer, their initial relationship of artist and patron steadily turned into one of a deep and lasting friendship. For the duke and duchess the appeal of having such a talented, affable and fun-loving young man around – who was, after all, only a few years older than Wriothesley – is clear, while for Landseer the friendship of a family such as the Bedfords provided a number of new opportunities, both professional and personal. Professionally, the duke provided introductions to new areas of patronage from both individuals and institutions, but more importantly, perhaps, on a personal level, Landseer felt welcomed into the warm rough and tumble of family life at Woburn, and he clearly enjoyed the colourful, light-hearted and humorous undercurrent that flowed beneath the pomp and formality of ducal life, an undercurrent driven by the complex and playful personality of Georgina.

One gets the impression that these were all things that had been missing from his own, very different, upbringing, dominated as it was by his father, John, a professional engraver. For the Landseer children, their father's single-minded dedication to their artistic training meant they never attended school and had little time or opportunity to enjoy childhood, or to develop as individuals outside the intense atmosphere of home. All the unmarried siblings continued to live together in the family home after their parents' deaths, and when the indulged child prodigy Edwin did leave and move into his own house in St John's Wood, he continued to be supported by a close-knit family, initially by his aunt Barbara Potts, who acted as companion and housekeeper, and a few years later by his sister Jessica, who remained with him for the rest of his life, aided when necessary by another sister, Emma.[362] Given all of this, although immensely talented as an artist whose early fame rested on his renderings of dogs and other animals, beyond this childhood precocity for drawing, it is simply not clear just how rounded a person Landseer was.

While he was clearly a very good and engaging companion to his group of male friends, none of them specify anything further about him, beyond the fact that he was very likeable, had a wicked sense of humour and fun, could tell endless anecdotes, drink with the best of them, and was a good sportsman. Certainly, throughout his life he needed strong individuals around him, both family and patrons, to organize his life and manage his business and money, and by the time the teenage Landseer met the Bedfords, while he seemed to be well on his way, one wonders just how ready he was for what was to come. He was a charming and handsome but naive and unworldly young man, lacking education or real experience of life, existing in a world formed entirely by his precocious gift. When in later life this gift began to burn less brightly and artistic tastes began to change, the structure of his world began to collapse.

As with his relationship with George Sinclair, meeting and working with Landseer provided the duke with the ideal individual with whom to explore a common interest: in this case, art. As with so much else, we know the duke lacked confidence in his own judgements, and Landseer seems to have offered him a non-judgemental sounding board for his ideas, someone who was happy to follow directions, who respected what the duke said, and who enabled him to put forward ideas about the details and processes of making art without fear of ridicule. For the duchess, these early years of their friendship meant that she found someone who shared her mischievous sense of humour and fun, who embraced her love of practical jokes, amateur theatricals and singing round the piano, and who took her interests and ambitions seriously, encouraging her to draw and teaching her to etch and engrave. Beyond this, the more time Landseer spent in Scotland with the Bedfords, the more his art developed as he explored the Highland landscapes, and the more he came to share what Georgina valued about life there, which drew them into a closer, more significant relationship. In addition to developing a friendship with the duke and duchess, however, Landseer also became friends with the children still at home and with members of the extended family: in particular, the duke's nephew William Russell, who, besides collecting his art, also became 'perhaps the closest and most loyal of Landseer's friends'.[363]

While at Endsleigh in May and June that year, the duke had been unwell, but he reported to Lady Holland that both he and Georgina had 'a delightful fishing day, and the Trout that we have caught have been excellent'. He continued to be excited about the developments there as work got underway on the Swiss Cottage and the Cold Bath in the river below. The completed plan, the setting and finished Swiss Cottage were described in 1842 as follows:

> At the end of the terrace is a grotto, which commands a view of the woods and meadows on the river's bank, and also a floating Bridge, governed by a rope and windlass. The neighbouring woods rise luxuriantly from the water's-edge, and are pierced by ascending walks, one of which, 'climbing the ridge in zig-zags,' conducts to the Swiss Cottage, a picturesque edifice in the midst of a sort of Alpine garden. An exterior staircase and gallery lead to the upper apartments … [where] an extensive prospect is obtained over the river, woodlands, and open downs, terminated by the distant hills and Tors of Cornwall. The home views … are exceedingly wild and picturesque. Rocks, woods, abrupt declivities, and the river, where it ceases to be navigable, tumbling and foaming over rude masses of stone, present some of the finest combinations a painter could desire.[364]

All of this was not, perhaps, what Repton had envisioned for the setting of a 'Gentleman's villa', but it illustrates clearly just what had drawn them to the site in the first place, what they meant by the phrase 'natural and picturesque beauties' (see opening quote to Chapter 6), and what would draw them to spend so much time in Scotland.

Also in 1820, as these developments began at Endsleigh, work was underway on the alterations and additions to Invereshie House, which delayed the family's first visit until the next year. The new additions were based on plans drawn up by 'Mr Grant the Younger at Rothiemurchus', referring to Elizabeth Grant's eldest brother, William, then twenty-two, who was at this time engaged in supervising improvements on the estate at Rothiemurchus. The Grant children actually had a surprising amount of experience in drawing up architectural plans, since along with William, Elizabeth and her sister Jane had assisted their father in the design of at least five new cottages built on the estate in 1814, most of which are still standing.[365]

It is quite possible that discussions of the plans for Invereshie were a part of the 'great chattering' that went on between the Bedfords and the Grant family in Liège the year before, and that William Grant had worked on them since then. Certainly, by March 1820, we hear that 'Mr Cameron is in daily expectation of getting directions from the Duke about building the western wing of the House at Invereshie,' and by April work had begun there and on the east end of the house, as the Ballindalloch factor, John McInnis, informed George Macpherson-Grant: 'Cameron has got a plan sent to him for another wing for the house at Invereshie … it is <u>to project in front of the old House</u>. The door in the Gable of the old house is to be opened, and to communicate with a sunk cellar, it is only to be 9 feet high above the ground and there is an idea of making it in wood … it seems the plan and instructions were sent Mr Cameron by the young laird of Rothiemurchus.' In May McInnis sent another update: 'the Duke of Bedford has commenced operations at Invereshie, the new building it appears is of no great extent, nor is it to be in any way uniform with the other wings … Andrew Davidson seems very ill pleased with the East Wing and is astonished you would have allowed his Grace to have spoiled the uniformity of the house … not with standing of all this, I should think they would among them make a tastie thing of it.' An enclosure sent with this letter was one McInnis had received from the Invereshie gardener, Donald Vass, who had been retained by the Bedfords, and was clearly keeping an eye on things for the factor. Vass wrote, 'The new building is begun last week with Mr Grant Younger of Rothiemurchus's plans and directions. He was here this day [helping lay out the building plot] with James Russell [the mason] … The extent of the new building is to be 45 feet by 21 feet, and the height of the walls 9 feet. A sunk cellar is to be underneath the building.'[366]

In the letters from John McInnis to George Macpherson-Grant in early 1820, we also get a fascinating glimpse of the duke's expectations for life at Invereshie and what interests he is looking forward to pursuing beyond the shooting. In anticipation of visiting that summer, the duke wrote a letter to Donald Vass in December 1819 with his queries and instructions for the year ahead. Touchingly, he treats Vass as he would George Sinclair or Andrew Wilson, the manager at Park Farm, Woburn – as an independent, authoritative figure – asking 'whether anything was done in respect of the pasture ground at Invereshie last season, either in feeding or manuring', what 'Vass would recommend as the best mode of treating it for its improvement previous to being pasture next season', and what stock the grazing could support. He also requested that Vass 'ensure the garden is planted with vegetables for the next summer', since he intends 'to be there with the family in the month of August', and asked that Vass 'write an answer to these questions'.

The visit did not happen, but Vass, clearly out of his depth, immediately passed the letter on to McInnis in January seeking his 'advice as to what answer he should give his Grace' and explaining that he could not read the duke's handwriting. McInnis wrote him out a suitable answer, informing 'his Grace' that 'respecting [the] pasture land at Invereshie … it was neither pastured nor mowed last season … [and] he is not aware of anything that can be done to improve the pasture for the next season, unless it were to get a top dressing with lime … It might also be advisable to carry off all the loose stones that are lying above ground,' and finally, that his 'orders shall be attended to in cropping the Garden for next season'.

Much debate then followed as to how best to apply 'the top dressing for the Duke's Park', Cameron advising forty bolls of lime shells and disagreeing with the duke's suggestion of 'hot lime' since 'it would burn up the moss.' McInnis concludes: 'My opinion is that this quantity will be of no use whatever and that the Duke will be disappointed in his object of improving the pasture'; Cameron, however, 'will appoint a proper person to purchase the Beasts' and 'thinks that 2 year olds will be the best to adapt'.

In the end, McInnis informed Macpherson-Grant that the duke had written to say he 'would be guided wholly by Mr Cameron's opinion with stocking and manuring of the Pasture'.[367] Clearly, everyone is getting used to the new situation – those at Invereshie having an entirely new 'owner' to deal with and having, for the first time, a duke actually living in their midst, and the duke himself learning to adjust to the implications of being a tenant rather than an owner and realizing that methods used at Woburn or Endsleigh would not necessarily work at Invereshie. Equally, not having total control over all the land and tenants around his home was something he was still getting used to at Endsleigh. While work on Invereshie House continued, we get our first glimpse of another project the duke and duchess have in mind with mention of the duke's proposed house in the glen.[368] It would seem that the lack of a farm or any buildings which had made it so hard to lease the Forest of Feshie in the first place remained a problem once the Bedfords arrived, and while initially proposing to build a 'hut', they subsequently negotiated access to the shieling huts at Ruigh Fionntaig, the closest buildings to the Forest of Feshie on Macpherson-Grant's land, to serve as a base for both family visits and for those heading up to shoot in the forest, a development which directly affected the tenant farmers.

While the process of the replacement of the small vertical farms with larger units and the introduction of sheep walks to the moors had removed the traditionally guaranteed rights of tenant farmers to access the summer grazing pastures, they were not totally excluded, and by agreement could still graze cattle or sheep. Similarly, when the first estates were established for grouse shooting in the later eighteenth and early nineteenth centuries, this activity was limited to a specific season in early autumn, and for the rest of the year tenant farmers had some access to grazing. However, the loss of access to the huts in the glen which had been used by the tenant farmers' families as a base during the months of summer grazing in the forest effectively ended this practice in this part of the glen. Rights to summer grazing on the moors largely remained in place until the late 1830s, when a growing number of estates were turned over to deer stalking, and this development meant that the moors were now maintained entirely free of any other individuals or livestock. Once this happened, a unique aspect of the traditional Badenoch farming lifestyle was destroyed, since the steady loss of access for the traditional farming communities to the high moors and the summer occupation of the shielings was not simply a matter of economics; it also changed forever the basic structures of the local communities as the practice of transhumance came to an end.

At the end of March 1820, the duke told Lady Holland that they were looking forward to taking possession of 'our new residence in St James' Square. I shall not like it as much as Hamilton Place for comfort and cheerfulness, but there we can lodge our servants and children, and with this, for a pied à terre we ought to be contented'; once back in London, Georgina began to plan another busy social season at the new and larger London house (Map 4). Tickets for parties up to nine people were bought for 'Almack's Rooms' for June and July's 'Dress Balls'; repeated visits were made to Holland House and a trip arranged to Vauxhall Gardens.[369] The central event, however, was a grand ball she planned to hold at the house on 18 July, just before the family were fully moved in, to celebrate the birthdays of her daughters, Georgiana and Louisa, and for which no expense was spared. The library was 'fitted up' with pink and white drapery, a 'platform for the Musicians and tiers of seats' installed, and '2 large Letters, "L" & "G", with artificial flowers' were hung over the library doors, while entertainment was provided by eight musicians and 'Monsieur Boisgiard, Master of the Dance'.

The grand pink and white extravaganza at St James's Square was then followed by another trip down the Thames to Richmond, this time on a steam boat, for a 'dinner, dessert with Ice Creams, tea and coffee' for forty-five people at the Castle Inn. This time entertainment on the boat was provided by the band of the Third Guards of '18 musicians and 3 Blacks'. It was a fitting finale, perhaps, to Georgina's summer season.[370]

Meanwhile, the duke, who had thoroughly enjoyed what he described as the 'ultra-retirement' of the three-week Endsleigh trip and would have been quite happy to remain at Woburn pursuing all his new projects, told Lady Holland, 'I am always well and always happy here, but I am not selfish in my nature and must consider [the family] as well as myself.'[371] Others were to disagree with the duke's perception of his 'nature', but at this time he seems to have been genuinely concerned about Georgina, both her health and her spirits, and so he planned to join her in Worthing, where she was to return for some peace and quiet and a chance to come to terms with recent news she had received from Scotland that summer, which seems to have deeply upset her, as reported by Countess Granville: 'We had a tremendous storm here yesterday. It came on at Holland House, where we dined. Georgy arrived in the midst of it galled at the Duke of Gordon's marriage.'

Her father's marriage meant that his mistress, Jean Christie, was now Duchess of Gordon, and that she and their five children moved into Gordon Castle, much to Georgina's surprise and 'fierce opposition from all his family'. As George Gordon goes on to say, 'The Duke's affair with Jean was already a twenty year old story, and hardly the latest news in Fochabers, but marriage! Jean as Duchess!' Opposition, it seems, was, and remained, widespread. Although there is no record that Jean Christie ever visited Kinrara, which had been left to the Marquis of Huntly, it is clear that Jane Maxwell's children found the changed circumstances and the idea of a new duchess cast a shadow over the memory of their mother, particularly for Georgina, who had been so close to her.[372]

Before leaving for Worthing, however, all the arrangements for the move from Hamilton Place to St James's Square were finalized, and in August the remaining furniture was moved. With this work underway, the Bedfords spent several weeks at Worthing, where the duke tells Lady Holland, 'A change of air and a change of weather have done wonders, and I feel quite different from being here from what I did in London. The Dss is particularly well.' They had initially been expected at Invereshie in late August, but Georgina's health, the fact that work on the Invereshie house was not yet finished, and quite possibly the unwelcome news of her father's marriage meant that their first visit came a year later. Some family members, however, did make the trip when, perhaps curious about Scotland and what drew his father there, Lord William and Bessy visited Kinrara, and once again it is Elizabeth Grant who catches the moment: 'We had great fun this Autumn; poney races at Kingussie and a ball at the cattle tryst, picnics in the woods, quantities of fine people at Kinrara,

Lord Tweeddale … the Ladies Cornwallis, kind merry girls … Mrs Rawdon and her clever daughter, Lady William Russell, who I do not think much liked her little shabby looking Lord … Mrs Rawdon, rather a handsome flirting widow, taking Uncle Ralph for a widower, paid him very tender attentions.'

While William would subsequently visit his father and Georgina at The Doune during the shooting season, this appears to have been Bessy's one and only visit, and she was not impressed. Writing to old Lord William a few years later, she commented, 'I am glad you were happy in Scotland … It is a horrid place I must own [and] the climate exceedingly disagreeable.'[373]

Just before joining Georgina in Worthing and perhaps encouraged by his experiences in Scotland, the duke participated in what is his only recorded stag hunt. There is no detail about where or with whom this hunt took place, but his comments about it are very interesting. Writing to Lady Holland in September he says, 'Holland will be amused to hear that I have been <u>stag</u> <u>hunting</u>, and after a run of 3¾ hours, was recompensed for my toil and trouble, by the glory of being in at the death.' Since the 'toil and trouble' of the chase does not seem to have figured in his pleasure that day, he seems only to have been recompensed for the effort by 'the glory' of witnessing the death of the stag, presumably when it was finally overwhelmed by dogs. The word 'glory' is noticeably different from any terms he ever used about the experience of bird shooting, and its meaning to the duke would seem to refer to a heightened sense of exultant pride he felt in himself for witnessing the scene, as if the event somehow brought honour and renown to him personally. Indeed, the experience appears to have been so powerful that he sought to relive it in the first major art work he commissioned from Edwin Landseer five years later, *The Hunting of Chevy Chase*. In this painting, mounted men with spears, a retainer with a bow and arrow, and another with spear and hunting dog join other dogs that have just killed a doe and are in the act of bringing down a stag at the end of the chase. The importance of creating a painting which, for the duke, accurately reproduced the circumstances of his own experience is indicated by his intimate involvement in its production, his letters to the artist at the time seeming to continue their ongoing conversations about title, subject, details and style.

In one letter, the duke specifies the species of deer to be shown, before telling Landseer how much he is looking forward to the finished painting:

the principal deer in your picture should undoubtedly be 'a powerful red stag', and all the hinds should be of the same species, as it would be an incongruity, and indeed an anomaly, to have an indiscriminate slaughter of red and fallow deer, as the two species do not herd together. Moreover, the red deer stags and hinds are much finer subjects for a picture than the fallow bucks and does.

We must therefore have all the Deer in your picture of the red species, but we must give it some other name than 'Chevy Chase'.

Bedford

Fully persuaded as I am that this Stag hunt will be one of the finest pictures in any collection of the works of British Artists, I naturally feel a more than common anxiety about it, and for your credit and fame, I wish it could have been ready for Somerset House next year, but that is now quite out of the question. B [374]

The sense of 'glory of being in at the death' of a beast, or of reliving the experience through a painting, was evidently the motive that lay behind the commissioning of *The Hunting of Chevy Chase*, which otherwise has been described as a 'cruel and violent scene', and comes as close as may be possible to explaining what the picture meant for the duke.[375] In addition, we see his sense of a hierarchy of subjects, deer being finer subjects than birds, and red deer being finer than fallow, stags finer than does – all presumably based on some correlation between size and potential to put up a 'noble' enough spectacle to promote the 'glory of being in at the death'. For Landseer, however, the motive for creating such images seems to have been a little different. After initially gaining attention for sentimental depictions of dogs, ponies and other pets, towards the time he met the duke Landseer had increasingly turned his attention to understanding animal physiology, visiting slaughterhouses and carrying out detailed dissections. While his studies revealed 'a keen scientific curiosity and a remarkable understanding of animal anatomy', the uses he put this understanding to indicate something more morbid at work, both in him and those who bought the images: a kind of fascination in witnessing an animal fight for its life against overwhelming odds, seemingly disengaged from the reality of what was happening.

This apparent fascination fuelled a steady stream of images throughout his career of dead and particularly dying animals being torn apart by dogs, dogs and deer locked in a fight to the death, shot and wounded animals in their death throes or crawling away to die, wounded birds falling from the sky, animals suffering varying degrees of cruelty and even torture, and the kind of violent deaths of which *Chevy Chase* was an example. All these came in stark contrast to his touching and sentimental portraits of both children and adults, family life, pet animals, faithful sheepdogs, rural life and country living. The year before he painted *Chevy Chase*, however, Landseer paid his first visit to Scotland, and this trip was to mark an interesting new direction in his art.

We have little indication as to the nature of Georgina's ill-health in the last few months of the year, but after his stag-hunting experience the duke joined her in Worthing and then for five weeks in Brighton, both places where she could rest and enjoy a change of air. These ongoing problems with her health, coupled with her growing interest in gardening, may well have been the reason that in November 1820 the duke took the lease on a small villa on Campden Hill, a short distance from their friends the Hollands at Holland House and the open spaces of Holland Park in Kensington. Until this point the Bedfords' London houses had been in terraces with little or no outside garden space, and in busy, fashionable and polluted areas of the city. The new villa, however, with its large open garden to the south and long views towards the Surrey hills beyond, felt much like being in the country – the air infinitely fresher, the surroundings quieter and greener – and offered them something far more peaceful. When in 1823 the duke actually bought the property they adopted the name Bedford Lodge, and so well did it suit Georgina that it remained her London home until she died.[376]

Following their stay in Brighton, the family arrived back at Woburn in early December, where they were greeted by two new arrivals, the keepers of the

Menagerie having taken delivery of two antelopes from Malta in October. The two remained favourite pets of the family, living out their lives in the Menagerie, and were there in 1824 when one visitor met 'a little Antelope which was so tame that it ate from my hand', and still there in 1836 when Dr Allen Thomson noted 'some peculiar deer' in the Menagerie.[377]

The Christmas holidays began at Woburn with a ball on 18 December attended by family and guests, of whom one is of particular interest: Harriet Cavendish, Countess Granville. This is because, in letters to her sister Lady Morpeth and her sister-in-law Lady Harrowby, she has left us a detailed description of her week's stay. It is worth noting by way of context, however, that Harriet was not a usual guest at Woburn, being neither a close relative nor a family friend, but was married to Granville Leveson-Gower, the duke's distant cousin through his grandmother Gertrude. In addition, her mother, Georgiana, Duchess of Devonshire, had been a fierce rival of Georgina's mother, Jane, both socially and politically, and was one of those so appalled at the thought of a Russell, whether Francis or John, marrying Georgina. Above all, perhaps, Harriet herself has been described as both 'reserved and prickly', and all these circumstances are reflected in her observations.[378]

To her sister, Harriet described the scene at Woburn on 19 December: 'The Duchess has not yet appeared. She has seen *tout ces dames*; but not me. You know I am not touchy therefore I take the goods the gods provide me and swallow the affront with a grateful heart. It is very comfortable here, no more nor less … In the evening the men play whist or billiards, and we sit in the saloon very well together, but Lady William Russell is the only one who really likes me.' She continues in a letter the next day:

> The Duchess appeared. She was to me just what I wish her to be, uncommonly cold and uncommonly uncivil … Lady William I like better every time I see her … I think very few people as agreeable as Lady William … The Duchess I do not see. Many of the men I like. I have a delightful room, and find the day too short for all I have to do in it … Why then, do I count the days till I can go? Why do I feel that I shall not be able to refrain from screaming with joy

when I drive off? It is no affront to Woburn. I do justice to its comfort, ease, splendour, and society.

Finally, she tells her sister-in-law:

We left Woburn yesterday, having spent there a week of as much pleasure as is compatible with seeing it end without any regret. The *locale* is itself a great source of enjoyment. There is so much space, so much comfort, such *luxe* and ease … Yet at the summing up I said 'Content'. I believe it was being obliged to dress very smart and sitting often at dinner between the Lords Tavistock and Worcester. These were my grievances; my pleasures were Lady William's society … The Duchess herself is very unwell and appeared but four times, only once at dinner, and when she did was very *souffrante* and out of spirits.

Finding her natural ally at Woburn to be Bessy, it is perhaps not surprising that Harriet was so prepared to be affronted by Georgina, in spite of being aware that she was 'very unwell'. She may not have been aware that Georgina had just discovered that she was pregnant with her eleventh child, Lord Alexander, who was born the following September. Following Harriet's departure, however, the celebrations continued, and in addition to the annual Servant's Ball, joiners created special scenery for 'Pantomimical Performances' held in the theatre at the Abbey, and at least one of the guests reported having enjoyed himself; Lord Thanet gave Henry Fox 'an account of Woburn, from whence he is just come and delighted with all there'.[379]

As the New Year of 1821 dawned and the duke looked back over the year just gone, there will have been one occurrence of particular significance to him: the retirement of Robert Salmon, the quiet, modest man who had worked so long for both himself and his brother, but whose health had finally failed and who died in his house across from Park Farm the next year. Described by Repton as 'the most ingenious man I have ever known', Salmon was buried in the churchyard of the old parish church at Woburn, where a plaque can still be seen today commemorating his 'unwearied zeal and disinterested integrity' in his service to the family. William Adam had retired in 1813 to his home at Blair Adam where, as he had told Repton, 'I purpose tarrying among my trees and my rocks, and my lakes and my rivulets';[380] with the loss of Salmon it marked the end of an era for the duke, as the long shadow of his brother finally passed away with the last of those who had worked with him. While there were not any dramatic changes, it was from this period on that, building on his work with George Sinclair, the duke turned increasingly to new interests, steadily creating a legacy of his own. Some of these interests, such as botanical science, were prompted by the success and recognition of the grass ground experiments, and others, such as family history and his collections, were to some extent prompted by the publication that year of Lord John's biography of their ancestor Lord William Russell, executed in 1683 for his part in the Rye House Plot. If the generation of Edwin, the hero of Beattie's poem *The Minstrel*, had approached the natural world and all its mysteries 'wrapp'd in wonder', the present generation now sought to use all the tools at their command – whether artistic, literary or, increasingly, scientific – to actively engage with those mysteries and integrate the processes of unlocking them into their cultural world through the traditional forms of art, poetry, literature and history.

The New Year ushered in new priorities, as it was confirmed that Georgina was pregnant and the duke became increasingly engaged with the Marquis of Tavistock's and Lord John's long commitment to the cause of parliamentary reform, which was dividing opinion among the Whigs, not as to whether but how it should be pursued. Henry Fox catches this mood in an entry in his journal in early January on a visit to Woburn with his father, Lord Holland: 'I went to Woburn for two days with my father, in order to attend the Bedfordshire meeting … The Duke spoke first. Nothing could be better; he was too warm about Reform, a silly, idle phantom which many adore because they do not understand … My father followed, and made a speech full of moderation, feeling and wit … Ld John's speech was short and full of point and neatness, for which he is always remarkable.'

In turn, Tavistock made one of his rare speeches to support the petition of parliamentary reform, declaring, 'nothing but meetings like the present could bring about any change in a system so long and fatally pursued … I am persuaded that no good could arise from a mere change of men without a temperate but effectual reform of parliament.' The duke, as with his cautious approach to the immediate and total abolition of slavery, gave his own, somewhat less committed, opinion to Lord Grey in February: 'I have read the plan for a Parliamentary Reform, which you were good enough to send me, with attention, and in some measure of satisfaction. The basics of the Plan – I think are good, tho' many alterations may be made with advantage to the details … Much is left undone in this Bill with regard to getting rid of corruption and expenses of contested elections, the duration of Parliament etc … It is much to be desired that some measure should be brought forward soon.'[381]

The duke, of course, like so many of his friends and fellow landowners, was nervous about the extent of the 'measures' which might be brought forward, since the implications of reform were the loss of their political patronage. The fact that the Tavistock constituency was not included in the schedule of those to be abolished first did not go unnoticed.

At Woburn, as work continued on the refurbishment of the covered way and the grass ground was given a new entrance gate (Colour Plate 20), the duke and Sinclair launched another significant botanical project when they started work on a collection of heaths. As he indicates in his introduction to Sinclair's catalogue of the collection, *Hortus Ericaeus Woburnensis*, published in January 1825, 'I have long been an admirer of that beautiful tribe of plants the *Genus Erica*, and have frequently lamented that so many of the species (chiefly natives of the Cape of Good Hope) should have been lost to this country … [and] had become *out of fashion* amongst our collectors.' Attracted by the 'variety and exquisite loveliness of their colour shades', the duke determined to start a comprehensive collection of heath species, a somewhat neglected plant with a reputation for being difficult to grow, since he thought them particularly beautiful when looked at carefully, and determined to understand and solve the technical problems that had led to this reputation and bring the plant to wider attention. He notes in the catalogue:

It is universally acknowledged that the genus … requires free exposure to the influence of light and air; and I therefore suggested a due attention to a circumstance of so much importance to the health and vigour of the plants, to my Architect, Mr. Jeffry Wyatt, who gave me a plan for the Heath House, elevated considerably above the level of the ground, by being erected over a covered walk within the pleasure-ground … lighted from both sides, as well as from the roof, and affording a fuller exposure of both light and air than would have been possibly obtained by other means.

In drawing attention to this circumstance, the duke was seeking to solve the difficulties and not simply accept conventional wisdom, because, as Paul Smith points out: 'The Duke thought their reputation for being difficult to grow was caused by the indifference shown by many nurserymen, characterised by an unwillingness to take the necessary precautions to ensure that these plants became well established.'[382] In this quote, Smith captures a key element of his character: once interested in something he was determined to understand it down the finest details. He did not simply set his employees the task of solving problems; he gave direction and understood that, if he wanted the team to succeed, he had to provide an atmosphere of curiosity and commitment to challenge received wisdom, and to provide the means by which investigation could move forward. His open-ended financial support in the late 1830s for William Hooker's plant hunters in Central and South America is typical of this unconditional commitment, and in the case of the heaths, he spent the money necessary to commission and build a special greenhouse to maximize the chances of success.

Work started on Wyatville's Heath House in 1821 and continued into 1822, when they were slating the roof, building flues and, outside, 'collecting ling mould and preparing ground' for the hardy heath garden, created to complement the indoor collection. The Heath House was completed in 1823 when it was 'fitted out', the display planters finished and the exterior stone stuccoed. Yet this was not just any greenhouse. Just as the duke's interest in grasses, and now heaths, was driven by a complex combination of aesthetic and scientific considerations, so was

'The Heath House', built 1823–5. Seen here in an image from J. D. Parry's *A Guide to Woburn Abbey* (1831), one of the figures points to the striking white stuccoed entrance to the Heath House. Following the elegant curve of the covered walkway it was built over, the Heath House, like the grass ground, was an early example of the duke's determination to integrate his scientific endeavours into the aesthetic experience of the pleasure ground.

the design and location of the Heath House, a spectacular and innovative structure set in the heart of the Abbey's complex of buildings, complete with a small library and reading alcove and painted window decorations:

The window facing the door of the ante-room, opening into the Pleasure Ground, is of an oval form, the margins of which are ornamented by 20 circular groups of different species of *Ericeæ*; and in the centre is a group of various kinds, represented in a basket; consequently, there are about 50 of the most beautiful flowering species painted on this window, which was executed by Mr. Andrews … The recesses are fitted up with shelves, in which are placed the splendid works of Mr. Andrews, on the *Ericeæ*, and various other botanical works.[383]

This was not just a place to admire the plants, but an opportunity to enter another world. Ahead was the anteroom with its extraordinary painted window, its coloured light bathing the book-lined shelves – a place to read, learn, discuss and reflect – and then the tall double doors opened to lose oneself in the world of colour, stretching away through the cool, scented air and out of sight round the long curve, the scene given an other-worldly feel by mirrors on three of the walls. On one side, the stepped planters rose up almost to head height, while on the other the low planters allowed a view out of the windows, down over the hardy heath garden below, and out towards the Menagerie in the gardens beyond (Colour Plate 21). The destruction of this building in 1949 was a huge loss, since its unique combination of the aesthetic world of art and design and the underlying science – the carefully regulated ventilation – pointed up a major element of the 6th Duke's legacy and the contemporary engagement with wonder. Appreciating the aesthetic qualities to be found in this pursuit of botanical science, he gained great pleasure and a deep satisfaction seeing his experiments unfold, and as these programmes continued through the 1830s, he increasingly sought to establish their place beside all the other indicators of culture and beauty. So it comes as no surprise that in 1823, on completion of the work, the duke published *Drawings of Heaths for the Heath House, Woburn Abbey* by Louis Parez and Henry Charles Andrews. The volume illustrates the painted window in a drawing by Parez and all the other images of the heaths by Andrews, and provides a tantalizing glimpse of just how spectacular this structure must have been.

In addition to the Heath House and continuing building work at Invereshie, a similar mood of engagement drove the duke's resumption of the Bloomsbury project at this time. Since the creation of Russell Square, Bedford Place (north) and the start of work on Tavistock Square, house building had largely stalled, largely due to wider economic factors, leaving those who had already purchased houses on Upper Bedford Place and the east side of the uncompleted Tavistock Square in a state of limbo. Beyond their houses to the east and north lay an unoccupied wasteland of waterlogged brick pits surrounded by scrub, building debris and piles of excavated soil. For several years the duke had been receiving letters of complaint from residents about these water-filled pits and night-time fly-tipping, dumping of sewage and lighting of bonfires across the unattended spaces. Donald Olsen quotes a letter from the duke to estate solicitor Thomas Pearce Brown in August 1817 of complaints he was already receiving from residents about 'the general nuisance which has caused so many representations to be made to me from that neighbourhood, and if there are any means of getting rid of these ponds without difficulty, it certainly must be a desirable object to the more respectable inhabitants of the vicinity.' Brown 'had replied that the ponds formed part of "the general nuisance which we are in daily hopes of getting rid of … What has impeded the matter is the large sum each proposer for the ground requires your Grace to expend in fencing, and in one plan these ponds are intended to be kept as objects of beauty."'[384]

This is the first time that we hear about considerations of 'objects of beauty' in terms of the developments, and although the ponds were not kept, it tells us that a new aesthetic sense was at play; as the duke re-engaged with the development of Bloomsbury, the old 1800 plan for development of the east and north sections of the estate was replaced by a new layout. Tastes had changed and the new plan – perhaps influenced by what he had seen of the second phase of Edinburgh's New Town, with its elongated gardens between Heriot Row and Queen Street – was drawn up.

By the 1820s, as building picked up again, Olsen tells us, these changes involved two new elongated oval squares, Torrington Square and Woburn Square, and, immediately north of the latter, the more traditional Gordon Square. While Torrington and Woburn squares 'were little more than widened streets with garden strips down the middle', Gordon Square was to be far grander, on a par with Russell Square, lined with first-rate houses and a showpiece central garden. The agreement for Torrington Square which emerged from extended negotiations between the builders and the Bedford office included not only an elevation for the houses, but also 'a detailed map of the garden, showing the precise location of the intended gravel paths, grass plots, shrubbery, trees and even benches. There was also an elevation of the dwarf wall and railing which were to surround the garden.'

By 1821 James Sim and Sons had begun work on Torrington Street and Torrington Square, both of which were finished by 1824, and Thomas Cubitt had finally completed Tavistock Square, before going on to sign a new contract covering 'all the remainder of your Grace's un-built upon land southward of the New Road [Euston Road]', undertaking to level the ground and lay out the sewers and roads 'in order to bring it into a proper state for building'. By 1829 this work was largely complete and the Sim family were able to begin work on Woburn Square, while Thomas Cubitt 'formed and enclosed the central gardens of the new square'.[385] Inevitably, perhaps, not all this development happened at once – Gordon Square was not completed until the mid-1830s, some thirty years after work began on Russell Square – but it seems clear that one key factor driving this new plan was the participation of the duke himself, who had begun to take the same interest in the designs and the contents of their gardens as he did in the development of Endsleigh and Woburn.

Also in London, it was to be another active social season for Georgina as she took on the task at which her mother had so singularly excelled: finding husbands for her girls. In this case, her 'adopted' daughter, Eliza Russell, who had been living with the family for some time now, had reached the age of seventeen. With a view to introducing Eliza to London society, and although she was heavily pregnant, Georgina purchased tickets for the two of them to evenings both at the Argyle Rooms and Almack's, to the opera and to performances at Astley's Royal Amphitheatre, a combination of theatre and circus, where a tip was required for the porter for 'keeping places for her Grace's party'.

Bloomsbury II, 1820s–30s: with Russell Square finished and Tavistock Square laid out, the second phase of building (outlined by dropped shadow) – Torrington, Woburn and Gordon Squares and the streets above Gordon Place – were completed up to the Duke of Grafton's Euston Square Gardens, which were bisected by the New Road (Euston Road).

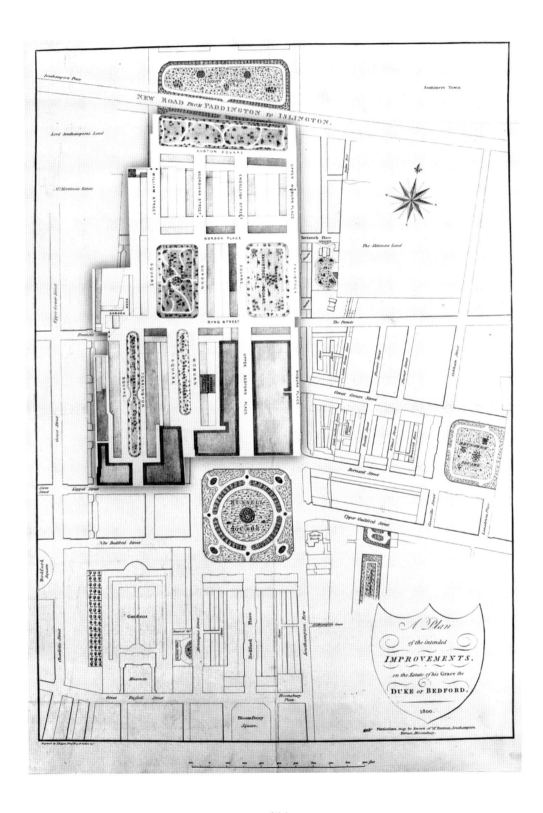

As Lady Holland told Lord William the next year, Eliza is 'one of the prettiest girls in town … so modest and innocently gay. I quite love her, and she is a great delight to both D. and Dss, the latter invariably kind to her.' In a remarkable survival from the time, we can catch a glimpse of Georgina and Eliza pictured at Almack's as two of the 152 named full-figure portraits in Charlotte Sneyd's *Panorama of Almack's* (Colour Plate 22). In this wonderful image on a scroll several metres long, a composite of attendees were painted in watercolour between 1821 and 1822; six pairs of dancers appear at one end and the rest stand in groups on the other side of a red rope – in one group we see the 'Duchess of Bedford' and 'Miss Eliza Russell'. While Almack's may appear to be simply another location for fashionable gatherings, as early as 1814 one observer had noted just how special it was:

> At the present time one can hardly conceive the importance which is attached to getting admission to Almack's, the seventh heaven of the fashionable world … the gates of which were guarded by Lady patronesses, whose smiles or frowns consigned men and women to happiness or despair. [These were] Ladies Castlereagh, Jersey, Cowper and Sefton, Mrs Drummond Burrell, now Lady Willoughby, the Princess Esterhazy, and the Countess Lieven … Many diplomatic arts, and a host of intrigues, were set in motion to get an invitation to Almack's.

He goes on to note that 'the dances at Almack's were Scotch reels and the old English country-dance; and the orchestra, being from Edinburgh, was conducted by the then celebrated Niel Gow,'[386] which must have provided an additional attraction for Georgina.

As well as attending society evenings, Georgina held her balls at St James's Square in late June and July, possibly less elaborate than the year before, but still with an orchestra of nine musicians, and then, in what perhaps was the most important social event that summer, the duke spent the night at the Seymours' house – Emily Byng and her husband, Henry Seymour – before attending the coronation of George IV at Westminster Abbey.[387] Finally, at the end of June, perhaps to everyone's relief, Lord William and Bessy left for the Continent, as the growing tensions between Bessy and Georgina persuaded Lord William to let his London house on a long lease and take his wife abroad, where they remained for the next two years.

By August, with the London season over, the duke, the heavily pregnant duchess and Eliza set off for their first visit to Invereshie House, where they were joined when school finished by Charles and Francis. Arriving in the second week of August, they remained until early September, leaving in time for Georgina to arrive back at Woburn in time for the birth of Lord Alexander on the 16th. The accounts suggest that Georgina spent the summer furnishing and fitting out the parts of the house that were complete, but given her pregnancy it cannot have been the relaxing visit she had perhaps been expecting. In fact, things at Invereshie had got off to rather a shaky start this year when in March the two staff members, Annie Cromie, the housekeeper, and Donald Vass, the gardener, suddenly 'eloped' after Annie became pregnant and 'no person in the vicinity can have any idea where they went.' The news was reported by Andrew Davidson to McInnis, who in turn told Mrs Macpherson-Grant: 'It is a most serious concern to see the house of Invereshie uninhabited and is very dangerous to have it so for fear of the property within it,' but because many of the contents belong to the Bedfords, Davidson is 'a little shy about looking into them … I feel a little doubtful whether any interference on my part would be agreeable.'

Fortunately, the issue was rapidly resolved by the return of the 'elopers' before the Bedfords arrived, and the duke was happy to forgive them, telling Macpherson-Grant, 'Thank you for your most obliging communication on the subject of the elopement from Invereshie. I wish to be guided wholly by you in the steps [to be taken] with regard to the Fugitives, who are now returned to their duties … if you think Donald Vass and Annie Cromie trustworthy, and fit to be retained in their situation, after a suitable admonition for their misconduct, I can have no possible objection to follow your example of leniency, and overlook the fault they have unquestionably committed.'[388]

Certainly, on arrival, the duke was determined to enjoy himself and kept meticulous notes of his shooting exploits. These indicate very mixed success, with the duke recording that he shot 'well', 'ill' or 'abominably ill' in about equal measure; he regularly overdid things and was 'too unwell to shoot'. Over the next few weeks, his efforts alternated between Invereshie's 'home muirs' and Mackintosh's Kincraig, where birds were 'plentiful, but not equal to what I saw on the same ground in 1818', before ending up at Kinrara 'to see Lord Huntly's dogs'. In spite of the days when he was too unwell or the weather was 'too hot' or 'stormy' to shoot well, he still managed to shoot almost a hundred grouse and 'Black Game' and '1 Snipe', but overall one gets the sense that he enjoyed the idea of going shooting more than the reality, and it lacked the rewards of that self-affirming sense of glory that had accompanied his stag hunt.

During this stay, the lack of any further mention of the duke's 'proposed house' in Glen Feshie is perhaps indicative of the fact that neither Georgina, whose pregnancy was nearing its end, nor the duke was very well during this trip. It is also likely that the suggestion that they would take over the buildings at Ruigh Fionntaig had met with considerable opposition from Macpherson-Grant's tenants, who depended on access to them for summer grazing, and that the task of letting some of the farms on the estate, complete with summer grazing, was still a priority for John McInnis. His concern is reflected in a letter of February 1821 to Macpherson-Grant in which he says, perhaps reflecting the new reality that so much forest and hill pasture had been hived off for the shooting leases, 'I did not think of going to Invereshie until about 1st April, but I see now there is a necessity of my going sooner that I may try to get these farms let.'[389] No clear date has been established for the Bedfords' eventual occupation of the buildings at Ruigh Fionntaig, but it may initially have been on a seasonal basis and for short periods while local farmers still utilized the grazing around them.

Back at Woburn, Lord Alexander Russell was born on 16 September, and although 'the birth was premature by some weeks … thank God both the Duchess and the infant are doing as well as possible.' Further excitement came when, much to the delight of the boys, Thomas Pratt, a long-serving groom at Woburn, arrived back at Woburn with '2 ponies from Huntly Lodge', gifts, no doubt, from Georgina's brother.[390]

Meanwhile, on 15 October Edwin Landseer paid his first recorded visit to Woburn. Perhaps the duke had invited him to make studies of the deer in the park in preparation for painting *The Hunting of Chevy Chase*, but it is another image, dated 1821, that indicates his presence at Woburn: a quick but extremely confident sketch of a large dog titled *Blue Cap*. This picture, much more finished than it may at first appear, seems likely to be the image recorded as *Old English Bloodhound* (1821), taken, as Algernon Graves notes, 'from a dog at Woburn'.

In December Georgina, taking stock of the furnishing of the various houses, put in a very large order for furniture and drapery for Endsleigh, St James's Square and the 'Boudoir', breakfast room and anteroom at Woburn Abbey. Unfortunately for the duke, however, his grand, end-of-year shooting party at Woburn did not go as smoothly as previous years, since, on 9 December, 'The Duke of York has hurt his arm, which is to break up the Woburn party,' and everyone went home.[391]

Also, in a sign of just how far things had moved by the end of this busy year, the duke took one more significant step when in December he resigned from the presidency of the Smithfield Club, stating that their objective – 'to improve the breeds of cattle, sheep and swine' – 'has been fully attained', a move which confirms just how far his priorities and interests had shifted from agricultural improvement to botany and horticultural science.

It is also important to note that after 1821 and the start of their regular visits to Scotland, the duke's engaged time at Woburn Abbey, beyond correspondence on estate management matters, became increasingly limited to the months from late November until late April or early May. After that, with the exception when ill health kept the family at Woburn, May to late June was largely spent at Endsleigh, from where they sometimes returned briefly to London or Woburn in July, but on occasion went straight up to Scotland where they would stay from August to October and, by the 1830s, November. As this cycle for the year became established, with the exception of trips abroad, the overall pattern of their lives also became increasingly private and introspective.

In early 1822, as Georgina was reporting to Lady Holland that 'I am recovering my health,' another of her sons left home when Francis, widely known as Frank or Franky, entered the navy at fourteen as Volunteer of the 1st Class, joining older brother Edward, still a midshipman, and his first cousin Commander John Russell on board HMS *Owen Glendower*. It is interesting that unlike Edward and, later, his brother Henry, Francis did not join as a midshipman and never rose in rank above commander; he always seems to have been something of an oddball in the family. In 1832, writing to his brother Lord William from Woburn, Tavistock described Frank in the hunting season: 'Frank also with the "unters and ack", all as strange as himself. He was sent to a private tutor to "study". When he returned, my Father asked him what he had been reading. History; ancient or modern? He didn't know, but believed it was ancient.'

Apart from the fact that he does not appear to have attended school (as the others had done) and was privately tutored, we do not know enough about Frank's life to challenge this image of him as 'strange and intellectually challenged', as Trethewey sums up Tavistock's opinion of him, but certainly his twenty-six-year naval career was nowhere near as successful his brothers', and his dropped 'h's, coarse language and manners, and a propensity for drunken brawling would seem to reflect his having grown up in the rough and tumble of the lives of the ratings rather than those of the officers of the navy. In June 1832 the horrified duke asked Lady Holland, 'Did you see the scandalous reports from Frank?: "Lord Francis Russell, of No.6 Belgrave Square, drunk with a black eye &c, &c, &c.." What a shame!' Even thirty years later, in 1866, when retired and living in Maidenhead, Frank twice appeared in court: in October he was found guilty of beating two horses, and then in November he was charged with assaulting his coachman, but was acquitted on the basis of self-defence – both, it seems, were drunk.[392] Certainly, whatever the cause, Frank was the one who confirmed for his three stepbrothers their reservations about the 'Gordon crop', the term they used for Georgina's children.

In January 1822 the duke recorded the following incident in his game books: 'I met with an accident on the 12th and was not able to go out before the 18th. I then found myself unable to walk and went home immediately.' There are no further details recorded, but whatever happened, it marked the first incident in a year which was to change his life and priorities forever. By the end of February the consequences of this accident became clear, as the duke's final comment in the game book for that month reads, 'I never shot well after the accident I had on the 12th Jan.'[393] Although he went on to shoot periodically over the coming years, particularly in 1823, this was the last detailed game book he kept, and there is no record of him participating in the increasingly fashionable sport of deer stalking; instead, his attention in Scotland was increasingly focused on the history and beliefs of the communities around him, and on the flora and fauna of the landscapes around them.

At Woburn that spring the structure for the Heath House was completed, while in the Sculpture Gallery they were by now 'unpacking and fixing Marble'. Also, at the south front of the Abbey, 'Her Grace's Garden' was fenced and the railings along the terrace in front of the library were cleaned and gilded. Beyond organizing the Sculpture Gallery, it is clear that the duke was also being actively encouraged to develop the collections by Lord William, who was in Italy with Bessy. Specifically, he suggested augmenting the collections with 'plaster casts of ancient statues', which he offered to buy for him. He considered that his father might 'easily get a place for them by heightening the covered way and covering it in on one or the other side of the Gallery', and that such acquisitions would be 'a fund of interest and pleasure to yourself who are so fond of sculpture'. In another letter he suggested that 'Casts of the Niobe family' and the 'dying gladiator, the listening slave and the Venus' would be interesting, before telling his father that 'I have picked up a beautiful bust of a Faun (antique),' and adding, 'I fear poor Canova is dying.' Beyond purchasing items, Lord William also sent his father in 1824 a highly detailed and scholarly description of stylistic elements to note on genuine 'ancient portrait busts' and how to spot a later fake.[394]

The other individual assisting with the collections and their arrangement at this time was Revd Philip Hunt, who had been in the duke's employment since 1806 when he accompanied the family to Dublin as private secretary. Since that time he seems to have been assisting Jeremiah Wiffen as a librarian and translator at the Abbey, while also serving as a magistrate in Bedford. Hunt's particular speciality, however, had been sourcing and acquiring a range of antiquities from statuary to ancient manuscripts from across the Middle East, and he had been a part of the team which removed the marbles from the Parthenon and transported them to England for Lord Elgin between 1802 and 1803.

The story of the removal of the marbles is famously murky, and the truth of what happened has never been fully explained. What started, apparently, as an exercise in recording the decorative friezes and pedimental sculpture in drawings and plaster casts soon included collecting many of the carved fragments lying around on the ground, and finally, most controversially, to the hurried removal of about half of those still *in situ* on the building, an undertaking which led to the destruction of some and the mutilation of the building. Those involved – Elgin, Hunt, the Italian artist Lusieri and Elgin's secretary, William Hamilton – claimed to have acquired a series of 'firmins', or written permissions, from the Turkish authorities, one of which, in 1801, they stated had given permission to actually remove marbles still *in situ*, while a further one in 1803 permitted their transportation to England. Unfortunately, no one was ever able to produce any of the original documentation, even to the subsequent House of Commons enquiry of 1816, which could explain what had really happened. Whether Elgin or Hunt ordered the removal of the friezes remains unclear, but Hunt was on the spot during the whole unedifying episode, an act, as one English eyewitness described it, of 'utter barbarism … Could anyone believe that this was done, and that it was done, too, in the name of a nation vain of its distinction in the Fine Arts?'[395] While the duke was clearly content to employ Hunt over a long period of time, and he left no opinion about Elgin's exploits or Hunt's part in them, it was a side to the trade in antiquities which seems to have made him increasingly uncomfortable, and may have contributed to his later decision to stop collecting.

In early summer 1822, the Bedfords were looking forward to another trip to Invereshie in August, but by late May not only were these plans put on hold, but everything had suddenly changed when two unforeseen but connected events occurred. First, the duke had participated in a local meeting in Bedford concerning measures to relieve agricultural distress, and had given an unusually critical speech attacking what he saw as corruption endemic in the current parliamentary system, claiming specifically that support for a 'great borough-proprietor, now a Noble Duke' had been 'purchased by Government … by conferring high offices on

[his] adherents'. The duke then asked 'whether, if a Reform had been effected by Parliament, such transactions could possibly happen?' The *London Gazette* reported what happened next: 'It seems the Duke of Buckingham took umbrage at these observations (which, it must be confessed, are somewhat strong), and personally demanded that the Duke of Bedford should retract them publically. The Noble Duke peremptorily refused to accede to this demand, and a challenge was the consequence.' Accompanied by Lord Lynedoch, the duke turned up for the duel early in the morning 'at a retired spot previously agreed upon' in Kensington Gardens. The ground was measured and

> on a signal given, the parties presented, but the Duke of Buckingham only fired; and his shot not taking effect, the Duke of Bedford instantly discharged his pistol in the air, upon which the Duke of Buckingham advanced towards his Grace and said, 'My Lord Duke, your Grace is the last man in existence I would wish to quarrel with; but you must be well aware that the life of a public man is not worth preserving, unless it be preserved with honour.' Whereupon the Duke of Bedford promptly replied, that upon his honour he meant no personal offence to the Duke of Buckingham … nor did he mean to impute in him, personally, any bad or corrupt motives whatever. Their Lordships then shook hands, and, as an evening paper stated, 'the whole business was terminated most satisfactorily.'[396]

'Terminated most satisfactorily' in terms of the two dukes perhaps, but it is probably just as well that there is no record of the remarks which passed between Georgina and her husband once she found out what had happened. There is a lot of concern for the gentlemen's 'honour' here, but had Buckingham's shot not missed, Georgina and her children would have lost everything and her future would have been as uncertain as her mother's; the price paid by her for her husband's honour could have been very high. The duke himself couched the affair as a 'necessity' in a letter to Lord William the next day informing him of the duel, adding that he 'escaped untouched', which may well reflect what he said to Georgina. William's reply was to ask for more details, before commenting: 'How could you resist putting a bullet into his fat guts, it would never have penetrated to a vital part.' Georgina's reply, however, is likely to have been very different.[397]

Following this incident the family travelled down to Endsleigh for the summer, but just how much stress the duel had really placed on the duke, and just how much tension remained, is reflected perhaps in the fact that in late June he suffered a 'severe apoplectic fit' – a major stroke – which, among other things, left half his face immobile. We can follow events and Georgina's mood in her letters to Lord Grey. By early July she writes her first update: 'he recovers slowly, but there is always a little pain within the head, the eyes, and the neck … enough to create and keep up a constant anxiety in my mind … [and] The paralised [sic] side of the face remains immovable.' Her initial plan in July had been that they would slowly make their way back to Woburn via a stay at Longleat, but by the end of August they were still at Endsleigh and the news was still not good: '[Dr] Halford is here, and thinks the Duke has been even more seriously ill than he apprehended … He is a melancholy and heart-breaking sight.' They eventually were able to return to Woburn in October, but Georgina was as anxious as ever, in spite of the duke himself trying to carry on as normal: 'Halford saw him last week and told me pressure still existed in the Brain, that the restoration of the face with natural form and powers would be evidence that the pressure no longer existed. As his face [remains] immovable, I cannot consider him as better. That he has been out shooting three times is true, but as he never has minded noise, it proves nothing. He has been less well for the last five days.'

Perhaps to minimize such activities, the family travelled to Hastings, from where Georgina reported to Grey of 'a return of all the disagreeable symptoms in his head … his pulse is not yet right,' before giving a glimpse of how she was dealing with this: 'My own health is good, and as long as I do not hear music, or meet with anyone … I appear cheerful and calm, but … what a revolution takes place in me when exposed to either of those things. I then feel all the horror I must go through … I fly out on something or other, to drive away thought.'[398]

With all the bad news, the Bedfords had, however, received some cheery news from their two sailors when, at the end of June, letters arrived from Edward and

Francis on board HMS *Owen Glendower* heading for Spithead after patrol off Copenhagen. The ship was to take on supplies before leaving for the Mediterranean and the West Africa Station, and Edward, now seventeen and a three-year veteran of the navy, was clearly in good spirits and looking after his younger brother: 'Dear Mama, … Frank is quite well and very happy, he was a little sick coming home, but I think he has nearly got over it … he goes up the rigging very well now and is not at all frightened. I do not know what will happen to us now.' He asks for news and refers to a senior officer 'Mr Russell', who he says 'sends his love', and ends, 'Give my love to Papa, Eliza and Sisters …'[399]

When the duke's brother, 'old' Lord William as he was known to avoid confusion with his nephew, arrived at Endsleigh to visit his sick brother, it was the first time they had all met for some time, but news of him had reached them in letters from Lord William. His life abroad appears to have become increasingly confused and aimless since the death of his wife and his retirement from Parliament, and writing from Florence, William had reported:

> *Old* Lord William lives in the house with us. He appears such an unhappy wandering spirit that I was glad to offer him a home, but he is too restless to remain in it & wanders about from tavern to tavern without knowing why or wherefore. I quite pity him … Lord William left us yesterday on his wanderings … I quite pity him, he appears quite destitute … so totally without interest about anyone or occupation of any sort … I feel much pity for him – he told me the other day with tears in his eyes that he had written a most affectionate letter to Francis [Tavistock], but that F had taken no notice of it. What a heartless beast he must be, only imagine yourself poor … widowed, alone, wandering from town to town … I imagine at the same time Tavistock living in all the idleness and luxury of London and Woburn Abbey.[400]

There is also an interesting hint here of William's own 'unhappy wandering spirit' and his growing bitterness about a system of inheritance which excluded him, as a second son, from the life that Tavistock had. He too was in exile on the

Continent, wandering between hotels and borrowed houses, disconnected from British politics, and searching for a role in life beyond gratifying his wife and her mother's needs. Fortunately for William, his shared interest in the Sculpture Gallery project provided a lasting connection with his father, and in 1822 this project went a step further when the duke, eager to establish the scope and quality of his collections, commissioned Philip Hunt to produce *Outline Engravings and Descriptions of the Woburn Abbey Marbles*, the first catalogue. It lists some seventeen items: reliefs, vases, busts and statue fragments of various sizes, some acquired by the 5th Duke, the others mostly bought by the 6th Duke in Rome during their visit of 1814–15. Hunt also records that it was with 'great difficulty' that the duke 'obtained permission from the Papal government to remove [the] ancient sculptures to England'.[401] This would seem to confirm that, whatever he may have thought about the ethics of Elgin and many of the other collectors, he at least went to great lengths to secure permission to take sculptures out of Italy; as we shall see, sometime later, when one of Hunt's Middle Eastern contacts offered him sculptures of dubious origin, he decided not to purchase them.

In February 1823, after an unusually quiet Christmas and New Year, the duke visited his doctors in London, and as Henry Fox tells us, 'I fear the account is not so good'; things were made considerably worse when in March he suffered a serious attack of gout which kept him in his room for several weeks. Generally, progress was painfully slow, and as Georgina explained in a letter to Grey in March concerning the duke's health and its effect on her: 'every symptom of his original complaint exists at present as strong as ever … [and] is aggravated by the Gout … to a state of health already but precarious. After this statement it is useless for me to tell you how nine months of constant watching and miserable anxiety has subdued the gaiety of my mind; but there is enough left to be always cheerful before him, and I thank God, also, for the power of making him quite happy.' She adds, 'I cannot understand the feeling, tho' the longer I live, the more things I see to astonish me, and none more than Lord Tavistock's conduct … neither Lord or Lady T, are kind to me,' but 'Lord John is all kindness to me, and all attention and affection to his father.'[402]

Dr Philip Hunt, 'The Sculpture Gallery', *Outline Engravings and Descriptions of the Woburn Abbey Marbles*, 1822. View east towards the Temple of Liberty. Following a busy period of collecting, the duke now had a collection of antique sculpture to rival what he had seen at Richard Worsley's Appuldurcombe in 1793. The reassembled pieces of the Ephesian Sarcophagus can be seen on the right.

As the long spring dragged on, the duke finally started to overcome the gout, and it seems his enforced confinement and life-changing stroke refocused his life and energies. He referred to these circumstances in his introduction to *Hortus Ericaeus Woburnensis* in 1825: 'In 1822, when I began to recover from a severe attack of illness, which had unfitted me for almost every other occupation, I determined on commencing a collection of Heaths, exotic as well as indigenous.'

In the Abbey, 1823 saw the start of work on the reception rooms to the north of the Saloon, starting with the redecoration of the West Drawing Room and the smaller Inner Drawing Room beyond. Redecoration included new wallpapers, new ceiling cornices, paint and gilding, new furniture and the refurbishment of the existing eighteenth-century sofas.[403] Outside, as noted above, work was completed on the Heath House, while in the Sculpture Gallery the duke began the work of arranging the exhibits – 'Fixing Basso Relievos', 'moving sculptures' – and organizing the installation of fragments of a mosaic pavement purchased by Lord William. In front of the library, the terrace garden was completed, while in the pleasure grounds 'new pens [were] added to the Menagerie' and elsewhere the gardeners were 'packing and crating seeds and plants for Endsleigh'.[404]

In April, as the gout subsided, they started to receive guests again, and one of the first to arrive was Edwin Landseer. Perhaps to recognize his debt to Georgina and to help cheer her up, the duke had commissioned a portrait of her, the first family portrait since Landseer had sketched Lord Cosmo on his pony and, indeed, the first written record of Landseer visiting the Abbey. This was followed in May by an even more significant gesture, as the duke announced to Lady Holland that, after years of leasing the property, 'I am now your neighbour, as I have bought Campden Hill Lodge.'[405] It would seem that with both of them needing fresh air and a quiet place to relax when in London, and no doubt at some urging from Georgina, the duke bought the villa, looking forward to enjoying not just the garden, but also the proximity of the Hollands.

In July 1822 Lord William had determined to return to England and attend Parliament, and the duke was anxiously hoping that it could mark a fresh start for all of them. Writing in December 1822 to Bessy he had said, 'It is an object near to my heart that all misunderstandings should be done away and I cannot help feeling anxious, *most* anxious about it – should I not get over this protracted illness, it will smooth the pillow of a dying man on his way to the tomb.' By March Lord William and Bessy were on their way, but Bessy was in no mood for reconciliation, as Henry Fox observed, 'To my great joy I found the Wm Russells on their way to England. She gave a delightful account of Italy, is quite miserable at going home, and kept no bounds about the Duchess of B.'[406]

By April Lord William was back in London, having left Bessy, who was heavily pregnant, in Paris while he looked for a place for them to stay. Before leaving France he must have written to his father about the antiquities he had purchased in Italy and the possibility of using the house in St James's Square, but it turned out that, when the duke bought Campden Hill, he had lent St James's Square to his niece Gertrude and her husband, where they had been joined by her sister Eliza. The duke replied: 'I am perfectly satisfied with the purchases you made for me in Italy … I sincerely wish it were in my power to offer my house in St James' Square to you and yours, but you know how it is occupied, and I must reserve my own rooms, as in the present uncertain state of my health, I am liable to be called up to town at any time … You were certainly guilty of imprudence in letting your own house for such a long time.' He ended his letter with the following, indicating things might not go smoothly:

> The concluding sentence in your letter gave me great pain. Why should you suppose that the Duchess dislikes you? I can assure you that the very reverse is the case … She is ever anxious to show every possible kindness to you, and your brothers, but her spirits are sometimes depressed, and this I think you may readily account for without any great stretch of the imagination. *She* indeed, imagines that neither you nor Tavistock, nor John like *her*, and in this I am sure that she is wrong, but the feeling arises from an excess of sensibility, and I cannot blame her.[407]

By July the duke was strong enough for the journey to Scotland, where they remained until September, while William and Bessy occupied rooms in the Abbey during their absence. As Blakiston tells us, 'Bessy, in the absence of the Duchess, was as happy at Woburn as it was in her nature to be. She was again with child and Lord William had a scheme for buying a house in London; but in August she had a miscarriage and her husband found he had no money for a house.' Things were going a lot better, however, in Scotland, where the Bedfords were enjoying a recreational few weeks in August and September, the duke shooting and Georgina pursuing her love for fishing: 'one day she hooked a fifteen and a half pound salmon with a fly and the next day caught a seventeen and a half pound one.'[408]

By October Georgina had taken a house for the family in Regency Square, Brighton, where, with a brief trip back to Woburn for Christmas, they stayed until early January. Writing to Grey from Woburn at the end of December 1823, it is clear that apart from a welcome visit from Lord Edward (or Teddy) on a brief shore leave, concerns about the duke's health, and the endless worries associated with it, were weighing heavily on Georgina's spirits. For her, Grey had become an essential friend and confidante: 'Though it is a long time since I have written to you, the time has not been passed without thinking of you, and I heard with pleasure that you were going to Plymouth … I do hope you will visit Endsleigh … The Housekeeper would make all comfortable, and the Scotch bailiff (Forester) is a most agreeable, tho' <u>rough Diamond</u>.' She goes on: 'as to the Duke, I have nothing satisfactory to say, he has been very unwell since we returned here … and I do not think he improves, particularly in his walking, he is so very weak on his legs. We have been quite alone, which in this large house is very melancholy. The arrival of my son Edward yesterday was a charming sight. I hope your son is as well and as handsome as Teddy; I am rather proud of him.' She then asked Grey about what would be a suitable allowance for Wriothesley at Cambridge, before concluding wistfully: 'I wish I could have a comfortable <u>chat</u> with you, a quiet walk at my dear Endsleigh, by the side of the River, or on the other side of the river on a wild common, with the rapid Tavy, moving through it, as bright as any Scotch stream; alas, I fear no such comfort is in store for me, and I must content myself with my <u>Mausoleum</u>, where all the inhabitants are cold, and the splendid magnificence very imposing and chilling.'[409]

This letter is a rare glimpse into the lives of the Bedfords and also into the role Woburn Abbey played in them. Clearly, for the duke the Abbey was the enduring embodiment of the Russell family; it represented some three hundred years of their history, their achievements, their taste and their vision of Britain. As such it provided the essential and appropriate stage upon which he could, in turn, display his contribution to this history, while also providing a gravitas to their endeavours that ensured they were taken seriously. The 6th Duke was extremely proud of his family history, which he would defend fiercely from any attacks, and he was determined that under his stewardship the Abbey, inside and out, would maintain the standards his brother had set, whatever the cost; debts could be paid off, and would ultimately cost far less than the necessity of attempting to bring back 'the splendid magnificence' should it ever be lost.

Yet, while Woburn was central to the duke's identity, for Georgina it was somewhere she had to learn to like, to find spaces within the edifice for herself and her children, and to warm up the 'imposing and chilling' mausoleum and make a home. Seen in the context of this letter, it is clear why Endsleigh, Invereshie, The Doune and Campden Hill became so important to her, and at this difficult moment it is not thoughts of Woburn but of 'a quiet walk at Endsleigh' or 'the rapid Tavy … as bright as any Scotch stream' that bring her comfort, because they lay at the heart of *her* identity. It is important to note, too, that this letter also indicates the extent to which the key individuals who were brought in to help the Bedfords realize their ambitions were also Scots: from William Adam to George Sinclair and, a few years later, James Forbes at Woburn and John Forester at Endsleigh, the 'rough diamonds' who brought fresh ideas and energy and, for Georgina, a link to home.

One bright spot that New Year was the 'Children's Ball' that George IV hosted at his recently completed Royal Pavilion at Brighton on 1 January 1824. Lady Granville records that 'the child's ball was beautiful. Near one hundred of them; the King was so engrossed in the Bedford Children … [and] the youngest Bedford girl [Louisa] beautiful, exactly like what Georgiana Gordon was.' Trethewey notes that not only was Louisa 'beautiful', but her particular success that night was her solo performance of the 'The Spanish Shawl Dance', which led the king to personally congratulate her.

With a full return to health still in the balance, and under strict doctor's orders to concentrate on his recovery, the duke spent the spring of 1824 at Woburn receiving visitors and furthering his new interests. In March, reflecting his new focus on British artists, he mentioned one such visit to Lord Holland: 'I have a lot of R.As coming here this week – Flaxman, Westmacott and Wyatt … have you bought any new prints? You and I are engaged in the same pursuit, and I begin to find it an amusing one.'[410]

Another pursuit the duke was engaged in was the purchase of several fragments of 'Ancient Sculpture' from neighbouring Battlesden Park. We are alerted to this by an account book entry for 1824, 'Sculpture Gallery: Loading and unloading marbles from Battlesden Park', and a description of what he had bought by Philip Hunt:

In the year 1824, four Fragments of Ancient Sculpture, in alto and basso relievo, were purchased by the Duke of Bedford at the sale of effects belonging to Sir G.P.O Turner at Battlesden Park, Beds … They had formerly been placed, with other fragments of sculpture, over the arch of a gateway at Ephesus: from whence they were taken, some years ago, by two Travellers, and bought to England for sale.

On arrival of these fragments at Woburn Abbey they were carefully inspected by an eminent sculptor [Westmacott], who soon ascertained that they had originally constituted one entire series, forming the four sides of a sculptured Sarcophagus, consisting of a single block of marble, and, under his superintendence they have been restored to their original relative positions, and reunited, as accurately as their injured and mutilated condition would permit ... The whole composition appears to be descriptive of Scenes and Events connected with the Trojan War.[411]

While the duke was busy with his collections, in the gardens the children's garden, built to Repton's plan of some years before, was completed, as was the addition next to it of a 'Rustic Grotto' designed by Wyatville. This dumpy, circular structure, built of rough rubble stone with openings to the east and west, was decorated on the inside with crystals, quartzes and strange rocks transported from the Devon estates, which were then lit by candle, creating, along with a small bubbling fountain in the centre, an other-worldly interior where the children were read to and told stories. The children's garden offered each one a small area of their own, where 'their names were marked on bits of China on a stick.' The only one we can identify now from the plan was Edward's, which featured an 'anchor made of Box planted in that shape'.[412]

During that year work also started on Wyatville's proposals from the year before for alterations to Campden Hill (Colour Plate 23). Between April and December, bricklayers and carpenters were creating new offices and servants' apartments on the east end of the house, while Georgina ordered a new flower garden layout to the west; a year later, to make the most of the new gardens, a new drawing room was added overlooking them. While building went on at Campden Hill, at Woburn the Inner Drawing Room, West Drawing Room, North-West Drawing Room and Small Drawing Room were all refurbished, with new gilded window cornices, bookcases, furniture and fittings. Thus, both houses were being worked on when the family set off for Invereshie in August, where they were joined by old Lord William, and in a landmark moment in their lives, the family met up with Landseer in September on his first visit to Scotland, which was to prove seminal in the development of his art.[413]

In early September, Landseer had travelled to Scotland to meet his friends and fellow painters, C. R. Leslie and G. S. Newton. They initially met up in Edinburgh, where Leslie was to paint Walter Scott, but finding Scott was away and with a few days to kill, Leslie and Newton travelled across to Glasgow and on up to Loch Lomond, Loch Katrine and Loch Earn, before returning to meet Scott at Abbotsford. Landseer, however, seems not to have gone with them, and instead made his way on his own visit to Blair Castle where he had a letter of introduction to John Crear, the Duke of Atholl's head gamekeeper, written for him by Professor Robert Jameson of Edinburgh University. Landseer spent ten days at Blair Castle making studies of deer, but at some point he also met up with the Bedfords, who seem to have made arrangements with the Duke of Atholl to spend a few days at his Forest Lodge in Glen Tilt. Since there is no record of the Bedfords taking a formal lease, no account of the trip or of them being there very long, the arrangements all seem to have been made at short notice, perhaps as soon as Landseer informed them where he was, but it must have been a wonderful moment for Georgina as she, the duke, Georgiana, Louisa, Francis and Cosmo set off on their ponies, each one led by a ghillie, following the old drove road up Glen Feshie to Ruigh Fionntaig, travelling over the tops to the pass at Minigaig, and down Glen Bruar to Bruar Lodge. Here they left the main drove road and headed east through the Atholl estate to Gilbert's Bridge, before heading up Glen Tilt to Forest Lodge – the kind of adventure she had so enjoyed as a child on similar trips round Glenfiddich and Kinrara (Colour Plate 34).

The impact of the Scottish landscape on Landseer's career was profound. As one biographer put it, 'It is no exaggeration to describe the year 1824 as the turning-point in Landseer's career,' since it was at this point that he began to paint landscapes – not the conventional views of famous places, but scenes in those remote glens he found himself in.[414] Most importantly, though, the images he began to create were attempts to reproduce what he was actually seeing, to catch the atmosphere and his emotional response to it, totally free of art historicism or stylization. In this context, three images that Landseer produced that year are of particular interest for this book.

The first is *Scene on the River Tilt, in the Grounds of His Grace the Duke of Bedford*, which not only shows an old Highland lady overseeing the four Bedford children, all in their Highland outfits, who are watching the cooking pot on an open fire set on the bank of the river Tilt, but also records in detail the wider setting – the river flowing down out of the backdrop of mountains which rise up behind the children (Colour Plate 24). Whether Landseer actually witnessed this scene, or whether the children were drawn elsewhere and then placed against a suitable background, we do not know, but the picture has a strong sense of place. We see Landseer working hard to capture the landscape of the glen, the rounded heather-covered hills, the sound and sparkle of the river tumbling over a fall under the bridge in the middle distance, and, closer to us, the details of the light on the water and of the riverbanks, rocks, shrubs and autumn-tinted birch trees. Clearly, Landseer's response to the Highlands was immediate and intense, producing what may be his 'first ever true landscape'.

The second image, also dated 1824, is an oil painting called *Lord Cosmo Russell on his Pony Fingal* (Colour Plate 25), and though it has a very similar title to the sketch of 1820 that hung in St James's Square, the two are likely to have been different images. Given that in 1820 Cosmo was only three, it seems more plausible that in the sketch the boy was sitting on a stationary pony held by a groom, and that it was not until Landseer's visit to Scotland that the subject became part of the full-blown Romantic scene we see in the oil painting. Although the horse and rider are 'said to have been painted in the riding school at Woburn Abbey', they are now placed in a Highland landscape, riding across open moorland, a wide glen opening up below, and the background filled with rising mountains whose tops are obscured by rain squalls and racing clouds. Such was Landseer's instinctive ability to capture what he saw – whether it was the look in a dog's eye, the minute gradations of softness in an animal's coat, or now the sense that someone could be at home in these immense wild and windswept places – it is hard to believe, looking at these pictures, that they were some of his first attempts to portray landscape.[415]

The third image is a little different, and less is known about it. It appears in C. S. Mann's catalogue as *Trout Fishing on the Daune*, dated 1824, and the finished oil painting was sold under the same title, but what the image actually shows is a scene on the Tamar at Endsleigh (Colour Plate 26). Whether Landseer never gave this image a title and Mann created it for the catalogue, or Landseer deliberately made up a name to obscure the actual location, is not clear, but it is obvious that we are looking upstream as the Tamar runs round under Leigh Woods, the view terminated by the great spur of rocks running down from the Swiss Cottage, clearly visible on the crest of the hill, and halfway up there is a suggestion of the openings between the pillars of the Rock Seat. In the foreground an unidentified young boy is fishing from a rock out in the river, a location still recognizable today, accompanied by a large white dog. Since the dog strongly resembles the dog bounding along beside his pony in the previous image, it is possible that this figure also shows Cosmo. We do not have a firm date for either Landseer's first visit to Endsleigh – it may well have been earlier that summer, before he set off Scotland – or this oil painting, in which indications of at least one change to the composition (what appears to be a painted out figure in front of the boy) suggest it may have been worked on after Landseer's return from Scotland. Certainly, the assured skill and quality of the picture indicate that Landseer had been practising and is able to produce an image that so clearly captures the different feel of the lush variety of the dense Devon woodlands compared to the open heather moorlands of the Highlands.

In these images, the colours capture a soft and Romantic glow, as though part of Landseer's vision of landscape is already shaped by Scott's tales and Georgina's memories, but they retain a sharp sense of realism, which in turn gives them a sense of the intimacy of the moment, as it was experienced. All three have a strong sense of rapidly realized studies, open air sketches capturing not just the shapes of the landscape, but the feeling of being there on a particular day: Landseer recording the atmosphere, learning to portray the interplay of light and shadow on the different elements of the view, developing the new element of landscape which became such an integral part of his later work and for which he is now remembered.

CHAPTER EIGHT
1825–1830

ALTHOUGH 1824 HAD BEEN AN EXCITING YEAR, particularly in Scotland, it had also seen the end of the year-long fragile peace between the duchess and Lady William Russell when simmering tensions suddenly blew up over a disputed incident. The way Lady William described it, she was 'going down to Woburn … before the Duke's going to Scotland … to take leave till next year', and had been about to leave when she heard from William, who was in Bedford, asking her 'to put off' her departure since 'his father had written him a note begging of him to prevent my coming and he gave as a reason a string of words evidently dictated by the Duchess … that while she, the Duchess, could not "command our affections but that a certain decorum and respect was due to her as mistress of the house etc, etc, etc.", in short that I have been rude and ungrateful.' She continued, 'The Duchess told everybody [at Woburn] that I had merely sent word by William the day before that I should be at Woburn to dinner, that the Duke thought it impertinent and forbid me the house.'

Neither the duke nor the duchess gave their side of the story, so what had really happened remains unclear, but they were both very upset, as is clear in a letter from the duke to Lady Holland: 'I confess I cannot comprehend William's conduct to the Duchess, he does not treat her with the common decency and decorum due from a man to a woman; much more from him to his father's wife … Surely the Dss. cannot be expected to make an *apology* for an offence denied and not committed!' In his final comment on the issue in a letter to Lord William, the duke says, 'During the nine months that you were [at Woburn], it was the constant wish of both the Duchess and myself, to make you and yours as comfortable as we could, and if we have failed in our endeavours, we can only lament it.'[416]

Had Georgina overreacted to a perceived slight? Quite possibly but whatever the truth of the affair, Lady William's description of what the duchess had said – that 'certain decorum and respect was due to her as mistress of the house' – is vividly reminiscent of her mother's words to the lawyer Farquharson during her bitter negotiations with the Duke of Gordon: 'as a Wife and Mistress of his family I never shall forget what I owe to myself.' Georgina's prickliness about station, respect and dignity seems to be directly related to her mother's treatment twenty years before, and the determination that this would never happen to her appears to have become a defining factor in her character. The result was perhaps inevitable, and by October Bessy was 'banished *par contumace*', as she put it, from Woburn. Lord William in turn refused to go without her, and the rift, which lasted some two years, was complete. In September 1825 the duke, always uncomfortable with tension and disagreement, attempted to draw a line under the whole sad issue: 'Whilst I regret that we should be compelled to think and feel differently on the unpleasant subject we have recently discussed … Let everything on so painful a subject be now forgotten, and completely blotted from our memories.' Ending this letter, the duke then says something very interesting. He is explicit about his frame of mind: 'What I have said with regard to myself is the settled conviction of my mind – others may think differently, but I feel the vital powers languish and decay, and the lamp of life is dimming, and must soon be extinguished.'[417]

Although he lived for another fourteen years, this view of his own prospects should be kept in mind, since it forms the background to everything that happened subsequently. From here on, there is a growing introspection around his activities as he turns from worldly matters – politics, agricultural improvements, committees and societies – to his private interests – family history, scientific horticulture and botany.

This trend in the duke's behaviour started to emerge in 1825. While his health remained fragile, he became increasingly preoccupied with research and study facilitated by cutting edge technology and dedicated collections of carefully monitored plantings. It is almost as though he had suddenly glimpsed an opportunity to take a place among the scientists and their patrons who were opening up the wonders and mysteries of the natural world, and for Woburn to take its place beside the institutions and new botanical gardens where these people were working. With widespread recognition of the value of his work with Sinclair on the grass ground and the establishment of his first serious scientific collection in the Heath House, we see a new focus driving his pursuit of this vision, as if the duke had glimpsed what could constitute his legacy. This prompted a new urgency to achieve it and required a kind of dedicated commitment that we have not seen manifested in his life so far; it represented an entirely new phase of his life. While the early years of their marriage had seen mostly shared endeavours and while they remained very close as a couple, this new phase saw them increasingly follow separate interests: the duke history and science, the duchess art and engagement with her Highland background, creating complementary and individual lives.

In many ways, this new phase really began in January 1825 with the publication of *Hortus Ericaeus Woburnensis* and the appointment of a new head gardener at Woburn a short time later. In the first case, this was the second publication marking the successful establishment of one of his personal projects, and furthered Woburn's reputation as a centre for groundbreaking science. In the second, publication of the book gave George Sinclair the opportunity to move on to new challenges, but before leaving Woburn he had given the duke an idea for the next project: a comprehensive collection of willows. Fortunately, his successor was already on hand in the form of James Forbes, another Scotsman, who had joined Sinclair's garden staff at Woburn the year before. Originally from Perthshire, and after training in Ireland, Forbes had become Deputy Curator to James Mackay and assistant at the Botanic Garden, Trinity College, Dublin, between 1820 and 1824. At Dublin, as Paul Smith writes, 'The Curator, James Townsend Mackay had established a valuable and systematically organised collection of English willows and his deputy must have become familiar with many varieties,' and Smith suggests that it may have been partly for his knowledge of willows that Forbes was chosen to replace Sinclair as head gardener at Woburn, a post he retained until 1861, dying while still in the service of the 7th Duke.

Sinclair had arrived at Woburn as an ambitious twenty year old with deep scientific interests and a confident independence that allowed him to develop projects with little input from the duke. By 1825, however, he was successful in his own right, having become a Fellow of the Horticultural Society in 1823 and of the Linnean Society in 1824, and, as reflected in the duke's introduction to *Hortus Ericaeus Woburnensis*, he had developed a growing reputation: 'Under the superintendence of my late Gardener, Mr George Sinclair, F.L.S., F.H.S., the accuracy of whose researches into Botany, and Vegetable Physiology, is too well known to need any encomium from me, I have been enabled to complete [this] catalogue.'

In a sense he probably outgrew Woburn, and while setting up and monitoring the grass ground experiments and the successful establishment of the heath collection had been challenges he had been eager to pursue, he was also ambitious to follow his own interests. He went into the plant and seed business, forming a successful partnership with John Cormack based at the New Cross Nursery in Surrey and Covent Garden. Interestingly enough, when Sinclair left Woburn as part of his new venture, 'he developed the principles that had been established in the grass garden experiments to develop lawn seed mixtures suited to different soil conditions,' a groundbreaking progression in the development of lawn grasses and the science of lawns.[418] Whether or not the duke ever learnt of this new work is not recorded, but if he did, he would no doubt have been both proud and delighted that the grass garden at Woburn continued to contribute to science, especially in an area that was to become such a dominant and enduring feature of gardens large and small.

In fact, now that he was increasingly engaged personally with the horticultural and botanical developments at Woburn, the duke too may have been ready for change. Sinclair may well have been his ideal partner at the beginning, but in many ways Forbes was exactly the kind of person he needed now. Unlike his predecessor, who at twenty was just getting into his stride and eager to make his mark in the world, Forbes was fifty-one when he arrived at Woburn, with an established reputation and career behind him as an estate gardener, horticulturalist and curator of collections, and as such was probably delighted to be offered a position that promised both security and interesting prospects for projects to come. One senses, too, that Forbes, like Landseer in the world of art, was someone the duke felt comfortable working collaboratively with.

Within weeks of Sinclair leaving, Forbes was appointed head gardener with responsibilities which included the kitchen gardens, and four years of work on the willow collection began. During that time the location and design of the collection, once again set within the pleasure grounds, altered several times, but the final result was described by Forbes in 1833 as 'consisting of the most numerous species and varieties of *Salices* in Britain … The larger growing kinds are planted round the outer beds, or circles of this grove, and the small, or dwarf species, occupy the centre circles. The whole is enclosed by a Holly-hedge, with the exception of the entrance, which is formed by an iron arch *trellis*, intertwined with some of the more flexible *salices*.'[419]

The collection had become another highly decorative display of serious scientific material, such as we have seen with the grass garden and the Heath House, yet it is also clear that for the duke the willow collection had a personal meaning. This was pointed out many years later by the botanist Sir William Hooker when he quoted from a letter of 11 November 1804 from the duke to the botanist Sir James Edward Smith thanking him for his letter naming *Salix russelliana*, and acknowledging his brother's interests in these things, adding that 'I have lately discovered … that my grandfather introduced the same willow into this country 40 or 50 years ago, and distributed it amongst his tenants.' This collection was partly created in homage to both his brother and his grandfather, the 4th Duke.[420]

Such recognition of his family became increasingly important to the duke, and as early as 1822 he had also turned his attention to their history when he commissioned Henry Bone to produce a series of miniature portraits of his Russell ancestors, twenty-five of which were framed in groups and displayed in the Abbey. Bone specialized in miniature portraits in enamel on ormolu (gilded bronze), and looking at the dates in his sketchbooks of images taken from portraits at Woburn, he seems to have begun work in 1822, completing the series in 1825. Decorative as these miniatures may have been, however, the real purpose behind this project became clear when in May 1825 the duke published *A Catalogue of Miniature Portraits in Enamel by Henry Bone Esq, RA, in the Collection of the Duke of Bedford at Woburn Abbey*, in which the twenty-five selected images are accompanied by biographies of the individuals, probably written by Jeremiah Wiffen with input from the duke and suitably exhortative quotations from classical writers to encourage his sons to do honour to the name of Russell: '"Et te, repetentum exempla tuorum, Et pater Æneas, et avunculus excitet Hector" Virg. Æn. Lib. XII.'[421]

Although the duke was modest about his new catalogue, telling Lady Holland, 'My little catalogue is at last printed and here it is … [it] is without pretentions and is, moreover, somewhat old fashioned,' it nevertheless meant a great deal to him, and he explained why when he sent a copy to Lord William: 'I am glad you like my Catalogue, I have endeavoured to prove that we are something better than the mere descendents of a minion of Henry VIII as Mr. Burke called us in a fit of spleen. I have inserted these lines from Virgil as an incitement to my sons, and to future Dukes of Bedford, to emulate the Conduct of their forefathers … and I have defended your Lucy against the severe observations of Walpole and Pennant.'

Edmund Burke's remarks had come in a written reply to the 5th Duke and Lord Lauderdale, who had both spoken in the House of Lords in opposition to the government's grant of a pension to Burke in 1796. In a furious 'letter' Burke called out the Duke of Bedford for criticizing the grant, pointing out that the duke's own fortune was built upon enormous crown grants: 'The first peer of the name, the first purchaser of the grants, was a Mr Russell, a person of an ancient family, raised by being a minion of Henry the Eighth,' and goes on to say that his own grant was 'from a mild and benevolent sovereign: his from Henry the Eighth'.[422]

While the duke does not comment directly on Burke or the letter or his brother's speech, he clearly never forgot this attack – it rankled and had struck a nerve. Never as thick-skinned as his elder brother, it seemed to shake his confidence in his own legitimacy, and even after publishing the *Catalogue of Miniature Portraits*, it was still on his mind, leading him to commission a full historical account of his ancestors from Jeremiah Wiffen in 1833 to prove that the family were never anyone's minions. Whatever Francis may have thought of Burke's letter, it seems John was deeply hurt, and no doubt this had exacerbated his disenchantment with the world of politics.

During this busy time at Woburn, it would seem that Georgina, while continuing to oversee the development of the parterres and flower beds in front of the Sculpture Gallery and in her own garden, was also starting to develop her interest in art, actively inspired by the presence of Landseer. In May 1824 he was starting to earn a good living and had finally moved out of his old family home to a house of his own in St John's Wood. Looked after by his sister and aunt, he also spent time at Woburn Abbey working on a series of three paintings of Alexander, aged four, with a variety of dogs, and one of Louisa, then thirteen, feeding a donkey. In addition, in 1828, Landseer also produced a 'sketch' showing family members and friends accompanying the duke on his horse through the park, entitled *Shooting Party at Woburn Abbey*, and showing the duke taking things easy following his stroke (Colour Plate 27). While all the images were done at Woburn, in two of them Alexander is wearing Highland dress, while that of Louisa has 'a Highland background added', giving us a strong indication of the growing importance of Scotland as a background to their lives.[423]

The fact that the next year Georgina produced an etched image, *Stag killed by the Duke of Gordon*, tells us that apart from encouraging her to draw, Landseer had also begun to teach Georgina to etch, an art form that firmly caught her imagination. She may also have watched as Landseer produced his series of 'Game Cards' for the Abbey, used for recording numbers of birds shot, and in this case decorated by etched images of game birds and animals.

During this period, work also continued on *The Hunting of Chevy Chase*, and given the new Scottish interests of Landseer and the duke, it should come as no surprise that Landseer's version of the stag hunt should by now have been wrapped in the romance of Walter Scott's poetry and novels and the history of the Scottish Borders. This was also something the duke had become interested in, and the year before, he had contacted Lord Grey searching for information about the grave site of his ancestor Lord Francis Russell, who had died at the skirmish of Windy Gale in the Cheviots in 1585: 'The case is simply this – one of my ancestors, Francis Lord Bedford, who was Warden of the Middle Marches, was killed in a border fray in the age of Elizabeth, and was buried in the Parish

Church of Alnwick. What I wish to know is whether there is any monument created to his memory in that Church, or any inscription. If you are acquainted with the incumbent, perhaps you will ask him to take the trouble of furnishing me with that information.' He was very disappointed to be told that no record of Lord Francis Russell in Northumberland appears to have survived, but in September he pursued his researches by contacting Scott. In a letter to Lady Holland from Invereshie on 26 September he said, 'I have had a correspondence with Sir Walter Scott upon a portion of Border history connected with my ancestors.' He added on 3 October: 'I have got deep into a correspondence with Sir Walter Scott … he has invited us to Abbotsford in our way home.'[424]

By June 1825 the family were back at Campden Hill, where Jeffry Wyatville had been completing the new building works, and where Georgina was preparing to host a ball. In addition, the duke and duchess enjoyed the company of more of Landseer's artist friends, George Jones and Augustus Wall Calcott, and during the visit, as the duke tells Lady Holland, 'We took our artists to the shady groves of Holland House this evening, to enjoy the cool walks of your beautiful gardens … Mr Jones was very much struck with the beauty and magnificence of the exteriors which he had never seen before.'

Following her ball, which seems to have been something of a social formality, Georgina was ready to leave for Scotland, and a letter in July to Lord Grey sums up her mood: 'I go to Woburn tomorrow where I wish you were coming [but] time is short, as we start for Scotland on Monday … My joy at leaving London is not to be expressed, for I find that I am <u>old</u> enough not to enjoy going out for going out sake … Kindest love to Lady Grey and the girls.'[425]

While Georgina and the children left for Invereshie almost immediately, the duke was not in quite such a hurry and he spent another month at Woburn, preoccupied with at least four new projects, before joining them. In the first case, in the Sculpture Gallery they were setting up new displays, while in the park 'Ivy Lodge' was built at the point where the 'Great Avenue' leading from the west front of the Abbey crossed the London road. Although there was no road into the park at this location, Ivy Lodge marked the point where a footpath led from the road towards the Abbey and the Cold Bath, and work done at this time included new fencing and repairing the 'Walk'.

In addition, Forbes began work that summer on a 'New Shrubbery' at the back of the tennis court, and quite possibly this represented the first phase of new collection of plants that Forbes later described as 'the American Banks … upwards of an acre of ground, the whole being richly planted with numerous species and varieties of Rhododendrons and Azalias [sic] etc.'. In the existing Evergreen Plantation, they were also 'forming new rides near Sand Hill', the first work done on the Evergreens since 1802, and represented an expansion of the access rides through woodlands planted by the 5th Duke after his enclosure of the northern section of the park in 1792.[426] Finally, and perhaps most significantly, the duke and Forbes began work on designs for their next major undertaking: a brand new, state of the art kitchen garden complex which would continue the integration of science and decorative design already underway in the pleasure grounds.

Unfortunately, the weather in Scotland when the duke arrived at Invershie in August was terrible, and he complained to Lady Holland of receiving no mail due to prolonged heavy rain, floods and damaged bridges. His spirits revived, however, when old friend Lord Lynedoch and Lord John arrived, and together they joined the Marquis of Huntly's shooting party at Kinrara on moors he had come to know well. Georgina, on the other hand, having escaped the social season in London and the formality of life at Woburn, had been enjoying visits to their wooden hut at Ruigh Fionntaig in the upper reaches of Glen Feshie. It would seem that she had first visited the site the year before, when the duke informed Lady Holland, 'The Dss is gone off to the Braes to prepare our bivouacaya [sic] for next week in a Peat cart! I wish you could see her in this gay and commodious equipage … Your little friend Cosmo looks well in his tartan dress and kilt, and seems to enjoy his freedom as much as a native Highlander.'

The image of Georgina setting off in her peat cart is one to savour, and adds to what she, in turn, wrote to Lord Grey. In what seems to be her first mention of Glen Feshie, she tells Grey they were surrounded by 'grand and wild scenery … in the Hills, where I have been for two days with the Duke, who went there to shoot … Salvator Rosa is the only person who could do justice to Glen fishie. I have enjoyed our solitude amazingly, and the absence of all <u>worries</u> has done my health, which was suffering severely in England, a great deal of good.'[427]

So much here is reminiscent of her mother's letters to Beattie, and it suggests she sensed that perhaps this could be as important to her as Glenfiddch and Kinrara had been to her mother: a place where she could finally recapture key elements of her identity. The year 1825 was also particularly significant in this process since it marked Landseer's first recorded visit to the landscape in which he was to spend so much time with Georgina, and which was to become central to his paintings. Rachel Trethewey quotes from a letter Landseer wrote to his friend William Ross that summer in which he explains that he had travelled 'further north this season and am a little crazy with the beauties of the Highlands'. The year before, during his first trip to Scotland, Landseer had stayed at Blair Atholl and met the Bedfords in Glen Tilt. This year he says he has gone 'further north', suggesting that he was part of the Marquis of Huntly's shooting party at Kinrara, since, following this, he says that he intends to visit Blair Atholl and then to 'revisit the Marques [sic] of Huntly', this time at Gordon Castle, after which his 'movements will be south'.[428]

While he reported to Ross that he had been 'working very hard and painting deer and grouse', other images he produced that year allow us to follow his progress, from the woodcut of *Glen Eirich, 1825*, presumably done on his way through Blairgowrie, and then three images from the Highlands. The first is another woodcut, *Highland Interior*, a simple drawing, perhaps his earliest, of the interior of a bothy and a young girl sitting beside the fire, while the second is a lively sketch, *Mountain Torrent*, which could easily be Glen Feshie, and finally a large study of an oil painting titled *A Scene in the Highlands, with portraits of Duchess of Bedford, Duke of Gordon, Lord Alexander and Stalker* (Colour Plate 28).[429] There are two versions of this painting: an earlier study in which the location is specific – showing huts by the distant river, indicating that the scene is likely based on Glenfeshie – and the second a tidied up version, the figures recomposed and the

Edwin Landseer, *Mountain Torrent*, 1825. Just a year after his first visit to Scotland, we see Landseer studying the details of the landscapes around him; the dogs and game are now part of a wider study of the natural world.

background more generic. The first appears to be Landseer's first identifiable Glen Feshie landscape, and the scene is used as a backdrop to a portrait group of Georgina, her son Alexander, her brother the Marquis of Huntly, who was Duke of Gordon by the time it was titled and exhibited in 1828, and a ghillie, the figures no doubt painted elsewhere, possibly at Kinrara.[430]

The other event of some importance was that in October, after a long and no doubt very welcome four-year break, Georgina discovered she was once again pregnant. The resulting child, her last, a girl named Rachel, has been the subject of much speculation about exactly who her father was – the duke or Landseer – and whether or not this proved that Georgina had embarked on a long-lasting affair with the young painter who became her constant companion during the years in Glen Feshie. So far it has proved impossible to uncover any evidence to settle this matter one way or another, and as Richard Ormond concludes, 'There is, however, no certainty that they were lovers, although in some circles it was assumed so.' Equally, even if they were, there is no certainty that Landseer was Rachel's father.[431] Had the duke not been in Scotland that year, it would be beyond doubt, but his arrival at Invereshie in late August removes any such certainty. Indeed, there is no hint of any scandal related to Rachel's parentage in any of the correspondence, and, as we shall see, the only thing which raises any questions about the circumstances of Rachel's life came following Georgina's death in 1853, when the trustees of her will discussed the 'problem of Rachel' and who should tell her the 'secret'. Although this secret was never revealed, either at the time or later, it appears to have revolved around an 'arrangement', and that word is perhaps more suggestive of a financial settlement than Rachel's parentage.

However, there is no doubt that the relationship between Georgina and Landseer became unusually intense and that, as the years went by, they spent more and more time together, albeit with staff and often the children, at The Doune and in Glen Feshie, and there can be no doubt that for both of them this location became a shared experience that enriched both their lives immeasurably, far beyond a mutual interest in art. Equally, while at least one of Landseer's portraits of Georgina suggests that the relationship may at one point have become physical, there is no evidence of tensions in the Bedfords' marriage beyond the occasional indication that, as his health deteriorated, the duke resented the amount of time his wife spent in Scotland, and we see no indication that the duke's friendship with Landseer changed in any way, as they continued to enjoy each other's company. He made no comment one way or another on Rachel's birth, except to be thankful that both were well and healthy, to any of his intimate correspondents, and there is no evidence he ever questioned her legitimacy.

Indeed, following the news Georgina was pregnant, everything carried on as normal, and in spite of the fact that she was initially very unwell, the duke continued with his plans for their trip to France, which was to last seven months. By 31 October the duke, duchess and Eliza were on their way to Paris, and in a letter to Lady Holland in December, he gives us a hint as to one reason for their trip, when he outlined his proposed 'Norman Excursion':

St Germaine en Laye	The Chateau
Rouen	Lillebonne, Court of William the Conquerer
Caen	Abbé de la Trinité
	Abbey & Cathedral of St Stephen [St Étienne]
Bayeux	Tapestry
Cherbourg	Ancient town & Port of Rossel
Évreux	Cathedral.

Looking at this itinerary it is clear that this excursion, which he took alone, leaving Georgina and Eliza in Paris, had a specific purpose, and a clue as to what it was can be found in some of the names, particularly 'Rossel'. Earlier that year at Woburn, the duke's librarian Jeremiah Wiffen had begun what he describes as 'the idea of collecting together all the records I could find, connected with the Russell family, in Normandy and England'. Encouraged by the duke, Wiffen worked over the next eight years gathering this material together and travelling on a research trip to Normandy before publishing the results in *The Historical Memoirs of the House of Russell* in 1833.[432] Although later historians have doubted how much of Wiffen's early research in Normandy was really factual, and how much was there to confirm the duke's theories of his family origins in the Norman Conquest, it created a lasting connection between the names 'Russell' and 'Rosel' or 'Rossel'. In 1825 Wiffen's ideas would have chimed with the duke's growing interest in the family history, and it seems likely that the trip became a pilgrimage to the places he believed to be associated with those ancestors, and perhaps to find their graves and memorials in one or another of the cathedrals.

Also in October, as the family left for France, work got underway at Woburn on the major new project, the new kitchen garden, which the duke had been planning since the summer. In July he had begun work on the plans, and in October William Atkinson paid his first visit to start on the designs when the family had left for France. Atkinson, an architect who had made his reputation as a specialist in the Gothic style, had first come to the duke's notice for his work on Walter Scott's house at Abbotsford between 1816 and 1823: indeed, the pair may have met there on one of the duke's visits, and he turned out to be an ideal collaborator, since he had also become well known for experimental work with hot-water heated greenhouses. The use of hot water pipes heated by a boiler was still new and had begun when 'it was understood that hot water would circulate in a closed circuit without external pumping, a fact not established until 1818,' and following this breakthrough the first installations in Britain were made in the early 1820s.[433]

From the very beginning of the collaboration in 1825, it was clear that these gardens, and the process by which they were designed, were going to be very different to anything that had gone before. Certainly, the duke called in one of the pioneering designers in the new world of water-heated greenhouses; however, Atkinson's role was not so much to present a finished scheme, but to collaborate with the duke and Forbes to produce something that utilized cutting edge technology, the latest horticultural and botanical science, new varieties of fruit and vegetables, and also met the practical needs of the Abbey and household. At the same time, however, it also reflected the duke's vision of a creating a garden which expressed his understanding of a fundamental unity between the sciences of physics and chemistry and the worlds of aesthetics, art, design and even literature; which would provide a comprehensive harvest of fruit and vegetables; and which people would want to visit and explore, spend time in and contemplate the wonders of the natural world in an idealized setting.

The time and effort that went into designing these kitchen gardens is evident from the fact that Atkinson's visits to discuss, survey and lay out the gardens carried on for the next seven years, some two years longer than it had taken to design and carry out Repton's proposals. During this time, working with assistants, he visited up to eight times a year, and delivered new or revised plans every year as new ideas were introduced and old ones further developed. Such was the process that, in the end, even the plan shown in *Hortus Woburnensis* in 1833 was out of date by the time it was published. The fact that both the duke and Forbes received copies of these plans seems to indicate just how collaborative it was, and after 1828 additional designs for decorative details

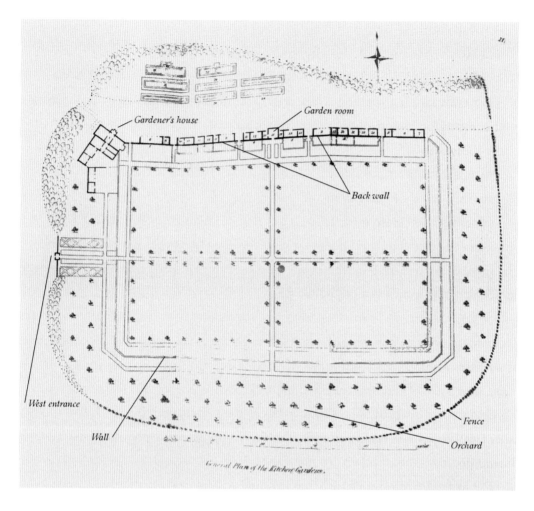

John Forbes, 'General Plan of the Kitchen Gardens', *Hortus Woburnensis*, Plate XVI, 1833. Top left is the gardener's house, with its wide bay window providing views of the whole kitchen garden. On the north side of the back wall we see the rows of storehouses, workshops, boiler rooms, open sheds and, in the centre, the garden room. On the south side of the back wall runs the sequence of hot walls, greenhouses and hot houses, and the grand west entrance, which still stands, provided access from the Abbey.

suggest how ornamental the finished structures were to be. This showcase of new technologies and horticultural techniques was expressed in the cool, utilitarian neoclassical style used by his brother at Park Farm over thirty years earlier, a very similar undertaking. Also like Park Farm, this would be a place that the duke could visit with his family and friends.

Forbes tells us:

The site ... is on the declivity of an eminence, or rising ground, where it slopes towards the South ... [laid out] in a parallelogram, which is the most convenient form for cropping ... Total area of the Garden is 4 acres. [Surrounding the garden was a broad belt of fruit trees.] A selection of the best sorts of *pears* and *apples* ... gives the exterior of the Garden the appearance of an Orchard.

The interior of the Garden is divided into four quarters, each of which is surrounded by a row of standard fruit trees, planted along the flower borders ... In the centre of the Garden, where the walks cross each other, is an iron *cupola*, which is covered with creepers, and forms a pleasing object to the eye from the different parts of the Garden.

Beyond the four quarters of vegetable garden, 'the range of *Forcing-houses* is erected against the South side of the North wall of the Garden' while on the north side of that wall was a range of 'Back Sheds' containing 'Coal-sheds, and Furnaces', fruit and vegetable storage rooms, seed room, office, foreman's quarters, workmen's room, storerooms, Root House and open sheds for 'mould, Flower pots &c'.[434]

By April 1826 the Bedfords were still in Paris, but anxious perhaps to be back in England to be nearer her doctors should any complications should arise with the pregnancy, Georgina returned to England, leaving the duke to complete his excursion to Normandy. At Woburn, while Lords Henry (ten) and Cosmo (nine) were away at school, Georgina rejoined Georgiana (now sixteen), Louisa (fourteen) and Alexander (five) as they waited for the birth of their new sibling. Work inside the Abbey was still ongoing, with the refurbishment of the north and west corner rooms on the principal floor. In the grounds, work continued on the kitchen gardens, in the pleasure grounds on the establishment of the willow garden, in the park on a new underground water reservoir on Stumps Cross Hill to ensure reliable water supplies for the new kitchen gardens, and in the distant Evergreens a new ride was laid out among the new plantations round Sand Hill.

It would appear that by this time there was a degree of reconciliation between the duke and duchess, Lord William and his wife, since Bessy tells us that when she saw the duchess, 'I thought her looking ill & immensely large, but in violent spirits.' The remark would seem to confirm that Georgina's pregnancy had continued to be difficult even after she got back from France, and so it must have been with some relief that Georgina, then forty-five, finally gave birth to her twelfth child and third daughter, Rachel, on 19 June. A few weeks later, however, in spite of her shaky health, Georgina travelled down to Devon for a brief visit to Endsleigh. During their short stay, with the newly completed Fly Bridge now providing access into the woods on the far side of the river, the duke and duchess spent time planning the development of the 'Rides and Drives on the Grounds above Wareham' which were to run along the far side of the river and up through the woods to the viewing points above.[435]

Since the birth of the baby had delayed their annual trip to Devon, the family did not stay long, and by the end of August, after a short visit to Woburn, they set off for Scotland. In a new departure, Georgiana, Henry, Cosmo, their French governess Mlle Migneron and the 'Ladies Woman', Sophia Smith, all travelled to Edinburgh by steam packet from Blackwall docks in London as far as Newhaven on the Forth, from where they took a coach to Kincraig; however, even as time went by, the duke could never be persuaded to travel 'by steam', whether by sea or later by rail, and always made the trip by coach. By 1 September, however, the family had all arrived and were looking forward to enjoying the Highlands, having been joined by William Adam, retired from his duties for the Bedford estate and enjoying his retirement at Blair Adam, where he in turn invited the duke to break his journey on his way south.[436]

So far, 1826 had been a very busy year for Landseer. Settled now in St John's Wood, where he was to live and work for the rest of his life, high on his agenda in the spring in his new studio had been completing the duke's commission, *The Hunting of Chevy Chase*, in time for the Royal Academy exhibition in May. It proved a success, and this was followed up by his being elected as an Associate of the Royal Academy at the age of twenty-four. This was 'an astonishingly early age', as Ormond has pointed out, and emphasizes just how fast Landseer's star had risen. With business in London taken care of, he too travelled to Scotland in September, paying another visit to Blair Atholl before moving north to stay at Kinrara again with the Huntlys. From here he paid a number of visits to Invereshie and joined the Bedfords as they travelled up Glen Feshie to spend time in the huts at Ruigh Fionntaig.

One result of Landseer's stay this year was drawings of *Forest Lodge* and *Keeper with Dogs* at Blair Atholl, and at Invereshie two of Rachel, one in her crib and one being held by Louisa, a sketch of *The Duchess of Bedford riding a Pony*, the head of a *Stag killed by the Duke of Gordon*, and the head of one of the dogs. These are of particular interest because, under Landseer's guidance, Georgina went on to produce

Etching by Georgina, Duchess of Bedford, *Forest Lodge*, 1826. Forest Lodge stood in Glen Tilt, and was where Landseer met up with the Bedfords on his first trip to Scotland in 1824. This was one of a series of etchings of drawings by Landseer that Georgina produced under his guidance a few years later.

'Rabbit Warren' or 'River Scene', signed 'GB', 1826. Another etching by Georgina of a Landseer drawing, almost certainly of a view in Scotland, and possibly somewhere on the Invereshie estate.

etchings of five of them. In addition, Landseer's image of the duchess on a pony alerts us to the fact that this year the family began to visit Ruigh Fionntaig much more frequently, enjoying the remote location and the rough and ready experience of the huts; getting there involved the kind of pony ride that Georgina had taken so many years before as a teenager herself. Clearly enjoying himself in the 'braes' at their 'bivouacaya', the duke tells Lady Holland, 'William Adam leaves us tomorrow, much invigorated by the Highland air … Pray tell him to describe our Highland Château to you,' before adding in a second letter from Dalwhinnie, 'I write to you from the highest inhabited house in Great Britain. I came here for two days shooting with no other companion than my little Louisa [fourteen],' an early indication of Louisa's interest and participation in Highland sports – hunting, shooting and fishing – which she was to pursue vigorously with her husband in later years.

On his return from Glen Feshie at the end of September from his 'wooden Château in the Hills', the duke turned his attention to improving his access to pasture at Invereshie, writing to Macpherson-Grant, 'much obliged to you for your desire to accommodate me with the acre of Pasture land below the garden at Invereshie … Bedford.'[437] In total, the duke's letters this summer indicate that, having got used to their surroundings, the family enjoyed themselves, experiencing for the first time that life in the hills Georgina remembered so fondly.

Leaving Invereshie in early October, the duke paid a visit to Blair Adam before meeting up with the duchess at Lord Grey's house at Howick, having assured Grey that 'our invasion is not likely to be a very formidable one as we propose to send the greater part of the children and the heavy baggage on before us.' Just how much he enjoyed this season in Scotland is clear from his final letter to Lady Holland that year from Edinburgh: 'I have left the blue mountains of Scotland [and the] pure air, healthy climate and cheerful scenery of our Highland abode with infinite regret.'

Determined, perhaps, to continue the run of good health, after a short stay at Woburn, the Bedfords visited Campden Hill for a week or so before travelling to Brighton for a stay until Christmas. As in previous years, they took two houses, one for themselves and one for the children. Before leaving for Brighton, Georgina wrote to Grey to give him an update on the duke's health: 'Even you would be pleased with this little Villa, it is so cheerful [as opposed to Woburn] and yet so quiet, and everything within so brilliant, so fresh, free from blacks and smoke. The Duke, apart from looking old … is otherwise looking well. He has for the last ten days been free from all Complaints.'[438]

The duke and duchess returned from Brighton for the usual Christmas and New Year celebrations at Woburn. While they were away, however, the Abbey received a distinguished foreign visitor who, after being shown round by staff, wrote an account of what he found in letters to his sister. Prince Hermann von Pückler-Muskau, as a landscape gardener himself, was particularly interested in the gardens and grounds, but also left some interesting comments on unusual things he found in the Abbey. Arriving on 20 December, during a tour undertaken with a succession of 'attendants', he particularly admired Bone's 'remarkable collection of miniature portraits of the family … [which] were arranged … in a long narrow gold frame, and set like medallions', and noted one other feature of the Abbey which had struck him: 'Round all the apartments of the great quadrangle runs an inner wide gallery … and a variety of collections, some open, some in glass cases … interspersed with stands of flowers, are set out. This affords a walk as instructive as it is agreeable in winter or bad weather.'

Leaving the Abbey by the library doors, he noted that 'the gardens appear to me peculiarly charming, so admirably interwoven with the buildings and so varied it is difficult to describe them adequately,' and following the 'unbroken arcade' joining the various buildings, he was very impressed when he caught sight of Georgina's parterre gardens in front of the Sculpture Gallery: 'In one place the bowery-walk leads quite through a lofty Palm-house, before which lie the most beautiful embroidered parterres, intersected by gravel walks.' Beyond this, he entered the magical world of the Heath House, and has left us a short but vivid description of this extraordinary building: 'Over the arcade are partly climbers, partly the prettiest little green-houses … one containing nothing but heaths, hundreds of which, in full blow, present the loveliest picture, endlessly multiplied by walls of mirrors.' Passing out into the pleasure gardens, he noted a fascinating aspect of such tours that is not apparent from the archive record when he remarked on reaching the Aviary, 'Here the fourth or fifth attendant awaited us (each of which expects a fee, so that you cannot see the establishment under some pounds sterling).' Finally, after admiring the variety of birds in the Aviary, the tour finished up with a visit to the Thornery, which he described as a 'wild sort of copse intersected with walks and overgrown with thorns and brushwood; in the midst of which stands a little cottage with the loveliest flower-garden'.[439]

In March came another event of some significance to the duke, when the architect P. F. Robinson published *History of Woburn Abbey*, the first volume of his monograph series 'Vitruvius Britannicus'. Robinson had been a pupil of Henry Holland, and the book takes the history of Woburn Abbey from the remodelling by Henry Flitcroft for the 4th Duke in 1747 to the work done by Holland for the 5th Duke in the 1780s. For the 6th Duke, this was a timely celebration not only of his grandfather's and his brother's work, but also of his own collections and additions, since the text also included a 'General Catalogue of the Paintings at Woburn Abbey' and a 'General Catalogue of the Marbles and Other Works in Sculpture at Woburn Abbey'.[440]

As work at Woburn picked up again in the spring of 1827, the development of the new kitchen gardens dominated the agenda. By April work was underway on the new gardener's house, and construction of the house and associated outbuildings lasted for the next eighteen months; completed in 1829, the house remains in use. Meanwhile, work got underway on the new garden layout and the 'Forcing Houses', the series of specialized heated plant houses laid out along the south side of the back wall. When completed these included a 'Range of Peach Houses', 'Citron House', 'Fig House', 'Range of Vineries' and 'Pinery'. By January 1828 Edward Crocker, the duke's steward at Woburn, was able to report to William Adam:

> The foundations of the West, South & East walls are now going on … Mr Forbes wishes the South and East Walls to be stopped, and the North and West proceeded with in preference, the ground being complete on these sides and not to the others. When they are finished he can then make his Walks and the Garden fit for Company to come in on that side, have all the carting done from the East side, and leave the Walls until next year. I think his remarks appear reasonable, and it would be the best way of proceeding, otherwise the Garden will be in no better state next Year.[441]

Clearly, even while they were being built, the duke and Forbes were concerned that the gardens should be 'fit for company', stressing their vision that they were to be seen, enjoyed and admired as a celebration of horticultural science. Over the following months Atkinson issued several different sets of plans as decisions were made about the contents of the gardens, including the addition of different 'Pits' for 'late melons' and 'fruiting pines', but then, in September, he submitted plans for two very significant additions: 'Plans and Elevations for Entrance to Garden' and 'Two sketches for Room, Centre of Garden'. While the earlier plans had been about the size and scope of the gardens, here we see the direct intervention of the duke as he sought to realize his vision for a place of science that was also a statement of taste and aesthetics.

While Forbes had stated that the 'Back Sheds' were 'not in view from the principal walks of the Gardens', this did not mean that they were not to be seen. On the contrary, the trouble the duke took to create a garden he was proud to show off to the family, friends, visitors and professionals is indicated by the elaborate designs for the entrance and the addition at the heart of the complex of a special 'Room, Centre of Garden', which Forbes described as follows: 'In the centre of the range of back Sheds, No. 15, is an apartment fitted up for the entertainment of company in the fruit season; the ceiling of the room is ornamented by several kinds of birds, and the floor is inlaid with different kinds of oak. On the walls are hung two magnificent fruit pieces by G. Lance, Esq, whose accuracy in the delineation of fruits is universally admired' (Colour Plates 29 and 30).

The small size of the room and its out-of-the-way location do little to suggest the importance it must once have had, but the remains of the painted ceiling, the coloured window glass, the descriptions below, and Atkinson's surviving plans give us some idea of its importance and the attention that was given to its design and ornamentation. In addition, the 'Plan of the Hot Houses' shows the room in the heart of the design (no. 15) carefully framed by the symmetrical layout of hot houses on either side. Built with the rest of the structures c.1828 'from the designs of William Atkinson, Esq. of Grove End, St. John's Wood', one visitor left this description of the room soon after it was completed: 'About the middle of the Hot-houses is a small sitting apartment for occasional use, neatly fitted up, with a painted ceiling, and an oak inlaid floor. Two remarkably beautiful Fruit-pieces by G. Lance, ornament the walls; and a fine collection of Fruit on China, is kept in two cabinets. The chimney-piece is of green Irish serpentine.'[442]

Just as the fruit and vegetable gardens were to be admired, so too was the range of back sheds leading from the gardener's house to the fruit room itself, which offered an opportunity to admire the both the new technology and the produce that it made possible. The neat gardener's 'villa' set the tone and a smart cobbled road ran

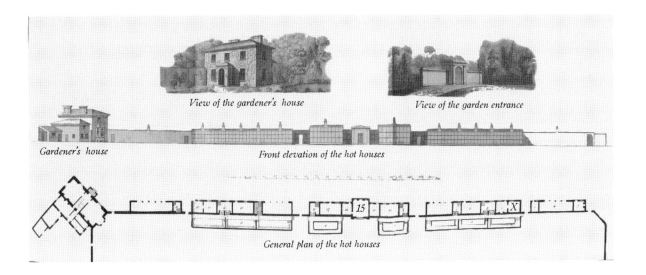

View of the gardener's house

View of the garden entrance

Gardener's house

Front elevation of the hot houses

15

X

General plan of the hot houses

John Forbes, 'General Plan of the Hot Houses', *Hortus Woburnensis*, Plate XVII, 1833. Detailed layout of the buildings in the kitchen gardens. Above the back wall we see (left to right) the open sheds, the smaller boiler rooms with their flues, offices, rooms for displaying cooking and eating apples, the garden room (No. 15), onion and mushroom sheds, the workmen's room on the far right and their entrance to the gardens next to the foreman's cottage, marked 'X'.

down the length of the back sheds, leading on one side past the first open shed, full of compost, decorative urns and flower pots, past an office, the large boilers and pipe works, the seed collections, the two apple rooms, one for kitchen apples and one for dessert apples, and on the other, the pine, melon and cucumber pits, all of which were to be visited, inspected and admired on both sides on the way down to the entrance to the waiting room and fruit room. Beyond this stretched the storage rooms for roots and onions, more open sheds for storage, 'mould' and soil mixes, the foreman's cottage, the workmen's room and their entrance to the gardens.

In turn great attention was also paid to the formal entrance: 'The principle [*sic*] entrance to the Garden is situated opposite to the centre of the West wall; its being in the most direct line from the Abbey ... The main entrance ... a handsome architectural building, is connected with the Garden by a neat iron arch trellissary ... covered with different kinds of creepers.' A comfortable walk from the Abbey, the gardens became a recreational and educational outing for the family, friends and visitors, but above all provided a place to see and eat a huge range of fruit. As Paul Smith points out, 'Exotic or out of season fruit were also a means of conferring prestige on country house owners. Fruit could be sent as an impressive gift to relatives or friends, and dinner guests would be fed with carefully nurtured pineapples, peaches, apricots, grapes and cherries from forcing ranges.'[443]

Today, out of season fruit is so ubiquitous it is scarcely noticed – it has no status or novelty – but in this context the 'Fruit Room' takes on special value. The room, dedicated to the appreciation of fruit, and the fruit decorations were not just 'decoratively' beautiful; they were also a reminder of what was on offer in these gardens: exotic fruit, out of season fruit, the peak of ripeness, colour and flavour, and a range of the best varieties available. It was a celebration of taste and of the dedication to innovation from new varieties of seeds and advances in cultivation to the structures of the greenhouses and the machines which provided the heat that made it all possible.

With this project underway, the family spent a rather 'cold and uncomfortable' few weeks at Endsleigh in April and May before returning to Woburn, from where Georgina was called to attend her father, who had suddenly fallen ill in London. The duke reported to Lady Holland, 'my poor wife never left his bedside from half past eleven last night till he breathed his last … this morning. This is too much for her.' While it is not clear if any of her sisters were there, her brother Huntly was abroad, but from the duke's account, it seems she might have been on her own when her father died on 17 June. For reasons of his own, the duke opted not to join her in London, telling Lady Holland, 'I shall not go to town this morning as I had intended.' Indeed, 1827 was proving to be a difficult year for Georgina. In February her niece Lady Emily, another of her sister Susan's children, who was living with the Huntlys, had died of a sudden illness, aged twenty-one, and then, barely a month after her father's death, on 11 July, a major fire destroyed the 'entire East Wing of Gordon Castle, which included the old Duke's own private apartments'.[444]

After some confusion due largely to Huntly's absence, funeral arrangements were made and the Duke of Gordon was interred in the family vault in Elgin at the end of the month. Given the fact that both Susan and James Hoy, her father's librarian and companion, both died the next year, Georgina must have felt that her old life was slipping away, and what she did next strongly suggests that she wanted to withdraw for a few weeks from her life as duchess to reconnect with memories and what remained of that old life. While the duke was too preoccupied with the work on the kitchen gardens to leave at that point, she went to Invereshie with Henry, Cosmo and Alexander, and stayed for the next four months. She spent much of that time in Glen Feshie (where she was joined by Landseer), fully expecting the duke to join them in August. In the end he did not come, and in his absence this was the first year that we start to see the close relationship between Georgina and Landseer attracting attention, when McInnis tells Macpherson-Grant, 'His Grace has not been at Invereshie this Season but the Duchess has been there since the end of July and spends her time in the Glen with Mr Landseer the painter.'[445]

What McInnis does not say, however, is that the children and staff were also 'in the Glen', and that rather than this time being some kind of a private rendezvous, it has the feel of quiet family holiday. Certainly, Landseer was very busy, and one interesting image he produced was a small drawing, rapidly executed and full of atmosphere, inscribed 'Glen Fishie/1827', the first that can be unequivocally linked to the glen. The image is taken from an unusual viewpoint, low down beside the river, and is brought alive by the snaking forms of the wind and flood-blasted pine trees set against the backdrop of a misty mountain peak. Images like this were a new departure, because, as Richard Ormond tells us, by now, 'Landseer's originality lay less in the fact of his sketching out-of-doors than in his choice of wild Highland scenery' and the fact that 'unlike more conventional topographical artists, he was not recording the great set-pieces of Highland scenery like Dunkeld, Blair Atholl, Loch Katrine, Glencoe, Loch Lomond and the Falls of Clyde,' but was choosing instead to record what caught his eye, those insignificant incidental elements that actually made up the landscape in front of him, to convey how the changing light and weather gave these artistic interest and significance, and, through them, to record his emotional response. Ormond concludes, 'He seems to have painted for his own pleasure and they were not known until his estate sale in 1874, when more than a hundred were put up for auction. None of the sketches are dated.'

Edwin Landseer, *Glenfishie*, 1827. This carefully observed pen and ink study is the earliest Landseer image that can be firmly dated to Glen Feshie. With not an animal or game bird in sight, we see Landseer exploring ways to capture the details and atmosphere of the glens – the peace and quiet of a summer's day revealing the turmoil that engulfs these places during fierce winter storms. Trees such as those in the foreground, battered and damaged, were to feature in a number of Landseer's later images.

Beyond the 'Glen Fishie/1827' sketch, there are at least six or seven others of Glen Feshie, all undated and untitled, and all done from 1827 onwards, a number relating specifically to the part of the glen where Georgina's huts were located. One other completed oil painting, which may also date from this year, *Highlanders returning from Deerstalking*, shows two ghillies leading a string of ponies, each carrying the carcass of a stag while the deerhounds run beside, an image which indicates Landseer's growing preoccupation with the narrative of Highland and sporting life that became the subject of so many of his Scottish paintings, and represents an early departure from depicting his aristocratic patrons out hunting.[446]

While it is clear that Georgina was enjoying her stay in Scotland, a letter to Grey in November confirms that she had not been expecting to be alone there: 'My widowhood is not the most agreeable part of my [sojourn?] here, but as the Duke promised to follow me in a fortnight, but preferred moving about with the rapidity of a steam engine here and there and everywhere, I have remained enjoying this wild country, with my children, who are quite as fond of the Highlands as their Mother.'

The duke had indeed been 'moving about'. After spending August at Woburn Abbey, working busily with Forbes and Atkinson on the kitchen garden project, he left in September for another visit to Leamington. While the usual reason given for visiting the spa was to take the waters in preparation for the winter ahead, another visitor the year before suggests that it was the seasonal social life of the town which was the real attraction: 'Leamington ... is now a rich and elegant town, containing ten or twelve palace-like inns, four large bath-houses with colonnades and gardens, several libraries, with which are connected card, billiard, concert and ball-rooms (one for six hundred persons) and a host of private houses, which are almost entirely occupied by visitors ... All here is on a vast scale, though the waters are insignificant. The same are used for drinking as for bathing, and yet it swarms with visitors.'[447]

After taking the waters and, no doubt, busily socializing, the duke returned briefly to Woburn in October before setting out to visit the Spencers, a trip which occasioned the following comment from Georgina: 'The Duke has been at Althorp for the first time in his life, but was to be at home on Monday to receive Lady P. Vernon and her charming husband,' adding, 'The duke, I hear, looking better than he has done in twenty years.' He then left for Brighton where he was expecting to be joined any day by Georgina and the children when they returned from Scotland.

Georgina, however, was in no hurry and decided to stay on at Invereshie for a while longer; her explanation for this in her letter to Grey in early November is very revealing: 'Your kind letter ought to have been answered sooner, but I received it just as dear Wriothesley arrived, which for a time put everything out of my head, and I thought by this time I should have settled my time for leaving the North, but I find the Duke so gay without me, visiting about and receiving young and gay parties at Woburn, that I shall remain amongst my Mountains till the snow drives me away.'

There is a sense in this letter of her withdrawal into a quieter internal world, her contentment with the company of close friends and family amidst the landscapes that felt like home, a new focus on herself after the years of childbirth; at forty-six she was embarked on the complex experience of the menopause.

One other reason for delaying her departure was that she had been expecting to meet her brother at Kinrara for the first time since their father's death and he became Duke of Gordon. However, business detained him at Gordon Castle, so she travelled up to visit for three days at the end of October instead; as we shall see, there was much for the two to discuss since all was not well in the world of Gordon finances.

In November she writes to Lord Grey: 'I never feel [as well] as I do here in England. I have not had one period of anything but perfect health, and own I shall be too happy, if possible, to pass the horrid gloomy month of November while the fogs and damps do not prevail … My movements depend … [on] the Duke's going [to] Brighton, where I have no wish to dance attendance, *dans la pays bas*, which does not suit my Highland blood.'[448]

Leaving Invereshie in late November, Georgina's party stopped off in Edinburgh, where they dined twice with Walter Scott, who left the following accounts in his *Journal*:

Nov 28th: I dined with the Duchess of Bedford at the Waterloo and renewed … an old acquaintance which began while her Grace was Lady Georgiana. She has now a fine family, two young ladies, silent just now but they will find their tongues or they are not right Gordons. A fine child, Alaster [Alexander], who shouted, sung and spoke gaelic with much spirit …

Nov 29th: Dined at the Lord C. Commissioner's [William Adam] to meet the Duchess and her party. She can be extremely agreeable but I used to think Her Grace *journalière*. She may have been cured of that fault or I may have turned less jealous of my dignity. At all events let a pleasant hour go by unquestioned and do not let us break ordinary gems to pieces because they are not diamonds. I forgot to say that Edwin Landseer was in the Duchesses train. He is to my mind one of the most striking masters of the modern school. His expression both in men and animals is capital. He shewed us many sketches of smugglers etc. taken in the Highlands, all capital.<end ext>

By 19 December Georgina and the children had joined the duke in Brighton, but it is clear from an entry in Lord William's diary in February 1828 that the duke's ongoing health problems and what the future held were a source of growing worry for Georgina: 'Had a curious conversation with Mrs Grundy [the nickname given Georgina by her stepsons]; appears sore and out of humour, complains of her husband, complains she knows nothing of her future prospects or of her children's.'[449]

As the duke's health continued to cause alarm, Georgina was becoming increasingly anxious about what settlements she could count on if he died – a situation exacerbated by the duke's apparent unwillingness to discuss it – and the situation her own father had left her brother in. Although their relationship survived, this issue remained an undercurrent of tension in their marriage, and Georgina remained in ignorance of the terms of his will until he died. Nevertheless, the following years saw a renewed and supportive closeness which only grew stronger as the duke's health continued to fail.

As if to emphasize this renewed family unity, the performances at the Abbey theatre in January 1828 were the most exuberant yet. On 3 January the playbill proudly announced: 'Woburn Abbey Theatre: Under the Patronage of Her Grace the Duchess of Bedford *The Liar* Foote's Admired Farce. Cast includes: Duke of Bedford, Lord Wriothesley Russell, Lord Charles Russell, Lord Henry Russell, Lord Cosmo Russell, Mr Shelley, Lady Georgiana Russell, Mlle Migneron, Lady Louisa Russell. N.B. During the recess great improvements have taken place in the interior of the Theatre, and no expense has been spared.'

Following this, when Lord Grey and his family had joined them, there were three more performances, '*Raising the Wind*, a Farce', for which Landseer joined the cast and Georgina replaced the duke, a repeat performance of *The Liar*, and on 31 January a performance of *The Midnight Hour*, 'with entirely new dresses and decorations'. And these were not just any 'decorations', because, as Lennie tells us, Landseer was not just performing: 'Edwin's duties were two-fold – to make up the ladies and paint the scenery,' which included indoor and outdoor scenes, deer and human figures.[450]

After this bright start, however, 1828 soon darkened. At Woburn that winter the duke's correspondence and conversations were dominated by the changing political landscape and the rising power of the ultra-Tories, a loose association of right-wing conservative politicians who came together to oppose any movement towards Catholic emancipation, which they saw as threatening the dominance of the Anglican Church across church and state. For the leading Whigs, many of whom, like the duke, had fought throughout their political careers to achieve this end, they watched this development with foreboding, fearing that such a movement was likely to jeopardize, if not defeat, not just their hopes for Catholic emancipation but also, beyond that, their hopes for parliamentary reform. Three Tory prime ministers in succession, Canning, Goderich and the Duke of Wellington, came and went between 1828 and 1830, and as the uncertainty spread, the Whig leaders sought to bring their party together to create a viable opposition which could counteract this threat and vie for power. Even Lord William, for so long adrift in Europe and absent from Parliament, left his wife and mother-in-law abroad to join his uncle, old Lord William (who also returned from the Continent), and his brothers in representing the Bedford interest.

In March, however, priorities suddenly changed for the Bedfords when the duke suffered a second stroke, not as devastating as the first, but this time his recovery was slower and less complete; indeed, his health was never robust again. Georgina, for whom the timing was terrible, was determined not to lose him and was quick to take control. She whisked him away from Woburn to the relative peace and quiet of Campden Hill, before removing him from the political scene altogether by taking him to Endsleigh. Accompanied by Georgiana, Louisa, Henry, Cosmo and Alexander, the family remained in Devon for the next two months.

Fortunately, most of the work at Endsleigh on the house, gardens and more distant grounds had largely been completed. There was a great deal of planting in the gardens, woods and the Dairy Dell still ongoing, but there were no major decisions to be made and the family were largely free simply to enjoy what had been created. Although the duke told Lady Holland in a letter at this time, 'It is useless to indulge in political speculating at this distance,' this is, of course, exactly what he loved to indulge in, and it was for the opportunity to do this, without fear of criticism or ridicule, as much as anything else, that he valued their correspondence. It allowed him to feel in touch with the world of Holland House even though he was in Devon or Scotland, but at a safe remove from the harsh realities of participating directly.

In late August, with the duke settled and out of further immediate danger, Georgina suddenly left him at Endsleigh and set off with the girls and Alexander for Scotland. Clearly, for her to leave the duke at this moment, something important must have come up, and he, in turn, seemed entirely sanguine about it, telling Lady Holland, 'I have … satisfactory accounts of her progress northwards … I hope she will be south again a little earlier than she was last year … You will find me blooming from Devonshire.'[451]

Later that month, he returned to Woburn, staying there until late October when he again travelled down to Brighton to await Georgina's return. With work well underway at Woburn on the kitchen garden, the duke spent much of this time negotiating the purchase of a house in one of London's newest developments: the recently completed No. 6 Belgrave Square. With the lease up on St James's Square and the Campden Hill villa too far from central London, the duke found himself a smart new address, large enough for the family to stay and with room for the staff, and went on to use this house for the rest of his life.

So sudden had been the decision to leave for Scotland that many of the staff were left to find their own way for what was to prove to be everyone's last trip to Invereshie. There appear to have been two possible motives for Georgina's sudden visit. In the first case, she could have got wind of the possibility of leasing new quarters for the family at The Doune, Rothiemurchus, home of her old childhood friends the Grants (Map 5). In the second, she could have been keen to be on hand to assist her brother if necessary, as he struggled to minimize the damage to the Gordon inheritance from the mountain of debt which he had inherited.

Serious financial problems also forced the Grants to let their ancestral home at this time. By Elizabeth Grant's account, their last carefree year at The Doune was 1825; with financial problems mounting relentlessly, by September 1827 the family had left for India, where they arrived in February 1828. The Grants' money problems dated back to unaddressed debts accumulated during her father's election campaign for Grimsby in 1812, a seat he had won at enormous cost; he had been unable to keep up with repayments on the loans he had taken. In 1826 the situation deteriorated steadily, as heavy bills went unpaid and new orders were refused, and so difficult was the situation that year that Elizabeth and her sister 'wrote a bundle of rubbish for the *Inspector*, and received £40 in return'. The final straw came later that year, when the Duke of Bedford required Grant's seat at Tavistock so he could return old Lord William, and this sudden loss of parliamentary privilege meant that Grant was now exposed to his creditors. Elizabeth Grant describes vividly the catastrophe that had befallen them: 'This enforced retirement closed the home world to my poor father; without this shield his person was not safe. He left us; he never returned to his Duchus. When he drove away to catch the Coach that lovely summer, he looked for the last time on those beautiful scenes … though he never valued his inheritance rightly. He first went to London and then abroad, taking John with him. Then came the news of his appointment to a judgeship in India – Bombay … and we were desired to proceed to London immediately for the voyage.'

Facing departure from The Doune, Elizabeth wrote that she and her sister Mary had taken a last walk 'down through the wood to the walk by the Spey … and so to the green gate under the beech tree … not a tear till we heard that green gate clasp behind us; then we gave way, dropt down on the two mushroom seats and cried so bitterly.' She adds, 'Even now I hear the clasp of that gate; I have heard it all my life, since I shall hear it till I die, it seemed to end the poetry of our existence.' In September 1827 they sailed for India, arriving in February 1828, but before they left, arrangements needed to be made for the property which it was hoped would save the family in the long term. As Elizabeth writes: 'There was a good deal to be done, for the house was to be left in a proper state to be let furnished with the shootings, a new and very profitable scheme for making money out of the bare moors of the highlands.'[452] With the family safely in India, over the next year the estate lawyers oversaw these arrangements and prepared the house and estate for rental.

It would seem that Georgina had heard this news, and after discussing it with the duke over the summer, she had hurried to Scotland to enquire about the lease on the house and lands that she knew so well. Georgina's efforts in Scotland to secure The Doune bore fruit the next year, and by 4 November she, Georgiana, Louisa and Alexander had joined the duke in Brighton before returning to Woburn for the festive season. Georgina, however, will have had a lot on her mind since her brother, the new Duke of Gordon, faced seemingly insurmountable debts. His situation is summed up in a letter from George Macpherson-Grant to his eldest son, John, in August 1827, in which he says the new duke might accept a foreign appointment since 'the late Duke has treated him cruelly, having invested the Estate in Trustees who are to give the Duke £12,000 a year out of the Estate but no provision being made for payment of his debts … The Duke is now at Kinrara … he feels his father's want of confidence in him very much. It is certainly a shameful settlement.' Georgina will certainly have shared this view of her father's settlement, as did Lady Stafford writing to Macpherson-Grant: 'One cannot help feeling for the distressing situation of the Duke of Gordon. With his own debts added to those of his father it will be difficult for him to subsist unless the Trustees find some method of relieving him by sales of parts of the estate.'

Such was the situation that by 3 December 1828 the following announcement appeared in *The Scotsman*, confirming that the years of expenditure had now caught up with the family: 'Extensive Estates for Sale: The Duke of Gordon's Lands in the southern division of the county of Inverness, lying in the parishes of Laggan, Kingussie and Alvie, with the exception of the Farms of Kinrara, and Easter and Wester Lynvully, adjoining Strathsprey, will be exposed to sale during the ensuing spring and summer.'

In an interesting letter the year before from George Macpherson-Grant to his son, he had written, 'There is a rumour that the Duke of Bedford is to buy

Badenoch and Lochaber,' which seems to suggest that the duke and Georgina had been aware of her brother's plight soon after their father died, and may briefly have considered making major purchases of Gordon lands. Macpherson-Grant, however, concluded, 'I think this is improbable,' and this was certainly the case.[453] For a moment, the duke may have harboured dreams of becoming laird of substantial estates in Strathspey and Georgina of reviving her family's traditional place in the Highlands, but fortunately for all concerned, cooler heads prevailed and the opportunity to lease Rothiemurchus may have come at the perfect moment.

By the start of 1829, the Whig party watched carefully as the ruling Conservative coalition began to show signs of strain. Sensing that there might finally be an opportunity for power on the horizon, the Whig leaders, including the duke, set about trying to persuade Lord Grey to step up and lead the party. The duke had already begun to take a more active role in the House of Lords, and over the summer of 1828 he had become involved in the unsuccessful attempt to reform the game laws, telling Grey of his concerns about 'the increasing severity and the inadequacy of the Game Laws, they certainly do not now answer to the purpose they were originally intended for.'[454]

While Lord Grey still hesitated to challenge for control of the Whigs, the Duke of Wellington's government opened a serious rift in the Tory party by finally passing the Roman Catholic Relief Bill in April 1829, with firm support from the Whig opposition. The goal, so long cherished by the leading Whigs, and the duke since his days in Ireland, caused a vicious backlash against the government by the ultra-Tories, the self-appointed guardians of Anglican supremacy, in the name of the Glorious Revolution of 1688. Thus, at the 1830 general election, with both parties seriously split, the result in the end was the emergence of a new administration with Wellington at the head of an uneasy coalition of Tories and some Whigs, in which Lord Grey and other leading Whigs refused to serve and remained in opposition. It was an unstable and unsatisfactory result for all. Nevertheless, when the administration fell a few years later over parliamentary reform, Grey was there ready to lead a new Whig-dominated government, and the Reform Bill, under Lord John Russell's management, was finally at the top of the agenda.

In town for the sessions of Parliament and meetings with friends and allies, the duke may have found that the brand new house in Belgrave Square needed some alterations to make it work for the family – indeed, the square, its roads, pavements and gardens were so new that much still needed finishing – and at this time he also took a lease on 11 Mansfield Street, and hired a cook and cleaner to staff it. Accounts indicate, however, that the family members who used the house most were Henry (thirteen), Cosmo (twelve), and Alexander (eight), and so it appears the house was taken partly as a base for them as they attended school. It was not long, however, before Henry left, and on turning fourteen that August he became the next Russell to join the navy. Described later by the duke's doctor, Allen Thomson, as 'one of the most good-humoured merry creatures I ever met with', Henry was much missed by the family.[455]

On the other hand, as one left, another son returned, when in March 1829 the Bedfords' eldest son, Wriothesley (twenty-five), having graduated in religious studies from Trinity College, Cambridge, and after travelling on the Continent, returned to England to marry his cousin Eliza Russell, old Lord William's daughter, who had been living with the family for some time. On his son's marriage, the duke had him appointed Rector of Streatham and then Chenies, two livings under his direct control, and we have a vivid image of Chenies at this time and the impact of Wriothesley's arrival from a memoir written by Revd Francis Dunne, his former clerk. At Chenies, Dunne says, 'The parish church was damp, dirty, and cold, in more senses than one; plaster covered the outside, whilst whitewash adorned the interior … Attendance at church was not very cheering, many following the then common resource of fishing to while away the time on Sundays … Chenies could boast no school whatsoever … and but few of the residents could read or write.' He adds: 'With a world of position and wealth open to him,' Wriothesley chose to 'surrender all [his] prospects for a few hundred souls and a benefice worth £400', and that after his appointment 'the change began'.[456]

During the spring of 1829 the duke turned his attention to estate matters, starting a new project when he became interested in the potential of a new 'Allotment and Cottage Garden System', an idea that promised to improve conditions for his estate tenants. This was being promoted by a group that became the Labourers' Friend Society in 1830, when the duke joined as a vice-president and he became an enthusiastic backer of the allotment project. In a memorandum to the society, the duke's steward, Thomas Bennett, reported in 1835: 'I should state first of all, that the labourers living in cottages, the property of the Duke of Bedford, had, in some cases, a plot of ground attached to their cottages, before the allotment system was begun. The first trial (as a system) was made at Maulden, in the winter and spring of 1829 and 1830, when 18 acres of land were divided into lots of 20 to 40 poles each, and divided among 70 to 80 agricultural labourers.' This was followed across the whole Bedfordshire estate, and between 1830 and 1832 some 600 allotments were created.

It seems to have been a popular and generally very successful programme with the exception, it seems, of Chenies: 'The Duke of Bedford has also tried the plan at Chenies, in Bucks, but the people are not alive to the advantages of it; and this year, I had some difficulty to persuade them to try it, on a *very small scale*.'[457] No doubt the arrival of the Revd Wriothesley soon encouraged a wider and more enthusiastic participation.

Meanwhile, there was a significant development in Scotland, as negotiations with the lawyers acting for the trustees of Grant's creditors resulted in a new lease for The Doune:

> The Tack betwixt Patrick Borthwick Esq. as Trustee of the Creditors of John Peter Grant and the Duchess of Bedford. 1829
>
> … [The Tack] lets to the said Duchess of Bedford … all and whole the mansion house of the Doune as lately possessed by Sir John Peter Grant, with the whole furniture presently contained in the said House, with Coach House and part of the Offices on the Doune Farm to be afterwards fixed … As also the Garden and Shrubbery belonging to the said House, the Gardener's House and the West Lodge, together with the Land adjoining to the said mansion house … with the right of shooting and fishing over the estate of Rothiemurchus and that for the space of Five years from and after Whitsuntide last.[458]

Looking back, it seems clear that Invereshie had served as the perfect beginning for the Bedfords' life in Scotland, a complete package of a house with staff and grounds, the shooting lease and the hut at Ruigh Fionntaig, but for the duke it had always lacked the spacious park and pastureland he really wanted, and for Georgina it lacked the emotional attachments that she had for the Kinrara and Rothiemurchus estates on the other side of the Spey. Kinrara, of course, remained in her brother's hands, but she may always have had her eye on the possibility of finding somewhere nearer the place that she knew so well. Initially, she had made enquiries about the Kincraig estate, about halfway between Invereshie and Kinrara, but now The Doune itself had become available, directly across the river from Kinrara, with a slightly larger house, more flat riverside pastures, farmland, woodlands and shooting (Colour Plate 31). It is noticeable that while the lease for Invereshie had been signed by the duke, that for The Doune was negotiated and signed by Georgina: this was a very personal vision.

By June it was clear, however, that the duke was not well enough to travel to Scotland that summer, and as Lady Holland reports, 'the Duchess is very attentive and miserable about him.' Nevertheless, the timing could not have been worse, since taking up this tack was a major priority for them, and when the duke's doctors recommended he spend a few weeks on the Isle of Wight, she left with Cosmo, Alexander, Rachel and staff to travel to The Doune, take over the house, set up the household and, having given up the huts at Ruigh Fionntaig, continue her negotiations to secure a new location they could visit in Glen Feshie. Travelling without the duke, as he notes, she took the opportunity to try the new form of transport: 'the Duchess goes to Edinburgh <u>by steam</u> – one of her cousins went in the same vessel … and gives her so favourable a report that she is determined to try it.'[459]

That summer, after exhibiting his new painting, *An Illicit Whiskey Still in the Highlands,* at the Royal Academy between May and July, Landseer also made his way to join Georgina and the children at The Doune. He had worked on the painting for some three years, and it indicates the extent to which Landseer's work in the Highlands had moved beyond animal and hunting scenes to far more intense concentration on the people and their lives, and the traditions of Scottish painting. Richard Ormond points out the influence of David Wilkie on Landseer through his 'startlingly realistic scenes of everyday life', and this influence can be seen in the new painting.[460] The representation of the little girl in this picture, later reproduced as *Rustic Beauty*, became an iconic image of sentimental romanticism, but the overall picture shows Landseer's determination to explore the full complexity of these lives – the harsh conditions, the hardscrabble existence on the peripheries of genteel society, survival on the edges of the law, poaching to feed a family – yet the action in the image is entirely focused on the tiny movements of the distiller's mouth as he savours a sip of the new batch of whiskey surrounded by his expectant family, whose immediate future is totally dependent on his skill and connoisseurship and the quality of the product.

Before leaving for Scotland that summer, when looking for alternatives to the hut at Ruigh Fionntaig, she had asked a neighbour at The Doune, James Clark of Dalnavert, for Mackintosh's address to 'ask about building a wooden house in the Glen' on his land (Colour Plate 34). Clark, it seems, was initially hesitant and with good reason. At Dalnavert Clark was a Mackintosh tenant, and as such he was dependent on the Mackintosh land in Glen Feshie for his summer grazing; Georgina's proposal to lease a part of this land must have been particularly unwelcome. Nevertheless, he passed on the address the second time, but not without also writing to Mackintosh in an attempt to limit any threat to his grazing rights: 'The duchess of Bedford made a second application to me … for your address in order to write to you about the shooting on this side of the Spey and also for leave to build a wooden house in Glenfeshie … It would perhaps at a future period save you trouble to have this house erected where her horses and dogs would do as little injury as possible to the tenants' cattle and sheep.'[461]

Having done his best to protect his grazing, Clark seems to have accepted that Mackintosh would give his permission and allow Georgina to take over some of the unimproved huts on his land at the township of Ruigh Aiteachan, on the east bank of the Feshie, and a short distance downstream from Ruigh Fionntaig. Although an agreement was made for her to create a wooden house on the site, she did not hold the lease on the area until 1836. Until that time she had to share the area with other tenants, including Charles Mackintosh, nominally a stalker but no doubt also a poacher, who dealt in firewood and who held the lease from 1835 to 1836. Even when she did take on the lease, she was still happy to share the area with other occupants of the area, farmers such as Clark, long-time residents of the old township, those working for the wood companies licensed to take timber off the Mackintosh land and float the harvest down the Feshie to the Spey, and visiting travellers following the roads over to Blair Atholl and Braemar. In addition she also rented one of the existing old 'cottages' from its tenant, Margaret Shaw, who lived further down the glen and was referred to as the 'old woman'. This circumstance alerts us to a key element of what Georgina was looking for in Glen Feshie, since it was not simply a Romantic idyll of remote isolation, but rather a nostalgic participation in a fading way of communal life with echoes of the seasonal occupation by women of the shielings, which she had witnessed in childhood but by now was largely lost.

In 1890 Alexander MacBain noted, 'The Ordnance Survey maps, 6 [inches] to the mile … contain for Badenoch some 1,400 names: but these do not form more than a tithe of the names actually in use or once used when the glens were full of people, and the summer shealings received their annual visitants.' Every knoll and rill, piece of moor, bog, clump of trees, rock or crag, tiny loch or river pool, 'each and all, however insignificant, had a name among those who dwelt there … But how many of these names are lost, with the loss of population, and the abandonment of … the summer migration to the hills.'[462]

Yet, in addition to the loss of names, for the women of these communities the end of the summer migrations meant the loss forever of something else very special: their own place in the landscape. Meryl Marshall has described this aspect of the migration in the context of Glen Feshie: 'In May or June the cattle and domestic stock would be taken to the fresh green pastures of the hills in order to keep them away from the growing crops in the valleys; a migration, known as transhumance … The womenfolk and children would take up residence in small roughly constructed shelters called shielings and the men would return to the valley.'

Another writer, Katherine Stewart, points out that 'as well as the dairying, much spinning was done, of wool and of flax. Lichens and roots had to be gathered for dyeing the wool,' concluding that 'the sojourn at the shielings, with the woman in charge, was a valuable part of the pattern of the year, beneficial in every way.' The poet Kathleen Jamie, visiting a remote, long-abandoned shieling site in the high hills, wrote:

> There were seven or eight huts straggling along the riverside, forming not a street, they were too spaced out for that, but a suggestion of neighbourliness … the Shielings, and the shieling grounds, were the high summer pastures, the places where the cattle were driven to graze … for a few weeks at the top of the year … the time of ease and plenty. The people would come up from the farmsteads below around the beginning of July – "the girls went laughing up the glen" as the poem says – and return at harvest time. Up here they made milk, butter and cheese, and it was women's work. What a loss that seems now: a time when women were guaranteed a place in the wider landscape … [today] the presence in this valley of another woman … would have surprised me.

Jamie concludes that the abandonment of the shielings marked the 'closure of life lived directly on the land'.

Anne MacVicar Grant also recognized this unique circumstance of the women's lives: 'the care of the cattle was peculiarly theirs. Changing their residence so often as they did in summer, from one bothy or glen to another, gave a romantic peculiarity to their turn of thought and language.' She concludes that, hard though this life was, 'the women find a degree of power or consequence in having such an extensive department, which they would not willingly exchange for the inglorious ease.'

In Glen Feshie the end of transhumance and the abandonment of the old shielings was under way by the late eighteenth century, and as Madeleine Bunting tells us, for those across the Highlands who had seasonally occupied them, 'Being forced off the land altogether was a catastrophic loss of identity bound up with place.' Once land in Badenoch, as elsewhere, was no longer the basis of identity, and 'was no longer expected to provide food or an income, it had instead become an opportunity for personal fantasy'.[463]

In her letter to Beattie in the autumn of 1792, Jane had written of her desire to build a 'shieling' in Badenoch. Kinrara was, of course, not a shieling site but rather the main farmhouse; however, Jane meant what she said. She wanted to create a location where she and her daughters could recapture that sense of removal to a summer place such as Glenfiddich, which she also referred to as a 'shieling', and the freedom it brought beyond the norms of their everyday life. It was where she had roamed, like Beattie's Edwin, 'wrapp'd in wonder', rediscovering the world of the rocks, trees and torrents.

Now for Georgina spending time again among the old locations in the glens at both Ruigh Fionntaig and later Ruigh Aiteachan – places which had long histories as shieling sites – those special circumstances survived in her memories, and in those of the older women she knew and learnt from. She was looking to fulfil the 'project so long held', which was certainly partly a 'personal fantasy' driven by a sense of nostalgia. A life in the shieling had little to do with who she was in 1829 when she wrote 'asking about building a wooden house in the Glen', but it was certainly a large part of a world she had known. She too shared that sense of place and identity and sought not so much to play at peasant life, but to create an environment which stimulated these ideas and revived those feelings for herself. Ruigh Aiteachan was her attempt to create the possibilities presented by Glenfiddich and Kinrara during her youth, echoing the 'romantic peculiarity' of the 'thought and language' and lifestyle of the shielings, a wish to reintroduce part of what had been lost to her own life and that of her children.

To a large extent the project was a product of personal Romantic sensibilities, of what one Scottish eighteenth-century poet described as 'everlasting longings for the lost', but, as such, it also provided the location in which, among other things, one of the country's leading artists could share the experience and develop a vision, style and subject matter that ultimately produced some the country's best loved works of art.[464]

Yet, as Georgina and Landseer arrived there in August 1829, beyond her friends and family, who perhaps understood its true nature, their relationship was starting to attract attention in the press. Rachel Trethewey quotes from a letter written by Tavistock to Lord William: 'The wicked world has been full of sad and scandalous reports, and so have the newspapers. It is very distressing.' One of the earliest sources for the story about an affair appears to be the artist Benjamin Haydon, who wrote in his diary, 'I never seduced the wife of my Patron and accepted money from the Husband while I was corrupting his Wife and disgracing his Family,' but he was not an entirely objective witness since he was dogged by serious financial problems and, having previously taught the young Landseer, seems to have been jealous of his extraordinary success. On the other side of the argument and perhaps equally telling is the fact that nowhere in any of the correspondence, including that of Bessy, Lord William's wife, do we find any comment on Rachel's birth or parentage, or Georgina and Landseer's behaviour, until nearly a decade later when Bessy wrote to Princess Lieven, 'Vous verrez je crois le Duc et la Duchesse à Paris. Son amant actuel n'est plus le peintre mais dit-on son valet de chamber Suisse.'

Indeed, by 1829, such were the 'libellous paragraphs against the Duchess' that the duke 'wanted to refute [them] by joining her' in Scotland, and was only prevented by his doctors from setting off immediately. In the end, though, it would seem that Lady Holland was right when she concluded, 'these matters are always best to be left to die a natural death.'

One other reference to newspaper reports of the affair comes in a letter written by the Earl of Clare in September 1829 to his friend Ralph Sneyd, who was also a friend of the Bedfords:

I heard from Lady Bath yesterday who has the Duke [& Dss] of B at Longleat, indignant with the gentlemen of the press for having calumniated the Duchess. He [the duke] is more devoted than ever to Her Grace and believes her to be the most virtuous of women and most exemplary of wives – so now remember you will be pleased to contradict these reports wherever you go … I hate scandal and how can these stories be true? Her Grace has long since put forth the midsummer short and in the autumn of her years t'would be too bad *de se racanaille*r [to be racy] with an artist, an ugly little whippersnapper creature as ever I saw.[465]

Aware of all the excitement in Scotland but prevented from travelling by his doctors, who had suggested instead a restorative seaside trip, the duke went to the Isle of Wight, where he could 'never remember a more cold, wet, damp and uncongenial *soi-disan*t summer than we have experienced', and spent his time moving between Ryde and Cowes, and worrying about his brother. He wrote to Bessy, 'I anxiously hope that you may fall in with my poor brother … I am afraid he is very ill.'[466]

The duke was back at Woburn by the time Georgina arrived home at the end of November, from where Lord John reports to Lord William: 'We have all the world just arrived – the Duke of Wellington, Fitzroy Somerset, Rosslyn, Aberdeen and last not least the Duchess herself, who has come from Scotland on purpose.'[467] It was to be another big Christmas at the Abbey, with Landseer very much involved in the theatrical activities and the duke's guests enjoying the 'rough shooting'. It is worth noting, however, that although Lord Grey's son, Lord Howick, was there, the other guests listed above were all Tories of one kind or another, indicating the fluidity of the times and symptomatic perhaps of the ongoing search for common ground and a sustainable coalition.

While Christmas and then the New Year of 1830 were spent alternating between Woburn and Brighton, little social activity was recorded, and by February the duke, who had clearly been unwell but was keeping up with political developments, told Lady Holland, 'I am sure you will be glad to hear that I have got quite well, and nothing of my illness remaining … I crawl every evening wrapped up in furs from my room to the Saloon, but this is all – however, I must have patience. Politicks are in a strange state.'

After their usual trip to Endsleigh, the family travelled to London for the summer season, during which Georgina 'and her party' visited Astley's theatre, and spent several evenings at Almack's and the opera, while the duke turned his attention to advising on some alterations at Holland House, as he reported to Lady Holland in June: 'I rode to Holland House today, but found you were both out. I looked at your Entrance from the Turnpike Road – the access with the Park is sufficiently easy, but I think the Turnpike Trustees ought to re-build the front of your lodge. Nothing can be worse than the present blank gable facing the road. They should throw out a bay window – the porter would then command the approach both ways – east and west. The Trust is bound to make good any injury they have done you and this I think you have a right to claim from them.'[468]

During this period the duke also turned his attention to a wide-ranging programme of investment in infrastructure across the Bedford estate. In London, this included a comprehensive update for Covent Garden Market, including a new conservatory and cellars, new well, lighting and gas fittings; in Woburn village a brand new Market House was commissioned, repairs carried out to the church tower, and the construction of new 'double cottages'; and at the long-neglected village at Chenies, Wriothesley's arrival prompted long overdue repairs and building work, both to the rector's house and the church buildings, as the village's fortunes started to change.

While the duke was busy at Woburn in June, Georgina travelled down to Brighton with Rachel and Lord Edward, now a twenty-five-year-old commander and on leave, where she purchased a 'Drawing in pencil of St Helen's point, Isle of Wight' from Louis Parez, the children's old art teacher who now worked from a studio in Regency Square. The image was later to appear as one of the illustrations for Jeremiah Wiffen's *Historical Memoirs of the House of Russell*, which appeared three years later.[469] Returning to London in July, she hosted her annual balls to celebrate Louisa's eighteenth birthday and Georgiana's twentieth at Campden Hill.

Also, while Lord Edward was home in June, William Adam reported to Edward Crocker that the duke asked him to perform 'some little ceremony at the laying of the foundation stone of the new Market House. His Grace will not be able to attend himself, but … he will send down Lord Edward to represent him. Let me know what you propose to do and … what would you wish Lord Edward to do. Lord E. is a <u>freemason,</u> I don't know if that fact is of any consequence.' Adam went on to say that he was 'anxious to have a thorough investigation of the condition of the Riding House and Tennis Court immediately. I do not think, and His Grace agrees, that it would be the best plan to send down an Architect as we should require no assistance in point of taste. It occurs to us that some experienced and practised builder – one who has been engaged in large buildings with roofs of a corresponding span – would be better able to advise us.'[470]

By early July, however, everyone's thoughts were turning to the imminent general election. The change in the political climate following the death of George IV in June placed the Whigs in a stronger position than they had been in for some time, but at Woburn there were real concerns about the Bedford interest, where all was not well. Foremost among the duke's and Tavistock's concerns was the fact that Lord William, although consistently returned for the duke's seat in Bedford, had failed to engage with his responsibilities, spending much time abroad, not attending Parliament, and, even more seriously, not attending the social and ceremonial dinners and meetings in Bedford which were so much a part of local political life. The result was that by this time he was so unpopular with officials and electors that his seat was coming under sustained pressure from his Tory opponents. Lord John somewhat unwillingly stood in his place but faced a losing battle, as he told Bessy: 'Here I am, standing in William's shoes, & very pinching shoes they are. A Tory candidate has started … relying on his money and beer to bring him in. I was canvassing all yesterday and shall be all tomorrow. We are likewise to have a contest in the county against Tavistock.' By 18 August their worst fears were realized, as Tavistock told Lord William in Geneva, 'Well, my dear William, the election is over, and we lost not only the seat of Bedford, but the seat of Huntingdon, too. Poor John's is a hard case.'[471]

The general election took place between July and August 1830, and, in the end, the Duke of Wellington was able to put together his fragile coalition, but in Bedfordshire and Northamptonshire the Bedford interest had taken a severe blow. Lord William's reaction to the loss of his Bedford seat was to shift the responsibility to others, noting in his diary, 'Letters from T. and John, still harping on Bedford; they have mismanaged but it is nothing to me,' and the duke, by then at The Doune, wrote a resigned letter to William: 'On Bedford I can say little … the

Borough is gone, and forever, unless … the Bedfordians should think better of their past conduct, and wish to renew their connection with my family – whether the fault has been mine, or yours, or John's.'

Once again, we sense just how sensitive the duke is to perceived criticism of 'my family', which, true to form, he takes personally, but his comments also provide a fascinating glimpse of the expectations and assumptions of the paternalistic landowning aristocrats of his day. Hurt and weary of the business of politics, he was soon safely removed to the Highlands, from where he wrote a somewhat more upbeat letter to Grey, 'I do not think I shall leave the Highlands until the end of October … We have had a very good year for Grouse in these Highlands, and I have been able to follow them with my gun, and kill my two brace daily without suffering from fatigue.'[472]

At The Doune that summer, while Georgina was preoccupied with bringing in new furniture and fittings, this year also marked the end of an era, as major change was underway across the river at Kinrara. Here, due to the new Duke of Gordon's ongoing financial problems, the house and estate, like The Doune before it, had been let for shooting, and instead of Georgina's brother and his family, their new neighbours during the season were Sir George and Susan Sitwell. The new tenants may have been from England, but they too seem to have fallen under the same spell that had captivated so many people before; they visited every year until the lease was terminated on the death of the Duke of Gordon in 1836, as their daughter Georgiana Sitwell wrote: 'we children thought Kinrara itself a perfect paradise … Here for six years we spent the summer and autumn, delighting in the wild scenery and in the little difficulties which only made the place more romantic in our eyes.'[473]

While the redecoration of The Doune went on in Scotland, work was also underway at Campden Hill, where construction had progressed on Wyatville's 1829 plan for a new dining room and Georgina's new flower garden layout beside the entrance court, while a 'Rustic Summerhouse' was added to the main gardens south of the house. While the building work on the new rooms was completed, outside workmen were 'Cleaning and repairing paving in the area', and specialist 'wire-workers' supplied and installed forty arches for the walks and baskets for the flower beds.[474]

The duke returned from Scotland in early November, and during his journey south he will have become increasingly aware of the looming political crisis and widespread unrest across the country that occurred in the wake of the rejection of the Reform Bill in the House of Lords. Following the general election, Wellington, as Antonia Fraser put it, 'remained obdurate on the question of Reform' and dismissed any calls for negotiation, believing that 'the Tories should be in belligerent mood' and 'unaffected by popular outcries for Reform from people of little sense and even less education'. His point-blank refusal to engage with the issue duly brought down his government by the middle of November, and the field was suddenly open for Lord Grey to form a new Whig administration. With the Whigs back in power, the patronage machine whirled into action, as the duke immediately set about the task of securing positions not just for family members, but also for others whose careers he was seeking to promote. In late November he wrote a superbly worded letter to Grey:

the friendship and affection which has subsisted between us for so many years, has I may truly assure you been the pride of my life … Looking solely at the interests of the Country, I feel most anxious that you may be able to form a strong and efficient government, and one that may most effectively secure and uphold those interests … John will, I am certain, be anxious to lend his services to your Government in any department in which you may judge him to be most useful … If you design any office in your administration to him, may I ask you to write a line to him yourself, as he is gone down to Tavistock for the Election.

In turn, on assuming office, Grey then nominated the duke as a Knight of the Garter in a gesture, perhaps, by which he sought to acknowledge the duke's unappreciated efforts all those years ago in Ireland. In an echo of his letter to Fox on accepting the Lord Lieutenancy, the duke replied, 'I have now totally made up my mind, and satisfactorily so, and my own feelings. I therefore lose no time in acquainting you that I accept the Garter, in full approbation of the principles on which your Administration is formed, and an entire confidence in you – on no other grounds could I accept it, and I consider that I owe it to you, and to you alone' (Colour Plate 32).[475]

After all this activity, the year ended quietly for the family, but not before one last surprise. While the duke had returned long since from The Doune, Georgina did not arrive back at Woburn until sometime later, and Rachel Trethewey explains what had happened: 'in December, when she was almost fifty, [Georgina] discovered that she was pregnant again … and while visiting Scotland she became ill and had to stay in Edinburgh.' In a letter to Lord Holland she wrote, 'I had felt very unwell for some time, but would not believe the worst, until Dr Hamilton confirmed my suspicions for I have been going on as ill as possible … I hope he will send me home when I am safe. If I go on I shall be confined in June.' To everyone's relief, perhaps, given how dangerous this pregnancy might have been for her, she miscarried the baby almost immediately, and was able to return home later that month. By January 1831 the duke could report to Lady Holland, 'my account of the Dss today is more satisfactory – her suspicions have vanished as they did in Paris in 1818. I rejoice at it, for at her age, the "perils of child-birth" are no light matter' (Colour Plate 33).[476] Christmas was particularly quiet that year, and instead of the usual theatrical productions over New Year, the family travelled to Chenies to join Wriothesley and Eliza in their refurbished rectory.

The New Year of 1831 saw the country in a state of unease. Politically, two issues which had been bubbling under the surface for some time were rapidly coming to a head – reform of Parliament and the abolition of slavery in the British colonies – and positions had steadily hardened as momentum swung in favour of both. To further unsettle the country, the year brought with it a rapidly spreading outbreak of cholera, which came close enough to Woburn for a payment 'to the Mother of the Child from whom The Ladies Russell were vaccinated'.

Also at Woburn, the year started badly for the duke when on 2 January he suffered an unspecified 'foolish accident' which seriously damaged his shoulder.

Edwin Landseer, *Little Red Riding Hood*, 1831. Rachel Russell, aged five, in one of her earliest appearances in the theatricals.

Two days later it had become too painful for him to write, and by the 7th he was in London for treatment. Although these circumstances meant that the festivities at Woburn were noticeably muted, a masque ball was held; with the duke away for treatment, he might well have missed one of his five-year-old daughter Rachel's earliest appearances, as 'Little Red Riding Hood'.[477]

CHAPTER NINE
1831–1836

⌒

I N EARLY 1831 the duke set about reviewing plans for the year ahead. In a series of
notes sent from the Abbey to Park Farm, he asked his steward, Edward Crocker,
for a plan which he had mislaid: 'Do you know anything of the Portfolio, with
Sir Jeffrey Wyatville's designs for altering the South Front? The Duchess thinks she
left them in the library, but I cannot find them.' These were ambitious plans which
also included designs 'for new entrances to the Abbey, at the West and North Fronts'.
In addition, he was looking for a plan by Repton 'of a Rustic Temple' which must
have been gathering dust in the Park Farm office for over fifteen years. The plan was
never found, but the duke supplied Crocker with a 'rough sketch'. Wyatville's grand
and very expensive plans were never carried through, but Repton's rustic temple
was 'erected at the top of the opening now made in the Evergreens opposite upper
drakeloe Pond … the seat will be Covered with Barke, and the floor paved with
tiles.'[478] The structure was laid out in early April and completed within a few months,
providing a view over Upper Drakelow, Repton's new pond which had subsequently
not received much attention. Although the original is long gone, the site has been
identified and the structure was temporarily reconstructed for the Woburn Abbey
Garden Show in 2016.

Further work was carried out once the family returned to Woburn in late May
from Endsleigh, when the duke commissioned extensive new buildings for the
Free School in Woburn and repairs to the church tower were completed, while
Georgina headed for Campden Hill and the London season. Since Georgiana had
now turned twenty-one and Louisa nineteen, Georgina was under some pressure
to find the girls suitable husbands, and was keen to use Campden Hill to host a
series of 'Breakfast' parties and accompany the girls on the usual visits to Almack's.

Edwin Landseer, *Lady Georgiana Russell*, 1834. One of the few images of Georgiana, this painting by Landseer was made three years after her battle with typhoid fever.

Even though the house was not in as fashionable a part of London as their previous homes in Hamilton Place and St James's Square, its large gardens made it a better venue than Belgrave Square, and in preparation for the first 'Breakfast' Georgina ordered a quantity of new 'Rustic' garden furniture and new linen decorated with 'Needle Work by design of Her Grace'.[479] Guests included Lord John, Lord William and their friend Thomas Moore, who later noted: 'The fine day, and the assemblage of pretty women in these green flowery grounds very charming.' Between these gatherings, the duke and duchess also selected a new venue on the Thames to celebrate the duke's birthday in July, when everyone travelled down by boat to the new 'Eel Pie House' set among pleasure grounds on the river at Twickenham.

A 'commodious … assembly-room' had been erected on the island the year before which had rapidly become 'a favourite resort for refreshment and recreation to water parties'.[480]

While all these family activities were going on, the movement to reform Parliament had gained a critical momentum, and all eyes were on Parliament when, in March, Lord John Russell presented the first Reform Bill. Opposition numbers soon forced it to be withdrawn, and although the second bill in late March passed the Commons by one vote, the government was defeated on a subsequent amendment, leading to a period of stalemate that lasted until 21 April when the king dissolved Parliament. In the subsequent general election held in June, the Whig government was returned with an enormous majority of 250 seats on a surge of support for reform; however, implacable opposition in the Lords meant that it took another year before the third bill was finally passed in June 1832.

The size of the government's majority and the changes it made possible meant that 1832 was also a landmark year for the abolitionists. Although the West India Interest had successfully blocked any progress throughout the 1820s, the loss of many of their supporters in the parliamentary election and the mood following the Reform Bill meant that at the start of Parliament in January 1833, the leading abolitionist Thomas Buxton could tell supporters: 'I have reason to hope that the King's Speech will declare that Government has resolved to effect the total and immediate emancipation of the slaves.' This would have been unimaginable just a few years before, and although, as with the Reform Bill, it took long negotiations and the payment of some £20,000,000 in 'compensation' to the slave owners for their loss of property, the bill passed its third reading in August 1833.[481]

During those tense months in early 1831, the duke had spent most of his time recuperating from his accident in Brighton and then at the Abbey while impatiently waiting for news of the Reform Bill, and while his mood was lifted by quiet and growing pride in Lord John's role, the bill was inevitably accompanied by the loss of traditional aristocratic political patronage and, for individuals like the duke, brought with it a sense that the world was changing. This was only strengthened the very next year when the abolitionists finally succeeded in overturning the traditional ideas of an inviolable right of property ownership, even when that property was a human being. The duke had, of course, believed in the arguments put forward that slaves, having been paid for, became the property of the purchaser, that slavery itself was essential to the success of the imperial project, British prosperity and the slave owners, and beneficial for the Africans themselves, a people who, without the guidance and example of Europeans, were not otherwise capable of achieving the degree of civilization that could enable them to benefit from freedom. This belief too had been challenged and overturned, and, coming so close together, these two bills combined to diminish and even eclipse the world that he, his brother, their parents and grandparents had known, taken for granted and never questioned.

It had been a challenging start to the year with the duke and the family not just experiencing the tension and dramas of introducing these bills and their fractious progress through Parliament, but also coming to terms with the social and political change in the air. So it must have been with great relief that in early August the duchess, Georgiana, Louisa and Rachel set off for The Doune. The duke joined them in the first week of September, but the visit was to be overshadowed by both Georgina and then Georgiana falling ill, and few details of the stay have emerged. Fortunately, Elizabeth Grant's sister Jane has left a vivid picture of Rothiemurchus that summer in her 'Travel Journal', when she visited for ten days in early August with her husband, James Gibson Craig of Riccarton. Staying at nearby Inverdruie, a house her family still had access to, Jane visited Loch an Eilein, noting 'the Duchess of Bedford's care of the place. She is … filling up the ruts and mending the … road.' The next day, Jane and her husband were moved by a visit to the old church at Rothiemurchus, and taken by surprise by a crowd of local people who rushed 'towards us as we left', which she put down to 'my being one of what they call the true blood; a descendant of Macalpine and of Macalpine's fathers whom they and their father's fathers had acknowledged for their chiefs, and had loved and honoured with all the wild devotion of Highland clansmen'. Deeply moved, she writes, 'And still in that distant valley lingers some rich bond between these people and their absent Laird. It was proved by the ardour with which they gathered round me, his daughter, and by the affection which I felt swell in my heart for them.' She goes on, 'We spent the afternoon … going over the house and gardens of The Doune … Everything … was in the highest order and much had been done and I think with great good taste to improve both house and shrubbery … They are painting the dining-room quite new … and Papa's study beautifully fitted up and furnished for the Duke with a glass door into the shrubbery and new flower garden. This occupies all the space that was gravel between the old house and … the new [wing] projects.'

After the walking through the 'quite beautiful' shrubbery, they then followed the 'river walk' to the West Lodge before heading back along the road to the kitchen gardens, also much improved. At the end of the week, Jane returned again to The Doune hoping to meet Georgina, but 'The Duchess was not at home … I was sorry I missed seeing her as I was anxious to let her know how grateful [are] the poor people she is so kind to and [they] speak of her goodness. The Duke put ten pounds [£600 today] into the poor box upon going away last year, and the Duchess has built a house for old John Mackintosh.'[482]

We do not know, of course, just how large the crowd which 'rushed towards' them was or who they were, but Jane's account throws some light on the mood on the Rothiemurchus estate just four years after the Grants had left, fleeing the bailiffs and leaving substantial local debts. However their lairds had behaved, old clan loyalties still ran very deep, and some of that 'rich bond' seems to have been extended to Georgina, daughter of one of the greatest lairds of them all, and whose gifts and attention to people's lives were able to ease to some degree the situation of those she and the duke felt moved to help.

Wherever she had been when Jane Grant called, in late September Georgina made a brief trip to Glen Feshie, and then on 1 October with Georgiana and Louisa attended a 'Grand Ball' at Balbirnie in Fife, home of General Robert Balfour and his wife, Eglantine Fordyce, Georgina's first cousin. The Balfours' daughters Eglantine and Elizabeth (Bessie) both spent many summers at the Ruigh Fionntaig huts with their father and his co-tenant, Edward Ellice, who had married their elder sister, Katherine (Janie). Unfortunately, soon after their return to The Doune, Georgiana developed typhoid fever and rapidly became very ill. By early November she was so ill that it left her temporarily blind and her hearing permanently damaged; much to Georgina's annoyance but true to form perhaps, the duke decided to leave and set out for home some ten days later, taking Louisa with him. It was to be almost seven weeks before Georgina was able to set out with her patient.

On 20 December the duke reported that the duchess 'is now on her road journeying homewards by easy stages, on account of her invalid who is still very weak'. Once home, Georgiana's health improved enough for her to play a small part in some of the most elaborate New Year theatricals ever staged. Over the month of January 1832 the Woburn theatre staged three farces and 'An Interlude', making the most of a revolving cast of family and friends, including the duchess, Georgiana, Louisa, their French governess, Mlle Migneron, Charles, their cousin Colonel Francis Russell, Mr Balfour (a cousin from Balbirnie) and others.[483]

Beyond painting the scenery and making comic sketches of the performers, Landseer was also very active over these years in the design and ordering of costumes, particularly the elaborate masks, and two of Landseer's drawings seem to illustrate just such a performance. One shows Louisa, soon to become Lady Abercorn, in the elegant masquerade costume, in animated conversation with a grotesquely masked figure in the hat and aprons of a chef or confectioner, while a small, blacked-up figure thumbs their nose at them.[484] In a second drawing, the same masked figure in hat and apron is shown listening to a town crier, acted by the duchess, who is unrecognizable in elaborate costume and what may well be the 'Nose & Eyes with specks' mask designed by Landseer. In a finished oil painting dated 1832, Landseer shows Louisa in her 'late 18th century' costume with a hand-held mask and another 'Nose & Eyes' mask lying on the ground in front of her.[485]

Other than the theatrical productions, the duke appears to have been short of company this winter, and early in the year he wrote to Landseer hoping he would visit and bring his artist friends:

I think I may say now for certainty that I shall be at the British Gallery on Saturday about 2 o'clock. Perhaps I may meet you there when you can point out some of the best things in the Exhibition, as I shall not have much time to spare. I rely on seeing you with your gun for the last days of shooting. Would any of your brother Artists like to come down for a few days country air – Wilkie, Leslie and Calcott? If so, I would ask them to come. Old Lewis is coming with his unfinished proof of Lady Louisa, and he would 'like to meet the fine gentlemen' you know.[486]

By April 1832, while everyone was following events in Parliament where the protracted and fierce battle for the Reform Bill was coming to a climax, the Bedfords spent the month in Brighton with the girls, where the duke was planning a visit to Landseer's studio to view Louisa's masquerade portrait and indulge in 'a little quiet artistic conversation': 'On … April 9th, I hope to see you in your in your studio at 11 o'clock, and to have the satisfaction of seeing my picture on your Easel. I shall invite my neighbours and your brothers of the R.A, Wilkie and Calcott … I'm afraid there is no chance of my being able to prevail upon you to come and eat at C. Hill on Sunday that we may have a little quiet artistic conversation. I have seen and heard so little of the arts in the last five months that I am really quite ignorant of all that is going on.'

Finally, on 4 June came the news they had been waiting for when the Reform Bill finally passed, but not without leaving opinion in the country and individual families seriously divided. Awkwardly, for Georgina, while her husband's family had had so much to do with the bill passing, her brother, the Duke of Gordon, true to his Tory roots, was 'bitterly hostile' and one of the few who voted against the third reading. Such problems, however, were soon swept aside by growing hints that Louisa's world was about to change, and the moment is caught for us by Lord William's thirteen-year-old son, Hastings. During the early summer, Lady William and her boys were still in London waiting to join William in his new diplomatic post in Lisbon, and Hastings passes on his observations in letters to his father. He recounts 'riding daily with my young aunts Georgiana and Louisa Russell', and becomes aware of something going on, 'What's in the wind about Abercorn and L? I don't twig but I know that she has ridden alone with him to Richmond Park … while I rode another way with Georgy.'

Soon after this, Hastings tells his father, 'This week the Duchess went to Woburn with the Duke, Abercorn and Louisa *soli*! To make him pop the question but he did not though everybody in town believed that he had.' For all Abercorn's hesitation, by August the duke told Lady William, 'I have received a very pleasing letter from Lord Abercorn asking my consent to his union to Louisa … it gives me the greatest satisfaction.' No doubt, Georgina was greatly satisfied too, a daughter soon to be married and to a marquis (who would eventually be a duke) – her mother would have been proud. Everyone was far less proud, however, of Louisa's brother Frank, who was in London on shore leave at this time and, to his father's despair, was getting himself into trouble. Writing to Lady Holland, the duke asks her, 'Did you see the scandalous reports from Frank?: "Lord Francis Russell, of No.6 Belgrave Square, drunk with a black eye &c, &c, &c.." What a shame! Stagg very properly went immediately to the Editor of the Times.'[487]

After her annual series of 'Breakfasts' at Campden Hill that Georgina hosted in tents on the lawn in late June – this year with lavish refreshments and music from a 'a Band of Scotch Musicians' – she left for Brighton before setting off in early August with the three girls and Alexander for The Doune, where the duke and Landseer joined them a month later. This summer two of Landseer's most charming drawings of Rachel were done: one, *The Little Actress at The Doune*, shows Rachel in full theatrical costume, while the other shows her with a pet deer called Harty.[488]

Great expectations hung in the air as everyone awaited Abercorn's imminent arrival, fresh from a meeting with his mother and the lawyers and the finalizing of the wedding arrangements. At one point the duke, who had just returned from a trip to the huts, leaving Georgina, Louisa and the others in Glen Feshie to enjoy a 'bonfire and dance', wrote a note to Louisa to update her on the news: 'My dearest Louisa, Got safe to my long journey's end … and sat down to my solitary dinner … I think it possible that Abercorn will not return tomorrow.' Fortunately, over the next few weeks the issues were resolved and the wedding set for 26 October at Gordon Castle. The choice of venue was evidently made by Abercorn's mother, since 'her ladyship, the Countess of Aberdeen, [was] in too delicate a state of health to permit her travelling to London, where it was at first intended the marriage should take place,' and the duke's agreeing to this marked a significant break in Russell family tradition. Among a host of Georgina's immediate family and Gordon relatives, only Louisa's parents and two sisters, Georgiana and Rachel, attended. Indeed, to some extent, the wedding itself was soon overshadowed by the celebrations that followed. After the brief ceremony in the private chapel at Gordon Castle, toasts were drunk and an elaborate cake cut for distribution in the drawing room before the happy couple left for a brief honeymoon at Huntly Lodge. After their departure the public celebrations began with a parade, music and 'copious libations', which were followed by two days and nights of bibulous festivities in and around Fochabers.

On their return to Gordon Castle, the couple set out with the Bedfords 'to his lordship's magnificent estates in Ireland'.[489] This too was a new departure for the family, and added a whole new dimension to their travels; a series of trips over the years were taken to visit Louisa and her husband at his ancestral home of Barons Court, County Tyrone, many of them, like this one, directly after their annual stay in Scotland. Visiting Northern Ireland, with its largely Protestant and Tory aristocracy, gave the duke and duchess different landscapes to explore and a very different perspective on the country to their experiences in Dublin. It is also interesting to note that the terms of the 'Contract of Marriage' between Abercorn and Louisa were drawn up 'with the special advice, consent, concurrence and approbation of her said father', and that two key provisions were Louisa's guaranteed personal allowance of one thousand pounds paid quarterly, and that Abercorn 'obliges himself and his Heirs, Executors and Successors … to make payments to the said Lady Russell, during all the days of her lifetime after the decease of the said James, Marquis of Abercorn in case she shall survive him … of £5,000 each year of her life after the decease of said James, Marquis of Abercorn'. While the duke is credited with advising on these terms, their definitive wording strongly suggests that Georgina, worried that her own settlement and that of her mother had noticeably lacked such a guarantee, played some role in formulating the advice. This issue had begun to haunt Georgina as the duke's health continued to fail.[490]

As the young couple arrived at Barons Court there was some work to be done. Abercorn had inherited the estates at the age of seven following his grandfather's death in 1818, and although the estates were in a good financial position, he had spent little time there, having been brought up during his minority at Bentley Priory, Middlesex. This meant that the house and grounds at Barons Court, barely used throughout the 1820s, were now a little rundown and in need of attention. The house sat at the centre of its parkland, which stretched out along a string of three lakes lying in a long, open valley and flanked by low rolling hills, and the family had lived there since the early 1740s, when Abercorn's great-grandfather built a Palladian villa and started a programme of tree planting. By 1751 he had created the deer park, and between 1767 and 1782 a larger house was built on the present site beside the central lake.

By the mid-1790s, new plantations had been added, along with new roads, walks and rides, and the lakes deepened and named, south to north, Fanny, Catherine and Mary, after his grandfather's daughters.[491] A plan from 1800 shows the extent of the expanded park, complete with two ruined castles, roads, lakes, bogs, plantations, pastures and buildings, and it also indicates that, with the exception of a driveway and forecourt on the north side, there were no formal gardens round the house at all. For Louisa, who had grown up amidst the endless gardening activity of her mother and father at both Woburn and Endsleigh, her new home must have appeared somewhat bare and neglected. As for the duke, he was decidedly underwhelmed by everything he saw, telling Landseer a few years later that 'there is nothing of the "beautiful and sublime", or even the Picturesque in this part of Ireland to compensate for the malaise and uncertainty of crossing the Irish Channel twice at this season of the year.'[492] In time, after the house and setting became familiar to him, his view mellowed and he even went so far as to replicate one of the buildings in the park at Woburn.

The visit started well with light-hearted 'Barons Court festivities', but early in the New Year of 1833, as Trethewey reports, things took a more serious turn when Georgina 'fell from a carriage on to her back and although she did not break any ribs, she developed a chest infection'. In his typical reaction to the presence of illness in the family, the duke, 'thinking his wife was being a hypochondriac', told Lady Holland that 'the Duchess is wonderfully well … and not willing to acknowledge herself better when she is so'; he decided that he needed to return to England, leaving Georgina and the children in Ireland.[493] Barely a week after he arrived home, however, news of the seriousness of Georgina's condition reached the duke, and on 15 January he left for Holyhead and Dublin to rejoin the duchess, who, as much as anything, was missing her husband. In the event, it took several more weeks for Georgina to be fit to travel, the family finally arriving home in early February.

Despite the way the year had begun, the duke's spirits were soon revived by the publication in March of the second edition of P. F. Robinson's *Vitruvius Britannicus: History of Woburn Abbey*, followed a month later by that of Jeremiah Wiffen's *Historical Memoirs of the House of Russell*, the result of his eight years of research into the family history. Wiffen's book represented a celebration of the family's pedigree as a whole, linking it to the earliest emergence of an aristocracy of which they were still such a central part. Even though he, like others, may have had doubts about some of the connections Wiffen made with pre-Conquest families in Normandy, the duke felt the book justified his pride in his ancestors, right up until his brother Francis. The memoir came out in two volumes and contained a series of Louis Parez's images done on their trip to Normandy in 1827, 'for an examination of Records and Libraries', and the picture of St Helen's Point on the Isle of Wight (see Chapter 8). It had been an enormous undertaking, and the duke immediately sent copies out to his friends, but, cautious as ever, he also seems to have had some reservations about the propriety of some of the content. In January, for example, when reviewing the book's contents before publication, he wrote to Lord Holland from Baron's Court, 'I wish to ask your opinion on one point, which pray give me by return of post – I mean the propriety of Wiffen's publishing his "Russell Memoirs" – which are now in [preparation for publication] … my grandfather's <u>secret</u> dispatches to the Secretary of State when he was Lord Lieutenant of Ireland … having in mind that 80 years have elapsed since that period.' In May he replied to Holland: 'I am pleased with your critique on Wiffen's work, and am glad to see that you approve what you have read.'[494] Indeed, the contents of the *Memoirs* featured in an ongoing discussion over the next few months between the duke, Wiffen, Lord Holland and John Allen over their different interpretations of history, particularly the Tudor and Stuart periods.

Outside the Abbey, although it is clear the duke had plans for the pleasure grounds, where he was keen to continue to develop his collections, all immediate work had to be put on hold when William George Adam, who had succeeded his father, William Adam, as Chief Agent, made it clear that economic retrenchment was necessary, and the duke came under pressure to minimize expenditure. In a letter replying to enquiries about possible economies, Robert Ireland, Head of Woods, wrote, 'On reducing my Establishment … It is as much my wish, as it is my duty, to accede to any plan of retrenchment commended by your Grace' and 'most readily to acquiesce in any regulation which your Grace thinks proper … but this I leave with your Grace.'[495] Inevitably, perhaps, leaving it to the duke was not really going to help, and the ensuing years saw the period of expenditure – and resulting debt – that was to so upset the 7th Duke on his succession in 1839, but for this year at least, the duke does seem to have put his more ambitious projects on hold.

Throughout late April and early May, the duke reports on the duchess's continuing poor health, and on 3 May tells Lord William, 'If the Duchess is well enough to move we shall probably go [to Endsleigh] this month, but she is much thrown back by a severe attack of the prevailing influenza, and her cough and sleepless nights are as bad as ever.' Although it does seem that Georgina held at least one of her breakfasts at Campden Hill, the family soon left for the peace and quiet of Endsleigh, and they were joined by the Abercorns and Edward, briefly ashore on leave. The duke writes to Lord Holland in June that while Georgina is 'in my opinion, much better, though (*entre nous*) she does not willingly own it', he has to admit that he had spent most of this time incapacitated by gout and had been getting around on crutches, but hopes 'to be able to go out on my Pony in a few days'.[496]

Back at Campden Hill, a revived Georgina attended Almack's and the theatre, and took Alexander on a visit to the Surrey Zoological Gardens, before setting

off for The Doune in August. It was during this London season that Sir Denis
Le Marchant described seeing Georgina and Georgiana, who had 'passed the day
with us' at Holland House, considering Georgina a 'bold, bad woman – with the
remains of beauty' and Georgiana as 'a dull dowdy'. He went on: 'Lord Ebrington
was also of the party … He has been one of the most handsome men of the day
and one of the most pleasing, as too many ladies know to their cost, and amongst
others her Grace of Bedford.' His comments illustrate just how carelessly unkind
'polite' London society could be, and his final remark reminds us just how little we
can ever know about the details of these people's lives.

Before leaving for Scotland in late August, Landseer helped Georgina to organize
a post-theatre supper at Belgrave Square, and decided to invite his friend Charles
James Mathews, at that time an art student and exhibitor at the Royal Academy, to
meet the family and help with the entertainment:

> Dear Mat,   Aug 1st, 1833
> Could you send your fiddle to No.6 Belgrave Square, during tomorrow? As
> the Duchess gives us a supper after the play, when we shall most likely have
> a lark. This is all *my* arrangement, and I hope you will not send your guitar
> to sup without the poor player, as I wish my good friends to become better
> acquainted with you, as they will most likely be bored by us for a month in
> the Highlands.[497]

Clearly, Georgina was delighted with Mathews's company since he was one of an
unusually large group of people who assembled at The Doune that summer. While
the duke remained at Woburn, possibly still subject to painful gout symptoms,
by the end of August the duchess, Charles, Georgiana, Cosmo, Alexander and
Rachel had all arrived at The Doune, where they were joined by 'Miss Balfour',
one of their Balfour cousins, the Abercorns, Landseer and Mathews, all ready for
some adventures; the unusual size of this year's house party was reflected in the
arrival of a large order for 'China, Glass, Crockery and Earthenware, chiefly for
The Doune'.[498] Once there, Mathews, who went on to become a successful comic

actor, was immediately swept up into the excitement and light-hearted fun that surrounded life at The Doune and in Glen Feshie.

In early September they were joined by Lord Tankerville, a friend of Colonel Ross, who had taken over the Invereshie lease, and Edward Ellice, who subsequently took the tenancy with General Balfour of Balbirnie. Tankerville tells us, 'It was unanimously proposed by the ladies and gentlemen to make an expedition to the top of Ben Avon [Macdui], the highest peak in the Cairngorms, from which a magnificent view of all these mountains of the mid-Highlands is to be seen.' Reading the account closely, it actually seems that the ultimate destination was not to climb the 'highest peak' but to visit Loch Avon, the 'very beautiful lake near its summit formed in the bed of its crater. Black precipices of porphyry and granite spring up sheer from its sides, straight like plummet lines from its water's edge till they reach the highest tops' (Colour Plate 34).

The trip, which involved camping overnight beside the lake, began soon after breakfast, the men on foot – Mathews got into the spirit by 'appearing in a smart tartan kilt with all the appointment of a Highlander' – while the ladies, 'the Duchess and her two daughters and two of her friends', rode their ponies. 'So the party set forward merrily through the old pine woods, where the path gradually wound its way above the base of the hill, till we came out into the open.' After a long climb up 'a zig-zag path of rolling stones', and after they were able to 'stop for breath and for luncheon in a panorama of the finest mountain scenery in these parts', they 'arrived at our destination on the plateau above, where the lovely lake lay before us, the bright sun giving splendid reflection of the peaks of Ben Avon frowning over it'.

Following a meal beside the campfire, they 'spent a pleasant hour or two in singing' and, when the pipes 'struck up', dancing, after which 'the ladies retired to their tents and the men to the Poachers Cave … amongst the boulders' for the night. The next morning, 'we made an early start … to return to the glen, bidding goodbye to [these] most charming scenes.'[499]

Following their return from Loch Avon, Mathews provides a vivid picture of the rest of his visit in further letters to his mother, capturing the free and easy atmosphere created by Georgina and the girls as he adapted to his 'wild' surroundings. On 21 September, following an expedition, he wrote, 'There is no moment which can be found for long letter writing. I have been living for the last three or four days in a tent, and am in a state of excitement … Everything here is wild; the weather is wild; the two young ladies who are here are wild as March hares; and I verily believe, if I stay another week here I shall be wild myself.'

To this letter one of the 'young ladies' added, 'The young ladies are not wild. So far from it, that's quite the reverse. The gentlemen *horrid bores*; and do nothing but boast of their shooting, throwing large stones, and having savage dogs; and I must say I shall not be sorry to get rid of their company.' Mathews then ended the letter: 'The above is written by one of the prettiest girls in the world, in red stockings, a short bedgown, grey petticoat, and a snood, by which you will see that I am well and in good spirits.'

Whichever of the girls wrote this wonderful passage, it tells us what Georgina, and now her daughters, valued about the lives they were creating in Glen Feshie. Although the men seem to have stayed a few nights at the huts on this occasion, this was unusual since most years the shooting parties would leave the glen after shooting and return to The Doune, where the hot bath, large living room, easy chairs, extensive cellar, roaring fires, billiard table and army of servants provided what was needed after a hard day on the moors. This year, looking forward to the quiet life in the glen, we catch a note of heartfelt impatience in the girl's comments, 'I shall not be sorry to get rid of their company.' That Georgina saw Glen Feshie in these terms is made clear when Mathews writes a further letter to his mother: 'A day or two after our return from the trip to Loch Avon, which I described to you in my last letter, preparations were made for flitting from The Doune, to take up our residence in a romantic glen about fifteen miles off, where the Duchess loves to dwell and lay out her pin money. Orders were given that all *grande toilette* should be suspended until further notice, and that those who were not prepared to rough it should stay behind.'[500]

Two things Mathews says here are interesting. First, the word 'flitting', associated with the annual departure to the shielings, is something he is only likely to have heard at The Doune, perhaps reflecting Georgina's use of the word to describe their departure for Glen Feshie. Second, it is telling that he should bother to add 'where the Duchess loves to dwell and lay out her pin money', emphasizing that it was the duchess rather than the duke who enjoyed staying in Glen Feshie, and picking up on the fact that the Glen Feshie enterprise was largely funded by Georgina out of her own money for herself and her daughters.

Leaving The Doune for Glen Feshie, the men 'set off on our shaggy ponies with the intention of shooting our way over the mountain tops to the glen', and arrived at the huts towards evening, where Mathews found 'the Duchess, Lady Rachel, and the maids had arrived a little before me in their tilt-cart; Miss Balfour and Lady Georgiana having, under the escort of a guide, walked all the way from The Doune.' Mathews tells his mother: 'The appearance was that of a small Indian settlement, consisting of one low building containing three or four bedrooms and the kitchen, &c., and two smaller ones of one room each, the one being the dining-room, parlour, drawing-room, and hall, and the other containing two beds for ladies' (Colour Plate 35). 'The rest of the settlement' was composed of tents, where he discovered 'the gentlemen's apartments', two to a tent, and here they stayed for a few days' shooting on the moors above.

Describing the huts, he says, 'The walls [are] made of turf and overgrown with foxglove, and the roof of untrimmed spars of birch … Everything of rough unpeeled birch, except the uncovered turf walls.' Inside, 'the beds of the ladies resembled small presses or chest of drawers, with mattresses stuffed with heather and pillows of the same,' while 'the gentlemen's apartments were in tents, each containing two small heather couches … one small table and a wash-hand-stand.' Mathews concludes that 'everything is picturesque in the extreme. It is without any exception the most delightful sort of life I have ever seen or experienced. Amusements of every sort are constantly going on. The guitar is in great request, and a small piano of two octaves, made on purpose for travelling, is constantly going. Lord Ossulton and Miss Balfour both sing beautifully, and we get up songs, duets, and trios without end.' However, he notes that outside, 'The weather has been very rough and stormy since our sojourn in the glen, and sketching and painting have been out of the question.' Mathews's description of the huts makes it clear that at this point the accommodation at Ruigh Aiteachan still consisted of the traditional bothies, and that they had not yet been improved, unlike the much more substantial huts at Ruigh Fionntaig with their wooden walls, fireplaces and chimneys.

Unfortunately the weather did not improve, and later in the stay, when invited by Ross and Ellice to cross the Feshie for a grand dinner at the Ruigh Fionntaig huts, Mathews relates that, 'The day turned out tremendous. Torrents of rain and tempests of wind succeeded each other, till we began to fear that the river would be too much swollen to allow us to attempt the fords, three of which were to be passed. At seven o'clock, however, in the midst of a hurricane we set off.' After much excitement, everyone arrived safely and they were rewarded by a 'profuse banquet … exceedingly gay, the piper playing all the time outside, and an enormous bonfire … kept constantly alive, in spite of the most tremendous unceasing hurricane which raged'. Their journey home was just as exciting as they braved the roaring river, and 'in spite of all difficulties we reached our own quarters in safety, and, within our tents that night, many were the glasses of whiskey toddy … consumed by the survivors.'

Undaunted by these adventures, the following night

we gave a ball, and all the lads and lassies in the neighbourhood (that is about a dozen in all, being the population of ten or twelve miles around) were invited. Two fiddlers and a piper worked away from right in the evening till six in the morning … The Duchess, notwithstanding a slight failing – from a previous accident – in her knee, danced as well as any one of the party, and in the reels decidedly beat all. The young ladies are sylphs. As to myself, I must own I am amazed. The manner in which I walk over the hills, ford the rivers, scale the rocks, and dance the reels is past belief.

Following this shared experience, a strong friendship grew up between Landseer, Mathews and Tankerville, which in the case of the first two lasted the rest of their lives, and at the end of the visit that year, the three of them travelled to Tankerville's home at Chillingham Castle, 'and it was not without reluctance that a return was made to London,' from where they travelled together to Woburn Abbey that Christmas to take part in the theatre productions.[501]

Mathews and Tankerville provide a vivid picture of life in Glen Feshie, but also a very rare one, since there are no other such accounts of large parties spending time at the huts in subsequent years or on a similar trek. It seems that after this unusually busy summer life became much quieter, focused around Georgina and the girls, the only known exception to this being Landseer, who stayed most years in the glen for extended periods 'sketching and painting', and had a tent, and then a hut, of his own. The storminess of the weather that summer is reflected in the atmospheric paintings and sketches Landseer produced during their time there, particularly his images of the Loch Avon expedition, *An Encampment on Loch Avon* (Colour Plate 36) and *Loch Avon and the Cairngorm Mountains*, also called *Lake Scene: Effect of a Storm*. Another Landseer image shows us the elaborate porch of Georgina's 'dining hut', and life in these huts in bad weather was captured by Tankerville when he described seeing 'The old Duke … sitting with an umbrella over his head, to save his soup from being watered by a dribble which was leaking from the roof above; quite happy and resigned to his fate – a wet seat in a wooden cabin instead of Woburn Abbey'.[502] Both Landseer's painting of the porch and Tankerville's description of the duke under his umbrella would seem to confirm that the Ruigh Aiteachan huts were still very basic.

Two further images from this period also reflect the troubled and stormy skies of the Loch Avon images and continue this new direction in Landseer's art: *Glenfeshie (Rainy Day in the Highlands)* and *A Highland Landscape*. The former shows the point where the Feshie emerges from the upper glen to sweep past Ruigh Fionntaig on its way north, a point where the masses of Creag na Gaibhre and Creag na Cailich face one another like guardians of the glen. It formed the gateway to the mysteries of the landscape beyond and seems to have particularly caught Landseer's imagination since he painted it repeatedly. The latter is a particularly interesting picture and shows a very different view of the glen. It is framed by a wooden post on the left and wooden balustrade along the bottom, suggesting it was the view from a duck shooting lodge of some sort looking over part of the Insh marshes and out across rolling moorland to what were at that time the open fields of lower eastern Glen Feshie, with the ridgeline of the east side of the glen running south across the horizon, its peaks all partially obscured by showers of rain from the dark low clouds above. If this is what it shows, an area now long lost to plantations, it provides a rare glimpse of the landscape of the Invereshie estate when it was still populated and farmed by tenant farmers, and as it was when the Bedfords were there.[503]

While all this activity was going on in Scotland, the duke was at Woburn in July to celebrate a landmark moment when he published *Hortus Woburnensis*. It is likely that the duke and Forbes gave it this title to link the book directly to the tradition of *Hortus Kewensis*, the catalogues of plants cultivated in the royal gardens at Kew that were published in 1768 and 1789. Yet in many ways, *Hortus Woburnensis* was different, an extraordinary and in some ways unique work, since although it is subtitled 'A Descriptive Catalogue of Upwards of Six Thousand Ornamental Plants cultivated at Woburn Abbey', unlike its predecessors it was not simply a catalogue of plants, and nor was it a detailed record of scientific endeavour and experiment.

Instead, the catalogue of plants (Part I) occupies just half the book, while the rest consists of detailed descriptions of the structures and contents of the pleasure grounds (Part II) and the kitchen gardens (Part III). The frontispiece, showing the 'South West View of Woburn Abbey', with the Abbey and the ranges of buildings beyond seen through the trees of the park, and the title page, featuring the recently completed 'London Entrance' topped by the impressive Bedford coat of arms, together set the scene: this book is about Woburn Abbey as a whole. As the pages unfold in Parts II and III, complemented by detailed architectural and artistic renderings and a list of some eighty-six entries of the 'Botanical books in the Library', Forbes discusses matters of design, aesthetic taste and historic architecture alongside new technology, horticulture and botany as he details the designs and contents of the main features of grounds around the Abbey and elsewhere in the park. In some sections, particularly those with a historical perspective, one can also detect the hand of the duke, and together they produced a book that in essence appears as a celebratory summary of what they had achieved at Woburn since the

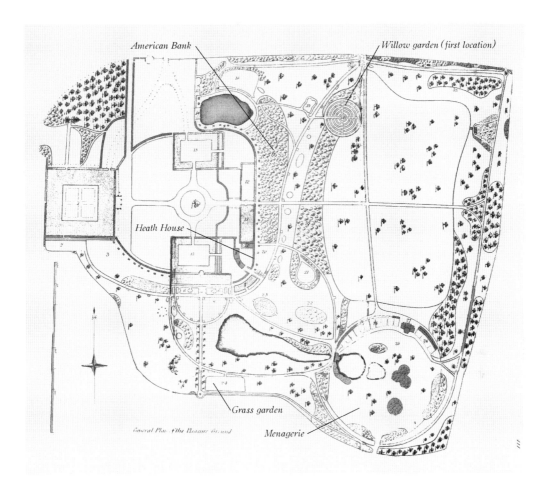

American Bank

Willow garden (first location)

Heath House

General Plan of the Pleasure Ground

Grass garden

Menagerie

John Forbes, 'General Plan of the Pleasure Ground', *Hortus Woburnensis*, Plate III, 1833. This plan helps to illustrate how the duke was now determined to combine his scientific interests with the recreational and aesthetic elements of the gardens. The 'American Bank' was the name given to the sloping area that was used to display the collection of plants from America.

mid-1820s through their efforts to combine experimental horticultural science with new and ground-breaking technologies (Map 6).

In addition, although it appears in the context of a book about new science and technologies, Plate III, 'General Plan of the Pleasure Ground', is the earliest and most complete record of the duke and duchess's priorities and taste in landscape gardening that we have. It was the first such plan to emerge since Repton's Red Book of 1805, and comparing the two, we can see just how far their vision had moved on from an eighteenth-century picturesque world filtered by art to one of direct engagement with the natural world as it actually was. This plan, and Wyatville's embellished version of it, which appeared in 1838, not only encapsulate these changes in taste and content, they also illustrate and explain the origins of the completed gardens that Queen Victoria was to enjoy in 1842. Beyond the book itself, one other aspect about its publication is worth noting: the list of subscribers. Although the duke was a member of at least nine of the leading scientific, botanical and horticultural societies based in London, none of them appear as subscribers or were presented with copies. Instead, the list of 179 names seems to reflect the spirit of this age of enquiry in that rather than comprising of established academic, scientific or botanic experts and the institutions to which they belonged, it consists of those – whoever and wherever they were – who shared a passion for the subject and who made up the duke's and Forbes's circle of family, friends, correspondents and contacts. It forms a broad list of professionals and amateurs, and includes the duke's peers and their families, friends, politicians, artists, a sculptor, professional gardeners (at thirty-six, by far the largest single group of subscribers), nurserymen, seedsmen and manufacturers of the new technologies from across England, Scotland and Ireland, along with eight of the garden staff from Woburn, Endsleigh and Campden Hill, and the directors or head gardeners of the new botanic gardens at Hull, Edinburgh, Glasgow and Dublin. With this book Forbes and the duke were staking Woburn's claim to a place among these people in the wider engagement with science and wonder that dominated the Romantic age.[504]

In spite of Adam's warnings, the duke launched a number of new projects in the pleasure grounds that August, starting with the creation of the Maze, or Labyrinth as it was known, based on the plan Lord William had brought back from Portugal, complete with a Chinese 'Temple' at its centre. The other pressing task which needed to be addressed was fixing the ongoing leaks in the roof of the riding house, but as work got underway, damage to that of the tennis court was also revealed, meaning both had to be removed and replaced over this year and next, before work began on extensive repairs to both interiors. With all this underway, the duke, encouraged by his growing list of contacts and his ever stronger relationship with James Forbes, then turned their attention to planning a new arboretum and separate pinetum in the pleasure grounds. Although by 1833 the plans were advanced enough to be included as part of *Hortus Woburnensis*, a possible lack of funds meant that it was not until

1835–6 that work was able to begin on the new collections. It was also this summer that another Scot, John Caie, joined Forbes's staff as an under gardener at Woburn Abbey, and he has left this account of what he found at Woburn:

> the new Kitchen garden and forcing-houses were finished and in good working order, as was afterwards shown in the fine fruit produced by Mr. Forbes, both for family use and for exhibition purposes. The plant-houses in the pleasure ground were being filled with collections of plants, such as Cacti and Orchids. Ericas held a very prominent place here, and these were placed under my care, with a degree of liberty to exercise my own judgment in their cultivation which seldom falls to the lot of one in such a situation. That success attended our hopes will be obvious from a remark made by the late Mr. McNab, of the Royal Botanic Garden, Edinburgh, in reference to the growths of Heaths, that 'our method was worth knowing.'[505]

In September, with the family still away in Scotland, and on the advice of his doctors to seek some relief from the gout, the duke returned to Leamington Spa to spend the month visiting the mineral springs, drinking the restorative waters, and hoping to see some old friends. It was a place where the duke felt very much at home, but not very mobile and, destined to sit in the baths for long periods of time, he was anxious for some friendly company. He urged the Hollands to join him, offering them a bed but suggesting they would be 'better off at the hotel, which is large, airy and spacious … I do not think you will like these small houses. You will have good air here, a pretty country, good roads and the agreeable society of Lord Essex and me.'[506] The Hollands duly arrived and joined the duke and Essex on their regular visits to the baths, where the gouty gentlemen would spend much of the day, gossiping, greeting friends, seeing and being seen; in the evenings they enjoyed the duke's weekly 'Hamper & Boxes of Grouse' and delivery of wine from Woburn. Yet, perhaps the most significant development during the stay in Leamington is that it marks the start of the duke's correspondence with William Hooker, then Professor of Botany at Glasgow University and Director of the Glasgow Botanical Gardens, on an issue that was to increasingly dominate the final years of his life. In what would appear to be a reply to a request by Hooker, the duke wrote, 'I will lose no time in making the necessary enquiries as to who has the appointment to the office of Director of the Royal Garden at Kew. I am fully convinced that were you to succeed Mr Aiton in that situation, it would be of the greatest advantage to the Science of Botany … You do me too much honour in calling me "a man of science" – I have no pretensions whatever to that appellation' but through a 'partiality to Botany' pursued it 'at a very humble distance'.

Hooker later recalled that their relationship dated from as early as 1816, when the duke had sent him a copy of *Hortus Gramineus Woburnensis*, and that he 'was particularly gratified to find myself in the number of the select few to whom, though personally unknown to His Grace, the Hort. Gramm was spontaneously sent', and from this point they remained in touch, largely through Forbes, on matters of plants, plant collections and other areas of mutual interest. For Hooker, the relationship provided an interested and influential patron who could help advance his career in the closed world of professional academic institutions and societies, as we see in his request to the duke, and he had taken steps to strengthen their personal relationship by dedicating a volume of *Curtis's Botanical Magazine* to the duke in fulsome terms.[507]

For the duke, of course, the relationship allowed him to feel a part of that world and to participate in its development. We can imagine, in spite of his protestations in the above letter, just how gratifying it must have been for the duke to be considered a 'man of science' by one of its rising stars. Although, at this time, there was little the duke could do for Hooker, their friendship grew over the next five years as they campaigned for the royal gardens at Kew to become a national collection, and later, when the gardens had passed to public ownership, the duke campaigned unstintingly, and ultimately successfully, to have Hooker appointed its first director.

Following the trip to Leamington, the duke was back at Woburn Abbey in early November to await the family's return from their adventures in Scotland. By the time he returned, the Abbey had been closed up for several months, and inspecting the Temple of Liberty, he was not at all pleased by what he found there. His subsequent note to Crocker leads one to wonder just how often anyone in the family visited the Sculpture Gallery during these busy years: 'I went to the Temple of Liberty in the Sculpture Gallery this afternoon, and was very sorry to see it in so neglected a state. The floor and ceiling of the Temple are covered with dirt, cobwebs hanging from the ceiling, part of the gilding peeling off &c. &c. It was very damp … Surely stoves ought to be lit in such damp weather as this! Be so kind as to look at this tomorrow morning.'

Georgina arrived back at Woburn with the children by mid-December, but in spite of their active outdoor summer in the glens, the duke reported to Lady Holland that the duchess was suffering from 'a very severe bilious attack and complete jaundice'. While his wife recovered, however, he was somewhat preoccupied by exchanging festive 'forget-me-nots' with Lady Holland: 'A thousand thanks … for your pretty "forget me not." I had written my thanks in doggerel rhymes, but, on reading them over, I threw them in the fire, and must therefore say in simple prose, I very sincerely thank you.'[508]

Soon enough a large party, including Princess Lieven and Lord Grey, began to assemble for the Christmas and New Year festivities, and the Abbey remained 'full of company' until early February 1834. An early highlight was a grand ball in January, as reported in the *Morning Post*: 'Woburn Abbey: During the whole of last week was a scene of extraordinary festivity. On Tuesday was a grand Ball, to which were invited all the neighbouring Nobility and Gentry … The Marquis of Abercorn, Lord John Russell, Lord and Lady Wriothesley Russell, and the Duchess herself joined in the mazy round. Each day from 28–30 dined at the great table, commencing on Christmas-Eve.'

Following the ball, Georgina joined Charles Mathews, Edward, Charles and Frank among others in the cast of *Simpson & Co.* and *Scan. Mag* at the Woburn Abbey theatre, but the limelight seems to have been stolen by little Rachel, then eight, who appeared on two nights in the intervals between shows; for the first, 'by the particular Desire of several of the Nobility of the First distinction', she sang the 'Favourite Song of "Buy a Broom", dressed in Character', and the next night, 'Between the two pieces, Lady Rachel Russell will sing the much admired songs of *The Railroad* and *The Lake of Killarney*.'[509]

Beyond the busy festive season, 1834 marked the start of a very exciting period for both duke and duchess. With the three boys at sea, Charles living in Woburn and entering Parliament for Bedford in the 1832 election, Cosmo and Alexander finishing school and headed for careers in the army, and Louisa married, life at Woburn had become a lot simpler, and this enabled their parents to follow up on their growing interests in botany and horticulture. As a result, the years 1834–9 were a period of intense activity, not least in the pleasure grounds and gardens at Woburn, where the duke sought to build on all the things he, Sinclair and Forbes had achieved as detailed in *Hortus Woburnensis*, to expand and consolidate Woburn's growing reputation as a serious centre for scientific botany and horticulture, and to create further unique and interesting exotic collections. With Atkinson's new kitchen gardens up and running, we see the duke and Forbes increasingly focused on four distinct areas of interest: continuation of the existing collections and the addition of at least eight new ones, the exploration of the native botany of Badenoch and the Cairngorms, an active engagement with William Hooker's growing network of overseas plant collectors, and, in the final years of the duke's life, his significant role in lobbying for the obsolete royal gardens at Kew to be saved and adopted by the government as a national garden, and Hooker's appointment as its first director. In turn, these activities went hand in hand with the duchess's growing interest in creating a 'British Flower Garden', her ambitions growing to match those of the duke, as she explored plant species that interested her and further possibilities for ornamental displays of both native plants and flowers across a spectrum of colours. Forbes alerts us to this new interest when writing to Hooker in May: 'We have been some time employed in forming a British Flower Garden which the Duchess is very anxious to have a full collection of British plants in, should you meet with any of the *Pyrolas* or other little showy plants when on your Botanical excursions, I know Her Grace would be much pleased by sending a few for her Gardens.'[510]

As is clear from the plan of the pleasure grounds in *Hortus Woburnensis*, in early 1834 Georgina's flower gardens were limited to the Sculpture Gallery parterres, her small formal layout around a fountain in her private garden, and the ribbon parterre on Repton's narrow terrace in front of the library windows. Now, in

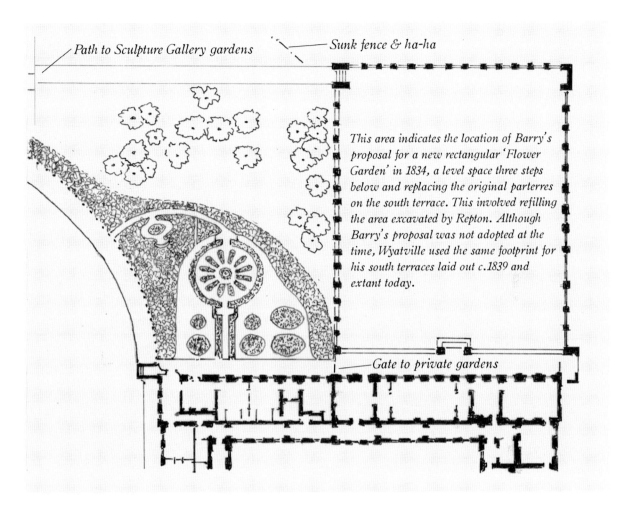

Path to Sculpture Gallery gardens

Sunk fence & ha-ha

This area indicates the location of Barry's proposal for a new rectangular 'Flower Garden' in 1834, a level space three steps below and replacing the original parterres on the south terrace. This involved refilling the area excavated by Repton. Although Barry's proposal was not adopted at the time, Wyatville used the same footprint for his south terraces laid out c.1839 and extant today.

Gate to private gardens

Charles Barry's plan for the south gardens, 1834. Added the year after the *Hortus Woburnensis* plan was drawn, Georgina's flower gardens are laid out in front of the private apartments and follow the curve of the walkway on the left. Barry's proposal for a new 'Flower Garden' in front of the libraries is shown on the right.

pursuit of more space for the 'British Flower Garden', the duke commissioned the architect Charles Barry to come up with plans for a new garden stretching south from the existing library terrace, reporting that 'Mr Barry is here and stakes out excellent ideas.' By early February Barry had submitted a comprehensive design not just for a new flower garden, but also one which integrated it with Georgina's original parterres in front of the Sculpture Gallery.[511]

The new rectangular flower garden stretched the width of the terrace and ran out to the south beyond Georgina's garden until it lined up with the facade of the Sculpture Gallery to the east. A new central opening in the terrace wall gave access to a short set of steps which led down to the garden a few feet below. A perimeter path led round the elaborately designed display beds and ribbon parterres, complete with a fountain, to the south end where it overlooked the park beyond, and gateways on the south-west and south-east corners provided access to the park on one side and to a wide straight path leading to the Sculpture Galley on the other. It was proposed that Georgina's garden should be enlarged to include the whole area bounded by the new garden and the straight path and be hidden from both by dense plantings, and that the old covered walkway should be made private. Thus, access for visitors and family went directly from the library door, round the new garden and directly to the Sculpture Gallery and pleasure grounds beyond, leaving the gardens in front of the apartments entirely private.

It was a deceptively simple plan, since constructing it would involve filling in much of Repton's original excavation, raising and levelling the ground inside new retaining walls on the west and south sides. The sheer expense of this garden may well have sealed its fate at this point, but an almost identical, if less elaborate, plan by Wyatville was installed four years later in the same footprint and remains essentially unchanged today. In the end, when Georgina did create her 'British Flower Garden', it was a completely new design, and was overlooked not by the library at the Abbey but by the drawing room at Campden Hill.

Another project they returned to that spring was the revitalization and expansion of the Evergreens, which had been largely untouched since 1826. The duke and duchess were drawn back to the network of paths that wound across the slopes through the dense trees, just wide enough for the pony carts, and reflected the kind of environment they enjoyed so much at Endsleigh and in Scotland. At Woburn, new trees, new places of interest and new destinations were all added over the next four years.[512] For the first of these features, the duke told Crocker, 'The site marked out in Evergreens for the ruined building from Ridgemont will do perfectly well … The stones should be placed exactly as they now are, without any attempt to

Woburn Abbey, south wing, east end, 1949. This is the only image of the private apartments in the Abbey's south wing that has come to light, taken in 1949 just prior to their demolition. Although it is not clear when the window shutters were added, the photograph still captures something of the more intimate scale of this part of the building, far more like a family home perhaps than the rest of the Abbey. In addition, the demolished covered walkway can also be seen on the right, covered in climbing plants.

clean or repair them, and if they can be fixed without cement, so much the better. Where cement is necessary, take care that the mortar is the same colour as the stone.' He insisted the finish should not be 'too neat and regular'. Following the installation of some new seats at the ruin, another destination was added the next year when the duke ordered work to start on the 'shelter carriage shed in Evergreens so that it may be completed and ready for thatching with straw and heather'. Both the colonnade from Ridgemont and the shelter shed were caught by Henry William Burgess, who produced his *Drawings of the Evergreens at Woburn Abbey* in 1837 and an album of 'Views in the Evergreens' in 1838 (Colour Plate 37).[513]

By March, the duke's and Forbes's attention had turned to the collections, specifically the Cactaceae, and in a sign of what is to come, the duke tells Hooker, 'I have purchased the whole of the <u>Cacteae</u> from Mr Hitchen's collection of Norwich, they form an interesting addition to mine.' Over the next year the collection grew rapidly, in part due to a successful eight-week European tour undertaken by Forbes to 'obtain cacti from botanic gardens, nurserymen and private collectors', and partly from donations, of which one in particular, from Hooker, made a deep impression on the duke: 'It is impossible for me to express how much gratitude I feel by your kindness in offering me a plant of your new Cactus, C. Napoleonis which you have described a "a most splendid plant". The value of it to me will be greatly enhanced by the consideration that it is a mark of your regard.'

Although the collection was still housed in a small greenhouse next to the Heath House, by the end of the following year the duke was sufficiently pleased with it to want to show it to Hooker: 'my collection of *Cactera* is now approaching to some value for its extent and variety, and I shall have great satisfaction in showing it to you when I have next the pleasure of seeing you at Woburn.'[514]

In April, to everyone's delight, another family milestone was reached when Lord Charles, now twenty-seven, married Isabella Clarissa Davies. The couple settled down at Bedford Lodge in Woburn, and while attending Parliament Charles also became central to life at Woburn; indeed his growing involvement with the running of the estate became a source of some irritation to Tavistock and his brothers. Isabella, however, became a firm favourite of the family, particularly because of her artistic skills. Dr Thomson recorded a few years later: 'I have been drawing a little in sepia under the superintendence of Lady Charles and the Duchess. Lady Charles draws trees both in pencil and sepia in the very best style. The Duchess knows a good deal about the art but does not execute much.'[515]

The family news continued to improve when the duke travelled to Endsleigh to meet Lord William, Bessy, her mother and the children, who had just arrived after sailing from Lisbon to Plymouth. The visit started well, as he told Lady Holland, 'William had a rough and very tortuous passage but I heard no "perils" except in Mrs Rawdon's imagination,' and the party was completed when Georgina and

Rachel arrived at the end of April. They were delighted to see each other. William noted in his diary, 'The Duchess arrived – what spirits, what a woman!' There were, however, underlying tensions and Georgina told Bessy of the duke's annoyance over some intercepted letters the latter had written while in Lisbon with William, which seemed to interfere with confidential diplomatic business. Bessy defended herself with typical vigour, explaining to Lord Holland: 'The Duke of Bedford has written me enigmatical innuendoes & the Duchess informed me at Endsleigh that he had been *very much annoyed* … that a political correspondence of mine was in the hands of *Ministers* … Notwithstanding the absurdity of the story … I am compelled to take notice of it.'[516] The duke evidently feared that these letters might be politically indiscreet, but the incident soon blew over.

Back at Woburn in late May, the family were joined by the French diplomat Charles-Maurice de Tallyrand-Périgord and his companion, Princess Dorothée, Duchess de Dino. The latter has left a particularly clear-eyed account of life at Woburn, and in many ways it sums up exactly the particular, and not always comfortable, role that the Abbey – as the enduring, formal and impersonal repository of the Dukedom of Bedford – played in the individual lives of the families who also lived there:

This house is certainly one of the finest, the most magnificent, and the greatest in England … There are Lord and Lady Grey … Mr. Ellice, Lord Ossulton, the duke and duchess, three of their sons, one of their daughters, Monsieur de Tallyrand and I … All these people are clever, well educated and well mannered, but, as I have observed before, English reserve is pushed further at Woburn than anywhere else, and this in spite of the almost audacious freedom of speech affected by the Duchess of Bedford, who is in striking contrast to the silence and shyness of the duke and the rest of the family. Moreover, in the splendour and magnificence, and the size of the house, there is something which makes the company cold and stiff.

It would seem as though the Abbey by its very nature imposed this atmosphere, no matter who occupied it, and this was certainly not people's experience of the family at the other houses – Campden Hill, Endsleigh or in Scotland – and helps explain why these other homes were so important to Georgina, and probably the duke, both of whom, for different reasons, enjoyed the privacy and freedom they provided.

De Dino goes on:

A party at Woburn in particular is as carefully arranged as a London dinner-party. Twenty or thirty persons who know each other, but not familiarly, are invited to be together for two or three days. The hosts go to their house for the special purpose of receiving their guests, and return to town after their departure. They have themselves the air of being on a visit. However, when all is said and done, there is so much to see and admire; the Duke of Bedford is so charming, such a perfect embodiment of the *grand seigneur*, the Duchess is so attentive, that it is impossible not to carry away with one the most pleasing impressions.[517]

De Dino's observation that the family has 'the air of being on a visit' at Woburn sums up the ephemeral nature of each generation's occupation of this and other such houses in the context of the weight of history each one carries.

Yet, if history hung heavy at Woburn, in London the houses continued to evolve. In 1834 'Gas lights, fittings, pipes and all the Apparatus for fitting the Basement at Belgrave Sq' were installed, and there were major developments in the gardens at Campden Hill. Perhaps because the flower garden designs had not been adopted at Woburn, Georgina spent this summer working with her gardener James Sanders to develop a new flower garden beside the house, where 'Rustic' stonework was installed. For the main garden to the south of the house, the duke had secured supplies the year before of 'some decayed vegetable mould formed by dead leaves' from Holland House, since, as the duke told Holland, the duchess has to 'sow in *terra pauperis*', and leaf compost is 'admirable for the

Campden Hill gardens plan, c.1838. The house and grounds at Campden Hill, dominated by the large orchard stretching south below the house, and Georgina's new 'British Flower Garden' laid out in front of the new reception room added to the west front. Decorative shrubberies featured on the lawns overlooked by the veranda and small summer houses were accessed by the path round the orchard.

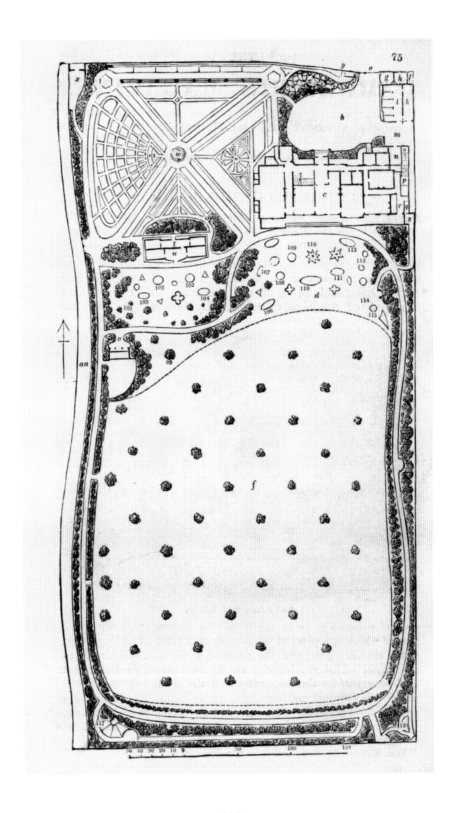

Campden Hill flower garden, c.1838. A view from the flower garden at Campden Hill, looking across the 'wall of vases' and 'baskets' to the trelliswork and the west front of the house.

growth of woody plants', which are 'the subject of the Duchess's hobby-horse at Campden Hill'.

The gardens took some four years to develop fully, mostly after John Caie, under gardener from Woburn, replaced James Sanders in 1835. By 1838 the layouts and plantings were complete and were recorded in some detail in an illustrated article by Caie in the *Gardener's Magazine* that September.[518] In this, Caie specifies three main garden areas: the decorative rockwork and arbour around the entrance court north of the house, the formal flower garden laid out to its west, and the lawn and orchard that ran south from the veranda of the house and down the slope to the southern garden wall. Mixed in between these areas were shrub beds, arbours, a three-part greenhouse, potting sheds, workshops, and a gravel pathway running round the perimeter of the orchard and lined by trees and shrubs. While the decorative mixed plantings of the flower garden, complete with a central fountain and elaborate iron trelliswork to support climbers, were the main feature of the view from the drawing room, the wide spaces of the carefully planted orchard hosted the shows and dances of the annual 'Breakfast' gatherings.

In February 1834 Edwin Landseer, who seems to have had some part in designing the rockwork beside the entrance court, procured 'Marble Blocks for Rock Work at Campden Hill', and in March a number of decorative iron-rod frames, including a 'Trainer 18 ft high with Umbrella top on alcove over the Fountain', and trellises for climbing plants were installed in the centre of the flower garden. These and a variety of other items, including the iron garden furniture, were then all painted in 'Olive Green'.[519]

By the summer, with the garden construction work largely complete, and after a trip to Astley's Amphitheatre to celebrate Rachel's birthday with thirty of her friends, further work got underway to prepare the house for one of Georgina's annual balls. The orchard was rolled and fresh gravel added to the paths, while carpenters were busy in the house creating a 'new staircase & platform to form way to Dining Room, moving furniture from the Drawing Room', 'preparing the Rooms for dancing & refreshments' and, afterwards, 'repairing fencing and the lights' and returning everything to normal. A succession of three balls took place on 9, 16 and 17 July, before the family set out for The Doune in late July. The duke arrived first, having visited Blair Adam, and was joined by the duchess, Georgiana, Rachel, Edward, Alexander and Landseer, the children travelling up by steam packet from Blackwall to Leith. Writing a day or two later, the duke tells Lady Holland: 'the Dss is now with me ... We Highlanders are all well here, including the Lowlanders and the Ellices ... the Dss is up in her Glen, or she would add her love ... I am unusually well and the Highland air has much improved both my health and spirits.'[520]

A few days later, the family were joined by the Abercorns and their new baby, Harriet, and if the previous summer had been memorable for expeditions and activities with friends, this summer was to prove memorable for the family themselves. It was now some four years since they has taken the leases on The Doune from the Grants and Ruigh Aiteachan from Mackintosh, and it is in the course of this summer that we see the duke and duchess adapting both sites to their needs. At The Doune, the duke now had at least seven full-time workers in the gardens and on the farm, and late that summer the wide meadows in front of the house were busy with people making hay. In the house, Georgina began an extensive freshening up, repainting the family rooms and whitewashing service rooms.[521]

By 1 August Georgina was 'up in her glen' where she was equally busy addressing the various issues that seem to have arisen the busy year before. While initially a tailor was set to 'repairing the Tents at Glenfeshie', action was also taken this year on the indoor accommodation at Ruigh Aiteachan. Perhaps due to the leaking roof reported by Tankerville, the lack of a proper kitchen or the general lack of space, this year saw 'Expenses for building a New House in Glenfeshie' (Colour Plate 38). Although the records refer to both a 'new House' and a 'new Cottage', the latter perhaps the term used by the Bedfords, this seems to have been the same building, stone built, with a fireplace, chimney, solid wooden roof and two or more rooms. Five masons and eight carpenters worked on the building, which included two large stones specially brought in for the fireplace, 'fitted out' rooms and beds, a new dining table, a new oven delivered from Inverness, and 'small trees' planted to form a 'flower fence' round the garden outside. But then, an entry in the accounts for 18 October records something different: 'Expense of a new Black House in Glenfeshie'.[522]

'Black House' is a term which seems to have come into widespread usage at this time, and was increasingly used to differentiate between the traditional Highland houses – the 'but and ben', shieling structures and bothies built of turf, thatched and often without a chimney – and the new structures: the wooden 'Huts', 'Houses' and 'Cottages', with fireplaces and chimneys, built to accommodate the needs of the sporting estates. Whether this 'Black House' was actually a 'new' building or the refurbishment of an existing structure is not clear, but another invoice from 1836, which tells us '5 men' worked on 'Repairs on Black House, Glenfeshie', suggests it may have been the latter.[523] This is also suggested by the fact that it was markedly different from the new 'House', being constructed of rough timber, turf and thatch

Edwin Landseer, *Hut in Glen Feshie*, c.1836. An interesting image of a ruinous hut, which could well show the 'Black House' that was repaired for Landseer to use for painting expeditions. This idea is perhaps supported by the landscape in the background, which would seem to show a 'narrow gorge' such as that which contained 'Landseer's Falls'.

and considerably less expensive to build. Indeed, while clearly built 'in Glenfeshie', it may not actually have been located with the others at Ruigh Aiteachan.

One of Landseer's paintings of this period, titled simply *Hut in Glen Feshie*, shows a rundown hut of exactly this 'black house' type, possibly the one that was rebuilt at this time, and it is of some interest to us because one account says that Landseer used a hut of his own for painting trips in upper Glen Feshie some distance from the duchess's huts. Information about Landseer's hut has come down to us in a descriptive guide to scenic drives into the countryside around Kingussie written in 1905. In a drive titled 'Excursion No. III: Kingussie to Manse of Insh and Glenfeshie', the author describes following the road from the Manse of Insh and Balnespick into Glen Feshie, where, after passing Druimcaillach, the farmstead of Achlean appears on the opposite bank of the Feshie: 'Achlean is the residence of the district fox-hunter ... the present tenant's father, "Callum Ruadh", was a friend of Landseer's, and he and his dogs frequently appeared in the artist's pictures.' Then, a little further on, just beyond Carnachuin and across the river from Glenfeshie Lodge, 'Macpherson-Grant's land is intersected on the south side by an extensive strip belonging to Mackintosh … On "The Island", on the south side of the Feshie, opposite the lodge, is the site of "the huts" … [These] were a series of semi-detached wooden shanties of a very primitive kind, but the Duchess and her party had an extraordinary fondness for living therein, and, as a recent writer says, "such steer and fun as used to be carried on are unknown now-a-days."' Further on, 'The glen is particularly picturesque between "The Huts" and Allt Coire Bhlair. The finest gorge in the glen is that of Allt Coire Bhlair on the right bank of the Feshie opposite Sron na Ban-righ (2406 ft). It is an exceedingly narrow gorge,

A sketch by Landseer illustrating a letter, showing dancers at The Doune, 1836. This tiny sketch vividly conveys something of the energy and excitement of the reels and fiddle music.

The Duke and Duchess of Bedford at The Doune, c.1830–35. Another of Landseer's rapidly executed sketches which catches a moment of great tenderness between the duke and duchess in Scotland.

rife with vegetation, and containing a linn, Landseer's Falls, over 150 feet in height. On the left bank of the burn, where it is crossed by the path, the *larach* [site, ruins] of a hut may be seen where Landseer occasionally painted.'[524]

Perhaps waiting for the 'hut' to be habitable, Landseer was also busy this year at The Doune painting the family, particularly Louisa and her first child. Images firmly dated to this year are an oil painting, *The Marchioness of Abercorn and her Eldest Child*, two pen and ink drawings of *The Duchess of Bedford and Lady Harriet Hamilton*, and, perhaps inspired by Louisa nursing baby Harriet, *A Highland Breakfast*, which Ormond considers 'one of Landseer's best'. Possibly also produced this year were a rapidly executed and very touching pen and ink wash drawing of Georgina standing behind the duke's chair as he reads a newspaper, her hand protectively on his shoulder, and some of the steady stream of images of Georgina, often drawn from slightly behind with the subject looking away, featuring the line of her neck and shoulders, which clearly both fascinated and attracted Landseer.

While Georgina was busy in the glen that summer, the duke was preoccupied with his own projects. In the first place, the accounts tell us that in September 1834 the duke had workmen busy 'Building a cairn on the Rock of Kinapole', to which an inscribed tablet with painted letters was added a few years later. The explanation for this cairn is recorded by Fraser-Mackintosh in his *Antiquarian Notes*: 'The Duchess [had] secretly erected a monument, with suitable inscription, in honour of her husband, near their favourite walk on Ord Hill. To this, all unconscious, the duke was led, and to the surprise of the Duchess said very little in appreciation of the compliment. But the Duke, though he said little, thought much, and the following season he led his wife to a monument in her honour, with a suitable inscription.'[525] This activity gives a clear indication of just how important this shared adventure in Scotland had become for the Bedfords, although sadly only the 'Duchess's Cairn' on Kinapole survives today.

In the second, the duke was eager to start exploring the geology and flora of the mountains around him. Not only had he arranged for Forbes to travel up from Woburn, he was also encouraged by 'my neighbour', Sir David Brewster, who was now living with his wife at Belleville, having taken over running the estate from his sister-on-law. Brewster was also, among other things, a keen botanist and interested in aspects of traditional Highland life, particularly beliefs in magic and second sight. Although a renowned scientist, born in Jedburgh and educated in Edinburgh, as a great believer in 'improvement' he became widely and deeply unpopular for his treatment of Belleville's Highland tenants.

Noticeably, this year's stay at The Doune was such a success because everyone was in good health at the same time. As the duke had told Lady Holland in August, he was feeling 'unusually well' due to the Highland air, and in September he tells her that he is a strong 'advocate of our Highland climate, for the clouds are never charged with that electric fluid which produces what we call thunder and lightning, during the many years that I have known the Highlands, I never remember but one thunder storm.' Inevitably, perhaps, the one cloud on the horizon at this time was the behaviour of Bessy, who with 'her children and the man she calls their tutor' had been staying at Woburn Abbey in the Bedfords' absence. As he tells Lady Holland, 'I know [this] only from correspondence – she has never written a line on any subject to the Dss or myself, nor could I <u>extract</u> one from her during William's illness just to tell me how he was going on … Is she not an extraordinary woman!' The rest of the letter is more cheerful, as he recounts being 'up the Glen for a couple of days', and this trip into the mountains may reflect the fact that Woburn head gardener John Forbes had joined them at The Doune, and that this was the duke's first period of serious botanizing as he and Forbes looked for certain species of plants to collect for both Woburn and Hooker's botanic gardens in Glasgow.

Given the general good health, the bright new rooms at The Doune, the new, improved hut in the Glen, the presence of their granddaughter and Landseer's genial company, this may have been one of the outstanding visits to The Doune for the family. Not highly sociable like the year before, it was very much a family gathering, complete with Lord Edward on a rare extended shore leave.[526] While the family travelled up and down from the glen, apart from his one visit, the duke spent most of his time at The Doune, where he enjoyed quiet visits from Edward Ellice, who had become a particularly close family friend, the two very much at ease in each other's company whether in conversation in his study or strolling in the gardens. In late September, while Forbes returned to Woburn, visiting the Glasgow Botanic Garden to drop off some of the plants they had collected on his way south, the duke, Landseer and Lord Alexander spent a week or so visiting the Duchess of Sutherland at her 'holiday home', Dunrobin Castle.

In October, on their way back to The Doune, the party visited the Duke and Duchess of Gordon at Gordon Castle, and in what seems to have been a first for the duke, they joined the Gordons on a visit to their 'romantic cottage at Glenfiddich'. There is no other record before this of the duke visiting the Glenfiddich lodge, something he would have heard all about and was no doubt curious to see. Following this visit, in late November, as the days began to draw in and the weather worsened, the duke travelled back to Woburn via Balbirnie. This year, even if they had been planning to visit Ireland, the trip would have been cancelled due to a lethal outbreak of cholera that was bad enough at Barons Court to require the furniture and fittings from some of the estate houses to be taken out and burned. Leaving Balbirnie the duke tells Lord Holland: 'Your letter came as I was getting into my carriage to leave the snow-clad Hills of the Highlands … we had some bad weather, or what the Dss would call "southern weather."'[527]

Arriving back at Woburn, the duke's attention immediately turned back to the somewhat neglected Sculpture Gallery, since one of the long awaited 'fragments of the Ephesian Sarcophagus' had finally arrived, along with a letter from Thomas Burgon, 'Turkey merchant': 'I rejoice very much to hear that the Ephesian Relievei are in such good hands and shall feel real pleasure in assisting to get the remaining fragments to England.' Burgon added that he would go ahead with shipment of these as soon as he got authority, indicating perhaps that the duke had been unwilling to engage with Arundell until he knew the proper authority was in place. After that, Burgon assured him, 'all that would be necessary, would be that I should be authorized by Mr Arundell to remove the marbles … from his House in Smyrna, and that you should add any hints or instructions … as to packing which you should think necessary.'

It was also at this time that Crocker sent the duke an estimate for 'sundry alterations' to the Sculpture Gallery, specifically, 'erecting a Chamber for the Mosaic pavement on the north side of the centre of the Gallery, and a Vestibule and Portico'. While the duke was by now very involved in the gardens and botany, it seems that items of antiquity that had been bought over the years were continuing to arrive, and that he was still keen on his wider collections. The year ended on something of a high when in due course the duchess and Georgiana, who may have stayed on at Balbirnie, arrived back safely from Scotland, and 'as the newspapers say "in good health and spirits"'.[528]

The start of 1835 was unusually quiet at Woburn, the family being preoccupied with other ongoing projects, including completing the refurbishment of Georgina's gardens at Campden Hill. Throughout February work went on in the gardens, laying new gravel paths, finishing the new vegetable house and shed, painting the interior of the main greenhouse and installing garden lights. Inside the house, the study and sitting room were repainted. The duke also had a new project at Woburn, telling Crocker in March of the 'new small cottage I intend building in the Park next summer'. This cottage, completed by the following summer, was Purrett's Hill Lodge, built in the style of the Elizabethan era, and was another historically accurate reconstruction along the lines of Repton's Aspley Lodge at Woburn Sands. It occupied an empty corner of the park just south of the Froxfield Gate overlooking the start of what had been the 4th Duke's 'Platoons' walk, and also provided an eye-catching focal point for the main views from the new kitchen garden and its garden room.[529]

At this time we also see Georgina establish a new pattern of visiting as she leaves London or Woburn to stay with either the Abercorns and the grandchildren at Bentley Priory, where a second daughter had been born, or with Wriothesley and Eliza and their growing family at Chenies, where they were busy with the small school they had founded in the rectory kitchen. In early April the duke and duchess, the Tavistocks, the Abercorns and Georgiana all travelled to St George's in Hanover Square to attend the wedding of Lord John (now forty-three) and Adelaide Lister at a ceremony performed by Wriothesley. Adelaide was the widow of Lord Ribblesdale, and while this was widely welcomed in the family, Lord William, now posted to Stuttgart, noted in his diary, 'John announces his marriage with a widow and four children – bold man, I hope he may be happy.'[530]

Soon after the ceremony, however, the mood darkened when in mid-April the duke suffered another paralytic stroke, serious enough to cause the left side of his face to droop. As soon as it was possible, the family set out for a month's stay at Endsleigh where, once again, it was hoped he could rest and recuperate. Progress was slow, and while he had recovered sufficiently to return to Woburn by July, the effects of the stroke were long lasting, as Lady Holland reported to Lord William: 'Your father is recovering his general health, his calm, sweet temper enables him to bear with composure, if not fortitude, the great annoyance of his eye which is drawn down upon his cheek so that he has not the power of closing it night or day and the tears excoriate his cheek, it is most distressing to see … however he continues to amuse himself and beguile the long hours.'[531]

Indeed, the duke had plenty with which to amuse himself, and while William George Adam had once again been forced to warn him about expenditure, he was eagerly trying to persuade Hooker to pay a visit to Woburn to see the new developments he and Forbes had completed. Writing in early June, 'I recover but slowly from my indisposition … must give up all thoughts of visiting Scotland this year,' but hopes to see Hooker at the Abbey in July. The enforced inactivity of the early summer saw the duke reviewing his collections, and just as he had found the Sculpture Gallery to be in a neglected state the year before, now he worried about the condition of some of the art collection. The result was that in July William Thane was paid for cleaning and repairing ten of the portraits, including Hoppner's portrait of his brother Francis and one of the portraits of his father as Marquis of Tavistock by Reynolds.

While the duke was preoccupied at Woburn, Georgina spent several weeks in June at Campden Hill working with Caie on the flower gardens. In addition, as we saw the year before, when a new ramp had to be built to access the gardens, the layout and size of the existing reception rooms, particularly the 'Sitting Room', proved inadequate for the large 'Breakfast' gatherings. Thus, in August Wyatville submitted plans for the new, larger drawing room at Campden Hill, running the width of the east side of the house, and complete with steps and terrace to provide easy access to and from the gardens.[532]

With the duke and duchess preoccupied at Woburn and Campden Hill respectively, perhaps the most socially active member of the family that summer was Georgiana. Now that Eliza, Wriothesley, Charles and Louisa were all married, the issue of when Georgiana might find a husband must have been very much in the air. Noted as a withdrawn and quiet girl, described by Lord William as 'short and awkward' when compared to the 'thin and graceful' Louisa, and declared 'dull and dowdy' by Le Marchant, Georgiana passed largely unnoticed. Still recovering from the lingering effects of her bout of typhoid fever, as her deafness increased, she became acutely embarrassed by the need to use an ear trumpet, which she tried to hide, but now, at twenty-five, she was under increasing pressure to meet someone. This summer, her mother encouraged her out again, and we see

Georgiana socializing, going to the theatre, visiting Almack's and attending the Epsom Races. At Almack's, while Lord and Lady Charles and Cosmo all visited once, Georgiana was there four times between May and July.[533]

For the duke, the highlight of the summer came on 8 August when he was able to host a visit by Hooker and Dawson Turner, giving him a chance at last to show them round his collections. This was a highly significant moment for the duke, and no doubt much was discussed and comments made and ideas suggested, but above all, the visit of two of the country's leading botanists gave real credibility to what the duke, Sinclair and Forbes had created. Unfortunately, the long-awaited visit did not quite work out as he would have liked since his continuing poor health made it impossible for him to accompany them on their tour of the gardens, and he was particularly disappointed when Hooker left earlier than expected, having to travel up to Newcastle later that day to deliver a lecture the next morning. Nevertheless, it had been an important day for the duke, and he wrote as much to Hooker: 'It has given me the great pleasure to make your acquaintance and I have only to regret the state of my health which compels me to abstract myself so much from society, and which has during your recent visit prevented me from enjoying and profiting by your conversation as much as I would have wished to do.'

Fortunately, by the end of the month, the duke's health improved enough for him to set out for Scotland with the duchess. Taking into account the need for him to take the journey in small stages, they planned what the duke described to Landseer as a 'Northern Tour', whereby they would travel in easy stages, visiting places of botanical and historic interest on their way. On 16 August, just before leaving, the duke wrote to Landseer, 'I thank you for your kind offer of coming here to finish the sketch of the Corsican Deer, but it would now be useless as we start from here early on Thursday morning on our Northern Tour. We shall be at Chatsworth on Sunday and Monday next, and then by what is called the Western Road to Glasgow.'[534]

There is no doubt that Landseer had by now become a central component in the Bedfords' seasonal occupation of The Doune and Glen Feshie. For Georgina he was a key contributor to the entertainments and activities at The Doune, but it was in Glen Feshie that his presence was really felt. Here he fitted seamlessly into the small community, making friends, as we have seen, with local people up and down the glen; fully embracing the world she had created, he returned faithfully year after year. Whatever the exact nature of their relationship, a central part of it was her fascination with his art; she liked to be around the artist, to see his reaction to scenery, listen to his comments, understand what he was viewing, and watch as it came to life in his quick sketches and finished paintings. For the first time, perhaps, here was someone who valued her experiences as a child growing up in these landscapes and who had the skills to capture in an image those emotional qualities and that Romantic sensibility for the world around them that had so far only been expressed in the words of people like James Beattie and her mother.

For Georgina's new, imperfect and widely misunderstood community at Ruigh Aiteachan, more than all the friends, politicians, philosophers, writers, poets and sportsmen who also visited, it was Landseer who, through his art, was able to provide that community with some sense of what the shielings and the landscape around them had meant emotionally to those who had spent their summers there, and just what had been lost when the practice of transhumance ended. It was the development during the 1830s of Landseer's small sketches in oil of the Glen Feshie landscapes, shown in ever changing light and weather conditions, which helped to reveal what the glen meant to Georgina and to capture a sense of the soul of the place, in a way that was perhaps never matched until Nan Shepherd distilled something similar a hundred years later in the prose of her celebration of the Cairngorm range, *The Living Mountain* (Colour Plate 39).[535]

The duke similarly enjoyed Landseer's company as an artist and as a shooting companion, but above all because in a social world predisposed to be critical and suspicious of both Georgina and her family, Landseer, like the duke, was one of the few people who embraced her unconditionally, who tolerated her eccentricities and valued what she had created at Endsleigh and in Scotland. While the duke does not seem to have shared long conversations in the quiet of his study with Landseer, as he did with Edward Ellice, he enjoyed his company when out shooting. Unlike his early ruminations on the 'glory' of stag hunting, the duke never commented on shooting, partly perhaps because his health meant that he had as many, if not more, 'bad' or 'very bad' shooting days than good ones, and so, rather than being an end in itself, he enjoyed a day out for the company and Landseer's shared interest in wildlife and birds.

On the 'Northern Tour', of the places they visited before joining the Western Road to Glasgow – including Chatsworth, Hardwick, Bolton Abbey and Naworth Castle in Cumbria – Chatsworth and Glasgow seem to have fired up the duke's growing passion for collecting plants. At Chatsworth, where the Duke of Devonshire had commissioned enormous new glasshouses to house his growing collections, the duke was delighted to be able to study the designs, and also to meet up with Joseph Paxton, Chatsworth's resident gardener and ground-breaking architect of glass plant houses. In 1833 the duke had begun to plan seriously for his next ventures at Woburn, including a new arboretum and pinetum in the pleasure grounds, and during this visit he discussed these ideas at length with Paxton. Work on them does not seem to have started until 1836, following the duke's visit to Chatsworth and his subsequent meeting with 'Mr Murray' at Glasgow, where he was 'amply compensated for dirt and filth and smoke and steam engines of Glasgow, by its truly rich and curious collection of plants in the botanic garden'. The duke summed up just how enjoyable this leisurely journey had been in a letter to Lady Holland: 'We arrived here safe and <u>tolerably</u> sound after 18 days leisurely travelling from Woburn in the most delightful weather, and thru' the most interesting and beautiful country. We saw all the Duchess of Devonshire's splendid domains at Chatsworth, Hardwicke [*sic*] and Bolton Abbey, and Lord Carlisle's old baronial castle at Naworth with all its feudal reminiscences still fresh upon it, and recalling the border forays of "t'olden time"' – just the kind of history he had always been interested in.

Once at The Doune, the duke settled into his study, but was missing the company of Edward Ellice, as he told Lady Holland: 'We miss our neighbour The Bear, or the "old gentleman" as the Highlanders call him, the young cub and his *sposa* do not compensate for his absence.' He did, however, have a new source of amusement, having been provided with a pedometer to encourage him to go on walks and record how much exercise he was taking for Georgina and the doctors. Soon enough, though, they were joined by Georgiana, Rachel, Cosmo, Alexander and Landseer, and the men set about enjoying a season's shooting of 'muirfowl' organized by Georgina: 'The Dss is the *grande maitress de la chasse* here, and I do not interfere.'[536] Interestingly enough, just as the duke's interest in botany and plant collecting was growing, he tells us later that 1835 was to be the last year he held a gun in his hand, as his health forced him to give up shooting across the land and to stop and study it instead.

In an echo of two years before, when the ladies found the 'gentlemen *horrid bores*' who 'do nothing but boast of their shooting, throwing large stones, and having savage dogs', Georgina and the girls soon headed off for the peace and quiet of Glen Feshie, where Landseer joined them, exchanging gun for brush. With the new 'Black House' completed, this may have been the first year Landseer was able to travel on to Ruigh nan Leum and spend time exploring the splendours of Allt Choire Bhair and the waterfalls of the gorge. In this context, 1835 is the suggested date for two lovely pen and ink wash drawings of Georgina on her pony, dressed in her customary Highland plaids, shawls and bonnet. In one image she is alone on her pony led by a ghillie, while the other shows three figures: Georgina on her pony following a figure who could well be Landseer, and in front a figure whose posture indicates it is another female riding side-saddle and led by a ghillie. While this picture is really a study of Georgina – the only part of the image completed to any degree – the small size of the party and the date both suggest that these pictures could have been one of the occasions when Georgina and Georgiana accompanied Landseer to his new hut.

Landseer's close relationship with the whole family is further illustrated by two other images from this summer, which, although very different in style and completion, are both closely observed and sympathetic portraits of Georgiana and Rachel. The former, a pen and ink wash drawing, is a carefully finished profile portrait and represents one of the few images we have of Georgiana; dressed in a low ball gown, her neck and shoulders bare, she looks very much like her mother. The portrait of Rachel is very different, being a completed oil on board study of the nine-year-old in a smart dress, her hair neatly arranged, sitting with a blanket over her knees, engrossed in a book – a fairly normal picture until one notices the background. In contrast to Rachel's neat appearance, we see behind her the wooden post and mud-plastered wall of one of the huts, in which Rachel is sitting propped up in her 'chest' bed and clearly totally at home. It is a picture that would have reminded her mother of her own childhood at Jane's 'but and ben' house in Kinrara, and that not only sums up what a confident and precocious child Rachel was, but also just how unusual were the circumstances of Georgina's small community.[537]

By the end of September, having given up shooting, the duke was now embarked on his career as a plant collector in Scotland, spurred on perhaps by Georgina's interest in the Pyrolas, evergreens that were native to Scotland, and as a patron of Hooker's plant collectors abroad. In a letter to Hooker, the duke asks whether he intends to send out 'a plant collector to succeed the late Mr Drummond' and, if so, 'I shall be happy to be a subscriber to such a mission.' This is the first mention of his interest in helping to facilitate overseas plant collecting, and the duke also says, '[if] I can be of any use in collecting our Highland production here, for your Botanic Garden, I beg you will freely command my services – I could convey them in a very short time to Glasgow.' The Doune and mountains around it had become a focus of the duke's botanical interests, and while he was hoping to persuade Hooker to spend a summer botanizing there with him, he was also working with his gardener and a 'laddie', busily engaged in collecting plants off the hills. He tells Hooker, 'My gardener here has collected a large quantity of plants of the *Lutus chamorous*, and the *Azalea procumbens* on Cairngorum … He is no botanist, but Mr Forbes when he was here last year, pointed [them] out to him.' In addition to the gardener, an invoice for 8 November records '2 days of a pony at Glenfeshie & Glenmore … 2 Boys, 2 days collecting plants'.[538]

Unfortunately, it was now late in the year and the duke was due to return to Woburn, meaning that it was too late in the season for him to make a detour heading south for a proposed meeting with Hooker at Roseneath to inspect the renowned plantation of silver firs beside Gare Loch. Before leaving Scotland, however, news reached them that the Abercorns had taken the shooting lease on the Ardverikie estate on nearby Loch Laggan, later extended to include Ben Alder Forest, and that work had started on building a lodge of 'good sound rubble work', 'polished stone floors' and a roof of 'dark blue slates'.[539] Louisa clearly had no inclination to follow her mother's lead and intended to be as comfortable as possible on her excursions to the Highlands. As life at The Doune and in Glen Feshie became even quieter and more introspective, Ardverikie steadily replaced it as the centre for sporting activities and noisy house parties for the younger family members and their friends.

Just before the family arrived back at Woburn, there had been an august visitor when the director of the Royal Art Gallery in Berlin, Dr G. F. Waager, arrived in October hoping for a tour of the collections. No doubt the duke would have thoroughly enjoyed guiding such a visitor round his art and sculpture collections, and indeed those in the gardens, but unfortunately the house was closed during the family's absence; instead, the housekeeper, Mrs Delbridge, 'suffered herself to be induced' to show him round the house, and a footman and one of the gardeners took him round the Sculpture Gallery and gardens. Writing an account of his visit as part of his *Works of Art and Artists in England* (1838), Waager says:

> the Revd Dean Hunt [Philip Hunt], who is very intimate at the Duke's, gave me a letter to the Housekeeper, who rules alone in the absence of the Duke. In fact, the very respectable-looking, corpulent woman, who, in her black silk gown, came rustling with much state to meet me, suffered herself to be induced by [the letter] to show me about the house. But this view was the most uncomfortable of all that I have had in England. With the curtains closed, and the gloomy weather, a Cimmerian darkness prevailed in the rooms which, at my earnest entreaty, she dispelled a little, for a few moments only, by drawing the curtains aside.

After then being shown by a footman into an anteroom of the 'Gallery of Antiquities', 'I was received by a gardener, who proved to be very civil, so that I could look at the works at my ease. As the rain had at length ceased, and there was more light … At one end of the gallery is the Temple of Liberty, at the other the

Temple of the Graces. The sculptures are placed partly along the wall, opposite to the windows, partly in 2 rows in the middle.' He then describes in detail seventeen of the sculptures, the reliefs on the sarcophagus from Ephesus, the Temple of Liberty and the Temple of the Graces:

> The small temple of the Graces, of a circular form, is adorned in front with two Ionic pillars of Verde Antico. It was built by the present duke in 1818, after a design of Mr Jeffery Wyatt. In the two niches of the vestibule there are two marble statues. One by Thorwaldsen, representing the duke's eldest daughter, Lady Georgiana Elizabeth Russell, as a child of four years of age, is extremely pleasing from the simple design, the natural infantile expression. The other, by Chantrey, representing Lady Louisa Jane Russell, a sister of the proceeding, who is caressing a dove, has a most studied and affected expression. The shift, which is drawn up, is treated in the manner of this artist, so admired in England, without any style … I then went out into the beautiful flower-garden, to look at the exterior of the building … [and] the bronze copies of the celebrated statues of the Borghese, and the Dying Gladiator.

Moving into the garden, he was impressed by the range and quality of the plant collections:

> I was highly delighted with the hot-houses. One of them contains only the greatest variety of heaths, of which many very beautiful ones were just in blossom. The collection of cactus and geranium is likewise uncommonly rich. In another hot-house there are palms and other rare tropical plants. An enclosed part of the garden has manifold species of grasses, the duke being … one of the most zealous and eminent agriculturalists.

During the months in Scotland, the duke had clearly been ruminating on the developments he had seen at Chatsworth and the discussion he had had with Paxton about the new plant houses, and just before his return to Woburn, he wrote to Hooker: 'I meditate erecting some new houses at Woburn for my tropical plants, and shall be thankful for any hints you may be [able] to give me.'[540]

These new structures to house and display the tropical plants were also to form the grand centrepiece for all their work at Woburn, and an ideal site already existed on the large area that had been levelled into a wide terrace by Repton thirty years earlier. It had remained essentially an open field, and one which both occupied the very centre of the grounds and allowed room for the new structure. Wyatville was duly commissioned to design a suitable building, which would run north–south and be centred on the main axis line of the Grand Avenue, the Abbey buildings, the north and south courts, and the path running straight up the gardens to the 5th Duke's little temple seat on the eastern boundary of the gardens. Once decided, things moved very fast and work began on the 'New Flower Houses in the Pleasure Grounds' in August 1836, although the size and scale meant that the project took three years to complete (Colour Plate 40).

The family had finally left The Doune, and after visits to Blair Adam and 'to see my old friend Mr McNab' at the Edinburgh Botanical Gardens, the duke, duchess and Georgiana arrived back at Woburn in early November, from where he updated Hooker on another of the collections. While he was 'proceeding well with my new Salictum (interrupted only by the severity of the frost)', once again, the expanding collection seems to have rapidly outgrown the concentric circle design of the original site, and in May 1836 it was moved to a larger site with a different design. Exactly what subsequently happened to this particular collection is unclear, since there is no 'Salictum' shown on Wyatville's plan of 1838, and it could be that, in the end, while particularly ornamental specimens may have been retained, these plants were simply not decorative or interesting enough to warrant the space required for a formal collection. The final item of concern for the duke this year was progress on his new cottage, and in his last note to Crocker that November he wrote, 'I hope you will take the time to expedite the completion of the cottage on Purrat's Hill, as I wish to put the labourer (Mrs Day) into it as soon as possible after Christmas.'

Yet beyond the collections, new plant houses and cottages, the duke was also eagerly following up on his other new interest – supporting Hooker's plant

PLATE 35: Charles Mathews, *The Duchess of Bedford's Dining Bothy at Glen Feshie*, 1833. The image makes it clear that, although the Bedfords took over existing huts at Ruigh Aiteachan and the walls were 'made of turf and overgrown with foxglove', as Mathews tells us, some were not without basic comforts. The stone chimney, on which Landseer painted an image of stags, is all that remains today of this building.

PLATE 36: Edwin Landseer, *An Encampment on Loch Avon*, *c*.1833. This picture captures the expedition to Loch Avon described by Charles Mathews, when after their meal they 'spent a pleasant hour or two in singing' before 'the ladies retired to their tents and the men to the Poachers Cave', among the boulders in the background.

PLATE 37: Henry William Burgess, 'New "Ruins" from Ridgemont in the Evergreens', from the album 'Views in the Evergreens', 1838. The 'ruins' were moved from Ridgemont and rebuilt in the Evergreens in 1834, as the duke sought to add interesting destinations for family and friends to visit while they walked or drove in donkey carts along the rides that wound through the trees.

PLATE 38: Frederick Richard Lee and Edwin Landseer, *Scottish Landscape: Bringing Home the Stag*, *c*.1836. By the time this was painted, the buildings at Glen Feshie no longer had turf walls and roofs, reflecting the building work that went on between 1834 and 1836. The building on the right would appear to be the duchess's dining bothy, the porch of which, decorated by stags' antlers, had been painted earlier by Landseer when it still had a turf roof.

PLATE 39: Edwin Landseer, *Glen Feshie View*, c.1830–35. One of the many small images in oil that Landseer made on his painting expeditions in Glen Feshie in the 1830s. The fact that these pictures were not sold until after his death, when hundreds of such studies were found in his studio, suggests they had a personal importance to the artist. So different from the earlier works on which his fame rested, here there is not a stag, rabbit or grouse in sight, just an atmospheric emotive image looking towards the upper Glen Feshie as the river flows down past the hut at Ruigh Fionntaig.

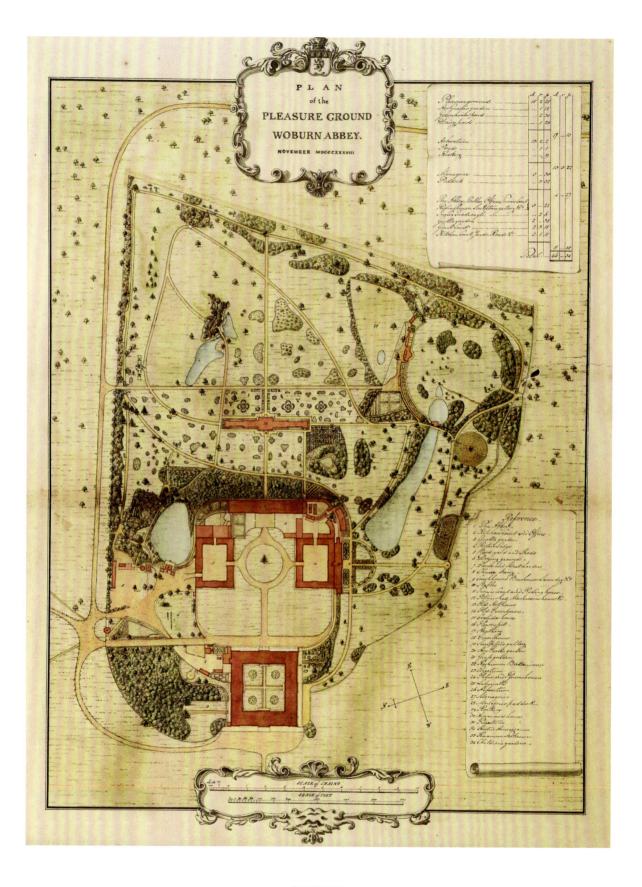

PLAN
of the
PLEASURE GROUND
WOBURN ABBEY.

NOVEMBER MDCCCXXXVIII

SCALE of CHAINS

SCALE of FEET

PLATE 40: Jeffry Wyatville, *Plan of the Pleasure Grounds, Woburn Abbey* (with key), 1838. With the additions of the maze, the new flower houses and the rock grotto and ponds, the pleasure grounds were more or less complete. The only major additions still to come were the south terraces in front of the library.

PLATE 41: 'A Sketch by Georgianna, Duchess of Bedford, for the Hundreds Cottage Gardens 1836'. This sketch represents a rare surviving example of Georgina's interest in flower gardens. Similar sketches were no doubt made for her ideas for parterres and formal flower gardens at Woburn Abbey, Campden Hill and Barons Court, where she helped her daughter Louisa lay out new gardens.

PLATE 42: Katherine Jane Ellice, 'Lady Rachel Russell, Glenfeshie', album of watercolours. No portraits of Rachel as an adult have been traced, but this drawing of her as a teenager catches her lost in thought, observing the world of Glen Feshie outside the window, and suggests the woman who went on to write historical novels, one of which, *Jesse Cameron*, concerns the landscapes and lives of the people she had grown up among in Badenoch.

collectors in Central and South America. In November he had assured Hooker that 'I am ready to in any way to contribute to the [expense] of sending out a collector,' specifically Mr Gardner, and in November he was busy making arrangements through Admiralty connections and his son Edward to secure a passage for Gardner on a Royal Navy vessel to Montevideo, but 'should pecuniary means be wanting towards furnishing Mr G. with everything requisite to his outfit on the expedition he is about to undertake I request that you will have the goodness to put down my name to any sum you may think fit towards promoting so interesting and rational an object.' In a final letter this year, the duke once again reassured Hooker of his total commitment to supporting the plant hunting: 'I fear I did not make myself quite explicit about Mr Gardner … I give you carte blanche to put down my name for any sum you please as soon as the plan is finally arranged. Should Mr Gardner go in the first instance to S. America, I will give him letters of introduction to my son, Lord Edward, who commands HMS Meteor, and will give every facility to his pursuit which his ship is able to afford.'[541]

While 1836 began with the usual New Year celebrations, within a few weeks the family had left the Abbey to spend most of the next three months in Dover. Here they had taken a house in the new and fashionable Waterloo Crescent, from which the view looked out over the esplanade to the sea beyond. The duke, writing to Lord William in December 1835, reported that 'I go to the sea side, in hopes that the bracing air of the sea may continue the benefits which I unquestionably received from the highlands in the Autumn,' and it seems that some quiet time for the family by the sea was the immediate priority. The duke and duchess were soon joined by Georgiana, Rachel and Henry, who was waiting to join his next ship, and by Lord William, who had spent a few weeks at Woburn Abbey, a short time later.

Although he had finally found some success in his diplomatic career in Berlin, William was a desperately unhappy man at this moment, as his relationship with Bessy fell apart and he began pursuing a doomed affair with a woman tentatively identified as Rebecca de Haber, whom he had met at Baden-Baden spa. Even though he had consistently criticized her over the past few years, once again Georgina was able lend him a sympathetic ear during this visit, as he noted in his diary, 'Jan, 1836. To Woburn Abbey … what splendid luxury, what refinement, what comfort. The Duchess spoke to me on the subject of marriage kindly & sensibly; kindness & sense always makes an impression on me.'

In March Landseer joined the others in Dover, where he caught an image of Georgina quietly seated at a window looking out towards the sea beyond the esplanade. She is fully dressed up as though waiting for guests to arrive, but in this quiet moment appears far away, lost in thought; for a short while, just herself and not a duchess.[542] It is a consistent theme of Landseer's growing number of portraits of Georgina that, rather than facing the artist, she is seen in profile or from behind, and while, as already noted, this emphasizes the line of her neck and shoulders, it also gives the subject an air of introspection.

Following his arrival in Dover, the duke was confined to his room by a 'smart attack of gout', where he was able to pursue his botanical studies. While reading Hooker's *Journal of Botany*, he came across 'a notice' of a recently published book, *Algae Danmoniensis or Dried Specimens of Marine Plants* by Mary Wyatt of Torquay, and noted that 'as the Duchess takes great pleasure in collecting [such] specimens she would have great pleasure in getting one of Mrs Wyatt's collections as far as she has proceeded with them.' He wrote to Hooker asking if he could order a copy for her. But his main concern at this time was ensuring Gardner's trip to South America went ahead, and to facilitate his travel there on a naval ship he promised to 'send [Gardner] a letter of introduction to my son Lord Edward', for which he enclosed 'a cheque [for] £50 which I proposed to give him'.

As a committed patron, we now see the duke using his influence to help Hooker both professionally and personally. Not only was he using contacts in the navy to arrange transport for Gardner and the subsequent shipping of his collected specimens back to England, he also increasingly turned to his political contacts to further Hooker's career – and not just with introductions. In March that year the duke told Hooker that should he be interested in 'the honour of a Knighthood, I will lose no time in applying to Lord John Russell as soon as your wishes are made known to me.' The answer came soon enough and the duke confirmed that Lord John was 'happy to recommend' the knighthood, 'but you must come to London to be personally knighted by the King.'[543] He hoped also to have the opportunity to meet up before Hooker returned to Glasgow. In April, after Georgina and Rachel travelled to Brighton to visit Louisa, who was expecting her third child, and being reassured that all was well, the family were able to set off for a break at Endsleigh.

Before the duke left that spring, the plans for Gardner's trip came to fruition as he left for Montevideo, and the duke was pleased to tell Hooker, 'I feel highly indebted to that gentleman for my copy he presented to me [of his *British Mosses*] which I have placed in the Duchess of Bedford's hands as far more worthy of possessing it than I can pretend to be.'

As they started for Endsleigh, Forbes had just started work on the pinetum and the new arboretum at Woburn, where he planned to arrange the new collections in clumps of the different species spread out along the length of the path which ran round the north and east boundaries of the gardens: the 'very complete Arboretum, surrounding the extremity of the grounds' and encompassing the existing temple/ seat near the north-east corner.

Unfortunately, even before it began, the visit to Endsleigh was overshadowed by the sudden and unexpected death of Jeremiah Wiffen at Woburn and, as Adam reports, 'The Duke is very much distressed by poor Wiffen's sudden death – it must be a heavy blow to anyone to be deprived of the person with whom he is in the habit of daily intercourse.'[544]

Indeed, in Wiffen the duke had lost a key figure in his ambitions for Woburn. Following this loss, almost as soon as they arrived at Endsleigh, Georgina went down with 'severe influenza' and remained unwell until the end of their stay, but then, on top of all of this, news arrived on 28 May that Georgina's brother, the 5th Duke of Gordon, had suddenly died. Although still not well, she left immediately for Scotland, not returning to Campden Hill for several weeks. Fortunately, in March, the family had been joined by another significant individual when, as the duke told Lady Holland, 'We are very pleased to be joined by a Scotch doctor … he is highly spoken of. Mr Allen must know something of him … by name of Allen Thomson. He has volunteered his services to us and having a history of high character we have gladly accepted him.'[545]

This marks an important moment for Georgina; it took some of the responsibility for the duke's health off her shoulders, and while the duke usually ignored his wife's advice on food and drink, she was hopeful that he would listen to professional advice. It is also a significant moment since Thomson, the godson of John Allen at Holland House, remained with the family for the next three years and he has left a particularly rich collection of letters to his parents and sister describing his life with the Bedfords, which include some of the most informed and objective descriptions of his 'ducal friends'. Thomson's arrival meant that Georgina could now leave at short notice for Scotland and not worry about the duke's care.

Back at Woburn in June, we see Allen Thomson getting used to his new surroundings and the routine of his new life. That month he wrote to his mother, 'The Duke is a regularly good natured old man, the Duchess at present much vexed about her brother's death and Lady Abercorn's health, yet joked a great deal and is extremely kind to me. Lady Georgiana is shy but pleasant, and Lady Rachel has already got over the terror with which she awaited my arrival.' He then added somewhat optimistically, 'The Duke's health is wonderfully good, and I believe that if he takes care I shall not have much to do in treating him.' Writing a little later to his father, Thomson tells him, '[Lady Georgiana] is rather a retired person but very good and with considerable talent and humour. The youngest is a lively girl of 10, a little spoilt, remarkably clever and the pet of the rest. Lord Charles Russell, an MP, is married and lives in a house in the Park … they are a good deal at the house.'

Throwing further light on some of the difficulties Georgina must have experienced, Thomson says of his patient, 'My difficulty is not the general treatment of the case which seems sufficiently simple, but … the Duke when he is ill does not think of eating and drinking less, which you may believe would be the first thing I should be disposed to recommend.' He then gives a rare glimpse of the depth and seriousness of the duke's interests when describing his study, where the duke has his books and 'every opportunity of dissecting and experimenting'. The study was no doubt well equipped with reference books old and new, microscopes, powerful lenses and all the tools necessary to dissect and investigate the intricacies of botanical specimens.

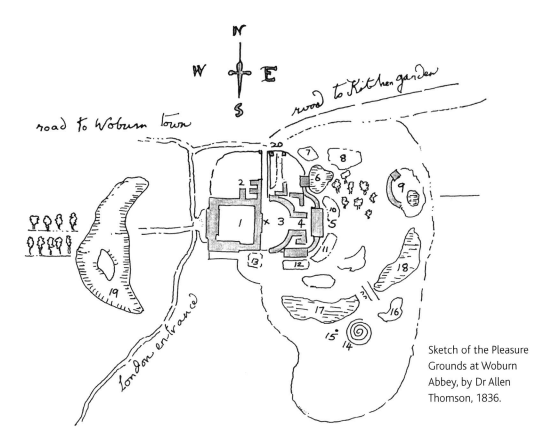

Sketch of the Pleasure
Grounds at Woburn
Abbey, by Dr Allen
Thomson, 1836.

Later that summer, in a long letter to his sister, Thomson goes into more detail:
'After breakfast, having asked the duke how he felt, I … joined the duke to accompany
him to church. He drove me there in a little chaise drawn by a beautiful white pony,
the servant riding on another pony behind … I then went out by myself to take my
walk. I sauntered for 3 hours in the pleasure grounds or ornamental garden which
surrounds the house … the extent of this is about 50 acres.'

Fortunately for us, he also includes in this letter a numbered sketch of the layout
of the features round the Abbey, complete with a key, which shows the gardens mid-
way between those of 1833 (*Hortus Woburnensuis*) and 1838 (Wyatville). In addition
to indicating the location of the new pinetum and arboretum, although it is not
topographically accurate, the sketch does perhaps suggest the experience of walking
round the gardens, emphasizing the difference between the long walk up the ponds
to the Menagerie, passing the Maze, swing and grass garden (numbers 14–18 and 9),
and the features grouped around Thomsons's favourite seat, which he described in
detail: 'I walked about … sat down and meditated. One spot I always return to with
great pleasure is between 6 & 8 on a seat at the side of the pond which is before the

Chinese Dairy, below a fine spreading oak in the neighbourhood of very fine horse chestnuts, ashes and other large trees … the Menagerie, which with the exception of some peculiar deer, a tortoise, is exclusively an aviary.'[546]

In July the duke received another series of letters from the collector Mr Arundell concerning the 'Ephesian Sarcophagus'. Arundell had returned to England after securing new fragments and was now eager to sell them. Although, in the end, these fragments never made it to Woburn, the letters throw an interesting light on the nature of the trade in antiquities at this time. Arundell tells the duke: 'In 1831 Sir Robert Gordon kindly procured me a special Firman [grant or permit] to make researches at Ephesas, but that permission was restricted to what was above the surface; and there was no leave given for removing anything'; while waiting for permission from authorities in Smyrna to remove items, he travelled to the site to see what was still there: 'On arriving … I was surprised to find the fragments more important, and much larger than I had anticipated … completing all that is deficient on that side of the Sarcophagus.' He was then summoned to meet the Great Pasha's nephew, Sadik Effendi, and 'after long discussion' Arundell persuaded Sadik to allow him to take a fragment down under 'the guarantee that it should not be taken away until permission was obtained'. He succeeded in removing it, but since 'it was so massy, that having no means whatever to remove it, nor time to do so,' he was forced to leave it there after protecting it with 'large walls of stone' and a 'Turk' to guard it. He then wrote to the English Consul of Scala Nova 'telling him what I had done', and requesting him 'to get it removed … to Smyrna, where my friends … were prepared to receive it, and to embark it on one of their vessels for London'.

After Arundell left the fragment 'in safety', however, it would appear that no one ever saw it again: it never arrived and Arundell had no idea what happened to it. He proposed going back to find out, clearly hoping the duke would fund such a venture or at least guarantee to buy it should he succeed, but in spite of his efforts, it had vanished without trace and was lost forever into the seedy world of dealers, middlemen and unscrupulous collectors.

Reacting to this news, the sculptor Richard Westmacott, who it seems was closely involved in the duke's collecting efforts and eagerly awaiting the arrival of the fragments, was 'vexed at what I conceived the management of the parties in the plans for extracting the fragment. It is now made an official business, whereas a few Piastres judiciously employed would have spared all trouble … I have no doubt from my conversation with Mr A[rundell] that this fragment will complete the whole of the front of the Sarcophagus.'[547]

Perhaps the duke had been naive about the realities of the antiquity trade he had dipped his toes into, or perhaps he had been happy not to know how the objects he bought had been collected or obtained, yet having such a close relationship with Revd Philip Hunt, it is hard to believe that he was unaware of the circumstances by which, for example, the Elgin Marbles were removed from the Parthenon and shipped to England, and the questionable role Hunt and Richard Hamilton, both working for Elgin, had played in the process. In addition, Westmacott's casual suggestion that all the irritating bureaucratic red tape could have been circumvented by 'a few Piastres judiciously employed' indicates that they were all fully aware of how these things were done. When personally involved in such transactions, however, such as when he was purchasing items in Italy, the duke had been careful to secure the necessary permissions, and one senses that he had never been entirely comfortable with the trade in antiquities, and that Arundell's persistence in involving him in the clearly murky saga of the fragment was the last straw. When Arundell later offered the duke another piece of equally dubious provenance, the duke turned it down and, perhaps with some relief, turned his full attention to the world of botany and horticulture.

In so doing, the duke was now totally engaged with plants, plant hunting and building new facilities to house his growing collections. Encouraged by what he had achieved with Sinclair and Forbes, by the support and validation provided by his expanding group of fellow botanists in England and Scotland, and with a new-found confidence in himself that stemmed from this support, the duke had found his true passion: exploring and helping to uncover that particular world of wonder, the mysteries and surprises of the world's plant life.

CHAPTER TEN
1836–1853

I N AUGUST 1836, while Georgina and Rachel returned to Brighton for the birth of Louisa's daughter, the duke, anxious to resume his botanical collecting activities and hoping to persuade Hooker to visit him, left for The Doune accompanied by Georgiana and Allen Thomson, travelling via Edinburgh, where he stopped off at the botanical gardens to meet with Professor Graham and Mr McNab. By 29 August he had reached his 'old highland quarters'; he was soon joined by Cosmo and Alexander on their school holidays, who were looking forward to the shooting season. Anticipating Landseer's arrival, the duke wrote to him, 'I trust we shall see you here to follow the grouse on the Muirs before the season gets too advanced. You will find plenty of Birds – my boys bagged 20 brace with ease the other day.'

In his first trip to The Doune and indeed to the Highlands, Thomson's letter to his sister conveys his excitement. For Thomson, as with so many travellers born and raised in Edinburgh and the Lowlands, the watershed moment in their journey north comes as they cross into the Highlands at the Pass of Drumochter, 'the bleakest and wildest ride I think I have ever passed through', but 'the desolate wildness of the scene quite charmed me,' and he finds 'the opening of the valley of the Spey … is very fine' as it 'opens into a wide strath'. Of The Doune itself, Thomson says:

> the largest part of the house in appearance fronts the south and seems to have been added to a much smaller house which is now behind it. There are two public rooms; in the old part of the house the Duke has two rooms and the Duchess one, and between them is an interesting little chamber 6 feet by 9

which lodges your humble servant … The Duchess with her ingenuity can accommodate a great number of people but they must be satisfied with country quarters. The two young Lords, and Lord Henry when he comes, sleep in one of the outhouses [west kitchen wing] … I chose the small room because I understood it was the warmest, had the morning sun and a pleasant look out into a flower garden on the Duchess's parterre … [We] keep ourselves warm by moving about a good deal. Sporting of course is our chief employment, and I am getting gradually used to its mysteries. My tartan and Shepherd's plaid will be home tomorrow when I shall be fit for the moors … We have a lot of fishing both with the rod in the Spey and with nets in the lochs.[548]

This is also the year that the McDonald family – John, a carpenter and odd-job man, his wife and their young son John, who seem already to have been living in the glen, possibly part of the wider Ruigh Aiteachan township – were formally hired to look after the huts full-time. Over the next few years, Mrs McDonald received bi-annual payments for 'taking charge of Glenfeshie cottage', while John McDonald, after working on the house, was retained to maintain the buildings, gardens, fences, flood defences and plantings with the help of his son John working as a labourer.

As well as 'moving about a great deal', pedometer in his pocket, the duke was in regular touch with Hooker, keeping him up to date with the plant hunting, inquiring about Gardner's progress in South America, and encouraging Hooker to join him. In fact, Hooker was already familiar with The Doune, having visited the Grants on at least two occasions in 1820 and 1822 after taking the Chair of Botany at Glasgow University.[549] Once there he had begun both to revitalize the department and to build Glasgow's botanical garden into a major collection, while also conducting plant hunting expeditions in the Highlands with students. At this time, however, in spite of repeated invitations from the duke over the coming years, Hooker does not seem to have visited again.

By 3 September, although the duke was disappointed Hooker would not be visiting, he was joined by Georgina and Rachel. Georgina then spent the next several weeks overseeing the completion of the new buildings and garden in Glen Feshie and having a formal opening of the new house, commissioning repairs to the road round Loch an Eilein and cleaning the Loch an Eilein cottage, but in addition, as in most years, she spent time visiting in the communities of Rothiemurchus. Here she interested herself in the lives and problems of the elderly, the widows of estate workers, schooling for the younger children, and comforted or intervened where she felt she could. While the sums of money the Bedfords donated to families, housing, churches or schools over the years were miniscule in the wider context, the following comments by Jane Grant and Dr Thomson suggest that part of the impact of Georgina's interest went beyond the economic. During her visit in 1831, as noted in the previous chapter, Jane had said, 'I was anxious to let her know how grateful [are] the poor people she is so kind to and [they] speak of her goodness,' while Thomson, writing to his sister in 1836, added some important detail. After commenting on the poverty of the 'common people's' diet in the area, the expense of fuel for the cottages and the uncertainty of income due to the nature of seasonal employment, he says, 'The duchess has done an immense deal in this immediate neighbourhood to better the condition of the poor and no greater proof of her tact and knowledge of the world can be given than the judicious way in which she has done so.'[550]

Both comments suggest that the impact of Georgina's efforts had little to do with money, but rather in an age of largely absentee landlords, for the first time in younger people's lives but within the memories of the eldest, somebody actually took an interest in them: visited, listened and sympathized. In a region where a sense of the old clan loyalties evidently still lingered, her attitude echoed the days of her own mother and a time when clan chiefs were duty bound to take a paternalistic interest in their people.

On 13 November the family finally left The Doune, and after delays due to very bad weather in the Irish Sea, they arrived at Barons Court (the duke stopped off in Belfast to visit its new botanical garden). Writing to his sister after meeting the Abercorns for the first time, Thomson notes that 'when one gets on rising ground one sees lakes and water everywhere,' but considers it as good a place 'as could

Barons Court, house and gardens, 1890s. The first parterre gardens beside the house were laid out with Georgina's help, and were subsumed in later extensions (shown here) until they reached the shore of Lough Fanny.

be found for a residence. The country above is undulating, the slopes gentle,' and he writes, 'Great changes are at present taking place in the arrangement of the property … It is all to be rebuilt and refitted next year.'

He considered the marquis to be 'a great dandy and agreeable enough in exterior manner and very affable', while the marchioness, who was already pregnant again, 'is very beautiful and one of the most amiable and agreeable persons I ever saw. She is neither quite like the Gordons nor the Russells but a happy medium between the both. She is not remarkably clever but has a good deal of quiet fun, and sets everybody quite at their ease … Everything here is of course, tory and protestant,' and reports finally: 'the Duke in good health, Duchess in low spirits.'

Writing to Lady Holland, the duke was even less impressed than Thomson by what he saw: 'There is nothing remarkable about this place, except that it is surrounded by bogs, which is not remarkable for Ireland. Altho' it is called Barons Court there is nothing in it to convince me of a baronial court of long ancestry. Everything is modern, a modern house tumbling down through want of repairs, and modern plantations, which in 2 or 3 hundred years will be fine woods. Abercorn is not disposed to lay out much money upon it, beyond making the house comfortable and habitable, which he will do.' In spite of this, however, he was impressed enough with the design of the boat house, built in the style of a North American log cabin, to have it recreated in the Woburn Evergreens between 1838 and 1839, a structure which stands to this day. It is also suggested in a piece of doggerel that Georgina had some hand in redesigning the flower gardens at Barons Court around this time, but to what extent this is true is not clear:

> We pride ourselves on Baronscourt,
> Its Lords, its Ladies fair,
> Its ruins grey, its islands,
> Its lakes, its gay parterre.
> For natural and artistic style,
> Old Erin has few such as
> Its walks for leisure, its grounds for pleasure,
> Designed by Bedford's Duchess.[551]

It would seem that so far Thomson had had as little success as Georgina in getting the duke to alter his diet and moderate his consumption of claret, since the start of 1837 saw him laid up at Barons Court where 'the new year has not begun very well for me … a bit of Gout.' Nevertheless, he recovered enough for Georgina to send an encouraging report to Lord William: 'I still have excellent accounts to give you of your Father and all here – We leave on the 11th, in Dublin the 12th – 14th, and by easy journeys arrive at the old Abbey, which I hope I shall find free from

Measles & Influenza, which have been severe and fatal there … And now Dearest William, Adieu & believe me always Yours Affectly, Georgy B' – suggesting that the two had finally been able to renew their former friendship.[552]

By late February the family and staff had arrived back at Woburn. The duke visited the Dublin Botanical Garden on his way, and was able to tell Hooker that he was very pleased with what he saw; the two corresponded regularly from this point on concerning the progress of Gardner's expedition and the regular deliveries of cactus plants. Over the next two years the duke wrote to Hooker at least once, if not twice, a week in spite of his uncertain health, entirely swept up in the activities and sheer excitement surrounding his new interests. In spite of feeling life's lamp dimming, it was possibly the happiest period of his life.

While the duke was busy, so was Woburn. Writing to his mother in late March, Thomson mentioned a great assembly of company at Woburn and a grand ball to celebrate the Easter holidays. Guests included Landseer with his fellow artists Calcott and Wilkie, and it is instructive that during this visit the duke adopted Landseer's suggestion that they should take all the cups and pieces of plate that he and the 5th Duke had won at the agricultural meetings over the years, melt them down, and create a single 'Commemorative silver Salver'.[553] This decision would not have been taken lightly, and it tells us just how far the duke's priorities had changed.

Beside organizing the ball, Georgina was also busy with more 'lying-in hospital duties', helping with the care of Wriothesley's wife, Eliza, who on 5 May gave birth to a daughter, Evelyn. While Georgina had by now helped both Louisa and Eliza on a number of occasions, it would seem that this one held some significance. Sending the news to Lord William, Georgina wrote, 'Forty-eight hours ago, Eliza was delivered safely of an enormous girl … "Good old Granny, with her specs upon her nose, working when she is not nursing babies." What an altered picture, the once lovely, charming, &c. &c. Georgy Gordon, to become a darling old soul, who is now, ever, Always affectionately yours.'[554]

It is an interesting letter because it suggests not only how close the two had become again, but also a new sense of mellowness in Georgina, as though, surrounded now by increasing numbers of grandchildren, she is coming to terms with – even embracing – her status now as 'Good old Granny'. Georgina was fifty-six when she wrote this, and we see reflected in this clear-eyed, dispassionate and humorous observation both the acceptance of herself as an older woman and the new inwardness – a retreat into self – that sets the older woman apart. She also became increasingly creative as her involvement in the design of flower gardens grew (Colour Plate 41). Between them, the silver salver and 'Good old Granny' indicate just how far the duke and duchess had moved on personally since the time when as newlyweds they drove into the park at Woburn.

The lavish entertainment of the visitors, however, soon took its toll on the duke, and in late May he told Hooker he was once again 'confined … by a severe attack of rheumatism … [and] a seizure of gout was superadded to the rheumatism'. However, a few days later he added that since he was still 'interested at all times on all subjects relating to Botany, I cannot delay thanking you for your very kind letter,' before going on to discuss the new cacti that had been arriving from Gardner in South America and to hope that Hooker had received his copy of Forbes's account of his 'Continental Tour'.[555] In June the duke's health started to gradually improve as the weather warmed up, and Thomson was able to report to his father: 'I ride or walk every day now that I am not required in so immediate attendance on the Duke. The grass ride round the park itself is about 12 or 14 miles long … The woods abound with a considerable variety of plants … and I have collected about 40 or 50 common plants the names of which I am teaching to Lady Rachel and myself. The gardens are just coming on. We have peaches, pineapples, grapes and strawberries from the hot houses, the cactuses are magnificent.'

Yet underlying Thomson's apparently idyllic existence a number of things were on his mind. He had a strong commitment to medicine and was anxious to continue his studies in Edinburgh while also hoping to get married before too long, but perhaps most importantly, he was increasingly concerned as to whether the Woburn position, and all that went with it, was really the best use of his time and skills. In a candid letter to his mother at this time he writes:

I remember you saying to me before I left home that I should probably think some of the points of manner I saw as bad or vulgar. You can have no idea to what an extent this is sometimes carried … I have before said in my letters that extreme case of manner in the high ranks (but especially among the young who are almost all made spoilt children by servants) too often takes the place of quiet politeness. And among the most polite aristocracy even, it is impossible not to perceive that that they look upon themselves as a superior class of beings. One can even distinguish this in the Duke who is I think the most gentlemanly nobleman I have ever seen.[556]

It is clear that such a close involvement in family life at Woburn was not always easy for Thomson, but the circumstance that brought things to a head for him was what he considered to be Georgina's overly zealous interference in his treatment of the duke. It reached such a point in June that he informed her he would like to leave. Her short reply speaks volumes about Georgina:

Whenever you are obliged to leave us, it will be a day of sincere regret to everyone, more particularly to the duke and myself. Still, great as our satisfaction would be could you remain in our family, neither of us would like you to make any sacrifice, either of a _private_, or public engagement, to promote our wishes.

  Having stated our feelings, let me add in the duke's name and my own, how much comfort and pleasure, we have derived from your Society, and how grateful I feel for your kind attention to Rachel, and how sensible the duke and I are, of your constant, unremitting, and cheerful attendance.

It worked and Thomson, who had clearly become an important figure in Rachel's life as much as anyone's, agreed to stay another year. Settled for now in his mind as to why he was there, he was infected by the Bedfords' enthusiastic engagement with their interests, writing to his sister: 'finding a good geological map at Woburn, I dabbled a little in the structure of the earth in the neighbourhood … Then I have been drawing a little in sepia under the superintendence of Lady Charles and the Duchess. Lady Charles draws trees both in pencil and sepia in the very best style. The Duchess knows a good deal about the art but does not execute much. On other days I went to the ponds to fish with Lady Rachel … We had little or no company at Woburn.' This did not mean, of course, that all the tensions and issues had been eased, and in this letter he also mentions a lecture he received from the duchess on etiquette, noting in his own defence, 'It is somewhat difficult to construct one's sentences so as to introduce "My Lord" and "Your Grace" at the proper time.'

By July the duke was mobile enough to travel briefly to Endsleigh, from where he was already arranging to meet Hooker and Dawson Turner at Woburn in August, and hoping, 'if I am tolerably well', to see him at The Doune: 'I flatter myself we might … do a little Highland botanizing. I wrote to Mr Dawson Turner some time ago to propose to him to meet you at Woburn.' Meanwhile, Dr Thomson seems to have remained at Campden Hill or to have just returned there, and so was on hand when Landseer suffered a serious injury in a carriage accident. He tells his sister, 'Two nights ago I had a surgical case. Mr Landseer the painter had been dining at Holland House and was upset in his gig a little way from Kensington. He is very intimate with the Bedfords and Lord Cosmo and I acted as Doctors and took him home, he had a severe cut on his head.'[557]

For a few days, Landseer remained at Campden Hill with Dr Thomson recuperating from the accident, but although Thomson describes the damage as a 'cut on the head', this may well have been accompanied by serious concussion, even some brain damage, and Landseer's breakdown a few years later may have been partly connected to this accident.

The duke's health, however, continued to improve and after a brief stop at Campden Hill, he returned to Woburn, where he appointed John Martin the new librarian. With his plans to meet Hooker and Dawson Turner having fallen through, however, he left for Scotland on 7 August, visiting the Abercorns at Bentley Priory on the way. Once at The Doune, the duke was disappointed, once again, to hear that Hooker would not be visiting, and so took his own 'short Highland Excursion', probably botanizing on the slopes above Glen Feshie, while, as Thomson tells his mother, the others have been 'fishing and sketching or taking any other of the amusements that are going … The Duchess joined us four days ago and brought a great accession of bustle and gaiety to our party … We are likely to see some more company here now. There are a great many of the nobility struggling about in the moors throughout the Highlands.'[558] Thomson's bemusement with the attractions of the moors is clear in a letter to his sister: 'This is a shockingly wet day … We have now settled into an idle sort of life which is generally led in these parts which consists of being engaged in outdoor amusements or in its higher title of sports of the field, for which the great folks migrate with so much trouble and expense to the north.'

Although his gout kept the duke and Thomson at The Doune, another overnight stay beside Loch Avon was organized, undertaken this time by the duchess, Lady Abercorn, Georgiana, one of the Miss Balfours, Cosmo and Alexander, Edward Ellice and others, each assigned a ghillie and a pony. Thomson also mentions Georgina: "The great joke against me just now is my objection to calomel which [the duchess] brings out upon all occasions, particularly at the dinner table … imitating my voice in the midst of the Dinner party she bawls out "Your grace must excuse me I am determined to give no calomel". She has completely regained her spirits and is a most astonishing woman, extremely clever, with information on all subjects, a great mimic and always ready for a joke.' He adds that she is 'affable to everyone, but rigidly tenacious of dignity and rank and formalities of manner and conversation, but forgetting it entirely in most other circumstances'. Most importantly for him, perhaps, 'She is extremely kind to me and I think on the whole, tho' she contradicts my practice, has considerable confidence in my judgement.'

It had been a consistently bad year for the duke's niggling health problems, and at some point over the course of this stay it was decided that the family would spend the winter in the south of France in the hope that the warmer weather would ease some of his enduring symptoms. After returning to Woburn at the end of October, the plans were finalized and, joined by Frank, Georgiana, Rachel and the Abercorns, Thomson reports that they would leave England in November and spend up to six months in Nice, travelling through Paris, Avignon and Toulon. As the duke told Lady Holland, 'travel, easy journeys, change of air and scene, will be of service to both body and mind.'[559]

On 22 November the party reached Paris and were preparing to leave for Avignon when news caught up with them that Henry, in Portsmouth for the refitting of the ship he was serving on, had been struck on the head by a block falling from the rigging and was seriously ill in hospital. Georgina and Frank immediately left for England, arriving at the Haslar Hospital in Portsmouth a few days later. They stayed until 22 December, travelling once or twice a day by boat from Gosport to the hospital, before going briefly to Woburn and setting out again for Paris. Henry was conscious while they were there and Georgina seems to have been reassured that he was out of immediate danger, even though he faced a long recovery. In the event, it was to be February 1838 before he left hospital, and even then, as Trethewey tells us, he 'suffered from epileptic fits which led to his premature death in 1842, aged just 26'.[560]

While Georgina was away, the duke, who seems to have been much recovered, entertained himself in Paris visiting friends, flirting with favourite ladies, and basking in the reflected glory of his sociable daughters. In one account, Harriet, Countess Granville, wrote, 'We are all charmed by Lady Abercorn, she is so unaffected, gay and graceful. Marie and Dody like Lady Georgiana, and say that she is amusing and original. The Duke is better … He calls our Lady Harcourt "Dearest Lizzie" before company, which causes surprise.'

When Georgina and Frank finally arrived back in Paris in early January, she was hurt deeply by the duke's offhand greeting, as she told Lord Holland, ' I left Dover at nine o'clock on Thursday and was with the Duke at six o'clock on Friday. All he said was: "Oh you are arrived" … I think he is more occupied with the beauty or beauties of Paris than is quite good for his health.'[561] His seeming lack of concern for her or Henry fit the established pattern of the duke's tendency to leave his wife to deal with family illness on her own.

After leaving Paris they faced an unusually difficult journey, as severe winter weather made progress slow, and it was some ten days before they finally met the warmth of Nice, where they took up residence at the Maison Guilia, with the Abercorns taking the villa next door. Thomson, writing to his mother, reports: 'I don't think the Duke is in very good spirits, but there are so many trifling outs and ins in his life that I do not know whether to ascribe this to bad health or simple ill humour. Perhaps after all the trouble we have had to bring him here, he is disappointed. Perhaps the circumstances in which he returns to Nice are so different to those of his former visit as to affect him. Fifty-two years ago he came to Nice with his first wife on account of her health and he has not been here since. I trust that exercise … and regular life will put him right.'

Yet by the end of month, it was, predictably, botany that 'put him right', and he reported excitedly to Hooker that, after a very cold journey, during which temperatures fell below -6 degrees, he was now delighted to say that he 'had the good fortune to find here Mr Risso, a native and zealous naturalist, and a most amiable man. Indeed, I may say *en passant* that I have almost uniformly through life found lovers of natural history to be amiable men. Mr Risso was named to me by your friend Mr Webb in Paris' and he is 'an excellent man and a zealous Botanist, I wish you knew him.'[562] We get a strong sense here of the duke's immense satisfaction that his endeavours and friendships have secured him a place in an international network of botanists and collectors; not only has he found his passion, he has found a place within its world.

Just as life was settling down in Nice, it was suddenly interrupted when the duke's footman and Rachel's maid both developed 'bilious fevers' and became 'dangerously ill'. A week later, when the Abercorns continued their planned trip to Italy, the duke decided he should accompany them as far as Genoa and took Cosmo and Thomson with him for company, telling Lady Holland that since the Abercorns were travelling that way, 'it would be foolish of me to be so near Genoa and the Corniche without seeing them. The Dss does not join me in Genoa. She will not leave Nice at present … Georgy, Rachel and Frank stay with her.'

In Genoa, the duke wrote to Hooker: 'I passed the morning yesterday with the Professor of Botany here – an intelligent young man. They are backward here in that science, but are about to open an Establishment on a more important scale. If you come to Nice next winter (as I hope you may) the communication with that place, across the Mediterranean Lake is an affair of only nine hours by steam, and Genoa is worth seeing. It is a wonderful place.'[563]

More importantly perhaps, this letter also marks the beginning of the campaign that came to dominate the last few years of the duke's life: the establishment of the national botanical garden at Kew with Hooker appointed as its first director. Following the death of William IV, the Treasury sought to rationalize the costs of the royal household, including the expense of the various royal kitchen gardens, looking to make substantial savings. To this end in January 1838 a working group was established led by John Lindley, Professor of Botany at University College London, to report on the situation. One key aspect of the report was to ascertain whether 'some practical public purpose' could be found for the extensive but neglected and unwanted botanic garden and pleasure grounds stretching out beyond the kitchen gardens at Kew. Lindley's 'Report on Royal Gardens' (1838) recommended that, if kept and slightly enlarged, the Kew kitchen gardens could supply all the palaces, while the area of the pleasure grounds should be taken over by the state and run as a national botanical institution. Specifically, Lindley wrote that it 'should either be at once taken for public purposes, gradually made worthy of the country, and converted into a powerful means of promoting national service, or it should be abandoned', and at the back of Lindley's mind was the possibility that he might be appointed as the first director of this new national garden.[564]

While the duke passionately shared Lindley's vision and spent the last years of his life fighting to make it happen, he was, however, firmly committed to the idea that Hooker was the obvious and most suitable candidate for the directorship and lobbied hard to support him. After two years of uncertainty, due partly to an alternative proposal to establish such a garden in a much smaller site in Regent's Park promoted by the Royal Botanical Society, the issue was laid before Parliament, and after finding support from Queen Victoria, the land at Kew became public property and the national gardens were established under the directorship of Hooker in 1840.

In his letter from Genoa in March this year, the duke wrote to reassure Hooker that he was actively pursuing this end: 'I look with hope and expectation to the prospect of seeing Kew Gardens and the whole surrounding demesne, converted into a great national Establishment … and you may be certain that I have not forgotten you.' In April, to get things moving, he advised Hooker to approach Lindley and enlist his help in persuading the government as a 'man of science and practical knowledge'.

By the time the duke returned to Nice, Georgina's patients were recovering and she had travelled to Cannes 'to be with Rachel who she sent there for a change of air'; preparations then began for their return to England.[565] Once everyone was fit and well, the family set out, arriving in Paris by 1 May and London a few days later, where excitement was growing as preparations got underway for the coronation of Queen Victoria. Spending a few days at Campden Hill, the duke was perplexed to discover that Lady Holland had had a new fence built which effectively blocked off the views of Holland Park from the recently completed drawing room at the villa. The reasons for this are not entirely clear – Queen Victoria ascribed it in her journal to Lady Holland's disapproval of the new room and her desire 'to vex the Duchess' – but the duke was able to defuse any potential row by treating it with humour. In a letter to Lady Holland, he writes she had 'completely cut off all communication between Holland House and poor little C. Hill. I saw with regret the formidable barricade you had erected on the top of your park paling, opposite the Dss's little garden so as to effectively exclude her view of your beautiful grounds … so we … must be content … with the [memory] of the view we once enjoyed … Notwithstanding all this, I shall still hope to find my way to Holland House somehow or other … I do assure you that I am most anxious to see you again, and shall make a point of going to see you as soon as I return to town, *nonobstant les Baricades*.'[566]

The family, however, soon travelled on to Woburn where Henry had been convalescing and was due to rejoin his ship in early June, and family life briefly resumed. While there, twelve-year-old Rachel wrote the following letter to her friend Dr Thomson, which gives us the first clear suggestion as to why she was such a favourite with family and friends:

Dear old Doctor,

We have had the plague here, in the shape of a young lady or tomboy schoolgirl vulgar Miss. This was Miss White, Mistress Delbrige's niece. Yesterday we had a small party on Georgey's birthday and amongst others she was asked. She is vulgar, ill-bred, dreadful spoiled, deceitful, and commanded us in a high voice 'Go there you, do this la! How dull you har' … Emily, Martin and all of us were whispering 'I don't like her, so vulgar'. I went to Miss Reddall's child's Christening today, Rachel Anne is her name. Mad Poozellie says that 'Miss White is everyone's Bête Noire'. Good bye, dear Doctor Tomty,

your own little friend, Rachel.

Rachel Anne, my god daughter, think o'that!!! I ought not to have blamed Miss White, though she is so vulgar it was not kind of me, pray excuse me.[567]

For Georgina, attending the coronation on 28 June provided only a brief diversion from family affairs, and by mid-July she had hurried down to Brighton, where Louisa was once again experiencing a difficult pregnancy. On 2 August the duke wrote to Lady Holland that 'The Dss says the sea at Brighton is "awfie" as the Scotch say … and she continues to watch over Louisa, with a maternal anxiety and solicitude which as you will know so eminently belongs to her.' By the end of August she had been joined by the duke, Georgiana and Rachel, who were all there when Louisa finally gave birth on 24 August, producing the Abercorns' anxiously awaited son and heir, James. This had been a tense and difficult time for all, and although it was late in the season, Georgina left for The Doune to join Cosmo and Alexander, who had been there shooting since early August. The duke told Lady Holland: 'The Dss was off to her native land travelling quite alone – as she would take no companion with her, I am convinced the journey and the Highland air will be of service to her. Her nerves were sadly shaken, though she would not complain.' During her absence, the duke occupied himself with the campaign for Kew and in October told Hooker he was expecting Lord John soon from Ireland and will discuss 'what are the Government intentions' for Kew with him. He restates his firm objections to the Regent's Park plan as 'quite unfit for purpose': bad soil, too near the city smoke and fog, and 'liable moreover, to the perpetual Cockney intrusion of the City, who do not care one farthing about Botany, or any other science, and would flock there merely as a Lounge'.

In mid-October the duke was joined in Brighton by Lord John and his wife, Adelaide, who was also nearing the end of a pregnancy. By the end of the month, Georgina had arrived back from Scotland, arriving just in time to be present for the devastating tragedy of Adelaide's death on 1 November following the birth of her second daughter, Victoria. The duke attended Adelaide's funeral at Chenies a week or so later, but noted sadly on his return to Brighton that 'the Dss does not rally as I hoped she would.'

Thus, a year which should have been so enjoyable as so many of their shared interests came to fruition in the gardens at Woburn and Campden Hill and in Scotland had instead been overshadowed from the very start with news of Henry's accident, the duke's ongoing health issues, staff illness, and now ended with Adelaide's death; at Woburn that winter, it was hoped that 1839 would be better.

Although the New Year celebrations were somewhat muted, a number of the family, including 'Edward, Charles, Cosmo, Georgy, Rachel … and old William, who chatters more and more to himself everyday,' were at the Abbey. In addition, the Abercorns were there to ensure that the theatre tradition was kept up. Small performances were staged, followed by 'A Comic Song in Character by that astonishing Child, Lady Rachel Russell!!!', and concluded with an 'Epilogue, written by Georgiana Duchess of Bedford, which began "Hush, hush! I beg you don't announce me now, I'll pop in, unawares, and make my bow"'.[568]

Meanwhile, events concerning Kew were moving on. In January Lindley delivered his report, with which the duke 'entirely agrees', concerning the viability of the site at Kew for a national garden, and warned of the next battle: convincing the Lords of the Treasury it was the right thing to do, as he wrote to Hooker: 'I sincerely hope Mr Spring Rice [Chancellor of the Exchequer] may soon find leisure from Corn Laws, and political warfare, to turn his attention to the Establishment of Kew Gardens.'

In February, eager to show them all the new developments at Woburn, the duke was hoping for another visit from Hooker and Dawson later in the year, but in the meantime was looking forward to the arrival of Mr Fitch, Hooker's 'illustrator' at Glasgow, for a few weeks to work with Forbes in the spring to catch the flowering season, when 'the Cactus House will afford a greater field for his graphic powers.' The duke was also delighted to be able to send Hooker a copy of his new catalogue, *Pinetum Woburnense*, which he hoped Hooker would 'receive with your usual indulgence to Pseudo-Botanists, who like me have thought their investigations into the Culture of that interesting tribe, the Genus Pinus, may be of some advantage in drawing the attention of land-owners to the growth of a family of trees', and apologized for the delay in its arrival, caused by the unfortunate fact that the 'Porter entrusted to carry it from Belgrave Square to the Coach Office, got drunken on the way, and lost it in an ale house. After some time, however, the publican found it, and had the honesty to return it to me, since when it has been unaccountably delayed in Edinburgh.'[569]

April and May were spent on a quiet, and no doubt very welcome, family retreat at Endsleigh, before Georgina returned to Campden Hill for her London season of 'Breakfasts' and a ball in July, while the duke made his way to Woburn. Having received a letter from Hooker inquiring about Kew on his way from Devon, his first priority on arriving was to try to contact the Chancellor of the Exchequer before his budget and get him to 'listen favourably to my projects as to Kew'. He had been encouraged by Lord Aberdeen, who 'tells me that he finds Spring Rice the most liberal Chancellor of Exch. he ever met with in promoting the well being of the arts and sciences'. Meanwhile, in a slightly gloomier letter, Forbes informed Hooker: 'I went out to Kew and had a long gossip with Mr. Aiton, but everything remains in the same state as when you were there. Mr. Aiton informed me that he cannot get away, although he has sent in his Resignation twice. None of the Court seem to take any interest in Kew Gardens. I hear His Majesty has only paid them one solitary visit.'

Closer to home the Woburn collections continued to grow as new plants arrived, particularly orchids. In April Forbes recorded that 'Mr. Skinner has forwarded by two different packets a large collection … states that the *Orchidium* is the most beautiful thing of the kind he ever met with, and, if new, he wishes it to be called *Russelliana*, but as that name is already preoccupied, I must beg of you to name it after the Duchess, who takes a greater interest in the *Orchidae* than His Grace does.' These plants were followed in August by 'a box of Orchidiae from Dr Schomburgh [in Demarara] containing … various other good things that are apparently different to any that we have got and have all arrived in excellent order'. By this time the duke had been pleased 'to receive Mr Fitch's new drawings of my Cactaceae here as soon as he has finished them', and it would seem, from the trouble they had taken to get these drawings, that the duke and Forbes had decided their next illustrated catalogue should record the cactus collection, especially now that they were installed in their new home in the flower houses.[570]

Whatever the longer term publishing plans were, in the event the next book the duke published was altogether different. As the introduction reads, 'These Memoirs were drawn up in my leisure moments; and thinking that some of my young friends might derive, in reading, a portion of the pleasure I have had in writing them, a few copies have been printed privately for their perusal. In drawing them up, I have been assisted by a young friend at that time living with me.' The little volume, titled *Memoirs of Two Favourites*, is dedicated 'To the Ladies Harriet, Beatrice and Louisa Hamilton, these pages are inscribed by their affectionate Aunt Rachel E. Russell. Woburn Abbey, 6th July 1839.'

Reading this, it is perhaps hard to believe that although the girls were five, four and three years old, their 'affectionate Aunt', at thirteen, was only a few years older. Confidently and fluently, even precociously, written, the book contains two stories, 'Memoirs of a Dormouse' and 'Memoirs of a Doll', and take us into Rachel's world: her pets, friends and cousins, the life and places she knew, idyllic sun-filled woodlands, country estates and cottages, town houses, toy shops and parties. We also enter the world of the pets and toys, as the mice and dolls are passed between 'pretty little girls' and badly behaved girls who mistreat and neglect them.[571]

In July, clearly proud of what Georgina and John Caie have achieved there, the duke invited Hooker to visit them at Campden Hill, and even if they have left for Scotland, 'the Gardener [John Caie], who is a Glasgow lad, and a protégé of Mr Murray, has full instructions to show you and your daughter every attention' and hoped they would enjoy 'the <u>gaiety</u> of the Flower Garden, and the brilliant flow of the <u>floral</u> creation, in which the Dss takes such delight. I start on 5th Aug to Scotland, but I fear there is no hope of your visiting the Highlands next autumn.' By 14 August they had arrived at The Doune, as the duke told Lady Holland, 'I am once more "over the hills and far away" without the slightest accident or even alarm from the dangers of the Rail-road [because] we did not go by Rail-road, but took the old-fashioned mode of travelling with post-horses.'[572] They were soon joined by Georgiana, Rachel and the staff, who did travel by the new train service, and later by Lord William, Landseer and Ellice, for what turned out to be the most beautiful early autumn – five weeks of uninterrupted fine weather.

While no doubt giving fresh instructions to his gardener and the two boys about new plants to look out for, the duke was also in his study writing to Hooker and, among other things, advising him to visit Mr Wells, one of Landseer's major patrons, at his 'beautiful little place at Redleaf … I am sure he cannot experience greater pleasure than in showing you his plants and his fir trees.' Georgina, on the other hand, headed for Glen Feshie and, unhappy with what she found, wrote the following letter to Mackintosh:

Dear Mackintosh,

I have already been to visit Glenfeshie, and grieved over the havoc made amongst the your beautiful trees, none within the Garth, but <u>close to it</u>, and some on the banks of the River <u>in front of my windows</u>, close behind the old woman's cottage – it is a sad pity as it gives a look of desolation to a lovely spot. I should think that the value of the Timber to those <u>who cut it as they do</u> would not be very great. I hope if you come to this country, we shall have the pleasure of seeing you and tho' I may not be able to lodge you in the House, I have hired Inverdruie to accommodate my friends that cannot find room here … Georgina Bedford.

The setting of the huts at Ruigh Aiteachan was clearly of primary importance to Georgina, and, according to one source, in a rare and early act of conservation she seems to have actually bought some of the trees to protect them and limit further desolation: 'G, Dss of Bedford was greatly attached to the place, and so much so that when Mackintosh proposed to sell some of the pine woods, she purchased most of the finest trees, and her mark, consisting of a tablet with her coronet and initials, may still be seen identifying some of them, horrible to relate, many of these badges have been removed by tourist visitors to the glen.'[573]

As late August passed 'in full enjoyment of the most heavenly weather', although he paid one visit to Glen Feshie 'to enjoy a little fresh Highland breeze', the duke soon returned to The Doune and 'remained quietly here in my valley of the Spey'. He wrote to Lady Holland that 'Ellice comes to us occasionally and gives me, as you may imagine, plenty of political gossip,' but even when Ellice hosted a Highland Games at Ruigh Fionntaig, the duke was content with his botanizing and to remain writing letters in his study. In one such, in reply to Lady William, we catch a glimpse of his frame of mind: 'You talk about my "grouse-shooting" on the hills here – all the recreations have been long since over with me. I have not had a gun in my hand for the last four years, and am now only an old and Miserable worn out individual.'

While he also remained in close touch with Forbes about plants that had arrived and the state of the collections, most of the letters were to Hooker, full of observations, questions and comments. In one such, on 14 September, after assuring Hooker that he will not let the Kew project fail, the duke brings up the subject of the Duke of Devonshire's developments at Chatsworth, a subject which came up repeatedly, and the letter indicates the respectful yet highly competitive spirit that existed between the two botanical establishments: 'I have received your letter from Chatsworth. Forbes had preceded you ... by a few days and his report co-insides [*sic*] exactly with yours. It will be a pity if the Duke should have built so very magnificent receptacle for plants, without having duly considered the means of heating it,' an observation that the duke can safely make, of course, in the full knowledge that he and Forbes had 'duly considered' everything and taken pains to install the most up-to-date heating technology in the Woburn kitchen gardens, hot houses, plant stoves and flower houses.[574]

Above all, though, along with ensuring Hooker had the necessary funding to support Gardner's collecting endeavours, the duke was most concerned with the future of Kew and how best to achieve their goals. On 15 October he wrote, 'I would therefore advise you to write a letter to Lord Melbourne (memorials are never attended to) stating fully and clearly the objects you seek, and your claims – Lord John will I am confident, have much pleasure in putting this letter into Lord Melbourne's hands … I will only add that I still fondly cling to the hope of seeing the establishment of Kew Gardens … with yourself, as the fittest and most efficient person, at the head of it.' The same day he told Lady Holland, 'The Dss is up in her favourite Glen – Mr Landseer arrived here 2 days ago, to quit his easel and get some holidays and recruit health and strength after a [busy] Painting Campaign.'[575]

On the morning of 18 October the duke was once again sitting at his desk, pen in hand. Outside the window, the autumn sun shone across the closely cropped grass of the hay meadow stretching away in front, picking out the little church on one side and the trees along the Spey on the other, the dark green of the conifers pierced by brown, red and gold. Beyond that lay Kennapole Hill, with its cairn dedicated to the duchess, and beyond that again the moors and mountains. It was the end of the year, but there was the promise of so much more to come. Georgina had arrived back from Glen Feshie a few days before, and so Landseer and all the family were in the house when suddenly the pen slipped from his fingers as the duke suffered another major stroke. Summoned by the footman who witnessed the moment, Georgina found the duke 'still sitting in his chair, but motionless and speechless; his head sunk upon his bosom, and one side paralysed'. Lifted on to the bed, 'after having uttered a few incoherent words, he fell into a stupor', and died two days later. At that moment Francis, Marquis of Tavistock, became 7th Duke of Bedford, and everything changed: for Georgina, as she faced the uncertainties of a future without the duke; for his three older sons, who now had proprietorial access to a place that had never been their

Edwin Landseer, *John Russell, 6th Duke of Bedford*. The duke, quill in hand, sketched writing at his desk.

home; and for Georgina's children, who became occasional visitors in a place that had been their lifelong home.[576]

After a delay due to bad weather that swept in, the duke's body was taken by steamer to London and then by hearse to Chenies. Although initially Georgina planned to accompany the coffin, the delay persuaded her to make her own way south, leaving The Doune on 3 November. The duke had requested a 'quiet and unostentatious' funeral with 'no pomp, no parade of following carriages', and on the 16th she attended the church service at Chenies, but due to her stepsons' opposition did not attend the procession to the family vault. Something of Georgina's mood can be seen in two letters she wrote to Lord Holland: 'My spirits are so broken and my heart so wounded that I can barely recollect anything,' she wrote in the first, and in the second, 'My loneliness is dreadful … I have not left my room … [and] cannot bear much and have no right or will to make others happy.'[577]

Following the funeral, it seems Georgina left Chenies immediately and set out for Barons Court, where she met up with the Abercorns, Georgiana and Rachel, who had all travelled there from The Doune, and they spent the next four difficult months together, necessarily far removed from the business of the new duke and duchess taking over the Abbey.

Although Georgina trusted that her husband would have taken care of financial arrangements for her and her children, it turned out that to some extent he had not, and there was some confusion about his instructions, which were left for the new duke to interpret. While Georgina had no claims to Woburn Abbey, except for a few personal items and those of her children, or to the contents of the settled estate, she was left Campden Hill and its contents for her lifetime. Endsleigh, however, was more ambiguous. She clearly had some expectation of future access and of her right to some of the custom-built furniture and fittings, but the new duke saw things differently. He considered the house and contents to be an inalienable part of the estate and that, having been given Campden Hill, she had no claim to anything at Endsleigh. Although she was aware that in the last few years of his life, the duke had intended to gift part of Endsleigh to her, an area on the Cornish side of the river opposite Innyfoot that included the fishing cottage, it would appear he failed to make any formal arrangements, and Georgina seems never to have visited the house or grounds at Endsleigh again. She did, however, fight for some of the house contents and when she sought legal advice, as Trethewey tells us, the duke, 'to avoid an embarrassing legal battle', was 'forced to allow [her] to take the plate and whatever else she wanted from Endsleigh'.[578] It was a sad end to the fairytale of a house that had not only brought the shared dream of a young couple to life, but provided, throughout their lives together, a place where such dreams could grow.

During her subsequent trip to Ireland to join her family, Georgina turned her attention to those things she could still control and, perhaps uncertain now about continuing access to The Doune, she contacted her friend Mackintosh telling him that she was hoping to keep it but enquiring about pasture and shooting facilities at Kincraig, where in addition to confirming the lease on the house, she wanted access to a house for her gamekeeper and a 'cow's grass'.

Returning to England in early April, she headed straight for Woburn for the difficult but necessary negotiations with the new duke. James Forbes described her arrival to Hooker: 'The Duke and Duchess came here Tuesday to meet the Dowager Duchess on her return from Ireland ... I saw [her] yesterday, when Her Grace also informed me that the Duke would use all his influence on your behalf, as he had been speaking to her also on the subject. I am grieved to say that Her Grace is very much altered ... I was, however, gratified to hear from her that the present Duke has acted in the most kind and liberal manner towards her.'

Part of the difficulty here was that the new duke and Georgina could not have been more different characters. Blakiston describes him as 'a man of great integrity but not much warmth of heart' and quotes John Cam Hobhouse: 'Lord Tavistock does not like company, but he does not like solitude either. He is a good man, but not a happy man.' Living at Oakley, his 'favourite pursuits were hunting, racing and shooting', and Blakiston notes his 'high sense of duty'; while labouring under 'the disability of ill health', he nevertheless 'drove himself mercilessly' and held others to similar standards.[579]

The difficulty of the task ahead was steadily becoming clear to the duke as he got to grips with the financial state of the estate:

It is marvellous to me how the estate ever can have got so encumbered [with debt]. Our great-grandfather ... was considered the richest man of his day ... he died without debt, leaving my uncle with a minority of 18 or 19 years before him. What *his* fortune must have been therefore, free and unencumbered on coming to the title, can hardly be calculated on – yet after having been in possession only 15 years – having in that time sold the great family estates in Surrey and Hants, he died leaving a debt of more than £200,000, that debt was increased by his successor to more than half a million, and the interest on 'encumbrances' is running at £40,000 a year. I do not know these things are done.[580]

As he pondered he made a list of things he had to do immediately:

I offer Endsleigh to Lord John to live there when he likes – instead of his hiring a Place.

Carriages, Horses, and any little things to the Duchess that she may fancy at the Houses.

To pay the Coachman … if the Dss does not like the expenses.

To each of her sons one of his Father's Horses.

To Charles to live in Bedford Lodge.

One hundred a year to Wrio.

Stables at Woburn for the Duchess's Sons … a Horse at Woburn for each when we are there.

Pensions for the old servants.

Keep all the Labourers and as many of the old Servants as possible.

Edward to remain in Belgrave Square till it is parted with, or the House in Spring Gardens.

And the bills kept coming in: old invoices from Paris, £2,454 for furniture and fittings, as well as '17 cases of plants from Mexico', 'expensive Botanical Works purchased by the late Duke', a similar sum for 'Botanical works,' and 'a magnificent collection of natural history, the same', totalling some £7–8,000.

Although the duke was assured that 'The rent roll of the Estate will increase … in Bedfordshire, Devon and Cambridgeshire, when the buildings and repairs are finished and the new works in the Fens come into full operation,' he wrote to his brother William that there must be a 'gradual diminution of charges, and a wholesale restoration of family affairs – but it will require persevering and long continued rather than severe economy, and forbearance. This is the task that has fallen upon me.' Worried about the level of debt and what further money was owing from unpaid bills, the duke felt 'almost overpowered by the responsibility that is before me', but 'I must try to do my best,' and warned him that 'It will be necessary to shut up the old Abbey for a time.'[581]

According to Trethewey, quoting the 7th Duke, 'On the Duke's death [Georgina] had £649 in her bank account,' and as far as she was concerned, the new duke followed his father's instructions to the letter, giving Georgina '£10,000, £5,500 which her husband had borrowed from her ... and £4,500 as a present'. In addition, Georgina was to receive an allowance for 'the maintenance and education of Rachel', the duke noting he had 'placed the whole of that allowance, viz £600 a year at the disposal of the Duchess ... The Duchess ... repeat[ed] her wish ... that I would make "an exception" in her favour, by paying her income tax ... I have yielded to her desire.'[582] Her husband's recognition of Rachel as a legitimate heir, and the 7th Duke's acceptance, would have come as a considerable relief to Georgina if there was any question about her daughter's paternity, and, on the face of it, the settlement would suggest that there was not.

Although the 7th Duke earnestly ensured that everyone received what was due to them, it is clear that the relationship between the elder sons and Georgina, while superficially cordial, was never going to be comfortable or close, and although no longer a regular visitor, Georgina seems to have been occasionally invited to Woburn over the following decade, where she also made a few appearances at the Woburn theatre. Largely, her life now became centred on Campden Hill and long spells at The Doune, where Alexander took over running the deer forest.

By 1842, however, there were clear tensions between the duke and his brothers and Georgina's other children. The duke wrote to William in March:

As for gratitude or thanks, I never expect them. I know the Duchess's children, except one or two, have no affection for any of us, and that they are glad to take advantages of Woburn, for the sake of their own conveniences and not from any feeling they have towards us. All this is very vexatious ... I wish ... I could place you in my shoes ... you would not manage the estate as well, but you would probably treat the Duchess and her belongings much more as they deserve. Charles has every quality that can make a man disagreeable, therefore it can be no pleasure to have him settled under my Park wall, but I have persuaded myself that it is right ... Recollect how the Duchess's children have been brought up, self – self – self, nothing else, and no good feeling.

It is not possible to know for sure which 'one or two' the duke is referring to, but his relationship with Georgina and the others clearly continued to be a difficult subject, as he explained to William in July: 'The Duchess, I know, exists and flourishes upon grievances … so we can't expect her to be without them now … my writing does no good … I have tried excess of kindness towards the Duchess and her sons, but have now got to the end of my tether in that direction.'

Yet, in spite of the apparently fatal estrangement of the families, two things should be noted. First, from January 1840 onwards, Georgina's children Edward, Charles, Cosmo and Alexander all continued to appear regularly in the Woburn Abbey theatricals and to hunt and shoot at Woburn, and, second, the duke continued to address the chronic gambling debts of both Edward and Alexander – clearing their obligations and urging them to address their addictions before they further disgraced the family – and to engage with Charles's ongoing grievances now that he was no longer in charge at Woburn.[583]

Equally, as far as the gloomy financial predictions were concerned, rather than the Abbey being shut down 'for a time', not only did the duke and duchess go on to host an elaborate honeymoon visit by Victoria and Albert in late July 1841, with Georgina and some of her children sharing the occasion, but Lord William was able to report from Woburn to Lady Holland in December that year, 'as to the style of living here … In point of magnificence it is equal to the old days, and in point of comfort there is an evident improvement … You will be glad to hear the old Abbey has come out of the fire of its purification with more splendour than ever, but pray consider this as a private communication.' It would seem, in the end, that neither interfamily relations nor finances were quite as bad as predicated.

In May 1840, however, a further tragedy struck the whole family out of the blue, when on 5 May old Lord William Russell, the eccentric but well-liked uncle, was murdered at his home in London by his butler, M. Courvoisier. Fearing, it seems, that he was about to be sacked for theft, Courvoisier told the trial: 'My character was gone and I thought murdering him was the only way to cover my fault.' Blakiston sums up what happened next: 'He was convicted and hanged two months later.'[584] The whole event had deeply shaken both family and friends, and on top of this, later that month, 'at the height of his powers and reputation', Landseer suffered a severe nervous breakdown.

The immediate causes remain obscure, but observing that 'his mother's death … in January may not be entirely unconnected,' Ormond writes: 'Lady Holland laid the blame on the fatigue and the mental anxiety of his being on the hanging committee of the Royal Academy,' quoting her: 'and then the shock of the murder of poor Ld William Russell, with whom he was very intimate … He [was] full of terror & horror … it is really very shocking.' The idea has also circulated, however, that his breakdown was due to Georgina refusing an impulsive proposal of marriage by him in spring 1840. If this did happen, it may well have been in reaction to seeing her so desperately unhappy in the aftermath of the duke's death, as he hints in a letter to Count d'Orsay, 'There is an old friend of yours here in the shape of a widow! – Tears and Crape always touch one's heart.' While not impossible, Ormond comments that 'it is by no means certain that he proposed,' but if it did happen, not only did she turn him down, but the moment could not be taken back – it had broken the spell, the illusion that their relationship, whether it was intimate or not, need not affect the wider family. In one of her last surviving letters to Landseer, Georgina tells him, 'I hope you have been able to execute your orders with comfort to yourself. If so, you will be relaxed and happy. I shall be at C. Hill on Monday, I believe,' which suggests that she accepted there now had to be some separation, but hoped they could still remain friends.[585]

We do know, however, that after doctors recommended rest and a change of scene, and Landseer's long-time friend and business manager, Jacob Bell, suggested they take a trip abroad together to find new people and places to paint, Georgina was 'unhappy and anxious enough' about Landseer's state of mind to ask Dr Hammick to visit him before he left and give her a report. Over the next two months, the trip took the pair to Belgium, France, Germany and Switzerland, and back through France, but although there was much to see and he made numerous drawings, the trip did not prove to be a new starting point,

since, as Campbell Lennie put it, in the end the 'Scottish Highlands remained Landseer's only magic place.'[586]

Once back in England, his relationship with Georgina and the children was clearly changed forever, and unable to look to the duke for patronage any longer, Landseer found new patrons and a new family to take him in: Victoria and Albert. From this time on he was busy with commissions at Windsor and Balmoral, but there are no more Bedford or Glen Feshie pictures. Although he remained close to the Abercorns and would still call in at The Doune to see Georgina some summers on his continuing visits to Ardverikie, it is unclear whether they ever visited Glen Feshie again together, and, if they did, it is likely the intimacy and excitement of the early days were gone.

Sadly enough, during this summer at Campden Hill, while she had enjoyed his company, Georgina's neighbour and very old friend Lord Holland, although still active in politics, had been periodically unwell, and this was to be the last time Georgina saw him, since he fell ill again and died on 22 October 1840. By then Georgina, Georgiana, Rachel and the Abercorns had been at The Doune for two months, where they were visited by Lord John, who of the three brothers was the only one to maintain a close relationship with Georgina throughout this period, and whose second wedding she attended the following year. He had spent the early summer with her at Campden Hill, and then visited her in Scotland, no doubt at her urging, staying at The Doune for the first time. It would seem that Georgina remained in Scotland for the rest of the year and became increasingly close to Edward Ellice, who was still leasing Invereshie, and was the 'the only person who stirred up our peaceful thoughts and led them "over the hills and far away"'.[587]

While Georgina, Georgiana and Rachel spent the spring and summer of 1841 at Campden Hill, continuing the usual round of 'Breakfasts', the highlight of everyone's year was the visit that July of the newly married Victoria and Albert to Woburn during their honeymoon. Anna Maria, Duchess of Bedford, was an

After Count Alfred D'Orsay, lithograph by Richard Lane, *Edwin Landseer*, 1843. Titled 'A Royal Academician', D'Orsay's portrait shows Landseer at the height of his career.

old friend of the queen and now a lady-in-waiting, and it seems the queen was looking forward to visiting the Bedfords' home. Arriving on 26 July, after being greeted at the west front of the Abbey by some four thousand 'well-dressed people', the royal couple spent four days at Woburn, during which time they toured the house, Sculpture Gallery, conservatories and hot houses, walked round the covered walkway to the Chinese dairy, and strolled through the pleasure grounds, the plant collections and round the Menagerie. They were also taken round the park to the Thornery and Evergreens, and drove through Woburn village, where they were almost overwhelmed by the excited crowds that 'thronged the way'. There among the illustrious guests to witness it all were both Georgina and Georgiana, the former telling Landseer: 'The Queen was most gracious to everyone, and particularly kind to me. The first day she came up and kissed me – Prince Albert has the most bewitching countenance I ever saw and appears a charming person.'[588]

From Woburn, Georgina left immediately for The Doune, where great uncertainty surrounded the renewal of her lease. Out in India the financial situation of the Grant family had steadily stabilized, and the future was looking a lot more secure since J. P. Grant and both his sons, William and J. P. junior, had been working consistently for the colonial administration and developing financial interests of their own. As a result, the eldest son, William, who had now been given responsibility for running the Rothiemurchus estate, drew up ambitious plans for its revitalization and improvement, and in the summer of 1841 his brother returned to Scotland on furlough, anxious to reoccupy The Doune and carry out as many of William's plans for the estate as possible. Once Georgina arrived at The Doune, she was offered accommodation at the much smaller Inverdruie House a short distance to the north, but fearing perhaps that this would then become a permanent arrangement, she refused, insisting that only The Doune was large enough for her needs. After suddenly losing access to Endsleigh, Georgina was now faced with the prospect of losing somewhere equally important to her and was determined to stand her ground. The fact that J. P. Grant agreed instead to take his family to Inverdruie suggests that, in the event, the brothers were not in a financial position to terminate her lease immediately, and although it briefly lapsed, Georgina was then able to negotiate an agreement that allowed her to use The Doune 'for several months each year', during which time the Grants would occupy Inverdruie. In return, she lost access to the farm, most of the pasture land, and the shooting and fishing rights on the estate; this was not perfect, but for now she had retained The Doune.

Although Georgina was joined by Rachel, Cosmo and Alexander that summer, after the negotiations with the Grants, she and Rachel were obliged to leave Scotland in early September to be in London for the marriage of Lord Henry to Henrietta Stopford at Greenwich. Notably, guests from all sides of the family attended, including Henry's stepbrothers the Duke of Bedford and Lord John, the Duchess of Bedford and William, Marquis of Tavistock, along with Georgina and Henry's brothers and sisters Louisa, Charles, Georgiana and Rachel, and the bride's parents and sisters.[589]

In November Georgina left for a trip through France to Italy accompanied by Georgiana and Rachel. They intended to meet up with Edward Ellice in Naples and then travel to Nice for the rest of the winter, but the trip was delayed in Pisa when Georgiana fell ill, so they did not reach Naples until early December. Illness was not the only problem, however, since, as Trethewey points out, there was clearly considerable tension by now between Georgina and Georgiana, who was thirty-one, still unmarried, worried about her own future, and increasingly out of place in her mother's and young Rachel's ongoing lives. In a letter at this time, Georgina confided to Lord John, 'Every hour I live, I feel the desolation of being alone, no one with whom I can exchange a thought or a word … Georgiana never does speak to me, nor does she show … the slightest interest about myself, [or] my plans … I feel how few are left to love me, and how very few understand me.'

Fortunately, much was to change once they reached Naples where they met up with not just Ellice but also Charles Romilly, an old family friend. Romilly, who was two years older, and Georgiana had grown up together as children of leading Whig families, and he was now a close friend and fellow Marylebone Cricket Club member of her brother Charles. How close the couple had been previously is not clear, but now, brought together in Italy, the two seem immediately to have recognized a fellow soul, both perhaps lonely and a little lost, and within weeks they announced their engagement. The two were married in Naples in early January 1842, the bride given away by Edward Ellice, and the Duke of Bedford sending £220 for her expenses.[590] Given this sudden change in circumstances, the rest of the stay seems to have been a lot more enjoyable, especially as Georgina had her old friend Ellice on hand, and so rather than moving on to Nice, it was not until April that Georgina, Rachel and the Romillys set off for home, travelling via Rome and Paris.

At Woburn the start of 1842 was a very difficult time for James Forbes as he worried about the new duke's intentions towards the botanical collections. Towards the end of January he had part of the answer, as he told Hooker, 'I am very sorry to have to tell you that the Duke of Bedford has come to the resolution of disposing of the Orchidea here, the collection now consists of about 850 plants amongst which are many fine specimens … I very much regret to be obliged to part with them … but his Grace not seeing any flowers on them, says they are not worth keeping, and when they would be in flower, they would not be at the Abbey, so I must dispose of them the best way I can.'

Although nothing further happened for a few months, in July Forbes wrote to Hooker, 'I assure you, however deeply I regret the parting with the collection of Orchidea, I rejoice that His Grace has at last offered them to Kew Gardens,' and a week later was happy to learn that 'Her Majesty has accepted the collection of Orchidea for Kew, where I know they will be appreciated by you … [and will] visit Kew when we can arrange about the best time for the removal of the plants.'[591]

The removal of the orchids started a process which saw almost the entire range of plant collections given away or destroyed over the next ten years or so. The redundant flower houses were demolished and special collections dispersed, until the entire achievement of the 6th Duke, Sinclair and Forbes was effectively eradicated with the sole exception of the kitchen gardens, which remained intact until the Second World War. The pleasure grounds, which had participated in the excitement and wonder of the new horticultural science and technology for two decades, steadily resumed a sleepier existence of manicured lawns, shrubberies and well-tended flower borders. By the time the orchids went to Kew, James Forbes was sixty-nine, knew Woburn like the back of his hand, and was clearly both liked and respected by the new duke and duchess as an individual and a highly skilled gardener. There is no indication that they wished him to retire or leave, or that Forbes was anxious to move on, so he remained at Woburn, seeing out the new era, and dying in post in 1861 at the age of eighty-eight, the same year as the duke himself.

After spending the spring and early summer of 1842 at Campden Hill, in late July Georgina and Rachel, accompanied once again by Lord John and his family, set off for The Doune, where it had been agreed she could stay until November even though her lease had lapsed. (She lived with this yearly negotiation until August 1844, when J. P. Grant junior returned to India. It soon became clear, however, that the Grants were not going to be able to return and use the house, and a new annual arrangement was made later that year by which Georgina regained the tenancy, annual occupancy from August to December, some pasture and the shooting. In the end, further financial problems for William Grant would mean that this arrangement was made permanent in 1846.) This particular year, Georgina stayed until late November and returned to London via Edinburgh and Howick, where she visited her old friend Lord Grey.

Landseer visited again this year, but soon moved on to join the Abercorns at Ardverikie, 'where he draws the large chalk cartoons on the walls of the lodge'; from there he went to Black Mount to visit another new patron, the Marquis of Breadalbane.[592] It seems likely, however, since Landseer was a famously social being, that from at least 1835 he had spent more and more time with the Abercorns as a key member of a regular crowd of young people, particularly young men, who gathered at Ardverikie every year to stalk deer, fish, roam the moors and participate in the lively social life hosted by James and Louisa; for Landseer, it had become, perhaps, a welcome break from the increasingly quiet and largely older company at The Doune.

The issue of the long-term future of The Doune rumbled on for several more years, and in June 1843 J. P. Grant junior and his family, who had been visiting his sister Elizabeth and her husband, Colonel Smith, at Baltiboys House, Co. Wicklow, left Ireland to return to Scotland. Elizabeth wrote at the time, 'Their plan is to see as much of Scotland as they can on their way to The Doune, which they must leave for Inverdruie by the 1st of August, as that vile Duchess of Bedford has this year The Doune again.' Clearly, those of the Grant family who were not far away in India were starting to resent Georgina's presence, and also, perhaps, the continuing circumstances which made her presence necessary to the upkeep of the estate. Certainly, the 'Highland Lady' is seldom as direct and harsh in her descriptions of people, and what she goes on to say perhaps explains her language: 'I should so love a few summer months there … we mountain children never lose the love of fatherland … our hearts turn ever to our heathery hills, the pine forests, the wild burn, the lonely loch, and the deep feudal love of our people. "Wherever we wander, wherever we rove, the hills of the highlands for ever we love."'[593]

Thus another autumn passed with Georgina and Rachel at The Doune, and the Grants – just up the road at Inverdruie House – were ready to move back into The Doune when she left in late October. After arriving back at Campden Hill in November, Georgina made plans for another trip to the Continent, once again staying in Paris in December and leaving for 'the Italian States', and then on to Nice. Reaching Nice in February 1844, Georgina and Rachel stayed until April, and while they were there news came of another impending wedding when the engagement of 'Captain Francis Russell, R.N.' to Elizabeth Peyton was announced. No doubt, Georgina was hoping very much the news meant that Frank would finally settle down and put his wild naval days behind him. The couple were duly married at St George's Hanover Square a few months later.[594]

Spending the London season at Campden Hill, Georgina busied herself with organizing a series of four 'Fêtes' – one a week through July – designed to celebrate Rachel's eighteenth birthday. While it is hard to believe that Georgina actually wanted Rachel to leave her, finding a potential suitor was no doubt on her mother's mind, and that meant she needed to be introduced to London society – hence the series of gatherings of London's young people among the lawns and flower beds of Campden Hill. In the event, it would seem that Rachel was not in any hurry to leave or marry, and after remaining with her mother until she died, it was to be another three years before Rachel married at the age of thirty.

Following the social season, the two left for The Doune, where they found that everything was about to change once again. J. P. Grant junior's furlough ended in August, at which point the family left for India, leaving The Doune to Georgina with a substantially larger area of pasture put at her disposal, largely for the ponies, and control of the Rothiemurchus shooting, something her sons, particularly Cosmo and Alexander, had long been hoping for. Although it was not certain at the time, the Grants' financial situation continued to deteriorate, and this meant that these arrangements were to stay in place for the next six years. At this time the Rothiemurchus estate was run for the Grants by Mr Caw, an interesting if slightly mysterious individual. He was first mentioned by Elizabeth Grant in 1817 when the Grants were in Edinburgh: 'My father and his new, very queer, clerk, Mr Caw, worked away in their law chambers till my father went up to London late in the spring.' While he ran J. P. Grant senior's law office in Edinburgh, Caw also seems to have steadily become central to the family's life, running their business affairs, and became fiercely protective of the girls, always allowing his displeasure to show if he did not approve of a potential suitor. He seems never to have married, but by 1825 he had also taken up the post of 'bookkeeper' at The Doune, and when the Grants left for India, they were joined by 'Mr Caw, that clever, good hearted oddity, who was going with us to India in the hope of being provided for, as his long, unwearied services deserved'.[595] Returning to England, he was at Rothiemurchus when J. P. junior returned on furlough in 1842, but his friendship with Georgina and Rachel suggests that they had known him well for some time. During this latter period Rachel became particularly attached to him, going to him for advice about her various projects, visiting him at Inverdruie, and Caw evidently became an important part of Georgina and Rachel's world at The Doune.

This year seems to have been a particularly quiet one at The Doune, with only Landseer visiting on his way to Taymouth Castle where he was completing the commissions for the Marquis of Breadalbane. Part of the reason there were so few

Edwin Landseer, *Georgina at The Doune*, 1841. This tender image was one of a last series Landseer made of Georgina following the duke's death and their relationship became steadily more distant. Her lease at The Doune continued until the year before she died, and in spite of growing ill health, it and Glen Feshie remained at the centre of her life.

visitors was the terrible weather, a prolonged period of cold and rain that kept everybody indoors and limited both travel and the sporting activities. By October, the weather had further deteriorated with thick snow and severe flooding, bad enough to take out a number of bridges and disrupt ferry crossings of the Spey.

Georgina and Rachel finally made it back to Campden Hill by the beginning of December, and made plans to travel abroad again to escape more winter weather. On his way to visit them, Landseer fell from his horse at full gallop, suffering another serious head injury. It seems Georgina immediately cancelled her plans and looked after him at Campden Hill, but while he initially seemed to recover, she was very aware that his mental health appeared to be just as fragile as his physical condition.[596]

Since they were in England over the Christmas and New Year period for the first time in a number of years, Georgina and Rachel were among the guests at the large gathering at Woburn, where they were also joined by Edward and William. The 'Woburn theatre' playbills suggest that this was a rare and successful family gathering that may also have caught something of the fun and festiveness of the old days when the whole family, and all generations, had been involved. Performers listed for a series of charades and comic pieces for New Year 1845 included 'the Dowager Duchess of Bedford', Rachel and Edward, with Rachel not only performing but also acting as stage manager. While this marked the last time Georgina would perform at Woburn, Rachel and some of the boys continued to appear, particularly in the years immediately after their mother's death.

Following their time at Woburn, Georgina and Rachel settled once again into the life of the London social season, preparing the house and gardens at Campden Hill for the July fetes, which this year seem to have been as successful as ever. Another neighbour, from a few doors down at Loudon Lodge, has left us a rare description of them. Writing to his friend Ralph Sneyd, Henry William Vincent reports, 'By the bye, the Duchess of Bedford had one of the prettiest little Balls I ever saw the other night. She seemed to have permitted none but the prettiest girls in London to come there.'[597] For Georgina, the point of inviting 'the prettiest girls' in London was the best way of ensuring that the cream of eligible young men would also attend, no doubt with Rachel's future in mind.

Once in Scotland again, Georgina immediately set about securing more control over her life there and ensuring that it could not, once again, be turned upside down by the uncertain plans of the Grant brothers. To this end she took the tack for seven years on Mackintosh's Dalnavert farm, becoming tacksman of land that was contiguous with the southern boundary of Rotheimurchus, and which came with 'the exclusive right to the game and shooting over said farmlands' from meadows by the Spey right up into the eastern side of the Cairngorms beside Loch Einich. At The Doune, meanwhile, they would have heard news from Mr Caw of the planned visit to Rothiemurchus by Elizabeth Grant and her husband, Colonel Smith, although at this point the exact date was still uncertain; it was likely to be an interesting occasion, since up to now Georgina had been dealing only with Grant's brothers and sister Jane, and had not seen the formidable Elizabeth for some thirty years.

In November, when Georgina and Rachel were in Brighton where Louisa was reaching the end of her eighth pregnancy, news reached them of Lady Holland's death, and with her passed a constant presence in Georgina's world in London and Woburn since her marriage. The death of Lady Holland, largely a close and caring friend but occasionally capricious and critical, brought one more element of Georgina's life with the duke to an end. Lady Holland had been the centre of controversy since the day she met Lord Holland and little changed when she died, when it was discovered that 'instead of leaving her property to her children, she left it to Lord John Russell … her particular favourite.'[598] Yet for all this, the year ended on a rather more joyful note when Louisa gave birth to her third son, George, on 17 December.

The summer of 1846 was marked by another death in the family when Lord William Russell died in July. Long separated from Bessy and drifting between diplomatic posts, William's life had been increasingly disconnected from the family since the death of his uncle old Lord William, the two of them leading similarly aimless peripatetic lives across Europe. William died in Genoa, his son Hastings doing his best to look after him, while Bessy lived on for another twenty-eight years, just long enough to see her son Hastings succeed as 9th Duke of Bedford in 1872. By a strange coincidence, William died on the same day that his brother John reached the zenith of his political career, finally becoming prime minister.

Due to Lord William's death, Georgina and Rachel did not travel up to Scotland until early August, by which time Elizabeth Grant, with her husband, two daughters and son, had been at Inverdruie for about a week, and she has left a detailed account of their stay. On 20 July Grant had arrived at the Rothiemurchus ferry: 'The rain fell in torrents. We entered the boat and were rowed silently across, and thus I returned to Rothiemurchus.' After visiting Inverdruie, they 'walked direct to The Doune, went all over the house … explained every picture to [the children], wandered over the hill on the lawn which was once a shrubbery.' From there they walked to Loch an Eilein, 'till we reached the point whence I always fancied the scene looked best – whence Mr Landseer has taken his celebrated painting, and whence an equally fine artist, of nature's own making, I believe, took one of his prettiest sketches. All my Uncle's framed drawings left at The Doune have been hung in the best lights by Mr Landseer, who greatly admires them.' On the wider estate, she notes, 'Almost all that has been done to the land is improvement … But the people have stood still, no schools, no doctor, an inferior clergyman, the want of a resident landlord very plainly to be seen.' A few days later they had 'spent our morning at Kinrara' and 'walked along the banks a mile to the Duchess [of Gordon's] grave, lost with its large obelisk in a clump of very fine evergreens extended to four times the original size by the good taste of her successor … I don't know why but there is not a spot in the world dearer to me than Kinrara: the mirth there in my childish days … and to find it desolate, the furniture faded, the books and pictures gone, yards empty, and the house let with the garden and shooting to half a dozen English Indians who come down there for six weeks in the Autumn.'

At The Doune, Grant writes far more sympathetically of Georgina, noting 'preparations were going forward for her Grace … there could not be a better tenant for she spends much upon the place and circulates large sums among the people, many of whom she employs – to many she is very charitable – to all very kind. There is a good feeling in all she does.' She was, perhaps, impressed by the respect the Bedfords showed to her family: 'Within, the old pictures remain in their old places excepting some of the family portraits which she has *framed* and promoted to the walls of the principal rooms … much comfort has been added in many ways; and among her many handsome chairs, sofas and ottomans, still stands the little low backed seat which was my grandfather's and then my father's. The Duke always used it.'

On Georgina and Rachel's arrival at The Doune, they almost immediately left for Glen Feshie, where Landseer joined them from Gordon Castle. Georgina certainly knew the visitors were there, but spent the next two weeks at the huts before returning to The Doune and reaching out to Inverdruie. Grant records that they 'walked to call on the Duchess who sent us three brace of grouse last night'. Two days later, 'The Colonel and I went to The Doune. The Duchess having gone to Glenfeshie and all else being out, we went in to look at the dear old library, now only a pretty drawing room … It has been new papered since the other day; more of the old pictures have been reframed and hung upon the walls.'

As when her sister Jane had visited:

The people generally had a great wish both to see us all and shew themselves … to us. They asked permission to meet and dance in the barn here … a few wore highland dress, smart handsome lads … attired magnificently – buckles in their shoes, fringe to their garters, velvet jackets, silver brooches, belts ornamented, handsome dirks, purses, etc. – nothing could be more beautiful; there were but some half dozen accoutred, pets of the Duchess's; the expense of this superior style is so great few can afford the outlay … My girls … caught up the Strathspey style after a reel or two and gave much satisfaction to their partners … The Colonel danced with the cook … it was a very merry night.

Once the ice had been broken, Georgina and Elizabeth seem to have got on very well. After church, the former 'called for me to wait for her a moment, when she came up all kindness, introduced her family, and then walked on with us to Inverdruie; sat a while to make acquaintance with Colonel Smith and then … we walked back with her.' Grant gives us a very rare glimpse of the nature of Georgina and Rachel's relationship, describing Georgina as

exceedingly agreeable, very much softened since her Duke's death … very unwilling to annoy Lady Rachel [now twenty] who don't approve of all her mother's former doings. She is a very interesting girl and she and Annie took so much to one another, talking of musical duets and pony rides here and there that there seemed mutual regret at the acquaintance being so soon to end. 'I hear', said the Duchess to me, 'that you are bringing up your girls charmingly. Accomplish them as you like but don't make fine ladies of them – that's a deplorable life, useless and miserable etc.' I told her there was no fear.

Finally, 'we talked over all the clans of the Highlands, all their southern allies, all that had happened since the last day I saw her when she carried off my Jacobite airs to sing them at Invereschie … She asked us to dine, asked the girls to an hour or two of music and luncheon, in short is all kindness.' Before the visitors left, 'The Duchess has just sent over five brace of grouse for my mother, and Lady Rachel has sent with them a pretty note of regret at our departure.'[599] Perhaps too, given how well this reunion had gone, Georgina regretted not having had a closer relationship with Elizabeth.

Before visiting Glen Feshie, Landseer had been on his usual Highland tour that summer, spending much of it at Gordon Castle and then Ardverikie. The fact that Elizabeth Grant does not mention Landseer may suggest that she too did not 'approve of all [Georgina's] former doings', or it could be that he did not stay long in Glen Feshie or visit The Doune but soon moved on to Ardverikie. Although Landseer's career continued to thrive, it had been a challenging year for the artist since he had faced unprecedented criticism of his work; suddenly, it seemed, the precocious talent and artistic judgement which had driven his entire life and allowed him to thrive were being questioned. Of this criticism, perhaps none came harder than that of John Ruskin, an early and enthusiastic supporter of the painter, who nevertheless reacted with horror to Landseer's *The Otter Speared, Portrait of the Earl of Aberdeen's Otter Hounds* (1842). In volume 2 of his *Modern Painters* (1846), Ruskin wrote, 'I would have Mr. Landseer, before he gives us any more writhing otters, or yelping packs, reflect whether that which is best worthy of contemplation in a hound be its ferocity, or an otter its agony, or in a human being its victory … over a poor little fish-catching creature, a foot long.'[600] It was a devastating comment on a painting that left critics and viewers alike struggling to find any hint of the much vaunted 'nobility' of the hunt, and contemplating a disturbing and morbid obsession with the death of wild creatures.

January 1847 saw Charles, Cosmo and Rachel making appearances at the Woburn Abbey theatre, where events were now held in the 'Queen's Drawing Room', but the playbill notes that the cast appeared in 'entirely Old Scenery, Dresses, and Decorations', suggesting that some of the excitement and enthusiasm had gone out of the proceedings now that Landseer was no longer artistic director. Nevertheless, the same cannot be said for the entertainments at Campden Hill that spring, which included 'a delightful *soirée dansante* on Monday ... A limited yet brilliant circle of the aristocracy assembled, and the festivity of the night was prolonged to an advanced hour.' This was followed in July by the usual weekly fetes, or 'Breakfasts' as the family tended to refer to them.[601]

By the end of July, Georgina and Rachel had arrived at The Doune for a five-month stay, and the great excitement this year was the arrival at Ardverikie of Queen Victoria and Prince Albert. They had visited Scotland twice before, in 1842 and 1844, but this year, as Elizabeth Grant tells us, the queen 'is going to Laggan to Lord Abercorn's Lodge with all her Court for the shooting season, and before that is to yacht round her islands – can't sit still, poor restless creature'. Once at Laggan, Grant notes that 'The Duchess of Bedford went up to Ardverikie to receive her, and then returned to The Doune, it is said to prepare for a royal visit.'[602] The royal visit to The Doune seems not to have happened or passed unrecorded, but it was this year, having also fallen under the spell of the Highlands, that the royal couple took their first lease on Balmoral before buying the property in 1852. Landseer had also joined the party at Ardverikie, painting *Queen Victoria Sketching at Loch Laggan* before going on to visit The Doune and Gordon Castle.

At The Doune, it became clear by the end of their stay that, rather than spending all her time with her mother, Rachel had created a place for herself, making friends of her own and pursuing her own interests (Colour Plate 42). Just before they left, she wrote the following letter to Mr Caw at Inverdruie:

I had quite set my heart on paying you a farewell visit, and I have a disagreeable cold which has taken away all my voice, so like a prudent young lady, I have stayed at home. I must beg you accept my best wishes for your health and happiness, and I hope you won't forget me before next summer. I shall be 'thinking long' till I see the Highland Hills and the dear Highland People again. I have copied the enclosed and I think the young lady was very determined about her Jamie Johnstone.

I shall come back Rachel Russell next year; Mind you watch us drive by your door tomorrow morning about ten o'clock –

Goodbye dear Sir, Yours very sincerely, Rachel Evelyn Russell

The letter indicates that Rachel had formed a friendship with Caw similar perhaps to that she had with Dr Thomson, her 'dear old doctor', and also suggests that one of the things she had been discussing with Caw was her future marriage. Whatever the 'young lady's' feelings had been for Jamie Johnstone, she seems at pains to tell Caw that she will not be marrying any time soon, in spite of all her mother's efforts in London. A further glimpse of Rachel's visit to Rothiemurchus this year is provided by the *Inverness Courier*, which reported after she had left, 'Lady Rachel, with unceasing kindness, spared neither personal fatigue nor money in her efforts to lessen the pressures of poverty and disease among the poor families – visiting the bedridden, relieving their wants and administering with her own hands the remedy deemed most efficacious. In the cause of education she takes a deep interest, and, by her ladyship's active exertions, it is hoped ere long that a school may be established in the district for the young of her own sex.' Once back at Campden Hill, they were joined by Alexander and his wife, who had 'just returned from Canada, where his Lordship has been on duty with his regiment, the Rifle Brigade'.[603]

In January 1848 Georgina and Rachel were in Brighton once again to visit the Abercorns and to meet their new daughter, Albertha, who had been born the year before. Returning to Campden Hill, although there were no recorded gatherings at the house that year, one event stands out: Georgina, Rachel and a party of friends paid a visit to the 'Qiying' or 'Keying', the first Chinese junk to visit Europe, which was causing quite a stir in London when it arrived at Blackwall in London in April after visiting New York.[604]

In Scotland that summer, Georgina discovered that her tenancy at The Doune was likely to be safe for the foreseeable future as news arrived that the Grants were again declared bankrupt. In January Elizabeth Grant had given a hint of the imminent financial catastrophe involving her father's and brothers' activities in the Union Bank of Calcutta that was about to envelop her family when she wrote, 'Pray heaven the Calcutta National Bank may be able to meet its obligations. I have had two packets from Jane grieving over the folly of my father and my brothers, the extent of whose ruin was not fully known to themselves when they first announced their crash.'

By February the extent of the disaster was becoming clear as Mr Caw, who had invested his savings in the bank on the Grants' advice, tells Elizabeth that he is 'annoyed by advances made to John and William which they cannot fully repay at present'. She concludes, 'William has certainly been speculating disastrously, though he will not own it.' By May, the losses of those she knew personally were revealed – her sister Jane's 'loss is seven thousand pounds and Mr Caw's five thousand pounds', 'half his hard earnings' – and Elizabeth discovers that her brother William 'appropriated twenty-thousand pounds of the [bank's] funds of which there is no account'. Caw was absolutely furious with the Grants, believing they had lied to him. As the collapse was ongoing, William, through the Rothie trustees, had been trying desperately to raise money by selling trees, with the result that by August 1848 there were 'few trees fit for the axe in that once fine forest'. Elizabeth concluded, 'The ruin is complete, fortune, character, station.' In the event, William returned from India in September 'penniless' and with debts of 72,000 pounds and 'with nothing to show for it'.

For Georgina, these misfortunes finally gave her a degree of security, since the Grants' financial problems meant that they could not afford to take back the Rothiemuirchus estate, and she was able to remain the tenant at The Doune until her death. This year, after a busy season, they stayed until December. Indeed, her confidence about future access to The Doune is reflected in a letter from William Grant to his brother following Georgina's death: 'of course you know that the Dss of Bedford is dead. Did I tell you that she mentioned to James Craig, her wish, in case anything happened to her, that the Abercorns might have the offer of The Doune.'[605]

Secure in her tenancy, it was this year that Georgina appointed William Collie, a local man from Glen Feshie, as 'her forester, and being then only 19 years and six months old, was the youngest man ever known to get charge of a deer forest'. Collie reports that 'Ann Rose [his future wife] was staying at the Duchess' gardener's house … The Duchess was very fond of her, and was delighted when she heard that her young forester was making love to her favourite.' Indeed, Georgina was fond enough of the girl to send 'from Venice a very pretty and costly trousseau to her Rosie, wishing us both all manner of happiness', when the couple married in 1852. It is also clear that Georgina was very fond of other individuals who made up her community at Ruigh Aiteachan. In another example, we hear of a 'a particularly fine watercolour' by Landseer which 'shows an old Highland woman, in a big black bonnet and an old stalker's tweed jacket miles too big for her. She clutches a long-handled spade,' and 'written at the bottom in Landseer's writing': 'Sarah. E.L. Feshie Cottage … sketched for the Dss of B'. Sarah was almost certainly one of the women Georgina hired to help with the gardens and other jobs at the huts, probably over an extended period of time, and it is telling that she should have wanted Landseer to make a sketch of her.

Soon after their departure from The Doune, the following note appeared in the *Inverness Courier*. Written in the inevitably flowery prose, it nevertheless indicates something of what Georgina's and Rachel's activities around Rothiemurchus meant to the local population:

During the stay in The Doune of those noble ladies, much of their time was occupied in visiting the cottages of the poor … endeavouring to alleviate the sufferings of the afflicted, and in clothing and feeding the destitute. So sensible were the people of the district of her Grace's and Lady Rachel's kindness to them and their poor neighbours … that they spontaneously assembled, to the number of 150, on the first morning of the New Year, in front of The Doune, to salute her Grace and Ladyship … A select body of young men afterwards proceeded to the lawn, where, during the remainder of the day, they did their best to amuse, by playing games of the country.

This year, after leaving The Doune, instead of returning straight to Campden Hill, Georgina and Rachel travelled to Woburn Abbey, where they remained until late January. While there, both took part in the theatricals: Georgina as Queen Elizabeth in 'Our Virgin Queen' and Rachel playing multiple roles in two productions, billed in the latter as 'Mlle Rachelini'.[606]

With the exception of the three July fetes at Campden Hill, 1849 was a noticeably quiet year, and after an uneventful trip to Scotland, Georgina and Rachel made their way to Torquay for the winter. The reason for this could be Georgina's health – she 'frequently suffered from chest infections' – and although due to leave by the start of February 1850, they are reported as 'prolonging their residence at Torquay'. The late summer and autumn saw them once more at The Doune, where they were visited by Landseer on his way to pay his first visit to Balmoral. Although they were joined by Alexander and his wife, things were a little different at Rothiemurchus that summer. It seems that Mr Caw had given up his post and returned to Edinburgh, to where Rachel writes to him in October, no doubt having missed his company: 'Dear Mr Caw, I have great pleasure in writing to you for I shall be very glad to hear how you are and that you have not forgotten me, and also Mama desires me to say with her kind remembrances, that by the mail tonight some Grouse will begin their journey to you and we hope they are good.'[607]

The great excitement in London during the spring of 1851 focused on the preparations for the Great Exhibition, the celebration of culture, trade, industry and the British colonial empire that was due to open at the Crystal Palace on 1 May. Although none of the family is recorded as attending, it is hard to believe that the duke, had he still been alive, would not have visited as often as he could. With its exhibits from around the world and its celebration of new ideas and new technologies, the Great Exhibition in some ways represented the culmination of that age of enquiry and discovery which had been such a part of his life, and the end of that relative innocence, or naivety, that gave it such a rosy glow before the true impact of colonialism on those subjected to it, and of industrialization on both people and the natural world, became clear.

In Scotland that summer, as William Collie remembered: 'In 1851 I gave even more satisfaction to the Duchess and her sons, the Lords Russell, than in the preceding year,' and just how much satisfaction he was able to give is summed up in the *Inverness Courier* in November: 'Lord and Lady Alexander Russell left The Doune on the 30th inst, after a successful campaign for three months by his lordship in the deer forest.' The article continues:

> her Grace … was particularly attentive to the aged and infirm, as also affording employment to a number of work people in the neighbourhood … Previous to her grace's starting for the south, an excellent dinner was given to about sixty people and children, when blankets and warm clothing for the winter were liberally distributed among them … Lady Russell, who might be seen daily, basket in hand, along with some of her friends, paying domiciliary visits to her poorer neighbours … gave a tea party to about forty children on the green, [and] distributed to them, after an amusing dance, little books suited to their capacity, and left a number more to be given … as prizes to the best scholars at the next examination of the school.

Their visit was, however, cut slightly short this year, as they left in mid-October to join the Abercorns at one final marriage: that of Cosmo, now thirty-four, to Annie Norbury.[608] Although he featured in a large number of Landseer's portraits of the family and Cosmo was clearly a popular boy, his voice is scarcely heard in the record and few people wrote about him at the time, except to note his fragile health. One cheerful anecdote about him, however, is recorded from the year he got married by his nephew, Lord Arthur Russell: 'My uncle Cosmo was a clever wag, and an extraordinarily cool fellow. Dining with his mother, at Campden Hill, he frightened us all by saying aloud, across the table: "I was so sorry to see that Lady Jocelyn has met with an accident: the papers this morning say she broke her fan and injured her bottom". The ladies looked very uncomfortable, nobody laughed and he went on talking. The Lady Jocleyn was a Channel Island screw steamer, and she had been injured by a collision in the manner the morning papers correctly reported.'[609]

Georgina and Rachel spent the first three months of 1852 in Brighton with the Abercorns once more before returning to Campden Hill, where they remained for the London season. One of the highlights this year was the Duke of Devonshire's 'sumptuous *dejeuner a la forchette* ... at the Burlington Villa, Chiswick, after his grace's guests had attended the first horticultural fête', where Georgina, Rachel and the Abercorns were part of the 'select party' of floral and horticultural enthusiasts. By the beginning of August, Georgina and Rachel arrived at The Doune for what turned out to be Georgina's last visit to Scotland. Although they stayed until the end of October, it seems that she was not in good health and by 1 December they had travelled on to Nice, losing no time to escape the oncoming winter.

Some superficial details of their stay in Scotland that summer were recorded by the *Inverness Courier*: 'The Duchess and the ladies busied themselves ... in providing labour for the industrious by the formation of walks, &c., and in distributing warm clothing among the poor ... Her Grace ... commenced the building of a new dwelling house for a teacher ... [which], with the excellent school-house erected last year, will furnish the parish with very suitable school accommodation.' But it is clear that this account does not tell us what was really going on; this is revealed by Trethewey, quoting from a letter Georgina wrote to Lord John when she first arrived at The Doune in August. From the start of the visit, something was very different: 'I cannot command the cheerful feelings I have always (with one sad exception) felt here ... I must pray, and hope that the Almighty, will allow us all to meet here next year,' and one senses that she has already accepted this may be unlikely. Seen in this light, Georgina's flurry of activity reported by the *Courier* appears as a kind of final gesture, and that rather than spending her time in Glen Feshie, she had sought to engage with the people who had made up the community which, in a sense, had taken her and her husband in.

In Nice they were soon joined by the Abercorns, and so both Louisa and Rachel were with Georgina when she died following a severe bout of influenza on 23 February 1853. Although in her will, signed 1849, she states that 'I desire to be buried at Chenies,' there was to be no return home for her; she either changed her mind or her family had reason to believe that the duke would not approve, and

This rare photograph, 'Strathspey from Kinrara Rock', c.1870, gives us a glimpse of The Doune and Strathspey some thirty years after the Bedfords had been there.

instead she was quietly buried at the Anglican church in Nice, where there is a record of her death. The grave site itself has been lost in subsequent reorganizations of the churchyard. In a letter to his friend Landseer, C. S. Leslie, who was in Nice at the time, described the end: 'She died composed and calm with her children that are here with her. Lady Rachel suffers most acutely.'[610]

Most of Georgina's will, drawn up by the solicitor William Nicholson, was straightforward: bequests of pictures, portraits, furniture, ornaments and jewellery to her daughters, her surviving sisters, the duke, Lord John and Landseer from among her belongings at The Doune and Campden Hill, and small bequests to long-serving staff, in particular to Mlle Migneron, Rachel's governess and travelling companion, 'as a testimony to my regard and respect'. Everything else was to be divided equally as thought best. Yet it soon became clear that parts of the will did not match some of the family's expectations, leading to some confusion for her active executors, Lord Wriothesley and Edward Ellice junior. On 4 March Wriothelsey wrote to Ellice, 'I cannot but fear that she [Georgina] has said more than she has written. Much that she told me not only does not appear, but is inconsistent with the Will – Poor Rachel is much to be pitied. Perhaps when we have ascertained fully how matters stand, you would be so kind as to write and explain fully her position. From me it might seem unkind, and a mere dry letter of business is grating – especially to a girl, and yet her eyes must be opened and if possible before she returns to Campden Hill.' To which Ellice replied the same day, 'I will not dwell upon the painful secret which leads thus to our correspondence … We are placed in a delicate and difficult position with regard to the trust imposed upon us both in the Will that has been produced by Mr Nicholson … Rachel I understand writes from Nice apparently in ignorance of the arrangement that we are now made aware of.'

He went on say that it was imperative that they take all steps to ascertain 'whether any alteration has been made in the Will of which Mr Nicholson has sent us a copy, or whether any subsequent one has been substituted for it'. They needed to check Campden Hill, since 'it would be cruel to you and your sisters in Nice to leave them in suspense upon the subject, and it is right that Edward who may be ordered to sea at any hour, should know anything which has been the final disposition of their mother.'

He added that, after the search was made, 'a letter should then be written to Nice, in order that your sisters may know exactly the state of the case before Lady Rachel returns home.' We still do not know what the 'secret' or 'the arrangement' was, and neither is it clear what the significance of alterations to the will might have been, but in the light the fact that Rachel was 'shocked' when she was finally told, it may have been about the lack of a financial settlement for her.[611] In the event, it fell to the duke to decide how to proceed, and perhaps because Rachel was one of the 'one or two' of the duchess's children that the 7th Duke actually liked, a financial settlement was made and her position in the family remained unchanged.

Reporting Georgina's death, the English newspapers focused on her marriage, her children, and on the role of Campden Hill in the fashionable world; only the

Scottish newspapers mentioned her mother or her time in Scotland. The obituary in the *Stirling Observer*, for example, noted:

> The fifth and youngest daughter of Alexander, 4th Duke of Gordon, by his Duchess the famous Jane Maxwell, Lady Georgina, the lady now deceased … was a lady of great simplicity of manners, and to the last retained a strong attachment to Highland customs. She regularly visited every autumn her beautiful Highland retreat at The Doune of Rothiemurchus, on the Spey, and there, following the custom now occasionally adopted by royalty, not infrequently retired to a shealing on a solitary glen or hillside, and would live there for days with scarcely an attendant.

On his mother's death it would seem that Wriothesley was pushing to take on the lease of The Doune for himself and his family, but Georgina's lawer William Nicholson, in a letter to Ellice, was 'convinced this is a mistake'. He also said there appeared to be 'some misunderstanding as to the removal of furniture from Glenfeshie', since they had discovered that Wriothesley's son had gone up to claim it. All of which seems to suggest that no prior discussions had taken place about the distribution of assets in Scotland: a sad and confused end to the whole Highland adventure.

In London things moved rapidly. By 5 July the duke had ordered the sale of Campden Hill, and the following announcement appeared: 'to the world of fashion the exquisite pictures, plate and furniture of her Grace … [including] pictures by Sir Edwin Landseer, Sir George Haytor, David Roberts, the late David Wilkie, Nasmyth, Bonnington, and other celebrities – magnificent silver-gilt plate, – rare china, including old Sèvres, Dresden, Berlin, Chelsea, and Oriental – furniture of the finest designs and the richest materials – curious specimens of old French marqueterie [sic], a select English and foreign library, in superb bindings, in short, objects so numerous as to occupy a week in the disposal of them.'[612]

Everything was soon sold or dispersed and – materially at least – it seems that Georgina, such a large presence in life, slipped away almost without trace. In many ways she was an outsider, and although she never wrote about or seems to have made an issue of it, her heartfelt plea to Elizabeth Grant to avoid making 'fine ladies' of her daughters alerts us to what appears to have been one of the dominant themes of her life: her determination to free herself and her daughters from the 'deplorable … useless and miserable' existence to which women were routinely condemned. Her words seem to sum up years of frustration, and there is a blunt clarity about them that suggests this issue had long been on her mind. With hindsight, we can perhaps identify here one of the key motives that lay behind the community she sought to create in Glen Feshie.

Yet, if this side of Georgina's life has been lost to sight, at Woburn, at Endsleigh and in Badenoch today her legacy is still very much alive. At Woburn Abbey, Georgina's great achievement as duchess was to humanize the formality of the dukedom, creating a family home where none had existed for so long, a place for herself, and a joint legacy with the duke of the grandest house, parkland and grounds ever to exist at the Abbey and of Woburn as a serious centre for scientific horticulture and botany, all of which was proudly displayed to Victoria and Albert by the 7th Duke. This legacy has survived and is still drawn on at Woburn, where ideas and designs from this period form the basis for much of the restoration work, both indoors and out, that is being undertaken today.

At Endsleigh, by building a new house she and the duke created something which not only broke with the Russell family traditions, but also drew on an entirely new source of inspiration: the picturesque landscapes of the distant Highlands of Scotland, which was unique at the time. The house they built, and the wider setting they created for it, combined to turn a remote valley in Devonshire into an enduringly special, even magical, place which, over two hundred years after it was created, still has the capacity to surprise, intrigue and captivate visitors; visits to Endsleigh were the direct inspiration for both Trethewey's pioneering biography of Georgina and, some years later, this investigation of her life with the duke.

At Invereshie, The Doune and in Glen Feshie, their legacy is more complex since their presence in Badenoch had ramifications beyond the impact on them personally. It was also part of a process that established the deer forests, and the culture that has grown up around them, as the dominant model of land use across large areas of Scotland – a model and a culture that remain contentious to this day. Clearly, this would not have happened if it was not economically beneficial to the landowners, but it came at a price to local communities which is still evident. Ironically, while Georgina's occupation of the sites at Ruigh Fionntaig and Ruigh Aiteachan found a seemingly permanent place for her Romantic vision of life in the Highlands as it was picked up by like-minded royalty and others, it was also part of the process which helped to erase that way of life and relegate it to history. Places such as Glenfiddich and Glen Feshie, while they had evolved as locations for summer grazing, had always been visited for hunting, and it is impossible to know if the Bedfords would have taken the leases, and spent as much time in Scotland, if there had been no shooting available, or whether the houses at Invereshie and The Doune and access to the hut sites could have become an end in themselves, as they might do today.

By the time Georgina visited Badenoch for the last time, deer forests cleared of people and all forms of livestock had become firmly entrenched across Scotland, and with them a new way of life in local communities – for individuals and families of the professional gamekeepers and stalkers such as Collie and the businesses which supported them – had become and remain firmly established. It is also true, however, that even within the lifetimes of individuals who had known those early days of the huts in Glen Feshie, a government commission, looking at the impact of these developments in 1912, had concluded, among other things, that 'the Committee do not accept that sport is the best use of land even though it may produce higher profit for the landowner.' The debate continues to this day.

Beyond these elements of their legacy, however, lies that sense of wonder which powered the Romantic ideal, which provided, as one historian has put it, 'the wider context of a mighty cultural effervescence, the nearest they came to the grand romantic sense of fruitful destiny in the 1840s. These visions may seem foolish in retrospect … but, all the same, they had a moral force, and moral force, in the end, is what history best celebrates.'[613]

Maps

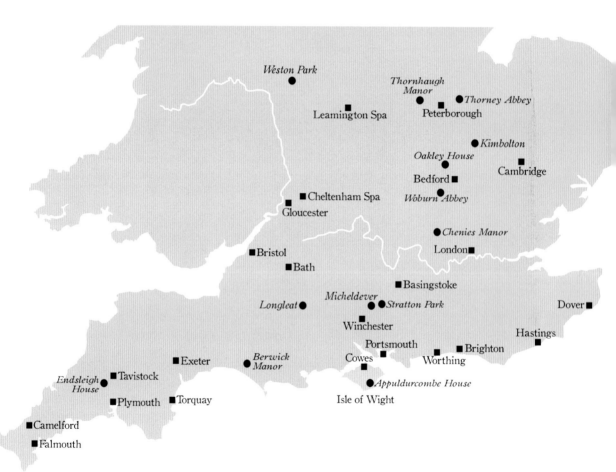

MAP 1
Southern England showing the location of the Russell family's properties.

MAP 2
Central Scotland showing Gordon family properties, Loch Laggan and Ardverikie Lodge, Strathspey,
and the route from Edinburgh to Inverness.

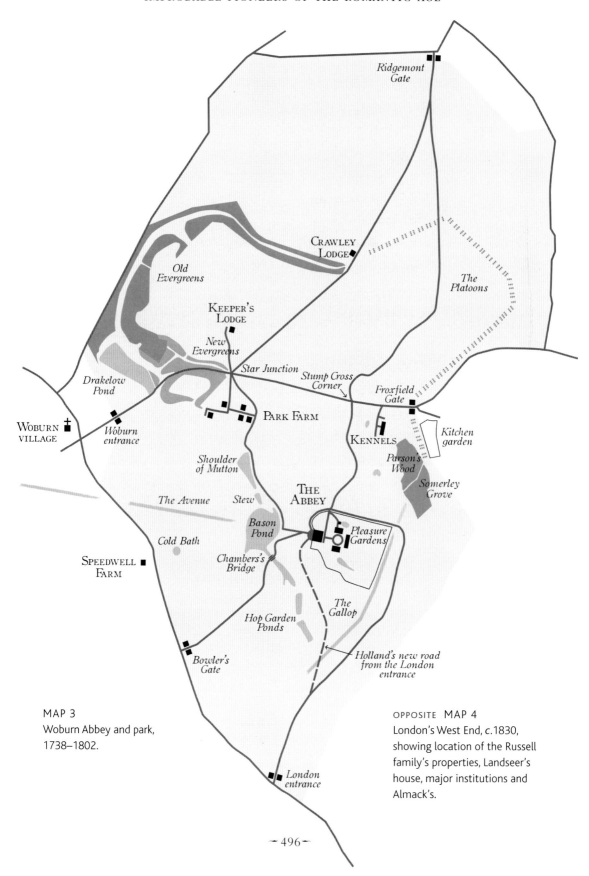

Ridgemont Gate

Old Evergreens

CRAWLEY LODGE

The Platoons

KEEPER'S LODGE

New Evergreens

Star Junction

Stump Cross Corner

Froxfield Gate

Drakelow Pond

PARK FARM

KENNELS

Kitchen garden

WOBURN VILLAGE

Woburn entrance

Shoulder of Mutton

Parson's Wood

Somerley Grove

The Avenue

Stew

THE ABBEY

Cold Bath

Bason Pond

Pleasure Gardens

SPEEDWELL FARM

Chambers's Bridge

The Gallop

Hop Garden Ponds

Bowler's Gate

Holland's new road from the London entrance

MAP 3
Woburn Abbey and park,
1738–1802.

London entrance

OPPOSITE MAP 4
London's West End, c.1830,
showing location of the Russell
family's properties, Landseer's
house, major institutions and
Almack's.

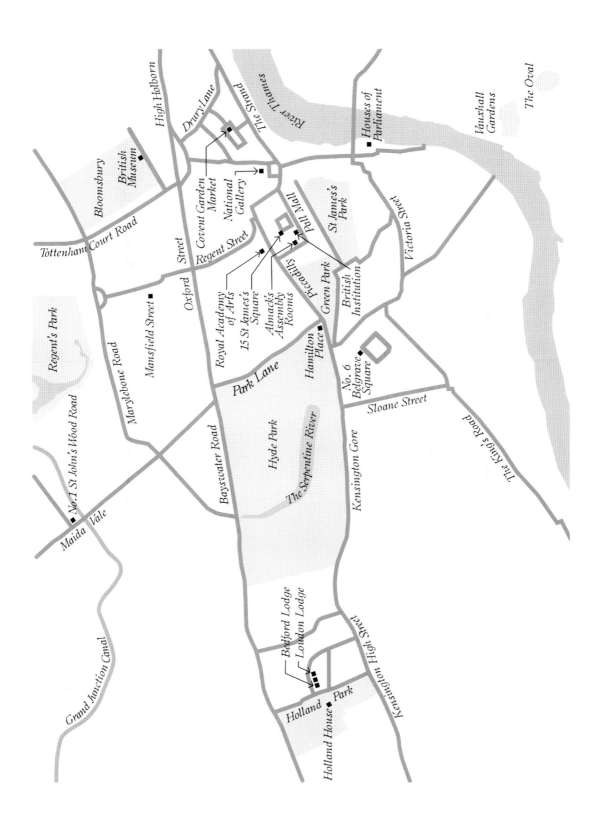

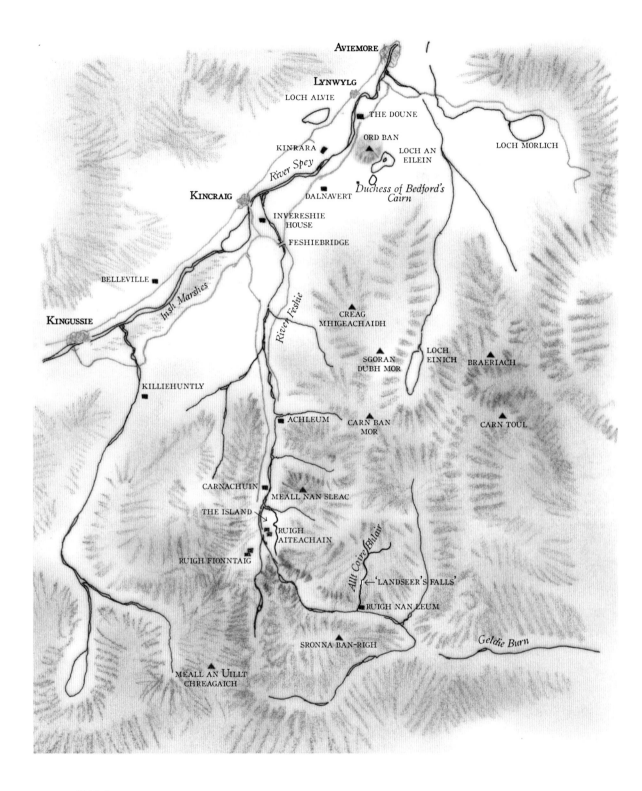

MAP 5

Glen Feshie and Strathspey from Aviemore to Kingussie, showing Kinrara and the properties leased by the Russell family on the Spey at Invereshie House and The Doune and the Feshie at Ruigh Fionntaig and Ruigh Aiteachan. See also the area known as 'The Island' and the location of Landseer's hut at Ruigh nan Leum.

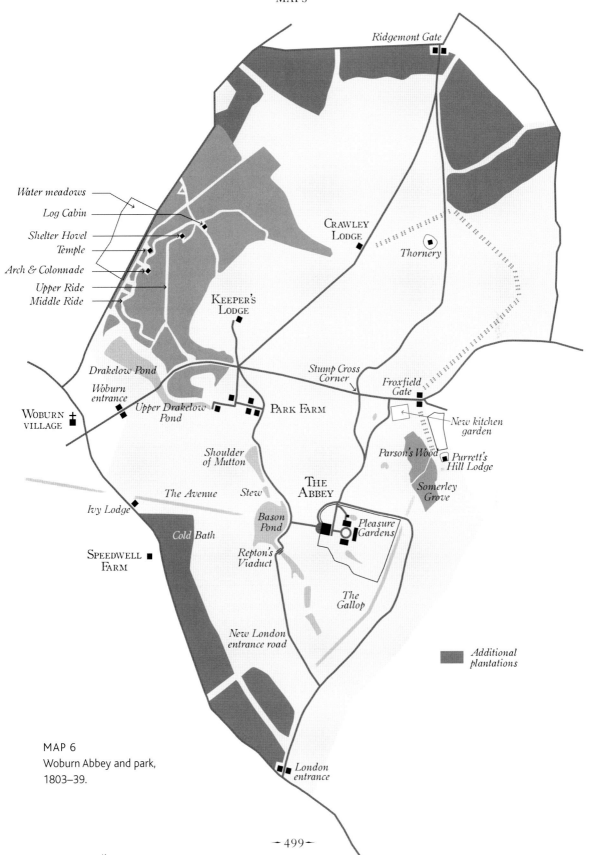

Water meadows

Log Cabin

Shelter Hovel

Temple

Arch & Colonnade

Upper Ride

Middle Ride

Ridgemont Gate

CRAWLEY
LODGE

Thornery

KEEPER'S
LODGE

Drakelow Pond

*Stump Cross
Corner*

*Froxfield
Gate*

*Woburn
entrance*

*Upper Drakelow
Pond*

PARK FARM

*New kitchen
garden*

WOBURN
VILLAGE

*Shoulder
of Mutton*

Parson's Wood

*Purrett's
Hill Lodge*

Stew

THE
ABBEY

*Somerley
Grove*

The Avenue

*Bason
Pond*

*Pleasure
Gardens*

Ivy Lodge

Cold Bath

*Repton's
Viaduct*

SPEEDWELL
FARM

*The
Gallop*

*New London
entrance road*

*Additional
plantations*

MAP 6
Woburn Abbey and park,
1803–39.

*London
entrance*

Notes

ABBREVIATIONS

AP: Abercorn Papers, PRONI

BARS: Bedford Archives and Records Service, Duke of Bedford/Russell Collection

DHC: Devon Heritage Centre, Bedford Estate Archive, Taunton

ELC: Edwin Landseer Correspondence, NAL

EP: Ellice Papers, NLS

GP: Grey Papers, University of Durham Library

GRP: Grant of Rothiemurchus Papers, Edinburgh and The Doune

GW: Goodwood Papers, WSRO

HHP: Holland House Papers, British Library, London

MGP: Macpherson-Grant Papers, Edinburgh and Ballindalloch

MM: Mackintosh Muniments, NRS

NAL: National Art Library, Victoria and Albert Museum, London

NLS: National Library of Scotland, Edinburgh

NRAS: National Register of Archives for Scotland, Edinburgh

NRS: National Records of Scotland, Edinburgh

PRONI: Public Records Office, Northern Ireland, Belfast

RBGK: Royal Botanical Gardens Kew, Archive Room, Director's Correspondence, English Letters

SC: Sneyd Correspondence, Keele University Library

SRO: Staffordshire Record Office, Stafford

WAC: Woburn Abbey Collection, Woburn Abbey

WRSO: West Sussex Record Office, Chichester

1   George Skene to Lord Fife, 28 June 1803, in *Lord Fife and his Factor, Being the Correspondence of James Second Lord Fife, 1729–1809*, ed. Alistair and Henrietta Tayler (London: William Heinemann, 1925), p. 174. Quoted by Mary Miers, *Highland Retreats: The Architecture and Interiors of Scotland's Romantic North*, New York: Rizzoli, 2017, p. 82.

2   While Lord John's first wife had been christened Georgiana, there is some confusion about Georgina Gordon's name because, after she married the duke, she too was also known as Georgiana. All the evidence suggests, however, that she was christened Georgina, and referred to as such, or as Georgy, by family members throughout her life, the more formal version of her name, Georgiana, being reserved for use in the context of her role as duchess.

3   Quotations from Osbert Sitwell, ed., *Two Generations* (London: Macmillan, 1940), p. viii, and Gavin de Beer, ed., *Autobiographies: Charles Darwin, Thomas Henry Huxley* (London: Oxford University Press, 1974), p. ix.

4   Curt Meine's reflections on biography in *Aldo Leopold: His Life and Work* (Madison: University of Wisconsin Press, 1988), p. xxix.

5   The manuscript of Gladys Scott Thomson's 'Life of the 5th Duke of Bedford' is held at Somerville College, Oxford, and a photocopy at the Woburn Abbey Archive, WAC GB-N11. Rachel Trethewey, *Mistress of the Arts: The Passionate Life of Georgina, Duchess of Bedford* (London: Review, 2002).

6   Richard Holmes, *The Age of Wonder* (London: HarperCollins, 2009), pp. 1, xvi, xx.

7   Quotations from publisher's cover description of Holmes, ibid.

8   NRAS, GD176/2226, letter Georgina to Mackintosh, 28 November 1838.

9   Queen Victoria, *Leaves from the Journal of our Life in the Highlands, from 1848 to 1861*, ed. Arthur Helps (London: Smith, Elder and Co., 1868), 'First Great Expedition, September 1860' and 'Third Great Expedition, October 1861'.

10   See Royal Collection Trust description of a drawing by Queen Victoria, 'Endsleigh Dated 13 August, 1856' (RCIN 980033), www.rct.uk: 'In her journal entry of 13 August, Queen Victoria describes the visit

to Endsleigh … "Endsleigh is approached by a pretty lodge and avenue of evergreens, & suddenly a most magnificent extensive view opens out before one." Trethewey, *Mistress of the Arts*, pp. 1, 2.

11   Marquis of Tavistock is the title given to the eldest son and heir apparent to the Duke of Bedford, and he is traditionally referred to as 'Tavistock' within the family.

12   Georgiana Blakiston, *Woburn and the Russells*, London: Constable, 1980, pp. 130–35. The Dunstable Hunt uniform featured the buff and blue colours of the Whig party.

13   Ibid., p. 130. See Lydia Figes, 'Decoding the Grand Tour portraits of Pompeo Batoni', 24 October 2019, www.artuk.org (accessed 1/11/2019). His work and style appealed to their 'mania for antiquities', and he was happy to give them what they wanted: a heroic portrait among the glorious ruins of Rome, particularly the Colosseum.

14   For details of the 4th Duke of Bedford's landscaping generally, and the Bason and New Ponds, and the Arch specifically, see Keir Davidson, *Woburn Abbey: The Park and Gardens*, London: Pimpernel Press, 2016, pp. 105 and 106.

15   J. H. Wiffen, *Historical Memoirs of the House of Russell*, 2 vols, London: Longman, Rees, Orme, Brown, Green, and Longman, 1833, vol. 1, pp. 547–9, letter Marquis of Tavistock to Earl of Upper Ossory, from Woburn Abbey, July 1764.

16   WAC A.2.Tav, vol. 1, p. 34.

17   The Duchess (of Marlborough) was Tavistock's sister, Caroline Russell. See H. W. Toynbee and P. J. Toynbee, eds, *Letters of Horace Walpole to Horace Mann*, 16 vols (Oxford: Clarendon Press, 1903), 19 March 1767, quoted in Gladys Scott Thomson, 'Life of the 5th Duke of Bedford', p. 3, WAC GB-N11.

18   WAC HMC8-57-32, 36 and 47.

19   WAC HMC8-57-58.

20   Adeline Marie Tavistock and Ela M. S. Russell, *Biographical Catalogue of the Pictures at Woburn Abbey*, 2 vols, London: Elliot Stock, 1890, vol. 1, p. 34.

21   Scott Thomson, 'Life', p. 7.

22   See Davidson, *Woburn Abbey*, pp. 84–111, for further details of all the architectural and landscaping features worked on by the 4th Duke. WAC HMC8-58-114, letter Duchess of Bedford to Duke of Bedford, from Woburn Abbey, 27 July 1769. See also Blakiston, *Woburn and the Russells*, p. 143. WAC HMC 58, 4th Duke of Bedford, Memorandum Books, 11 August 1769.

23   Scott Thomson, 'Life', pp. 135 and 7. WAC HMC8-57 and 58, letters Gertrude, Duchess of Bedford, to Duke of Bedford.

24   Walpole quoted in Tavistock and Russell, *Biographical Catalogue*, vol. 2, pp. 52–3.

25   John Langton Sanford and Meredith Townsend, *The Great Governing Families of England*, 2 vols, Edinburgh: William Blackwood and Sons, 1865, vol. 2, p. 50. Tavistock and Russell, *Biographical Catalogue*, vol. 2, 51–2, 55–7, 153 and 161. The authors of the *Biographical Catalogue* also warn us that Horace Walpole 'detested' the duke, having never forgiven him for his opposition to his father, Robert Walpole.

26   Quoted in Scott Thomson, 'Life', p. 5.

27   Ibid., pp. 4A, 5 and 6.

28   SRO D1287/18/20 (P/898), letter 6th Duke of Bedford to Dr Francis Randolph.

29   Scott Thomson, 'Life', p. 102.

30   Lord Holland quoted ibid., p. 109.

31   *The World and Fashionable Advertiser*, 3 February 1787, quoted in Scott Thomson, 'Life'. Stanley's memoir is included in Jane H. Adeana, ed., *The Early Married Life of Maria Josepha, Lady Stanley, with Extracts from Sir John Stanley's 'Præterita'*, London: Longmans, Green and Co., 1899, pp. 2–6. In later life, Stanley seems to have maintained some contact with the Russell family, and applied to stand for the 1790 election to Parliament as a candidate for Okehampton in the Bedford interest.

32   Georgiana Blakiston, *Lord William Russell and his Wife, 1815–1846*, London: John Murray, 1972, p.154.

33   Currency conversion: it is notoriously difficult to pin down an accurate equivalence between the value of a sum of money in the early nineteenth century and today; adjustment suggestions vary between ×50 and ×100. In this book, where an equivalence is suggested in the text, the original sum has been multiplied by ×60 to give a relatively conservative estimate of today's values.

34   Scott Thomson, 'Life', pp. 8, 12, 88–90. All the financial details are taken from Scott Thomson's exhaustive calculations, but because the manuscript is a first draft, complete with handwritten alterations and additions, there are a few gaps and anomalies which would no doubt have been sorted had the work been taken further.

35   Letter Horace Walpole to Sir H. Mann, 2 February 1752, quoted by Scott Thomson, 'Life', p. 7. Gerald le Grys Norgate, 'Dictionary of National Biography, 1885–1900/Vernon, Richard (1726–1800)', www.en.wikisource.org (accessed 25/5/2021).

36   WAC HO-C2-3, letters Robert Palmer to Duke of Bedford, Letter Book of Robert Palmer, p. 152 (3 June 1780), p. 282 (15 October 1782) and p. 303 (11 March 1783).

37   Göttingen University: quotations and details of the university's history, academic focus and names associated with it are taken from Gordon M. Stewart, 'British Students at the University of Göttingen in the Eighteenth Century', *German Life and Letters*, 33:1, October 1979, www.onlinelibrary.wiley.com (accessed 28/1/2020). This includes the quotation from Baron Munchausen which begins 'It is my intent', and an invaluable list of British students who enrolled at Göttingen between 1740 and 1800.

    For further details on Göttingen, see website of Georg-August-Universität. Articles include a general introduction and 'History of the University – an Overview' by Dr Ernst Böhme, www.uni-goettingen.de (accessed 27/1/2020).

38   George Hanger, *The Life, Adventures, and Opinions of Col. George Hanger*, London: J. Debrett, 1801, vol. 1, pp. 27–31, www.archive.org (accessed 28/1/2020).

39   Letters Robert Palmer to Lord John Russell, Dr Erxleben and William Rohloff, Letter Book of Robert Palmer, pp. 231, 253, 254, 255, 281 and 291 (January, April and November 1782).

40   The Lakagigur eruptions lasted from June 1783 until February 1784. The dense hydrofluoric acid and sulfur dioxide cloud haze was so toxic that it killed both livestock and people and caused one of the hottest summers, followed by one the coldest winters, ever recorded. Gilbert White described the effects he saw that summer in his *Natural History of Selborne*, London: Dent, 1976, p. 279.

41   Letter Robert Palmer to Francis Randolph, Letter Book of Robert Palmer, p. 516 (5 November 1784).

42   WAC bundle of Bedford estate papers, letter William Rohloff to Robert Palmer, Angouleme, 24 July 1784, and letter Francis Randolph to Robert Palmer, Bordeaux, 12 August 1784.

43   *Morning Herald and Daily Advertiser*, 16 October 1783, quoted in Scott Thomson, 'Life', p. 16.

44   *Morning Herald and Daily Advertiser*, 26 April, 24 May and 19 October 1784.

45   *Morning Post*, quoted in Scott Thomson, 'Life', p. 19A. *General Advertiser*, 20 January 1785. It is likely that this 'anonymous' dowager duchess was Gertrude, renowned for her attention to expenses.

46   Letter Lord John to Palmer (June 1785), quoted in Scott Thomson, 'Life', p. 22.

47   See undated letters Lord John Russell to an unknown friend: WAC LOC, Curator 6 (uncatalogued), loose bundle of bound items, three letters. Perhaps the most likely recipient is Francis Randolph. If Lord John and Randolph were this close, it would explain why two key clerical appointments within the Bedford patronage, Chenies and St Paul's Covent Garden, were later given to him.

48   WAC LOC 31-17-2, three letters Lord John Russell to Robert Palmer, December 1785. Tavistock and Russell, *Biographical Catalogue*, vol. 2, p. 173. For the 'opposition of relatives', see Scott Thomson, 'Life', p. 23. Letters Robert Palmer to Lord John Russell and Lord Torrington, Letter Book of Robert Palmer, pp. 78 and 79 (both 13 December 1785).

49   WAC LOC 66-180, Box No. 7, folder 1, letter Duke of Bedford to Lord John Russell, January 1786.

50   Letter Book of Robert Palmer, letters Robert Palmer to Duke of Bedford, p. 81 (20 December 1785), to Lord John Russell, p. 89 (24 December 1785), and to Mr Rohloff, p. 89 (25 December).

51   Letter Book of Robert Palmer, letters Robert Palmer to Duke of Bedford, p. 91 (13 January 1786), to Lord John Russell, pp. 99 (14 February 1786), 100 (21 February 1786) and 102 (28 February 1786.

52   'the house of the British Minister in Brussels': WAC NMR 4/4/1, large box of mostly legal papers, certificates, etc. Letters of 15 August and September 1786 from the duke to John Fitzpatrick, Earl of Ossory (a cousin through Evelyn Leveson-Gower), Fitzpatrick MSS, National Archives of Ireland, Dublin Castle, quoted in Scott Thomson, 'Life', p. 26. Letter Robert Palmer to Duke of Bedford in France, Letter Book of Robert Palmer, p. 127 (20 July 1786).

53   WAC LOC66-180, Box No. 7, folder 1, letters.

54   Box No. 7, folder 1, letter Lord William Russell to Lord John Russell, Plombieres, 1 July 1786.

55   George Spencer, the 4th Duke of Marlborough, a keen amateur astronomer, had built an observatory on the south-east tower of Blenheim Palace in 1789 equipped with the latest reflecting telescopes, and later added a second observatory on the south-west tower ('Oxfordshire Observatories', https://shasurvey:wordpress.com, accessed 27/2/2020).

56   Donald E. Ginter, *Whig Organization in the General Election of 1790*, Berkeley and Los Angeles: University of California Press, 1967, pp. xx–xxi, xxiii.

57   Box No. 7, folder 1, letter Lord William to Lord John, Oxford, 19 October 1786.

58   WAC NMR 3/7/2, Diary of Georgiana Russell, 10 August 1793 to 8 November 1793, 12 September 1793.

59   Box No. 7, Georgiana Russell, Letter Book, 1786.

60   Ginter, *Whig Organization*, p. 197, n. 6. The constituency may have been selected for Lord John due to its proximity to Bulstrode and Portland's influence in the area. Tavistock was the administrative centre for the Russell estates in Devon, which were formerly the lands of the dissolved Tavistock Abbey and which had been granted to John Russell, 1st Earl of Bedford, by Henry VIII in 1534 on his appointment as 'Lord President of the Council of the West'. The Russells had secured control of the parliamentary seat following the upheavals of the Civil War, creating a secure pocket borough, and returned candidates for the Russell interest until the late 1860s. Richard Rigby, the 4th Duke of Bedford's political agent and manager, had held the seat from 1754 to 1788, and Lord John, joining the parliamentary session running November 1787 to August 1789, served 1788–90 and 1790–1802, at which point he was elevated to the Lords on becoming 6th Duke of Bedford.

61   WAC 6D-C1-3, Bundle 1, 1790, undated letter Georgiana to Lord John at Woburn Abbey.

62   WAC 5D-A1-2-36, box of 5th Duke of Bedford era business, 5D253.

63   WAC 6D-C1-3, Bundle 9, 1790, letter Georgiana in Harley Street to Lord John in Winchester, 20 February 1790.

64   Bundle 7, April? 1790, letter Georgiana in Streatham to Lord John in Newport. The pressed flowers are still intact in the folds of the letter.

65   Ginter, *Whig Organization*, p. 112.

66   Bundle 7, May 1790, letter Georgiana in Streatham to Lord John at Stratton Park.

67   Bundle 7, 1 June 1790, Streatham to Stratton Park and Highclere to Stratton Park. Highclere Castle was the home of Lord Porchester, later 1st Earl of Carnarvon. Porchester, as a leading Whig politician and later member of the 'Ministry of All Talents', was central to Portland and Adam's election efforts in Hampshire in 1790, encouraging candidates to stand in constituency contests.

68   Hants RO 20M64/7, quoted in 'Russell, Lord John (1766–1839)', Member Biographies, www.histparl.ac.uk (accessed 6/6/2021).

69   Bundle 7, June 1790, Highclere to Stratton Park. For details of the occupation of Stratton Park by successive generations of the Russell family, see Keir Davidson, *Woburn Abbey: The Park and Gardens*, London: Pimpernel Press, 2016, pp. 68–70, 78–80.

70   Ginter, *Whig Organization*, p. 197, n. 6.

71   Ibid., p. 196, letter Portland to Adam, 30 June 1790, and p. 197, notes.

72   WAC 6D-C1-3, Bundle 10, 1790. Kempshot House, near Basingstoke, was rented by the Prince of Wales in 1788 as a hunting lodge and private getaway from London, where he could entertain both his male friends and his mistress, Mrs Fitzherbert. Lord John is recorded as being there on several occasions while they lived at Stratton. The building was demolished when the M3 motorway was built.

73   WAC 6D-C1-3, Bundle 6, 1791, letters Georgiana to Lord John.

74   Georgiana's eldest brother had died as a baby, and now, besides her mother, she lost both her young brothers. She became increasingly close to her three sisters. Lucy Elizabeth had married Orlando Bridgeman, 1st Earl of Bradford, in 1788 and was living at Weston Park, Shropshire; it would seem that her father had left Brussels when his wife died and was living with Georgiana's younger sisters Isabella (19) and Emily (14) at Southill before selling the house in 1795. With her mother, brothers and the family home all gone, everything was now invested in her marriage.

75   Diary of Georgiana Russell, 10 August 1793 to 8 November 1793. The entries about Cowes and the Isle of Wight begin 12 August.

76   Sir Richard's and Georgiana's mothers, Elizabeth Boyle and Lucy Boyle, respectively, were half-sisters. He later retired to his smaller Sea Cottage, Undercliff, St Lawrence, on the coast south of Appuldurcombe.

77   Diary of Georgiana Russell, 10 August 1793 to 8 November 1793, journey to Lisbon. Diary of Georgiana Russell, November 1793 to April 1794, stay in Lisbon.

78   Diary of Georgiana Russell, April 1794 to November 1794, and Diary of Georgiana Russell, 6 December 1794 to 4 August 1795, Cintra, their return to England and resumption of life at Stratton Park.

79   John Boyle, 5th Earl of Cork, was a leading Irish writer who listed among his personal friends Jonathan Swift, Alexander Pope and Samuel Johnson.

80   Diary of Georgiana Russell, 10 August 1793 to 8 November 1793, Isle of Wight.

81   Lady Ann Fitzroy, sister of the Duke of Wellington, married to Henry Fitzroy, was freed from detention in Quimper in 1795.

82   Diary of Georgiana Russell, 6 December 1794 to 4 August 1795, the journey home.

83   WAC 6D-C1-3, Bundle 3. The letters are undated, but the watermark on the paper is 1794. The fact that they were still in Cintra that year – and a loose sheet in the bundle from August 1795 tells us Lord John's trip to Devon with the duke was delayed – suggest that the letters date from early September 1795, when Lord John visited Tavistock and Georgiana wrote to him from Bristol. Rachel Trethewey identified Lord John's pattern of behaviour in *Mistress of the Arts* (London: Review, 2002), and it seems to have been a feature of his character throughout his life.

84   Francis Randolph, Lord John's old friend from Göttingen, was from Bristol and was there in 1793 as prebendary at Bristol Cathedral.

85   WAC 6D-C1-3, Bundle 5, November 1795 to February 1796. Twenty-one largely undated letters written from Stratton Park to Lord John at various locations, including 'Reddish's Hotel', St James's St, London, during the parliamentary session (October 1795 to May 1796).

86   His little note gives a clear indication of young Francis's interests: 'No Sport, Too many Foxes. I saw Lee as soon as he saw me he galloped up to see me. I was too late. I thank you for your kind letter and I hope you will come to us soon. Your dutiful son, Francis Russell.' By 19 November she informs Lord John that Francis, aged seven, 'was out this morning with the Prince's Hounds in Treefolkwood'. The Prince of Wales's Hounds were based at his hunting lodge at Kempshott Lodge, Basingstoke.

87   The much criticized Treasonable Practices Act and the Seditious Meetings Act were both passed this month.

88   WAC HMC 91, Day Book of Lord John Russell's farm, 1 February 1796 to 7 October 1797, for details of Lord John's farming activities at Stratton Park at this time.

89   WAC 6D-C1-3, Bundles 4 and 5, 12 March and undated, 1796, letters Bedford House to Stratton Park.

90   Bundle 5, November 1795 to February 1796, letters Georgiana to Lord John, 3 and 9 February 1796.

91   November 1795 to February 1796, loose, undated sheet; WAC 6D-C1-3, Bundle 4, March to April 1796, letters 8 and 9 March.

92   Bundle 4, March to April 1796, letter Bedford House to Stratton Park, 12 March.

93   WAC 6D-C1-3, Bundle 2, 1797 and 1798, letters Stratton Park to hotels in London.

94   WAC 6D-C7, transcription of letters contained in WAC B.2 D.6.RUS and *Letters of Lady John Russell to her Husband, 1798–1801*, London: Chiswick Press (for private circulation), 1913, p. 5.

95   There were, of course, a number of other pressing issues, such as the attacks on free speech, repressive legislation such as the Sedition Act, assessed taxes and Catholic emancipation, but this discussion is limited to the two which severely challenged the assumptions of politicians, the landed aristocracy and their incomes.

96   Ginter, *Whig Organization*, p. l.

97   'Russell, Lord John (1766–1839)'. It took another thirty-four years, but the Russell family remained central to the issue, and the Bills when ready were taken through the House by Lord John Russell.

98   Basil Davidson, *African Civilization Revisited*, Trenton, N.J.: Africa World Press, 1991, pp. 3–4.

99   Abdul Mohamed and Robin Whitburn, 'Britain's Involvement with New World Slavery and the Transatlantic Slave Trade', 21 June 2018, www.bl.uk (accessed 2/11/2019).

100   WAC LOC21-24-5 6DOB, Misc. Box: items in loose bundle, all relating to Lord John Russell, 1780s and 1790s, quotation from a 'Copy of Gov[nr] Ellis's Letter to Lord Hawkesbury concerning the Slave trade, dated Marseilles, 12th March, 1788' (Henry Ellis to Lord Hawkesbury, later 1st Lord Liverpool). Ellis was a former slave trader and pre-revolution governor of Georgia, where he had also owned plantations, and Hawkesbury had been charged by the government with issuing a report on the practicalities of abolishing the slave trade. Lord John, and probably his brother the duke, were clearly influenced by Ellis's arguments. For Lord John Russell's speech in this debate, see 'Russell, Lord John (1766–1839)', Member Biographies, www.histparl.ac.uk (accessed 6/6/2021).

101   *Letters of Lady John Russell*, p. 15.

102   Ibid., p. 27.

103   Ibid. p. 28. Thomas Whately's *Observations of Modern Gardening* (ed. Michael Symes, Woodbridge: Boydell & Brewer, 2016), first published in 1770, 'was instantly successful and in the same year a second edition appeared: it reached a third the following year … and the fourth edition appeared in 1777 and the fifth in 1793 … and the sixth, illustrated, followed in 1801' (p. 5). WAC HMC 92, Lord John Russell, Day Book and Accounts, 15 February 1799 to 2 October 1802, Oakley House.

104   Quoted in Georgiana Blakiston, *Woburn and the Russells*, London: Constable, 1980, p. 190. Also see Davidson, *Woburn Abbey*, ch. 3, n. 29.

105   WAC uncatalogued, 6th Duke of Bedford's personal diary, 'Oakley, Jan 1802'.

106   WAC PP-GeorgBY-3, autopsy result, 'Appearances on the Dissection of Lady John Russell, Oct 11, 1801'. I am much indebted to Dan Henderson for his professional opinion concerning the autopsy result.

107   SRO D1287/18/20 (P/900), extract of a letter from Francis, 5th Duke of Bedford, to unknown recipient, 18 November 1801.

108   WAC 6DOB LOC, Curator 6, Lord John Russell, Diary, 1 January to 30 March 1802.

109   Pattishall is now known as Patshull, Staffordshire. Major elements of Lancelot Brown's landscaping, *c.*1765, are still visible at Patshull today.

110 WAC 5D–WS6, 6th Duke of Bedford's will: the 5th Duke's illegitimate children were recognized and provided for in his will.

111 WSRO Goodwood MS 1171/002322–2323, letter Duchess of Gordon to James Beattie, 14 December 1785. WSRO Goodwood MS 1171/002273–2275, letter Duchess of Gordon to James Beattie, 1783.

112 John Malcolm Bulloch, *The Gay Gordons: Some Strange Adventures of a Famous Scotch Family*, London: Chapman and Hall, 1908, pp. 4, 12.

113 George Gordon, *The Last Dukes of Gordon and their Consorts: A Revealing Study*, Aberdeen: G. Gordon, 1980, p. 13.

114 Bulloch, *Gay Gordons*, pp. 7, 9. Gordon, *Last Dukes*, p. 33. The Batoni portrait is now in the National Gallery of Scotland, and for commentary on it, see Pompeo Batoni, *Alexander Gordon, 4th Duke of Gordon (1743–1827)*, www.nationalgalleries.org (accessed 12/3/2020).

115 See commentary on Angelica Kauffmann, *Alexander Gordon, 4th Duke of Gordon (1743–1827)*, www.nationalgalleries.org (accessed 12/3/2020).

116 WSRO Goodwood MS 1170/000749, Microfilm, Box MF 1218, 'Diary of Events at Gordon Castle, 1766–1776'.

117 From the introduction to *An Autobiographical Chapter in the Life of Jane, Duchess of Gordon (1864)*, 'Privately Printed'. The introduction is initialled 'J.W.G.', thought to be J. Wylie Guild of Glasgow. WSRO Goodwood MS 1171/2357, letter Duchess of Gordon to James Beattie, Glenfiddich, undated: 'I beg you may ask for the Latin poem Huntly sent – the translation the Duke made this morning.'

118 WSRO Goodwood MS 1172/000530, Microfilm, Box MF 1238. See, for example, the letter from the Duke of Gordon of 1789, in which, after helping a member of Charles Gordon's family financially, he now calls on Gordon 'to give John Belches your support in the Mearns, and as I hear he will be hard pushed, I hope it will not be inconvenient to you to attend the election.'

119 See Holden Furber, *Henry Dundas, First Viscount Melville, 1742–1811: Political Manager of Scotland, Statesman, Administrator of British India*, London: Oxford University Press, 1931, p. 202. Gordon, *Last Dukes*, p. 33.

120 James Boswell's journal, 24 September 1762, quoted in Biographies, William Maxwell, 3rd Baronet of Monreith, Life with Boswell, www.jamesboswell.info (accessed 28/6/2021).

121 Robert Chambers, *Traditions of Edinburgh*, new edn, London and Edinburgh: W. & R. Chambers, 1847, pp. 297–8.

122 'Lady Jane Maxwell', www.clanmaxwellsociety.com (accessed 28/6/2021).

123 WSRO Goodwood MS 1170/000780 and 000781, letter Henry Home to Duchess of Gordon, November 1767. WSRO Goodwood MS 1170/000789, 000791 and 000792, letter Home to Duchess of Gordon, January 1768. WSRO Goodwood MS 1170/000794 and 000796, letter Duchess of Gordon to Home, 5 February 1768.

124 WSRO Goodwood MS 1170/000778, Microfilm, Box MF 1218, letter Sir William Maxwell to Jane, 6 September 1767. It would appear that there were two versions of her name, 'Jane' and 'Jean', and that they were pretty much interchangeable, 'Jean' or 'Jeany' reflecting Scots dialect and 'Jane' more anglicized.

125 This definition of the Highland Line is taken from David Johnson, *Music and Society in Lowland Scotland in the 18th Century*, London: Oxford University Press, 1972, p. 3.

126 William Marshall: all quotations from www.ibiblio.org/fiddlers/marshall (accessed 31/8/16).

127 Dr Gregory was 'one of the most cultured persons in Scotland at the time, a Professor at both Edinburgh and Aberdeen': see Johnson, *Music and Society*, p. 111.

128 Ibid., p. 120. The Scots 'snap' was 'a short-long rhythmic structure, or in other words the preceding note should be of a shorter note value.' The strathspey is known for its 'dotted rhythm', which creates a

'snapping' effect: quoted from www.musicinvestigation.wordpress.com, 'Scotch Snap' (accessed 9/9/16). The snap had long been associated with Gaelic song, and to a degree the rhythms of Gaelic speech. This account of the origins of the strathspey is based on the online debate between William Lamb and Robert Newton on the origins of the Strathspey dance form. Sourced from virtualgael.wordpress.com/2014/01/04/the-origins-of-the-strathspey-a-rebuttal (accessed 9/9/16 but deleted by authors and no longer available). Broadly put, the minuet + snap = strathspey. For 'nostalgic in character', see Johnson, *Music and Society*, p. 128.

129   For Hoy, see Margaret Forbes, *Beattie and his Friends* [1904], Bristol: Thoemmes, 1990, p. 191. These details of Hoy's life and career are taken from John Wilson, *The Works of Robert Burns, with Dr. Currie's Memoir of the Poet*, vol. 2, Glasgow: Blackie & Son, 1844, p. 194, n.1.

130   Forbes, *Beattie*, p. 242, letter Duchess of Gordon to James Beattie, 1788.

131   WSRO Goodwood MS 1170/000749, 'Diary of Events'.

132   'Jane Maxwell's Daughter – Parish Register of Bellie, J.M.B.', *Scottish Notes and Queries*, second series, VII (August 1905), p. 29. Jane's mother, Magdalen Blair, seems to be have used her own name after separating from William Maxwell.

133   Goodwood MS 1171 (no folio number), Microfilm, Box MF 1218, letter Duchess of Gordon to Henry Home, 19 November 1768.

134   Forbes, *Beattie*, p. 139. WRSO Goodwood MS 1170/000751, 'Diary of Events', June 1769. WSRO Goodwood MS 1170/000762, 'Diary of Events', June 1773.

135   WSRO Goodwood MS 1170/000752, 'Diary of Events', August 1769. WSRO Goodwood MS 1170/000750, 'Diary of Events', September 1768. WSRO Goodwood MS 1170/000759, 'Diary of Events', August 1772. 'Loch Cathness': this word is very hard to read; it may be a specific loch somewhere, but it may simply mean the lochs of Caithness, visible across the Moray Forth.

136   WSRO Goodwood MS 1170/000764 and 000766, 'Diary of Events', Autumn 1774 and December 1775. Rosemary Baird, *Goodwood: Art, Architecture, Sport and Family*, London: Frances Lincoln, 2007, p. 217.

137   WSRO Goodwood MS 1170/000750 and 000751. WSRO Goodwood MS 1170/000803, letter Duchess of Gordon to Henry Home, 1769.

138   All quotes from Charles Fraser-Mackintosh, *Antiquarian Notes, Historical, Genealogical and Social*, second series, Inverness: A. and W. Mackenzie, 1897, pp. 396 and 397. Confusingly, on the opposite bank of the river stood another farm also called Kinrara, and the two have generally been distinguished as either 'Kinrara north' (on Gordon land) or 'Kinrara south' (on Mackintosh land), but not always.

139   To Jane her son George (1770–1836) became 'My George' as opposed to the 'Duke's George' (an illegitimate son of the 4th Duke, also called George Gordon (1766–1835), born to Bathia Largue, a Gordon Castle servant, just before the duke's marriage to Jane.

140   WSRO Goodwood MS 1170/000759, Microfilm, Box MF 1218, 'Diary of Events', August 1772.

141   WSRO Goodwood MS 1171/002311–2317, letter Duchess of Gordon to James Beattie?, from Gordon Castle, August 1784.

142   All quotes from Forbes, *Beattie*, pp. 23–7.

143   Ibid., p. 71.

144   WRSO Goodwood, MS 1171/002377, letter Duchess of Gordon to Henry Home, from Gordon Castle, 5 March 1776. WSRO Goodwood MS 1171/002161 and 2172, letters Duchess of Gordon to James Beattie, from Gordon Castle, 1778 (neither fully dated).

145   James 'Fingal' Macpherson was a writer, collector of traditional Scottish poetry and politician, 'Editor' and 'translator' of the *Ossian* cycle of epic poetry. He claimed to have discovered the fragments of 'ancient poetry' on his travels in the Highlands, and their publication caused a sensation, but inconsistencies in the texts and his inability to produce the original documents led ultimately to his claims being largely dismissed and the poetry declared forgeries.

146   WSRO Goodwood MS 1171/002198 and 2199, letter William King to Duchess of Gordon, from Elgin, 13 June 1779.

147   WSRO Goodwood MS 1171/002097 and 2098, letter Duchess of Gordon to James Beattie, from Gordon Castle, July 1775.

148   Richard Grenville-Temple, 2nd Earl Temple. His brother, George Grenville, served as Prime Minister 1763–5; Temple remained loyal to his brother's faction of the Whig party following the latter's split with Pitt in 1761.

149   For the Grotto, see Benton Seeley, *A Description of the Garden of Viscount Cobham, at Stow, in Buckinghamshire* (Northampton, 1744) (one of the first such guidebooks ever written), and 'J. De. C.', *Les Charmes de Stow* (1748). For the texts of both, see G. B. Clarke, ed., *Descriptions of Lord Cobham's Gardens at Stowe 1700–1750*, Aylesbury: Buckinghamshire Record Society, 1990, pp. 136 and 167.

150   'The Complaint, or Night Thoughts on Life, Death and Immortality' by Edward Young was published between 1742 and 1745 following the death of Young's wife, Elizabeth, and other family members in 1740.

151   Claud Nugent, *Memoir of Robert, Earl Nugent, with Letters, Poems and Appendices*, Chicago: Herbert S. Stone & Co., 1898, p. 25. WSRO Goodwood MS 1171/002106, letter Lord Temple to Duke of Gordon, from Stowe, 5 July 1776; 002108–2110, letter Lord Temple to Duchess of Gordon, or the 'Dear Duchess', as her husband calls her, 4 August 1776; 002115, letter Lord Temple to Duchess of Gordon, from Stowe, 25 August 1776; 002117–2119, letter Lord Temple to Duchess of Gordon, 1 September 1776.

152   On Jane's charms, see 'Duchess of Gordon', *Public Characters*, London: R. Phillips, 1799, p. 391. (The contributors to *Public Characters* are anonymous, although some of the articles are initialled. The 'Advertisement' at the beginning is written by 'the editor' and refers simply to 'the various writers'.) One such anecdote is recalled here, after a group of people had met the duchess at the inn in Blair Athol. Asked what was so 'enrapturing about her', one commented on 'her careful forbearance of her display of superiority of rank in the distribution of her attentions … giving everyone an opportunity of speaking on a subject on which he supposed he could speak well'.

153   Johnson, *Music and Society*, p. 123.

154   'Duchess of Gordon', *Public Characters*, p. 510. The orchestra of the Duke of Athol is likely at this time to have been a relatively modest affair, and, as at Gordon Castle, probably consisted of one or two fiddles, a cello, and possibly a piano or harpsichord. I am much indebted to Jack Campin, musician and musicologist, for his thoughts on this. The piece Gow played at Blair Athol was 'Lament for James Moray of Abercairney', written following the death of Moray that year, a 'most liberal patron' of Gow's. The Leith races were held annually on the sands at Leith, four to five days in the last week July and the first week of August. Race weeks represented a major holiday for Edinburgh's population, and the Gordons and their friends attended regularly and sponsored many of the prize purses.

155   David Taylor, *The Wild Black Region: Badenoch, 1750–1800*, Edinburgh: John Donald, 2016, p. 186.

156   Bulloch, *Gay Gordons*, p. 11.

157   All quotes from Furber, *Henry Dundas* (in order), pp. 202, ix, xi, 149, 293.

158   Lord Alexander Gordon joined the 10th Dragoons in 1801, then the Coldstream Guards, 59th Foot, and in 1807 moved to the Aberdeen Militia. Finally, in 1808, while at Musselburgh Barracks he fell seriously ill and died aged just twenty-three.

159   Mary Miers, *Highland Retreats: The Architecture and Interiors of Scotland's Romantic North*, New York: Rizzoli, 2017, p. 80.

160   WRSO Goodwood MS 1171/002313, letter Duchess of Gordon to unknown correspondent (but probably Beattie), from Gordon Castle, August 1784. M. Bentham-Edwards, ed., *Autobiography of Arthur Young with Selections from his Correspondence*, London: Smith, Elder, 1898, pp. 334–5. Alexander Ross, 'The Fortunate Shepherdess', 1780.

161   WRSO Goodwood MS 1171/002198 and 002199, letter William King to Duchess of Gordon, from Elgin, 13 June 1729.

162   WRSO Goodwood MS 1171/002311–2318, letter Duchess of Gordon to unknown correspondent (but probably Beattie), from Gordon Castle, August 1784.

163   WSRO Goodwood MS 1171/002191–2193, Microfilm, Box MF 1218, letter Henry Home to Duchess of Gordon, from Edinburgh, 8 March 1779. WSRO Goodwood 1171/002234, letter Duchess of Gordon to Lady Anne Gordon, from Kinrara Cottage, summer? 1782. Anne married Revd Alexander Chalmers, Minister of Cairnie, Huntly, in 1782. Chalmers was twice her age, and she outlived him and died childless at Huntly in 1816.

164   Matthias D'Amour worked for the family until 'after 1796': see Matthias D'Amour, *Memoirs of Mr Matthias D'Amour*, London: Longman, Rees, Orme, Brown, Green, & Longman; Sheffield, Whitaker, 1836, p. 142.

165   Ibid., pp. 144–5.

166   Ibid., p. 200. D'Amour is wrong about Georgina's age – she must have been four by then – and he is also using the formal version of her name, Georgiana, which seems also to have been adopted after her marriage to the Duke of Bedford. WSRO Goodwood MS, 1171/002322–2323, letter Duchess of Gordon to Beattie, 1785.

167   Alexander Ferguson, *Henry Erskine: His Kinsfolk and his Times*, Edinburgh: n.p., 1882, p. 287.

168   See 'Memoirs and Correspondence of Mrs Grant of Laggan', p. 177, www.electricscotland.com/history/women/mrsgrant.pdf (accessed 20/9/2016).

169   George Gordon, *The Last Dukes of Gordon and their Consorts: A Revealing Study*, Aberdeen: G. Gordon, 1980, p. 64. D'Amour, *Memoirs*, pp. 146, 151.

170   NRAS, Douglas-Home MSS TD95/54, diary of Lady Mary Coke, 29 June and 18 July 1787, quoted in Amanda Foreman, *Georgiana: Duchess of Devonshire*, London: HarperCollins, 1998, p. 219. For the quote by the Earl of Fife's brother, see letter Major Lewis Duff to Lady Grant, from Blervie, May 1787, in Sir William Fraser, *Chiefs of Grant, Volume II: Correspondence*, Edinburgh: n.p., 1883, p. 495. For '… points of great delicacy', see Gordon, *Last Dukes*, p. 64. For '… her phrase obscene', see Foreman, *Georgiana*, p. 219.

171   Alexander Ross, the 'Poet of Loch Lee', visited Gordon Castle in 1776.

172   Margaret Forbes, *Beattie and his Friends* [1904], Bristol: Thoemmes, 1990, p. 241. It is not entirely clear just who was still at home, but if they were all there, the children would have been: Charlotte, now twenty, marries the next year (Duke of Richmond); Madelina, now sixteen, marries the next year (Sir Robert Sinclair, Lieutenant Governor of Fort George, Inverness); Susan, now fourteen, marries 1793 (5th Duke of Manchester); Louisa, now twelve, marries 1795 (2nd Marquis of Cornwallis); Georgina, now seven, marries 1803 (6th Duke of Bedford); and Alexander was now three.

173   Falkirk Museum, Forbes of Callendar Papers, NRS 171/263/8, letter Duchess of Gordon to Major Ross, from St James's Square, London, June 1789. Unfortunately, Sir Robert died in 1795, and Madelina went on to marry Charles Fysche Palmer at her sister Susan's home, Kimbolton Castle, in 1805. The 'Fish Palmers', as they are later referred to, lived not far from Woburn Abbey and this meant that Georgina had three sisters, including Louisa, Lady Cornwallis, whose husband's seat was at Culford, within visiting distance once she married, and the Fish Palmers shared the duke's interest in classical art and antiquities.

174   D'Amour, *Memoirs*, p. 184.

175   Gordon, *Last Dukes*, p. 63.

176   As David Taylor has established, 'Between 1791–1793 the family's personal expenses totalled over £27,000,' while Jane's expenditure ran to '£112,000 between 1791–1809'. NRS GD44/51/405/62, Accounts, 1791–1809, quoted in David Taylor, *The Wild Black Region: Badenoch, 1750–1800*, Edinburgh: John Donald, 2016, pp. 185–7.

177 Quoted in Forbes, *Beattie*, p. 191.

178 Gordon, *Last Dukes*, p. 56.

179 Quoted in Forbes, *Beattie*, p. 247, letter Mr Gordon of Cluny to Beattie, 3 December 1789. Other sources agree, and 1789 is given as the year of the Gordons' estrangement by Historic Environment Scotland, entry GDL00246.

180 The relationship between Jane and Jean does not appear to have been hostile, and they seem to have got along when necessary. Perhaps there was a degree of mutual respect, since the duke also had three other children by two, or possibly three, other women, so both Jane and Jean had to accept serial infidelity. Ann Thomson was another employee of the castle to catch the eye of one of the Gordon males, and went on to have two children with George, Marquis of Huntly, before his marriage to Elizabeth Brodie in 1813.

181 Colonel William Montagu, 5th Duke of Manchester, was a soldier, colonial administrator, Governor-General of Jamaica (1808–27) and politician. He married Susan in 1793. Forbes, *Beattie*, p. 271, letter Duchess of Gordon to Beattie, from Gordon Castle, autumn 1792. This marks Jane's return to Kinrara. The 'solitary shore' probably refers to Peterhead, Aberdeenshire, where Jane and Mr and Mrs Beattie would often visit.

182 Falkirk Museum, Forbes of Callendar Papers, NRS 171/263/15, 'Correspondence of Duchess of Gordon to General John Ross, 1786', letter Duchess of Gordon to General Ross, Glenfiddich, September? *c.*1792. These letters are undated, but the content reflects that of letters to Beattie from this period, and Jane's known movements.

183 John Malcolm Bulloch, ed., *The Gordon Book*, Fochabers: Bazaar of the Fochabers Reading Room, 1902, p. 26. Gordon, *Last Dukes*, p. 78.

184 Forbes, *Beattie*, p. 277. Two examples of how Jane took care of family and friends are as follows: letter Duchess of Gordon to Colonel (later General) Ross from Milhead, 1786. In this letter, Jane is asking Ross for a position when he goes to India, to serve under Lord Cornwallis, for her maid's brother. Ross went out in April 1786 (Falkirk Museum, Forbes of Callendar Papers, NRS 171/263/1). Letter Duchess of Gordon to Colonel Ross, from Gordon Castle, December 1789: here Jane is looking for a post for George Gordon, and writes, 'I introduce Mr George Gordon to your protection' (Falkirk Museum, Forbes of Callendar Papers, NRS 171/263/10).

185 'But and ben' was the traditional name of the old two-room farmhouses, the 'but' being the kitchen/ sleeping area, and the 'ben' the living room. Each had a fireplace and chimney. For '… small farm *cabin*', see Elizabeth Grant, *Memoirs of a Highland Lady*, ed. Andrew Tod, Edinburgh: Canongate, 2005, vol. 1, p. 45. See NRS GD2497 (a map, part of which includes Kinrara, Wester Lynwlg, Kanloch, etc., in 1771 and the existing buildings and surrounding fields at Kinrara) and 'A Project to Identify, Survey and Record the Archaeological Remains of a farmstead at North Kinrara', June 2006–January 2011, North of Scotland Archaeological Society, and Meryl M. Marshall, *Glen Feshie: The History and Archaeology of a Highland Glen*, 2nd edn, [Conon Bridge:] North of Scotland Archaeological Society, 2013, Chapter 10. I am particularly indebted to Meryl both in correspondence and conversation for her generous sharing of knowledge and materials on both Kinrara and Glen Feshie.

186 'Memoirs and Correspondence of Mrs Grant of Laggan'. Quotations from Anne MacVicar Grant, *Letters from the Mountains*, 3 vols, London: Longman, Hurst, Rees and Orme, 1807: vol. 2, letter XII to Miss Ourry, Laggan, July 1779, pp. 67, 78, and letter XIII to Mrs Smith, Fort George, July 1786, p. 118.

187 Grant, *Letters*, vol. 1, letter VI, 1773, p. 48.

188 Grant, *Letters*, vol. 2, letter IX, 1778, p. 52: she mentions writing out 'some of Beattie's poems'.

189 'Memoirs and Correspondence of Mrs Grant of Laggan'. In 1806 Grant published the two-volume collection of her letters, *Letters from the Mountains*, to some acclaim, and further success came in 1808 with her best-selling account of her early life in America, *Memoirs of an American Lady*. The financial security

which resulted from these sales led to a final move to Edinburgh in 1810. Anne Grant and Jane continued to meet up on occasion, both in Stirling and Edinburgh, linked partly she tells us by 'a joint interest in an orphan family in the Highlands, which creates a kind of business between us'.

190 The financial success of his books enabled Macpherson to buy the Badenoch estate of Raitts for 8,000 guineas in 1787, and to spend a further £4,000 on a new house by Robert Adam. A year later he renamed the house Belleville and purchased the Phones and Etteridge estates. Falkirk Museum, Forbes of Callendar Papers, NRS 171/265/5, letter Duchess of Gordon to Ross, February 1787, and letter Elizabeth Grant to Mrs Brown (formerly Miss Jane Ewing), Laggan, October 1788, in Grant, *Letters*, vol. 2, letter XXVI, p. 134.

191 Taylor, *Wild Black Region*, p. 219, and John Stoddart, *Remarks on the Local Scenery & Manners in Scotland, during the Years 1799 and 1800*, vol. 2, London: William Miller, 1801, p. 156.

192 Taylor, *Wild Black Region*, p. 221. Jane Gordon, Duchess of Gordon, *An Autobiographical Chapter in the Life of Jane, Duchess of Gordon (1864)*, Glasgow: privately printed, 1864, letter V, June 1805. In contrast to the situation that developed on the Gordon estates, Taylor points to management of the nearby Invereshie estate by George Macpherson and his son Captain John Macpherson, where they created 'individualised leases … detailing the exact reforms and labour required from each farmer'. In addition to nineteen-year leases, further incentive was provided by 'The first seven years [being] rent free … [and afterwards] the rent increasing in proportion to the improvement'. See Taylor, *Wild Black Region*, pp. 117–18.

193 Isobel Williamson's son, Alexander Gordon, was one of the nine 'natural' children the duke had by five different women. All were recognized by the duke, given the Gordon name, and provided for. Thomas Young was a British polymath and physician. Description of the birthday party from Bence Jones, *The Royal Institution: Its Founders and its First Professors*, London: Longmans, Green and Co., 1871, p. 229.

194 Gordon, *Last Dukes*, pp. 91–2. WSRO Goodwood MS 1172/524, Microfilm, Box MF 1238, letter Lord Brome to Duke of Gordon, March 1797.

195 'Agricultural Survey', in George Robertson, *A General View of Kincardineshire; or, The Mearns*, London: Richard Phillips, 1810, pp. 356–60. Forbes, *Beattie*, p. 298.

196 WAC 6D-C7: Georgiana Russell, *Letters of Lady John Russell to her Husband, 1798–1801*, London: printed for private circulation at Chiswick Press, 1913, p. 11; transcription of letters contained in WAC B.2 D.6.RUS.

197 *The Times*, 12 February 1799.

198 The following quotations are all from Stoddart, *Remarks*, pp. 154–8.

199 Grant, *Memoirs of a Highland Lady*, vol. 1, pp. 45–6.

200 Sarah Murray, *A Companion and Useful Guide to the Beauties of Scotland*, vol. 2, 3rd edn, London: printed for the author, 1810, p. 343. WSRO Goodwood MS 1171/002373, letter Duchess of Gordon to Beattie, from 'Glen Fidich', 1776?

201 WSRO Goodwood MS, 1176/002102–2104, Microfilm, Box MF 1238, letter 554, Duchess of Gordon to Charles Gordon of Cluny, from Margate, 7 June 1801.

202 Foreman, *Georgiana*, p. 296, n. 42: see *Bon Ton*, no. 56 (October 1795). The friendship between Bedford and the Duchess of Devonshire had foundered on her defaulting on a loan of £6,000. Foreman goes on, 'When he realized that no payments would be forthcoming his sympathy turned to anger. He was furious, thinking she had used him, and … resolved never to speak to her again.' See Foreman, *Georgiana*, pp. 329 and 352.

203 Castalia, Countess Granville, ed., *Private Correspondence of Lord Granville Leveson Gower, 1781 to 1821*, 2 vols, London: John Murray, 1899, vol. 1, p. 336. Culford Park, Suffolk, was the home of Georgina's sister Louisa, married to the Marquis of Cornwallis. Louisa was five years older than Georgina and the two, along with Susan, Duchess of Manchester, living at Kimbolton, seem to have been close and to have visited each other once Georgina moved into Woburn Abbey.

204   HHP Add MS 51661, fol. 5, letter 6th Duke of Bedford to Lord Holland, 18 March 1802.

205   WAC 6D LOC21-27-1, NMR 3/22/4, Bundle 2, No. 1, letter Duchess of Gordon to Duke of Bedford, July 1802.

206   Bundle 2, No. 2, copy of a letter Duke of Bedford to Duchess of Gordon, undated but clearly *c.* July 1802. Bundle 1, No. 1, letter Georgiana Gordon to Duke of Bedford, from Piccadilly, 12 August 1802.

207   Quoted in Rachel Trethewey, *Mistress of the Arts: The Passionate Life of Georgina, Duchess of Bedford*, London: Review, 2002, pp. 56 and 60.

208   BP D1287/18/12 (P/938), letter Duke of Bedford to Lady Bradford, from Trentham, 11 March 1802.

209   Ibid., letter Duke of Bedford to Lady Bradford, from Paris, February? 1803. WAC 6D-ART 139-44, receipt for clothing bought in Paris, 1803, and 139-35, 36 and 37, invoices for items bought in France, 1803.

210   WSRO Goodwood MS 1173/848 and 850, letter Duke of Bedford to Duke of Gordon, from Arlington Street, 2 May 1803, and letter Duke of Gordon to Duke of Bedford, 21 May 1803.

211   BP D1287/18/12 (P/938), letter Duke of Bedford to Lady Bradford, from Arlington Street, 20 May 1803.

212   Gordon, *Last Dukes*, p. 110. The event is quoted from Lady Charlotte Bury, *The Diary of a Lady in Waiting*, ed. A. Francis Steuart, London: Bodley Head, 1908, vol. 2, p. 338. WAC NMR 44/4/1, marriage certificate (large box of mostly legal papers, certificates, etc.). *The Times*, 8 July 1803; this must have been a very long day since the barge trip itself was about 13 kilometres/8 miles.

213   Forbes, *Beattie*, p. 307, letter Duchess of Gordon to Mr Glennie, the husband of Beattie's niece, August 1803. The line of poetry is from *The Minstrel*, Book II, Stanza XVII.

214   James Beattie, *Essay on the Nature and Immutability of Truth, in opposition to Sophistry and Scepticism* [1770], 6th edn, Edinburgh: Denham & Dick, 1805 (all quotations from his discussion of the role of intuition).

215   Forbes, *Beattie*, p. 115, letter Beattie to Dr Blacklock, 1766.

216   Sources for this summary include: Richard Holmes, *The Age of Wonder: How the Romantic Generation Discovered the Beauty and Terror of Science*, London: HarperCollins, 2009, and Simon Winchester, *The Map that Changed the World*, Harmondsworth: Penguin, 2001. Quotations from James Hutton's Theory of the Earth (1788) in 'James Hutton', en.wikipedia.org/wiki/James_Hutton (accessed 06/05/2020).

217   Samuel Taylor Coleridge, *Biographia Literaria*, London: R. Fenner, 1817. Malcolm Elwin, *The First Romantics: Wordsworth, Coleridge, Southey*, London: Macdonald & Co., 1947, p. 44, quoting from a letter by Dorothy Wordsworth in 1793 (*The Early Letters of William and Dorothy Wordsworth*, ed. E. De Selincourt, Oxford: Clarendon Press, 1935, p. 93). Roger Robinson, 'Beattie, Wordsworth and Coleridge', *Coleridge Bulletin*, new series, no. 4 (Autumn 1994), pp. 9, 11, 12 and 13.

218   For a detailed account of these walks, see Keir Davidson, *O joy for Me! Samuel Taylor Coleridge and the Origins of Fellwalking in the Lake District, 1790–1802*, London: Wilmington Square Books, 2018. Quotations (in the order they appear) pp. 97, 88, 127, 149.

219   Taylor, *Wild Black Region*, p. 220.

220   Grant, *Letters from the Mountains*, vol. 2, p. 142, letter Anne Grant to Mrs Furzer, July 1798, quoted in Marshall, *Glen Feshie*, p. 84. For '… singular place', see James Robertson, *General View of the Agriculture of the County of Inverness,* London: B. McMillan, 1808, p. lix. For '… advanced in growth', see *The New Statistical Account of Scotland, Vol. XIV: Inverness-shire, Ross and Cromarty*, Edinburgh and London: William Blackwood and Sons, 1845, p. 84, www.electricscotland.com (accessed 9/2/2019).

221   Grant, *Memoirs of a Highland Lady*, vol. 1, p. 46. Stoddart, *Remarks*, pp. 154–8. NRS GD2497, Wester Kinrara, plan of Kinrara, Wester Lynwylg, Kanloch, etc., 1771. This plan, recording in detail the existing condition of the farm at Kinrara, may well have been drawn up at the time of the initial 'warning out'

of the occupants, and shows, to the west of the farm buildings, the outline of the 'morass' running down the side of the knoll from an area marked 'water', presumably a spring head, down to the Spey. The size of the area, and its being prone to flooding 'occasioned by the River Spey', would have made any attempt to ornament it very challenging, if not futile.

222 Eata of Hexham (d.686) trained under Aidan at Lindisfarne and was 'chosen as one of the 12 monks selected to found … the monastery at Melrose'. In 661 he became Abbott of Melrose before moving to Ripon. An opponent of the reforms of the Synod of Whitby (663), he rejected the changes made to the traditional Celtic Church to bring it in line with Roman practice, and returned to the more conservative practice at Melrose ('Eata of Hexham', www.en.wikipedia.org [accessed 8/5/2020]). It could be that his cult came north with the original Gordon settlers from Melrose and the Border region, and became established in some of the Highland regions they occupied.

223 Although totally missing today, in the late eighteenth century the farm site at Kinrara and the area around it must have had a much stronger sense of connection to historic spiritual worlds, since in addition to whatever survived from the cult of St Eata, beside the southern access road to the farm stood a cluster of prehistoric tumuli in which 'Human Remains, Sword Blades & Buckles Etc. were found in A.D.1800' according to the Ordnance Survey in 1869 (while Jane was living there), and a short distance away in fields across the Aviemore-Kingussie road stood a stone circle and standing stone at Delfour (now largely destroyed). See maps.nls.uk/view/74427095, First Edition Ordnance Survey 'Inverness-shire (Mainland), sheet LXXIII (includes Alvie, Duthil and Rothiemurchus)', survey date 1869.

224 Keir Davidson, *Woburn Abbey: The Park and Gardens*, London: Pimpernel Press, 2016, p. 114. For '… status quo', see Paul Smith, 'The Landed Estate as Patron of Scientific Innovations: Horticulture at Woburn Abbey, 1802–1839', Phd thesis, Open University, 1983, p. 111. I have found Paul Smith's thesis invaluable in understanding these aspects of the duke's life, and many of the threads in this book have been drawn from it along with useful facts.

225 'Virgil, *The Georgics: A Poem of the Land*', trans. Kimberly Johnson, Harmondsworth: Penguin, 2010, pp. xiv, xvi, xv.

226 WAC 5D-WS2, letter 5th Duke of Bedford to Lord John Russell, 1–2 March 1802. WAC LOC21-24-6 6D, Correspondence Bundle, Middlesex, Mssrs Gotobed & Brown, letter John Gotobed, Norfolk Street, to Joseph Davis, Swyre, 23 July 1802. John Gotobed, the senior partner, seems to have died sometime in early 1804, and was succeeded by Brown.

227 John Martin Robinson, 'Estate Buildings of the 5th and 6th Dukes of Bedford at Woburn 1787–1839', *Architectural Review*, November 1976, pp. 277–81 (BARS CRT 130 Woburn 29).

228 Elizabeth Grant, *The Highland Lady in Ireland: Journals 1840–50*, ed. Patricia Pelly and Andrew Tod, Edinburgh: Canongate, 1991, p. 75.

229 See Matthew Hirst, 'The Realisation of a Regency Palace: The 6th Duke of Bedford and the Redecoration of Woburn Abbey', *Furniture History*, LIII (2017), pp. 225–42. I am much indebted to Matthew and Victoria Poulton in the Curator's office at Woburn for their assistance in all matters to do with the collections and redecoration of the Abbey at this time.

230 Ibid, p. 225. BARS R5/1348, Fortnightly Account Books, Extraordinary Works, October 1803.

231 WAC LOC24-26-2, Box of Notebooks, Diaries and Account Books, two brown leather notebooks for 1802 and 1804. Both record journeys made by William Adam. All quotations which follow, unless otherwise indicated, are from 'Notebook 1802'.

232 Between 1845 and 1851, for example, once the copper mines were fully open, the Bedford estate received enormous royalties of £44,000 (*c.* £2,640,000 today). See Thomas Spargo, *Statistics and Observations on the Mines of Cornwall and Devon* (1864), quoted in 'Devon Great Consols', www.en.wikipedia.org, accessed 2/7/2021.

233   WAC LOC21-24-6 6D, Correspondence, Bundle: Middlesex, Messrs Gotobed & Brown, letters Adam to Gotobed, 27 August 1802, and Gotobed to Adam, 30 August 1802. Robert Adair, a Whig and relative of the duke, was elected 1802–10. The constituency was abolished in 1832.

234   Letter Duke of Bedford to William Adam, 15 November 1802, quoted in 'Camelford', historyofparliamentonline.org, accessed 2/1/2021 (article and n. 8).

235   Quoted in Georgiana Blakiston, *Woburn and the Russells*, London: Constable, 1980 , p. 172.

236   William Pontey, *The Forest Pruner*, Huddersfield: private printing, 1805, p. viii, and *The Profitable Planter*, Huddersfield: private printing, 1800.

237   George Biggin, 'Experiments to determine the Quantity of Tanning Principle and Gallic Acid contained in the Bark of Various Trees', *Philosophical Magazine*, first series, 5:20 (1800), pp. 321–5. Richard Holmes, *The Age of Wonder: How the Romantic Generation Discovered the Beauty and Terror of Science*, London: HarperCollins, 2009, p. 142. *London Chronicle*, 8–10 April 1784.

238   William Smith, *Observations on the Utility and Management of Water Meadows, and the draining and irrigating of peat bogs; with an account of Prisley Bog, and other extraordinary improvements, conducted for His Grace the Duke of Bedford, Thomas William Coke MP and others*, London: Longman, 1806. For '… a medal', see Simon Winchester, *The Map that Changed the World*, Harmondsworth: Penguin, 2001, p. 203. For 'Sir Humphry Davy', see Jane Margaret Strickland, *A Memoir of Edmund Cartwright, Inventor of the Power Loom*, London: Saunders and Otley, 1843, p. 205.

239   *Morning Chronicle*, 20 June 1804.

240   For details of the architectural changes to the Abbey, the new areas around the building and the new road system, see Davidson, *Woburn Abbey*, pp. 115–19.

241   Humphry Repton, *Fragments on the Theory and Practice of Landscape Gardening*, London: J. Taylor, 1816, p. 149. For detailed discussion of Repton's designs for Woburn, see Keir Davidson, *Humphry Repton and the Russell Family, Featuring the Red Books for Woburn Abbey and Endsleigh Devon*, London: Pimpernel Press for the Bedford Estates, 2018, and for a wider account of Repton's career, see Stephen Daniels, *Humphry Repton: Landscape Gardening and the Geography of Georgian England*, New Haven and London: Yale University Press, 1999 (quote on p. 173).

242   For a full discussion and images of these changes, see Davidson, *Woburn Abbey*, pp. 95, 100–1.

243   The duke's middle son – Lord George William – was more commonly known as William or Billy, and in turn the duke's brother became known as 'old Lord William'.

244   Georgina was actually pregnant twelve times during this period, but one little boy, born 1813, died the next day, and another who was born in 1819 died two months later.

245   Donald J. Olsen, *Town Planning in London: The Eighteenth & Nineteenth Centuries*, 2nd edn, New Haven and London: Yale University Press, 1982, p. 51.

246   Dana Arnold, *Rural Urbanism: London Landscapes in the Early Nineteenth Century*, Manchester: Manchester University Press, 2005, Table 1.2, p. 29. This emphasis on high-end development on the Bedford estate at this time is made clear in figures produced by Arnold which indicate that in the years 1798–1803, out of 166 'first-rate' houses built by James Burton across Bloomsbury, 132 of them were built for the Bedford estate, 29 for the Foundling Hospital estate, 4 for the Skinner's estate and just 1 for the Lucas estate. Standards for house building in London were consolidated by the Building Act of 1774, which established a four tier 'rate' for house construction: 'First Rate' were houses of more than 900 sq. ft with a value over £850. 'Second Rate' were those of 500–900 sq. ft with a value of £350–850, 'Third Rate', 350–500 sq. ft and valued at £150–300, and 'Fourth Rate', less than 350 sq. ft and valued below £150. In terms of location, the higher the rating, the grander the streets and squares they were built in, with the lower ratings lining minor streets and areas around the stables and mews complexes.

247   In keeping with the precedent of Bedford Square, the Bedford Office was responsible for the

surveying and layout of the streets and squares, the construction of the sewers, the laying of road surfaces and providing outline guidance for the rating and style of the housing. In turn, the builders themselves were responsible for the specific architectural details of the houses and the pavements in front.

248   James Peter Malcolm, *Londinium Redivivuim* (1802–7), quoted in Olsen, *Town Planning in London*, p. 53.

249   Earl of Ilchester, ed., *The Journal of Elizabeth, Lady Holland (1791–1811)*, 2 vols, London: Longmans, Green & Co., 1908, vol. II, p. 107.

250   Daniels, *Humphry Repton*, p. 181.

251   Humphry Repton, *Enquiry into the Changes in Taste in Landscape Gardening*, London: J. Taylor, 1806, pp. 60–64. Russell Square and Bloomsbury Square were the 'two squares'. For the Repton quotations in the following paragraph, see ibid.

252   Quoted in Olsen, *Town Planning in London*, p. 55.

253   Elizabeth Hervey was the only legitimate child of Francis Marsh (or March) and Maria Hamilton; she was the residual heir to her father's estates, and in 1774 married Colonel Thomas Hervey. Hervey died four years later, but not before he had gambled away most of her inheritance. Between 1792 and 1820, Elizabeth wrote a series of journals, and all quotations here are taken from Journal 60 (entries 17 August – 3 September 1804) and 61 (entries 18–23 October 1804): © SRO D6584/C/101 and 102, Mrs Elizabeth Hervey Journals, 1792–1820. I am much indebted to Dr Diane Barr's work on the transcriptions of these journals, for bringing this material to the attention of Nicola Allen, Woburn Abbey Archivist, and for her thoughts and comments.

254   For details of the work on Repton's Red Book designs, see Daniels, *Humphry Repton*, and Davidson, *Woburn Abbey* and *Humphry Repton and the Russell Family*. Lord Lieutenant of Ireland: in Ireland the chief 'governor' was known as the 'lord deputy' until 1640, when the title was raised to 'Lord Lieutenant of Ireland' or 'Viceroy'. Following the Act of Union, emphasis was laid on latter title to add a royal sheen to the authority of the post in line with nineteenth-century colonial policy.

255   WAC 6D-Ireland, Box 2, letter Duke of Bedford to Charles James Fox, 1806.

256   GP GRE/BE/17, letter Duke of Bedford to Lord Howick, 19 September 1806, quoted in Rachel Trethewey, *Mistress of the Arts: The Passionate Life of Georgina, Duchess of Bedford*, London: Review, 2002, p. 80.

257   Charles O'Mahony, *The Viceroys of Ireland: The Story of the Long Line of Noblemen and their Wives Who Have Ruled Ireland and Irish Society for Over Seven Hundred Years*, London: J. Long, 1912, p. 210. For '… pointedly conservative', see Laura Engel and Elaine M. McGirr, eds, *Stage Mothers: Women, Work and the Theater, 1660–1830*, Lewisburg, Pa.: Bucknell University Press, 2014, p. 202. *Dublin Evening Post*, 12 April 1806, quoted in Trethewey, *Mistress of the Arts*, pp. 82–3.

258   WAC 6D-Ireland, Box 2, ceremonial arrangements for receiving Duke of Bedford, April 1806.

259   Ibid., 'Private Instructions' from George III to Duke of Bedford, 1806.

260   HHP Add MS 51661, fol. 20, letter Duke of Bedford to Lord Holland, from Phoenix Park, 15 May 1806.

261   See Trethewey, *Mistress of the Arts*, pp. 84–7, for a detailed account of that summer.

262   HHP Add MS 51661, fol. 26, letter Duke of Bedford to Lord Holland, from Phoenix Park, 28 September 1806. GP GRE/B6/17/1, letter Duke of Bedford to Lord Howick, from Phoenix Park, 29 September 1806.

263   WAC 6D LOC21-27-1, Bundle 3, Nos 8 and 5, letters Georgina to Duke of Bedford from Phoenix Park, 4 and 9 October 1806.

264   Ibid., No. 10, letter Georgina to Duke of Bedford, from Clontarf, 13 October 1806.

265   WAC HMC 96C2/14–19, letter Duke of Bedford to Lord Spencer, from Phoenix Park, 20 November 1806.

266   GP GRE/B6/17/1/34 and 35, April 1809 and August 1809, letters Duke of Bedford to Lord Grey, from Stanhope Street, 14 May 1809.

267   WAC 6D LOC21-27-1, Bundle 23, No. 17, Duke of Bedford's *Reflections*, 12 August 1807.

268   Ilchester, *Journal*, vol. II, p. 232.

269   WRSO Goodwood MS 1176/000619, Duchess of Gordon to Charles Gordon, from Ayton, 26 October 1807.

270   HHP Add MS 51665, fol. 4, letter Duke of Bedford to Lady Holland, from Edinburgh, 18 October 1807. Dr John Allen was treated at Holland House as one of the family, and he became indispensable to the Hollands as their librarian for the next forty-two years. For '… entered the household', see Sonia Keppel, *The Sovereign Lady: A Life of Elizabeth, Third Lady Holland, with her Family*, London: Hamilton, 1974, p. 118.

271   Smith, 'The Landed Estate as Patron of Scientific Innovations', pp. 145–6.

272   WAC, loose sheet 'List of Company expected at the Sheepshearing, 1808', including bedroom allocations. The '2 Mr Reptons' are likely to be Humphry and his son, the architect John Adey Repton, and this suggests that they were working with the artist Agostino Aglio on the interior designs for the cottage in the Thornery. See in particular WAC AHB-3, 'Agricultural Papers 1802–12'.

273   HHP Add MS 51661, fol. 86, letter Duke of Bedford to Lord Holland, from Woburn Abbey, January 1808. WAC, 'Biographical Catalogue', vol. 2, p. 179.

274   WAC 6D LOC21-27-1, Salmon Reports, Pleasure Grounds, March 1808. For the quote, see WAC, James Forbes, *Hortus Woburnensis*, London: J. Ridgway, 1833, p. 239.

275   All quotations Smith, 'The Landed Estate as Patron of Scientific Innovation, pp. 145–6. Interestingly enough, one other person running such tests was the duke's acquaintance from Ireland, the Earl of Hardwicke at Wimpole Hall, but no one else produced anything like Sinclair's book. Sir Humphry Davy, *Elements of Agricultural Chemistry in A Course of Lectures for the Board of Agriculture*, London: Longman, Hurst, Rees, Orme and Brown; Edinburgh: A. Constable and Co., 1813.

276   Kathleen Coburn, ed., *Inquiring Spirit: A New Presentation of Coleridge*, London: Routledge & Kegan Paul, 1951, p. 27.

277   Quoted from Davy, *Elements* (2nd edn, 1814), 'Advertisement', pp. v, vi. Forbes, *Hortus Woburnensis*, Plate III, 'General Plan of the Pleasure Ground'.

278   Quotations from Phyllis Mary Hembry, *British Spas from 1815 to the Present Day: A Social History*, London: Athlone, 1997, p. 9. See Alan Griffin, 'Leamington History', 9 July 2013, www.leamingtonhistory. co.uk/some-early-aristocratic-residents (accessed 10/2/2017), for details of Jane Maxwell's house.

279   For details of the new landscaping, see Davidson, *Woburn Abbey*, pp. 126, 136–8, and Davidson, *Humphry Repton and the Russell Family*, p. 41.

280   WAC 6D LOC21-24-5, Misc. Box, formal ornamental letter to the duke from the Secretary of the Society of Antiquaries, Nicholas Carlisle, 23 June 1809. WAC (no archive accession no.), Red Pocket Diary, 'The Ladies Museum, or, Complete Pocket Memorandum Book for the year 1810', diary kept by Lady Gertrude Francis Russell, daughter of Lord William Russell, entries for 3 and 11 April 1810. Repton, *Fragments*, pp. 13–16.

281   J. D. Parry, M.A., *A Guide to Woburn Abbey* (Woburn: printed by S. Dodd, 1831), p. 136. The guide is dedicated to both 'John, Duke of Bedford' and to 'Georgiana, Duchess of Bedford'.

282   Derek Linstrum, *Sir Jeffry Wyatville: Architect to the King*, Oxford: Clarendon Press, 1972, p. 93, n.5.

283   See listing 1105547, 'Well House Stone Pier and Rustic Seat in the Dairy Dell', historicengland. org.uk, accessed 17/7/2020: 'A picturesquely irregular inscription panel on the gable reads "This simple structure enclosed the holy well which served as a baptismal font to the Abbots of Tavistock at their hunting lodge in this parish."'

284   HHP Add MS 51674, letter Duke of Bedford to Lady Holland, December 1810, quoted in Rachel Trethewey, *Mistress of the Arts: The Passionate Life of Georgina, Duchess of Bedford*, London: Review, 2002,

p. 112. HHP Add MS 51674, fol. 1, letter Duchess of Bedford to Lord and Lady Holland, from Woburn Abbey, 16 March 1810.

285   WAC (no archive accession no.), Red Pocket Diary, 'The Ladies Museum, or, Complete Pocket Memorandum Book for the year 1810', diary kept by Lady Gertrude Francis Russell, daughter of Lord William Russell, entry for 15 August 1810. Lord Le Despencer: this description of Knowle Cottage and all quotations are from research done by Christine and Rab Barnard, and images from the Sidmouth Museum collection, published in Christine and Rab Barnard, *The Knowle, Sidmouth: A Stately Pleasure Dome*, Sidmouth Museum, 2013.

286   DHC L1258M/E/A/E8, Cash Accounts and Account Books for Endsleigh, 1810–15.

287   WAC, Red Pocket Diary, entries for 19 and 20 January 1811 and 25 December 1810.

288   WAC 6D DE-E5-4-1-1B, 4, 5, letters William Walker to Edward Bray, from Longbrook Lodge, February, 25 March and 8 April 1811.

289   WAC 6D DE-E5-4-1-6, 9, 11, 13, letters Walker to Bray, from Endsleigh, May, 5 June, 16 and 30 July 1811.

290   HHP Add MS 51674, letter Duchess of Bedford to Lady Holland, May 1811, quoted in Trethewey, *Mistress of the Arts*, p. 112.

291   HHP Add MS 51661, fol. 166, letter Duke of Bedford to Lord Holland, 16 November 1810.

292   GP GRE/B6/17/39, letter Duke of Bedford to Lord Grey, from Woburn Abbey, 9 September 1811.

293   WAC HMC 130, Volume 2, Game Book 1804–22. WAC 6D LOC21-24-5 6 DOB, Misc. Box, certificate and seal for the Freedom of the City of Aberdeen, presented to John, Duke of Bedford, 15 October 1811.

294   DHC 1943M/E/15, letter Duke of Bedford to Richard Edgcumbe Esq. of Edgcumbe House, Milton Abbott, Tavistock, from Woburn Abbey, 15 March 1812.

295   John Malcolm Bulloch, ed., *The Gordon Book*, Aberdeen: Rosemont Press, 1902, p. 31 ('Prepared for: The Bazaar of the Forchabers Reading Room, Sept 1902'). Bulloch quotes the description of funeral procession from Alexander Macpherson in his *Glimpses of Church and Social Life in the Highlands in Olden Times* (1893).

296   Elizabeth Grant, *Memoirs of a Highland Lady*, 2 vols, ed. Andrew Tod, Edinburgh: Canongate, 2005, vol. 2, p. 37.

297   John Stoddart, *Remarks on the Local Scenery & Manners in Scotland, during the Years 1799 and 1800*, vol. 2, London: William Miller, 1801, p. 154.

298   Grant, *Memoirs*, vol. 1, pp. 198, 215 and 333.

299   Trethewey, *Mistress of the Arts*, p. 124. WAC 6D LOC21-27-1, Bundle 4, No. 3, letter Lady Jane Montagu to Duke of Bedford, 20 January 1812.

300   WAC 6D LOC21-27-1, Bundle 4, No. 1, letter Lord William Russell to Duke of Bedford, from Edinburgh, sent to Hamilton Place and redirected to Woburn Abbey, 18 September 1812.

301   WAC NMR 4/8, Cash Book A, 9 August 1812: 'Her Grace the Duchess of Bedford, from John Pringle (on behalf of the executors of the late John Fordyce) for "Fortnights Rent of the House & Garden belonging to Mrs Fordyce £26.5.0"', plus 'Dilapidations: "Goblets, 1 Candlestick, 1 Breakfast Cup, 1 Wine Glass: £0.3.3".' WAC NMR 4/8, Cash Book A, 10 February, 2 April and 22 June 1812, 'Botanical Publications'.

302   Richard Edgecumbe, *The Diary of Frances Lady Shelley, 1787–1817*, London: John Murray, 1912, pp. 49–50, letter Lady Shelley to Lady Spencer at Althorp, from Woburn Abbey, December 1812.

303   DHC W1258M/CP4, Bundle 1, No. 26, Endsleigh, Samuel Facey & Partner, site work and quarrymen, 13 February 1813.

304   DHC W1258M/LP4/9, September 1813, building the pheasant house in Leigh Wood. DHC W1258M/LP4/15, new trees. DHC E8, Cash Book for Endsleigh, Abstract of Expenditure, February 1811 to October 1815. In modern terms £21,741.18.4 = £1,304,460 [×60].

305   *Monthly Review*, vol. 74 (June 1814), p. 205, Monthly Catalogue, Poetry: 'Woburn Abbey Georgics; or, The Last-Gathering', introductory remarks to the review.

306   Quotations from Trethewey, *Mistress of the Arts*, pp. 124–5, on which this account is based. Hundreds Farm House: Lord John occupied the house between 1815 and 1832. Sir Robert Inglis, MP, son of Sir Hugh Inglis of Milton House, Milton Bryant, was among the visitors and recorded the remark 'the place in which his mind was formed.' See Spencer Walpole, *The Life of Lord John Russell*, 2 vols, London: Longmans, Green and Co., 1889, vol. 1, p. 163, n.1.

307   WAC 6D LOC21-27-1, Bundle 9, No. 1, letter Revd Mr Greenwood to Duke of Bedford, 21 December 1807.

308   HHP Add MS 51661, fol. 148, letter Duke of Bedford to Lord Holland, 4 March 1810. WAC HMC 110, three pocket books, 1838–9, of Anna Maria Stanhope, daughter of General Charles Stanhope, 3rd Earl of Harrington. Georgiana Blakiston, *Lord William Russell and his Wife 1815–1846*, London: John Murray, 1972, p. 24. John Cam Hobhouse, *Recollections of a Long Life by Lord Broughton*, 6 vols, London: John Murray, 1909, vol. 3, p. 166.

309   E. F. Leveson-Gower, ed., *Letters of Harriet, Countess Granville, 1810–1845*, 2 vols, London: Longmans, Green and Co., 1894, vol. 1, p. 100, letter Harriet, Countess Granville, to Lady Morpeth, from Paris, June 1817.

310   GP GRE/B6/17/37, letter Duke of Bedford to Lord Grey, from Longleat, 24 August 1809.

311   See David R. Fisher, 'Russell, Lord George William (1790–1846)', www.historyofparliamentonline.org, accessed 18/8/2020.

312   Blakiston, *Lord William Russell*, p. 9. WAC 6D LOC21-27-1, Bundle 4, No. 3, letter Lady Jane Montagu to Duke of Bedford, 20 January 1812.

313   Blakiston, *Lord William Russell*, p. 25. For the Duke of Gloucester's Band, see WAC NMR 4/8, Cash Book B, party at Richmond, 16 July 1813.

314   HHP Add MS 51665, fol. 150, letter Duke of Bedford to Lady Holland, from Cintra, 24 June 1814.

315   GP GRE/B6/16/1, letter Duchess of Bedford to Lord Grey, from Lisbon, 19 October 1814.

316   WAC 6D-ART 154, Duke of Bedford, Travel Diary, pp. 8 and 10.

317   Trethewey, *Mistress of the Arts*, p. 137.

318   WAC 6D-ART 154, Travel Diary, pp. 10–12.

319   Ibid., pp. 13–14. WAC NMR 4/8, Cash Book B, the duke's birthday.

320   WAC 6D-ART 154, Travel Diary, p. 14.

321   DHC Bedford MSS L1258 E/12, 'Report concerning Endsleigh Cottage', 11 August 1814.

322   Repton's suggestions for work on the far side of the river were somewhat premature since in 1814 the duke had still not secured the lease for the woodland, and work could not have gone ahead. The fact that this work remained undone, even three years later when the lease was secured, suggests that the duke and duchess simply did not share Repton's vision of a picturesque landscape.

323   DHC W1258M/CP4, Bundle 4, October 1814 to February 1815, materials from the 'Freestone Quarry', much of it for the 'Wall in front of the buildings'.

324   Stoddart, *Remarks*, p. 157. HHP Add MS 51666, fol. 16, letter Duke of Bedford to Lady Holland, from Paris, October 1815. WAC NMR 4/8, Cash Book B, 6 May 1815, 'Capt. William Forrester, of the ship "Brilliant Star" from Leghorn to London. Customs dues for 4 packages.' The Fysche Palmers were neighbours in Bedfordshire, living at the Old House, Ickwell Green and Northill estate, and frequent visitors to Woburn. J. D. Parry, *A Guide to Woburn Abbey*, Woburn: printed by S. Dodd, 1831, p. 10. WAC 6D-ART 10, inventory in Italian.

325   WAC NMR 4/8, Cash Book B, 27 November 1815.

326   WAC NMR 8/11/9 BE-RB1, William Adam, Bedford estates annual reports, 1815–30.

327   WAC 6D LOC21-27-1, Bundle 24, No. 15, 'Proposed Regulations for the Lords Russell at Endsleigh'.

328   All quotes from Matthew Hirst, 'The Realisation of a Regency Palace: The 6th Duke of Bedford and the Redecoration of Woburn Abbey', *Furniture History*, LIII (2017), pp. 233–4.

329   The duke and Sinclair continued to pursue these experiments by refining techniques, adding varieties and improving data collection until Sinclair left in 1825, and the ongoing results were added to the third edition of *Hortus Gramineus Woburnensis* in 1826. William Jackson Hooker, 'Copy of a Letter Addressed to Dawson Turner … on the occasion of the Death of the Duke of Bedford, particularly with reference to the services rendered by His Grace to Botany and Horticulture', Glasgow: printed by George Richardson, 1840, p. 3. Charles Darwin, *The Origin of the Species*, London: Harper Press, 2011, p. 111, as part of his discussion of 'Divergence of Character'. See Andy Hector and Rowan Cooper, 'Darwin and the First Ecological Experiment (Perspectives on Ecology)', *Science*, 295:5555 (2002), p. 639. The authors rightly identify the experiments with grasses noted by Darwin as those conducted at Woburn, and go on to claim that these experiments can be seen retrospectively as the world's first ecological experiments. RBGK DC A–B, vol. 7, fol. 77, letter Duke of Bedford to William Hooker, from The Doune, 13 September 1836.

330   GP GRE/B6/17/57 and 58, letters Duke of Bedford to Lord Grey, from Woburn, 22 and 31 December 1816.

331   Sonia Keppel, *The Sovereign Lady: A Life of Elizabeth, Third Lady Holland, with her Family*, London: Hamilton, 1974, p. 232, quoting from the journal of the Hon. H. E. Fox, and p. 247, quoting HHP Add MS 51645, letter Duke of Bedford to Lady Holland.

332   All quotations from Blakiston, *Lord William Russell*, pp. 1–4, 15, 17, 2 and 29. Blakiston's comments carry considerable weight, since she was a direct descendant of William and Elizabeth, the curator of their papers and their main biographer.

333   Ibid, p. 44, letter Lady William Russell to Antonio Canova, from Woburn Abbey, July 1818.

334   Ibid., p. 38, letter Lord William Russell to Mrs Rawdon, from Woburn Abbey, 17 July 1817.

335   Leveson-Gower, *Letters*, vol. 1, p. 127, letter Harriet, Countess Granville, to Lady Morpeth, from Paris, June and August 1817.

336   WAC 6D LOC35-23-4, Bundle 18, William Adam Correspondence, letter Mr Gray (Duchy of Cornwall) to William Adam, 28 May 1818. See Moses Bawden, 'Mines and Mining in the Tavistock District (1914)', paper read at Tavistock, 22 July 1914, www.devonassoc.org.uk, accessed 27/8/2020. DHC W1258M/LP4, Bundle 7/149, August 1817, Joseph Williams, bills for 'the removal of the small boat from the river to the canal'.

337   DHC W1258M/CP4, Bundle 5, two receipts, July and August 1817, subscriptions for Tavistock Public Library and Tavistock Dorcas Society. Dorcas societies were local church-based groups organized to distribute clothing to the poor. DHC W1258M/CP4, Bundle 5, July 1818, *Western Luminary* and *Exeter Flying Post* and Tavistock Lying-in Society, £5 for twelve months.

338   DHC W1258M/LP4, Bundle 7, John Shepherd, stonemason, Plymouth, 'Lion's Head'. DHC E22, Account Book, 24 October 1820, 'John Deacon for Engraving and Painting an inscription in the Stable Yard at Endsleigh Cottage'. DHC W1258M/LP4, Bundle 7, June 1817, and DHC W1258M/LP4, Bundle 15, September 1817, cherry and apple trees.

339   WAC 6D LOC21-27-1, Bundle 8, Nos 1–3, letters Lord Grantham to and from the Duke of Bedford, January 1818. WAC NMR4/13, Bundle 12, J. P. Neale's 'Woburn Abbey'. HHP Add MS 51666, fols 183 and 184, letters Duke of Bedford to Lady Holland, from Paris, 9 and 13 April 1818.

340   Blakiston, *Lord William Russell*, p. 42, letter Lord William Russell to Lady Holland, from Dover, 25 June 1818.

341   AP D623/A 251/1, letter 11 June 1818, from Paris. AP D623/A 251/4, no date or address but Calais notepaper; 'Mamselle Clarisse' was Clarisse Bernard, French governess 1818–19. AP D623/A 251/2 and 3, letters 8 and 27 July 1818, from Milan and Calais.

342   WAC NMR 4/17/3, Bundle 3, Nos 38 and 39.

343   MGP, NRAS 771, Bundle 485, letter James Carnegy to George Macpherson-Grant, Edinburgh, 11 December 1818, concerning the lease. WAC NMR 4/9/1, Bundle 5, No. 17, November–December 1818, George Hunter & Co., Clothiers and Mercers, Edinburgh.

344   All quotations from David Taylor, *The Wild Black Region: Badenoch, 1750–1800*, Edinburgh: John Donald, 2016, pp. 117–21.

345   For quote ending 'for this purpose', see Meryl Marshall, *Glen Feshie: The History and Archaeology of a Highland Glen*, 2nd edn, [Conon Bridge:] NOSAS, 2013, p. 52. For quote ending 'Loch Ericht', see Mary Miers, *Highland Retreats: The Architecture and Interiors of Scotland's Romantic North*, New York: Rizzoli, 2017, p. 46. NRAS 771, Bundle 1202, accounts for work at Invereshie House, 1806.

346   All quotations from Taylor, *Wild Black Region*, pp. 45–8.

347   NRAS 771, Bundle 1203, letter Alex Bell, Invereshie, to Captain George Macpherson-Grant, Ballindalloch, 1807.

348   I am particularly grateful to Alan Marshall at Invereshie House for his time and interest, and for supplying the material on which this account is based.

349   Georgiana Blakiston, *Woburn and the Russells*, London: Constable, 1980, p. 178, and Blakiston, *Lord William Russell*, p. 135, letter Lord William Russell to Lord Tavistock, from Richmond Park Farm, 15 September 1825.

350   WAC NMR 4/9/1, Bundle 5, No. 44, invoices to Duchess of Bedford from Jeremiah Wiffen, 1818–19. WAC NMR 4/8, Cash Book C: 'For Instruction in Writing, Arithmetic & Latin. Lord Wriothesley [age sixteen], 18 lessons, Lord Edward [fifteen], 7 lessons, Lord Charles [thirteen], 24 lessons, Lord Francis [twelve], 20 lessons.'

351   HHP Add MS 51667, fol. 1, letter Duke of Bedford to Lady Holland, from Woburn Abbey, 5 January 1819. Edward went on to become an admiral and, like his brother Frank, was to prove very useful to his father, transporting botanical specimens from plant collectors in South America and elsewhere to England.

352   BARS R5/1352 (1809–15), R5/1353 (1816–21), for details of the garden accounts for Woburn Abbey during this period.

353   For details of their activities in London, see WAC 6D A1-2-18-1, Bundle 3, Nos 4, 7, 10, May–June, Almack's; No. 14, Buckingham Palace Drawing Room; No. 15, 'Concert at Hamilton Place'; WAC NMR 4/12/7/3-1, boat trips, 25 June, 5 and 16 July. Locations in both Richmond and Twickenham were used several times by the duke and duchess for such outings; the family sometimes also travelled down from central London by boat.

354   WAC 6542, folder, 'Original Drawings for Woburn and Endsleigh', Jeffry Wyatville, 'River Tamar – Seat in Leigh Woods and Swiss Cottage on the summit, Endsleigh. J.W. Aug 1819'.

355   DHC E21, Account Book, 1819 – February 1820, Endsleigh gardens, buildings, garden walls, Swiss Cottage, 10 September and December 1819.

356   WAC 6542, 'Original Drawings for Woburn and Endsleigh' (folder of drawings), Jeffry Wyatville, for Rustic Seat and Castle Head ruin. For a view of house from the Rock Seat, see F. C. Lewis, *The Scenery of the Rivers Tamar and Tavy, in Forty-Seven Subjects, Exhibiting the Most Interesting Views on their Banks*, London: John and Arthur Arch, and R. Triphook, 1823, No. 16. For images of the Ferryman's Cottage, see WAC PA 11 (nineteenth-century photograph album).

357   Georgiana Blakiston, *Lord William Russell and his Wife 1815–1846*, London: John Murray, 1972, p. 45, letter Lady William Russell to Lady Holland, 8 August 1819. Ibid, p. 46. Elizabeth Grant, *Memoirs of a Highland Lady*, 2 vols, ed. Andrew Tod, Edinburgh: Canongate, 2005, vol. 2, pp. 124–5.

358   Blakiston, *Lord William Russell*, pp. 45–6, letter Duke and Duchess of Bedford to Lord William Russell, from Vienna, 9 November 1819. ('Jobation' is a rebuke or a scolding.) Ibid., p. 46.

359   Matthew Hirst, 'The Realisation of a Regency Palace: The 6th Duke of Bedford and the Redecoration of Woburn Abbey', *Furniture History*, LIII (2017), pp. 225–42 (WAC), p. 236.

360   HHP Add MS 51667, fol. 44, letter Duke of Bedford to Lady Holland, from Endsleigh, 16 March 1820.

361   *The Times*, 29 June 1827, 'The Duke of Bedford's pictures at Christie on view prior to sale'.

362   For details of Landseer's early life, see Richard Ormond, *Sir Edwin Landseer*, London: Tate Gallery, 1981, pp. 1–5; Campbell Lennie, *Landseer: The Victorian Paragon*, London: Hamilton, 1976, pp. 3–14.

363   Ormond, *Landseer*, p. xiii.

364   HHP Add MS 51667, fol. 46, letter Duke of Bedford to Lady Holland, 15 May 1820. J. Britton and E. W. Brayley, *Devonshire Illustrated in a Series of Views*, London: Fisher and Jackson, 1842, pp. 55–6, 'Endsleigh Cottage, Milton Abbot'.

365   Grant, *Memoirs*, vol. 1, p. 286. In 1814 Elizabeth, Jane and William helped to design the West Gate Cottage, The Croft (rebuilt after a fire 1813), the 'Widow's Cottage' (possibly Milton Cottage), the Boat Man's House (beside the ferry point) and alterations to Polchar. The next year they drew up a design for Loch Eilein Cottage ('Mother's Cottage').

366   GRP, NRAS 771, Bundle 716, letter John McInnis to George Macpherson-Grant, March 1820. Ibid., letter John McInnis to George Macpherson-Grant, April 1820. (It is not quite clear who 'Mr Cameron' was, but he is likely to have been Angus Cameron, a ground officer for Macpherson-Grant in Badenoch.) Ibid., letter John McInnis to George Macpherson-Grant, 16 May 1820, enclosing a letter from Donald Vass, gardener at Invereshie. (Andrew Davidson was a Macpherson-Grant tenant farmer at nearby Farr who also seems to have had responsibility as local ground officer for Invershie.) The author is grateful to David Taylor for this information and the suggestion concerning the identity of Mr Cameron.

367   Ibid., letters John McInnis to George Macpherson-Grant, January (concerning the letter the duke had written to Vass in December 1819), 19 March, 11 April and 8 May 1820.

368   NRAS 771, Bundle 591, letter John McInnis to George Macpherson Grant, 24 June 1820.

369   HHP Add MS 51667, fol. 50, letter Duke of Bedford to Lady Holland, from Endsleigh, 29 March 1820. WAC 6D A1-2-18-1, Bundle 8, Samuel Avery, Footman, Vauxhall Gardens, miscellaneous and travelling expenses, June and July 1820.

370   WAC NMR 4/12/4/3-63 and WAC NMR 4/8, Cash Book B, Thomas Downing and Sons, decorations. WAC NMR 4/8, Cash Book B, 18 July 1820, 'Master of the Dance'. WAC NMR 4/8, Cash Book B, 25 July 1820, day trip to Castle Inn, Richmond, boat hire, and 'Edward Hopkins, Master of the Band of his Highness the Duke of Gloucester or Third Guards, for attending Her Grace the Dss of Bedford and party in the Richmond Steam Boat to Richmond and back on Tuesday 25th. 18 musicians and 3 Blacks.' These '3 Blacks' may have served a similar musical role to those shown in an image of *c*.1790 'depicting the relief of the guard at St James's Palace, London, [which] shows three black musicians [two drummers and a percussionist] among the band': see Porchester Castle, History and Stories, Black People in Late 18th-Century Britain, english-heritage.org.uk, accessed 14/09/2020.

371   HHP Add MS 51667, fol. 54, letter Duke of Bedford to Lady Holland, from Woburn Abbey, 2 July 1820.

372   E. F. Leveson-Gower, ed., *Letters of Harriet, Countess Granville, 1810–1845*, 2 vols, London: Longmans, Green and Co., 1894, vol. 1, p. 154, letter Harriet, Countess Granville, to Duchess of Devonshire, from London, 30 July 1820. The Duke of Gordon married his long-time mistress and mother of five of his children, Jean Christie. George Gordon, *The Last Dukes of Gordon and their Consorts: A Revealing Study*, Aberdeen: G. Gordon, 1980, p.158.

373   HHP Add MS 51667, fol. 56, letter Duke of Bedford to Lady Holland, from Worthing, 15 August 1820. Grant, *Memoirs*, vol. 2, p. 161. The 'Ladies Cornwallis' were Georgina's nieces, daughters of Louisa Gordon and Charles, Marquis Cornwallis. Blakiston, *Lord William Russell*, p. 123, letter Lady William Russell to old Lord William Russell, from Weymouth, 6 October 1824.

374   HHP Add MS 51667, fol. 57, letters Duke of Bedford to Lady Holland, from Woburn Abbey, September 1820. ELC 1316/23, letter Duke of Bedford to Edwin Landseer, from Endsleigh, 5 April 1825. ELC 1316/25, letter Duke of Bedford to Edwin Landseer, from St James's Square, 21 July 1825.

375   Ormond, *Landseer*, p. 66.

376   Bedford Lodge, Campden Hill, was one of seven houses built on fields immediately east of Holland Park between 1812 and 1817. Letters and records invariably refer to the property as Campden Hill, although it appears on maps as Bedford Lodge. Over the years, Wyatville was to make various alterations and additions for the Bedfords, and the house remained in existence until demolished in the 1950s as part of the development of Holland Park School. The present day 'Duchess of Bedford Walk' runs along the line of the south end of the gardens.

377   WAC 6D A1-2-18-1, Bundle 8, No. 6, two antelopes. Anon., *Journal of a Tour into Derbyshire, Warwickshire &c. made in the Vacation of 1824*, Folger Shakespeare Library, Miranda Digital Asset Platform, M.b20, collections.folger.edu (accessed 3/8/2021). WAC NMR 4/23/11 Ph-MSS 35-10, letter Dr Allen Thomson, from Woburn Abbey, *c.*1836.

378   Leveson-Gower, *Letters*, vol. 1, pp. 196–9, letters Harriet, Countess Granville, to Lady Morpeth, 19 and 20 December 1820, and to Lady Harrowby (Susan Leveson-Gower), 21 December 1820. Amanda Foreman, *Georgiana: Duchess of Devonshire*, London: HarperCollins, 1998, p. 285.

379   WAC NMR 4/8, Cash Book B, 26 January 1821. Henry Fox, *The Journal of the Hon. Henry Edward Fox, afterward Fourth and Last Lord Holland, 1818–1830*, ed. the Earl of Ilchester, London: Thornton Butterworth, 1923, p. 57.

380   Ann Gore, and George Carter, eds, *Humphry Repton's Memoirs*, Norwich: Michael Russell, 2005, p. 55, letter William Adam to Repton, 1812.

381   Fox, *Journal*, p. 60. 'Russell, Francis, mq. of Tavistock (1788–1861), of Oakley, Beds. and 18 Arlington Street, Mdx.', Member Biographies, www.histparl.ac.uk, accessed 16/09/2020. GP GRE/B6/17/75, letter Duke of Bedford to Lord Grey, St James's Square, February 1821.

382   WAC *Hortus Ericaeus Woburnensis*, London: printed by J. Moyes, 1825, intro. Duke of Bedford. Paul Smith, 'The Landed Estate as Patron of Scientific Innovation: Horticulture at Woburn Abbey, 1802–1839', Phd thesis, Open University, 1983, p. 184.

383   BARS R5/1354, 1819–21, and R5/1355, 1822–6, Fortnightly Account Books. WAC *Hortus Ericaeus Woburnensis*, p. 272.

384   Donald J. Olsen, *Town Planning in London: The Eighteenth & Nineteenth Centuries*, 2nd edn, New Haven and London: Yale University Press, 1982, p. 57, letter Duke of Bedford to T. P. Brown, 25 August 1817.

385   Olsen, *Town Planning*, p. 58. For the new layout, see 'Plan showing intended buildings between Russell Square and the New Road', *c.*1838, which also includes the final element of the development, the three new blocks of houses between Gordon Square and Euston Square, along Georgiana Street and Endsleigh Street. For quote ending 'proper state for building', see Olsen, *Town Planning*, p. 59, n.55, from Christopher Haedy's 1851 report to the duke, p.11.

386   WAC NMR 4/8, Cash Book B, July 1821. Visits to Astley's became increasingly popular with the children as they grew up. Blakiston, *Lord William Russell*, p. 63, letter Lady Holland to Lord William, 14 May 1822. For Sneyd Papers, see Keele University Library Special Collections, *Panorama of Almack's* by Charlotte Augusta Sneyd, 1821–2. Georgina and Eliza feature as Nos 123 and 124 on the numbered key. For Almack's, see Rees Howell Gronow, *Reminiscences of Captain Gronow*, Gloucester: Dodo Press, 2008, vol. 1, pp. 27–8.

387   WAC NMR 4/8, Cash Book B, 3, 14 and 22 July 1821.

388   NRAS 771, Bundle 503, letter John McInnis to Mrs George Macpherson-Grant, from Dandaleith, March 1821, and letter Duke of Bedford to George Macpherson-Grant, from Woburn Abbey, 19 March 1821.

389   WAC HMC 130, vol. 2, Game Books, Invereshie, August–September 1821. NRAS 771, Bundle 503, letter John McInnis to George Macpherson-Grant, from Ballindalloch, February 1821, letting farms.

390   Blakiston, *Lord William Russell*, p. 59, letter Duke of Bedford to Lord William Russell, from Woburn Abbey, December 1821. WAC NMR 4/8, Cash Book B, 'To Thomas Pratt, Groom, Freight & expenses for 2 ponies from Huntly Lodge to Woburn Abbey, [billed] March 17, 1822'.

391   WAC HMC 111, 'Album of Anna Maria, Duchess of Bedford'. NAL, Algernon Graves, *Catalogue of the Works of the Late Sir Edwin Landseer R.A.*, London: H. Graves & Co., 1876. WAC NMR 4-11-7, Bundle 3, No. 16, furnishings. Fox, *Journal*, p. 90.

392   Georgiana Blakiston, *Woburn and the Russells*, London: Constable, 1980, pp. 187–8. Rachel Trethewey, *Mistress of the Arts: The Passionate Life of Georgina, Duchess of Bedford*, London: Review, 2002, p. 243. HHP Add MS 51671, fol. 39, letter Duke of Bedford to Lady Holland, from Endsleigh, 14 June 1832. *Reynold's Newspaper*, 7 October 1866: 'Charge of Cruelty against Lord Francis John Russell: At the Maidenhead Borough Petty Sessions, before the magistrates Mssrs J. Higgs and J. Smith. Lord Francis John Russell was charged "that on the 18th day of September he did cruelly beat and ill-use … two horses, in the High street, Maidenhead … the magistrates considered the case proved on the evidence of one of the witnesses, who said he had never seen a horse beaten so badly in his life.' *Sheffield Daily Telegraph*, 9 November 1866: 'A Singular Charge of Assault Against Lord F. J. Russell: At Maidenhead petty sessions, Lord Francis John Russell appeared before the bench charged with assaulting Joseph Wise.'

393   WAC HMC 130, vol. 2, Game Book, February 1822.

394   BARS R5/1354, 1819–21, Fortnightly Account Books, Sculpture Gallery. WAC 6D LOC21-27-1, Bundle 15, No. 5, letter Lord William Russell to Duke of Bedford, from Florence, 26 October 1822, and No. 6, letter Lord William Russell to Duke of Bedford, from Florence, 16 October 1822. The 'beautiful bust of a Faun' was 'Antico', *c.*1503, by Pier Jacopo Alari-Bonacolsi, a bronze bust with mercury gilding and inlaid with silver eyes, which became one of the star attractions of the Sculpture Gallery. WAC 7D-JM17, Memorandum: 'Observations on ancient portrait busts by Lord Geo. Russell, 1824'.

395   Edward Daniel Clarke, *Travels in Various Countries of Europe, Asia and Africa*, vol. 6, part 2: Greece, Egypt and the Holy Land, London: T. Cadell and W. Davies, 1818. His experiences in Athens and at the Parthenon can be found on pp. 196–227.

396   WAC Russell family portraits, etc., large red scrapbook, *London Gazette*, May 1822, newspaper cutting.

397   Blakiston, *Lord William Russell*, p. 62, letter Duke of Bedford to Lord William Russell, from London, 3 May 1822. WAC 6D LOC21-27-1, Bundle 15, No. 4, letter Lord William Russell to Duke of Bedford, from Florence, 5 June 1822.

398   GP GRE/B6/16/2-5, letters Duchess of Bedford to Lord Grey, 5 and 22 August from Endlseigh, 29 October from Woburn and 26 November from Hastings, all 1822.

399   WAC 6D LOC21-27-1, Bundle 15, No. 2, letter Lord Edward Russell to Duchess of Bedford, 25 June 1822, on board HMS *Owen Glendower*. 'Mr Russell' refers to Commander John Russell, son of old Lord William and the boys' first cousin.

400   Blakiston, *Lord William Russell*, p. 64, letter Lord William Russell to Lady Holland, from Florence, May 1822. WAC 6D LOC21-27-1, Bundle 15, No. 4, letter Lord William Russell to Duke of Bedford, from Florence, 5 June 1822.

401   Philip Hunt, *Outline Engravings and Descriptions of the Woburn Abbey Marbles*, drawings by Henry Corbould, engravings by Henry Moses and others, London: printed by William Nicol, Shakespeare Press, 1822.

402   Fox, *Journal*, p. 157. GP GRE/B6/16/6, letter Duchess of Bedford to Lord Grey, from Woburn Abbey, 6 March 1823.

403   WAC *Hortus Ericaeus Woburnensis*, Introduction, p. 1. Hirst, 'The Realisation of a Regency Palace', pp. 236–7.

404   BARS R5/1355, 1822–6, Fortnightly Account Books. The mosaic pavement: in a letter from the duke to Lord William, January 1823, he asks for the 'size and pattern' of the pieces to know 'how it shall be put together', and a footnote tells us these were a 'Portion of a floor discovered near Rome in 1822 … on Mount Rosario. Several pieces were obtained by the Duke.' See WAC, *Letters to Lord G. William Russell 1817–1845*, 3 vols, London: printed for private circulation, 1915, vol. 1, p. 10.

405   HHP Add MS 51667, fol. 158, letter Duke of Bedford to Lady Holland, from Woburn Abbey, 26 May 1823.

406   Blakiston, *Lord William Russell*, pp. 75 and 80. Fox, *Journal*, Genoa, 28 March 1823, quoted in Blakiston, *Lord William Russell*, p. 80.

407   Blakiston, *Lord William Russell*, pp. 80 and 81, letter Duke of Bedford to Lord William Russell, from Woburn Abbey, 1823.

408   Ibid., p. 103. Trethewey, *Mistress of the Arts*, p. 184.

409   GP GRE-B6-16/13, letter Duchess of Bedford to Lord Grey, from Woburn Abbey, 29 December 1823.

410   Leveson-Gower, *Letters*, vol. 1, pp. 242–5, letter Harriet, Countess Granville, to Lady Morpeth, 3 January 1824. Trethewey, *Mistress of the Arts*, p. 187. HHP Add MS 5166819, letter Duke of Bedford to Lord Holland, from Woburn Abbey, 7 March 1824. 'R.As': Royal Academicians.

411   BARS R5/1355, 1822–6, Fortnightly Account Books. WAC 6D-JM20, Philip Hunt, 1824 description of the ancient sculptured sarcophagus (the Ephesian Marbles), purchased from Sir G. Page-Turner, Battlesden Park.

412   Anon., *Journal of a Tour into Derbyshire*.

413   Hirst, 'The Realisation of a Regency Palace', pp. 237–9. *Morning Post*, 15 September 1824: 'The Duke and Duchess of Bedford and "Old" Lord William Russell are at Invereshie, Badenoch, where they will remain during the shooting season.'

414   James A. Manson, *Sir Edwin Landseer*, London: Walter Scott Publishing Co., 1902, p. 55.

415   For Landseer's 'first ever true landscape', see Lennie, *Landseer*, p. 45. Richard Ormond, *Edwin Landseer: The Private Drawings*, Norwich: Unicorn Press, 2009, p. 35,

416   Georgiana Blakiston, *Lord William Russell and his Wife 1815–1846*, London: John Murray, 1972, pp. 117–24, quoting letters Lady William Russell to Lord Lynedoch, 11 October 1824; Duke of Bedford to Lady Holland, from Campden Hill, 1824; and Duke of Bedford to Lord William Russell, 1824.

417   Ibid., p. 133, letter Duke of Bedford to Lord William Russell, 8 September 1825.

418   Paul Smith, 'The Landed Estate as Patron of Scientific Innovation: Horticulture at Woburn Abbey, 1802–1839', Phd thesis, Open University, 1983, pp. 195–6. I am very grateful to Paul Smith for pointing out this important connection between the grass garden and Sinclair's work on lawn seed mixtures.

419   WAC James Forbes, *Hortus Woburnensis*, London: J. Ridgway, 1833, p. 237. The collection of willows was catalogued by Forbes in *Salicetum Woburnense*, published by the duke in 1829.

420   William Jackson Hooker, 'Copy of a Letter addressed to Dawson Turner on the occasion of the Death of the Duke of Bedford …', Glasgow: printed by George Richardson, 1840.

421   HHP Add MS 51668, fol. 143, letter Duke of Bedford to Lady Holland, from Woburn Abbey, 6 May 1825. Three volumes of drawings by Henry Bone, R.A., are held in the National Portrait Gallery's Reference Collection, and the portraits can be seen online at npg.org.uk. The Latin quotation can be translated as 'and you look back over your models / Aeneas, the father, and Hector the uncle.'

422   HHP Add MS 51668, fol. 153, letter Duke of Bedford to Lady Holland, from Woburn Abbey, 26 May 1825. WAC 6D-ART 131, letter Duke of Bedford to Lord William via Lady Holland, 1825. 'Your Lucy' refers to Lucy Harrington, wife of Edward Russell, 3rd Earl of Bedford, in whom Lord William seems to have taken a particular interest. Lucy was a renowned courtier of her time, friend of the poet John Donne

and often accused of extravagance. Thomas Pennant had written of her 'boundless vanity and extravagance' (*The Journey from Chester to London*, Dublin: printed for Luke White, Dame-Street, 1783, p. 356), and Horace Walpole, Lord Orford, wrote that 'the estate of her Lord, a weak man, was considerably impaired by her ostentation' (WAC 6D-ART 135, description of the portraits at Woburn Abbey, Lord Orford, 1791). Edmund Burke, *A Letter from the Right Honourable Edmund Burke to a Noble Lord: On the attacks made upon him and his pension, in the House of Lords, by the Duke of Bedford and the Earl of Lauderdale, early in the present sessions of Parliament*, London: printed for J. Owen, F. and C. Rivington, 1796.

423   Caleb Scholefield Mann, interleaved copy of the Landseer exhibition catalogue at the Royal Academy of Arts, 1874, with photographs of all recorded Landseer prints and extensive annotations, 4 vols, NAL, MSS86BB.19, vol. 4: *The Lesson (*showing Alexander with a pug dog), *Recompense* (showing Alexander in tartan with a spaniel), *Hours of Innocence: Lord Alexander and his dog Nevill* and *Lady Louisa feeding a Donkey*, oil paintings and engravings. Annotation ('a Highland background added') by Mann.

424   GP GRE/B6/17/83, letter Duke of Bedford to Lord Grey, from Woburn Abbey, 17 June 1824. HHP Add MS 51668, fol. 52, letter Duke of Bedford to Lady Holland, from Invereshie, 26 September 1824; fol. 56, letter Duke of Bedford to Lady Holland, from Invereshie, 3 October 1824.

425   HHP Add MS 51668, fol. 159, letter Duke of Bedford to Lady Holland, from Campden Hill, 18 July 1825. GP GRE/B6/16/15, letter Duchess of Bedford to Lord Grey, from Campden Hill, 24 July 1825.

426   BARS R5/1355, 1822–5, Fortnightly Account Books, Sculpture Gallery displays. BARS R Box 818, plans for 'Ivy Lodge', 1825. NMR 3/6/1, Farey accounts, 'Avenue Lodge'. BARS R5/1355, 1825, 'repairing the "Walk"'. For further details on Ivy Lodge and the Cold Bath, see Keir Davidson, *Woburn Abbey: The Park and Gardens*, London: Pimpernel Press, 2016, pp. 124–6. Known as 'Ivy Lodge', plans suggest it may actually have been a substantial redesign of an earlier building known as 'Avenue Lodge' that had been designed by Repton. BARS R5/1355, 1825, new shrubbery. Forbes, *Hortus Woburnenis*, p. 236, American banks. BARS R5/1355, 1825, 'new rides'. For the locations of the 5th Duke's new plantations, see Davidson, *Woburn Abbey*, p. 123.

427   HHP Add MS 51668, fol. 48, letter Duke of Bedford to Lady Holland, 18 August 1825. GP GRE/B6/16/14, letter Duchess of Bedford to Lord Grey, from Invereshie, 20 September 1825.

428   Rachel Trethewey, *Mistress of the Arts: The Passionate Life of Georgina, Duchess of Bedford*, London: Review, 2002, p. 203, letter Edwin Landseer to William Ross, September 1825.

429   For *Glen Eirich, 1825* (Glenericht, Blairgowrie) and *Highland Interior* (1825), see W. Cosmo Monkhouse, *Landseer's Works: Comprising Forty-Four Steel Engravings and about 200 Woodcuts, with a History of his Life and Art*, London: Virtue & Co. Ltd, 1892, p. 54 (WAC Curator's Office, bound book, annotated 'Mary Bedford, 1892'). *Mountain Torrent*, etching, in NAL, Mann, 'Interleaved catalogue', vol. 3.

430   *A Scene in the Highlands, with portraits of Duchess of Bedford, Duke of Gordon, Lord Alexander and Stalker*, version 1, oil on canvas, sketch, *c.*1825–8. *A Scene in the Highlands, with portraits of Duchess of Bedford, Duke of Gordon, Lord Alexander and Stalker*, version 2, oil on canvas, *c.*1825–8 (Richard Ormond, *The Monarch of the Glen: Landseer in the Highlands*, Edinburgh: National Galleries of Scotland, 2005, fig. 35, p. 45).

431   Ibid., p. 41.

432   HHP Add MS 51668, fol. 212, letter Duke of Bedford to Lady Holland, from Paris, December 1825. J. H. Wiffen, *The Historical Memoirs of the House of Russell*, 2 vols, London: Longman, Rees, Orme, Brown, Green, and Longman, 1833, Preface.

433   Anthony Huxley, *An Illustrated History of Gardening*, London: Macmillan, 1983, p. 246.

434   Description of the garden in Forbes, *Hortus Woburnensis*, pp. 297–9.

435   BARS R5/1355, Fortnightly Account Books, work at Woburn. Blakiston, *Lord William Russell*, p. 138, letter Lady William Russell to Lady Holland, from Brighton, 1826. DHC E26, Account Book, Lady Day (25 March) 1824 – Lady Day 1825, 'Grounds above Wareham'.

436   HHP Add MS 51669, fol. 7, letter Duke of Bedford to Lady Holland, from Invereshie, 1 September 1826. For details of the journey made by boat, see WAC NMR 4/9/3-17, voucher bundles.

437   HHP Add MS 51669, fol. 26, letters Duke of Bedford to Lady Holland, from Invereshie, 21 September 1826; fol. 27, Duke of Bedford to Lady Holland, from Dalwhinnie, 21 September 1826; fol. 31, Duke of Bedford to Lady Holland, from Invereshie, 29 September 1826. MGP NRAS 771, Bundle 683, letter Duke of Bedford to George Macpherson-Grant, from Blair Adam, 11 October 1826.

438   GP GRE/B6/17/87, letter Duke of Bedford to Lord Grey, from Invereshie, 5 October 1826. HHP Add MS 51669, fol. 31, letter Duke of Bedford to Lady Holland, from Edinburgh, 15 October 1826. GP GRE/B6/16/18, letter Duchess of Bedford to Lord Grey, from Campden Hill, 16 November 1826.

439   Hermann von Pückler-Muskau, *Tour in England, Ireland, and France in the years 1826, 1827, 1828, and 1829 … in a series of letters by a German prince*, Philadelphia: Carey, Lea and Blanchard, 1833, letter VIII, pp. 68–70.

440   P. F. Robinson, *History of Woburn Abbey: Illustrated by Plans, Elevations, Internal Views of the Apartments, from actual measurement*, London: James Carpenter and Son, 1827. Plates included 'View of the House from the Park', 'The Library', 'The Portrait Gallery', 'The Sculpture Gallery', 'Plan of the Principal Story', 'General Plan', 'Elevation of West Front', 'Exterior of Sculpture Gallery'. This was the first in Robinson's series of five such volumes conceived as a continuation of Colen Campbell's *Vitruvius Britannicus* (1715, 1717 and 1725), which would include Woburn Abbey, Hatfield House, Hardwicke Hall, Castle Ashby and Warwick Castle.

441   BARS R5/1356, 1827–30, Fortnightly Account Books. BARS R3/2256, 21 January 1828, Crocker to Adam report on progress on new kitchen garden.

442   Forbes, *Hortus Woburnensis*, 1833, Plate XVII, pp. 298 and 299. For the Irish serpentine 'chimney-piece', see J. D. Parry, *History & Description of Woburn and its Abbey*, Woburn: printed by S. Dodd, 1831. Parry's work is dedicated to both 'John, Duke of Bedford' and to 'Georgiana, Duchess of Bedford'. The fruit on china is a set of thirty-three Davenport plates, each painted with a vignette of fruits, with the name of the species inscribed on the reverse; these are still in the Abbey collections: WAC Box 34 107–108 JPGs. The Lance pictures measured *c*.107 × 71 cm/*c*.42 × 28 inches and they remained in the 'Fruit Room, Kitchen Gardens' until at least 1910. They are dated 1829, and were sold in 1951 as 'Fruit on Stone Ledges' by Lance, Christie's Old Masters Sale, lot 185. Georgina had a picture by Lance of fruit at Campden Hill. I am indebted to Victoria Poulton, Assistant Curator, for all these details.

443   Forbes, *Hortus Woburnensis*, p. 300. Smith, 'Landed Estate', p. 28.

444   HHP, letter Duke of Bedford to Lady Holland, 17 June 1827, quoted in Trethewey, *Mistress of the Arts*, p. 209. George Gordon, *The Last Dukes of Gordon and their Consorts: A Revealing Study*, Aberdeen: G. Gordon, 1980, p. 170. MGP NRAS 771, Bundle 683, letter John McInnis to George Macpherson-Grant, 28 September 1827.

445   MGP NRAS 771, Bundle 683, Letter John McInnis to George Macpherson-Grant, 28 September 1827.

446   Ormond, *Monarch of the Glen*, p. 81. For *Highlanders returning from Deerstalking*, see ibid., fig. 44, p. 51.

447   GP GRE/B6/16/20, letter Duchess of Bedford to Lord Grey, from Invereshie, 1 November 1827. Von Pückler-Muskau, *Tour in England*, p. 76.

448   GP GRE/B6/16/19, letter Duchess of Bedford to Lord Grey, from Invereshie, 16 October 1827. GP GRE/B6/16/20, letter Duchess of Bedford to Lord Grey, from Invereshie, 1 November 1827.

449   W.E.K. Anderson, ed., *The Journal of Sir Walter Scott*, Oxford: Oxford University Press, 1972, pp. 385 and 386. *Journalière*: banal, mundane. Blakiston, *Lord William Russell*, p. 154, diary of Lord William Russell.

450   Campbell Lennie, *Landseer: The Victorian Paragon*, London: Hamilton, 1976, p. 55.

451   HHP Add MS 51669, fol. 156, letters Duke of Bedford to Lady Holland, from Endsleigh, 30 June 1828; fol. 162, Duke of Bedford to Lady Holland, from Endsleigh, 17 August 1828.

452   All quotations from Elizabeth Grant, *Memoirs of a Highland Lady*, 2 vols, ed. Andrew Tod, Edinburgh: Canongate, 2005, vol. 2, pp. 195–203. 'Duchus': a traditional land holding within the clan system.

453   MGP NRAS 771, Bundle 161, letter George Macpherson-Grant to John Macpherson-Grant, August 1827; Bundle 683, letter Lady Stafford to George Macpherson-Grant, September 1827; Bundle 16, letter George Macpherson-Grant to John Macpherson-Grant, from Ballindalloch, 28 September 1827.

454   GP GRE/B6/17/115, letter Duke of Bedford to Lord Grey, from Endsleigh, 19 August 1828.

455   WAC Ph-Mss 35-30, letter Allen Thomson to Dr John Thomson (father), from The Doune, 12 September 1837.

456   WAC B.5 D6. Rus Dun, F.W.B. Dunne, *Personal Recollections of Lord Wriothesley Russell and Chenies*, London: Elliot Stock, 1888, pp. 12 and 16.

457   'Statement from Thomas Bennett, Esq, Steward at Woburn', in *The Labourers' Friend: A Selection from the Publications of the Labourers' Friend Society*, London: published for the Society, 1835, p. 225. For the wider context of the allotment movement, see Smith, 'Landed Estate', pp. 24–5.

458   MGP NRAS 102, Bundle 289, 'The Tack betwixt Patrick Borthwick Esq. as Trustee of the Creditors of John Peter Grant and the Duchess of Bedford. 1829'.

459   Blakiston, *Lord William Russell*, p. 196, letter Lady Holland to Lord William Russell, from Holland House, 3 July 1829. GP GRE/B6/17/17/130, letter Duke of Bedford to Lord Grey, from Woburn Abbey, 2 August 1829. See also WAC NMR 4/7/2, Bundle 1, No. 2, 7 August 1829, William Allen, valet, invoice for travel expenses: 'Boats to the Steam Packet at Greenwich for Her Grace and the luggage and waiting. 2 Baskets to take with Her Grace on board.'

460   Ormond, *Monarch of the Glen*, p. 601. Lennie, *Landseer*, p. 52: 'Landseer had himself no doubt sampled the raw and fiery product of those clandestine shebeens.'

461   MM NRS GD176/2149, letter James Clark to Mackintosh of Mackintosh, from Dalnavert, 21 July 1829.

462   Alexander MacBain, *Badenoch: Its History, Clans and Place Names*, Inverness: Northern Chronicle, 1890.

463   Meryl Marshall, *Glen Feshie: The History and Archaeology of a Highland Glen*, 2nd edn, [Conon Bridge:] NOSAS, 2013, p. 15. Katherine Stewart, *Women of the Highlands*, Edinburgh: Luath Press, 2006, pp. 31–3. Kathleen Jamie, *Findings*, London: Sort of Books, 2005, pp. 121–3. Anne MacVicar Grant, *Letters from the Mountains; Being the Real Correspondence of a Lady, between the Years 1773 and 1807*, 2 vols, Sligo: HardPress Publishing, 2012, vol. 2, pp. 123–4, letter XXIV, from Laggan, 27 August 1787. Madeleine Bunting, *Love of Country: A Hebridean Journey*, London: Granta Books, 2016, p. 154.

464   John Logan, 'Ode written on a Visit to the Country in Autumn', allpoetry.com (accessed 17 August 2021).

465   Trethewey, *Mistress of the Arts*, p. 215, letter Lord Tavistock to Lord William Russell, 1829, and letter Lady Holland to Lord William Russell, 22 September 1829. W. B. Pope, ed., *Diary of Benjamin Haydon*, 5 vols, Cambridge, Mass.: Harvard University Press, 1960–63, vol. 3, p. 404, quoted Ormond, *Monarch of the Glen*, p. 41. Blakiston, *Lord William Russell*, p. 372, letter Lady William Russell to Princess Lieven, from Stuttgart, 23 February 1836: 'Her current lover is no longer the painter but is said to be his Swiss valet de chambre.' SC6/15, letter John, Earl of Clare, to Ralph Sneyd, from Mount Shannon, 10 September 1829.

466   Blakiston, *Lord William Russell*, p. 196, letter Duke of Bedford to Lady William Russell, from Ryde, 24 August 1829.

467   Ibid., p. 202, letter Lord John Russell to Lord William Russell, from Woburn Abbey, 27 November 1829.

468   HHP Add MS 5167, fol. 15, letter Duke of Bedford to Lady Holland, from Woburn Abbey, 7 February 1830; fol. 51, letter Duke of Bedford to Lady Holland, from Belgrave Square, 9 June 1830. The letter includes one of the very few drawings done by the duke, in which he outlines his proposal for the bay window.

469   Covent Garden: WAC 6D-E10-1-62, E10-1, 'Act for the Improvement and Regulation of Covent Garden Market, Royal Assent, 27 June 1828 from George IV'; E10-4, ground plan for the new Covent Garden Market layout; E10-6, 'Covent Garden Market: Rules, Orders, and Bye-laws, 1828'. St Helen's Point: according to Wiffen, this location had significance for the family because in 1341, in the reign of Edward III, a French invasion force landed there, only to be defeated by local inhabitants led by a distant fourteenth-century ancestor, Sir Theobold Russell, one of the wardens of the Isle of Wight who was mortally wounded in the battle (Wiffen, *Historical Memoirs*, vol. 1, p. 140.

470   BARS R3/2867, letter William Adam to Edward Crocker, 8 June 1830.

471   Blakiston, *Lord William Russell*, p. 215, letter Lord John Russell to Lady William Russell, from Bedford, 4 July 1830. Ibid., p. 220, letter Marquis of Tavistock to Lord William Russell, 18 August 1830. If it wasn't for the fact that the duke had considered Lord John the most popular candidate to retain Bedford, he could have stood again for Huntingdon, which he was likely to have won.

472   Ibid., p. 221, Lord William's diary, 1 September 1830; p. 223, letter Duke of Bedford to Lord William Russell, from The Doune, 16 October 1830. GP GRE/B6/17/141 and 141A, letter Duke of Bedford to Lord Grey, from The Doune, 8 September 1830.

473   Osbert Sitwell, ed., *Two Generations*, London: Macmillan, 1940, pp. 81 and 82.

474   WAC NMR 4/5/4, Bundle 3, No. 26, Campden Hill Accounts, John Parker, Wire Worker, August to October 1830, 'Wrought iron frame for basket wired with Trellis wire work & upright, 40 wrot. iron arches … 91 wrot. iron 5 bar light cattle hurdles, 42 wrot. iron braces prepared for round standards of arches'.

475   Antonia Fraser, *Perilous Question: Reform or Revolution? Britain on the Brink, 1832*, New York: Public Affairs, 2013, p. 94. GP GRE/B6/17/142, letter Duke of Bedford to Lord Grey, from Belgrave Square, 17 November 1830. GP GRE/B6/17/143, letter Duke of Bedford to Lord Grey, from Belgrave Square, 19 November 1830. The appointment was ceremonial, awarded to those who had served in public office and contributed to public life, and carried no commitment to engage in political activity, which is probably why the duke contemplated it at all.

476   HHP, letter Duchess of Bedford to Lord Holland, 22 December 1830, quoted in Trethewey, *Mistress of the Arts*, pp. 220–21. HHP Add MS 51667, fol. 110, letter Duke of Bedford to Lady Holland, 2 January 1831.

477   WAC Cash Book D, March 1831, vaccination. HHP Add MS 51667, fol. 116, letter Duke of Bedford to Lady Holland, from Belgrave Square, 7 January 1831, regarding treatment for his shoulder in London.

478   BARS R3/2407 and 2410, letters Duke of Bedford to Edward Crocker, 16 and 25 March 1831. Edward Crocker was the resident steward of Woburn Park and Farms from 1828 to 1839, following Robert Salmon's retirement a few years earlier.

479   WAC NMR 4/16/10, Bundle 1, August 1831, tickets to Almack's. WAC NMR 4/11/4, Bundle 1, No. 23, 21 June 1831, 'Rustic' garden furniture. WAC NMR 4/8, Cash Book D, 24 June 1831, 'Needle Work by design of Her Grace'.

480   Thomas Moore, *Memoirs, Journals and Correspondence of Thomas Moore*, quoted in Rachel Trethewey, *Mistress of the Arts: The Passionate Life of Georgina, Duchess of Bedford*, London: Review, 2002, p. 221. Samuel Lewis, *National Gazetteer*, 1848, quoted in Wikipedia, 'Eel Pie Island', en.wikipedia (accessed 3/8/2018).

481   See Michael Taylor, *The Interest: How the British Establishment Resisted the Abolition of Slavery*, London: Bodley Head, 2020, p. 253. As Taylor points out, so large was the government debt incurred by this compensation that it was 2015 before it was finally paid off by British taxpayers.

482   GRP, The Doune, Jane Grant, 'Travel Journal', August 1831.

483   WAC, loose playbills and two bound volumes, 'Woburn Abbey Theatricals, Vols 1 & 2, John Martin, Librarian, 1844'. Richard Ormond, *Edwin Landseer: The Private Drawings*, Norwich: Unicorn Press, 2009, p. 110.

484   WAC Cash Book D, January 1830, payment to Landseer for masks for 'Abbey theatre'.

485   Ormond, *Edwin Landseer*, p.110, quoting Louisa's son Lord Frederic Hamilton, *The Days Before Yesterday*, London: Hodder and Stoughton, 1920, p. 326. WAC NMR 4/15/9, Bundle 1, No. 64, Christmas 1829 (billed 19 May 1830), masks included '5 masks with moving chins', '1 Ladies mask with moving chin', '1 Monkey mask with moving chin', '1 Child's Mask', '1 Man's Character mask with Beard, '1 Nose & Eyes', '1 Nose & Eyes with specks'. See Ormond, *Edwin Landseer*, fig. 72, 'Lady Abercorn in a Twelfth Night masquerade, *c.*1832 (pen and ink and wash)', fig. 74, 'The Duchess of Bedford in a masquerade costume, *c.*1832 (pen and ink and wash, and red crayon)' and fig. 73, 'Lady Abercorn in masquerade costume, 1832 (oil on canvas). Exhibited Royal Academy, 1836'. For 'late 18th century' costume, see Ormond, *Edwin Landseer*, fig. 73 caption.

486   ELC 1316/31, letter Duke of Bedford to Edwin Landseer, from Woburn Abbey, 23 January 1832. 'Old Lewis' was Frederick Christian Lewis, engraver, landscape painter and portraitist, who had produced an engraving of Lord John Russell in 1825; see npg.org.uk (accessed 19/12/2020).

487   ELC 1316/33, letter Duke of Bedford to Edwin Landseer, from Brighton, 3–7 April 1832. Georgiana Blakiston, *Lord William Russell and his Wife 1815–1846*, London: John Murray, 1972, pp. 251, 252 and 257, letters Hastings Russell to Lord William Russell (undated) and Duke of Bedford to Lady William (undated). HHP Add MS 51671, fol. 39, letter Duke of Bedford to Lady Holland, from Endsleigh, 14 June 1832. John Stagg was the Woburn house steward.

488   NAL, Caleb Scholefield Mann, interleaved copy of the Landseer exhibition catalogue at the Royal Academy of Arts, 1874, with photographs of all recorded Landseer prints and extensive annotations, 4 vols, vol. 1, no. 11, Edwin Landseer, *Lady Rachel Russell with her Pet Faun, Harty*, and vol. 3, no. 58, *The Little Actress at The Doune*.

489   PRONI D623/A/251/5, letter Duke of Bedford to Lady Louisa Russell, from The Doune, 1832, 'To the Lady Louisa J. Russell, Glenfeshie'. PRONI D623/A/251/8, '27th October 1832, Report of the Marriage of the Marquis of Abercorn', *Aberdeen Journal*, 30 October 1832.

490   PRONI D623/B/2/44, 'Contract of marriage between the Most Hon. the Marquis of Abercorn & Earl of Abercorn … and the Right Hon. Lady Louisa Jane Russell, daughter of the most noble John, Duke of Bedford, 1832'.

491   William J. Roulston, *Abercorn: The Hamiltons of Barons Court*, Belfast: Ulster Historical Foundation, 2014, p. 78, and for full details of the history of Barons Court.

492   PRONI D623/D/1/72, plan of Barons Court Park, 1777, and PRONI D623/D/1/21, plan of Barons Court Park, 1800. ELC 1316/36, letter Duke of Bedford to Edwin Landseer, from Barons Court, 1 December 1836.

493   PRONI D/A/251/17, 1832, 'Baron's Court festivities'. Trethewey, *Lord William Russell*, p. 236. HHP, letter Duke of Bedford to Lady Holland, 7 January 1833.

494   HHP Add MS 51664, fol. 30, letters Duke of Bedford to Lord Holland, from Barons Court, 25 January 1833. and fol. 50, Duke of Bedford to Lord Holland, from Endsleigh, 31 May 1833.

495   BARS R3/2252, letter Robert Ireland to Duke of Bedford, from Park Farm, 7 March 1833. Ireland had succeeded Salmon as Head of Woods and served 1820–39.

496   HHP Add MS 51664, fol. 54, letters Duke of Bedford to Lord Holland, from Endsleigh, June 1833, and fol. 172, Duke of Bedford to Lady Holland, from Endsleigh, 10 June 1833. Edward was commander of the *Nimrod*, twenty guns, on the Lisbon station, a post he held until August, when he was invalided home.

497   WAC NMR 4/11/10, Bundle 2, No. 48, 'Surrey Zoological Gardens'. Arthur Aspinall, ed., *Three Early Nineteenth Century Diaries*, London: Williams and Norgate, 1952, p. 366. Hugh Fortescue, Viscount Ebrington, was a reforming Whig politician. Charles Dickens, ed., *The Life of Charles James Mathews*, vol. 2, London: Macmillan, 1879, p. 57.

498   WAC NMR 4/8, Cash Book E, 'Thomas Sharpey, £87'.

499   Charles Tankerville, *The Chillingham Wild Cattle: Reminiscences of Life in the Highlands*, Kingston: printed at the 'Surrey Cornet', 1891. The account of this expedition comes from a short memoir by Charles Bennet, Lord Ossulton, later 6th Earl of Tankerville, written some sixty years after the events. In this the author appears to run together a series of memories drawn from visits he made to Glen Feshie from 1829 until the late 1830s, and to the Abercorns' hunting lodge at Ardverikie on Loch Laggan until at least 1846, if not later. Due to this apparent conflation of years and events, it is difficult to confirm either the few dates or the details of the incidents recounted. Unfortunately, the letter in which Mathews describes this trip does not appear to have survived, so there is no way to verify the details of Tankerville's account.

500   Dickens, *Mathews*, Chapter 2, 'The District Surveyor', pp. 45–57.

501   Ibid., p. 57.

502   For the Landseer paintings, see Richard Ormond, *The Monarch of the Glen: Landseer in the Highlands*, Edinburgh: National Galleries of Scotland, 2005, figs 96 and 97, p. 89; fig. 83, p. 82. Tankerville quoted in Meryl Marshall, *Glen Feshie: The History and Archaeology of a Highland Glen*, 2nd edn, [Conon Bridge:] North of Scotland Archaeological Society, 2013, p. 48. As with the rest of Tankerville's memoir, it is not possible to date this specific anecdote.

503   For *Glenfeshie (Rainy Day in the Highlands)*, see Ormond, *Monarch of the Glen*, fig. 93, p. 87. For *A Highland Landscape*, ibid., fig. 106, p. 93.

504   James Forbes, *Hortus Woburnensis*, London: J. Ridgway, 1833. It cost subscribers £1.10s.0d, or £2.2s to non-subscribers. List of Contents: Part I, 'Catalogue of Plants', pp. 1–213; Part II, 'Pleasure Ground &c', pp. 233–93; Part III, 'Kitchen Garden Department', pp. 297–439.

505   John Caie, 'A Sketch of his Horticultural Career', *Gardeners' Chronicle*, October 1875, p. 453, archive. org (accessed 13/7/2019). John Caie was born in Scotland, trained at the Glasgow Botanical Garden under Hooker and Murray before working at Chiswick House in London. He worked at Woburn as an under gardener between 1833 and 1835, when he was appointed Georgina's head gardener at Campden Hill.

506   HHP Add MS 51671, fol. 196, letter Duke of Bedford to Lady Holland, from Leamington Spa, 5 September 1833.

507   RBGK, A–B, vol. 3, no. 162, letter Duke of Bedford to William Hooker, from Leamington Spa, 24 September 1833. Hooker held the Chair of Botany at Glasgow University between 1820 and 1841, where he revitalized both the department and built up Glasgow's botanical garden into a major collection. He also created a major herbarium, which eventually became the basis for the national herbarium at Kew. William Jackson Hooker, 'Copy of a Letter Addressed to Dawson Turner … on the occasion of the Death of the Duke of Bedford, particularly with reference to the services rendered by His Grace to Botany and Horticulture', Glasgow: printed by George Richardson, 1840, p. 3. For *Curtis's Botanical Magazine*, see Ray Desmond, *The History of the Royal Botanical Gardens, Kew*, London: Harvill Press, 1995, p. 152. Hooker had been editor of the magazine since 1827, and the dedication read: 'To John, Duke of Bedford, &c. &c. A Nobleman no less distinguished for his private than his public virtues, and who, by the various splendid works which he has fostered, patronized and published, has eminently deserved well of Botany and the Arts, the present volume is dedicated.'

508   BARS R3/2455, letter Duke of Bedford to Edward Crocker, from Woburn Abbey, 17 November 1833. HHP Add MS 51671, fols 247 and 255, letter Duke of Bedford to Lady Holland, from Woburn Abbey, 29 December 1833.

509   WAC, *Morning Post*, 6 January 1834, and loose playbills and two bound volumes, 'Woburn Abbey Theatricals, Vols 1 & 2, John Martin, Librarian, 1844'.

510   WAC Ph-MSS 33/4, letter James Forbes to William Hooker, from Woburn Abbey, 3 May 1834.

511   Sir Charles Barry was Joseph Paxton's son-in-law, had worked at Chatworth, and at this time had also established himself as a pioneering designer of 'elaborate architectural flower-gardens'; see Howard Colvin,

A Biographical Dictionary of British Architects 1600–1840, London: John Murray, 1978, p. 90. WAC HMC 152, Sir Charles Barry, 'plans/drawings for enlarging terrace of Library, 1834', photocopies of RIBA Image Disc 97/B: SC34/II (i) Designs for Flower Garden, Woburn Abbey 'View' ('Sketch of the Proposed Flower Garden as it will be seen from the Library Windows') and SC34/II (ii) Designs for Flower Garden, Woburn Abbey 'Plan'.

512   See Keir Davidson, *Woburn Abbey: The Park and Gardens*, London: Pimpernel Press, 2016, pp. 168–9.

513   BARS R3/2461, letter Duke of Bedford to Edward Crocker, 12 March 1834; BARS R3/2466, letter Duke of Bedford to Edward Crocker, 31 March 1834; and BARS R3/2486, letter Duke of Bedford to Edward Crocker, 8 May 1835. Henry William Burgess became a landscape painter and produced the *Eidodendron: Views of the General Character and Appearance of Trees Foreign and Indigenous as connected with Picturesque Scenery* (1827), and a sketch of the 'Johnson Willow' as a frontispiece for *Salictum Woburnense* (1829). WAC *Drawings of the Evergreens at Woburn Abbey* (1837), and 'Views in the Evergreens' (1838).

514   RBGK A–B, vol. 3, no. 163, letter Duke of Bedford to William Hooker, from Woburn Abbey, 29 March 1834. It should be noted that the duke uses a number of variations of this scientific name in his letters. Ibid., no. 178, letter Duke of Bedford to William Hooker, from The Doune, 7 October 1835. Ibid., no. 183, letter Duke of Bedford to William Hooker, from Woburn Abbey, 26 November 1835.

515   WAC Ph-MSS 35-25, letter Allen Thomson to Margaret Thomson (his sister), from Campden Hill, 9 July 1837.

516   HHP Add MS 51672, fol. 37, letter Duke of Bedford to Lady Holland, from Endsleigh, 20 April 1834. Blakiston, *Lord William Russell*, pp. 294 and 295.

517   Dorothée, Duchesse de Dino, *Memoirs of the Duchesse de Dino (Afterwards Duchesse de Tallyrand et de Sagan), 1831–1835*, ed. The Princess Radziwill, New York: Charles Scribner's Sons, 1909, Chapter 4.

518   WAC NMR 4/5/2, Bundle 5, No. 34, 8 March 1834, gas fittings at Belgrave Square. HHP Add MS 51664, fol. 66, letter Duke of Bedford to Lord Holland, from Woburn Abbey, 18 October 1833. John Caie, 'Descriptive Notice of Bedford Lodge, the Suburban Villa of His Grace the Duke of Bedford, at Campden Hill', *Gardener's Magazine*, 14:102 (September 1838), pp. 401–10. Figures 74–9 show views of the house and gardens and the 'General Plan of the entire place' (fig. 75) and that of the flower garden (fig. 79).

519   Campden Hill garden work: WAC NMR 4/16/4, Bundle 6, No. 34, 10 February 1834, marble blocks; NMR 4/5/2, Bundle 5, No. 34, 13 May 1834, John Parker, wire fence maker; and No. 18: Edward Oliver, plumber, painter and glazier, 2 June 1834.

520   WAC NMR 4/26/4, Bundle 2, No. 19, 18 June 1834, 'Astley's Theatre, 30 tickets and keeping places on the occasion of the Lady Rachel Russell's Birthday'; NMR 4/26/4, Bundle 2, No. 35, 5 July 1834, 'William Lamb, Carpenter, C. Hill'; NMR 4/26/4, Bundle 4, No. 6, 'Julien Baatard, Groom of the Chambers, for travelling exp to The Doune. August 1'. HHP Add MS 51672, fol. 52, letter Duke of Bedford to Lady Holland, from The Doune, 1 August 1834.

521   WAC NMR 4/13/7, Bundle 9, No. 85, 14–15 July 1834, to 'His Grace at Doune of Rothiemurchus, by Grantown', John Grant, painter and glazier.

522   Ibid., No. 66, tent maker; Nos 10, 21–30 and 64, July–8 October 1834, 'New House in Glenfeshie'; No. 26, 'Black House in Glenfeshie'.

523   Ibid., No. 34, October 1836, 'Her Grace. To Repairs on Black House, Glenfeshie. 5 men: Charles McIntosh, William Munro, John Shaw, John Martin, James Munro.'

524   *Kingussie and Upper Speyside (Badenoch): A Descriptive Guide to the District*, Kingussie: George Crerar, 1905, Excursion No. III, pp. 69–73, electricscotland.com/history/Inverness/Kingussie.pdf (accessed 13/12/2020). 'Steer': in this context 'activities' or 'course of action'. The *larach* is that recorded as Ruigh nan Leum at the mouth of Allt na Leuma (OS Explorer 4032), and is shown on the Thomson map (1830) as Rea Leame and Alten Leame. 'Landseer's Falls' are in the ravine above as it runs down from Allt Coire Bhlair.

525   *The Marchioness of Abercorn and her Eldest Child*, 1834, oil on copper: see Ormond, *Monarch of the Glen*, fig. 34, p. 45. *The Duchess of Bedford and Lady Harriet Hamilton* (two images), 1834–5, pen and ink wash on paper: Ormond, *Edwin Landseer*, fig. 53, p. 90, and fig. 58, p. 96. *A Highland Breakfast*, 1834, oil on panel: Ormond, *Monarch of the Glen*, fig. 65, p. 68. Ormond comments on this painting: 'delicacy of feeling is underscored by the subtle treatment of the interior, one of Landseer's best.' For Georgina standing behind the duke's chair, Ormond, *Edwin Landseer*, fig. 54, p. 91. For the images of Georgina's neck and shoulders, ibid., fig. 55 p. 93, and fig. 56, p. 94. Charles Fraser-Mackintosh, *Antiquarian Notes, Historical, Genealogical and Social: Second Series, Inverness-shire Parish by Parish*, Inverness: A. & W. Mackenzie, 1897, p. 415, and WAC NMR 4/13/7, Bundle 9, No. 58, Bundle 8, No. 29 and Bundle 6, No. 79, cairn on Kinapole.

526   HHP Add MS 51672, fol. 63, letters Duke of Bedford to Lady Holland, from The Doune, 8 September 1834, and fol. 66, Duke of Bedford to Lady Holland, from The Doune, 10 September 1834.

527   WAC *Inverness Courier*, 8 October 1834, Glenfiddich. PRONI D623/C/6/1, Accounts for John Humphreys (Barons Court agent from 1833), 1833, compensation paid to cottagers for loss of 'furniture burned during the prevalence of Cholera'. HHP Add MS 51664, fol. 105, letter Duke of Bedford to Lord Holland, from Balbirnie, 13 November 1834.

528   WAC 6D-ART 105, letter Thomas Burgon, Turkey merchant, to Duke of Bedford, 8 December 1834, shipping a fragment of the Ephesian Sarcophagus. Mosaic pavement: WAC NMR 2/3/3 7D-JM1-131-15, 'Letters collected by the Librarian at Woburn Abbey in the time of the 6th Duke: Nos 1–89', letter Edward Crocker to Duke of Bedford, December 1834. HHP Add MS 51672, fol. 103, letter Duke of Bedford to Lady Holland, from Woburn Abbey, 15 December 1834.

529   WAC NMR 4/16/11, Bundle 5, No. 1, February and March 1835. BARS R3/2480, letter Duke of Bedford to Edward Crocker, 12 March 1835. For detailed discussion of Purrett's Hill Lodge and its location, see Davidson, *Woburn Abbey*, pp. 152–3.

530   WAC B.5 D6, Rus Dun., F.W.B. Dunne, *Personal Recollections of Lord Wriothesley Russell & Chenies*, London: Elliot Stock, 1888, p. 20. WAC *Northamptonshire Mercury*, 18 April 1835, for details of marriage. Diary of Lord William Russell quoted in Blakiston, *Lord William Russell*, p. 325.

531   Adeline Marie Tavistock and Ela M. S. Russell, *Biographical Catalogue of the Pictures at Woburn Abbey*, 2 vols, London: Elliot Stock, 1890, vol. 2, p. 180. Blakiston, *Lord William Russell*, p. 337, letter Lady Holland to Lord William Russell, July 1835.

532   RBGK, A–B, vol. 3, no. 170, letter Duke of Bedford to William Hooker, from Woburn Abbey, 2 June 1835. WAC 6D-ART 132 and 133, portrait of the Marquis of Tavistock by Reynolds. Campden Hill Garden Accounts: WAC 6D-A1-1-7, Cash Book E, 1835, 1 August. WAC 'New Drawing Room, Campden Hill', J. Wyatville, August 1835.

533   Lord George William Russell's diary, March 1827, quoted in Blakiston, *Lord William Russell*, p. 157. WAC NMR 4/5/2, Bundle 7, No. 21, tickets for Almack's.

534   RBGK, A–B, vol. 3, no. 175, letter Duke of Bedford to William Hooker, from Woburn Abbey, 8 August 1835. The 'Northern Tour': ELC 1316/34, letter Duke of Bedford to Edwin Landseer, from Woburn Abbey, 16 August 1835.

535   Nan Shepherd, *The Living Mountain*, Aberdeen: Aberdeen University Press, 1977, reissued Edinburgh: Canongate, 2011. Although the manuscript was written in the late 1940s, Shepherd did not submit it for publication until 1977.

536   NRAS 1454, Bundle 426, letter Duke of Bedford to William Adam, from The Doune, 1 September 1835. Mr Stuart Murray was Curator of Glasgow Botanic Garden. HHP Add MS 51672, fol. 132, letter Duke of Bedford to Lady Holland, from The Doune, 3 September 1835. WAC Cash Book E, May 1835, 'William Payne for a Pedometer for His Grace taken to The Doune.', 16 May. HHP Add MS 51672, fol. 141, letter Duke of Bedford to Lady Holland, from The Doune, 8 October 1835.

537 Blakiston, *Lord William Russell*, p. 431, letter Duke of Bedford to Lady William Russell, from
The Doune, 21 September 1839. *Duchess of Bedford on a Pony, with a Ghillie, c.*1835: Ormond, *Edwin
Landseer*,
fig. 28, p. 59. *Duchess of Bedford on a Pony, with Other Riders, c.*1835, ibid., fig. 29, p. 60. *Lady Georgiana Russell
and a Highlander, c.*1835, ibid., p. 63, fig. 31. *Lady Rachel Russell, c.*1835, oil on board (untraced), Ormond,
Monarch of the Glen, fig. 29, p. 42.

538 RBGK, A–B, vol. 3, no. 16, no. 177, letter Duke of Bedford to William Hooker, from The Doune,
20 September 1835. WAC NMR 4/13/7 Bundle 7, No. 14, 8 November 1835, The Doune gardener and
lads collecting plants.

539 PRONI D623/A/268/1, Ardverikie Lodge.

540 Dr G. F. Waagen, *Works of Art and Artists in England*, London: John Murray, 1838, vol. 3, pp. 344–56.
RBGK, A–B, vol. 3, no. 178, letter Duke of Bedford to Hooker, from The Doune, 7 October 1835.

541 RBGK, A–B, vol. 3, no. 183, letter Duke of Bedford to William Hooker, from Woburn Abbey,
26 November 1835, the Salictum. BARS R3/2495, letter Duke of Bedford to Edward Crocker, from The
Doune, 3 November 1835. RBGK, A–B, vol. 3, no. 187, letters Duke of Bedford to William Hooker, from
Edinburgh, 11 November 1835, and no. 189, Duke of Bedford to William Hooker, from Woburn Abbey,
2 December 1835.

542 Waterloo Crescent, Dover, was built between 1834 and 1836 by Philip Hardwick. Blakiston, *Lord
William Russell*, p. 367, letter Duke of Bedford to Lord William Russell, from Woburn Abbey, 24 December
1835. For Rebecca de Haber, see Blakiston, *Lord William Russell*, p. 336. For Lord William's diary entry, ibid.,
p. 367. WAC (not yet catalogued), Edwin Landseer, *Georgiana, Duchess of Bedford, Looking Out of a Window*,
coloured chalk over pencil drawing.

543 *Journal of Botany*, Part II for April 1834. RBGK, A–B, vol. 7, no. 64, letter Duke of Bedford to William
Hooker, from Dover, 10 March 1836. *Algae Danmoniensis or Dried Specimens of Marine Plants, principally
collected in Devonshire; carefully named according to Dr. Hooker's British Flora and sold by Mary Wyatt, dealer
in shells, Torquay*, Torquay: Cockrem for the author, 1834–40. RBGK, A–B, vol. 7, no. 65, letter Duke of
Bedford to William Hooker, from Dover, 18 March 1836. In this he also thanks Hooker for securing both
a copy of Gardner's *British Mosses* for himself and Mrs Wyatt's book for the duchess. Ibid., nos 67 and 68,
letters
Duke of Bedford to William Hooker, from Dover, 31 March and 10 April 1836.

544 RBGK, A–B, vol. 7, no. 72, letter Duke of Bedford to William Hooker, from Endsleigh, 20 May 1836.
For 'very complete Arboretum', see Forbes, *Hortus Woburnensis*, p. 238. RBGK, A–B, vol. 7, no. 72, letter
Duke of Bedford to William Hooker, from Endsleigh, 20 May 1836. BARS R3/2970, letter W. G. Adam to
Edward Crocker, 5 May 1836.

545 HHP Add MS 51672, fol. 174, letter Duke of Bedford to Lady Holland, from Dover, 29 March 1836.
Allen Thomson, a Scottish doctor, served as private physician to the duke from 1837 to 1839. He was the
son of Dr John Thomson of Edinburgh, and half-brother of William Thomson, Professor of Medicine at the
University of Glasgow.

546 WAC Ph-MSS 35-1, letter Allen Thomson to Mrs John Thomson (his mother), from London,
23 June 1836. The immediate family were the duke (seventy), duchess (fifty-five), Georgiana (twenty-six)
and Rachel (ten). WAC Ph-MSS 35-2, letter Allen Thomson to Dr William Thomson, from Woburn Abbey,
28 June 1836. WAC Ph-MSS 35-10, letter Allen Thomson to Margaret Thomson, from Woburn Abbey,
1836.

547 WAC NMR 2/3/3 7D-JM1-131-22 and 23A, 'Letters collected by the Librarian at Woburn Abbey
in the time of the 6th Duke', letters from Revd F. V. Jago Arundell to Duke of Bedford, 1836. WAC NMR
2/3/3 7D-JM1-131-25, letter Sir Richard Westmacott to Duke of Bedford, 1836.

548   ELC 1316/35, letter Duke of Bedford to Edwin Landseer, from The Doune, 2 September 1836. WAC Ph-MSS 35-4, letter Allen Thomson to Margaret Thomson, from The Doune, 26 August 1836.

549   WAC NMR 4/13/7, Bundle 4, No. 21, letter Duchess of Bedford to Mrs John McDonald, from Glenfeshie, 11 November 1836. Elizabeth Grant, *Memoirs of a Highland Lady*, 2 vols, ed. Andrew Tod, Edinburgh: Canongate, 2005, vol. 2, p. 160.

550   Letter Jane Grant to William Grant, 7 April 1831 (private collection). WAC Ph-MSS 35-5, letter Allen Thomson to Margaret Thomson, from The Doune, 23 October 1836. It is worth noticing that Thomson also had a typical Lowlander's reaction to the life and people he met, stating in the same letter that 'the Highland character' is 'in every way inferior to that of the Lowland Scot'.

551   WAC Ph-MSS 35-9, letter Allen Thomson to Margaret Thomson, from Barons Court, 5 December 1836; this letter also contains a sketch map of the grounds. HHP Add MS 51672, fols 222 and 228, letters Duke of Bedford to Lady Holland, from Barons Court, 7 and 16 December 1836. Alister Rowan, *North West Ulster: The Counties of Londonderry, Donegal, Fermanagh & Tyrone*, Buildings of England, rev. edn, New Haven and London: Yale University Press, 1979, p. 135.

552   HHP Add MS 51673, fol. 1, letter Duke of Bedford to Lady Holland, from Barons Court, 1 January 1837. WAC LOC66-233, copies of various letters 1824–69, No. 229, letter Duchess of Bedford to Lord William Russell (in Berlin), from Barons Court, 5 February 1837.

553   WAC Ph-MSS 35-15, letter Allen Thomson to Mrs John Thomson, from Woburn Abbey, 26 March 1837. For Landseer's salver, see Richard Ormond, *Sir Edwin Landseer*, London: Tate Gallery, 1981, fig. 96, p. 140. The silver salver is inscribed on the reverse: 'This salver was formed from various cups and other pieces of plate obtained as premiums by Francis, Duke of Bedford and awarded to him at Agricultural meetings in 1799, 1800 and 1802, and by John, Duke of Bedford, his successor, in 1802, 1803, 1804, 1805, 1806, 1807, 1808, 1809, 1810, and 1811 for livestock, cattle sheep and swine, for ploughing and for cloth manufactured from wool grown at Park Farm at Woburn. 1837'.

554   Letter Duchess of Bedford to Lord William Russell (in Berlin), from Belgrave Square, 9 May 1837, quoted in Georgiana Blakiston, *Lord William Russell and his Wife 1815–1846*, London: John Murray, 1972, p. 394.

555   For quote ending 'to the rheumatism', see RBGK, A–B, vol. 9, no. 39, letter Duke of Bedford to Sir William Hooker, from Woburn Abbey, 23 May 1837. Ibid., no. 40, letter Duke of Bedford to Sir William Hooker, from Woburn Abbey, 28 May 1837.

556   WAC Ph-MSS 35-18, Letter Allen Thomson to Dr John Thomson, from Woburn Abbey, June 1837. WAC Ph-MSS 35-27, letter Allen Thomson to Mrs John Thomson, from Woburn Abbey, 1837.

557   WAC Ph-MSS, 35-19, letter Duchess of Bedford to Allen Thomson, from Woburn Abbey, 3 June 1837. WAC Ph-MSS 35-25, letter Allen Thomson to Margaret Thomson, from Woburn Abbey, 9 July 1837. RBGK, A–B, vol. 9, no. 54, letter Duke of Bedford to Sir William Hooker, from Endsleigh, 17 July 1837. WAC Ph-MSS 35-25, letter Allen Thomson to Margaret Thomson, from Campden Hill, 9 July 1837 (Landseer's accident).

558   WAC Ph-MSS 35-28 and 29, letters Allen Thomson to Mrs John Thomson, from Woburn Abbey, 10 August and 4 September 1837. WAC Ph-MSS 35-32, letter Allen Thomson to Margaret Thomson, from The Doune, 1837.

559   WAC Ph-MSS 35-33 and 29, letters Allen Thomson to Mrs John Thomson, from The Doune, 1837 (4 September for travel to Nice). HHP Add MS 51673, fol. 42, letter Duke of Bedford to Lady Holland, from The Doune, 19 August 1837.

560   WAC NMR 4/26/2, Bundle 5, No. 27, visits to hospital. Rachel Trethewey, *Mistress of the Arts: The Passionate Life of Georgina, Duchess of Bedford*, London: Review, 2002, p. 262.

561   E. F. Leveson-Gower, ed., *Letters of Harriet, Countess Granville, 1810–1845*, 2 vols, London: Longmans,

Green and Co., 1894, vol. 2, p. 252, letter Harriet, Countess Granville, to Lady Carlisle. 'Lizzie' was Lady Elizabeth Bingham, wife of George Granville Harcourt of Nuneham. Also known as Lady Sandwich, she was a long-time favourite of the duke. HHP Add MS 51674, letter Duchess of Bedford to Lord Holland, 8 January 1838.

562   WAC Ph-MSS 35-36, letter Allen Thomson to Mrs John Thomson, from Nice, 4 February 1838. RBGK, A–B, vol. 9, no. 34, letter Duke of Bedford to William Hooker, from Nice, 20 February 1838.

563   HHP Add MS 51673, fol. 78, letter Duke of Bedford to Lady Holland, from Nice, 6 March 1838. RBGK, A–B, vol. 10, no. 36, letter Duke of Bedford to William Hooker, from Genoa, 23 March 1838.

564   See Ray Desmond, *The History of the Royal Botanical Gardens, Kew*, London: Harvill Press, 1995, Chapter 9, for details of this period at Kew.

565   RBGK, A–B, vol. 10, no. 36, letter Duke of Bedford to William Hooker, from Genoa, 23 March 1838, and no. 37, letter Duke of Bedford to William Hooker, from Nice, 14 April 1838. HHP Add MS 51673, fol. 84, letter Duke of Bedford to Lady Holland, from Nice, 14 April 1838.

566   For quote from Queen Victoria, see Sonia Keppel, *The Sovereign Lady: A Life of Elizabeth, Third Lady Holland, with her Family*, London: Hamilton, 1974, p. 331. HHP Add MS 51673, fol. 96, letter Duke of Bedford to Lady Holland, from Woburn Abbey, 29 May 1838.

567   WAC Ph-MSS 35, letter Lady Rachel Russell to Allen Thomson, from Woburn Abbey, 1 June 1838.

568   HHP Add MS 51673, fols 122 and 129, letters Duke of Bedford to Lady Holland, from Woburn Abbey, 2 August and 13 September 1838. RBGK, A–B, vol. 10, no. 55, letter Duke of Bedford to William Hooker, from Brighton, 3 October 1838. HHP Add MS 51673, fol. 143, letter Duke of Bedford to Lady Holland, from Brighton, 1 November 1838. WAC LIB447 (B.2.D7.Rus), letter Duchess of Bedford to Lord William Russell, from Woburn Abbey, 20 December 1838.

569   RBGK, A–B, vol. 12, no. 40, letter Duke of Bedford to William Hooker, from Woburn Abbey, 11 January 1839. Ibid., no. 50, letter Duke of Bedford to William Hooker, from Woburn Abbey, 15 March 1839. Ibid., vol. 10, no. 55, letter Duke of Bedford to William Hooker, from Brighton, 3 October 1838. Ibid., vol. 12, nos 46 and 47, letter Duke of Bedford to William Hooker, from Woburn Abbey, 10 and 22 February 1839.

570   Ibid., nos 62 and 63, letters Duke of Bedford to William Hooker, from Ilminster, 16 and 26 June 1839. WAC Ph-MSS-33-30, letter James Forbes to William Hooker, from Woburn Abbey, 9 May 1839. WAC Ph-MSS-33-29, letter James Forbes to William Hooker, from Woburn Abbey, 26 April 1839. WAC Ph-MSS-33-31, letter James Forbes to William Hooker, from Woburn Abbey, 16 August 1839. RBGK, A–B, vol. 12, no. 63, letter Duke of Bedford to William Hooker, from Woburn Abbey, 26 June 1839.

571   Rachel E. Russell, *Memoirs of Two Favourites*, London: printed by Samuel Bentley, 1839. Book measures 14 × 11 cm, green leather cover, illustrated. British Library, London, BL 12805.aa.28.

572   RBGK, A–B, vol. 12, no. 66, letter Duke of Bedford to William Hooker, from Campden Hill, 12 July 1839. HHP Add MS 51673, fol. 194, letter Duke of Bedford to Lady Holland, from The Doune, 14 August 1839.

573   RBGK, A–B, vol. 12, no. 69, letter Duke of Bedford to William Hooker, from The Doune, 14 August 1839. NRS GD 176/2230, letter Duchess of Bedford to Mackintosh of Mackintosh (in Inverness), from The Doune, 18 August 1839. A. Grimble, *The Deer Forests of Scotland*, London: Kegan Paul & Co., 1896, p. 166, babel.hathitrust.org (accessed 28/10/2020). I am much indebted to David Taylor for mentioning this source.

574   HHP Add MS 51673, fol. 198, letter Duke of Bedford to Lady Holland, from The Doune, 22 August 1839. Blakiston, *Lord William Russell*, p. 431, letter Duke of Bedford to Lady William Russell, from The Doune, 21 September 1839. RBGK, A–B, vol. 12, no. 71, letter Duke of Bedford to William Hooker, from The Doune, 14 September 1839.

575   RBGK, A–B, vol. 12, no. 76, letter Duke of Bedford to William Hooker, from The Doune, 15 October 1839. HHP Add MS 51673, fol. 214, letter Duke of Bedford to Lady Holland, from The Doune, 15 October 1839.

576   Quotations from William Jackson Hooker, 'Copy of a Letter Addressed to Dawson Turner … on the occasion of the Death of the Duke of Bedford, particularly with reference to the services rendered by His Grace to Botany and Horticulture', Glasgow: printed by George Richardson, 1840, p. 24. After the duke's death, everything also changes for the way this particular book can be written. From the moment the estate stopped paying Georgina's bills, she effectively vanishes from the archive material. In addition, her personal papers and letters received, if any survived, have not been traced, so it is no longer possible to follow her life in the same detail as before, and the narrative becomes much more dependent on external and secondary sources.

577   For the duke's funeral, see Trethewey, *Mistress of the Arts*, p. 273. Ibid., p. 272. HHP Add MS 51673, two letters Dowager Duchess of Bedford to Lord Holland, from The Doune, October and November 1839.

578   Trethewey, *Mistress of the Arts*, p. 274.

579   NRS GD 176/2217, letter Dowager Duchess of Bedford to Mackintosh of Macintosh, 1840. WAC Ph-MSS-33-41, letter James Forbes to William Hooker, from Woburn Abbey, 9 April 1840. Blakiston, *Lord William Russell*, pp. 23–4.

580   Blakiston, *Lord William Russell*, p. 432, letter Duke of Bedford to Lord William Russell, from Woburn Abbey, from Oakley, 3 December 1839. Rough modern equivalents: £200,000 (c.£12,000,000), half a million (c.£30,000,000) and £40,000 (c.£2,400,000). WAC LOC30-1-1, box labelled '7th Duke Woburn Abbey Book Room' (Belgrave Square Series), package marked 'Copies of the Duke & Duchess of Bedford letters, collected 1861. 6th & 7th Dukes. Item: Envelope 1: Blue envelope "Without dates".'

581   WAC NMR 15/9/1, Bundle 9, Nos 84–116, abstracts of outstanding bills due in France. £2,454 (c.£146,700) and £7–8,000 (c.£480,000) for plants and books, etc. WAC LOC30-1-1, box labelled '7th Duke Woburn Abbey Book Room' (Belgrave Square Series), package marked 'Copies of the Duke & Duchess of Bedford letters, collected 1861. 6th & 7th Dukes. Item: Envelope 1: Blue envelope "Without dates"'. Blakiston, *Lord William Russell*, p. 442, letter 7th Duke of Bedford to Lord William Russell, from Oakley, January 1841, and p. 432, letter 7th Duke of Bedford to Lord William Russell, from Woburn Abbey, November 1839.

582   Trethewey, *Mistress of the Arts*, pp. 274–5. Equivalent values today: £649 (c.£38,940), £600 (c.£36,000). WAC LOC30-1-1, box labelled '7th Duke Woburn Abbey Book Room' (Belgrave Square Series), blue envelope 1840–49, letter 7th Duke of Bedford to Lord Duncannon, from Oakley, 4 March 1843.

583   Blakiston, *Lord William Russell*, p. 467, letters 7th Duke of Bedford to Lord William Russell, from Oakley, March and July 1842. WAC LOC30-1-1, box labelled '7th Duke Woburn Abbey Book Room' (Belgrave Square Series), blue envelope 1840–49, letters 7th Duke of Bedford to Lord Edward Russell, from Belgrave Square, 14 June 1842, to Lord Alexander Russell, from Belgrave Square, 21 April 1846, and to Lord Charles Russell, from Belgrave Square, 21 April 1845.

584   Blakiston, *Lord William Russell*, p. 455, letter Lord William Russell to Lady Holland, from Woburn Abbey, 25 December 1841. Ibid., p. 435.

585   Ormond, *Sir Edwin Landseer*, p. 10. ELC, letter Edwin Landseer to Count d'Orsay, 13 July 1840. Ormond, *Sir Edwin Landseer*, p. 10. NAL Eng. MS, 86 RR, vol. 1, 1962/1316/46, letter Dowager Duchess of Bedford to Edwin Landseer, from Woburn Abbey, 30 July 1841.

586   Ormond, *Sir Edwin Landseer*, p. 10. Campbell Lennie, *Landseer: The Victorian Paragon*, London: Hamilton, 1976, pp. 110–11.

587   Ormond, *Sir Edwin Landseer*, p. 10. Lennie, *Landseer*, pp. 110–11.

588   *Morning Post*, 30 July 1841, for the royal visit to Woburn. NAL Eng. MS, 86 RR, vol. 1, 1962/1316/46, letter Dowager Duchess of Bedford to Edwin Landseer, from Woburn Abbey, 30 July 1841.

589   *Bell's Weekly Register*, 26 September 1841, for Lord Henry's marriage.

590   PRO Kew PRO/22/4A, letter Dowager Duchess of Bedford to Lord John Russell, 1841, quoted in Trethewey, *Mistress of the Arts*, p. 283. Ibid., p. 284, for Georgiana's expenses.

591   WAC Ph-MSS-33-58, 62 and 61, letters James Forbes to William Hooker, from Woburn Abbey, 19 January, 4 and 17 July 1842.

592   Ormond, *Sir Edwin Landseer*, p. 187.

593   Elizabeth Grant, *The Highland Lady in Ireland: Journals 1840–50*, ed. Patricia Pelly and Andrew Tod, Edinburgh: Canongate, 1991, pp. 177 and 197. 'My Heart's in the Highlands' is a poem and song by Robert Burns (1789), of which these lines are part of the first verse.

594   For the trip to the Italian States, see *Bucks Gazette*, 6 January 1844, and *Freeman's Journal*, 11 March 1844.

595   Grant, *Memoirs*, vol. 2, pp. 66 and 215.

596   See Trethewey, *Mistress of the Arts*, p. 287.

597   SC 15/105, letter Henry William Vincent to Ralph Sneyd, from Loudon Lodge, 2 July 1845. Vincent, a clerk in the Treasury, who was also appointed Queen's Rembrancer, leased the house on Campden Hill in 1824, from which he could see both Bedford Lodge and Holland House, and in 1833 bought Thornwood Lodge, which he renamed Loudon Lodge.

598   NRS MM GD176/1465, 1845, 'Agreement of Tack between Mackintosh of Mackintosh, Daviot House, Inverness, and Alexander Stewart, Dalnavert, 1846'. 'Tacksman': gentry holding land from landowner as principal tenant and subletting it to peasant farmers; see David Taylor, *The Wild Black Region: Badenoch, 1750–1800*, Edinburgh: John Donald, 2016, Glossary, p. 263. For Lady Holland's legacy, see Trethewey, *Mistress of the Arts*, p. 288.

599   Grant, *The Highland Lady in Ireland*, 1991, pp. 239–53. Elizabeth's uncle, the 'equally fine artist', was Dr James Griffith, Fellow of University College, Oxford, who married his cousin, Mary Ironside, a relative of Grant's mother.

600   Ormond, *Sir Edwin Landseer*, p. 187, quoted from John Ruskin, *Modern Painters*, 1846, vol. 2, part III, sec. 1, ch. xii.

601   *Exeter and Plymouth Gazette*, 6 March 1847. For 'The Duchess (Dowager) of Bedford's *Fete Champetre*' at Campden Hill, see *Morning Chronicle*, 3 July 1846. 'The Dowager Duchess has commenced her morning parties at Bedford Lodge. Her Grace's entertainments will be continued daily': *Western Times*, 17 July 1847.

602   Grant, *Highland Lady in Ireland*, p. 339. For further details of Victoria and Albert in Scotland and at Balmoral, see Mary Miers, *Highland Retreats: The Architecture and Interiors of Scotland's Romantic North*, New York: Rizzoli, 2017, pp. 105–6.

603   GRP NRAS 102, Bundle 216, letter Rachel Russell to John Caw, from The Doune, 12 November 1847. *Inverness Courier*, 26 November 1847. *Morning Post*, 19 November 1847. Alexander had married Anne Emily Worsley Holmes, daughter of Sir Leonard Worsley Holmes, 9th Baronet, in 1844. In 1847 Alexander had been appointed aide-de-camp to the governor general of Canada. Following this Alexander saw active service in the Crimean War, particularly the Siege of Sevastapol, before eventually returning to Canada as commander of British troops.

604   *Morning Post*, 8 June 1848.

605   All quotes Grant, *Highland Lady in Ireland*, pp. 364–417. GRP NRAS 102, Bundle 216, letter William Grant to J. P. Grant junior, from Edinburgh, April 1853.

606   William Collie, *Memoirs of William Collie* [1908], Inverness: Highland Printers, 1992, pp. 76 and 77. Paul Johnson, 'What did the Duchess get up to in her Wood and Turf Hut?', *Spectator*, www.spectator.co.uk (accessed 12/08/2021). *Inverness Courier*, 11 January 1849. For the theatricals, see WAC, *Exeter & Plymouth Gazette*, 22 January 1849.

607 Trethewey, *Mistress of the Arts*, p. 289. For Torquay, *Morning Post*, 8 February 1850. GRP NRAS 102, Bundle 579, letter Rachel Russell to John Caw, from The Doune, 22 October 1850.

608 Collie, *Memoirs*, p. 77. *Inverness Courier*, 13 November 1851. For Cosmo's marriage, see *Exeter and Plymouth Gazette*, 25 October 1851.

609 WAC GB N37 and N38, 'Miscellaneous Observations', 1839–89, by Lord Arthur Russell, second son of Lord William Russell. Arthur was in London at this time serving as private secretary to Lord John Russell, then prime minister.

610 ELC, letter C. S. Leslie to Edwin Landseer, from Nice, February 1853, quoted in Trethewey, *Mistress of the Arts*, p. 293.

611 NLS EP MS 15051, fol. 1, 'The Last Will and Testament of The Most Noble Georgiana Duchess Dowager of Bedford, 29th May 1849'. Ibid., fol. 9, letter Lord Wriothesley Russell to Edward Ellice junior, 4 March 1853, on Rachel and the ambiguous terms of the will. Ibid., fol. 9, letter Edward Ellice junior to Lord Wriotheseley Russell, from Arlington Street, 4 March 1853. Ibid., fol. 13, letter Lord Wriothesley Russell to Edward Ellice junior, 5 March 1853.

612 *Stirling Observer*, Obituary, 17 March 1853. NLS MS 15051, letter William Nicholson to Edward Ellice, July 1853. *Morning Post*, 5 July 1853.

613 *Scottish Land: The Report of the Scottish Land Enquiry Committee* (1912; London: Hodder and Stoughton, 1914), p. 161. Basil Davidson, Notebook, 1988, private collection.

Select Bibliography

Anderson, W.E.K, ed., *The Journal of Sir Walter Scott*, London: Oxford University Press, 1972

Arnold, Dana, *Rural Urbanism: London Landscapes in the Early Nineteenth Century*, Manchester: Manchester University Press, 2005

Aspinall, Arthur, ed., *Three Early Nineteenth Century Diaries*, London: Williams and Norgate, 1952

Baird, Rosemary, *Goodwood: Art, Architecture, Sport and Family*, London, Frances Lincoln, 2007

Beattie, James, *Essay on the Nature and Immutability of Truth, in opposition to Sophistry and Scepticism* [1770], 6th edn, Edinburgh: Denham & Dick, 1805.

Bentham-Edwards, M., ed., *Autobiography of Arthur Young with Selections from his Correspondence*, London: Smith, Elder, 1898

Blakiston, Georgiana, *Lord William Russell and his Wife 1815–1846*, London: John Murray, 1972

—, *Woburn and the Russells*, London: Constable, 1980

Bulloch, John Malcolm, ed., *The Gordon Book*, Fochabers: Bazaar of the Fochabers Reading Room, 1902

Bunting, Madeleine, *Love of Country: A Hebridean Journey*, London: Granta Books, 2016

Coburn, Kathleen, ed., *Inquiring Spirit: A New Presentation of Coleridge*, London: Routledge & Kegan Paul, 1951

Collie, William, *Memoirs of William Collie* [1908], Inverness: Highland Printers, 1992

Colvin, Howard, *A Biographical Dictionary of British Architects 1600–1840*, London: John Murray, 1978

D'Amour, Matthias, *Memoirs of Mr Matthias D'Amour*, London: Longman, Rees, Orme, Brown, Green, & Longman; Sheffield: Whitaker, 1836

Daniels, Stephen, *Humphry Repton: Landscape Gardening and the Geography of Georgian England*, New Haven and London: Yale University Press, 1999

Davidson, Keir, *Woburn Abbey: The Park and Gardens*, London: Pimpernel Press, 2016

—, *Humphry Repton and the Russell Family, Featuring the Red Books for Woburn Abbey and Endsleigh Devon*, London: Pimpernel Press for the Bedford Estates, 2018

De Beer, Gavin, ed., *Autobiographies: Charles Darwin, Thomas Henry Huxley*, London: Oxford University Press, 1974

Desmond, Ray, *The History of the Royal Botanical Gardens, Kew*, London: Harvill Press, 1995

Dickens, Charles, ed., *The Life of Charles James Mathews*, vol. 2, London: Macmillan, 1879

Dorothée, Duchess de Dino, *Memoirs of the Duchesse de Dino (Afterwards Duchesse de Tallyrand et de Sagan), 1831–1835*, ed. The Princess Radziwill, New York: Charles Scribner's Sons, 1909

Dunne, F.W.B., *Personal Recollections of Lord Wriothesley Russell and Chenies*, London: Elliot Stock, 1888

Edgecumbe, Richard, ed., *The Diary of Frances Lady Shelley, 1787–1817*, London: John Murray, 1912

—, *The Diary of Frances Lady Shelley, 1818–1873*, London: John Murray, 1913

Elwin, Malcolm, *The First Romantics: Wordsworth, Coleridge, Southey*, London: Macdonald & Co., 1947

Forbes, Margaret, *Beattie and his Friends* [1904], Bristol: Thoemmes, 1990

Forbes, William, *An Account of the Life and Writings of James Beattie, LL.D, including many of his Original Letters*, 1807 [archive.org, 'An Account of the Life and Writings of James Beattie by Sir William Forbes' (accessed 16/06/2011)]

Foreman, Amanda, *Georgiana: Duchess of Devonshire*, London: HarperCollins, 1998

Fox, Henry, *The Journal of the Hon. Henry Edward Fox, afterward Fourth and Last Lord Holland, 1818–1830*, ed. the Earl of Ilchester, London: Thornton Butterworth, 1923

Fraser, Antonia, *Perilous Question: Reform or Revolution? Britain on the Brink, 1832*, New York: Public Affairs, 2013

Fraser-Mackintosh, Charles, *Antiquarian Notes, Historical, Genealogical and Social: Second Series, Inverness-shire Parish by Parish*, Inverness: A. & W. Mackenzie, 1897

Furber, Holden, *Henry Dundas, First Viscount Melville, 1742–1811*, London: Oxford University Press, 1931

The Gay Gordons: Some Strange Adventures of a Famous Scotch Family, London: Chapman and Hall, 1908

Ginter, Donald E., *Whig Organization in the General Election of 1790*, Berkeley and Los Angeles: University of California Press, 1967

Gordon, George, *The Last Dukes of Gordon and their Consorts: A Revealing Study*, Aberdeen: G. Gordon, 1980

Gore, Ann, and George Carter, eds, *Humphry Repton's Memoirs*, Norwich: Michael Russell, 2005

Grant, Anne MacVicar, *Letters from the Mountains; Being the Real Correspondence of a Lady, between the Years 1773 and 1807*, 2 vols, Sligo: HardPress Publishing, 2012

Grant, Elizabeth, *The Highland Lady in Ireland: Journals 1840–50*, ed. Patricia Pelly and Andrew Tod, Edinburgh: Canongate, 1991

—, *Memoirs of a Highland Lady*, 2 vols, ed. Andrew Tod, Edinburgh: Canongate, 2005

Griffin, Alan, 'Leamington History', 9 July 2013, www.leamingtonhistory.co.uk/some-early-aristocratic-residents (accessed 10/2/2017)

Gronow, R. H., *Reminiscences of Captain R. H. Gronow*, 4 vols, Dodo Press, Volume 1

Hembry, Phyllis Mary, *British Spas from 1815 to the Present Day: A Social History*, London: Athlone, 1997

Hirst, Matthew, 'The Realisation of a Regency Palace: The 6th Duke of Bedford and the Redecoration of Woburn Abbey', *Furniture History*, LIII (2017), pp. 225–42 (WAC)

Holmes, Richard, *The Age of Wonder: How the Romantic Generation Discovered the Beauty and Terror of Science*, London: HarperCollins, 2009

Hooker, William Jackson, 'Copy of a Letter Addressed to Dawson Turner … on the occasion of the Death of the Duke of Bedford, particularly with reference to the services rendered by His Grace to Botany and Horticulture', Glasgow: printed by George Richardson, 1840

Ilchester, Earl of, ed., *The Journal of Elizabeth, Lady Holland (1791–1811)*, 2 vols, London: Longmans, Green & Co., 1908

Jamie, Kathleen, *Findings*, London: Sort of Books, 2005

Johnson, David, *Music and Society in Lowland Scotland in the 18th Century*, London: Oxford University Press, 1972

Keppel, Sonia, *The Sovereign Lady: A Life of Elizabeth, Third Lady Holland, with her Family*, London: Hamilton, 1974

Lennie, Campbell, *Landseer: The Victorian Paragon*, London: Hamilton, 1976

Leveson-Gower, E. F., ed., *Letters of Harriet, Countess Granville, 1810–1845*, 2 vols, London: Longmans, Green and Co., 1894

Linstrum, Derek, *Sir Jeffrey Wyattville: Architect to the King*, Oxford: Clarendon Press, 1972

Mack, Robert L., *Thomas Gray: A Life*, New Haven and London: Yale University Press, 2000

Manson, James A., *Sir Edwin Landseer*, London: Walter Scott Publishing Co., 1902

Marshall, Meryl, 'Report of the Archaeological Surveying and Recording Project in Upper Glen Feshie', August 2005, North of Scotland Archaeological Society

—, 'A Project to Identify, Survey and Record the Archaeological Remains of a Farmstead at North Kinrara', June 2006–January 2011, North of Scotland Archaeological Society

—, *Glen Feshie: The History and Archaeology of a Highland Glen*, 2nd edn, [Conon Bridge:] North of Scotland Archaeological Society, 2013

Miers, Mary, *Highland Retreats: The Architecture and Interiors of Scotland's Romantic North*, New York: Rizzoli, 2017

Monkhouse, W. Cosmo, *Landseer's Works: Comprising Forty-Four Steel Engravings and about 200 Woodcuts, with a History of his Life and Art*, London: Virtue & Co. Ltd, 1892

Olsen, Donald J., *Town Planning in London: The Eighteenth & Nineteenth Centuries*, 2nd edn, New Haven and London: Yale University Press, 1982

O'Mahony, Charles, *The Viceroys of Ireland: The Story of the Long Line of Noblemen and their Wives Who Have Ruled Ireland and Irish Society for Over Seven Hundred Years*, London: J. Long, 1912

Ormond, Richard, *Sir Edwin Landseer*, London: Tate Gallery, 1981

—, *The Monarch of the Glen: Landseer in the Highlands*, Edinburgh: National Galleries of Scotland, 2005

—, *Edwin Landseer: The Private Drawings*, Norwich: Unicorn Press, 2009

Parry, J. D., *A Guide to Woburn Abbey*, Woburn: printed by S. Dodd, 1831 and 1845

Phillips, R., *Public Characters*, London, October 1799. The contributors are anonymous, although some of the articles are initialled. The 'Advertisement' at the beginning is written by 'the editor' and refers simply to 'the various writers'. [archive.org/stream/public characters 1799 (accessed 2/9/16)]

Repton, Humphry, 'Red Book for Woburn Abbey', 1805

—, *An Enquiry into the Changes in Taste in Landscape Gardening*, London: J. Taylor, 1806

—, 'Red Book for Endsleigh', 1814

—, *Fragments on the Theory and Practice of Landscape Gardening*, London: J. Taylor, 1816

Robinson, John Martin, 'Estate Buildings of the 5th and 6th Dukes of Bedford at Woburn 1787–1839', *Architectural Review*, November 1976, pp. 277–81 (BARS CRT 130 Woburn 29)

Roulston, William J., *Abercorn: The Hamiltons of Barons Court*, Belfast: Ulster Historical Foundation, 2014

Sitwell, Osbert, ed., *Two Generations*, London: Macmillan, 1940

Smith, Paul, 'The Landed Estate as Patron of Scientific Innovation: Horticulture at Woburn Abbey, 1802–1839', Phd thesis, Open University, 1983

—, 'Woburn Abbey Gardens, 1822–39: A Locus of Horticultural and Botanical Innovation', *Garden History*, vol. 48, no. 1 (Summer 2020), pp. 47–58

Stewart, Katherine, *Women of the Highlands*, Edinburgh: Luath Press, 2006

Stoddart, John, *Remarks on the Local Scenery & Manners in Scotland, during the Years 1799 and 1800*, vol. II, London: William Miller, 1801

Taylor, David, *The Wild Black Region: Badenoch, 1750–1800*, Edinburgh: John Donald, 2016

Taylor, Michael, *The Interest: How the British Establishment Resisted the Abolition of Slavery*, London: Bodley Head, 2020

Trethewey, Rachel, *Mistress of the Arts: The Passionate Life of Georgina, Duchess of Bedford*, London: Review, 2002

Virgil, *The Georgics: A Poem of the Land*, trans. Kimberly Johnson, Harmondsworth: Penguin, 2010

Von Pückler-Muskau, Hermann, *Tour in England, Ireland, and France in the Years 1826, 1827, 1828, and 1829 … in a series of letters by a German prince*, Philadelphia: Carey, Lea and Blanchard, 1833

Waagen, Dr G. F., *Works of Art and Artists in England*, 3 vols, London: John Murray, 1838

Winchester, Simon, *The Map that Changed the World*, Harmondsworth: Penguin, 2001

Index

Acknowledgements

AUTHOR'S ACKNOWLEDGEMENTS

This book is the result of a special collaboration with Robin Russell, whose passion for the history of the Russell family has been a constant source of inspiration. Following a discussion at Endsleigh some ten years ago at which we determined that the story of the house and grounds and the people involved in it needed telling in detail, Robin's determination that this book should get written and published, his continued support and encouragement during the process, and his company on research trips over the past eight years or so have all played a crucial role. At every turn this story became richer and more interesting, and the opportunity to research and write it has been both very rewarding and a great pleasure, and Robin's dedicated commitment to the book has made it possible.

Many thanks are also due for the interest and assistance provided by their Graces the Duke and Duchess of Bedford and the Trustees of the Bedford Estates, for access to the collections and archives at Woburn Abbey and for permission to use material from both for publication in the text and as illustrations.

For providing a starting point for research and an understanding of the people involved in the story, grateful acknowledgement goes to the research and writing undertaken by the late Gladys Scott Thomson, (Academic and Archivist at Woburn Abbey 1927–40), for her *Life of the 5th Duke of Bedford* (unpublished), and that of Rachel Trethewey, for both her 2002 biography of Georgina Gordon, *Mistress of the Arts: The Passionate Life of Georgina, Duchess of Bedford*, and for her insights in conversation into Georgina's personality and her thoughts and suggestions for the present book. Both authors provided reliable chronologies and any number of important details and ideas.

At Woburn Abbey, for their patience, continued help, suggestions and encouragement, many thanks go to Archivist Nicola Allen, her assistants Natasha Kikas and Michaela Bilton, and the Woburn Arts Society volunteers. In the Curator's Office to Matthew Hirst and Victoria Poulton, and in the Gardens to Martin Towsey and his staff. We would also like to give a big thank you to Olga Polizzi and all her team at Endsleigh Hotel, and to John Dennis and the Endsleigh Fishing Club, for their help and assistance.

IN ENGLAND:

Particular thanks go to Richard Ormond, whose knowledge of Landseer's work has provided so many insights and lines of enquiry to guide and further the research. Richard has been most generous with both his time and his knowledge and has provided the kind of active support and patient responses to questions and enquiries that made this book possible.

Many thanks also go to Paul Smith for his great contributions, in both his written work and in conversation, to a fuller appreciation of the 6th Duke's interest in and promotion of new horticultural and botanical science. I would also like to thank Paul for reading some of the text and his thoughtful comments. The expertise of both Richard and Paul has made this a better book in so many ways and the process of writing it so much more enjoyable.

Thanks also go to the many staff members at Bedford Archives and Record Services, the British Library Manuscripts Room, Devon Heritage Centre, Durham University Library, James Piell, Curator of the Goodwood Collections, Helen Burton at the Special Collections, Keele University Library, and staff at the National Art Library Reading Room and Victoria and Albert Museum, National Portrait Gallery, the Archives at the Royal Botanical Gardens Kew, Tate Gallery, Staffordshire Record Office and West Sussex Record Office. Others who have helped along the way, in conversation or with materials, include Rosemary Baird, Gilly Drummond, Clare Greener, Warin and Sophie Kelly at Kelly House, Dianne Long and Wendy Page. Thanks also to Dr Diane Barr for alerting us to the journals of Mrs Elizabeth Hervey.

ACKNOWLEDGEMENTS

We would also like to acknowledge the owners of various private collections of paintings who would prefer to remain anonymous, and to thank them for their interest in the project and for providing us with images and publishing permission.

IN SCOTLAND:

My sincere thanks go to David Taylor, author of *The Wild Black Region*, who knows more than anyone about the history of Badenoch, and who, in conversation and by email over several years, helped me develop a clearer understanding of the social and economic background to the Bedfords' lives in Scotland in addition to providing sources and materials that helped bring this into focus and correcting errors. It has been a real pleasure to exchange ideas and information while we were both working on books whose subject matter explored a similar time and place, if from different perspectives. David's new book, *'The People are Not There': The Transformation of Badenoch, 1800–1863* will be published in 2022. Equally, thanks go to Meryl Marshall and the North of Scotland Archaeological Society for their fieldwork, for Meryl's excellent history of Glen Feshie and her generous sharing of material and ideas. Particular thanks also to Mary Miers for her encouragement and interest in this book and, on the ground, for her guidance, for critical introductions which made much of the research possible, and for her hospitality.

In addition, this book would not have been possible without the generous and encouraging help and hospitality offered by the Earl and Countess of Dysart at The Doune, which made visits to Rothiemurchus so instructive and enjoyable. We are also particularly grateful to Claire and Oliver Russell and Guy Macpherson Grant at Ballindalloch, and to Alan Marshall at Invereshie House. I would also like to acknowledge the contribution of the late Annie Maclaren at Kinrara, Ron Dutton at Kinrara, Thomas McDonell at Wildland, and the staff at Killiehuntly Farmhouse.

Thanks also to the staff of National Records Scotland at Register House, Olive Geddes and Rachel Beattie at the National Library of Scotland, Jean Jamieson at the Falkirk Community Trust and Dan Cottam at Grantown Museum and Heritage Trust for all their help over a number of years.

Finally, I must also thank Grenville and Virginia Irvine-Fortescue for their time, help and hospitality on a number of occasions, and their interest and help in so many ways, including keeping the car on the road. Thanks too to Andrew Tod for sharing his encyclopaedic knowledge of Elizabeth Grant, the Highland Lady, and her family, for his interest in the book, his suggestions and comments and for his wonderful company.

IN IRELAND:

I am particularly grateful for the help of William Roulston, both for his detailed history of the Abercorn family and Barons Court itself, and for guiding me through the Abercorn Papers at the Public Record Office of Northern Ireland, and to the many staff members who helped there.

I would also like to thank the Duke of Abercorn at Barons Court, and Keith and Elizabeth Adam of Blair Adam, who extended invitations to visit that I was unable to follow up on due to the pandemic, but who still helped as much as they could.

At Pimpernel Press, heartfelt thanks go to Jo Christian, Gail Lynch, and Emma O'Bryen for taking on this project. Thanks also go to Nancy Marten and Anne Wilson respectively for their patience and skill in copy-editing and designing the book. Additional thanks go to James Davidson for creating the endpapers, maps, figures and special artwork, and not least for the work which went into re-creating the views of the Garden Room.

Finally, great thanks, as ever, to my wife, Linda Crockett, both for everything she has contributed and specifically for her reading of the text and help in understanding Georgina.

PICTURE ACKNOWLEDGEMENTS

With the exception of those listed below, all photographs and illustrations in this book form part of the Woburn Abbey Collection and are reproduced by permission of His Grace, The Duke of Bedford and the Trustees of the Bedford Estates.

Author: Plates 14, 30. Pages 29, 199, 243, 286, 407

For permission to reproduce the images listed below, the publishers wish to thank:
Duke of Abercorn, collections at Barons Court, Northern Ireland: Plates 24, 32. Pages 419, 476
Elgin Public Library: Page 125
Grantown Museum and Heritage Trust: Page 489
Historic England: Page 409
Trustees of the Goodwood Collection: Plate 6. Page 123
Directors of the Irvine Burns Club: Plate 7. 'This painting by Charles M. Hardie of "Burns in Edinburgh, 1787" is the property of the Irvine Burns Club who have granted reproduction rights for it to be used in this publication. The original can be viewed in The Wellwood Burns Centre & Museum in Irvine, Scotland'
Keele University Library, Special Collections: Plate 21
Mary Bourne: Page 129
National Library of Scotland: Plate 40
National Portrait Gallery: Pages 461, 468
Private Collections: Plates. 8, 10, 17, 18, 23, 25, 26, 31. Pages 78, 285, 418, 443
©Tate Gallery: Plate 36
Victoria and Albert Museum, London: Pages 342, 381, 383
Wolverhampton Art Gallery / Bridgeman: Plate 27
Untraced: Plate 34. Pages 358, 417

The publishers have made every effort to contact holders of copyright works. Any copyholders we have been unable to reach are invited to contact the publishers so that full acknowledgement may be given in subsequent editions.

GORDON

Cosmo *1720-1752* m. Katherine Gordon *1719-1779* m. 1756 Staats Long Morris *1728-1779*
3rd Duke of Gordon   *of Haddo*   *no children*

William *1744-1823*   Anne *1748-1816*   George *1752-1793*   **Alexander** *1743-1827*
1 daughter   *d. at Huntly*   *d. unmarried in London*   *7th Marquis of Huntly*
                       no children   *Led the Gordon Riots 1780*   *4th Duke of Gordon*

Susan *1746-1814*   Katherine *1750-1797*

Charlotte *1768-1842*   George *1770-1836*   Madelina *1772-1849*   Susan *1774-1828*
m.   *8th Marquis of Huntly*   m.   m.
Charles Lennox *1764-1819*   *'my George'*   1 Sir Robert Sinclair *1774-1795*   William Montague *1771-18[?]*
4th Duke of Richmond   *no children*   *of Murtle*   *5th Duke of Manchester*
7 sons, 7 daughters   *1 son*   *2 sons, 5 duaghters*
                                      2 Charles Fsyche Palmer *d.1843*
                                            no children

4th Duke of Gordon's 'natural' children

—— *by* Bethia Largue ——   —— *by* Jean Christie *1770-1824* ——   *by* Isobel Williams ——
                              later Duchess of Gordon

George Gordon *1766-1835*
of Glentromie   6 children   1 child
'the Duke's George'

Revd Wriothesley *1804-1886*   Lt-Col. Charles *1807-1894*   Georgiana *1810-1867*
m.1829   m.1834   m.1842
Eliza Russell *1803-1886*   *Isabella Clarissa Davies d.1884*   Charles Romilly *1808-1887*
2 sons, 1 daughter   *2 sons, 3 daughters*   *6 sons*

Edward R.N. *1805-1874*   Francis R.N. *1808-1869*   Louisa *1812-1905*
m.*1860*   m.*1844*   m.1832
Mary Ann Taylor   *Elizabeth Peyton 1811-1888*   James *1811-1885*
no children   *no children*   *1st Duke of Abercor[?]*
                                                             7 sons, 7 daughters

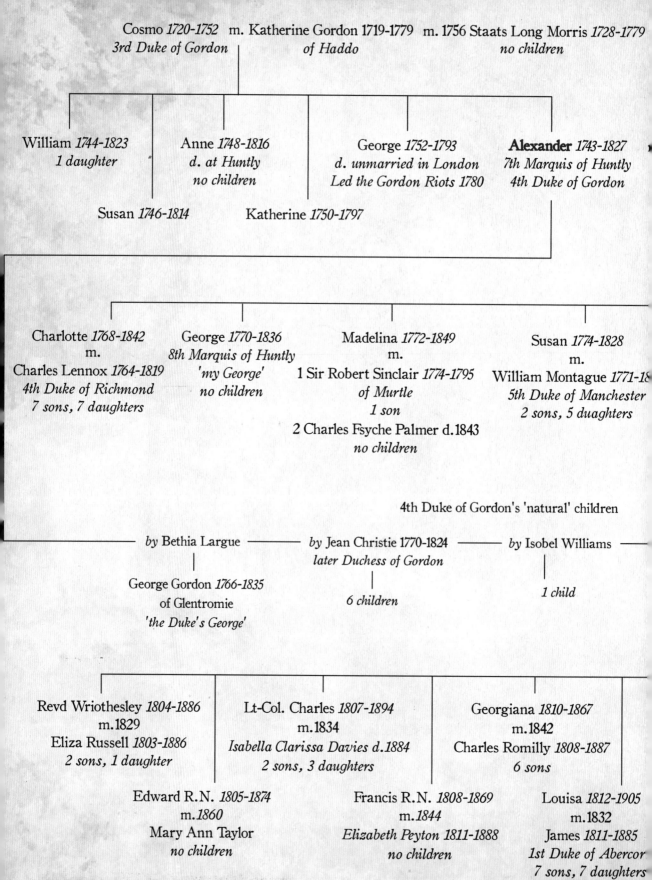